The Complete Encyclopedia
of
Television Programs
1947-1976

The Complete Encyclopedia

of

Television Programs

1947-1976

Volume 1

A - K

Vincent Terrace

EXCLUSIVE LIBRARY DISTRIBUTORS:

classic publications

P.O. Box 1228
Covina, Calif. 91722
PHONE: AREA CODE 213
332-1194

South Brunswick and New York:
A. S. Barnes and Company
London: Thomas Yoseloff Ltd

© 1976 by A. S. Barnes and Co., Inc.

A. S. Barnes and Co., Inc.
Cranbury, New Jersey 08512

Thomas Yoseloff Ltd
108 New Bond Street
London W1Y OQX, England

Library of Congress Cataloging in Publication Data

Terrace, Vincent, 1948-
   The complete encyclopedia of television programs,
1947-1976.

   1. Television programs—United States—Catalogs.
I. Title.
PN1992.3.U5T46   015   74-10022
ISBN 0-498-01561-0

Printed in the United States of America

For my parents

Preface

The Complete Encyclopedia of Television Programs is a detailed, alphabetical anthology that traces the medium of television from the pioneering programs of the middle forties to the established programs of the seventies.

Contained within these pages are nostalgic excursions into a time past—thirty years of television programming from January 1, 1946 — January 1, 1976; more than 2,700 network and syndicated entertainment programs: comedy, mystery, crime drama, serial, adventure, children's series, drama, documentary, anthology, game, variety, western, educational, science fiction, animated cartoon, spy drama, and discussion-variety.

My purpose is to acquaint the reader with these programs and the personalities involved in them. My intent to trace this evolution and evoke long-forgotten and long-neglected memories has fostered the first complete encyclopedia of television.

Acknowledgments

Individuals:

Bob Elliott, Ray Goulding, Albert Stangler, Mary Stangler, Bart Polin, Tim Faracy, Phil Foley, James Robert Parish, Paula Patyk, Stu Grossman, Roy Bright.

Organizations:

I.T.C. (Independent Television Corporation; and ATV Company); especially Arnold Friedman.

Hanna-Barbera Productions; especially John Michaeli.

Screen Gems (Columbia Pictures Television); especially Jerome Gottlieb.

Walt Disney Productions; especially, Rose Mussi, and Tom A. Jones.

A.S.C.A.P.; especially Lenore Terry.

The Television Information Office; especially Leslie Slocum.

B.M.I.; Hal Seeger Productions; Ken Snyder Enterprises; The New York Public Library at Lincoln Center; Emil Asher, Inc.; ABC-TV.

Photographs:

Independent Television Corporation: "The Adventurer"; "The Champions"; "Department S"; "The Julie Andrews Hour"; "My Partner the Ghost"; "The Persuaders"; "The Protectors"; "The Saint"; "Shirley's World"; "Thriller"; "U.F.O."

Hanna-Barbera Productions: "The Banana Splits Adventure Hour"; "The Flintstones"; "Help, It's the Hair Bear Bunch"; "Huckleberry Hound"; "The Jetsons"; "Moby Dick"; "Quick Draw McGraw"; "Samson and Goliath"; "Shazzan"; "Scooby-Doo, Where Are You?"; "Top Cat"; "Yogi Bear."

Screen Gems: "Bewitched"; "Camp Runamuck"; "Casey Jones"; "Circus Boy"; "The Donna Reed Show"; "The George Burns & Gracie Allen Show"; "Gidget"; "The Farmer's Daughter"; "Father Knows Best"; "Hazel"; "I Dream of

Jeannie"; "The Interns"; "Love on a Rooftop"; "Mr. Deeds Goes to Town"; "The Monkees"; "The Partridge Family"; "Route 66"; "The Second Hundred Years"; "Tallahassee 7000"; "The Three Stooges"; "Tightrope"; "The Ugliest Girl in Town"; "The Wackiest Ship in the Army"; "Wild Bill Hickok"; "The Young Rebels."

Walt Disney Productions: "Davy Crockett"; "The Mickey Mouse Club"; "The Nine Lives Of Elfego Baca"; "The Swamp Fox"; "Texas John Slaughter"; "Zorro."

Joe Franklin: "The Joe Franklin Show."

Others: *Movie Star News;* The Memory Shop.

Author's Notes

Networks:

Domestic:

ABC: The American Broadcasting Company.
CBS: The Columbia Broadcasting System.
NBC: The National Broadcasting Company.
DuMont: The DuMont Network; defunct.
NET: National Educational Television.
PBS: The Public Broadcasting Service.

Foreign:

The B.B.C.: The British Broadcasting Corporation.
A.B.C.: Associated British Corporation.
C.B.C.: The Canadian Broadcasting Corporation.

Program exclusions: Religious, sport, news, and specials (excluding those broadcast as a series).

Syndicated. This is a term that indicates programs that are sold or rented to local stations. A network program is broadcast by a key station and picked up by affiliated member stations across the country on a specific day and time. A syndicated program is broadcast by a local station according to its particular needs and is seen only in its coverage area. There are two main types of syndication.

Type One: First Run Syndication. This indicates programs that are made specifically for sale to any station that wants to buy it. Because these programs do not appear on a network, a station will not appear in its write-up. These types of programs are indicated as follows (for example):

DUSTY'S TRAIL—30 minutes—

Syndicated 1973.
MY PARTNER THE GHOST—
60 minutes—Syndicated 1974.

Type Two: Off-Network Syndication. After programs have completed their network runs, some are placed into syndication—sold or rented to any station that wants to buy the reruns for airing at any time. These types of programs are listed as follows (for example):

THE DEPUTY—30 minutes—NBC—September 12, 1959 - September 16, 1961. Syndicated.

THE FLINTSTONES—30 minutes—ABC—September 30, 1960 - September 2, 1966. Syndicated.

When the term *syndicated* appears after a network program it indicates that these series have been placed into syndication.

Dates. Dates are based on what information was available. All first-run syndicated programs are listed by their first year of distribution only. It would be impossible to provide years of resyndication, because programs of this type are constantly being sold over and over again.

Length or Time (pertaining to programs under thirty-minutes duration). Programs in this category are cartoon series. The length listed for each is the original produced length. In cases where programs are only four or six minutes per episode, stations are permitted to run these back to back to fill fifteen-minute or half-hour time periods.

Supermarionation. Developed by Sylvia and Jerry Anderson, it is a technique through which puppets receive locomotion through electronic means.

The phases:

Dialogue: Six artists are used; between them, they create the voices to the ten or fifteen characters that each film contains. The recording is then edited to remove pauses, particularly where an artist is playing two characters in one scene.

Puppet Creations:

Heads: Heads are sculptured in clay and copied in the form of fiberglass shells with provisions allowing for eyes and mouth mechanisms.

Brains and eyes: An electronic mechanism, controlled by the prerecorded dialogue, is inserted into the head. It enables the puppet character to speak in direct synchronization with the recorded voices. The eyes, constructed by optical experts, are capable of movement and expression through electronics.

Hair: Male figures are fitted with wigs. For female figures, human hair is used, and each strand is separately fixed to the head, gradually building up the tresses and giving each puppet an individualistic style.

Bodies: Produced in plastic, they are constructed in correct human proportion (between twenty-two and twenty-four inches in height), discarding the tradition that heads should be bigger than bodies.

Faces: Faces are first roughly

painted until the exact image is captured. They are then made up just as if they were human.

Clothing: Clothes are hand-made with the finest lightweight material to prevent bulkiness and weight.

Testing: Completed marionettes are wired with specially developed 0.005-inch-thick wire that is strong and straight, yet black enough not to photograph and matte enough not to reflect light. Each figure is controlled by nine eight-foot-long wires fixed to a control and worked by a human manipulator who stands on a bridge above the set. Electric current is passed through the control wires to activate the puppet's lip-sync mechanism.

Sets: Sets are constructed one-third the normal size. Through ingenious special effects the illusion of life is given.

Filming: Because five camera crews and two sets are constantly used, an identical twin to each character has to be made. When the film is completed, it goes to the new editorial department where the music score is added and the twelve tracks of sound effects and dialogue are blended to form the film soundtrack.

Supermarionation Series (Produced by The Independent Television Corporation; and ATV Company): "Captain Scarlet and the Mysterons"; "Fireball XL-5"; "Stingray"; "Supercar"; and "Thunderbirds." See "Thunderbirds" for photograph.

a

THE ABBOTT AND COSTELLO SHOW

Comedy. Background: Hollywood, California. The misadventures of comedians Bud Abbott and Lou Costello. Stories relate their attempts to acquire work and relieve monetary burdens.

CAST

Bud Abbott	Himself
Lou Costello	Himself
Sidney Fields, their landlord, the owner of the Fields Rooming House	Himself
Hillary Brooke, Lou's girlfriend	Herself
Mike the Cop	Gordon Jones
Stinky, Lou's friend	Joe Besser
Mr. Botchagalup, a friend	Joe Kirk
Mrs. Bronson, a tenant	Renie Riand
Hercules, a short bald man, a friend of Lou's	Bobby Barbar
Bingo the Chimp, Lou's pet monkey	Himself

Stock performers: Joan Shawlee, Veda Ann Borg, Iris Adrian, Joe Sawyer, Gloria Henry, Joyce Compton.

Music: Raoul Kraushaar.

THE ABBOTT AND COSTELLO SHOW—30 minutes—CBS—1952 - 1954. Syndicated.

Animated Version:

THE ABBOTT AND COSTELLO SHOW—05 minutes—Syndicated 1966. A Hanna-Barbera production.

Characters' Voices

Bud Abbott	Himself
Lou Costello	Stan Irwin

Music: Hoyt Curtin.

ABC ALBUM

Anthology. Adaptations of works by noted authors.

Host: Donald Cook.

Included.

Justice. The story of a young, impoverished wife who seeks help from the Legal Aid Society when she believes her husband is being blackmailed.

CAST

Lee Grant, Paul Douglas.

Hogan's Daughter. The story of an office girl who suddenly sees her slow, unimaginative boyfriend in a new light when she discovers lipstick on his collar.

CAST

Sheila Bond, Joshua Shelley.

Jamie. The story of the relationship between a lonely boy and an old man. The pilot film for the series of the same title.

CAST

Brandon DeWilde, Ernest Truex.

Mr. Glencannon Takes All. The story of Colin Glencannon and his attempts to win the trade of a whiskey manufacturer for his shipping company.

CAST

Robert Newton, Melville Cooper, Myron McCormick.

ABC ALBUM—30 minutes—ABC—April 12, 1953 - July 5, 1953. Also known as: "Plymouth Playhouse."

THE ABC COMEDY HOUR

See title: "The Kopycats."

THE ABC AFTERNOON PLAYBREAK

Anthology. Dramatic presentations.

Included:

Alone with Terror. The story of Susan Maroni, a police lieutenant's widow, who attempts to prove that her husband was not on the take at the time of his apparent suicide.

CAST

Susan Maroni: Juliet Mills; Marian Webb: Virginia Vincent; Leonard Walters: Colby Chester.

A Mask of Love. A biographer's ardent search for a deceased novelist's personal papers — a treasure now jealousy guarded by his last mistress.

CAST

Tina Bordereau: Barbara Barrie; John Connors: Harris Yulin; Juliana Bordereau: Cathleen Nesbitt; Mary Prest: Geraldine Brooks.

Last Bride of Salem. A young mother struggles to prevent demonic forces from possessing her husband and daughter.

CAST

Jennifer Clifton: Lois Nettleton; Matt Clifton: Bradford Dillman; Kelly Clifton: Joni Bick; Sebastian Mayhew: Paul Harding.

The Other Woman. The story of an unwed pregnant woman who wants to keep her baby despite embarrassment to her and the child's married father.

CAST

Liz Cunningham: Katherine Helmond; Dr. Miller: Pat O'Brien; Dave Collins: Joel Fabiana; Larraine Collins: Beverlee McKinsey.

THE ABC AFTERNOON PLAYBREAK—90 minutes—ABC—Premiered: October 30, 1973. Broadcast monthly.

THE ABC AFTERSCHOOL SPECIAL

Anthology. Programs relating various aspects of the world to children.

Included:

My Dad Lives in a Downtown Hotel. The story centers on a young boy as he struggles to understand and accept his parents' separation.

CAST

Joe Grant: Beau Bridges; June Grant: Margaret Frye; Joey Grant: Ike Eisenmann.

The Runaways. The story of two runaways, a teenage girl and a street-smart boy, and their struggle for survival.

CAST
Cindy Britton: Belinda Balaski; Francis: Claudio Martinez; Louis Britton: Patricia Blair; John Turner: Anthony Eisley.

Alexander. The story of a retired clown and his undying love for children.

CAST
Alexander: Red Buttons; Sue: Jodie Foster; Raymond: Robbie Rist; Tom: Kerry MacLane.

Cyrano. An animated adaptation of Edmond Rostand's romantic tragedy. The story of soldier-poet, Cyrano de Bergerac.

Voices: Cyrano: Jose Ferrer; Roxanne: Joan Van Ark; Rogueneau: Kurt Kaszner.

THE ABC AFTERSCHOOL SPECIAL—60 minutes—ABC—Premiered: October 4, 1972. Broadcast on the first Wednesday of each month.

THE ABC MONDAY NIGHT SPECIAL

Specials. Entertainment and news presentations.

Included:

Hollywood: The Dream Factory. The story of filmmaking featuring clips from MGM movies.

Narrator: Dick Cavett

The Robinson Crusoe Ice Spectacle. A musical variety hour set on ice.

Starring: Reg Park, Lorna Brown.

The Undersea World of Jacques Cousteau: The Forgotten Mermaids.

Narrator: Jacques Cousteau, Rod Serling.

In Search of the Lost World. An expedition's search for the artifacts and remnants of early man.

Narrator: E.G. Marshall.

THE ABC MONDAY NIGHT SPECIAL—60 minutes—ABC—January 10, 1972 - August 14, 1972.

THE ABC MOVIE OF THE WEEK
THE ABC TUESDAY MOVIE OF THE WEEK

Movies. Feature films produced especially for television.

Included:

Playmates. The story of two divorced men who make secret plays for each other's ex-wives.

CAST
Patti Holvey: Connie Stevens; Marshall Burnett: Alan Alda; Lois Burnett: Barbara Feldon; Kermit Holvey: Doug McClure.

Divorce His/Divorce Hers. The incidents, separate interests, and marital indifferences that destroy the marriage of a sophisticated couple.

CAST
Jane Reynolds: Elizabeth Taylor; Martin Reynolds: Richard Burton; Diane Proctor: Carrie Nye; Donald Trenton: Barry Foster.

The Sex Symbol. The rise and fall of Kelly Williams, a glamorous but neurotic Hollywood film star.

CAST

Kelly Williams: Connie Stevens; Agatha Murphy: Shelley Winters; Manny Foxe: Jack Carter; Grant O'Neal: Don Murray.

Call Her Mom. Background: The Alpha Rho Epsilon Fraternity of Beardsley College. The story of Angie Bianco, its housemother, a beautiful ex-waitress, as she struggles to supervise the all-male frat house.

CAST

Angie Bianco: Connie Stevens; Chester Hardgrave: Van Johnson; Dean Walden: Charles Nelson Reilly; Jonathan Calder: Jim Hutton.

Two on a Bench. The efforts of a federal investigator to discover which of two people—a beautiful but far-out girl, or a handsome but square young man—is working for a spy.

CAST

Marcy Kramer: Patty Duke; Preston Albright: Ted Bessell; Brubaker: Andrew Duggan.

The Night Stalker. Background: Las Vegas. A newspaper reporter attempts to prove that the murders of several young women were committed by a vampire. Pilot film for the series "The Night Stalker."

CAST

Carl Kolchak: Darren McGavin; Gail Foster: Carol Lynley; Vincenzo: Simon Oakland; Vampire: Barry Atwater.

THE ABC MOVIE OF THE WEEK—

90 minutes—ABC—Premiered: September 23, 1969. Later titled: "The ABC Tuesday Movie of the Week."

THE ABC MOVIE OF THE WEEKEND
THE ABC WEDNESDAY MOVIE OF THE WEEK

Movies. Feature films produced especially for television.

Included:

If Tomorrow Comes. Background: California during World War Two. The tender story of the love between an American girl and a Japanese-American boy—a love overshadowed by the fear and hatreds of war.

CAST

Eileen Phillips: Patty Duke; David: Frank Liu; Frank Phillips: James Whitmore; Miss Cramer: Anne Baxter.

In Broad Daylight. A blind actor attempts to dispose of his unfaithful wife.

CAST

Anthony Chapel: Richard Boone; Kate: Suzanne Pleshette; Elizabeth: Stella Stevens; Detective Bergman: John Marley.

Every Man Needs One. The complications that ensue when a male chauvinist is forced to hire a beautiful militant women's liberationist.

CAST

Beth: Connie Stevens; David: Ken Berry; Nancy: Carol Wayne; Wally: Henry Gibson; Louise: Louise Sorel.

The Daughters of Joshua Cade. A fur

trapper attempts to win a homesteading claim by recruiting three shady women to pose as his daughters.

CAST

Joshua Cade: Buddy Ebsen; Charity: Karen Valentine; Ada: Sandra Dee; Mae: Leslie Warren; Bitterfoot: Jack Elam.

Family Flight. The story of four people and their struggle for survival after their plane crash lands in the remote regions of Baja California.

CAST

Jason: Rod Taylor; Florence: Dina Merrill; Carol: Janet Margolin; David: Kristopher Tabori.

THE ABC MOVIE OF THE WEEK-END—90 minutes—ABC—September 18, 1971 - May 27, 1972. Returned, September 13, 1972, as: "The ABC Wednesday Movie of the Week."

ABC MOVIES

Movies. Theatrical features.

Titles:

THE ABC SUNDAY NIGHT MOVIE —2 hours—ABC—Premiered: September 20, 1963.

Included:

The Last Picture Show. Background: A fictitious Texas prairie town in the early 1950s. A tender portrait of life and love and of growing up and growing old in a small town.

CAST

Sonny: Timothy Bottoms; Duane: Jeff Bridges; Jacy: Cybil Shepherd; Ruth: Cloris Leachman; Sam: Ben Johnson.

The Heartbreak Kid. While honeymooning, a newlywed meets the girl of his dreams and decides to marry her. The story centers on his attempts to break the news to his wife.

CAST

Lenny: Charles Grodin; Lila: Jeannie Berlin; Kelly: Cybil Shepherd.

The Valachi Papers. A violent look at organized crime in America from 1929 to the 1960s, as revealed by Brooklyn mobster Joseph Valachi.

CAST

Joseph Valachi: Charles Bronson; Vito Genovese: Lino Venturo; Morra Valachi: Jill Ireland.

Can Can. Background: Paris during the 1890s. A lawyer defends a beautiful café owner accused of presenting the scandalous Can Can dance.

CAST

Francois: Frank Sinatra; Simone: Shirley MacLaine; Paul: Maurice Chevalier; Claudine: Juliet Prowse.

Do Not Disturb. Background: England. An American wife attempts to adjust to a new homeland.

CAST

Janet Harper: Doris Day; Mike Harper: Rod Taylor; Paul Bellari: Sergio Fantoni.

THE ABC MONDAY NIGHT MOVIE —2 hours—ABC—Premiered: January 1970. (The mid-season replacement for "ABC Monday Night Football"; Movies air each season from January through September.)

Included:

Marilyn. A documentary tracing Marilyn Monroe's film career.

Narrator: Rock Hudson.

The Bliss of Mrs. Blossom. A marital farce depicting the life of Harriet Blossom, an unfaithful wife.

CAST

Harriet Blossom: Shirley MacLaine; Robert Blossom: Richard Attenborough; Ambrose Tuttle: James Booth.

Woman Times Seven. Vignettes depicting variations on the female psyche—from would-be prostitute to housewife.

CAST

Shirley MacLaine, Peter Sellers, Rossano Brazzi.

UNSOLD PILOTS (Three):

The Barbara Eden Show. The harassed life of a beautiful young serial writer.

CAST

Barbara: Barbara Eden; Bradford: Joe Flynn; Barry: Lyle Waggoner.

Catch 22. A video adaptation of the novel by Joseph Heller. The antics of a company of fliers during World War Two.

CAST

Yossarian: Richard Dreyfus; Colonel Cathcart: Dana Elcar.

The Karen Valentine Show. The misadventures of a beautiful young Girl Friday in a public relations firm.

CAST

Karen: Karen Valentine; Buddy: Charles Nelson Reilly; Eddie: Kenneth Mars; Chic: Henry Gibson.

THE ABC WEDNESDAY NIGHT MOVIE—2 hours—ABC—1968 - 1969.

Included:

The Pumpkin Eater. A woman's desperate and destructive search for love.

CAST

Jo: Anne Bancroft; Jake: Peter Finch; Conway: James Mason.

The Trouble With Angels. Background: Saint Francis Academy. The story of two mischievous students, Mary Clancy and Rachel Devery.

CAST

Mary Clancy: Hayley Mills; Rachel Devery: June Harding; Mother Superior: Rosalind Russell.

Ride The Wild Surf. Background: Oahu Island, Hawaii. The story of three young men and their attempts to participate in an international surfing competition.

CAST

Steamer Lane: Tab Hunter; Brie Matthews: Shelley Fabares; Augie Poole: Barbara Eden; Lilly: Susan Hart; Jody: Fabian Forte.

The Slender Thread. A man attempts to save the life of a would-be suicide.

CAST

Inga: Anne Bancroft; Alan: Sidney Poitier; Dr. Coburn; Telly Savalas.

THE ABC SATURDAY SUMMER MOVIE—2 hours—ABC—June 3, 1972 - August 26, 1972.

Included:

Day of the Evil Gun. The story of an ex-gunfighter and his search for his wife and children.

CAST

Lorn Worfield: Glenn Ford; Owen Forbes: Arthur Kennedy.

Fireball 500. Background: South Carolina. A story of young people involved in racing, moonshine, and murder.

CAST

Jane: Annette Funicello; Dave: Frankie Avalon.

A Boy Ten Feet Tall. Aided by a diamond smuggler, a young boy attempts to find his only living relative.

CAST

Wainwright: Edward G. Robinson; Sammy: Fergus McCelland.

ABC Stage '67. Marilyn Monroe, the subject of the presentation, "The Legend of Marilyn Monroe."

ABC STAGE '67

Anthology. Original productions, both comedic and dramatic.

Included:

The Legend of Marilyn Monroe. A documentary tracing the life of actress Marilyn Monroe from her childhood sorrows to her adult heartaches and death.

Narrator: John Houston.

The Confession. A detective attempts to discover the truth behind a girl's reported suicide.

CAST

Lt. Hammond: Arthur Kennedy; Carl: Brandon de Wilde; Bonnie: Katherine Houghton.

Olympus 7-000. Background: A New England College. The story of football coach Todd Bronson and his attempts to organize a professional team from a group of fumbling recruits.

CAST

Todd Bronson: Larry Blyden; Hermes: Donald O'Connor; Mary: Phyllis Newman; Dean Severance: Fred Clark; Featured: The New York Jets.

Music: Richard Adler.

On The Flip Side. The story of a young singer, Carlos O'Connor, and the effect on his life when he is saved from obscurity by a quartet of spirits, the Celestials.

CAST

Carlos: Rick Nelson; Angie: Joanie Sommers.

Music: Burt Bacharach.

Lyrics: Hal David.

Orchestra: Peter Matz.

ABC STAGE '67—60 minutes—ABC—September 14, 1966 - May 11, 1967.

THE ABC SUSPENSE MOVIE

Movies. Suspense features produced especially for television.

Included:

Runaway. The story centers on an engineer's desperate attempts to halt a brakeless train that is cascading down a mountain.

CAST
Holly Gibson: Ben Johnson; Ellen Staffo: Vera Miles; Nick Staffo: Ed Nelson; Carol Lerner: Darleen Carr.

The Alpha Caper. The planning and execution of a thirty million-dollar gold heist from six armored cars.

CAST
Mark Forbes: Henry Fonda; Mitch: Leonard Nimoy; Tudor: Larry Hagman; Hilda: Elena Verdugo.

Double Indemnity. The conspiracy of a woman and an insurance man to kill her husband and collect on his policy.

CAST
Walter Neff: Richard Crenna; Phyllis Dietrickson: Samantha Eggar; Barton Keyes: Lee J. Cobb; Lola Dietrickson: Kathleen Cody.

Live Again, Die Again. The story of a woman who is brought back to life after being frozen for thirty-four years.

CAST
Caroline: Donna Mills; Susie: Geraldine Page; Thomas Carmichael: Walter Pidgeon; Marcia: Vera Miles.

Linda. A suspense drama that details a woman's carefully laid plot to set her husband up as a murderer.

CAST
Linda Reston: Stella Stevens; Paul Reston: Ed Nelson; Jeff Braden: John Saxon; Anne Braden: Mary Robin-Redd.

Mousey. A biology teacher attempts to wreak vengeance on his ex-wife.

CAST
George: Kirk Douglas; Laura: Jean Seberg; David: John Vernon.

THE ABC SUSPENSE MOVIE—90 minutes—ABC—September 29, 1973 - August 31, 1974.

ABC WIDE WORLD OF ENTERTAINMENT

Variety. Various entertainment programs occupying the ABC weeknight 11:30 P.M.-1:00 A.M. (E.S.T) time period.

Announcer: Fred Foy.

Included:

VARIETY:
The Dick Cavett Show (see title "Dick Cavett"). Aired one week each month.

Jack Paar Tonight (see title "Jack Parr"). Aired one week each month.

In Concert. Rock Music. Guests performing and hosting. Aired Friday evenings.

MYSTERY-SUSPENSE:
The Screaming Skull. The story of a woman who returns from the dead to avenge her death.

CAST
David McCallum, Carrie Nye.

Nightmare Step. The story centers on a woman as she plots to rid herself of her domineering husband.

CAST
Claire: Louise Sorel; Rafe: Don Stroud; Allan: John Vernon; Carol: Sue Anne Langdon.

Frankenstein. A video adaptation of the classic story. A scientist's unleashing of disaster by creating a living being from the remains of the dead.

CAST
Dr. Frankenstein: Robert Foxworth; Elizabeth: Susan Strasberg; The Monster: Bo Svenson; Henri: Robert Gentry.

Lady Killer. A suspense drama that details a man's carefully laid plot to murder his young wife.

CAST
The man: Robert Powell; his wife: Barbara Feldon; Toni: Linda Thorson.

This Child Is Mine. The custody battle between a child's natural and foster parents.

CAST
Elizabeth Thatcher: Rosemary Prinz; Shelley Carr: Robin Strasser; Judge: Marjorie Lord.

COMEDY:
Madhouse 90. Topical sketches performed by a cast of regulars:

CAST
J.J. Barry, Michael Bell, Tom Denver, Kay Dingle, Danny Flanigan.

Comedy News. A satirization of network news broadcasting.

CAST
Robert Klein, Stephanie Edwards, Mort Sahl, Dick Gregory, Bob and Ray, Kenneth Mars, Marian Mercer, Fannie Flagg.

Honeymoon Suite. Background: California, Room 300 of the plush Honeymoon suite of the Beverly Hills Hotel. Vignettes depicting brief incidents in the lives of newlywed couples.

CAST
Maggie, the housekeeper: Rose Marie; Charlie, the bellboy: Morey Amsterdam (also played by Henry Gibson); Duncan, the hotel manager: Richard Deacon.
Music: Jack Elliott, Allyn Ferguson.

ABC WIDE WORLD OF ENTERTAINMENT—90 minutes—ABC—Premiered: January 8, 1973.

ABE BURROWS ALMANAC

Satire.

Host: Abe Burrows.
Orchestra: Milton DeLugg.

ABE BURROWS ALMANAC—30 minutes—CBS 1950.

ABOUT FACES

Game. Competing: Specially selected studio audience members. The contestants are placed opposite each other and presented with clues concerning incidents in their past lives. The player first to correctly associate his relationship with the person opposite him, is the winner and receives a merchandise prize.

At home participation segment: "Place the Face." Viewers, chosen through a post card drawing, are telephoned and asked to identify the silhouette of a famous celebrity. If able, a merchandise prize is awarded.

Host: Ben Alexander.

ABOUT FACES—30 minutes—ABC— January 4, 1960 - June 30, 1961.

ACAPULCO

Adventure. Background: Acapulco. Dissatisfied with life in the States, Patrick Malone and Gregg Miles, Korean War veterans, retreat to Southern Mexico. Adopting the life-style of a beachcomber, they begin a search for an idyllic existence. Stories relate their experiences as they en-counter and assist people in distress.

CAST

Patrick Malone	Ralph Taeger
Gregg Miles	James Colburn
Chloe, a nightclub hostess	Allison Hayes
Bobby Troup, the club owner	Himself
Mr. Carver, a retired criminal lawyer	Telly Savalas

Music: Bobby Troup.

ACAPULCO—30 minutes—NBC— February 27, 1961 - April 24, 1961.

ACCIDENTAL FAMILY

Comedy. Jerry Webster, widower and Las Vegas nightclub entertainer, is awarded custody of his eight-year-old son, Sandy, providing that the boy not live in Vegas. Jerry, who owns a farm in the San Fernando Valley, relocates and encounters a problem when he finds he is unable to evict his tenants: Susannah Kramer, a young divorcee; her daughter, Tracy; and her uncle, Ben McGrath, an ex-vaudevillian. The situation is resolved by a decision to share the house — Jerry will reside there on weekends, and Susannah will care for Sandy and not pay rent.

The story of two mischievous children and the inevitable problems that befall an "Accidental Family."

CAST

Jerry Webster	Jerry Van Dyke
Susannah Kramer	Lois Nettleton
Sandy Webster	Teddy Quinn
Tracy Kramer	Susan Benjamin
Ben McGrath	Ben Blue
Marty, Jerry's manager	Larry D. Mann

ACCIDENTAL FAMILY—30 minutes —NBC—1967-1968.

ACCUSED

Courtroom Drama. Based on actual case files.

CAST

Judge	Edgar Allan Jones, Jr.
Clerk	Jim Hodson
Bailiff	Tim Farrell
Reporter-Announcer	Violet Gilmore

ACCUSED—30 minutes—ABC—December 31, 1958 - September 30, 1959.

ACROSS THE BOARD

Game. Two competing players. Object: To complete crossword puzzles from a series of picture and word clues.

Host: Ted Brown.

ACROSS THE BOARD—30 minutes —ABC 1959.

ACROSS THE SEVEN SEAS

Travel. Films depicting the people and customs of various countries around the world.

Host/Narrator: Jack Douglas.

ACROSS THE SEVEN SEAS—30 minutes—Syndicated 1962.

ACTION IN THE AFTERNOON

Western. Background: The town of Huberie, Montana, during the 1890s. Stories depict the differences placed on values then as compared with those of the 1950s. Broadcast live from Suburban Philadelphia.

CAST
Jack Valentine, Mary Elaine Watts, Blake Ritter, Phil Sheridan, Creighton Stewart, Kris Keegan, Jack V. Harriss Forest.
Music: The Tommy Ferguson Trio.

ACTION IN THE AFTERNOON—30 minutes—CBS—February 9, 1953 - January 29, 1954.

ACTION TONIGHT

Anthology. Rebroadcasts of dramas that were originally aired via other filmed anthology programs.

Included:

The Woman On The Bus. Fleeing from two gunmen, a woman takes refuge with a family in a remote area. Suddenly, she realizes that she has jeopardized their lives. The story centers on her attempts to escape without causing any harm to her protectors.

CAST
Dorothy Green, Ross Elliott, Linda Sterling, Onslow Stevens.

My Son Is Gone. The story of a man who retreats to a world of self-pity when his son is killed in a hunting accident.

CAST
Dean Jagger, Fay Wray, Sammy Ogg.

The Enchanted. The owner of a roadhouse has acted as guardian to a girl since she was twelve years old intending to marry her when she grows up. The story revolves around the conflict that ensues when the girl, now a young woman, falls in love with a musician.

CAST
Anna Maria Alberghetti, Kurt Kasznar, John Ericson.

ACTION TONIGHT—30 minutes— NBC—July 15, 1957 - September 27, 1957.

ACT IT OUT

Game. A scene that can be described by a single word is performed on stage by a group of actors. When it is completed, a telephone call is placed to a home viewer. If the participant can state the word that explains the scene, he receives a prize.

Host: Bill Cullen.

Regulars: Patty Adair, Roc Rogers, Monte Banks, Jr., Leon Kay, Ed Casey.

ACT IT OUT—30 minutes—DuMont 1947.

ACTOR'S HOTEL

Musical Variety. Background: A small rural boarding house.

CAST
Carlo Corelli,
   the proprietor   William Edmunds
Uncle Antonio   Alan Dale

ACTOR'S HOTEL—30 minutes—ABC —September 25, 1951 - May 13, 1952.

ACTOR'S STUDIO

Anthology. Dramatizations based on stories by Hemingway, Steinbeck, and Saroyan. Varying casts and presentations.

ACTOR'S STUDIO—30 minutes—CBS 1949.

ADAM'S RIB

Comedy. Background: Los Angeles, California. The story of the relationship between Assistant District Attorney Adam Bonner and his wife, Amanda, a lawyer with the firm of Kipple, Kipple, and Smith. Episodes relate Amanda's crusade for women's rights and the clash that ensues when she as the defense attorney and Adam as the prosecuting attorney are assigned to the same case. Adapted from the movie of the same title.

CAST
Adam Bonner (nickname:
   "Pinky")   Ken Howard
Amanda Bonner (nickname:
   "Pinkie")   Blythe Danner
Kip Kipple, Amanda's
   employer   Edward Winter
Grace Peterson, Amanda's
   secretary   Dena Deitrich
Roy Mendelsohn,
   Adam's partner   Ron Rifkin
Francis Donahue,
   the District
   Attorney   Norman Bartold

Music: Perry Bodkin, Jr.

ADAM'S RIB—30 minutes—ABC— September 14, 1973 - December 28, 1973.

ADAM-12

Crime Drama. Background: Los Angeles, California. After his partner is killed in a gun battle, patrol car (Adam-12) officer Pete Malloy, bitter and disillusioned, is teamed with an over-eager rookie, Jim Reed. Malloy feels responsible and is determined to keep his young partner safe and alive. Stories involve their assignments, their close teamwork, and police law enforcement procedures.

CAST
Officer Pete Malloy
   (Badge No. 2430) Martin Milner
Officer Jim Reed
   (Badge No. 744)   Kent McCord
Sergeant MacDonald   William Boyett
Officer Ed Wells   Gary Crosby
Officer Woods   Fred Stromsoe
Music: Frank Comstock.

ADAM-12—30 minutes—NBC—Premiered: September 21, 1968.

ADAMS OF EAGLE LAKE

Crime Drama. Background: The resort

town of Eagle Lake. The story of Sheriff Sam Adams and his attempts to maintain law and order in a small, peaceful town.

CAST

Sheriff Sam Adams	Andy Griffith
Margaret Kelly, his assistant	Abby Dalton
Officer Jubal Hammond	Iggie Wolfington
Officer Jerry Troy	Nick Nolte

Music: Jerry Goldsmith.

ADAMS OF EAGLE LAKE—60 minutes—ABC—August 23, 1975 - August 30, 1975.

THE ADDAMS FAMILY

Comedy. Background: The macabre Addams's home on North Cemetery Ridge. The story of its eccentric residents, the Addams family — Gomez, a wealthy lawyer; his beautiful wife, Morticia; their children, Pugsley and Wednesday; and a variety of odd relatives. Living in their own funeral world and believing themselves normal, the family struggles to cope with the situations that foster their rejection by the outside world. Based on the characters created by Charles Addams.

CAST

Morticia Addams	Carolyn Jones
Gomez Addams	John Astin
Uncle Fester, Morticia's relative	Jackie Coogan
Lurch, the zombie-like butler	Ted Cassidy
Wednesday Addams	Lisa Loring
Pugsley Addams	Ken Weatherwax
Grandmama Addams, Gomez's mother	Blossom Rock
Ophelia Frump, Morticia's sister	Carolyn Jones
Cousin Itt, four feet tall, completely covered with blonde hair	Felix Silla
Mr. Briggs, the postman	Rolf Sedan
Esther Frump, Morticia's mother	Margaret Hamilton
Thing, the family's servant, a human right hand	Itself

Addams Family pets: Kit Kat, a lion; Cleopatra, Morticia's African Strangler (a man-eating plant); Aristotle, Pugsley's octopus; Homer, Wednesday's Black Widow Spider.

Music: Vic Mizzy.

THE ADDAMS FAMILY—30 minutes—ABC—September 18, 1964 - September 2, 1966. Syndicated.

The Addams Family. Carolyn Jones (center), Lisa Loring (left), John Astin (standing), and Ken Weatherwax (right).

Animated Version: "The Addams Family."

The Addams's two-story home is converted into a camper, and the family leaves Cemetery Ridge on a motor tour of America. Stories relate their attempts to cope with the variety of con artists they encounter.

Characters: Gomez Addams, Morticia Addams, Uncle Fester, Lurch, Wednesday Addams, Pugsley Addams, Grandmama Addams, Thing.

Voices: Josh Albee, Janet Waldo, Jackie Coogan, Ted Cassidy, Cindy Henderson, Pat Harrington, Jr., Bob Holt, John Stephenson, Don Messick, Herb Vigran, Howard Caine, Lennie Weinrib.

Music: Hoyt Curtin.

THE ADDAMS FAMILY—30 minutes—NBC—Premiered: September 8, 1973.

THE AD-LIBBERS

Game. Object: For a group of actors to ad-lib their way through story ideas that are submitted by home viewers. For each suggestion that is used, the sender receives a case of the sponsor's product.

Host: Peter Donald.

Regulars: Jack Lemmon, Charles Mendick, Patricia Hosley, Joe Silver, Cynthia Stone, Earl Hammond.

THE AD-LIBBERS—30 minutes—CBS—August 3, 1951 - September 1, 1951.
Copy of a local New York program entitled "What Happens Now?" (WOR-TV, Ch. 9, 1949).

Host: Nelson Olmstead.

CAST
Ross Martin, Carol Omart, Larry Blyden, Cecily Burke, Joyce Gordon, Thorton DeCosta.

Announcer: Nelson Olmstead.

Music: Recorded.

ADVENTURE

Educational. Set against the background of the American Museum of Natural History, the program stresses the accomplishments of outstanding men of science.

Host: Mike Wallace.

Reporter: Charles Collingwood.

ADVENTURE—30 minutes—CBS 1953.

ADVENTURE AT SCOTT ISLAND

See title: "Harbourmaster."

ADVENTURE CALLS

Adventure. Films depicting the exploits of various adventurers, e.g., mountain climbers, hunters, explorers.

Host-Narrator: Richard Simmons.

ADVENTURE CALLS—30 minutes—Syndicated 1966.

THE ADVENTURER

Adventure. The exploits of United States Government Espionage Agent

The **Adventurer.** Barry Morse (left) and Gene Barry.

Gene Bradley, a multimillionaire businessman who adopts the guise of an international film star. Produced by I.T.C.

CAST

Gene Bradley	Gene Barry
Mr. Parminter, his contact, an agent posing as his producer	Barry Morse
Diane Mash, a contact	Catherine Schell
Gavin Jones, an agent posing as Bradley's accompanist, Wildman Jones	Garrick Hagon
Also (various roles)	Stuart Damon

Music: John Barry.

THE ADVENTURER—30 minutes—Syndicated 1972.

THE ADVENTURERS

Adventure. The global exploits of newspapermen.

CAST

Newspaperman	Edward Meeks
Newspaperman	Yves Renier

THE ADVENTURERS—30 minutes—Syndicated 1966. European title: "The Globetrotters."

ADVENTURES IN PARADISE

Adventure. Background: The South Pacific. The experiences of Adam Troy, skipper of the schooner *Tiki.*

CAST

Adam Troy	Gardner McKay
Clay Baker	James Holden
Oliver Kee	Weaver Levy
Chris Parker	Guy Stockwell
Renee	Linda Lawson
Kelly	Lani Kai
Lovey	Henry Slate
Penrose	George Tobias
Sondi	Sondi Sodsai
Inspector Bouchard	Marcel Hillaire

Music: Lionel Newman.

ADVENTURES IN PARADISE—60 minutes—ABC—October 5, 1959 - April 1, 1962. Syndicated.

THE ADVENTURES OF A JUNGLE BOY

Adventure. Background: Nairobi, Africa. The exploits of Boy, the young, orphaned survivor of an airplane crash, as he and Dr. Laurence, a research scientist, battle the sinister forces of evil.

CAST

Boy	Michael Carr Hartley
Dr. Laurence	Ronald Adam

THE ADVENTURES OF A JUNGLE BOY—30 minutes—Syndicated 1957.

THE ADVENTURES OF BLACK BEAUTY

Adventure. Background: England, 1877. Based on the classic children's story, *Black Beauty* by Anna Sewell. The love, devotion, and adventures shared by a young girl, Victoria Gordon, and her horse, Black Beauty. British produced.

CAST

Victoria Gordon	Judi Bowker
Dr. James Gordon, her father	William Lucas
Kevin Gordon, her brother	Roderick Shaw
Amy Winthrop, their housekeeper	Charlotte Mitchell

Music: Dennis King.

THE ADVENTURES OF BLACK BEAUTY—30 minutes—Syndicated 1972.

THE ADVENTURES OF CAPTAIN HARTZ

Adventure. Stories relating the sea adventures of Captain Hartz. Geared for young children.

CAST

Captain Hartz (the host and story teller)	Philip Lord

Also: Tony Mercern, Jerry Garvey.

Versions:

ABC—15 minutes—1953.
Syndicated—30 minutes—1955.

THE ADVENTURES OF CHAMPION

Western. Background: America's Southwest during the 1880s. The adventures of twelve-year-old Ricky North, and his stallion, Champion, a once-mighty leader of a herd of wild horses.

CAST

Ricky North	Barry Curtis
Sandy North, his uncle	Jim Bannon

Ricky's German Shepherd: Rebel.

Music: Norman Luboff, Marilyn Keith.

THE ADVENTURES OF CHAMPION—30 minutes—CBS—1955-1956. Syndicated.

THE ADVENTURES OF
FU MANCHU

Adventure. London, England. Dr. Fu Manchu, a respected Chinese physician, is awarded custody of Lia Elthram, a young Caucasian girl. Shortly after, during the Boxer Rebellion, his wife and son are inadvertently killed by Jack Petrie, a British officer. The doctor, who is unable to properly adjust to the circumstances, becomes deranged and vows to avenge the death of his family by destroying the Petrie family and the entire white race. He raises and teaches the young girl to share his hatred.

Retreating to Tibet, he establishes *SUBTLY*, his sinister organization of evil through which he provokes tension between East and West. Stories depict his attempts to achieve vengeance; and the efforts of Scotland Yard Inspector Sir Dennis Nayland Smith to thwart his plans.

CAST

Dr. Fu Manchu	Glenn Gordon
Lia Elthram	Laurette Luez
Sir Dennis Nayland Smith	Lester Stevens
Dr. Jack Petrie	Clark Howat
Malik, the French detective	Lee Matthews
Karameneh, the slave girl	Carla Balenda
Also	John George

THE ADVENTURES OF FU MANCHU—30 minutes—Syndicated 1956.
Originally planned as a network (NBC) series in 1950, but sponsor disappointment in scripts fostered only a televised pilot film.

CAST
Fu Manchu: John Carradine; Nayland Smith: Sir Cedric Hardwicke.

THE ADVENTURES OF GULLIVER

Animated Cartoon. Era: The 18th century. Adapted from Jonathan Swift's classic novel, *Gulliver's Travels*, which told of the voyages of Lemuel Gulliver.

Believing his father is missing, Gary Gulliver sets sail to find him. Caught in a tropical storm, he and his dog, Bib, are shipwrecked on the island of Lilliput. Winning Lilliputian friendship by defeating a dreaded foe, Gary, assisted by the six-inch people, begins the search for his father. Stories relate his adventures and his attempts to overcome the foul deeds of the evil Captain Leech, who seeks to acquire Gulliver's treasure map.

THE ADVENTURES OF GULLIVER—30 minutes—ABC—September 14, 1969 - September 5, 1970. Syndicated.

THE ADVENTURES
OF HIRAM HOLLIDAY

Comedy. Correcting a story and averting a multi-million dollar libel suit, Hiram Holliday, a meek and mild-mannered newspaper proofreader, is awarded a one-year-round-the-world tour by his publisher. Stories depict his adventures as he stumbles upon and attempts to foil the dealings of unscrupulous characters.

CAST

Hiram Holliday	Wally Cox
Joel Smith, his friend and reporter sent along to cover his activities	Ainslie Pryor

THE ADVENTURES OF HIRAM HOLLIDAY—30 minutes—NBC—October 3, 1956 - February 28, 1957.

THE ADVENTURES OF JIM BOWIE

Adventure. Background: The territory from New Orleans to Texas in the era following the strife of the Louisiana Purchase. The exploits of frontiers-man-pioneer Jim Bowie, as he crusades for and defends liberty.

Starring:
Scott Forbes as Jim Bowie (the inventor of the Bowie Knife).

Music: Ken Darby.

THE ADVENTURES OF JIM BOWIE —30 minutes—ABC—September 7, 1956 - August 29, 1958. Syndicated.

THE ADVENTURES OF JONNY QUEST

Animated Cartoon. The global expeditions of Dr. Benton Quest and his young son, Jonny, as they search for the unexplained answers to scientific mysteries.

Characters' Voices

Dr. Benton Quest	John Stephenson
Jonny Quest	Tim Matthieson
Roger "Race" Bannon, their bodyguard	Mike Road
Hadji, their traveling companion	Danny Bravo
Bandit, their dog	Don Messick

Music: Hoyt Curtin.

THE ADVENTURES OF JONNY QUEST—30 minutes. ABC—September 18, 1964 - September 9, 1965; CBS—September 9, 1967 - September 5, 1970; NBC—September 11, 1971 - September 2, 1972. Syndicated.

THE ADVENTURES OF KIT CARSON

Western. Background: The Frontier during the 1880s. The exploits of Christopher "Kit" Carson, Frontiersman and Indian scout, and his Mexican sidekick, El Toro.

CAST

Kit Carson	Bill Williams
El Toro	Don Diamond

THE ADVENTURES OF KIT CARSON—30 minutes—Syndicated 1956.

THE ADVENTURES OF OZZIE AND HARRIET

Comedy. Background: 822 Sycamore Road, Hillsdale, the residence of the Nelson family — Ozzie*; his wife, Harriet; and their children, Dave and Ricky. Stories relate the events that befall an American family—the good times and the bad.

CAST

Ozzie Nelson	Himself
Harriet Hillard Nelson	Herself

*On television, Ozzie's occupation was never identified; on radio, he was, as in real life, a bandleader and Harriet, a vocalist. In the feature film HERE COME THE NELSONS, Ozzie is seen as an executive for the H. J. Bellows and Company Advertising Agency.

Ricky Nelson	Himself
David Nelson	Himself
Kris Nelson, Ricky's wife	Herself
June Nelson, Dave's wife	Herself
Mr. Thornberry, a neighbor	Don DeFore
Joe Randolph, Ozzie's friend	Lyle Talbot
Clara Randolph, his wife	Mary Jane Croft
Darby, a friend	Parley Baer
Doc Williams, a friend	Frank Cady
Wally, Dave and Ricky's friend	Skip Young
Ginger, Wally's girlfriend	Charlene Salern
Melinda, a friend	Diane Sayer
Sally, Kris's friend	Kathy Davies
Miss Edwards, Dave and Ricky's secretary (establishing a law firm after college)	Connie Harper
Dean Hopkins, the college head	Ivan Bonar

Also: Barry Livingston, Kent Smith, James Stacy.

Announcer: Verne Smith.

Music: Basil Adlam.

THE ADVENTURES OF OZZIE AND HARRIET—30 minutes—ABC—October 3, 1952 - September 3, 1966. Syndicated.

THE ADVENTURES OF POW WOW

Animated Cartoon. The story of Pow Wow, a young Indian boy, as he learns about life.

THE ADVENTURES OF POW WOW —05 minutes—NBC 1957.

THE ADVENTURES OF RIN TIN TIN

Adventure. Background: California during the 1880s. While on patrol, the 101st Cavalry discovers the survivors of an Apache Indian raid on a wagon train — a young boy, Rusty, and his dog, Rin Tin Tin. Brought back to Fort Apache, they are unofficially adopted by Lieutenant Rip Masters.

Fearing a general's forthcoming inspection will cause the boy and his dog to be banished from the fort, Masters places them in the care of Sergeant Biff O'Hara. In seeking a place to hide, they uncover and ultimately foil an Indian plot against the colonel's life. In gratitude the colonel grants Rusty the title of Corporal to ensure his and the dog's continued presence on the post in accordance with regulations.

The story of a young boy, Corporal Rusty, his dog, Rin Tin Tin, and their efforts to assist the cavalry in maintaining law and order.

CAST

Corporal Rusty	Lee Aaker
Lt. Rip Masters	James L. Brown
Sgt. Biff O'Hara	Joe Sawyer
Corporal Randy Boone	Rand Brooks
The Colonel	John Hoyt

THE ADVENTURES OF RIN TIN TIN—30 minutes—ABC—October 15, 1954 - September 1958; ABC—September 28, 1959 - September 22, 1961. CBS—30 minutes—September 29, 1962 - September 19, 1964. Syndicated.

THE ADVENTURES
OF ROBIN HOOD

Adventure. Background: England, 1191. When King Richard the Lion-Hearted sets forth for the Crusades in the Holy Land, he presents the regency of the kingdom to his trusted friend, Longchamps, and angers his brother, Prince John. While visiting Austria, Richard is seized by Prince John's cohort, Sir Leopold, and held captive in Vienna. Assuming control of Nottingham, the evil Norman, Prince John, heavily burdens the Saxons with taxes—pay or suffer cruel consequences.

Appalled by the Norman mistreatment of Saxons, Sir Robin of Locksley opposes Prince John and finds himself declared a wanted outlaw (Robin Hood). Retreating to the Gallows Oak in Sherwood Forest, he organizes a small band of free-born Englishmen (the Merry Men). Stories relate their attempts to usurp Prince John and restore the throne to its rightful king, Richard the Lion-Hearted.

CAST

Robin Hood	Richard Greene
Friar Tuck (Francis Tucker)	Alexander Gauge
Little John (John Little)	Archie Duncan
Maid Marian Fitzwater, a ward of King Arthur's court	Bernadette O'Farrell
Prince John	Donald Pleasance
The Sheriff of Nottingham	Alan Wheatley
Sir Richard the Lion-Hearted	Ian Hunter
Lady Genevieve	Gillian Sterrett
Will Scarlet (Will of Winchester)	Paul Eddington

Music: Carl Sigman.

THE ADVENTURES OF ROBIN HOOD—30 minutes—CBS—September 26, 1955 - September 22, 1958. Syndicated.

THE ADVENTURES
OF THE SEA HAWK

Adventure. Background: The Caribbean Islands. The research undertakings of the schooner *Sea Hawk*, a floating electronics lab.

CAST

Commander John Hawk	John Howard
His aide, an atomic scientist	John Lee

THE ADVENTURES OF THE SEA HAWK—30 minutes—Syndicated 1958.

THE ADVENTURES
OF THE SEASPRAY

Adventure. Background: The South Pacific. The exploits of Australian writer John Wells, skipper of the eighty-three-foot sailing schooner *Seaspray,* as he searches for story material.

CAST

John Wells	Walter Brown
Mike Wells, his son	Gary Gray
Sue Wells, his daughter	Susanne Haworth
Noah Wells, his son	Rodney Pearlman
Willyum, their Fugian crewman	Leoni Lesinawai

THE ADVENTURES OF THE SEASPRAY—30 minutes—Syndicated 1968.

THE ADVENTURES OF SIR LANCELOT

Adventure. Background: Twelfth-century England. The exploits of Sir Lancelot du Lac, a Knight of King Arthur's Round Table, and the paramour of Queen Guinevere.

CAST

Sir Lancelot du Lac	William Russell
Queen Guinevere	Jane Hylton
Merlin the Magician	Cyril Smith
King Arthur	Ronald Leigh-Hunt
	Bruce Seton
Squire Brian	Robert Scroggins

Music: Bruce Campbell, Alan Lomax.

THE ADVENTURES OF SIR LANCELOT—30 minutes—NBC—September 24, 1955 - June 29, 1957; ABC—October 1, 1957 - September 26, 1958. Syndicated.

THE ADVENTURES OF SUPERMAN

Adventure. Faraway, in the outer reaches of space, there exists a planet known as Krypton, which is inhabited by superintelligent people. Suddenly, due to radioactive chain reactions, the planet begins to experience minor earthquakes. Jor-El, a leading scientist, approaches the Council of Scientists and states his belief that their world, which is being drawn closer to the sun, is doomed. Marked as a fool,

The Adventures of Superman. George Reeves and Phyllis Coates.

Jor-El returns home and begins preparations to save his family, his wife, Lara, and their infant son, Kal-El, from the approaching disaster.

Shortly after, when completing only a miniature experimental rocket, the planet begins to explode. Because the ship cannot hold all three, Jor-El and Lara decide to save Kal-El. Wrapping him in red and blue blankets, Lara places him in the craft. Jor-El sets the controls and directs the ship to a planet he knows to be inhabited, Earth. Moments following its take-off, Krypton explodes and scatters billions of radioactively charged particles of Kryptonite, the only substance that is able to destroy Kal-El, into the universe.

Landing in Smallville, U.S.A., the space craft and its infant passenger are discovered by Eben and Martha Kent, a childless farm couple. Fearing that no one will ever believe their fantastic story, they adopt the baby as their own and name him Clark Kent.

As the years pass, each bestows evidence of his remarkable powers: "super strength, super breath and super speed; the ability to fly; X-ray, telescopic and microscopic vision. . . super memory, super hearing and super thinking."

Clark, now twenty-five years of age, is urged by his mother to use his great powers to benefit mankind. Shortly after Martha fashions an indestructible costume for him from the blankets that were originally wrapped around him, Clark moves to Metropolis, where he takes up residence at the Standish Arms Hotel, Apartment 5-H. To conceal his true identity as Superman, he adopts the guise of mild-mannered Clark Kent. To learn of disasters immediately, and to be readily available to combat crime as Superman, he acquires a position as reporter for *The Daily Planet,* a crusading newspaper.

Editor Perry White and reporters Lois Land and Jimmy Olsen quickly become his friends.

Stories relate Clark's relentless battle against crime as the mysterious figure for justice, Superman.

The 1930s saw, through the efforts of Mort Weisinger, Forrest J. Ackerman, Jerry Siegel, and Joe Shuster, the emergence of the magazine *Science Fiction,* from which the first Superman evolved. In 1938, writer Siegel and artist Shuster introduced the character in D.C. Publications' *Action Comics.* Its instant success led to the evolvement of *Superman* magazine. Worldwide distribution was obtained through its purchase by the McClure Syndicate.

The first "live" Superman was the voice of Bud Collyer, heard over the Mutual Radio Network in the 1940s. (His was also the voice in the animated TV version.) An animated theatrical version, produced by Paramount Pictures, appeared in the late 1940s. A fifteen-episode serial was produced in 1948 by Columbia Pictures and featured Kirk Alyn as "The Man of Steel." In 1950, the first feature-length film, *Atom Man vs. Superman,* was produced by Columbia Pictures; and also starred Alyn. In 1951, Lippert Pictures introduced George Reeves as Earth's mightiest hero in *Superman and the Mole Men.* Reedited, it served as the video series pilot and became the only two-part episode.

Theatrical Cast:
Clark Kent/Superman: Kirk Alyn; Perry White: Pierre Watkin; Lois Lane: Noel Neill; Jimmy Olsen: Tommy Bond.

TV CAST

Clark Kent/Superman   George Reeves
Lois Lane   Phyllis Coates

Noel Neill

Perry White	John Hamilton
Jimmy Olsen	Jack Larson
Inspector Bill Henderson	Robert Shayne
Professor J.J. Pepperwinkle, a scientist, a friend of Clark's	Phillips Tead
Sy Horton, a Mob leader	Herb Vigran

Program open:
Scene: Metropolis. Superman is seen flying above a crowd of people.
Voices: "It's a bird! It's a plane! It's Superman!"
Announcer: "Yes, it's Superman, strange visitor from another planet who came to Earth with powers and abilities far beyond those of mortal men. Superman, who can change the course of mighty rivers, bend steel in his bare hands; and who, disguised as Clark Kent, mild-mannered reporter for a great metropolitan newspaper, fights a never ending battle for truth, justice, and the American Way."

THE ADVENTURES OF SUPERMAN
—30 minutes—Syndicated 1953.

Animated Version:

The New Adventures of Superman—30 minutes—CBS—September 10, 1966 - September 2, 1967.

Format: Two cartoons relating the adventures of Clark Kent and Lois Lane, and one relating the adventures of Superboy.

Characters' Voices
Clark Kent/Superman	Bud Collyer
Lois Lane	Joan Alexander

Narrator: Jackson Beck.

Program open:
Announcer: "Superman, rocketed to Earth as an infant when the distant planet Krypton exploded, and who, disguised as Clark Kent, mild-mannered reporter for *The Daily Planet,* fights a never ending battle for truth, justice and freedom with super powers far beyond those of ordinary mortals."

Also presented as a segment of the following programs:

The Superman-Aquaman Hour—Animated Cartoon—60 minutes—CBS—September 9, 1967 - September 7, 1968.

The Batman-Superman Hour—Animated Cartoon—60 minutes—CBS—September 14, 1968 -September 6, 1969.

The Super Friends—Animated Cartoon—55 minutes—ABC—Premiered: September 8, 1973.

THE ADVENTURES OF WILLIAM TELL

Adventure. Background: Fourteenth-century Switzerland. The efforts of William Tell, the leader of the Confederation of the Forest Cantons, to liberate his country from the rule of the tyrannical Austrian Empire Army. Based on the story by Johann von Schiller.

CAST
William Tell	Conrad Phillips
Walter Tell	Richard Rogers
Hedda	Jennifer Jayne
Gessler	Willoughby Goddard
The Bear	Nigel Green

THE ADVENTURES OF WILLIAM TELL—30 minutes—Syndicated 1957.

ADVENTURE THEATRE

Anthology. British-produced suspense dramas.

Host: Paul Douglas.

Included:

Thirty Days To Die. Blaming his failure on a much-hated critic, a disappointed playwright seeks to disgrace him.

CAST
Sidney Marvel: Hubert Gregg; Harcourt Garrett: Laurence Naismith.

The Marriage Trap. Background: London, England. The grim police hunt for a modern-day Jack the Ripper.

CAST
Inspector Mathew: Maurice Denham; Dr. Ingram: Cameron Hull; Della: Jo Huntley-Wright.

The Missing Passenger. A man, dating two sisters, attempts to jilt both of them.

CAST
Patrick Barr.

ADVENTURE THEATRE—60 minutes—NBC—June 16, 1956 - September 1956.

THE AFRICAN PATROL

Adventure. Background: Kenya, East Africa. The cases of the African Police Patrol, a unit of specially trained men organized to combat crime.

Starring:
John Bently as Inspector Derek, chief of the African Patrol.

THE AFRICAN PATROL—30 minutes—Syndicated 1957.

THE AFTERNOON FILM FESTIVAL

Movies. Theatrical features.

Host: Don Gordon.

Included:

Holiday Champ. A drama about the lives of several people at an English resort.

CAST
Flora Robson, Dennis Price, Jack Warner, Hazel Court.

Turn the Key Softly. A penetrating drama revealing the struggles of three women as they face their first day of freedom after serving lengthy prison sentences.

CAST
Yvonne Mitchell, Joan Collins, Kathleen Harris.

The Girl in the Painting. The story of an Austrian refugee and his search for his daughter, who is suffering from amnesia.

CAST
Mai Zetterling, Herbert Lom, Guy Rolfe.

THE AFTERNOON FILM FESTIVAL 90 minutes—ABC 1956.

THE AGE OF KINGS

History. Dramatizations based on eighty-six years of British history, beginning with the reign of Richard II. Based on the plays of William Shakespeare and performed by the British Broadcasting Repertory Company.

CAST

King Richard II	David Williams
Harry Percy (Hotshot)	Sean Connery
John of Gaunt	Edgar Wreford
Henry Bolingbroke	Thomas Fleming
Thomas Mowbray	Noel Johnson
Edmund Langley	Geoffrey Bayldon
The Duke of Aumerle	John Greenwood
Northumberland	George A. Cooper

THE AGE OF KINGS—Two hours—Syndicated 1961.

AIR POWER

Documentary. The history of aviation from its beginnings at Kitty Hawk to its progress with missiles in the 1950s.

Host-Narrator: Walter Cronkite.

AIR POWER—30 minutes—CBS 1958.

AIR TIME

Musical Variety. Presented by the U.S. Air Force Reserve.

Hosts: Vaughn Monroe, Merv Griffin.

Music: The Bobby Hackett Jazz Group; The Elliott Alexander Orchestra.

AIR TIME—30 minutes—ABC—1956-1957.

THE AL CAPP SHOW

Discussion. Discussions on various topical issues with guests whose opinions inevitably differ from those of the host.

Host: Al Capp.

THE AL CAPP SHOW—90 minutes—Syndicated 1971.

THE ALAN BURKE SHOW

Discussion. Unusually strong conversations between the host, his guests, and members of the studio audience on topics infrequently discussed on television at that time (1966); e.g. sex-change operations, abortion, civil rights, underground movies.

Host: Alan Burke.

THE ALAN BURKE SHOW—2 hours—Syndicated 1966. Originally produced in New York as a ninety-minute program for Metromedia-owned stations. Daily thirty-minute syndicated title: "Dear Alan."

ALAN YOUNG

Listed: The television programs of comedian Alan Young.

The Alan Young Show—Comedy—30 minutes—CBS—April 6, 1950 - June 1953.

Host: Alan Young.

Regulars: Polly Bergen, Fran Warren, Joseph Kearns, Ben Wright, Connie Haines, David Alpert, Mabel Paige, Phillips Tead, Dawn Adams, Russell Gaige, The Rodney Bell Dancers (Jane

The Alan Young Show. Center: Alan Young. Left: Jan Hollar, Tom Mahoney (dancers). Right: Jerry Antes, Jean Mahoney (dancers).

Hollar, Jerry Antes, Tom Mahoney, Jean Mahoney).

Orchestra: Lud Gluskin.

Format: Two to three vignettes depicting the misadventures of Alan Young, a well-meaning, good-natured man. Segments are alternated with songs by popular vocalists.

The Alan Young Show—Musical Variety—60 minutes—Associated Redifussion Television from London (British produced and broadcast)—1958.

Host: Alan Young.

Regulars: Ellen Drew, Laurie Payne, Nion Yonson, Daniele Roma, The Young Lovelies, The Brisas de Mexico.

Orchestra: Billy Ternet.

Format: Various comedy sketches, musical numbers, and songs.

Mr. Ed—Comedy—30 minutes—CBS—1961 - 1966. (See title).

ALARM

Drama. Background: California. The work of Paramedics, the men of the Los Angeles County Fire Department.

CAST
The Captain	Richard Arlen
Fireman	J. Pat O'Malley

ALARM—30 minutes—Syndicated 1954.

THE ALASKANS

Adventure. Background: Skagway, Alaska, 1898. Infatuated with Rocky Shaw, a beautiful saloon entertainer, a prospector reveals the location of a sled holding gold to her. Soon after, he is killed in a desperate attempt to retrieve it himself. When Miss Shaw learns of an expedition to the area, she persuades two prospectors, Reno McKee, a rugged cowpoke, and his fast-talking partner, Silky Harris, to let her join them. Her attempts to uncover the gold fail as an avalanche buries it beneath tons of snow. The three continue their journey and establish an operational base in Eagle City.

Stories relate the adventures of Rocky Shaw, Silky Harris, and Reno McKee as they search for gold in the beautiful but dangerous Ice Palace of the Northland.

CAST
Rocky Shaw	Dorothy Provine
Silky Harris	Roger Moore

Reno McKee   Jeff York
Nifty Cronin, a saloon
     owner and swindler   Ray Danton
Music: Paul Sawtell.

THE ALASKANS—60 minutes—
ABC—October 4, 1959 - September
25, 1960. Syndicated.

ALCOA PREMIERE

Anthology. Dramatic presentations.

Host: Fred Astaire.

Included:

Blues for a Hanging. When her
boyfriend insists that he killed a man
while he was drunk, a nightclub singer
begins an investigation to discover the
truth.

CAST
Connie Rankin: Janis Paige; Ted
Miller: Fred Astaire; Theresa Summer:
Lurene Tuttle.

The Town Budget. After the sheriff of
a small town resigns, two fleeing
criminals make the town their hide-
out. The story centers on the towns-
people and their desperate attempts to
acquire help.

CAST
Earl Sherwood: James Whitmore;
Fran Sherwood: Marilyn Erskine;
Jona: Timothy Carey.

The Boy Who Wasn't Wanted. A
young boy attempts to regain the
affections of his bickering parents.

CAST
Father: Dana Andrews; Mother:
Marilyn Erskine; Son: Billy Mumy.

The Girl with a Glow. When a movie
director sees a beautiful girl leave the
Hollywood library, he realizes that she
would be the perfect girl for the lead
in his next picture. After his attempts
to find her fail, he haunts the library
in hopes she'll return.

CAST
Peter Bronson: John Forsythe; June
Baker: Patricia Crowley.

ALCOA PREMIERE—60 minutes—
ABC—October 11, 1961 - September
12, 1963.

ALCOA PRESENTS

See title: "One Step Beyond."

ALCOA THEATRE

Anthology. Dramatic presentations.
Music: Frank DeVol.

Included:

The Broken Year. A story of bitter-
ness and guilt that threaten a marriage
after the wife blames herself for the
accident that crippled her husband.

CAST
Eric Green: Kier Dullea; Hilary Green:
Shirley Knight; Mr. Green: Leif
Erickson; Mrs. Green: Katharine Bard.

The Incorrigibles. The story of an
elder con artist and his attempts to
discourage a younger deliquent who
wants to follow in his footsteps.

CAST
Harvey Otis: Paul Douglas; Steve:
Danny Richards.

Show Wagon. A man attempts to

prove himself innocent of a murder charge.

CAST
Steve Emerson: Luke Anthony; Phoebe Malloy: Connie Hines; Pop: Jack Albertson.

Eddie. The story of a hoodlum and his desperate struggle to raise one thousand dollars or face death at the hands of gangsters.

Starring: Mickey Rooney as Eddie.

ALCOA THEATRE—60 minutes—NBC—October 14, 1955 - September 30, 1957; 30 minutes—NBC—October 7, 1957 - September 1960.

THE ALDRICH FAMILY

Comedy. Background: The town of Centerville. The trials and tribulations of the Aldrich family: Sam, the district attorney; his wife, Alice; and their teenage children, Mary and Henry. Stories depict the problems that befall Henry, a young, inexperienced and trouble-prone high-school student who one day hopes to become a lawyer. Based on the characters created by Clifford Goldsmith.

CAST
Henry Aldrich	Bob Casey (1949)
	Richard Tyler (1950)
	Henry Gerard (1951)
	Bobby Ellis (1952-1953)
Sam Aldrich	House Jameson
Alice Aldrich	Lois Wilson
	Barbara Robbins
	Jean Muir
Mary Aldrich	June Dayton
	Mary Malone
Homer Brown,	
Henry's friend	Jackie Kelk
	Robert Barry

Also: Peter Griffith, Nancy Carroll.

THE ALDRICH FAMILY—30 minutes—NBC—October 2, 1949 - May 29, 1953.

ALFRED HITCHCOCK PRESENTS
THE ALFRED HITCHCOCK HOUR

Anthology. Mystery and suspense presentations.

Host: Alfred Hitchcock.

Music: Frederick Herbert; Stanley Wilson; Lyn Murray.

Included:

Voodoo. Background: An oil-mining camp in the Amazon. A wife, who is in love with her husband's partner, pretends to be stricken with fever. Unaware of deceit and believing his wife's sanity is threatened, the husband arranges for a native servant to take her down river to a psychiatrist. Uncomprehending, he takes her to his people, "the best head shrinkers in the world." "I do what you tell," he says and returns her shrunken head to his master.

CAST
Marie Jensen: Cara Williams; Jeff Jensen: Nehemiah Persoff; Mike: Mark Richman.

DeMortius (Latin: About the Dead). Two friends visit the home of an aging college professor. When they believe that the professor found out about his unfaithful wife's activities and killed her, they devise an air-tight alibi for him. Taking advantage of the situation, the professor kills his beautiful young wife and buries her beneath the cellar floor. The closing narration states only one fact: that his act was discovered when he remarried.

CAST

Irene Rankin: Cara Williams; Professor Rankin: Robert Emhardt; Wally Long: Henry Jones.

Arthur. Arthur Williams, the owner of a chicken farm, is embittered after his fiancée jilts him to marry another. When a year later, she leaves her husband and returns to Arthur, he kills her. Although the police are suspicious, they are unable to find a body, prove a murder, or connect Arthur in any way.

Mr. Hitchcock, in the closing narrative, states that Arthur, who made his own chicken feed through the use of a large grinding machine, prepared a special mixture and added one extra ingredient — Helen. One of the very few episodes in which the criminal is undiscovered and unpunished.

CAST

Arthur Williams: Laurence Harvey; Helen: Hazel Court; Sgt. Farrell: Patrick Macnee.

Man from the South. Background: The Golden Nugget Gambling Palace in Las Vegas. The plot centers on a bet over the ability of a ninety-nine-cent cigarette lighter to light ten straight times. If it does, the challenger will lose his car; if it does not, the owner will forfeit the pinky on his left hand. Tension mounts as the hand is tied to a table, the challenger holds an ax, and the lighter is lit seven times.

The bet is cancelled, the hand untied when the challenger's wife enters and announces her husband has nothing to bet with as she has managed to win it all. As she picks up the car keys from the table the viewer sees the evidence of her having beaten him —two fingers remaining upon one hand, the thumb and the pinky.

CAST

The man with the lighter: Steve McQueen; the challenger: Peter Lorre.

ALFRED HITCHCOCK PRESENTS —30 minutes. CBS—October 2, 1955 - September 1960; NBC—September 13, 1960 - June 1962. Syndicated. THE ALFRED HITCHCOCK HOUR—60 minutes—NBC—September 1962 - May 10, 1965. Syndicated.

ALIAS SMITH AND JONES

Western. Background: Kansas during the 1890s. After infamous bankrobbers Jed Kid Curry and Hannibal Heyes, the leaders of the Devil Hole gang, find themselves incapable of cracking the newly developed safes, they decide to "go straight." They seek amnesty from the Governor and hope to have their slates wiped clean.

The Governor's decision, which is related by their friend Sheriff Lom Trevors, is a granting of provisional amnesty. It will become a complete pardon within twelve months if they end their life of crime and prove themselves worthy. However, in the meantime, the decision remains a secret among them, the Sheriff, and the Governor.

They leave their gang and adopt the aliases Thaddeus Jones (Curry) and Joshua Smith (Heyes). Stories center on two of the West's most wanted men and their attempts to stray from the troublesome situations that could threaten the granting of their amnesty.

CAST

Jed Kid Curry/	
Thaddeus Jones	Ben Murphy
Hannibal Heyes/	
Joshua Smith	Peter Duel
	Roger Davis

Sheriff Lom Trevors	James Drury
	Mike Road
Harry Briscoe, a Batterman detective	J.D. Cannon

Acquaintances of Heyes and Curry:

Big Mac McCreedy, a wealthy rancher	Burl Ives
Clementine Hale	Sally Field
Silky O'Sullivan	Walter Brennan
Blackjack Jenny, a card shark	Ann Sothern
Georgette Sinclair	Michele Lee
Winford Fletcher, a real estate broker	Rudy Vallee

The Devil Hole Gang:

Wheat	Earl Holliman
Lobo	Read Morgan
Kyle	Dennis Fimple

Music: Billy Goldenberg.

ALIAS SMITH AND JONES—60 minutes—ABC—January 21, 1971 - January 13, 1973.

THE ALICE PEARCE SHOW

Variety.

Hostess: Alice Pearce.

Pianist: Mark Lawrence.

THE ALICE PEARCE SHOW—15 minutes—ABC—January 28, 1949 - April 4, 1949.

ALL ABOUT FACES

Game. Two competing celebrity teams, composed of husband and wife or boy and girlfriend. Each team receives fifty dollars betting money. A previously filmed sequence involving people confronted with unexpected situations is played and stopped prior to its conclusion. After the teams wager any amount of their accumulated cash, they have to predict its outcome. The tape is played again and answers are revealed. Correct predictions add the bet amount to the player's score. A wrong answer deducts it. Winning teams, the highest cash scorers, donate their earnings to charity.

Host: Richard Hayes.

Candid film sequence cast: Glenna Jones, Ken Deas, Andy Kunkel.

Music: John Michael Hill.

ALL ABOUT FACES—30 minutes—Syndicated 1971.

ALL ABOUT MUSIC

Musical Variety. A three-week interim series.

Host: Milton Cross.

Week One: Calypso.
Guests: Johnny Banacuda, Helen Ferguson, Pearl Gonzalez, The Duke of Iron, the Trini Dancers, The Versatones.

Music: The King Carib Stud Band.

Week Two: American Folk.
Guests: Susan Reed, Jack Dabodoub, Buzz Miller, Rudy Tronto, Gomez Delappe, Bruce King, Bill Bradley, The Nelle Fisher Dancers.
Orchestra: Al Rickey.

Week Three: Jazz.
Guests: Lawrence Winters, The Nelle Fisher Dancers.

Orchestra: Paul Whiteman.

ALL ABOUT MUSIC—30 minutes—ABC—April 7, 1957 - April 21, 1957.

ALLEN LUDDEN'S GALLERY

Variety.

Host: Allen Ludden.

ALLEN LUDDEN'S GALLERY—90 minutes—Syndicated 1969.

ALL IN FUN

Variety. A two-week interim series.

First Week:

Host: Charles Applewhite.

Guests: The Fontaine Sisters, The Step Brothers, Lou Marks, Al Fisher, Jim Jeffries.

Second Week:

Host: George DeWitt.

Guests: Johnny Mercer, Bill Hayes, Lou Fisher, Al Marks, The Goofers.

ALL IN FUN—30 minutes—CBS—April 2, 1955 - April 9, 1955.

ALL IN THE FAMILY

Comedy. Background: 704 Houser Street, Queens, New York, the residence of the Bunkers, a White Middle-Class Anglo-Saxon American family: Archie, a dock foreman for the Prendergast Tool and Dye Company, a prejudiced, uncouth, loud-mouthed, hardhat conservative who is unable to accept the aspects of a progressing world; Edith, his dim-witted, sensitive, and totally honest wife; Gloria, their married daughter, beautiful and completely independent; and Mike Stivic, Gloria's husband, an unemployed, idealistic college student, representative of the radical, outspoken youth of today. (In later episodes, after graduation, Mike acquires employment as a college instructor, and he and Gloria move into their own home, next door to the Bunkers.)

Through the events that befall and test the reactions of the Bunker and Stivic families, American television comedy was led out of infancy and into maturity. The series, which reveals the little traces of Archie Bunker that are within everyone, allows the viewer to laugh at his own flaws as it presents life as it is—rampant with bigotry and racism.

CAST

Archie Bunker	Carroll O'Connor
Edith Bunker ("Dingbat")	Jean Stapleton
Gloria Stivic	Sally Struthers
Mike Stivic ("Meathead")	Rob Reiner
Lionel Jefferson, their neighbor	Mike Evans
George Jefferson, Lionel's father	Sherman Hemsley
Louise Jefferson, Lionel's mother	Isabel Sanford
Henry Jefferson, Lionel's uncle	Mel Stewart
Irene Lorenzo, Archie's neighbor, his co-worker	Betty Garrett
Frank Lorenzo, Irene's husband	Vincent Gardenia
Bert Munson, Archie's friend, a cab-driver	Billy Halop
Tommy Kelsey, Archie's friend, the owner of Kelsey's Bar	Brendon Dillon
Justin Quigley, a friend of the Bunkers	Bert Mustin
Jo Nelson, Justin's girlfriend	Ruth McDevitt

Stretch Cunningham, Archie's
co-worker   James Cromwell

Music: Roger Kellaway.

ALL IN THE FAMILY—30 minutes—
CBS—Premiered: January 12, 1971.
Based on the British series "Till Death
Us Do Part." Starring Warren Mitchell,
Pandy Nichols, Anthony Booth, and
Una Stubbs in the story of a son-in-
law who lives in his father-in-law's
home.

ALL MY CHILDREN

Serial. Background: The community
of Pine Valley. The dramatic story of
the Tyler family. Episodes depict the
incidents that befall and affect individual members.

CAST

Phoebe Tyler	Ruth Warrick
Amy Tyler	Rosemary Prinz
Ann Tyler	Diana de Vegh
	Judith Barcroft
Paul Martin	Ken Rabat
	Bill Mooney
Mary Kennicott	Susan Blanchard
Kate Martin	Kay Campbell
	Christine Thomas
Ruth Brent	Mary Fickett
Jeff Martin	Christopher Wines
	Charles Frank
Dr. Charles Tyler	Hugh Franklin
Tara Martin	Karen Gorney
	Stephanie Braxton
Lois Sloane	Hilda Haynes
Mona Kane	Frances Heflin
Nick Davis	Larry Keith
Erica Kane	Susan Lucci
Lincoln Tyler	Paul DuMont
	Nick Pryor
Dr. Joseph Martin	Ray MacDonnell
Sydney Scott	Deborah Soloman
Charles Tyler II	Jack Stauffer
	Chris Hubbell

Kitty Shea	Francesca James
Jason Maxwell	Tom Rosqui
Edie Hoffman	Marilyn Chris
Bill Hoffman	Michael Shannon
Margo Flax	Eileen Letchworth
Clyde Wheeler	Kevin Conway
Philip Brent	Richard Hatch
	Nicholas Benedict
Dr. Hoffman	Peter Simon
Franklin Grant	John Danelle
Tad Gardiner	Matthew Anton
Ted Brent	Mark Dawson
Bobby Martin	Mike Bersell
Lois Sloane	Hilda Hayne

Music: Aeolus Productions.

ALL MY CHILDREN—30 minutes—
ABC—Premiered: January 5, 1970.

THE ALL—STAR REVUE
THE FOUR—STAR REVUE

Variety. Varying program formats
styled to the talents of its guest hosts.

Included:

The Olsen and Johnson Show.

Hosts: Ole Olsen, Chick Johnson.

Guests: June Johnson, J. C. Olsen,
John Melina, Marty May, The
Dunhills.

Orchestra: Milton DeLugg.

The Jimmy Durante Show.

Host: Jimmy Durante.

Guests: Jules Buffano, Bob Crozier,
Eddie Jackson, Phil Leeds, Helen
Traibel, Candy Candito.

Orchestra: Roy Bargy; Jack Roth.

The Danny Thomas Show.

Host: Danny Thomas.

Guests: Kay Starr, Bunny Leubell, The Hurricaines.

Orchestra: Lou Bring.

The Victor Borge Show.

Host: Victor Borge.

Guests: Lauritz Melchior, Verna Zorina, June Hutton, Phil Leeds

The Martha Raye Show.

Hostess: Martha Raye.

Guest: Robert Cummings.

Orchestra: George Bassman.

The George Jessel Show.

Host: George Jessel.

Guests: Ray McDonald, Tony Martin, Dorothy Kirsten, The Skylarks.

The Ritz Brothers Show.

Hosts: The Ritz Brothers—Al, Jimmy, Harry.

Guests: Mimi Benzell, John Ireland, Bill Skipper.

Orchestra: Lou Bring.

The Ed Wynn Show.

Host: Ed Wynn.

Guests: Dinah Shore, Pat O'Brien, Ben Wrigley, Lucille Ball.

Also Hosting: Ezio Pinza, Jack Carson, Jane Froman, Herb Shriner, Phil Foster, Tallullah Bankhead.

Additional Orchestrations: Allan Roth.

THE FOUR–STAR REVUE (Original Title)—60 minutes—NBC—November 1, 1950 - May 16, 1951.

THE ALL–STAR REVUE (Retitled) —60 minutes—NBC—September 8, 1951 - April 18, 1953.

THE ALL–STAR SUMMER REVUE

Musical Variety. Summer replacement for "The All-Star Revue."

Hosts: Carl Ballantine, Oliver Wakefield.

Regulars: Georgia Gibbs, The Paul Steffin Dancers, The Acromaniacs.

Orchestra: Dean Elliot.

THE ALL STAR SUMMER REVUE —60 minutes—NBC—June 28, 1952 - September 1952.

THE AL PEARCE SHOW

Variety.

Host: Al Pearce

THE AL PEARCE SHOW—30 minutes—CBS—July 10, 1952 - September 1952.

ALUMNI FUN

Game. Two competing teams, each composed of three celebrity college alumni members. The host states a question. The player first to identify himself (through a buzzer signal) receives a chance to answer. If the response is correct, money is awarded. The winners, highest cash scorers, donate their earnings to their college alumni.

Host: Peter Lind Hayes.

ALUMNI FUN—30 minutes—CBS— 1964 - 1965.

THE ALVIN SHOW

Animated Cartoon. The misadventures of songwriter Dave Seville, the manager of the Chipmonks (Alvin, Theodore, and Simon), a group of singing animals. Plots revolve around his reluctant involvement in their unpredictable antics.

Additional segments:
"The Adventures of Clyde Crashcup." The attempts of world famous inventor Clyde Crashcup to perfect his discoveries, e.g., the bed, the safety match, the wheel.

"Sinbad Jr." The adventures of sailor Sinbad Jr., and his parrot, Salty.

Characters' Voices
Dave Seville	Ross Bagdasarian
The Chipmonks	Ross Bagdasarian
Clyde Crashcup	Shepard Menken
Sinbad	Tim Matthieson
Salty	Mel Blanc

Additional voices: June Foray, Lee Patrick, Bill Lee, William Sanford, Res Dennis.

Music: Ross Bagdasarian.

THE ALVIN SHOW—30 minutes—CBS—October 14, 1961 - September 12, 1962. Syndicated.

A.M. AMERICA

News-Information. Broadcast from 7:00 a.m. - 9:00 a.m., E.S.T.

East Coast Hosts: Bill Beutel, Stephanie Edwards.

West Coast Hosts: Ralph Story, Melanie Noble.

Guest Hostess: Jessica Walter, Barbara Feldon, Lynn Redgrave, Rene Carpenter, Candice Bergen, Barbara Howar.

Newscaster: Peter Jennings.

Regulars: Roger Caras, Dr. Sonya Friedman, Dr. Tim Johnson.

Music: Recorded.

A.M. AMERICA—2 hours—ABC—January 6, 1975 - October 31, 1975. Revised as "Good Morning, America." See title.

THE AMATEUR HOUR

See title: "Ted Mack."

THE AMATEUR'S GUIDE TO LOVE

Game. A taped, prearranged romantic situation, which involves unsuspecting individuals, is played and stopped prior to its conclusion. Two of the subjects involved in the situation appear opposite a panel of three guest celebrities, "The Guidebook Experts." The celebrities first advise as to what the outcome of the situation should be, then predict the subjects' answers—whether or not they actively involved themselves in it. The tape is played to reveal the answers. If the celebrities have predicted correctly, the subject receives two hundred dollars; if not, he receives one hundred dollars.

Host: Gene Rayburn.

Announcer: Kenny Williams.

Appearing in candid sequences: Barbara Crosby; guests.

Music: Recorded.

THE AMATEUR'S GUIDE TO LOVE—30 minutes—CBS—March 27, 1972 - June 23, 1972.

THE AMAZING CHAN
AND THE CHAN CLAN

Animated Cartoon. The investigations

of Charlie Chan, a Chinese detective who specializes in solving baffling crimes. Plots concern the intervention of his ten children and their meaningful, but disasterous efforts to assist him. A Hanna-Barbera production. Based on the famous movie character.

Characters' Voices

Charlie Chan	Keye Luke
Henry Chan	Bob Ito
Stanley Chan	Stephen Wong
	Lennie Weinrib
Suzie Chan	Virginia Ann Lee
	Cherylene Lee
Alan Chan	Brian Tochi
Anne Chan	Leslie Kumamota
	Jodie Foster
Tom Chan	Michael Takamoto
	John Gunn
Flip Chan	Jay Jay Jue
	Gene Andrusco
Nancy Chan	Debbie Jue
	Beverly Kushida
Mimi Chan	Leslie Kawai
	Cherylene Lee
Scooter Chan	Robin Toma
	Michael Morgan
Chu Chu, the clan dog	Don Messick

Additional voices: Lisa Gerritsen, Hazel Shermit, Janet Waldo, Len Wood.

Music: Hoyt Curtin.

THE AMAZING CHAN AND THE CHAN CLAN—30 minutes—CBS—September 9, 1972 - September 22, 1974.

THE AMAZING MR. MALONE

Crime Drama. Background: Chicago. The investigations of John J. Malone, a light-hearted criminal attorney.

Starring:
Lee Tracy as John J. Malone.

THE AMAZING MR. MALONE—30 minutes—ABC—August 27, 1951 - September 24, 1952.

THE AMAZING THREE

Animated Cartoon. Background: Twenty-first century Earth. The exploits of three celestial beings, creatures who have adopted the identities of a horse, a dog, and a duck to protect themselves, and Earthling Kenny Carter, as they battle the sinister forces of evil.

THE AMAZING THREE—30 minutes —Syndicated 1967.

THE AMAZING WORLD OF KRESKIN

Variety. Feats of mind reading, E.S.P., and sleight of hand.

Starring: Kreskin.

Host-Announcer: Bill Luxton.

Music: Recorded.

THE AMAZING WORLD OF KRESKIN—30 minutes—Syndicated 1972.

AMERICA

History. A thirteen-episode "personal history" of the United States. The country is explored through historical paintings and commentary from its founding to the twentieth century. Filmed by the B.B.C.

Host-Narrator: Alistair Cooke.

Music: Charles Chilton.

Episodes:
1. "The New Found Land." America's discovery.

2. "Home from Home." The seventeenth and eighteenth centuries.
3. "Making a Revolution." The American Revolution.
4. "Inventing a Nation." The American Constitution.
5. "Gone West." The Pioneers and the beginning of Western settlement.
6. "A Fireball in the Night." The Civil War.
7. "Domesticating a Wilderness." The taming of the West.
8. "Money on the Land." The development of American technology.
9. "The Huddled Masses." The influx of immigration.
10. "The Twenties." The songs, the sports, and the events of the twenties.
11. "The Arsenal." America's development and emergence as a military giant.
12. "Dixieland Jazz." A profile of the New England States.
13. "America Today." An analysis of American life.

AMERICA—60 minutes—NBC—November 14, 1972 - May 15, 1973. Syndicated.

AMERICA AFTER DARK

See title: "The Tonight Show."

AMERICAN ADVENTURE

Adventure. Films relating the experiences of various adventurers, e.g., mountain climbers, hunters, racers, etc.

Narrator: Gary Merrill.

Music: James Fagas.

AMERICAN ADVENTURE—30 minutes—Syndicated 1972.

AMERICAN BANDSTAND

Variety. Music and entertainment geared to teenagers.

Host: Dick Clark.

Appearing: Annette Funicello, Will Jorden, Stonewall Jackson, The Falcons, Kathy Linden, Ray Vernon, Frankie Ford, Romance Wilson, Gordon MacRae, Fats Domino, The Four Aces, Dave Appel, The Fontaine Sisters, Beverly Ross, The Chiffons, Jerry Vale, The Vibrations, Brenda Lee, Roy Hamilton, The Earls, The Fireballs, Dick and Dee Dee, Donna Loren, Johnny Mathis, Connie Stevens, Connie Francis, Paul Peterson, Shelley Fabares, The Hondells, Mel Carter, The Ventures, Paul Revere and the Raiders, Bobby Vinton, Paul Anka, The Hardy Boys, Frankie Avalon, Johnny Tilotson, Jerry Reed, Buffy Sainte-Marie, The Osmond Brothers, Davey Jones.

Music: Recorded.

Featured: Performances by top music personalities; dancing contests, undiscovered professional talent.

Featured Segment: "Rate-A-Record." Selected studio audience members are asked to rate a record from a thirty-five to a ninety-eight.

AMERICAN BANDSTAND—60 minutes—ABC—Premiered: October 7, 1957. Originally boradcast as a local program in Philadelphia from 1952 to 1957 before becoming a network attraction.

AMERICAN LIFESTYLE

Documentary. The story of America's past, present, and future. Emphasis is placed on the men and women who had the greatest impact on the development of the country.

Host-Narrator: E.G. Marshall.

Music: Michael Shapiro.

AMERICAN LIFESTYLE—30 minutes—Syndicated 1972.

AMERICAN MUSICAL THEATRE

Music. Guests, discussions, and demonstrations on the various types of American music.

Host: Earl Wrightson.

Vocalists: Christine Spencer, Ralph Curtis.

Music: The CBS Orchestra, conducted by Alfredo Antonini.

AMERICAN MUSICAL THEATRE—30 minutes—CBS—1961-1965.

AMERICANS

Drama. Background: Virginia during the Civil War. The wartime activities of two brothers, both farmers and in conflict against each other: Ben Canfield, a Union loyalist, and Jeff Canfield, a Confederate loyalist.

CAST
Ben Canfield	Darryl Hickman
Jeff Canfield	Dick Davidson
Pa Canfield	John McIntire

AMERICANS—60 minutes—NBC—January 23, 1961 - September 1961.

THE AMERICAN SPORTSMAN

Sport. Films depicting the experiences of famous American hunters and/or fishermen. Microphones, worn by hunters, pick up their whispers as they close in for the kill.

Host: Curt Gowdy.

Assisting: Joe Foss, Joe Brooks.

THE AMERICAN SPORTSMAN—60 minutes—ABC—Premiered: January 31, 1965.

THE AMERICAN WEST

Travel. Tours of America's present-day frontier.

Host-Narrator: Jack Smith.

THE AMERICAN WEST—30 minutes—Syndicated 1966.

AMERICA'S TOWN HALL MEETING

Interview. Background: A simulated Town Hall.

Hosts: George V. Denny; John Daly.

Guests: Political figures.

AMERICA'S TOWN HALL MEETING—30 minutes—ABC—October 5, 1948 - July 6, 1952.

THE AMES BROTHERS SHOW

Musical Variety. The format follows that of a fan magazine wherein highlights of the Ames Brothers career is injected into each program.

Hosts: The Ames Brothers: Ed, Vic, Joe, and Gene.

Orchestra: Harry Geller.

THE AMES BROTHERS SHOW—15 minutes—Syndicated 1955.

THE AMOS AND ANDY SHOW

Comedy. Background: New York City. The story of three men: Andrew Halt Brown, the naive and dim-witted president of The Fresh Air Taxi Cab Company of America, Amos Jones, his level-headed partner, the cab driver, and George "Kingfish" Stevens, an inept con artist, the head of "The Mystic Knights of the Sea" fraternity.

Stories relate Andy's romantic involvements and efforts to stray from the paths of matrimony; and, finding Andy the perfect sucker, George's endless attempts to acquire money from the cab company, despite Amos's warnings and efforts to protect his investment and keep the company solvent. Adapted from the radio program created by Freeman Gosden and Charles Correll.

CAST

Andrew Halt Brown	Spencer Williams, Jr.
George "Kingfish" Stevens	Tim Moore
Amos Jones	Alvin Childress
Sapphire Stevens, George's wife	Ernestine Wade
Mama, Sapphire's mother	Amanda Randolph
Lightnin', the cab company janitor	Horace Stewart
Algonquin J. Calhoune, the inept lawyer	Johnny Lee
Ruby Jones, Amos's wife	Jane Adams
Arabella Jones, Amos and Ruby's daughter	Patty Marie Ellis
Madame Queen, Andy's former romantic interest	Lillian Randolph
The Old Maid Gribble Sisters (3)	Monnette Moore Zelda Cleaver Willa P. Curtis
Miss Genevieve Blue, the cab company secretary	Madaline Lee

Orchestra and Chorus: Jeff Alexander

THE AMOS AND ANDY SHOW—30 minutes—CBS—June 28, 1951 - June 11, 1953. Withdrawn from syndication in 1966. The first television series to feature an all-Negro cast.

AMOS BURKE, SECRET AGENT

Mystery. The global investigations of Amos Burke, a former millionaire police captain turned United States government undercover agent. Stories depict his attempts to infiltrate crime organizations and expose high-ranking officials. A spin-off from "Burke's Law."

CAST

Amos Burke	Gene Barry
The Man, his superior	Carl Benton Reid

Music: Herschel Burke Gilbert.

AMOS BURKE, SECRET AGENT— 60 minutes—ABC—September 15, 1965 - January 12, 1966. Syndicated.

AMY PRENTISS

See title: "NBC Sunday Mystery Movie," *Amy Prentiss* segment.

AN AMERICAN FAMILY

Documentary. A cinema-verité portrait of the Louds: husband, William; his wife, Patricia; and their children, Kevin, Lance, Michele, Delilah, and Grant—an American family residing at 35 Wood Dale Lane, Santa Barbara, California. Of the three hundred hours of film used to record their daily lives, only twelve aired, which were presented in segments over a three-month period.

AN AMERICAN FAMILY—PBS—60 minutes—January 10, 1973 - March 28, 1973.

THE ANDY GRIFFITH SHOW

Comedy. Background: Mayberry, North Carolina. The story of the relationship between two friends: Sheriff Andy Taylor, widower, and his bachelor cousin, Deputy Barney Fife. Episodes depict Andy's attempts to raise his young son, Opie, and his and Barney's efforts to maintain law in a virtually crime-free town.

CAST

Andy Taylor	Andy Griffith
Barney Fife	Don Knotts
Opie Taylor	Ronny Howard
Bee Taylor, Andy's aunt	Frances Bavier
Ellie Walker, a druggist, Andy's first girl-friend	Elinor Donahue
Mary Simpson, the county nurse	Sue Ane Langdon / Julie Adams
Irene Fairchild, the county nurse (later episodes)	Nina Shipman
Helen Crump, the fifth-grade school teacher, later Andy's wife	Anita Corseaut
Thelma Lou, Barney's girlfriend	Betty Lynn
Otis Campbell, the town drunk	Hal Smith
Howard Sprague, the county clerk	Jack Dodson
Briscoe Darling, a hillbilly	Denver Pyle
Charlene Darling, his daughter	Margaret Ann Peterson
Briscoe Darling's Boys	The Dillard Brothers
Ernest T. Bass, a trouble-making hillbilly	Howard Morris
Gomer Pyle, the naive gas station attendant at Wally's Filling Station	Jim Nabors
Malcolm Merriweather, an Englishman, a friend of the Taylor's	Bernard Fox
Goober Pyle, Gomer's cousin	George Lindsey
Clara Edwards, Bee's friend	Hope Summers
Floyd Lawson, the barber	Howard McNair
Deputy Warren Ferguson, Barney's replacement	Jack Burns
Mayor Pike (early episodes)	Dick Elliot
Mayor Stoner (later episodes)	Parley Baer
Jim Lindsey, a friend of Andy's	James Best
Captain Barker, the State Police Chief	Ken Lynch
Emma Brand, the town hypochondriac	Cheerio Meredith
Sam Jones, the town councilman, a widower	Ken Berry
Millie Swanson, Sam's girlfriend	Arlene Golonka
Mike Jones, Sam's young son	Buddy Foster
Emmet Clark, the owner of the Fix-it-Shop	Paul Hartman

Skippy, a fun-loving girl
　　from Raleigh, sweet
　　on Barney　　　　Joyce Jameson
Daphne, her girlfriend,
　　sweet on Andy　　　Jean Carson

Music: Earle Hagen.

THE ANDY GRIFFITH SHOW—30 minutes—CBS—October 3, 1960 - September 16, 1968. Syndicated. Also titled: "Andy of Mayberry." Spin-off series: "Mayberry R.F.D." See title.

ANDY OF MAYBERRY

See title: "The Andy Griffith Show."

ANDY'S GANG

Children's Variety. Music, songs, comedy, and stories set against the background of a clubhouse.
　　Original title: "The Buster Brown TV Show with Smilin' Ed McConnell and the Buster Brown Gang." Later titled: "Smilin' Ed McConnell and His Gang." In 1955, after the death of Mr. McConnell, Andy Devine became its host under the title, "Andy's Gang."

Characters: Squeaky the Mouse; Midnight the Tabby Cat; Froggie the Gremlin, a mischievous frog; Old Grandie, the talking piano.

Story segment: "Gunga, the East India Boy." Background: The village of Bakore. The adventures of Gunga and his friend Rama, young men who perform hazardous missions for their leader, the Maharajah.

CAST
Ed McConnell (Host)	Himself
Andy Devine (Host)	Himself
Gunga Ram	Nino Marcel
Rama	Vito Scotti

The Maharajah	Lou Krugman
Algernon Archibald Percival Shortfellow, the Poet	Alan Reed
The Teacher	Billy Gilbert
Buster Brown	Jerry Marin
The Sound of his dog Tige	Bud Tollefson
Froggie the Gremlin	Ed McConnell

Also: Joe Mazzuca, Peter Coo, Paul Cavanaugh, Billy Race

Announcer: Arch Presby.

THE BUSTER BROWN TV SHOW WITH SMILIN' ED McCONNELL AND THE BUSTER BROWN GANG —30 minutes—NBC—September 23, 1950 - August 4, 1951.

SMILIN' ED McCONNELL AND HIS GANG—30 minutes. NBC—August 11, 1951 - August 15, 1953. ABC—August 22, 1953 - April 16, 1955. NBC—April 23, 1955 - August 13, 1955.

ANDY'S GANG—30 minutes—NBC— August 20, 1955 - September 1960.

ANDY WILLIAMS

Listed: The television programs of singer Andy Williams:

The Andy Williams-June Valli Show— Musical Variety—15 minutes — NBC—July 2, 1957 - September 5, 1957.

Host: Andy Williams.

Hostess: June Valli.

Orchestra: Alvy West.

The Chevy Showroom—Musical Variety—30 minutes—ABC—1958.

Host: Andy Williams.

Regulars: Dick Van Dyke, Jayne Turner, Gail Kuhr.

Music: The Bob Hamilton Trio.

The Andy Williams Show—Musical Variety—60 minutes—CBS—July 7, 1959 — September 22, 1959.

Host: Andy Williams.

Regulars: Michael Storm, The Peter Gennaro Dancers, The Dick Williams Singers.

Orchestra: Jack Kane.

The Andy Williams Show—Musical Variety—60 minutes—NBC—September 22, 1962 - September 3, 1967.

Host: Andy Williams.

Regulars: Randy Sparks and the New Christy Minstrels, The Osmond Brothers, The Good Time Singers, The George Wyle Singers, The James Starbuck Dancers, The Nick Castle Dancers.

Orchestra: Colin Romoff; Allyn Ferguson; Dave Grusin.

The Andy Williams Show—Musical Variety—60 minutes—NBC—September 20, 1969 - July 17, 1971.

Host: Andy Williams.

Regulars: Janos Prohaska (The Cookie-Seeking Bear), Irwin Corey, Charlie Callas, The Jaime Rogers Singers, The Earl Brown Dancers, The Archie Tayir Dancers.

Orchestra: Mike Post.

AN EVENING WITH . . .

Variety. Background: A simulated nightclub atmosphere. Programs are tailored to the personalities of its guests.

Appearing: Julie London, Gretchen Wyler, Xavier Cougat, Pete Fountain, Marty Allen and Steve Rossi, The King Sisters, Louis Prima, Gene Pitney.

AN EVENING WITH. . .—30 minutes —Syndicated—1965-1967.

ANGEL

Comedy. Background: Suburban New York. The trials and tribulations of young marrieds: John Smith, an architect; and his French wife, Angel. Stories depict Angel's difficulties as she struggles to cope with the bewildering American lifestyle.

CAST

Angel Smith	Annie Fargé
John Smith	Marshall Thompson
Susie, Angel's friend, a neighbor	Doris Singleton
George, Susie's husband	Don Keefer

ANGEL—30 minutes—CBS—October 6, 1960 - September 20, 1961.

ANIMAL KINGDOM

Documentary. Wildlife films depicting the animal struggle for survival.

Host-Narrator: Bill Burrud.

ANIMAL KINGDOM—30 minutes—NBC—June 16, 1968 — September 1968.

ANIMAL SECRETS

Documentary. Wildlife films depicting the animal struggle for survival.

Host-Narrator: Loren Eisley.

ANIMAL SECRETS—30 minutes—NBC—1966-1967.

ANIMAL WORLD

Documentary. Wildlife films depicting the animal struggle for survival.

Host-Narrator: Bill Burrud.

ANIMAL WORLD—30 minutes. CBS—May 8, 1969 - September 18, 1969; ABC—May 1970 - September 1970; CBS—July 11, 1971 - September 12, 1971. Syndicated.

ANNA AND THE KING

Comedy-Drama. Background: Siam, 1862. Anna Owens, a young widowed American school teacher, is hired to educate and introduce Western culture to the royal children of the King of Siam. His Majesty, the absolute Monarch, rules all but Anna. Independent and forthright, she is prompted to defy rules and customs, hoping to enlighten him to the principles of freedom and justice. Based on the movie of the same title.

CAST
The King of Siam	Yul Brynner
Anna Owens	Samantha Eggar
Prince Kralahome	Keye Luke
Louis Owens, Anna's son	Eric Shea
The Crown Prince Chulolongkorn	Brian Tochi
Lady Thiang, the King's head-wife	Lisa Lu
Princess Serana, the King's eldest daughter	Rosalind Chao
Child (unnamed), the King's daughter	Wendy Tochi
Kai-Lee Ling, the King's daughter	Tracy Lee

Music: Richard Shores.

ANNA AND THE KING—30 minutes —CBS—September 17, 1972 - December 31, 1972.

ANNIE OAKLEY

Western. Background: The town of Diablo during the 1860s. The exploits of Annie Oakley, woman rancher and expert sharpshooter, as she attempts to maintain law and order.

CAST
Annie Oakley	Gail Davis
Sheriff Lofty Craig	Brad Johnson
Tagg Oakley, Annie's kid brother	Jimmy Hawkins
Annie's horse: Buttercup.	

ANNIE OAKLEY—30 minutes—ABC —1953-1958. Syndicated.

THE ANNIVERSARY GAME

Game. Three husband-and-wife teams compete for merchandise prizes.

Rounds One and Two: One member of one team is subjected to a prearranged situation. The spouse is asked to predict the outcome. If correct, points are awarded. Each couple participates in turn, and each spouse has the opportunity to predict his or her partner's reaction.

Round Three: One stunt involving the three couples. The one player that remains wins points for his or her team.

Round Four: "The Lightning Fast Round." Couples are seated and asked general knowledge questions. The player first to sound a bell signal and be recognized receives a chance to answer. If correct, one point is awarded; incorrect, no penalty.

Winners are the highest scoring couple.

Host: Al Hamel.

Announcer: Dean Webber.

THE ANNIVERSARY GAME—30 minutes—Syndicated 1969.

THE ANN SOTHERN SHOW

Comedy. Background: New York City. The misadventures of Katy O'Connor, the assistant manager of the fictitious Bartley House Hotel.

CAST
October 6, 1958 - March 2, 1959:

Katy O'Connor   Ann Sothern
Jason Maculey, the hotel
    manager   Ernest Truex
Flora Maculey, his
    wife   Reta Shaw
Olive Smith, Katy's
    secretary   Ann Tyrrell
Paul Martine, the
    bellboy   Jacques Scott

Music: Thomas Adair.

CAST
March 9, 1959 - September 25, 1961:

Katy O'Connor   Ann Sothern
James Devery, the hotel
    manager   Don Porter
Olive Smith   Ann Tyrrell
Dr. Delbert Gray, the hotel
    dentist   Louis Nye
Woody, the bellboy   Ken Berry
Oscar Pudney, Katy's
    nemesis   Jesse White

Music: Thomas Adair.

THE ANN SOTHERN SHOW—30 minutes—CBS—October 6, 1958 - September 25, 1961. Syndicated.

ANOTHER WORLD

Serial. Background: The town of Bay City. The dramatic story of two families, the Randolphs and the Matthews. Episodes relate the conflicts and tensions that arise from the interactions of the characters.

CAST
Jim Matthews   John Beal
                       Leon Janney
                       Shepperd Strudwick
                       Hugh Marlowe
Mary Matthews   Virginia Dwyer
Grandma Matthews   Vera Allen
Alice Matthews   Jacqueline Courtney
Pat Matthews   Susan Trustman
                       Beverly Penberthy
Russ Matthews   Joey Trent
                       Sam Groom
                       Robert Hover
                       David Bailey
Janet Matthews   Liza Chapman
Liz Matthews   Sara Cunningham
                       Audra Lindley
                       Nancy Wickwire
Bill Matthews   Joe Gallison
Melissa Palmer   Carol Roux
Ken Baxter   William Prince
Tom Baxter   Nicholas Pryor
Gerald Davis   Walter Matthews
Helen Moore   Muriel Williams
Dr. John Bradford   John Crawford
Susan Matthews   Fran Sharon
                       Lisa Cameron
John Randolph   Michael M. Ryan
Lee Randolph   Gaye Huston
                       Barbara Rodell
Danny Fargo   Anthony Ponzini
Michael Dru   Geoffrey Lumb
Wayne Addison   Robert Milli
Walter Curtin   Val Dufour
Cindy Clark   Leonie Norton
Ted Clark   Steve Bolster
Michael Bauer   Garry Pillar
Alex Gregory   James Congdon
Karen Gregory   Ellen Watson
Dr. Ernest Gregory   Mark Lenard

Peggy Harris	Micki Grant
Mrs. Hastings	Mona Burns
Flo Murray	Marcella Martin
Hope Bauer	Elissa Leeds
Cathryn Corniny	Ann Sheridan
The Assistant District	
Attorney	Billy Dee Williams
	Alex Wipf
Lenore Moore	Judith Barcroft
	Susan Sullivan
Luella Watson	Dorothy Blackburn
Dr. David Thornton	Joseph Ponazecki
	Colgate Salisbury
Ellen	Irene Biendie
	Gail Dixon
Andy Cummings	Jim Secrest
Bernice Addison	Janis Young
Chris Tyler	Steve Harmon
Fred Douglas	Charles Baxter
Ernie Downs	Harry Bellaver
Dan Shearer	John Cunningham
Barbara Shearer	Christine Cameron
Jane Overstreet	Frances Sternhagen
Belle Clark	Janet Ward
Marianne Randolph	Tracy Brown
Michael Randolph	Christopher Corwin
Rachel Davis	Robin Strasser
	Margaret Impert
	Victoria Wyndham
Mark Venable	Andrew Jarkowsky
Prof. Philip	
Lessner	Ed Bryce
Mrs. McCrea	Nancy Marchand
Raymond Scott	James Preston
Dr. Philbin	Charles Siebert
Jamie Matthews	Aidan McNulty
Robert Delaney	Nick Coster
Zack Richards	Terry Alexander
Gil McGowen	Dolph Sweet
Linda Metcalf	Vera Moore
Gloria Metcalf	Rosetta LeNoire
Ada Downs	Constance Ford
Eliot Carrington	James Douglas
Denis Carrington	Mike Hammett
Iris Carrington	Beverlee McKinsey
Louise Goddard	Anne Meachan
Lahoma Vane	Ann Wedgeworth
Dr. Paula McCrea	Beverly Owen
Stephen Frame	George Reinholt

Frank Chadwick	Robert Kya-Hill
Tom Albini	Pierrino Mascorino
Gil McGowen	Charles Durning
Madge Murray	Doris Belack
Lefty Burns	Larry Keith
Walter Curtin, Jr.	Scott Firestone
	Denis McKiernan
	Jason Gladstone
Janice Frame	Victoria Thompson
Tim McGowen	Christopher Allport
MacKenzie Corey	Robert Emhardt
Sam Lucas	Jordan Charney
Dr. Curt Landis	Donald Madden
Olga Bellin	Ann Fuller

Also: Edmund Hashem, Elspeth Eric, Tom Ruger, Stephen Bolster, Bobby Doran, Jill Turnbull, Glenn Zachar, Tiberia Mitori.

Music: Chet Kingsbury.

ANOTHER WORLD—30 minutes—NBC—Premiered: May 4, 1964. Also titled: "Another World in Bay City."

ANOTHER WORLD IN SOMERSET

See title: "Somerset."

ANSWER YES OR NO

Game. Contestants are presented with a situation dilemma and asked to secretly choose a yes or no card, indicating whether or not he would or would not become involved. A celebrity panel of four then predict the contestants' answers. Each correct guess awards that contestant a merchandise prize.

Host: Moss Hart.

Panelists: Arlene Francis, Jane Pickens, Peter Lind Hayes, Mary Healy.

ANSWER YES OR NO—30 minutes—NBC 1950.

ANYBODY CAN PLAY

Game. A panel of four contestants compete for points. They are seated opposite a guest who possesses a concealed object. By means of indirect questions the panelists have to identify the object. The highest point accumulators are the winners and receive merchandise prizes.

Host: George Fenneman.

ANYBODY CAN PLAY—30 minutes —ABC—July 6, 1958 - December 8, 1958.

ANYONE CAN WIN

Game. Players: A panel of four celebrities — three regulars and one guest. Object: to identify an anonymous celebrity-guest whose face is hidden behind a rubber mask of the Al Capp character, Hairless Joe. Each panelist is given an allotted time to ask questions and foster a guess. A preselected studio audience member is then asked to back one of the panelists. The mystery guest is revealed and the contestant receives a cash prize if his choice is correct.

Host: Al Capp.

Panelists: Patsy Kelly, Ilka Chase, Jimmy Dykes.

ANYONE CAN WIN—30 minutes— CBS 1950.

ANYTHING YOU CAN DO

Game. Two three member teams, men vs. women. Located above each team is a category board containing three physical and/or mental stunts. The men select from the women's side and vice versa. Each team must perform the activities within a specified time limit (usually 90 seconds). The team accumulating the least amount of overall time is declared the winner and receives merchandise prizes.

Hosts: Gene Wood; Don Harron.

Announcer: Bill Luxton.

ANYTHING YOU CAN DO—30 minutes—Syndicated 1971.

ANYWHERE, U.S.A.

Anthology. Stories depicting the overlooked and often neglected health problems of people.

CAST
Doctor   Edward Dowling
Doctor   Robert Preston

ANYWHERE, U.S.A—30 minutes— ABC—November 9, 1952 - December 14, 1952.

APARTMENT 3-C

Comedy. Background: 46 Perry Street, New York City, Apartment 3-C. The trials and tribulations of young marrieds: John Gay, a writer, and his scatterbrained wife, Barbara.

CAST
John Gay   Himself
Barbara Gay   Herself

APARTMENT 3-C—15 minutes—CBS —September 1949 - December 1949.

APPLE'S WAY

Drama. Background: The small town of Appleton, Iowa. The dreams, frustrations, and ambitions of the Apple family: George; his wife, Barbara; and their children, Paul, Cathy, Patricia, and Steven. Stories depict George's attempts to recapture for himself and his family the treasured memories of his childhood: "the wonders of streams and woods. . .the mystery of growing crops and days filled with adventure. . .with participation in good and comforting things."

CAST

George Apple	Ronny Cox
Barbara Apple	Lee McCain
Paul Apple	Vincent Van Patten
Cathy Apple	Pattie Cohoon
Patricia Apple	Franny Michel
	Kristie McNichel
Steven Apple	Eric Olsen
Aldon Apple, George's father	Malcolm Atterbury

Apple family pets: Dogs: Muffin, Sam and Bijou; snake: Ruby.

Music: Morton Stevens.

APPLE'S WAY—60 minutes—CBS—February 10, 1974 - January 12, 1975.

APPOINTMENT WITH ADVENTURE

Anthology. Dramatizations based on the actual experiences of ordinary people in all walks of life.

Included:

Minus Three Thousand. Background: The Pyrenees Mountains between France and Spain. The story of two friends who decide to explore a cave; the conflict; one loves the other's wife.

CAST
Louis Jourdan, Claude Dauphin, Mala Powers.

Five In Judgement. A group of people are forced to remain in a roadside diner during a tornado. As they listen to the radio, a broadcast describes two men wanted for murder. The story depicts the desperation that arises when it is realized that two of their number resemble the description.

CAST
Paul Newman, Henry Hull, James Gregson, Jeff Harris.

The Fateful Pilgrimage. The story of an ex-G.I. who returns to the German village he helped capture during World War II to find the girl who nursed him back to health when he was wounded.

CAST
William Prince, Viveca Lindfors, Theodore Bikel.

APPOINTMENT WITH ADVENTURE—30 minutes—CBS—April 3, 1955 - March 25, 1956.

APPOINTMENT WITH LOVE

Anthology. Rebroadcasts of episodes that were originally aired via other filmed anthology programs. Dramatizations stressing the gentleness of life and the goodness of Nature.

Included:

Autumn Flames. The story of a wife who falls in love with another man after fourteen years of marriage.

CAST
Maria Palmer, Onslow Stevens.

Some Small Nobility. Believing her husband has only one year to live, a wife strives to make the year the happiest.

CAST

Joan Banks.

This Little Pig Cried. The story of a young couple's first marital spat.

CAST

Frances Rafferty, Robert Rockwell.

APPOINTMENT WITH LOVE—30 minutes—ABC—December 23, 1952 - September 25, 1953.

AQUAMAN

Animated Cartoon. Aquaman, born of an Atlantian mother and a human father (a lighthouse keeper), establishes himself as the ruler of the Seven Seas. He is capable of commanding all sea creatures through telepathic, radiating brain waves. Stories concern his battle against the sinister forces of evil as he attempts to protect the Kingdom of Atlantis.

Additional characters: Aqualad, his aide; Minnow, Storm, and Tadpole, their sea horses; and Tusky the walrus.

AQUAMAN—07 minutes—Syndicated 1970. Originally broadcast as part of "The Superman-Aquaman Hour"—60 minutes—CBS—September 9, 1967 - September 7, 1968.

THE AQUANAUTS

Adventure. Background: Honolulu, Hawaii. The cases of Drake Andrews, Larry Lahr, and Mike Madison, professional divers.

CAST

Drake Andrews	Keith Larsen
Larry Lahr	Jeremy Slate
Mike Madison	Ron Ely

Their boat: The *Atlantis.*

Music: Andre Previn.

THE AQUANAUTS—60 minutes—CBS—September 14, 1960 - May 1961.

ARCHER

Crime Drama. Background: Melrose, California. The investigations of private detective Lew Archer. Based on the character created by Ross Macdonald.

CAST

Lew Archer	Brian Keith
Lt. Barney Brighton	John P. Ryan

Music: Jerry Goldsmith.

ARCHER—60 minutes—NBC—January 30, 1975 - March 14, 1975.

THE ARCHIE SHOW

Animated Cartoon. The misadventures of a group of high school students in the mythical town of Riverdale. Based on the comic "Archie," by Bob Montana.

Characters: Archie Andrews; Jughead Jones; Betty Cooper; Veronica Lodge; Reggie Mantle, Sabrina, the teenage witch; Hot Dog, the gang pet; Salem, Sabrina's cat; Mr. Weatherby, the school principal; Aunt Hilda and Cousin Ambrose, Sabrina's realtives; Big Ethel; Ophelia; Spencer; Harvey.

Voices: Jane Webb, Dallas McKennon, Howard Morris.

Music: George Blais, Jeff Michael.

Versions:

The Archie Show—30 minutes—CBS—September 14, 1968 - September 9, 1969.

Format: Two ten-minute sketches and a dance-of-the-week-selection.

The Archie Comedy Hour—60 minutes—CBS—September 13, 1969 -September 5, 1970.

Format: Various sketches and musical numbers.

Archie's Funhouse Featuring the Giant Joke Box—30 minutes—CBS—September 12, 1970 - September 4, 1971.

Format: Dances and comedy sketches centered around a "Giant Joke Box" (which resembles and operates like a juke box).

Archie's TV Funnies—30 minutes—CBS—September 11, 1971 - September 1, 1973.

Format: The Archie Gang, operators of a television station, present animated adaptations of eight comic strips: "Dick Tracy," "The Captain and the Kids," "Moon Mullins," "Smokey Stover," "Nancy and Sluggo," "Here Come the Dropouts," "Broom Hilda," "Emmy Lou."

Everything's Archie—30 minutes—CBS—September 8, 1973 - January 26, 1974.

Format: Various comedy sketches and musical numbers.

The U.S. of Archie—30 minutes—CBS—Premiered: September 7, 1974.

Format: Stories of the accomplishments of great Americans.

ARE YOU POSITIVE?

Game. Celebrity panelists attempt to identify well known personalities from their baby pictures. The panelists, representing a home viewer who is selected by a postcard drawing, forfeit five dollars to that person if they are unable to identify the photograph.

Hosts: Bill Stern; Frank Coniff.

Panelists: Frank Frisch, Lefty Gomez (plus guests).

ARE YOU POSITIVE?—30 minutes—NBC 1952.

ARLENE DAHL'S BEAUTY SPOT

Women. Beauty and cosmetic tips.

Hostess: Arlene Dahl.

Music: Recorded.

ARLENE DAHL'S BEAUTY SPOT—05 minutes—ABC—September 27, 1965 - June 24, 1966.

ARLENE DAHL'S PLAYHOUSE

Anthology. Dramatic presentations.

Hostess: Arlene Dahl.

Included:

The Night Light at Vordens. The story of a possessive mother who attempts to dominate her daughter's life.

CAST
Craig Stevens, Jean Byron.

Death Has A System. A story of violence and retribution behind the scenes of a gambling casino.

CAST
Kim Spaulding, Sally Mansfield, Ian MacDonald.

The House Nobody Wanted. The fear that confronts a wife when she begins to suspect that her husband is a murderer.

CAST

Marilyn Erskine, Craig Stevens.

Claire. The story of a woman who constantly neglects her family to further her career.

CAST

Marguerite Chapman, Marilyn Erskine.

ARLENE DAHL'S PLAYHOUSE—30 minutes—ABC—1953 - 1954.

THE ARLENE FRANCIS SHOW

Variety. Guests, interviews, music, and songs. Comments on books, movies, and current events.

Hostess: Arlene Francis.

Music: The Norman Paris Trio.

THE ARLENE FRANCIS SHOW—30 minutes—NBC—August 12, 1957 - February 21, 1958.

ARMCHAIR DETECTIVE

Game. Selected studio audience members compete. A criminal case is reenacted and stopped prior to the denouncement. The first player to solve the case, based on script clues, is the winner and receives a merchandise prize.

Host: John Milton Kennedy.

Assistants: Jerome Sheldon, Cy Kendall.

ARMCHAIR DETECTIVE—30 minutes—CBS 1949.

THE ARMSTRONG CIRCLE THEATRE

Anthology. Dramatizations based on true incidents.

Included:

Crisis On Tangier Island. The story centers on the efforts of a priest to find a doctor who is willing to remain on a remote island.

CAST

Reverend Richel: Kent Smith; Mrs. Richel: Frances Reid; Sam Parker: Frank M. Thomas.

Assignment: Junkie's Alley. Background: Philadelphia. The story of the Narcotics Squad and their attempts to curtail the drug market through the use of police women.

CAST

Ann Rosen: Monica Lovett; Freddie: Addison Powell; Jimmy: James Congdon.

John Doe Number 154. The story of an amnesiac as he searches for his real identity.

CAST

George Applegate: John Napier; Mrs. Gentile: Ruth White; Dr. Kryslot: William Prince.

Have Jacket Will Travel. The story of three foreign children adopted by American families.

CAST

Gina: Patty Duke; Aristides Andros: Martin Brooks; Lewis Stidman: Don Briggs.

THE ARMSTRONG CIRCLE THEATRE—60 minutes—NBC—1953 - 1957; CBS—1957 - 1963.

ARNIE

Comedy. Background: Los Angeles, California. After twelve years as a dock boss for Continental Flange, Inc., Arnie Nuvo is promoted to the position of "New Head of Product Improvement." Stories concern Arnie's struggles as he attempts to adjust to the responsibilities of an executive position.

CAST

Arnie Nuvo	Herschel Bernardi
Lillian Nuvo, his wife	Sue Anne Langdon
Andréa Nuvo, their daughter	Stephanie Steele
Richard Nuvo, their son	Del Russell
Hamilton Majors, Jr., the company president	Roger Bowen
Julius, a friend of Arnie's	Tom Pedi
Neil Ogilvie, the plant supervisor	Herbert Voland
Fred Springer, the advertising head	Olan Soule
Felicia Farfas, Arnie's secretary	Elaine Shore
Randy Robinson, Arnie's neighbor, TV's "The Giddyap Gourmet."	Charles Nelson Reilly

ARNIE—30 minutes—CBS—September 19, 1970 - September 9, 1972.

ARREST AND TRIAL

Crime Drama. Background: Los Angeles, California. A depiction of two aspects of justice: The Arrest — police apprehension methods; and the Trial — the courtroom hearing.

CAST

Sgt. Nick Anderson	Ben Gazzara
John Egan, the defense counselor	Chuck Connors
Pine	John Kerr
Jake	Joe Higgins
Miller	John Larch
Kirby	Roger Perry

ARREST AND TRIAL—90 minutes— ABC—September 15, 1963 - September 13, 1964. Syndicated.

AROUND THE WORLD IN 80 DAYS

Animated Cartoon. England, 1872. After Phileas Fogg and Balinda Maze are unable to be married because her uncle, Lord Maze, objects, Fogg accepts Lord Maze's challenge to travel around the world in eighty days to prove himself worthy of the girl. Believing him incapable of the feat, Lord Maze wagers twenty thousand pounds against him and hires, unbeknown to Fogg, the evil Mister Fix to foil the attempt and ensure his winning the bet.

After a letter granting them permission to leave is acquired from the queen, Fogg and his aide, Jean Pasepartout, depart in a traveling balloon. Episodes depict their attempts to overcome the foul deeds of Mister Fix and complete their journey within the allotted time. Adapted from the novel by Jules Verne.

Characters' Voices

Phileas Fogg	Alistair Duncan
Jean Passepartout	Ross Higgins
Mister Fix	Max Obistein

Additional Voices: Owen Weingott.

Music: John Sangster.

AROUND THE WORLD IN EIGHTY DAYS—30 minutes—NBC—September

9, 1972 - September 1, 1973. Syndicated. Australian produced.

THE ART FORD SHOW

Musical Game. After a musical selection is played, the host asks a panel of three disc jockeys a related question. If panelists, who play for a home viewer selected by a postcard drawing, fail to answer correctly, they forfeit five dollars to that person.

Host: Art Ford.

Assistant: Arlene Cunningham.

Panelists: Freddie Robbins, Johnny Syme, Hal Moore.

Music: The Archie Koty Trio.

THE ART FORD SHOW—30 minutes —NBC 1951.

ARTHUR GODFREY

Listed: The television programs of radio and television personality Arthur Godfrey.

Arthur Godfrey's Talent Scouts—Variety—30 minutes—CBS—December 6, 1948 - July 7, 1958. Showcased: Undiscovered professional talent.

Host: Arthur Godfrey.

Substitute Hosts: Joe E. Brown, Steve Allen, Guy Mitchell.

Vocalists: The Holidays.

Announcer: Tony Marvin.

Orchestra: Archie Bleyer.

Arthur Godfrey and Friends—Musical Variety—60 minutes—CBS—January 12, 1949 - June 6, 1956.

Host: Arthur Godfrey.

Substitute Hosts: Robert Q. Lewis; Herb Shriner.

Regulars: Pat Boone, The McGuire Sisters (Christine, Phyllis, and Dorothy), Marion Marlowe, Janette Davis, Julius LaRosa, Johnny Nash, Lu Ann Simms, Allen Case, Frank Parker, Bill Lawrence, Haleloke (Dancer), Carmel Quinn, Stan Noonan, The Chordettes (Janet Erlet, Dottie Schwartz, Jimmy Osborn, Carol Hagedorn), The Mariners (James Lewis, Nathaniel Dickerson, Martin Karl, Thomas Lockard).

Announcer: Tony Marvin.

Orchestra: Archie Bleyer; Neil Hefti.

Arthur Godfrey and His Ukelele—Musical Variety—30 minutes—CBS—April 4, 1950 - June 30, 1950.

Host: Arthur Godfrey.

Announcer: Tony Marvin.

Orchestra: Archie Bleyer.

Arthur Godfrey Time—Musical Variety—30 minutes—CBS—January 7, 1952 - April 24, 1959.

Host: Arthur Godfrey.

Announcer: Tony Marvin.

Orchestra: Archie Bleyer.

The Arthur Godfrey Show—Musical Variety—60 minutes—CBS—September 23, 1958 - February 24, 1959.

Host: Arthur Godfrey.

Regulars: Johnny Nash, Lani Nill.

Announcer: Tony Marvin.

Orchestra: Dick Hyman.

1960-1961: The host of "Candid Camera." See title.
1969: The host of "Your All-American College Show." See title.

ARTHUR MURRAY'S DANCE PARTY

Variety. Dance instruction, dancing contests (judged by three guest celebrities), songs, and sketches.

Hostess: Kathryn Murray.

Regulars: Arthur Murray, Arnold Stang, Jack Norton, Teresa Brewer, Victor Borge, Joyce Bulifant, Lauritz Melchoir, Mary McCarthy, Bill and Cora Baird, Fran Warren, David Street, Jeri Gale, Mary Beth Hughes, Nelson Case, The Pastels, The Arthur Murray Dancers.

Choreographer: June Taylor.

Orchestra: Ray Carter; Emil Coleman.

ARTHUR MURRAY'S DANCE PARTY—30 minutes. DuMont—October 15, 1950 - March 18, 1951; CBS—July 11, 1952 - August 29, 1952; NBC—June 1953 - September 1953; NBC—June 1954 - September 1954; NBC—July 1955 - September 1955; NBC—June 1956 - September 1956; NBC—April 9, 1957 - September 16, 1957; NBC—September 29, 1958 - September 6, 1960.

ART LINKLETTER

Listed: The television programs of radio and television personality Art Linkletter.

Program nature: Interviews, points of interest, discussions, music, and audience participation.

Life With Linkletter—Variety—30 minutes—ABC—October 6, 1950 - April 25, 1952.

Host: Art Linkletter.

Announcer: Jack Slattery.

Music: The Muzzy Marcellino Trio.

House Party—Variety—30 minutes—CBS—September 1, 1952 - September 5, 1969. Later titled "The Linkletter Show."

Host: Art Linkletter.

Announcer: Jack Slattery.

Music: The Muzzy Marcellino Trio.

People Are Funny—Comedy—30 minutes—NBC—1951-1961. 150 of 246 filmed episodes are syndicated.

Format: Selected people attempt to cope with unusual situations.

Host: Art Linkletter.

Announcer: Pat McGeehan.

The Art Linkletter Show—Variety—30 minutes—NBC—February 18, 1963 - September 23, 1963. Humorous glimpses (recorded on film) of everyday life. Game portion: Selected studio audience members are presented with various minor emergencies. Those best at solving them receive a merchandise prize.

Host: Art Linkletter.

Life With Linkletter—Variety—30 minutes—NBC—December 29, 1969 - September 25, 1970.

Host: Art Linkletter.

Co-Host: Jack Linkletter (his son).

THE ASPHALT JUNGLE

Crime Drama. Background: New York City. The investigations of the Metropolitan Squad, an elite team of plainclothes detectives designed to corrupt the workings of the underworld.

CAST

Matthew Gower, the Deputy Police Commissioner	Jack Warden
Captain Gus Honocheck	Arch Johnson
Sergeant Danny Miller	Bill Smith

THE ASPHALT JUNGLE—60 minutes—ABC—April 2, 1961 - September 29, 1961. Syndicated.

ASSIGNMENT: DANGER

See title: "Martin Kane, Private Eye."

ASSIGNMENT: FOREIGN LEGION

Anthology. Dramatized: The role of the French Foreign Legion during the North African campaign of World War Two. Stories depict the events in the lives of its men and officers.

Starring: Merle Oberon as The Correspondent.

ASSIGNMENT: FOREIGN LEGION —30 minutes—CBS—September 15, 1957 - December 24, 1958. Syndicated.

ASSIGNMENT: UNDERWATER

Adventure. Background: Florida. The story of Bill Greer, ex-marine, widower, professional diver, and his daughter, Patty, the operators of the charter boat, the *Lively Lady*. Episodes depict Bill's investigations into acquired cases.

CAST

Bill Greer	Bill Williams
Patty Greer	Diane Mountford

ASSIGNMENT: UNDERWATER—30 minutes—Syndicated 1960.

ASSIGNMENT: VIENNA

See title: "The Men," *Assignment: Vienna,* segment.

AS THE WORLD TURNS

Serial. Background: Oakdale, U.S.A. Dramatic incidents in the lives of the Hughes and Lowell families.

CAST

Grandpa Hughes	Santos Ortega
Chris Hughes	Don McLaughlin
Nancy Hughes	Helen Wagner
Penny Hughes	Rosemary Prinz
	Phoebe Dorin
Lisa Miller	Eileen Fulton
Tom Hughes	Peter Link
	Peter Galman
	Paul O'Keefe
	David Colson
Bob Hughes	Don Hastings
	Bobby Alford
Hank Barton	Gary Sandy
Susan Stewart	Marie Masters
	Jada Rowland
Dr. Douglas Cassen	Nat Polen
Alma Miller	Ethel Rainey
Judge Lowell	William Johnstone
Ellen Lowell	Patricia Bruder
	Wendy Drew
Donald Hughes	Peter Brandon
Dr. John Dixon	Larry Bryggman
Julia Burke	Fran Carlon
Dan Stewart	John Reilly
	John Colenback
Jennifer Ryan	Geraldine Cort
	Gillian Spencer
Dawn Stewart	Jean Mazza
Carol Ann Stewart	Ariane Muenker
	Barbara Jean Ehrhardt
	Carol Ann Stewart
Betsy Stewart	Tiberia Mitri
	Susan Davids
	Simone Schacter

Dr. Rick Ryan	Con Roche
Paul Stewart	Dean Santoro
	Stephen Mines
Charles Shea	Pip Sarser
	Roger Morgan
Sara Fuller	Gloria DeHaven
Jack Davis	Martin Sheen
Barbara Ryan	Donna Wandry
Grant Coleman	Konrad Matthaei
	James Douglas
Jay Stallings	Dennis Cooney
Kim Reynolds	Kathryn Hays
Marty	Don Scardino
Amy Hughes	Yah-Ling Sun
Carol Demming	Rita McLaughlin
Peggy Reagan	Lisa Cameron
Dr. Flynn	Sidney Walker
Simon Gilbey	Jerry Lacey
Meredith Harcourt	Nina Hart
Claire Shea	Anne Burr
	Nancy Wickwire
	Barbara Berjer
David Stewart	Henderson Forsythe
Dr. Michael Shea	Roy Schumann
Martha Wilson	Anna Minot
Carl Wilson	Martin Rudy
Dick Martin	Edward Kemmer
Roy McGuire (early role)	Konrad Matthaei
Jimmy McGuire	Michael Cody
Karen Adams	Doe Lang
Mrs. Brando	Ethel Everett
Alice	Jean McClintock
Sandy McGuire	Dagne Crane
Sally Graham	Kathleen Cody
Dr. Jerry Turner	James Earl Jones
Neil Wade	Michael Lipton
Franny Brennan	Toni Darnay
Wally Matthews	Charles Siebert
Jeff Baker	Mark Rydell
Bruce Elliott	James Pritchett
Elizabeth Talbot	Jane House
Edith Hughes	Ruth Warrick
Jim Lowell	Les Damon
Dr. Tim Cole	William Redfield
Betty Stewart	Pat Benoit

Also: Joyce Van Patten, Teri Keane, Conrad Fowkes, Barbara Hayes.

Announcer: Dan McCulla.

Music: Charles Paul.

AS THE WORLD TURNS—30 minutes—CBS—Premiered: April 2, 1956.

ASTRO BOY

Animated Cartoon. Background: Twenty-first-century Earth. After his wife and son are killed in an automobile accident, a scientist, Dr. Boynton, creates Astro Boy, and indestructible, super-powered robot for companionship. Episodes depict their and Dr. Elefun's battle against evil. Japanese produced.

ASTRO BOY—30 minutes—Syndicated 1963.

THE AT HOME SHOW

Musical Variety.

Host: Earl Wrightson.

Music: The Norman Paris Trio.

THE AT HOME SHOW—15 minutes—CBS 1950.

THE AT LIBERTY CLUB

Musical Variety.

Hostess: Jacqueline.

Regulars: Gordon Gaines, Shara DeVries.

Orchestra: D'Artega.

THE AT LIBERTY CLUB—15 minutes—NBC 1948.

THE ATOM ANT/SECRET SQUIRREL SHOW

Animated Cartoon. The adventures of Atom Ant, the world's mightiest insect, and Secret Squirrel, the animal kingdom's most dauntless undercover agent. Episodes relate their battle against crime and corruption. Produced by Hanna-Barbera Productions.

Additional segments: "Precious the Dog"; "The Hillbilly Bears"; "Squiddly Diddly" (an octopus).

Characters' Voices

Atom Ant	Howard Morris
	Don Messick
Secret Squirrel	Mel Blanc
Morroco Mole	Paul Frees
Precious Pup	Don Messick
Granny Sweet	Janet Waldo
Squiddly Diddly	Paul Frees
Chief Winchley	John Stephenson

HILLBILLY BEARS:

Paw Rugg	Henry Corden
Maw Rugg	Jean Vander Pyl
Flora Rugg	Jean Vander Pyl
Shag Rugg	Don Messick

Music: Hoyt Curtin.

THE ATOM ANT/SECRET SQUIRREL SHOW—30 minutes—NBC—October 2, 1965 - September 7, 1968. Syndicated.

THE ATOM SQUAD

Spy Drama. Background: New York City — the operational base of the Atom Squad, a secret government organization established to combat cosmic invaders and safeguard U.S. atomic secrets. Episodes depict their attempts to protect the western world from the sinister forces of evil.

CAST

Steve Elliot, the squad leader	Bob Hastings
His assistants	Bob Courtleigh
	Bram Nossem

THE ATOM SQUAD—15 minutes—NBC 1953.

AUDUBON WILDLIFE THEATRE

Documentary. Wildlife films depicting the animal struggle for survival.

Host: Bob Davidson.

Narrator: Robert C. Hermes.

Music: Ron Harrison.

AUDUBON WILDLIFE THEATRE—30 minutes—Syndicated 1971.

AUTHOR, AUTHOR

Panel Discussion. Critical analysis of authors' works.

Host: Marc Connelly.

Panel: Gilbert Seldes, Dorothy Fields, Charles Sherman, Robert Lattor; plus guests.

AUTHOR, AUTHOR—30 minutes—ABC 1951.

THE AVENGERS

Adventure. Distinguished by four formats. The background for each is London, England.

Format One: March 18, 1961 - March 1962.

A gangster mistakenly delivers heroin to the fiancée of Doctor David Keel. She is killed by the dope ring when they discover their error and

The Avengers. Diana Rigg and Patrick Macnee.

The Avengers. Linda Thorson (Patrick Macnee's partner in later episodes.)

fear she will identify the messenger. Embittered, Keel vows to avenge her death. Investigating, he meets Steed, a mysterious individual seeking to infiltrate and expose the ring. Through Steed's guidance, Keel penetrates the ring. Exposed, and about to be killed, Steed, assisted by the police, intervene and save him, but—and in a rare moment in television—the ring leader escapes undetected. Vowing to avenge crime, the two men team, and on an alternating basis, battle criminal elements.

An actors strike ended the series. When first introduced, Steed's full name and occupation were not revealed. No one knows for whom he works except that his cover is that of a dilettante man about town and a purveyor of old-world courtesy.

Format Two: September 1962 – September 1965.

Following settlement of the strike in May of 1962, series production resumed. In September of that year, the program returned to the air with a complete change in format. Stories now concern the investigations of two British Government Ministry Agents: the dashing and debonair John Steed, and his glamorous female assistant, a widow, Mrs. Catherine Gale.

Format Three: September 1965 - March 20, 1968.

Shortly after Mrs. Gale resigns, Steed meets and befriends the "lovely and delectable" Emma Peel, widow of a test pilot, when they are involved in a minor automobile accident. Emancipated and independently wealthy, she teams with Steed for the sheer love of adventure. Stories depict their investigations as they attempt to solve baffling crimes.

Format Four: March 20, 1968 - May 26, 1969.

Emma's husband Peter Peel, believed to have been killed in an airplane crash in the Amazon, is found alive and flown back to England. As Emma returns to him, Steed is teamed with a beautiful and shapely brunette, Ministry agent Tara King. Stories relate their attempts to avenge bizarre crimes perpetrated against the British Government.

CAST

John Steed   Patrick Macnee
Dr. David Keel   Ian Hendry
Mrs. Catherine Gale   Honor Blackman
Mrs. Emma Peel   Diana Rigg
Tara King   Linda Thorson
Mother (a man), Steed's
    invalid superior   Patrick Newell
Rhonda, Mother's aide (a
    woman; a nonspeaking
    part)   Screen credit is not given

Steed's Other Partners:

Venus Smith (six episodes
    during the Catherine
    Gale era)   Julie Stevens
Also (three episodes during
    the Catherine Gale
    era)   Jon Rollason
Olga Volousby (one episode
    during the Emma Peel
    era)   Anna Quayle
Georganna Price Jones (one
    episode during the
    Emma Peel era)   Liz Fraser
Lady Diana Forbes Blakney
    (one episode during the
    Tara King era) Jennifer Croxton
Jimmy Merlin (one episode
    during the Tara
    King era)   Peter Barksworth
Frequently Cast:
Julian Glover, Peter Bowles, Christopher Lee, Talfryn Thomas, Bernard Cribbings, Warren Mitchell (as Ambassador Valdimer Brodney, Steed's friend, although an enemy agent).

Steed's home address: Number Three Stable Mews, City of London.

Tara's home address: Number Nine Primrose Crescent, City of London.

Music: Johnny Dankworth; Laurie Johnson; Howard Blake.

THE AVENGERS–60 minutes–ABC –March 28, 1966 - September 15, 1969. Syndicated. Premiered in London, ABC-TV (Associated British Corporation) on March 18, 1961. The episodes telecast from 1961 to 1965 were never seen in the U.S.

AWARD THEATRE

Anthology. Rebroadcasts of dramas that were originally aired via "Alcoa Theatre."

Included:

Hello, Charlie. The story of two safe-crackers and their attempts to release a little girl who is trapped in a locked vault.

CAST
Tony Randall, John Dehner, Joe E. Ross.

Shadow Of Evil. The story of an ex-alcholic who attempts to run for governor.
CAST
Cliff Robertson.

Any Friend of Julie's. After the death of a well-know playwright, a man tries to prove that he was the ghostwriter of all of his plays.
CAST
Leslie Neilson.

AWARD THEATRE–30 minutes– Syndicated 1958.

AWAY WE GO

Musical Variety. Songs, dances, and comedy sketches.

Host: Buddy Greco, George Carlin.

Regulars: Buddy Rich, his band; The Miriam Nelson Dancers.

Orchestra: Allyn Ferguson.

AWAY WE GO—60 minutes—CBS—June 3, 1967 - September 2, 1967.

B

THE BABY GAME

Game. Three husband-and-wife teams compete in a game designed to test their knowledge of childhood behavior. A specific situation that involves a child is explained. Players then bet points and state what they believe is the child's reaction to the situation. A previously filmed sequence is shown and the results are determined. Points are awarded if players are correct; deducted if they are wrong. Winners, the highest scorers, receive merchandise prizes.

Host: Richard Hayes, "America's favorite baby sitter."

THE BABY GAME—30 minutes—ABC—December 4, 1967 - July 12, 1968.

BACHELOR FATHER

Comedy. Background: 1163 Rexford Drive, Beverly Hills, California, the residence of Bentley Gregg, a bachelor-attorney; his Chinese houseboy, Peter Tong; and his orphaned thir-teen-year-old niece, Kelly, who became his legal ward after her parents were killed in an automobile accident.

Stories relate Bentley's attempts to adjust to the responsibilities of life as a Bachelor Father.

Special note concerning the cast. Kelly's friend, Ginger, is distinguished by three last names:

1957-1958: Ginger Farrell. Her mother, Louise, is a widow.

1958-1960: Ginger Loomis. Catherine McLead, who played her mother, was dropped, and Whit Bissel and Florence MacMichael were added as her parents, Bert and Amy Loomis. It should also be noted here that Whit Bissel, before portraying Ginger's father, played Steve Gibson, the father of a friend of Kelly's.

1960-1962: Ginger Mitchell. For unknown reasons, Whit Bissel and Florence MacMichael were dropped, and Del Moore and Evelyn Scott added as her parents, Cal and Adelaide Mitchell.

CAST

Bentley Gregg	John Forsythe
Kelly Gregg	Noreen Corcoran
Peter Tong	Sammee Tong
Howard Meechim, Kelly's boyfriend	Jimmy Boyd
Ginger Farrell	
Ginger Loomis	
Ginger Mitchell	Bernadette Winters
Louise Farrell	Catherine McLead
Bert Loomis	Whit Bissel
Amy Loomis	Florence MacMichael
Cal Mitchell	Del Moore
Adelaide Mitchell	Evelyn Scott
Vickie, Bentley's first secretary	Alice Backes
Kitty Deveraux, Bentley's second secretary	Shirley Mitchell Jane Nigh
Kitty Marsh, Bentley's third secretary	Sue Ane Langdon

Connie, Bentley's fourth
    secretary   Sally Mansfield
Chuck Forest, Bentley's
    friend, a bandleader Pat McCaffrie
Elaine Meechim, Howard's
    sister   Joan Vohs
Charles Burton, Bentley's
    friend   Karl Swenson
Gloria Gibson (later, Lila
    Gibson), Kelly's
    friend   Cheryl Holdridge
Steve Gibson, her
    father   Whit Bissel
Charlie Fong, Peter's
    conniving cousin Victor Sen Yung
Grandpa Ling, Peter's
    relative, the world's
    "oldest juvenile
    delinquent"   Beal Wong
Harry, the delivery
    boy   Sid Melton
Frank Curtis, Bentley's
    neighbor   Harry Von Zell
Warren Dawson, Bentley's
    law partner   Aaron Kincaid
Blossom Lee, Peter's
    niece   Cherlyene Lee
Susie, Peter's romantic
    interest; employed in
    a supermarket   Frances Fong
Horace Dawson, Warren's
    father   Davis Lewis
Myrtle Dawson, Warren's
    mother   Sheila Bromley
Aunt Rose, Peter's
    relative   Beulah Quo
Also, various roles: Mary Tyler Moore,
    Donna Douglas, H.W. Gim, Benson
    Fong.

Gregg family dog: Jasper.

Music: Conrad Salinger; Johnny
    Williams.

BACHELOR FATHER—30 minutes.
CBS—September 15, 1957 - June 11,
1958. NBC—June 18, 1958 - September 19, 1961. ABC—October 3, 1961 -
September 25, 1962. Syndicated.

BACK THE FACT

Game. Contestants are interviewed by the host and asked personal background questions. Players can answer truthfully or bluff. If a false statement is believed to have been made, an off-stage voice interrupts the procedings and asks the player to back the fact. If he is able, he presents the proof (e.g., a newspaper clipping) and wins a prize. However, should his bluff be called, he relinquishes his post to another player.

Host: Joey Adams.

Announcer-Offstage Voice: Carl Caruso.

BACK THE FACT—30 minutes—ABC 1955.

BAFFLE

Game. Two teams, each composed of a celebrity captain and a noncelebrity contestant. After one member of each team is placed in an individual soundproof booth, the sound is turned off in one. The other team plays the game. The outside player stands before a table containing large plastic letters which spell out a phrase. At six-second intervals, he places one letter at a time on a wall rack. The object is for his partner to correctly identify the phrase in the shortest amount of time. The sound is then turned on in the other booth and the other team plays the same phrase. The team accumulating the least amount of time each round receives the at-stakes merchandise prize. The team accumulating the least amount of time, in two out of three games is the overall winner. The noncelebrity contestant receives a chance at "The Solo Round."

First half. Object: the identification of ten words within thirty seconds. Parts of the words (e.g. PRT — Pretty; FRM — From) are displayed one at a time. Each correct identification awards the player fifty dollars and three seconds in the second half. *Second half.* Displayed: several letters of one word (e.g. MDY — Monday). The time a player has to identify it is determined by the number of words he correctly guesses in the first half. If the player correctly identifies the word he receives a new car.

Revised format: "All Star Baffle." Four celebrities play for selected studio audience members. The winning team's contestant receives a chance to play "The Solo Round."

Host: Dick Enberg.

Announcer: Kenny Williams.

Music: Mort Garson.

BAFFLE—30 minutes—NBC—March 26, 1973 - October 5, 1973.
ALL STAR BAFFLE—30 minutes—NBC—October 8, 1973 - March 29, 1974.

BAILEY'S COMETS

Animated Cartoon. The saga of a global skating race and of the seventeen competing roller derby teams who are seeking the million-dollar first prize. Clues to the prize are presented through an endless trail of poetic rhymes; and episodes depict the attempts of one team, Bailey's Comets, to overcome the diabolical schemes of the other teams as they attempt to eliminate them from the competition.

Teams: Bailey's Comets; The Broomer Girls; The Roller Bears; The Doctor Jekyll/Hydes; The Hairy Madden Red Eyes; The Duster Busters; The Yo Ho Ho's; The Mystery Mob; The Rambling Rivits; The Cosmic Rays; The Roller Coasters; The Texas Flycats; The Stone Rollers; The Gusta Pastas; The Rock 'N' Rollers; The Black Hats; The Gargantuan Giants.

Bailey's Comets Team Members: Barnaby, Dee Dee, Bunny, Wheelie, Pudge, and Sarge.

Helicopter Reporters: Dooter Roo, the pilot; and Gabby, the race commentator.

Voices: Don Messick, Sarah Kennedy, Daws Butler, Jim Brigg, Karen Smith, Bob Halt, Kathy Gori, Frank Welker.

Music: Doug Goodwin. Score: Eric Rogers.

BAILEY'S COMETS—30 minutes—CBS—September 8, 1973 - January 26, 1974.

THE BAILEYS OF BALBOA

Comedy. Background: Bailey's Landing, Balboa Beach, California. The story of the bickering relationship between two men: Sam Bailey, the captain of a noisy and decrepit character boat, the *Island Princess,* and his objecting neighbor, Cecil Wyntoon, the commodore of the high-class Balboa Yachting Club.

CAST

Sam Bailey	Paul Ford
Cecil Wyntoon	John Dehner
Barbara Bailey, Sam's daughter	Judy Carne
Jim Wyntoon, Cecil's son	Les Brown, Jr.
Buck Singleton, Sam's shipmate	Sterling Holloway

BALANCE YOUR BUDGET—30 minutes—CBS 1952.

BANACEK

See title: "NBC Wednesday Mystery Movie," *Banacek* segment.

The Bailey's of Balboa. Paul Ford.

THE BAILEYS OF BALBOA—30 minutes—CBS—September 24, 1964 - March 29, 1965.

BALANCE YOUR BUDGET

Game. Selected female members of the studio audience compete. Players first state the amount of money that is required to run their household for one year, then attempt to replenish it. The host reads a general-knowledge type of question. The player who is first to identify herself through a buzzer signal receives a chance to answer. If correct cash is scored. The winner, the highest scorer, receives the opportunity to compete again. Contestants end their play when they have balanced their budget or are defeated by another player.

Host: Bert Parks, "The keeper of the Horn of Plenty."

Assistant: Lynn Connor.

THE BANANA SPLITS ADVENTURE HOUR

Children. The misadventures of the Banana Splits, four live-action animals: Fleegle, the dog; Drooper, the lion; Bingo, the gorilla; and Snorky, the runt elephant. A Hanna-Barbera production.

Characters' Voices

Fleegle	Paul Winchell
Bingo	Daws Butler
Drooper	Allan Melvin
Snorky	Don Messick

The Banana Splits Adventure Hour. Left to right: Drooper (seated), Bingo, Snorky, and Fleegle. *Courtesy Hanna-Barbera Productions.*

Cartoon segments:

The Three Musketeers

Character's Voices

D'Artagnan	Bruce Watson
Porthos	Barney Phillips
Aramis	Don Messick
Athos	Jonathan Harris
Tooly	Teddy Eccles
The Queen	Julie Bennett
Constance	Julie Bennett

The Arabian Knights

Characters' Voices

Bez	Henry Corden
Evil Vangore	Paul Frees
Raseem	Frank Gerstle
Princess Nidor	Shari Lewis
Turban	Jay North
Fariik	John Stephenson

The Hillbilly Bears

Characters' Voices

Paw Rugg	Henry Corden
Maw Rugg	Jean VanderPyl
Flora Rugg	Jean VanderPyl
Shagg Rugg	Don Messick

Film segments:

The Micro Venture. Life in the world of microscopic creatures.

Characters' Voices

Professor Carter	Don Messick
Jill Carter	Patsy Garrett
Mike Carter	Tommy Cook

Danger Island. The adventures of archeologist/explorer, Professor Irwin Hayden.

CAST

Professor Irwin Hayden	Frank Aletter
Leslie Hayden, his daughter	Ronnie Troup
Link Simmons, his assistant	Michael Vincent
Morgan, the castaway	Rockne Tarkington
Chongo	Kahana
Mu-Tan	Victor Eberg
Chu	Rodrigo Arrendondo

Music: Hoyt Curtin; Jack Eskrew.

THE BANANA SPLITS ADVENTURE HOUR—60 minutes—NBC—September 7, 1968 - September 5, 1970. Syndicated title: "Banana Splits and Friends." Official title: "Kellogg's of Battle Creek Presents the Banana Splits Adventure Hour."

BAND OF AMERICA

Musical Variety.

Host: Paul Lavalle.

Regulars: Ray Crisara, Ross Gorman, Chauncey Moorehouse.

Announcer: Ford Bond.

Music: The Green and White Quartet.

BAND OF AMERICA—30 minutes—NBC 1949.

BANDSTAND

Musical Variety.

Host: Bert Parks.

Music: The Tex Beneke Band.

BANDSTAND—30 minutes—NBC—July 30, 1956 - August 23, 1956. Also known as "NBC Bandstand."

BANK ON THE STARS

Game. Two competing two member teams. Basis: The answering of questions drawn from the observation of film clips. Each correct response awards that team one point. The highest scoring team is declared the winner and receives fifty dollars for each point. The losing team's earnings correspond to what is obtained by dipping one hand into a barrel of silver dollars.

Hosts: Jack Paar; Jimmy Nelson.

Orchestra: Ivan Ditmars.

BANK ON THE STARS—30 minutes —CBS 1953.

BANYON

Crime Drama. Background: Los Angeles, California, 1937. The investigations of private detective Miles C. Banyon.

CAST

Miles C. Banyon	Robert Forster
Sgt. Peter McNeil, L.A.P.D.	Richard Jaeckel
Peggy Revere, a friend, the owner of the Revere Secretarial School	Joan Blondell
Abby Graham, a singer, a friend of Banyon's	Julie Gregg

BANYON—60 minutes—NBC—September 15, 1972 - January 12, 1973.

THE BARBARA COLEMAN SHOW

See title: "Here's Barbara."

The Barbara McNair Show. Left to right: Gordon MacRae, Barbara McNair, and Rich Little. © *Screen Gems.*

THE BARBARA McNAIR SHOW

Musical Variety. Staged as an informal concert.

Hostess: Barbara McNair.

Assistant-Announcer: Ronald Long.

THE BARBARA McNAIR SHOW—60 minutes—Syndicated 1969.

THE BARBARA STANWYCK THEATRE

Anthology. Dramatic presentations.

Hostess-Frequent Performer: Barbara Stanwyck.

Music: Earle Hagen.

Included:

Ironback's Bride. A woman, married to a shiftless outlaw, struggles to prevent her son from following in his father's footsteps.

CAST
Ella Cahill: Barbara Stanwyck; Isaiah Richardson: Charles Bickford; Charlie Cahill: Gerald Mohr.

No One. A producer's attempts to convince the backer of a Broadway play to hire a talented but unknown actress for the lead.

CAST
Cara Lester: Barbara Stanwyck; Tracy Lane: Susan Oliver; Jack Harrison: Alan Hewitt.

House In Order. A woman, told she may have only a short time to live, struggles to regain the love of her husband and daughter.

CAST
Elizabeth Moury: Barbara Stanwyck; Susan Moury: Yvonne Craig; Bill Moury: Shepperd Strudwick.

Discreet Deception. A tale of the deceptive romance between a woman and her late husband's married brother.

CAST
Amelia Lambert: Barbara Stanwyck; Simon Lambert: Patric Knowles; Vivian Lambert: Virginia Gregg.

THE BARBARA STANWYCK THEATRE—30 minutes—NBC—September 19, 1960 - September 11, 1961.

BARBARY COAST

Adventure. Background: San Francisco during the 1880s. The story of Jeff Cable, an undercover agent for the governor of California, and Cash Canover, his partner, the owner of Cash Canover's Golden Gate Casino. Episodes relate their attempts to apprehend lawbreakers on San Francisco's notorious Barbary Coast.

CAST
Jeff Cable	William Shatner
Cash Canover	Doug McClure
Moose, an employee of Canover's	Richard Kiel
Thumbs, an employee of Canover's	Dave Turner
Brandy, one of the dance girls	Francine York
Rusty, one of the dance girls	Brooke Mills
The Bartender	John Dennis
	Eddie Fontaine

Music: John Andrew Tartagla.

BARBARY COAST—60 minutes—ABC—Premiered: September 8, 1975.

BAREFOOT IN THE PARK

Comedy. Background: New York City. 49 West 10th Street, Manhattan, Apartment 5-B, the residence of the Bratters; Paul, an attorney with the firm of Kendricks, Kein, and Klein, and his wife, Corie. Episodes relate the struggles of a young couple as they attempt to survive the difficult first years of marriage. Based on the Broadway play and movie by Neil Simon.

CAST

Paul Bratter	Scoey Mitchell
Corie Bratter	Tracy Reed
Honey Robinson, their friend, the owner of "Honey's Pool Hall"	Nipsey Russell
Mabel Bates, Corie's mother	Thelma Carpenter
Arthur Kendricks, Paul's employer	Harry Holcombe

Music: J. J. Johnson; Charles Fox.

BAREFOOT IN THE PARK—30 minutes—ABC—September 24, 1970 - January 14, 1971.

BARETTA

Crime Drama. The investigations of Tony Baretta, an undercover police detective with the 53rd Precinct who has little respect for standard police procedures.

CAST

Tony Baretta	Robert Blake
Billy Truman, his friend, the house detective at the King Edward Hotel	Tom Ewell
Inspector Schiller	Dana Elcar
Lt. Hal Brubaker	Edward Grover
Rooster, Baretta's information man	Michael D. Roberts
Fats, Baretta's informant	Chino Williams

Tony's parrot: Fred.

Music: Dave Grusin; Tom Scott.

BARETTA—60 minutes—ABC—Premiered: January 17, 1975.

THE BARKLEYS

Animated Cartoon. The main characters are dogs who are modeled after the characters in "All in the Family." Episodes relate the life of Arnie Barkley, an outspoken, opinionated and loud-mouthed bus driver as he attempts to cope with life, understand his progressive children, and bridge the generation gap that exists between them.

Characters' Voices

Arnie Barkley	Henry Corden
Agnes Barkley, his wife	Joan Gerber
Terri Barkley, their daughter	Julie McWhrither
Chester Barkley, their son	Steve Lewis
Roger Barkely, their son	Gene Andrusco

Additional voices: Frank Welker, Bob Halt, Don Messick, Bob Frank, Michael Bell.

Music: Doug Goodwin; Score: Eric Rogers.

THE BARKLEYS—30 minutes—NBC—September 9, 1972 - September 1, 1973.

BARNABY JONES

Crime Drama. Background: Los

Angeles, California. The investigations of private detective Barnaby Jones. Tragically forced out of retirement by the murder of his partner-son, he represents the new image in detectives—an older man with a quaint country charm and trigger wit.

CAST

Barnaby Jones   Buddy Ebsen
Betty Jones, his
     daughter-in-law-
     assistant   Lee Meriweather
Lieutenant Biddle,
     L.A.P.D.   John Carter

Music: Duante Tatro; Jerry Fielding; Jeff Alexander; John Elizade.

BARNABY JONES—60 minutes—CBS—Premiered: January 28, 1973.

BARNEY BLAKE, POLICE REPORTER

Crime Drama. Background: New York City. The investigations of police reporter Barney Blake as he seeks to ascertain the facts behind criminal cases.

Starring: Gene O'Donnell as Barney Blake.

BARNEY BLAKE, POLICE REPORTER—30 minutes—NBC 1948.

BARNEY MILLER

Comedy. Background: Greenwich Village in New York City. The trials and tribulations of Captain Barney Miller, the chief of detectives of the 12th police precinct.

CAST

Captain Barney
     Miller   Hal Linden
Elizabeth Miller, his
     wife   Barbara Barrie
Sergeant Chano   Gregory Sierra
Sergeant Phil Fish   Abe Vigoda
Sergeant Wojehowicz   Max Gail
Sergeant Yemana   Jack Soo
Detective Harris   Ron Glass
Police Inspector Luger   James Gregory
Bernice Fish, Phil's
     wife   Florence Stanley

Music: Jack Elliott, Allyn Ferguson.

BARNEY MILLER—30 minutes—ABC—Premiered: January 23, 1975.

THE BARON

Mystery. Background: London, England. The story of John Mannering, a wealthy American antique dealer known as The Baron. Episodes depict his investigations into crimes associated with the art world.

CAST

John Mannering   Steve Forrest
Cordella, his
     assistant   Sue Lloyd
David, his
     assistant   Paul Ferris

Music: Edwin Astley.

THE BARON—60 minutes—ABC—January 20, 1966 - July 14, 1966. Syndicated.

BARRIER REEF

Adventure. Background: Australia. The explorations of the marine biologists assigned to investigate and study the Great Barrier Reef.

CAST

Captain Chet King	Joe James
Kip King	Ken James
Joe Francis	Richard Meikle
Steve Goba	Howard Hopkins
Tracy Dean	Rowena Wallace
Dr. Elizabeth Hanna	Ihab Nafa
Diana Parker	Elli MacLure
Elizabeth Grant	Sussana Brett
Ken	Peter Adams
Jack	George Assang
Professor Barnard	Peter Carver

Their ship: The *Endeavor,* a two-hundred-twenty-ton windjammer.

BARRIER REEF—30 minutes—NBC —September 11, 1971 - September 2, 1972.

BATMAN

Adventure. Background: Gotham City. Inheriting a vast fortune after his parents are killed by a gangster, ten-year old Bruce Wayne vows to avenge their deaths by spending the rest of his life fighting crime.

Cared for by Alfred, the family butler, he works in total isolation and

Batman. Left to right: Burgess Meredith (The Penguin), Cesar Romero (The Joker), Burt Ward (Robin), Adam West (Batman), Frank Gorshin (behind Batman, The Riddler), and Lee Meriweather (Catwoman).

becomes a master scientist. Fourteen years later, after constructing the world's greatest crime lab beneath Wayne Manor, he adopts the guise of the mysterious caped crusader, "Batman," a figure designed to strike fear into the hearts of criminals.

Bruce Wayne adopts the orphaned, teenaged Dick Greyson after the tragic death of his parents in a circus high-wire act. Dick is taught to perfect his mental and physical skills, and adopts the guise of "Robin, The Boy Wonder." Joining Batman they form "The Dynamic Duo."

Several years later, when Police Commissioner Gordon's daughter, Barbara, returns home following her college graduation, she acquires employment in the Gotham City Library and adopts the guise of the mysterious "Batgirl." Though operating independently, she forms "The Terrific Trio" when working with Batman and Robin.

Stories relate their crusade against the sinister forces of evil.

Created by Bob Kane, "Batman" first appeared in *Detective Comics* in May 1939. In the Spring of 1940, *Batman Comics* evolved.

In the 1940s, Batman and Robin, through the voices of Stacy Harris and Ronald Liss, respectively, occasionally made guest appearances on the Mutual Radio Network program, "Superman."

The first fifteen-chapter serial, "Batman," produced by Columbia Pictures, was released to theatres in 1943.

CAST

Batman: Lewis Wilson; Robin: Douglas Croft; Dr. Daka: J. Carroll Naish; Linda: Shirley Patterson; Martin Warren: Gus Glassmire.

In 1949, the final theatrical serial, "The New Adventures of Batman and Robin," produced by Columbia, appeared.

CAST

Batman: Robert Lowry; Robin: Johnny Duncan; Police Commissioner Gordon: Lyle Talbot; Jane Adams: Vickie Vale.

TV CAST

Bruce Wayne/Batman	Adam West
Dick Greyson/Robin	Burt Ward
Barbara Gordon/ Batgirl	Yvonne Craig
Alfred, the Wayne family butler	Alan Napier
Commissioner Gordon	Neil Hamilton
Police Chief O'Hara	Stafford Repp
Harriet Cooper, Bruce's aunt	Madge Blake
Criminals:	
The Penguin	Burgess Meredith
Dawn Robbins, his aide	Leslie Parrish
Lola Lasagne	Ethel Merman
Gluten, her aide	Horace McMahon
The Joker	Cesar Romero
Cornelia, his aide	Kathy Kersh
Venus, his aide	Terry Moore
The Riddler	Frank Gorshin
	John Astin
Molly, his aide	Jill Saint John
Anna Gram, his aide	Deanna Lund
The Archer	Art Carney
Maid Marilyn, his aide	Barbara Nichols
Crier Tuck, his aide	Doodles Weaver
The Catwoman	Julie Newmar
	Lee Ann Meriweather
	Eartha Kitt
Pussycat, her aide	Lesley Gore
Leo, her aide	Jock Mahoney

Lady Penelope Peasoup	Glynis Johns
Lord Marmaduke Ffogg	Rudy Vallee
Colonel Gumm	Roger C. Carmel
Pinky, his aide	Diane McBaine
The Black Widow	Tallulah Bankhead
Egghead	Vincent Price
Olga, his aide	Anne Baxter
Chicken, his aide	Edward Everett Horton
Dr. Cassandra	Ida Lupino
Cabala, her aide	Howard Duff
Falseface	Malachi Throne
Blaze, his aide	Myrna Fahey
The Sandman	Michael Rennie
The Puzzler	Maurice Evans
Rocket O'Rourke, his aide	Barbara Stuart
Sophie Starr	Kathleen Crowley
Eagle Eye, her aide	Harvey Lembeck
Chandell	Liberace
Jervis Tetch, the Mad Hatter	David Wayne
Mr. Freeze	George Sanders
Ma Parker	Shelley Winters
Clock King	Walter Slezak
The Minstrel	Van Johnson
The Siren	Joan Collins
Shame	Cliff Robertson
Marsha, Queen of Diamonds	Carolyn Jones
Louie the Lilac	Milton Berle
The Bookworm	Roddy McDowall
The Devil, his aide	Joan Crawford
Lydia, his aide	Francine York
King Tut	Victor Buono
Minerva	Zsa Zsa Gabor

Batman and Robin's car: The *Batmobile.*

Batgirl's mode of transportation: The *Batcycle.*

Music: Nelson Riddle; Billy May; Neil Hefti.

BATMAN—30 minutes—ABC—January 12, 1966 - March 14, 1968. Syndicated.

THE BATMAN/SUPERMAN HOUR

See individual titles: "The Adventures of Superman;" "Batman."

BAT MASTERSON

Western. Background: The territory from Kansas to California during the 1880s. The exploits of William Bartley "Bat" Masterson, a wandering law enforcer. Legend associates him with several trademarks: a gold-tipped cane, a derby hat, and a custom built gun—items presented to him by the greatful citizens of Dodge City during his service as sheriff.

Starring: Gene Barry as Bat Masterson.

Announcer-Narrator: Bill Baldwin.

BAT MASTERSON—30 minutes—NBC—October 8, 1957 - September 21, 1961. Syndicated.

BATTLELINE

Documentary. The key battles and campaigns of World War II are traced through film.

Host-Narrator: Jim Bishop.

BATTLELINE—30 minutes—Syndicated 1963.

BATTLE OF THE AGES

Game. Two talent teams compete: The Show Business Veterans and The

Youngsters. The teams compete in a series of talent contests designed to determine the better of the two. Winners, which are determined by off-stage judges, receive cash prizes.

Hosts: Morey Amsterdam; John Reed King.

Announcer: Norman Brokenshire.

Orchestra: Al Fennelli.

BATTLE OF THE AGES—30 minutes—DuMont 1951; CBS 1952.

THE BEACHCOMBER

Adventure. Pressured by society, John Lackland, a wealthy merchandising executive, departs San Francisco and retreats to Amura, a tropical island paradise in the South Pacific. Adopting the life of a beachcomber, he searches for the true meaning of life and happiness. Episodes relate his struggles as he encounters and assists people in distress.

CAST

John Lackland	Cameron Mitchell
Captain Huckabee, his friend	Don Megowan
Andrew Crippen, the Commissioner	Sebastian Cabot

Music: Joseph Hooven.

THE BEACHCOMBER—30 minutes—Syndicated 1961.

BEACON HILL

Serial. Background: Boston during the 1920s. Dramatic incidents in the lives of the Lassiters, a rich, powerful Irish-American family; and their servants, Irish immigrants, who live below them in a fashionable home on Louisburgh Square. Based on the British series, "Upstairs, Downstairs," which was broadcast in the United States via "Masterpiece Theatre." (See title.)

CAST

The Lassiter Family:

Benjamin Lassiter, an attorney	Stephen Elliott
Mary Lassiter, his wife	Nancy Marchand
Emily Bullock, their married daughter	DeAnn Mears
Trevor Bullock, Emily's husband	Roy Cooper
Betsy Bullock, their daughter	Linda Purl
Maude Palmer, Ben and Mary's married daughter	Maeve McGuire
Richard Palmer, Maude's husband	Edward Herrmann
Rosamond Lassiter, Ben and Mary's daughter	Kitty Winn
Fawn Lassiter, Ben and Mary's daughter	Kathryn Walker
Robert Lassiter, Ben and Mary's son	David Dukes

The Servants:

Mr. Hacker, the head butler	George Rose
Emmaline Hacker, his wife	Beatrice Straight
William Piper, the cook	Richard Ward
Brian Mallory, the chauffeur	Paul Rudd
Terence O'Hara, Mr. Hacker's assistant	David Rounds
Eleanor, a maid	Sydney Swire
Maureen, a maid	Susan Blanchard

Kate, a maid   Lisa Pelikan

Music: Marvin Hamlisch.

BEACON HILL—60 minutes—CBS—August 25, 1975 - November 4, 1975.

THE BEAGLES

Animated Cartoon. The misadventures of Stringer and Tubby, canines who comprise The Beagles, a Rock and Roll duo.

THE BEAGLES—30 minutes—CBS—September 10, 1966 - September 2, 1967. ABC—September 9, 1967 - September 7, 1968. Syndicated.

BEANIE AND CECIL

Children. The global misadventures of a small boy, Beany; his pet sea serpent, Cecil; and Huffenpuff, the captain of their boat, the *Leakin' Lena.* Based on the characters created by Bob Clampett.

Versions:

Time For Beany—Puppet Adventure—15 minutes—Syndicated 1950.

Characters: Beany, Cecil, Captain Huffenpuff, Moon Mad Tiger, Jack Webfoot, Dizzy Lou and Hey You, the Double Feature Creature with the Stereophonic Sound, Marilyn Mongrel, Louie the Lone Shark.

Voices: Stan Freberg, Daws Butler, Jerry Colona.

The Beany and Cecil Show—Animated Cartoon—30 minutes—Syndicated 1961.

Characters: Beany, Cecil, Captain Huffenpuff, Crowy the lookout, Dishonest John.

Voices: Daws Butler, Don Messick, Joan Gerber.

Music: Jack Roberts, Hoyt Curtin, Eddie Brandt, Melvyn Lenard.

BEARCATS!

Adventure. Background: the turbulent Southwest, 1914. The experiences of free-lance troubleshooters Hank Brackett and Johnny Reach. Episodes depict their battle against the early breed of twentieth-century criminal.

CAST

Hank Brackett   Rod Taylor
Johnny Reach   Dennis Cole

BEARCATS!—60 minutes—CBS—September 16, 1971 - December 30, 1971.

THE BEATLES

Animated Cartoon. The songs and misadventures of the famous Liverpool rock group, the Beatles.

Characters' Voices
John Lennon   Himself
Ringo Starr   Himself
George Harrison   Himself
Paul McCartney   Himself

Music: Recorded Beatle songs.

THE BEATLES—30 minutes—ABC—September 25, 1965 - September 7, 1969. Syndicated.

BEAT THE CLOCK

Game. Contestants, usually married

Beat the Clock. Guest Sheila MacRae and host Jack Narz.

couples, attempt to perform stunts and beat the amount of time shown on a ticking sixty-second clock. Cash and/or merchandise prizes are awarded.

Versions:

CBS—30 minutes—March 23, 1950 - February 16, 1958.
ABC—October 13, 1958 - September 26, 1962.

Host: Bud Collyer.

Assistant: Dolores Rosedale (Roxanne).

Syndicated—30 minutes—1969.

Hosts: Jack Narz; Gene Wood.

Assistants: Gail Sheldon, Betsy Hirst, Ellen Singer, Linda Somer, Diane Mead.

Announcers: Gene Wood; Dick Holenberg.

Music: Dick Hyman.

BEAT THE ODDS

Game. Two competing contestants. The game revolves around a large electronic spinning wheel which contains the first and last letters of numerous word possibilities and a point reclaimer, Mr. Whamie. After the host spins the wheel one player at a time presses a button and stops it. If two letters appear (e.g. S.....E) he must give a word corresponding to it (e.g. *Singl*E). Acceptable words earn the player ten points. However, should Mr. Whamie appear (the odds are four to one) the contestant loses his turn at play and any points he has accumulated. The only way a contestant can retain points is to freeze his score when he feels safe. When a score is frozen it cannot be affected by Mr. Whamie on that player's next turn. The player first to score one hundred points is the winner and he receives that amount in dollars.

Host: Johnny Gilbert.

Announcer: Bill Baldwin.

BEAT THE ODDS—30 minutes—Syndicated 1969.

THE BEAUTIFUL PHYLLIS DILLER SHOW

Variety. Various comedy sketches satirizing world problems.

Hostess: Phyllis Diller.

Regulars: Norm Crosby, Rip Taylor, Dave Willock, Bob Jellison, Merryl Jay and the Curtin Calls, The Jack Regas Dancers.

Announcer: Norm Crosby.

Orchestra: Jack Elliott.

The Beautiful Phyllis Diller Show. Phyllis Diller.

THE BEAUTIFUL PHYLLIS DILLER SHOW—60 minutes—NBC—September 15, 1968 - December 22, 1968.

BEHIND CLOSED DOORS

Anthology Drama. Tales of international intrigue based on the files of Admiral Zacharies, a World War II Naval Intelligence Chief.

Host-Narrator (appearing as Commander Matson): Bruce Gordon.

BEHIND CLOSED DOORS—30 minutes—ABC—May 25, 1959 - September 20, 1960.

BELIEVE IT OR NOT

Anthology. Dramatizations based on unusual but actual incidents compiled by Robert Ripley for his newspaper column, "Believe It Or Not."

Host: Robert Ripley.

BELIEVE IT OR NOT—30 minutes—NBC 1950.

THE BELL TELEPHONE HOUR

Music. A documentary style presentation wherein outstanding guests appear in distinguished programs devoted entirely to the music fields of opera, ballet, jazz, popular, and classical.

Music: The Bell Telephone Orchestra.

Conductor: Donald Voorhees.

THE BELL TELEPHONE HOUR–60 minutes–NBC–January 12, 1959 - June 1968.

BEN CASEY

Medical Drama. Background: County General Hospital. The victories and defeats of Ben Casey, a chief resident in neurosurgery.

CAST

Dr. Ben Casey	Vincent Edwards
Dr. David Zorba, his mentor, the neurosurgical chief	Sam Jaffe
Dr. Freeland, the neurosurgical chief (later episodes)	Franchot Tone
Dr. Maggie Graham, Casey's romantic interest	Bettye Ackerman
Nurse Willis	Jeanne Bates
Dr. Ted Hoffman	Harry Landers
Orderly Nick Kanavars	Nick Dennis
Dr. Terry McDaniel	Jim McMullan

Music: George Bassman.

BEN CASEY–60 minutes–ABC– October 2, 1961 - March 21, 1966. Syndicated.

BEN JERROD

Serial. Background: The town of Indian Hill. The dramatic story of two lawyers: John P. Abbott, a retired judge, the elder, set in his ways; and Ben Jerrod, his assistant, a Harvard-educated youth. Their first and only case: "The Janet Donelli Murder Trial." Episodes relate their defense of a woman who is accused of murdering her husband.

CAST

Ben Jerrod	Michael Ryan
John Abbott	Addison Richards
Janet Donelli	Regina Gleason
Jim O'Hara	Ken Scott
Engle, the coroner	William Phillips
The District Attorney	John Napier
Peter Morrison	Peter Hansen
Lieutenant Choates	Lyle Talbot
Lil	Martine Bartlett

BEN JERROD–30 minutes–NBC– April 1, 1963 - June 28, 1963.

THE BENNETS

Serial. Background: A small midwestern town. The dramatic story of attorney Wayne Bennet and his wife Nancy.

CAST

Wayne Bennet	Don Gibson
Nancy Bennet	Paula Houston

Also: Jerry Harvey, Roy Westfall, Sam Gray, Kay Westfall, Jim Andelin, Viola Berwick, Beverly Younger, Jack Lester, Sam Siegel.

THE BENNETS–15 minutes–NBC– July 6, 1953 - January 8, 1954.

BEN VEREEN . . . COMIN' AT YA

Variety. Music, songs, dances, and comedy sketches.

Host: Ben Vereen.

Regulars: Arte Johnson, Avery

Schreiber, Liz Torres, The Louis DaPron Dancers.

Ben's Dancing Partner: Lee Lund.

Orchestra: Jack Elliott, Allyn Ferguson.

Special Musical Material: Ray Charles.

BEN VEREEN . . . COMIN'AT YA—60 minutes—NBC—August 7, 1975 - August 28, 1975.

THE BERT PARKS SHOW

Variety. Music, songs, guests, and interviews.

Host: Bert Parks.

Regulars: Betty Ann Grove; Bobby Sherwood; The Heathertones: Bix Brent, Marianne McCormick, Nancy Overton, Jean Swain, and Marray Scholmann.

Music: The Bobby Sherwood Quintet.

THE BERT PARKS SHOW—30 minutes—NBC—November 1, 1950 - January 11, 1952.

THE BEST IN MYSTERY

Anthology. Rebroadcasts of suspense dramas that were originally aired via other filmed anthology series.

Hostess: Polly Bergen.

Included:

Lost Kid. The story of a grandmother who uses every possible device to keep her juvenile deliquent grandson from embarking on an adult life of crime.

CAST

Elizabeth Patterson, Mary Field, Harry Harvey, Jr.

Death Makes A Pair. The story of a businessman who finds himself with gambling fever after becoming involved with an associate.

CAST

Lloyd Corrigan, Jay Novello, Margia Dean.

The Watchers And The Watched. The story of three people who set out on an evil mission: to drive someone out of his mind; the motive: robbery.

CAST

Fay Roope.

THE BEST IN MYSTERY—60 minutes—NBC—July 16, 1954 - September 1954.

THE BEST IN MYSTERY

Drama. Background: San Francisco, California. The story of Willie Dante, former gambler turned owner of Dante's Inferno Nightclub. Episodes relate his struggles to overcome the situations that occur when his past reputation attracts unscrupulous characters. Originally broadcast as occasional episodes of "Four Star Playhouse."

CAST

Willie Dante	Dick Powell
Jackson, his aide	Alan Mowbray
Monte, his aide	Herb Vigran
Lieutenant Waldo, S.F.P.D.	Regis Toomey

THE BEST IN MYSTERY—60 minutes—NBC—July 13, 1956 - August 31, 1956.

THE BEST OF EVERYTHING

Serial. Background: New York City. The dramatic story of three young women: April Morrison, Linda Warren, and Kim Jordan, secretaries at Key Publishing. Episodes relate their experiences as they struggle to fulfill their lives.

CAST

April Morrison	Julie Mannix
Linda Warren	Patty McCormack
Violet Jordan	Geraldine Fitzgerald
Amanda Key	Gale Sondergaard
Ed Peronne	Vice Arnold
Ken Lamont	Barry Ford
Kim Jordan	Kathy Glass
Johnny Lomart	Stephen Grover
Randy Wilson	Ted La Platt

Also: M'el Dowd, Terry O'Sullivan, Jill Melody, Jane Alice Brandon.

THE BEST OF EVERYTHING—30 minutes—ABC—March 30, 1970 - September 24, 1970.

THE BEST OF THE POST

Anthology. Dramatizations based on stories appearing in the *Saturday Evening Post*.

Included:

Treasury Agent. The story of treasury agents Don Kearns and Paul Corbin and their attempts to apprehend the infamous gangster Vince Lewis.

CAST
Michael Higgins, Richard Arlen, Joe Mell.

The Baron Loved His Wife. The story of a Viennese nobleman who attempts to trail a British agent despite the constant hindrance of his wife.

CAST
Pete Lorre, Ingrid Goride.

Frontier Correspondent. Background: The Old West. The story of an Eastern newspaper reporter as he attempts to take a picture of Jesse James.

CAST
Bert Douglas.

THE BEST OF THE POST—30 minutes Syndicated 1959.

THE BETTY CROCKER STAR MATINEE

Variety. Guests, interviews, and dramatic vignettes.

Hostess: Adelaide Hawley.

THE BETTY CROCKER STAR MATINEE—30 minutes—ABC—November 3, 1951 - April 26, 1952.

THE BETTY HUTTON SHOW

Comedy. Background: New York City. Goldie Appleby, manicurist, one-time vivacious show girl, accepts a dinner invitation from a customer, a lonely millionaire. His sudden death finds her the unaccountable beneficiary of his will — head of the Strickland Foundation, the executrix of his sixty-million-dollar Park Avenue estate, and guardian of his three orphaned children.

Episodes concern her struggles to adjust to new responsibilities, run the ' foundation, and care for and secure the affections of Patricia, Roy, and

Nicky, the spendthrift Strickland children.

CAST

Goldie Appleby	Betty Hutton
Patricia Strickland	Gigi Perreau
Nicky Strickland	Richard Miles
Roy Strickland	Dennis Joel
Lorna, Goldie's friend	Joan Shawlee
Howard Seaton, the Strickland attorney	Tom Conway
Rosemary, the maid	Jean Carson
Hollister, the butler	Gavin Muir

THE BETTY HUTTON SHOW—30 minutes—CBS—October 1, 1959 - June 30, 1960. Also known as: "Goldie."

THE BETTY WHITE SHOW

Variety. Music, songs, guests, and interviews.

Versions:

NBC—30 minutes—1954.

Hostess: Betty White.

Announcer: Del Sharbutt.

Orchestra: Frank DeVol.

ABC—30 minutes — February 5, 1958 - April 30, 1958.

Hostess: Betty White.

Regulars: John Dehner, Chill Wills.

Orchestra: Frank DeVol.

BEULAH

Comedy. Background: New York City. The trials and tribulations of the Henderson family: Harry, an attorney; his wife, Alice; their son, Donnie; and their maid, Beulah, the irrepressible Queen of the Kitchen. Stories relate Beulah's attempts to solve arising household crises and the problems that are created by her unpredictable girlfriend, Oriole and her boyfriend, Bill Jackson, a fix-it-shop owner.

CAST

1950-1952:

Beulah	Ethel Waters
	Hattie McDaniel
Harry Henderson	William Post, Jr.
Alice Henderson	Ginger Jones
Donnie Henderson	Clifford Sales
Oriole	Butterfly McQueen
Bill Jackson	Percy "Bud" Harris

1952-1953:

Beulah	Louise Beavers
Harry Henderson	David Bruce
Alice Henderson	June Frazee
Donnie Henderson	Stuffy Singer
Oriole	Butterfly McQueen
Bill Jackson	Dooley Wilson

BEULAH—30 minutes—CBS—October 10, 1950 - September 22, 1953. Syndicated. Withdrawn.

THE BEVERLY HILLBILLIES

Comedy. Background: 518 Crestview Drive, Beverly Hills, California, the residence of the Clampett family: Jed, a widowed mountaineer; his beautiful and unmarried daughter, Elly May; his mother-in-law, Daisy "Granny" Moses; and his not-too-bright nephew, Jethro Bodine — a simple backwoods family who became multimillionaires when oil was discovered on their property in the Ozark community of Sibly. Stories relate their struggles to adjust to the fast, sophisticated, modern life of the big city.

Jed, though content, longs for life

as before. Granny, unable to practice her unlicensed mountain doctoring (Dr. Roy Clyburn has threatened to press charges), make her ly soap (the process pollutes the air), or find needed ingredients in city stores (e.g., "possum innerds") is miserable and wants to return home.

Elly May, determined to prove herself superior to any man, is unable to find a steady beau, and prefers life with her countless "critters." Jethro, educated and graduated from the sixth grade, delights in the excitement of the big city and endlessly attempts to attract the opposite sex and "find...a sweetheart."

CAST

Jed Clampett	Buddy Ebsen
Daisy Moses (Granny)	Irene Ryan
Elly May Clampett	Donna Douglas
Jethro Bodine	Max Baer
Jethrene Bodine, his sister	Max Baer
Milburn Drysdale, the President of the Commerce Bank, which houses Jed's money	Raymond Bailey
Jane Hathaway, his secretary	Nancy Kulp
Margaret Drysdale, Milburn's wife, a woman determined to rid her life of her unsavory neighbors, the Clampetts	Margaret MacGibbon
Pearl Bodine, Jethro's mother	Bea Benaderet
John Brewster, the president of the O.K. Oil Company	Frank Wilcox
Isabel Brewster, his wife	Lisa Seagram
Lester Flatt, a friend of the Clampetts	Himself
Earl Scruggs, a friend of the Clampetts	Himself
Gladys Flatt, Lester's wife	Joi Lansing
Louise Scruggs, Earl's wife	Midge Ware
Homer Winch, a backwoods oldster, fond of Pearl (a widow)	Paul Winchell
Jasper DePew, Jethrene's boyfriend	Phil Gordon
Ravenscott, the Drysdale's butler	Arthur Gould Porter
Marie, the Drysdale's maid	Shirry Steffin
Dash Riprock (Homer Noodleman), a movie star, Elly May's beau	Larry Pennell
Mark Templeton, Elly May's beau (later episodes)	Roger Torrey
Homer Cratchit, the bank bookkeeper	Percy Helton
Elverna Bradshaw, Granny's nemesis	Elvia Allman
Sonny Drysdale, Milburn's son, in his 19th year in college	Louis Nye
Janet Trego, a bank secretary	Sharon Tate
Dr. Roy Clyburn, Granny's nemesis	Fred Clark
The Psychiatrist	Richard Deacon
Harry Chapman, a movie producer at Mammoth Studios	Milton Frome

Announcer: Bill Baldwin.

Music: Perry Bodkin; Curt Massey.

THE BEVERLY HILLBILLIES—30 minutes—CBS—September 26, 1962 - September 7, 1971. Syndicated.

BEWITCHED

Comedy. Background: 1164 Morning Glory Circle, West Port, Connecticut, the home of Darrin Stevens, a mortal and advertising executive with the Manhattan firm of McMann and Tate;

Bewitched. Left to right: Erin Murphy, Dick York, Elizabeth Montgomery, and Agnes Moorehead. © *Screen Gems.*

and his wife, a beautiful witch, Samantha. Episodes relate Samantha's attempts to adopt the role of housewife, and Darrin's struggles to curtail and conceal his wife's powers and cope with his disapproving mother-in-law, Endora, who, when angered, delights in casting spells upon him.

CAST

Samantha Stevens	Elizabeth Montgomery
Serena, her beautiful, funloving cousin	Elizabeth Montgomery (credited: Pandora Sparks)
Darrin Stevens	Dick York
	Dick Sargent
Endora	Agnes Moorehead
Larry Tate, Darrin's employer	David White
Louise Tate, his wife	Irene Vernon
Gladys Kravitz, the Stevens's nosey neighbor	Alice Pearce
	Sandra Gould
Abner Kravitz, her husband	George Tobias
Maurice, Samatha's father	Maurice Evans
Uncle Arthur, a warlock, Samantha's relative	Paul Lynde
Doctor Bombay, Samantha's family physician	Bernard Fox
Aunt Clara, an aging, bumbling witch	Marion Lorne
Tabitha Stevens, the Stevens daughter, a witch	Erin & Diane Murphy (identical twins)
Frank Stevens, Darrin's father	Robert F. Simon
	Roy Roberts
Phyllis Stevens, his wife	Mabel Albertson
Esmeralda, a shy witch	Alice Ghostley
Adam Stevens, the Stevens son, a warlock	David & Greg Lawrence (identical twins)
Betty, Darrin's secretary	Marcia Wallace

Music: Warren Barker; Jimmie Haskell.

BEWITCHED—30 minutes—ABC—September 17, 1964 - July 1, 1972. Syndicated.

BICENTENNIAL MINUTES

History. A series of 732 sixty-second programs celebrating the birth of America. Personalities relate authenticated aspects of America's past — obscure or well-known incidents that occurred two hundred years prior to that particular evening's broadcast.

BICENTENNIAL MINUTES—01 minute (12 hours total)—CBS—July 4, 1974 - July 4, 1976. Broadcast each evening at either 8:27 or 8:28 P.M., (E.S.T.) depending on whether the previous program is a half hour or an hour.

BIFF BAKER, U.S.A.

Adventure. Background: The Soviet Union. The cases of Biff and Louise Baker (man and wife) American export buyers secretly working for the United States Government. Stories relate their attempts to investigate the secrecy barriers behind Iron Curtain rule.

CAST
Biff Baker   Alan Hale, Jr.
Louise Baker   Randy Stuart

BIFF BAKER, U.S.A.—30 minutes—CBS—1952-1953.

THE BIG ATTACK

Anthology. Backgrounds: The European Front during World War Two, and Korea during the 1950s. True stories of Americans in combat. Dramas relate the lives of particular individuals on missions; the driving forces that enable a person to accomplish amazing feats of daring.

Narrator: The actual person featured in each episode.

Music: Bert Grund.

THE BIG ATTACK—30 minutes— Syndicated 1957. Also known as "Citizen Soldier."

THE BIG BANDS

Musical Variety. Performances by the personalities of the Big Band Era.

Appearing: Tommy Dorsey, Count Basie, Glenn Miller, Harry James, Guy Lombardo, Buddy Rogers.

THE BIG BANDS—30 minutes—Syndicated 1965.

BIG EDDIE

Comedy. Background: New York City. The misadventures of Big Eddie Smith, a former gambler turned legitimate entrepreneur as the owner of the Big E Sports Arena. Created by Bill Persky and Sam Denoff.

CAST
Eddie Smith   Sheldon Leonard
Honey Smith, his
    wife   Sheree North
Ginger Smith,
    Eddie's grand-
    daughter   Quinn Cummings
Monty "Bang Bang"
    Valentine, Eddie's
    cook   Billy Sands
Jessie Smith, Eddie's
    brother   Alan Oppenheimer
Raymond McKay, an
    employee of
    Eddie's   Ralph Wilcox

Music: Jack Elliott, Allyn Ferguson, Earle Hagen.

BIG EDDIE—30 minutes—CBS— August 23, 1975 - November 7, 1975.

BIG GAME

Game. Two competing contestants. Undertaken: the big African game hunt (played similar to "Battleships.") Each player sets three translucent animals on a board concealed from the other. The host asks a general knowledge question. The player first to identify himself through a buzzer signal receives a chance to answer. If the response is correct, he receives the opportunity to hunt his opponent's game. A position is called and marked on a peg board. If the number called indicates the spot on which one of his opponent's animals is located, a hit is called. The player continues calling numbers until a miss is indicated. When that occurs, the questions resume and the game follows as before. The player first to "shoot" his opponent's animals is the winner and receives a cash prize.

Host: Tom Kennedy.

BIG GAME—30 minutes—NBC—June 13, 1958 - September 1958.

THE BIG PARTY

Variety. An informal gathering of celebrities at a personality's home. An old piano is the center of attraction with the guests milling about, exchanging talk, and performing.

Included Parties:

Host: Rock Hudson. *Guests:* Tallulah Bankhead, Esther Williams, Mort Sahl, Sammy Davis, Jr.

Hostess: Greer Garson. *Guests:* Martha Raye, Sal Mineo, Walter Slezak, Mike Nichols, Elaine May, Peter Lind Hayes, Mary Healy.

Hostess: Irene Dunne. *Guests:* Gypsy Rose Lee, Jack Carter, Pearl Bailey.

Hostess: Eva Gabor. *Guests:* Carol Channing, Sir John Gielgud, The Benny Goodman Trio.

Commercial Spokeswoman: Barbara Britton.

Musical Director: Gordon Jenkins.

THE BIG PARTY—90 minutes—CBS—1959-1960.

THE BIG PAYOFF

Variety. A combination of music, songs, dances, and game contests. Players, selected studio audience members, compete for furs, trips, and clothing via general knowledge question and answer or stunt rounds.

Hosts: Bert Parks; Randy Merriman; Mort Lawrence; Robert Paige.

Hostesses: Bess Myerson; Betty Ann Grove (Sandy Grove); Denis Lor; Dori Anne Grey.

Music: The Burt Buhram Trio.

THE BIG PAYOFF—30 minutes—CBS—1952 - 1960.

THE BIG PICTURE

Documentary. The history and development of the United States Army.

Host: George Gunn.

Narrator: Leonard Graves.

Announcer: Captain Carl Zimmerman.

THE BIG PICTURE—30 minutes—Syndicated 1951.

THE BIG RECORD

Variety. The recording industry's top entertainers perform the material that made them famous.

Hostess: Patti Paige.

Orchestra: Vic Schoen.

THE BIG RECORD–60 minutes–CBS–September 18, 1957 - June 11, 1958.

THE BIG SHOWDOWN

Game. Three competing contestants. A playoff point is established (e.g., 8) and an accompanying money value (from twenty-five to five hundred dollars) appears. The host reads a toss-up question. The player who is first to identify himself by a light-buzzer signal receives a chance to answer. If correct, he receives one point and control of a board that contains six subjects, each worth points (1,2,3,4,5, or 6). After the player chooses a subject, the host reads an accompanying question. The player who is first to identify himself receives a chance to answer. If correct, the points are added to his score; if incorrect, no penalty, and a new toss-up round begins. The player who is first to score the playoff points exactly receives the money. Additional rounds follow the same format with the playoff point increased by seven each time, each with a different amount of money. The two highest scoring players then compete in "Final Show Down."

A category board, which contains three subjects, each distinguished by points (1,2, or 3) is displayed. The playoff point is established at seven. The player with the highest score from the previous round chooses one subject. The question is asked and the player who first identifies himself receives a chance to answer. If correct, he chooses the next category. The player who is first to score seven points is the winner, receives two

hundred and fifty dollars, and the opportunity to win $10,000 in cash.

The player is escorted to a dice board. Two dice, which contain the word "Show" and "Down" on one side each are used. The player receives one roll. If he rolls "Show Down" he wins ten thousand dollars. If not, he receives thirty seconds to roll the dice. If "Show Down" appears, he receives five thousand dollars. If not, his original round earnings are won, and he returns to compete again.

Host: Jim Peck.

Announcer: Dan Daniels.

Music: Score Productions.

First Champion: Sharon Diamond.

THE BIG SHOWDOWN–30 minutes–ABC–December 23, 1974 - July 4, 1975.

BIG STORY

Anthology. Dramatizations based on the journalistic achievements of newsmen. Reporters receive five hundred dollars for the use of their stories.

Hosts-Narrators: William Sloane; Ben Grauer; Burgess Meredith.

Orchestra: Wladimar Selinsky.

Included:

Theory And Practice. A reporter attempts to find the murderer of a policeman.

Starring: Wesley Addy.

The Smell Of Death. A reporter attempts to free two youngsters who are being held hostage by a berserk gunman.

Starring: Peter Turgeon, Tom Carlin.

A Madman Is Loose. After two cab drivers are killed by a psycopathic killer who has an obsession for canaries, a reporter attempts to apprehend the murderer by exploiting his quirk.

Starring: Bernard Grant, Leonardo Cimino.

Nightmare. A reporter investigates the methods of treatment used by a psychiatrist in North Carolina.

Starring: Sara Seeger.

BIG STORY–30 minutes–NBC– 1949 - 1955. Syndicated.

THE BIG SURPRISE

Human Interest. People, chosen for a particular act of kindness, tell of their unselfish deeds. The program then unites the humanitarian with the recipient, and awards the former an item that he has wanted, but was unable to afford.

Host: Jack Barry.

THE BIG SURPRISE–30 minutes– NBC–1955 - 1956.

THE BIG TOP

Variety. American and foreign circus acts, "the biggest circus show on the air."

Ringmaster: Jack Sterling.

Clowns: Ed McMahon, Chris Keegan.

Regulars: Circus Dan, the Muscle Man; Lott and Joe Anders; La Paloma.

Music: The Quaker City String Band; Joe Basile's Brass Kings.

THE BIG TOP–60 minutes–CBS– July 1, 1950 - September 21, 1957.

BIG TOWN

Crime Drama. Background: Big Town, U.S.A. The story of two Illustrated Press newspaper reporters: Steve Wilson, an intrepid crime reporter, and Lorelei Kilbourne, the society reporter. Episodes relate their attempts to acquire headline-making and newspaper-selling stories.

Special note. Episodes from 1950 to 1954 portrayed Wilson as the ex-managing editor of the paper, a man observing people and their problems. For the duration of the series, 1954 to 1956, Wilson is returned to the position of managing editor and becomes actively involved in investigations.

CAST

Steve Wilson	Patrick McVey (1950-1954)
	Mark Stevens (1954-1956)
Lorelei Kilbourne	Margaret Hayes (1950-1951)
	Mary K. Wells (1951)
	Jane Nigh (1951-1953)
	Beverly Tyler (1953)
	Trudy Wroe (1954)
	Julie Stevens (1954-1955)
Diane Walker, I.P. reporter	Doe Averdon (1955-1956)
Charlie Anderson, the city editor	Barry Kelly
Lt. Tom Gregory	John Doucette

Music: Albert Glasser.

BIG TOWN–30 minutes–NBC– October 5, 1950 - September 23, 1956. Syndicated titles: "By Line– Steve Wilson"; "City Assignment"; "Crime Reporter"; "Headline Story" and "Heart of the City."

THE BIG VALLEY

Western. Background: The San

The Big Valley. Left to right: Peter Breck, Barbara Stanwyck, and Richard Long.

Joaquin Valley in Stockton, California, 1878. The saga of the close-knit Barkley family, cattle ranchers: Victoria, widow of Tom (killed by railroad officials in a stubborn defense of his independence), a woman of beauty and courage, a strong-willed matriarch; Jarrod, her eldest son, a lawyer; Nick, her second born, quick tempered and two fisted, the ranch foreman; Audra, her daughter, young, beautiful, proud, sensuous, and impulsive, a woman yet to be tamed by the love of a man; Heath, Tom's illegitimate son (born of an Indian maiden), a man who struggled, fought, and ultimately achieved his birthright—the name of Barkley—a man, troubled by the memories of a difficult childhood, still reaching out for the love that he never had; and Eugene, her youngest, shy and sensitive (dropped early in the series).

Stories depict the life, struggles,

and loves of the Barkley's as they attempt to maintain and operate their thirty-thousand-acre cattle ranch in an era of violence and lawlessness.

CAST

Victoria Barkley	Barbara Stanwyck
Jarrod Barkley	Richard Long
Nick Barkley	Peter Breck
Heath Barkley	Lee Majors
Audra Barkley	Linda Evans
Eugene Barkley	Charles Briles
Silas, their servant	Napoleon Whiting
Sheriff Steve Madden (also referred to as Fred Madden)	Douglas Kennedy
	James Gavin
	Mort Mills
Harry, the bartender	Harry Swoger
Frequently cast, various roles	Gene Evans
	James Gregory

Music: George Duning; Joseph Mullendore; Elmer Bernstein.

THE BIG VALLEY—60 minutes—ABC—September 15, 1965 - May 19, 1969. Syndicated.

BILCO

See title: "You'll Never Get Rich."

THE BILL ANDERSON SHOW

Musical Variety. Performances by Country and Western entertainers.

Host: Bill Anderson.

Regulars: Lou Brown, Jan Howard, Jimmy Gately, The Po' Boys.

THE BILL ANDERSON SHOW—30 minutes—Syndicated 1966.

THE BILL COSBY SHOW

Comedy. Background: The mythical Richard Allen Holmes High School in Los Angeles, California. Stories depict the trials and tribulations of Chet Kincaid, its physical education instructor and athletic coach; a man who gives of himself to help others.

CAST

Chet Kincaid	Bill Cosby
Marsha Patterson, the school guidance counselor	Joyce Bulifant
Brian Kincaid, Chet's married brother, a garbage collector	Lee Weaver
Verna Kincaid, Brian's wife	Olga James
Roger Kincaid, Brian's son	Donald Livingston
Rose Kincaid, Chet's mother	Lillian Randolph Beah Richards
Mr. Kincaid, Chet's father	Fred Pinkard

Music: Quincy Jones.

THE BILL COSBY SHOW–30 minutes–NBC–September 14, 1969 - August 31, 1971. Syndicated.

THE BILL DANA SHOW

Comedy. Background: The Metropolitan Hotel in New York City. The struggles of José Jiménez, a bewildered Latin American. Episodes depict his attempt to tend guests, enhance regular establishment services, and adjust to the American way of life.

CAST

José Jiménez	Bill Dana
Byron Glick, the fumbling house detective	Don Adams

The Bill Dana Show. Guest Virginia Kennedy and star Bill Dana.

Mr. Phillips, the hotel manager	Jonathan Harris
Susie, the hotel coffee shop waitress	Maggie Peterson
Eddie, José's co-worker	Gary Crosby
Mrs. Phillips	Amzie Strickland

Music: Earl Hagen.

THE BILL DANA SHOW–30 minutes–NBC–September 1963 - January 1965.

THE BILL GOODWIN SHOW

Variety. Music, songs, guests, and interviews.

Host: Bill Goodwin.

Vocalists: Eileen Barton, Roger Dann.

Music: The Joe Bushkin Trio.

Featured: "The Nostalgia Game." In return for prizes, selected studio audience members reenact the incidents in their lives that were affected by popular songs.

THE BILL GOODWIN SHOW—30 minutes—NBC—September 11, 1951 - March 27, 1952.

THE BILLY DANIELS SHOW

Musical Variety.

Host: Billy Daniels.

Featured: Jimmy Blaine.

Music: The Benny Payne Trio.

THE BILLY DANIELS SHOW—15 minutes—ABC—October 5, 1956 - December 28, 1956.

BILLY ROSE'S PLAYBILL

Anthology. Dramatizations based on stories appearing in the newspaper column, "Pitching Horseshoes."

Host: Billy Rose.

BILLY ROSE'S PLAYBILL—30 minutes—NBC 1951.

THE BING CROSBY SHOW

Comedy. Background: Los Angeles, California. The trials and tribulations of the Collins family: Bing, a former singer-musician turned building engineer; his wife, Ellie; and their children, Joyce (fifteen years of age) and Janice (ten).

CAST

Bing Collins	Bing Crosby
Ellie Collins	Beverly Garland
Joyce Collins	Carol Faylen
Janice Collins	Diane Sherry
Willie Walters, their live-in handyman	Frank McHugh

Orchestra: John Scott Trotter.

THE BING CROSBY SHOW—30 minutes—ABC—September 14, 1964 - June 14, 1965.

BIOGRAPHY

Documentary. The lives of outstanding figures of twentieth-century history are traced via newsreel footage, stills, and interviews.

Host-Narrator: Mike Wallace.

Music: Jack Tillar.

BIOGRAPHY—30 minutes—Syndicated 1962.

BIRDMAN

Animated Cartoon. An American, Ray Randall, is saved from a firey death by the goodness of the Egyptian Sun God, Ra. Bestowed with amazing powers, he becomes the crime-fighting Birdman and unites with the Galaxy Trio (Vapor Man, Galaxy Girl, and Meteor Man). Stories depict their battle against the sinister forces of evil. A Hanna-Barbera production.

Characters' Voices

Ray Randall (Birdman)	Keith Andes
Falcon 7	Don Messick
Birdboy	Dick Beals
Vapor Man	Don Messick
Galaxy Girl	Virginia Eiler
Meteor Man	Ted Cassidy

Music: Hoyt Curtin.

BIRDMAN—30 minutes—NBC—September 9, 1967 - September 14, 1968.

BIRTHDAY HOUSE

Children. Three children, each accompanied by two or three friends, celebrate their birthdays.
Host: Paul Tripp.
Assistants: Jan Leonakis, Kay Elhart.
Music: Kathryn Lande.

BIRTHDAY HOUSE—60 minutes—Syndicated 1963.

THE BLACK ROBE

Courtroom Drama. Reenactments based on actual metropolitan night-court cases. The program uses ordinary people as it mirrors the struggles of life.
Judge: Frankie Thomas, Sr.

THE BLACK ROBE—30 minutes—NBC 1949.

BLACK SADDLE

Western. Background: Latigo, New Mexico during the late 1860s. The cases of Clay Culhane, an ex-gunfighter turned circuit lawyer.

CAST
Clay Culhane — Peter Breck
Marshal Gib Scott — Russell Johnson
Nora Travis, the operator
of the Marathon
Hotel — Anna-Lisa
Music: Herschel Burke Gilbert.

BLACK SADDLE—30 minutes—ABC—October 2, 1959 - September 28, 1960.

BLACKSTONE MAGIC SPOTS

Variety. Short video sequences featuring magic tricks performed by Harry Blackstone.
Host: Harry Blackstone.

BLACKSTONE MAGIC SPOTS—03 minutes—Syndicated 1952.

THE BLACK TULIP

See title: "Family Classics Theatre," *The Black Tulip* segment.

BLIND DATE

Game. Players: six men, representing two universities, and three women, leading Manhattan models. Two men are seated on one side of a wall and one female on the other. The males, the Hunters, telephone the girl, the Hunted, and attempt to talk her into accepting a date with him. On the basis of voice and specially prepared questions, she chooses the most impressive one. The couple receives an all-expense paid romantic evening, including an invitation to the Stork Club. Three such rounds are played per broadcast.
Hostess: Arlene Francis.
Host: Jan Murray.
Announcers: Walter Herlihy, Rex Marshall.
Orchestra: Glenn Osser.

BLIND DATE—30 minutes—ABC. May 9, 1949 - March 9, 1950; March 16, 1950 - June 8, 1950; June 7, 1952 - July 19, 1952; June 1953 - September 1953.

BLONDIE

Comedy. The trials and tribulations of the Bumstead family: Dagwood, an architect with the Dithers Construction Company; his wife, Blondie; and their children, Alexander and Cookie.

Faced with an ever-present lack of financial resources, Blondie's ineffable sense of logic, and a tightwad boss, Julius C. Dithers, Dagwood, the simple-minded bumbler, struggles to cope with life and ease his monetary burdens. Based on the comic by Chic Young.

Versions:
NBC—30 minutes—January 4, 1954 - December 5, 1954; July 5, 1958 - October 4, 1958.

CAST

Blondie Bumstead   Pamela Britton

Blondie (CBS 1968). Left to right: Peter Robbins, Will Hutchins, Patricia Harty, Pamelyn Ferdin, and Daisy.

Blondie Bumstead (on radio and in features)	Penny Singleton
Dagwood Bumstead	Arthur Lake
Alexander Bumstead	Stuffy Singer
Cookie Bumstead	Ann Barnes
Julius C. Dithers	Florenz Ames
Cora Dithers, his wife	Lela Bliss-Hayden
	Elvia Allman
Eloise, Dithers's secretary	Pamela Duncan
Herb Woodley, Dagwood's neighbor	Hal Peary
Georgia Woodley, his wife	Lois Collier
Foghorn, Alexander's friend	George Winslow
Mr. Beasley, the postman	Lucien Littlefield

Bumstead family dog (both versions): Daisey, "the purebred mongrel."

CBS—30 minutes—September 26, 1968 - January 9, 1969.

CAST

Blondie Bumstead	Patricia Harty
Dagwood Bumstead	Will Hutchins
Alexander Bumstead	Peter Robbins
Cookie Bumstead	Pamelyn Ferdin
J.C. Dithers	Jim Backus
Cora Dithers	Henny Backus
Tootsie Woodley, the Bumstead neighbor	Bobbie Jordan

Music: Bernard Green.

THE BLUE ANGEL

Musical Variety. A revue set against the background of New York City's Blue Angel Supper Club.

Host: Orson Bean.

Songstress: Polly Bergen.

Music: The Norman Paris Trio.

THE BLUE ANGEL—30 minutes—CBS—July 6, 1954 - October 12, 1954.

THE BLUE ANGELS

Adventure. The experiences of Wilbur Scott, Hank Bertelli, Zeke Powers, and Cort Ryker, the pilots of the Blue Angels, a team of four precision U.S. Naval Jets.

CAST
Cdr. Arthur Richards	Dennis Cross
Lt. Russ MacDonald	Mike Galloway
Captain Wilbur Scott	Warner Jones
Pilot Hank Bertelli	Don Gordon
Pilot Zeke Powers	Robert Knapp
Pilot Cort Ryker	Ross Elliott

THE BLUE ANGELS—30 minutes—Syndicated 1960.

BLUE LIGHT

Adventure Serial. Era: World War II. David March, foreign correspondent, the last remaining agent of Blue Light Control, an American organization of eighteen men designed to destroy the Nazi High Command, renounces his citizenship and poses as a traitor. His plan to accomplish its objectives takes effect when he joins the ranks of the German Command and is assigned to its intelligence division in Berlin.

Episodes detail his suicide mission as he attempts to destroy the Third Reich from within under the code name Blue Light.

CAST
David March	Robert Goulet
Suzanne Duchard, his assistant	Christine Carere

Music: Lalo Schifrin; Joseph Mullendore.

BLUE LIGHT—30 minutes—ABC—January 12, 1966 - August 31, 1966.

BOB AND BETTY IN ADVENTURELAND

Animated Cartoon. The adventures of a boy and a girl as they travel throughout the world.

BOB AND BETTY IN ADVENTURELAND—05 minutes—Syndicated 1959.

BOB & CAROL & TED & ALICE

Comedy. Background: Los Angeles, California. The story of two families: Bob and Carol Sanders, a young, progressive couple in their late twenties; and their neighbors, Ted and Alice Henderson, an older, conservative couple in their thirties. Episodes relate the incidents and situations that test their reactions, their values, and their marriages. Based on the movie of the same title.

CAST
Bob Sanders, a film director	Robert Urich
Carol Sanders	Anne Archer
Ted Henderson, a lawyer	David Spielberg
Alice Henderson	Anita Gillette
Elizabeth Henderson, Ted and Alice's twelve-year-old daughter	Jodie Foster
Sean Sanders, Bob and Carol's six-year-old son	Bradley Savage

Music: Artie Butler.

BOB & CAROL & TED & ALICE—30 minutes—ABC—September 26, 1973 - November 7, 1973.

BOB AND RAY

Listed: The television programs of comedians Bob Elliott and Ray Goulding.

The Bob and Ray Show—Satire—15 minutes—NBC—November 1951 - May 1952.

Hosts: Bob Elliott and Ray Goulding.

Regulars: Audrey Meadows, Bob Denton.

Announcer: Bob Denton.

Music: Paul Taubman.

Format: Two or three three-minute vignettes; and a four- to five-minute soap opera, "The Life and Loves of Linda Lovely."

The Bob and Ray Show—Satire—30 minutes—NBC—July 1952 - September 1952.

Hosts: Bob Elliott and Ray Goulding.

Featured: Cloris Leachman.

Announcer: Durwood Kirby.

Music: The Alvy West Band.

Club Embassy—Satire—15 minutes—NBC—1952-1953.

Starring: Bob Elliott and Ray Goulding.

Hostess: Julia Meade.

Featured: Audrey Meadows, Florian ZaBach.

The Bob and Ray Show—Satire—15 minutes—ABC—1953 - 1954.

Hosts: Bob Elliott and Ray Goulding.

Regulars: Marion B. Brash, Charles Wood.

Announcer: Charles Wood.

BOBBIE GENTRY'S HAPPINESS HOUR

Variety. Music, songs, dances, and comedy sketches.

Hostess: Bobbie Gentry.

Regulars: Valri Bromfield, Michael Greer, Earl Pomerantz.

Orchestra: Jack Elliott, Allyn Ferguson.

Featured Sketch. "The Chorus Girls." The misadventures of two chorus girls (Bobbie and Valri).

BOBBIE GENTRY'S HAPPINESS HOUR—60 minutes—CBS—June 5, 1974 - June 26, 1974.

THE BOBBY DARIN AMUSEMENT COMPANY

Variety. Music, songs, dances, and comedy sketches.

Host: Bobby Darin.

Regulars: Dick Bakalyon, Tony Amato, Steve Landesberg, Charlene Wong, Rip Taylor, Kathy Cahill, Sarah Frankboner, Dorrie Thompson, Geoff Edwards, The Jimmy Joyce Singers.

Announcer: Roger Carroll.

Orchestra: Eddie Karam.

Sketches:
"The Old Neighborhood." Angie (Bobby) and his friend, Carmine

(Dick), in a weekly discussion over changing times.

"The Wisdom of Dustin John Dustin." The philosophy of a far-out poet (Bobby).

"An Encounter with the NBC Network Psychiatrist." Steve Landesberg as Dr. Buck Schmidt, who aides NBC employees through analysis.

"Los Angeles Traffic Reports." The helicopter reporting of Skyway Silverman (Rip Taylor).

"Musical Salutes" to cities around the country.

THE BOBBY DARIN AMUSEMENT COMPANY—60 minutes—NBC—July 27, 1972 - September 7, 1972. Returned as "The Bobby Darin Show" —60 minutes—NBC—January 19, 1973 - April 27, 1973.

THE BOBBY GOLDSBORO SHOW

Musical Variety.

Host: Bobby Goldsboro.

Featured: Calvin Calaveris, a frog muppet voiced by Peter Cullen.

Announcer: Peter Cullen.

Musical Director: Robert Montgomery.

THE BOBBY GOLDSBORO SHOW— 30 minutes—Syndicated 1973.

THE BOBBY LORD SHOW

Musical Variety. Performances by Country and Western entertainers.

Host: Bobby Lord.

Music: The Jerry Byrd Band.

THE BOBBY LORD SHOW—30 minutes—Syndicated 1965.

THE BOBBY VINTON SHOW

Variety. Music, songs, and comedy sketches.

Host: Bobby Vinton.

Regulars: Billy Van, Arte Johnson, Freeman King, Jack Duffy.

Orchestra: Jimmy Dale.

THE BOBBY VINTON SHOW—30 minutes—Syndicated 1975. Produced in Canada.

THE BOB CRANE SHOW

Comedy. Background: Los Angeles, California. The story of Bob Wilcox, a forty-two-year-old executive who quits his job as an insurance salesman to pursue a medical career.

CAST

Bob Wilcox	Bob Crane
Ellie Wilcox, his wife, a real estate saleswoman	Trisha Hart
Pam Wilcox, their daughter	Erica Petal
Ernest Busso, their landlord	Ronny Graham
Lyle Ingersoll, the dean of the City Medical School of University Hospital	Jack Fletcher
Marvin Sussman, a medical student	Todd Sussman
Jerry Mallory, a medical student	James Sutorius

Music: Mike Post and Pete Carpenter.

THE BOB CRANE SHOW—30 minutes—NBC—March 6, 1975 - June 19, 1975.

BOB CROSBY

Listed: The television programs of singer-musician Bob Crosby.

The Bob Crosby Show—Musical Variety—60 minutes—CBS—1953 - 1954.

Host: Bob Crosby.

Regulars: Joan O'Brien, The Modern-aires.

Announcer: Steve Dunne.

Music: Bob Crosby's Bob Cats.

The Bob Crosby Show—Musical Variety—60 minutes—NBC—June 14, 1958 - September 6, 1958.

Host: Bob Crosby.

Regulars: Gretchen Wyler, The Clay Warnick Singers, The Peter Gennaro Dancers.

Orchestra: Carl Hoff.

THE BOB CUMMINGS SHOW, LOVE THAT BOB

See title: "Love That Bob."

THE BOB CUMMINGS SHOW

Comedy. Background: California. The misadventures of bachelor-pilot Bob Carson. Stories relate his attempts to acquire charter flights and terminate his monetary burdens.

CAST

Bob Carson	Bob Cummings
Lionel, his side-kick	Murvyn Vye
Hank Geogerty, Bob's neighbor, a pretty teenage tomboy	Roberta Shore

THE BOB CUMMINGS SHOW—30 minutes—CBS—October 5, 1961 - March 1, 1962.

THE BOB HOPE CHRYSLER THEATRE

Anthology. Dramatic and comedic productions.

Host: Bob Hope.

Music: Johnny Williams.

Included:

The Enemy On The Beach. Era: World War II. The efforts of a team of demolition experts to disarm newly developed German mines.

CAST
Robert Wagner, Sally Ann Howes, James Donald.

Corridor 400. A nightclub singer attempts to trap a narcotics kingpin for the F.B.I.

CAST
Suzanne Pleshette, Andrew Duggan, Joseph Campanella.

Murder In The First. The tense trial of a law student accused of murdering a married woman.

CAST
Janet Leigh (her dramatic TV debut), Bobby Darin, Lloyd Bochner.

The Reason Nobody Hardly Ever Seen A Fat Outlaw In The Old West Is As Follows. The saga of the Curly Kid as he attempts to make a name for himself.

CAST
The Curly Kid: Don Knotts; the

Sheriff: Arthur Godfrey: his daughter: Mary Robin Reed.

Holloway's Daughters. The story of two teen-age girls and their attempts to assist their detective father on a jewel robbery case.

CAST
Robert Young, David Wayne, Brooke Bundy, Barbara Hershey.

THE BOB HOPE CHRYSLER THEATRE—60 minutes—NBC— October 4, 1963 - September 6, 1967. Preempted one week per month for presentation of "The Bob Hope Special."

THE BOB HOPE SHOW

Variety. A basic format unchanged since Mr. Hope's radio programs: an opening monologue and various comedy sketches with his guest stars. Most notable of his presentations has been the yearly Christmas programs for American servicemen in remote regions of the world.

Host: Bob Hope.

Featured: The Nick Castle Dancers.

Announcer: Frank Barton.

Orchestra: Les Brown.

THE BOB HOPE SHOW—60 minutes —NBC—Premiered: October 12, 1952. Broadcast as a series of specials. Also titled: "Chrysler Presents a Bob Hope Special"; and "The Bob Hope Special."

BOB NEWHART

Listed: the television programs of comedian Bob Newhart.

The Bob Newhart Show—Variety—30 minutes—NBC—October 11, 1961 - June 13, 1962.

Host: Bob Newhart.

Announcer: Dan Sorkin.

Orchestra: Paul Weston.

The Entertainers—Variety—60 minutes—CBS—1964. See title.

The Bob Newhart Show—Comedy—30 minutes—CBS—Premiered: September 16, 1972.

Background: Chicago. The home and working life of psychologist Robert Hartley.

CAST
Robert Hartley (Bob)	Bob Newhart
Emily Hartley, his wife, a third-grade school teacher at Gorman Elementary School	Suzanne Pleshette
Howard Borden, their friend, a 747 navigator	Bill Daily
Jerry Robinson, their friend, an orthodontist	Peter Bonerz
Carol Kester, Bob and Jerry's secretary	Marcia Wallace
Margaret Hoover, Emily's friend	Patricia Smith
Elliott Carlin, Bob's patient	Jack Riley
Mrs. Bakerman, Bob's patient	Florida Friebus
Michelle, Bob's patient	Renne Lippin
Mr. Peterson, Bob's patient	John Fiedler
Mr. Gianelli, Bob's patient	Noam Pitlik
Dr. Bernie Tupperman	Larry Gelman
Ellen Hartley, Bob's sister	Pat Finley
Howard Borden, Jr., Howard's son	Moosie Drier

Music: Pat Williams.

THE BOB SMITH SHOW

Musical Variety.

Host: Bob Smith.

Music: Enoch Light and the Light Brigade Orchestra.

THE BOB SMITH SHOW—30 minutes—NBC 1948.

BOLD JOURNEY

Travel. The filmed explorations of various adventures.

Hosts: John Stevenson; Jack Douglas.

BOLD JOURNEY—30 minutes—ABC —July 16, 1956 - August 31, 1959 (Stevenson); Syndicated 1958 (Douglas).

THE BOLD ONES

Drama. The overall title for four rotating series: "The Doctors," "The Lawyers," "The Protectors" and "The Senator."

The Doctors. Background: Los Angeles, California, the Benjamin Craig Institute, a medical research center founded by Dr. Benjamin Craig, a renowned neurosurgeon. Stories depict the pioneering of his protégés, Dr. Paul Hunter, research head, and Dr. Ted Stuart, surgical chief, as they attempt to break the barriers of ignorance and fight disease.

CAST

Dr. Ben Craig	E.G. Marshall
Dr. Ted Stuart	John Saxon
Dr. Paul Hunter	David Hartman
Dr. Cohen	Robert Walden

Music: Richard Clements.

The Lawyers. Background: Los Angeles, California. The cases and courtroom defenses of attorney Walter Nichols and his protégés Brian and Neil Darrell, brothers.

CAST

Walter Nichols	Burl Ives
Brian Darrell	Joseph Campanella
Neil Darrell	James Farentino

The Protectors. Also called: "The Law Enforcers." Background: California. The story of the relationship between two men — Deputy Police Chief Sam Danforth, and District Attorney William Washburn. Episodes relate their attempts to maintain law and order in a city beset by urban crises.

CAST

Sam Danforth	Leslie Nielsen
William Washburn	Hari Rhodes

The Senator. Background: California. The life of Senator Hays Stowe, a progressive politician who attempts to meet and understand the needs and desires of the people he represents.

CAST

Hays Stowe	Hal Holbrook
Ellen Stowe, his wife	Sharon Acker
Norma Stowe, their daughter	Cindy Elibacher
Jordan Boyle, his assistant	Michael Tolan

THE BOLD ONES—60 minutes—NBC —September 14, 1969 - January 9, 1973. Syndicated.

BOLD VENTURE

Adventure. Summoned to the bedside of a dying friend, Duval, adventurer

Slate Shannon agrees to become the legal guardian of his daughter, the beautiful Sailor Duval. Shannon, bored with his sophisticated life style, leaves the United States accompanied by Sailor, who is reluctant to abide by her father's wish. They retreat to Trinidad, where they purchase *The Bold Venture,* a hotel and boat. Episodes relate their varied island charters and attempts to assist the distressed. Based on the radio program of the same title.

Bonanza. Left to right: Pernell Roberts, Dan Blocker, Lorne Greene, and Michael Landon.

CAST

Slate Shannon	Dane Clark
Sailor Duval	Joan Marshall

Slate's girl crew: Jerri Bender, Joyce Taylor, Barbara Wilson, Narda Onyx.

BOLD VENTURE—30 minutes—Syndicated 1959.

BONANZA

Western. Era: The nineteenth century. The saga of the Cartwright family. Returning to New England after months at sea, First Mate Ben Cartwright and his fiancée, Elizabeth Stoddard, marry. Possessing a dream to settle in the West, but lacking the money, Ben settles down and establishes a ship chandler's business.

Shortly after giving birth to their son Adam, Elizabeth dies. Motivated by Elizabeth's desire for him to seek his dream, Ben journeys west and settles in Saint Joseph, Missouri where, after eight years, he marries a Swedish girl named Inger.

Still determined to establish a life in California, he organizes a wagon train. During the hazardous journey, Inger gives birth to a son named Eric Hoss after her father and brother Gunner.

Shortly thereafter, during an Indian attack, Inger is killed. Abandoning his dream, Ben settles in Virginia City, Nevada, and establishes the Ponderosa Ranch in the Comstock Lode Country.

When a ranch hand, Jean DeMarné, is fatally injured after saving Ben's life, his last request prompts Ben to travel to New Orleans to inform his mother and his wife, Marie, of his demise. Speaking first to Mrs. DeMarné, then to Marie, Ben hears a troublesome story. He discovers that Marie was supposed to have had an affair with another man. Jean, believing the incident true, had fled his home in disgrace. Investigating further, Ben uncovers the fact that Mrs. DeMarné had arranged the incident to discredit Marie, who she felt was not worthy of her son.

Ultimately Ben and Marie marry. Shortly after the birth of their son,

Joseph, Marie is killed when her horse steps in a chuckhole and throws her.

Stories relate the struggles of the Cartwright family as they attempt to maintain and operate their one-thousand-square-mile timberland ranch, the Ponderosa, in an era of violence and lawlessness. Building a reputation for fairness and honesty, they are admired and respected and often beseeched by those in distress to see that justice is done.

CAST

Ben Cartwright	Lorne Greene
Adam Cartwright	Pernell Roberts
Hoss (Eric) Cartwright	Dan Blocker
(Little) Joe Cartwright	Michael Landon
Hop Sing, their houseboy	Victor Sen Yung
Sheriff Roy Coffee	Ray Teal
Deputy Clem Poster	Bing Russell
Jamie Cartwright, the adopted son	Mitch Vogel
Mr. Canaday (Candy) the ranch foreman	David Canary
Griff King, a ranch hand	Tim Matheson
Dusty Rhodes, a ranch hand	Lou Frizzell
Elizabeth Stoddard (flashback; "Elizabeth, My Love")	Geraldine Brooks
Inger (flashback; "Inger, My Love")	Inga Swenson
Marie (flashback; "Marie, My Love")	Felicia Farr

Music: David Rose.

BONANZA—60 minutes—NBC—September 12, 1959 - January 16, 1973. Syndicated. Rebroadcasts (NBC), under title: "Ponderosa"—May 12, 1972 - August 29, 1972.

BONINO

Comedy. Background: New York City. Having spent little time with his family due to concert commitments, and feeling himself a stranger to his six children, Babbo Bonino impulsively decides to give up his operatic career and adopt the role of active father. Stories relate his attempts to raise his motherless children and solve the problems that he encounters.

CAST

Babbo Bonino	Ezio Pinza
Martha, his housekeeper	Mary Wickes
Rusty, his valet, confidant	Mike Kellin
Walter Rogers, his concert manager	David Opatoshu
Allentuck, the butler	Francis Butler
Andrew Bonino	Van Dyke Parks
Doris Bonino	Lenka Paterson
Edward Bonino	Conrad Janis
Terry Bonino	Chet Allen
Francesca Bonino	Gaye Huston
Carlo Bonino	Oliver Andes

Orchestra: Donald Voorhees.

BONINO—30 minutes—NBC—1953 - 1954.

THE BONNIE PRUDDEN SHOW

Women. Exercises, guests, interviews, health, and nutritional tips.

Hostess: Bonnie Prudden

THE BONNIE PRUDDEN SHOW—30 minutes—Syndicated 1968.

THE BONTEMPIS

Variety. The preparation of Italian meals; songs, guests, and interviews.

Hosts: Fedora and Pino Bontempi.

Pianist: Pino Bontempi.

THE BONTEMPIS—30 minutes—Syndicated 1952. Also called: "Breakfast Time" (1958) and "Continental Cookery" (1966).

BON VOYAGE

Game. Two contestants compete. Object: To identify geographical locations through stills and rhyming clues. The player with the most correct identifications is the winner and receives a trip to the place of his desire.

Host: John Weigel.

BON VOYAGE—30 minutes—ABC—April 24, 1949 - May 8, 1949. Also known as "Treasure Quest."

BOOTS AND SADDLES

Western. Background: Fort Lowell during the 1870s. The life and times of the American Fifth Cavalry.

CAST
Captain Shank Adams   Jack Pickard
Luke Cummings, the trail
    scout   Michael Hinn
Colonel Hays   Patrick McVey

BOOTS AND SADDLES—30 minutes —Syndicated 1957.

BORN FREE

Adventure. Background: Kenya, East Africa. The experiences of Game Warden George Adamson and his wife and assistant, Joy. Derived from and continuing where the books and the films *BORN FREE* and *LIVING FREE* ended. A story of man-animal friendship as depicted through the Adamsons' raising, conditioning (to face the rigorous life of her native habitat), and releasing of a young lioness, Elsa. Emphasis is placed upon conservation in contemporary Africa.

CAST
George Adamson   Gary Collins
Joy Adamson   Diana Muldaur
Makedde, their senior
    scout   Hal Frederick
Nuru   Peter Lukoye
Kanini   Joseph de Graft

Music: Dick De Benedicks; Richard Shores

BORN FREE—60 minutes—NBC—September 9, 1974 - December 30, 1974.

BOSS LADY

Comedy. Background: California. The story of Gwen F. Allen, owner and operator of the Hillendale Homes Construction Company. In the pre-Women's Lib era, Ms. Allen struggles to cope with and overcome abounding obstacles in a male-oriented field.

CAST
Gwen Allen   Lynn Bari
Jeff, her general
    manager   Nicholas Jay
Mr. Allen, her
    father   Glenn Langan
Also: Richard Gainer, Lee Patrick, Charley Smith.

BOSS LADY—30 minutes—DuMont—1952 - 1953; NBC—1953 - 1954.

BOSTON BLACKIE

Mystery. Background: New York City. The investigations of Boston Blackie, one-time master thief turned private detective. Based on the minor character originally appearing in the novels by George Randolph Chester.

CAST

Boston Blackie	Kent Taylor
Mary Wesley, his girlfriend	Lois Collier
Inspector Faraday, N.Y.P.D.	Frank Orth

Music: Joseph Hooven.

BOSTON BLACKIE—30 minutes—NBC—1951 - 1953. Syndicated.

Rex Randolph	Richard Long
Melody Lee Mercer, their secretary	Arlene Howell
Ken Madison, their junior assistant	Van Williams

Music: Paul Sawtell.

BOURBON STREET BEAT—60 minutes—ABC—October 5, 1959 - September 26, 1960. Syndicated.

BOURBON STREET BEAT

Mystery. Background: The French quarter of New Orleans, Louisiana. The investigations of private detectives Cal Calhoun and Rex Randolph.

CAST

Cal Calhoun   Andrew Duggan

BRACKEN'S WORLD

Drama. Background: Century Studios in Hollywood California. A behind-the-scene look at the world of film producing as seen through the eyes of studio head John Bracken, a man making and/or breaking careers. Filmed at 20th Century Fox Studios.

Bracken's World. Left to right: Karen Jansen, Linda Harrison, Laraine Stephens.

CAST

John Bracken	Leslie Nielsen
Sylvia Caldwell, his executive secretary	Elinor Parker
Kevin Grant, a producer	Peter Haskell
Marjorie Grant, his alcoholic wife	Madlyn Rhue
Laura Deane, head of the New Studio Talent School	Elizabeth Allen

THE YOUNG HOPEFULS:

Davey Evans	Dennis Cole
Tom Hutson	Stephen Oliver
Rachel Holt	Karen Jensen
Paulette Douglas	Linda Harrison
Diane Waring	Laraine Stephens

Music: David Rose.

BRACKEN'S WORLD—60 minutes—NBC—September 19, 1969 - January 1, 1971. Syndicated.

The Brady Bunch. Bottom, left to right: Ann B. Davis, Florence Henderson, Michael Lookinland, Maureen McCormick. Top, left to right: Eve Plumb, Barry Williams, Susan Olsen, Robert Reed, Christopher Knight.

THE BRADY BUNCH

Comedy. Background: Los Angeles, California. Architect Michael Brady, widower and the father of three sons, Greg, Peter, and Bobby, and Carol Martin widow, and the mother of three daughters, Marcia, Janice, and Cindy, marry and establish housekeeping on Clinton Avenue in the four-bedroom, two-bathroom Brady home. Aided by their housekeeper, Alice, Mike and Carol attempt to cope with the problems and chaos that exist in trying to raise six children.

CAST

Carol Brady	Florence Henderson
Mike Brady	Robert Reed
Alice	Ann B. Davis
Marcia Brady	Maureen McCormack
Janice Brady	Eve Plumb
Cindy Brady	Susan Olsen
Greg Brady	Barry Williams
Peter Brady	Christopher Knight
Bobby Brady	Michael Lookinland
Oliver, Alice's nephew	Robbie Rist

Music: Frank DeVol.

THE BRADY BUNCH—30 minutes—ABC—September 26, 1969 - August 30, 1974.

THE BRADY KIDS

Animated Cartoon. A spin-off from "The Brady Bunch." The story of the Brady children: Marcia, Greg, Janice, Peter, Cindy, and Bobby, and their attempts to independently solve problems without help from the adult world.

Characters' Voices

Marcia Bardy	Maureen McCormick
Greg Brady	Barry Williams
Janice Brady	Eve Plumb
Peter Brady	Christopher Knight
Cindy Brady	Susan Olsen
Bobby Brady	Michael Lookinland

Additional Voices: Larry Storch, Jane Webb.

Background Music: Yvette Blais.

The Brady Kids pets: Marlon, the magical bird; and Ping and Pong, talking Panda Bears.

THE BRADY KIDS—30 minutes—ABC—September 9, 1972 - August 31, 1974.

BRAINS AND BRAWN

Game. Two competing teams, each composed of four contestants – the Brain, which includes a professional expert, vs. the Brawn, which encompasses a professional athlete. The Brain portion of the program is broadcast from the network's studios and involves the players' attempts to answer difficult questions. The Brawn portion, broadcast from a remote location, puts the contestants through a series of physical-dexterity contests. The segments, though different in concept, are equal in difficulty. Teams are judged and awarded prizes according to their ability to complete assigned tasks.

Hosts:
Fred Davis (the Brain portion).
Jack Lescoulie (the Brawn portion).

BRAINS AND BRAWN—30 minutes—NBC—September 13, 1958 - December 27, 1958.

BRANDED

Western. Background: Southwestern Wyoming, 1870s. During the Battle of Bitter Creek, Jason McCord, army captain, is knocked unconscious when Comanches attack his division. Awakening, he finds that the conflict has ended and that he is the lone survivor. His story, which is disbelieved by military brass, fosters a court-martial. Stripped of his rank and dishonorably discharged, he is branded a coward—"scorned as the one who ran."

Thinking and hoping that someone else may have survived the battle, McCord undertakes a trek to clear his name. Episodes relate his difficulties as he encounters the hatred of men in a country torn by war.

Starring: Chuck Connors as Jason McCord.

Music: Dominic Frontiere.

BRANDED—30 minutes—NBC—January 24, 1965 - September 4, 1966. Syndicated.

BRAVE EAGLE

Western. Background: The early settlement days of the Old Frontier. The hardships of the American Indian as he struggles to safeguard his homeland from settlers is seen through the eyes of Brave Eagle, a young Cheyenne Chief, and his foster son, Keena.

CAST

Brave Eagle	Keith Larsen
Keena	Keena Nomleena
Morning Star, a Sioux maiden turned Cheyenne	Kim Winona

Smokey Joe, a half-
breed   Bert Wheeler

BRAVE EAGLE—30 minutes—CBS—
1955 - 1956.

BRAVE STALLION

See title: "Fury."

BREAKFAST CLUB

See title: "Don McNeill's TV Club."

BREAKFAST IN HOLLYWOOD

Variety. Adapted from the radio program. Broadcast from the Sun Club of
the Ambassador Hotel in Hollywood,
California.

Host: Johnny Dugan.

Features: Audience participation contests; a guest hostess of the week;
a tribute to the oldest lady in the
audience; the traditional Good
Neighbor Award.

BREAKFAST IN HOLLYWOOD—60
minutes—NBC 1954.

BREAKFAST PARTY

Variety. Music, songs, guests, and in-
terviews.
Hosts: Mel Martin, Eileen Martin.
Featured: Larry Downing.
Music: The Bell Airs Trio.

BREAKFAST PARTY—30 minutes—
NBC 1951.

BREAKING POINT

Drama. Background: Los Angeles, California. The work of two psychiatrists: Dr. Edward Raymer, director of
York Hospital's Psychiatric Clinic, and
Dr. McKinley Thompson, a resident
psychiatrist. Episodes relate their
attempts to assist the distressed—those
reaching the breaking point of human
emotion.

CAST

Dr. McKinley Thompson Paul Richards
Dr. Edward Raymer   Eduard Franz
Music: David Raksin.

BREAKING   POINT—60   minutes—
ABC—September 16, 1963 - September 7, 1964. Syndicated.

BREAK THE BANK

Game. Players are quizzed in a category of their choice. Each correct
response earns cash, which increases
with the difficulty of the question.
Eight straight answers break the bank,
and its cash amount is awarded to the
player. Two misses in a row defeat the
player and his funds are forfeited and
added to the bank.

Hosts: Bert Parks; Bud Collyer.

Assistant: Janice Gilbert.

Announcer: Win Elliott.

Orchestra: Peter Van Steeden.

BREAK THE BANK—30 minutes—
ABC—October 22, 1948 - September
23, 1949. NBC—October 5, 1949 -
September 1, 1953.

Spin-off: **BREAK THE $250,000
BANK.**
Basically the same format, the change
being to allow contestants to choose

an expert to assist in the answering of questions.

Host: Bert Parks.

Announcer: Johnny Olsen.

Orchestra: Peter Van Steeden.

BREAK THE $250,000 BANK—NBC —1956 - 1958.

BRENNER

Crime Drama. Background: New York City. The story of two policemen: Detective Lieutenant Roy Brenner, head of the Confidential Squad, a special crime-busting detective force, and his son, Patrolman Ernie Brenner.

CAST
Lt. Roy Brenner	Edward Binns
Officer Ernie Brenner	James Broderick
Captain Laney	Joseph Sullivan

BRENNER—30 minutes—CBS—June 6, 1959 - September 1959; June 19, 1961 - September 1961; June 7, 1962 - September 1962; May 10, 1964 - September 1964.

THE BRIAN KEITH SHOW

See title: "The Little People."

BRIDE AND GROOM

Wedding Performances. Actual services performed in a chapel setting in New York City.

Hosts: Byron Palmer; Bob Paige; Phil Hanna; Frank Parker; John Nelson.

Orchestra: Paul Taubman.

BRIDE AND GROOM—30 minutes— CBS—1946 - 1958.

BRIDGET LOVES BERNIE

Comedy. Background: New York City. Bridget Fitzgerald, an elementary grade school teacher, and Bernie Steinberg, a struggling writer and cabdriver, marry. Religious and social differences are dramatized.

Bridget's parents, Walter and Amy Fitzgerald, are wealthy socialites. Walter is a staunch Irish-Catholic; Amy, pleasant and rather naive; and their son, Michael, a liberal, realistic priest.

Bernie's parents, Sam and Sophie Steinberg, are Jewish and own a delicatessen in lower Manhattan, where they live over the store, as do Bridget and Bernie. They are simple, unpretentious, and unsophisticated.

A rich Catholic girl and a poor Jewish boy attempt to overcome family opposition and bridge the ethnic gap existing in their lives.

CAST
Bridget Fitzgerald Steinberg	Meredith Baxter
Bernie Steinberg	David Birney
Walter Fitzgerald	David Doyle
Amy Fitzgerald	Audra Lindley
Sam Steinberg	Harold J. Stone
Sophie Steinberg	Bibi Osterwald
Moe Plotnic, Sophie's brother	Ned Glass
Father Michael Fitzgerald	Robert Sampson
Otis Foster, Bernie's friend	William Elliott
Charles, the Fitzgerald's Butler	Ivor Barry

Music: Jerry Fielding.

BRIDGET LOVES BERNIE—30 minutes—CBS—September 16, 1972 - September 8, 1973.

A BRIGHTER DAY

Serial. Background: The small Midwestern town of New Hope. The dramatic story of Reverend Richard Dennis. Episodes depict the conflicts and tensions that arise from the interactions of the characters.

CAST
Reverend
  Richard Dennis   William Smith
                        Blair Davies
Sandra Talbot   Gloria Hoye
Vince Adams   Forrest Compton
Mrs. Jarrett   Abby Lewis
Crystal Carpenter   Vivian Dorsett
Larry   Del Hughes
Randy   Larry Ward

Also: Patty Duke, Lois Nettleton, Hal Holbrook, Mary Lynn Beller, Jack Lemmon, Lori March, Joe Sirola, Mona Burns, June Dayton, Santos Ortega, Mary K. Wells, Bill Post, Sam Gray.

A BRIGHTER DAY—15 minutes—CBS—January 4, 1954 - September 28, 1962.

BRIGHT PROMISE

Serial. Background: Bancroft, a college community beset by contemporary crises. Stories dramatize the private and professional lives of its president, Thomas Boswell, his faculty, students, friends, and family.

CAST
Professor Thomas
  Boswell   Dana Andrews

Professor William
  Ferguson   Paul Lukather
Ann Boyd Jones   Coleen Gray
                        Gail Kobe
Sylvia Bancroft   Regina Gleason
                        Anne Jeffreys
Jennifer   Nancy Stevens
Chet   Gary Pillar
Red Wilson   Richard Eastham
Gypsy   Annette O'Toole
Bob Cocharan   Philip Carey
Jody Harper   Sherry Alberoni
Martha Ferguson   Susan Brown
Dr. Tracy Graham   Dabney Coleman
Dr. Brian Walsh   John Considine
Charles Diedrich   Anthony Eisley
David Lockhart   Tony Geary
Henry Pierce   David Lewis
Samantha Pudding   Cheryl Miller
Howard Jones   Mark Miller
Sandra Jones Pierce   Pamela Murphy
Stuart Pierce   Peter Ratray
Dr. Amanda Winninger   June Vincent
Isabel Jones   Lesley Woods
Clara   Ruth McDevitt
Sandy   Susan Darrow
Dean Pierce   Tod Andrews
Professor Townley   Nigal McKeard
Bert   Peter Hobbs
Alice   Synda Scott
Fay   Kimetha Laurie

BRIGHT PROMISE—30 minutes—NBC—September 29, 1969 - March 31, 1972.

BRINGING UP BUDDY

Comedy. Background: Los Angeles, California. The trials and tribulations of Buddy Flower, a bachelor investment broker. Stories concern his efforts to overcome the plotting of his meddlesome and spinster aunts, Iris and Violet, as they attempt to find him a wife.

CAST

Buddy Flower	Frank Aletter
Violet Flower	Enid Markey
Iris Flower	Doro Merande

BRINGING UP BUDDY—30 minutes —CBS—October 10, 1960 - September 25, 1961. Syndicated.

BROADSIDE

Comedy. Background: The South Pacific during World War II. New Caledonia, a tropical island paradise untouched by war and women, is chosen to be a United States Navy supply depot. Four beautiful WAVES, Lieutenant Anne Morgan and Privates Molly McGuire, Roberta Love, and Selma Kowalski, assigned to attend the motor pool, disrupt the island serenity and the life of its commander, Adrian. Unable to rescind their orders, Adrian deviously attempts to rid the island of women by discrediting Anne and her WAVES. Determined not to be underminded by a man, the girls counterscheme, attempting to foil his efforts and remain on the island. A spin-off from "McHale's Navy."

CAST

Lt. Anne Morgan	Kathleen Nolan
Private Molly McGuire	Lois Roberts
Private Roberta Love	Joan Staley
Private Selma Kowalski	Sheila James
Commander Adrian	Edward Andrews
Lt. Maxwell Trotter, Anne's romantic interest	Dick Sargent
Marion Botnick, a male WAVE, by clerical error	Jimmy Boyd
Lieutenant Beasley, Adrian's aide	George Furth
Admiral Whitehead	Paul Byan
Nicky	Don Edmonds

Music: Axel Stordhal.

BROADSIDE—30 minutes—ABC— September 20, 1964 - September 5, 1965.

BROADWAY GOES LATIN

Musical Variety. Latin arrangements for Broadway songs.

Host: Edmundo Ross.

Regulars: Margie Ravel, Hector de San Juan, Chi Chi Navaroo, The Arnoldo Dancers, The Ros Singers.

Orchestra: Edmundo Ross.

BROADWAY GOES LATIN—30 minutes—Syndicated 1962-1963.

BROADWAY OPEN HOUSE

Variety. Music, songs, dances, and comedy sketches. Network television's first late-night entertainment show. Broadcast from 11:00 PM-12:00 PM, E.S.T., Monday through Friday.

Hosts: Jerry Lester, Morey Amsterdam, Jack E. Leonard.

Regulars: Dagmar (real name: Virginia Ruth Egnor, known also as Jennie Lewis), Barbara Nichols (portraying Agathon), David Street, Ray Malone, Buddy Greco, Frank Gallop, Andy Roberts, Jane Harvey, The Eileen Barton Dancers, The Kirby Stone Quintet, The Mello-Larks.

Announcer: Wayne Howell.

Orchestra: Milton DeLugg.

Broadway Open House. Jennie Lewis (Dagmar).

Format: Headline resumes of world affairs, Hollywood gossip, celebrity interviews, and quizzes.

Quiz Segment: The Host telephones a viewer and asks him a question based on a news event. If the question is correctly answered, the player receives a prize.

BROADWAY TO HOLLYWOOD HEADLINE—30 minutes—DuMont 1949.

BROADWAY OPEN HOUSE—60 minutes—NBC—May 22, 1950 - August 24, 1951.

BROADWAY TO HOLLYWOOD

Variety. Music, songs, and dances.

Host: Bill Slater.

Regulars: Dorothy Claire, Jerry Wayne, Earl Barton.

Music: The Al Logan Trio.

BROADWAY TO HOLLYWOOD—30 minutes—DuMont—1951 - 1953.

BROADWAY TO HOLLYWOOD HEADLINE

Variety.

Host: George Putnam.

BROADWAY TV THEATRE

Anthology. Condensed versions of Broadway plays.

Included:

Adam and Eva. A comedy depicting the misadventures of the wealthy head of a spoiled family.

CAST
Hugh Riley, Katherine Bard.

The Acquitted. A reporter attempts to uncover the murderer of an aged, wealthy man.

CAST
Judith Evelyn, John Baragrey.

R.U.R. A depiction of the world of the future — a state in which robot slaves rebel against their human masters.

CAST
Dorothy Hart, Hugh Riley.

Smilin' Through. A feud between two families and its effect on their children who want to be married.

CAST
William Prince, Beverly Whitney, Wesley Addy.

Death Takes A Holiday. Death visits Earth in an attempt to discover why mortals fear him. During his sojourn, there is no death anywhere. Conflict occurs when he falls in love.

CAST
Nigel Green, Wendy Drew.

BROADWAY TV THEATRE—60 minutes—Syndicated 1952.

as guilty as the Indian in frontier outrages.

CAST

Tom Jeffords	John Lupton
Cochise	Michael Ansara

Narrator: John Lupton

Music: Stanley Wilson; Paul Sawtell; Ned Washington.

BROKEN ARROW—30 minutes—ABC—September 25, 1956 - September 18, 1960. Syndicated.

BROKEN ARROW

Western. Background: Tucson, Arizona, 1870s, the era of the Apache Wars — the Indian and White Man struggling over the possession of land.

Tom Jeffords, an army captain, is assigned to resolve the constant Indian attacks on mail carriers. He studies the ways of the Apache and tries to persuade officials to understand the plight of the Indian, not slaughter him. In his attempt to accomplish through talk what weapons cannot, he confronts Apache Chief Cochise. Mutual respect leads the Chief to guarantee the safety of the Pony Express riders through Apache Territory.

Army officials, seeking to open the territory to settlers, acquire through Jeffords efforts, a treaty with the Apache and a Broken Arrow — the Indian symbol of peace, friendship, and understanding. Appointed as an Indian Agent to the Apaches, Jeffords becomes the blood brother of Cochise.

Stories relate Jeffords fight against the blindly prejudiced attitudes toward the Apache in the Southwest, fully believing that the White Man is

BRONCO

Western. Background: The Texas Plains during the 1860s. The exploits of Bronco Layne, a wandering ex-Confederate army captain.

Starring: Ty Hardin as Bronco Layne.

Music: Paul Sawtell.

BRONCO—60 minutes—ABC—October 20, 1959 - September 20, 1960. Syndicated.

BRONK

Crime Drama. Background: Ocean City, California. The investigations of Alex "Bronk" Bronkov, a police lieutenant operating under special assignment to the city's mayor, Pete Santori. Created by Carrol O'Connor.

CAST

Lt. Alex Bronkov	Jack Palance
Pete Santori	Joseph Mascolo
Ellen Bronkov, Alex's daughter, crippled in an accident that killed his wife	Dina Ousley

Sgt. John Webster, Alex's
    partner   Tony King
Harry Mark, a former
    cop who operates
    the M and B Junk
    Yard, Alex's infor-
    mation man   Henry Beckman
Marci, Pete's
    secretary   Marcy Lafferty
Mrs. Moury, Ellen's
    nurse   Peggy Rea

Music: Lalo Schifrin; George
    Romanis; Robert Dransin.

BRONK—60 minutes CBS Pre-
miered: September 21, 1975.

THE BROTHERS

Comedy. Background: San Francisco,
California. Inexperienced and desperately in need of money, Harvey and
Gilmore Box, brothers, pool their
resources and purchase a photography
studio. Stories relate their misadventures as they attempt to succeed in
the business world.

CAST

Harvey Box   Gale Gordon
Gilmore Box   Bob Sweeny
Marilee Dorf, Gilmore's
    girlfriend   Nancy Hadley
Carl Dorf, her
    father   Oliver Blake
Barbara, Harvey's
    girlfriend   Barbara Billingsley
Captain Sam Box, the brothers'
    father, a retired sea
    captain   Howard McNair
                      Frank Orth
Barrington Steel, a friend,
    a playboy   Robin Hughes

THE BROTHERS—30 minutes—CBS
—October 4, 1956 - March 27, 1957.

THE BROTHERS BRANNAGAN

Crime Drama. Background: Phoenix,
Arizona. The investigations of private
detectives Mike and Bob Brannagan,
brothers.

CAST

Mike Brannagan   Steve Dunne
Bob Brannagan   Mark Roberts

THE BROTHERS BRANNAGAN—30
minutes—Syndicated 1960.

THE BUCCANEERS

Adventure. Background: The Caribbean Colony of New Providence during the 1720s. The exploits of
buccaneer Dan Tempest as he battles
the injustices of Spanish rule.

CAST

Captain Dan Tempest   Robert Shaw
Lieutenant Beamish, his
    aide   Peter Hammond
Governor Woodes Rogers Alec Clunes

Tempest's ship: The *Sultana.*

THE BUCCANEERS—30 minutes—
CBS—September 22, 1956 - September 14, 1957. Syndicated. Also known
as "Dan Tempest."

BUCK OWENS TV RANCH

Musical Variety. Performances by
Country and Western artists.

Host: Buck Owens.

Regulars: Susan Raye, Merle Haggard,
    Kenni Huskey, Tommy Collins,
    Mayfi Nutter, Buddy Alan, The
    Stamp Quartet.

Music: The Buckaroos; The Bakers-
    field Brass.

BUCK OWENS TV RANCH—30 minutes—Syndicated 1968.

Host: Buck Weaver.

Animals: Pom Pom, the trained stallion; Dixie, "the world's smartest Doberman."

BUCKAROO 500—30· minutes—Syndicated 1963.

BUCK ROGERS IN THE 25th CENTURY

Adventure. Pittsburg, 1919. A young United States Air Force veteran, Buck Rogers, begins surveying the lower levels of an abandoned mine. When the crumbling timbers give way, the roof from behind him caves in. Unable to escape, he is rendered unconscious by a peculiar gas that places him in a state of suspended animation.

As the Earth shifts, fresh air enters and awakens Buck. Emerging from the cave, he finds himself standing in the midst of a vast forest. Meeting Lieutenant Wilma Deering of the Space General's staff, he discovers that it is the year 2430 and the place is no longer Pittsburg, but Niagra, America's capitol. Stories depict Buck's attempts to aid Wilma and the scientific genius, Dr. Huer, in their battle against evil. Based on the comic strip and radio versions.

CAST
Buck Rogers	Kem Dibbs
Wilma Deering	Lou Prentis
Dr. Huer	Harry Sothern
Barney Wade	Harry Kingston

Also: Sanford Bickart, Robert Pastene.

BUCK ROGERS IN THE 25th CENTURY—30 minutes—ABC—April 15, 1950 - January 30, 1951.

BUCKAROO 500

Children. Variety set against the background of a Western ranch.

BUCKSKIN

Western. Background: Buckskin, Montana, 1880s. The story of Annie O'Connell, widow and owner and operator of the town hotel. Episodes relate her attempts to provide a decent life for herself and her son, Jody. Jody, seated atop a corral fence, plays his harmonica and narrates each story — stories of struggle in a lawless territory.

CAST
Annie O'Connell	Sallie Brophie
Jody O'Connell	Tommy Nolan
Sheriff Tom Sellers	Mike Road
Ben Newcomb, the school teacher	Michael Lipton

Music: Stanley Wilson; Mort Green.

BUCKSKIN—30 minutes—NBC—July 3, 1958 - September 1958; NBC rebroadcasts: July 1965 - September 1965.

BUFFALO BILL, JR.

Western. Background: Wileyville, Texas, 1890s. The story of Buffalo Bill, Jr., and his sister, Calamity, orphans adopted by Judge Ben Wiley, the founder of the town. Appointed marshal, and aided by his sister Calamity, Bill attempts to maintain law and order.

CAST

Buffalo Bill, Jr.	Dick Jones
Calamity	Nancy Gilbert
Judge Ben Wiley	Harry Cheshire

BUFFALO BILL, JR.—30 minutes—Syndicated 1955.

THE BUFFALO BILLY SHOW

Western Puppet Adventure. Era: The 19th century. The exploits of Buffalo Billy, a young seeker of adventure as he journeys West with a wagon train.

Characters: Buffalo Billy; Ima Hog, his aunt; Pop Gunn, an Indian fighter; Blunderhead, Billy's horse; Dilly, the armadillo.

Voices: Don Messick, Bob Clampett, Joan Gardiner.

THE BUFFALO BILLY SHOW—30 minutes—CBS 1950.

THE BUGALOOS

Comedy. Background: Tranquility Forest. The story of the Bugaloos, Harmony, Joy, Courage, and I.Q., human-formed singing insects, the protectors of the forest and its creatures. Episodes concern the evil Benita Bizarre's disasterous attempts to destroy their "disgusting goodness."

CAST

Benita Bizarre	Martha Raye
Joy	Caroline Ellis
Harmony	Wayne Laryea
Courage	John Philpott
I.Q.	John Mcindoe

Characters (The Sid and Marty Krofft Puppets): Sparky, the firefly; Flunky, Benita's chauffeur; Tweeter and Woofer, Benita's aides.

Music: Charles Fox.

THE BUGALOOS—30 minutes—NBC—September 12, 1970 - September 2, 1972.

THE BUGS BUNNY SHOW

Animated Cartoon. The antics of Bugs Bunny, a rabbit who excells in causing misery to others. Often depicted: The attempts of Elmer Fudd and Yosemitte Sam to shoot that "darned wabbit" and end his relentless pranks.

Additional Segments:

"Sylvester the Cat." A hungry cat attempts to catch a decent meal — Tweety Pie, the canary.

"The Road Runner." A hungry coyote's determined efforts to catch a decent meal — the Road Runner, an out-foxing bird.

Voice Characterizations: Mel Blanc.

Music: Carl Stalling; Milt Franklin; William Lava; John Celly.

THE BUGS BUNNY SHOW—30 minutes—ABC—October 11, 1960 - September 25, 1962.

THE BUGS BUNNY-ROAD RUNNER HOUR—60 minutes—CBS—September 14, 1968 - September 4, 1971.

THE BUGS BUNNY SHOW—30 minutes—CBS—September 11, 1971 - September 1, 1973.

THE BUGS BUNNY SHOW—30 minutes—ABC—September 8, 1973 - August 30, 1975.

THE BUICK CIRCUS HOUR

Variety. Music, songs, dances, and circus variety acts.

Host: Jimmy Durante.

Regulars: Dolores Gray, John Raitt.

Announcer: Frank Gallop.

Orchestra: Victor Young.

THE BUICK CIRCUS HOUR—60 minutes—NBC—October 7, 1952 - June 16, 1953. Presented every fourth week in place of Milton Berle's "Texaco Star Theatre."

THE BULLWINKLE SHOW

See title: "Rocky and His Friends."

Burke's Law. Left to right: Gene Barry, Ellen O'Neal, Gary Conway.

BURKE'S LAW

Mystery. Background: Los Angeles, California. The investigations of Amos Burke, multimillionaire police captain of the Metropolitan Homicide Squad.

CAST

Amos Burke	Gene Barry
Detective Tim Tillson	Gary Conway
Detective Sergeant Lester Hart	Regis Toomey
Henry, Burke's houseboy-chauffeur	Leon Lontoc
Sergeant Ames, policewoman	Ellen O'Neal

Music: Herschel Burke Gilbert.

BURKE'S LAW—60 minutes—ABC—September 20, 1963 - August 31, 1965. Syndicated. Spin-off series: "Amos Burke, Secret Agent" (see title).

THE BURNS AND SCHREIBER COMEDY HOUR

Variety. Low-key, physical comedy.

Hosts: Jack Burns and Avery Schreiber.

Regulars: Teri Garr, Fred Willard, Pat Croft, Frank Leaks, Fred Welker.

Announcer: Dick Tufel.

Orchestra: Jack Elliot, Allyn Ferguson.

Sketches:

"The Taxi Routine." Avery as the harassed hackie who is plagued by Jack, the loud-mouthed passenger.

"The Monestary Sketch." Avery as Brother Timothy, and Jack as Brother Jasper, men who became monks to escape the evils of city life. The sketch revolves around the struggles of the younger Brother, Timothy, to adjust to the new life.

"The B & S Report." A satirization of newscasting.

"The Detective Sketch." Avery as Detective Kravitz, and Jack as Detective Honeywell, inept homicide detectives. The sketch centers on their efforts to solve crimes.

THE BURNS AND SCHREIBER COMEDY HOUR—60 minutes—ABC —June 30, 1973 - September 1, 1973.

BUS STOP

Drama. Background: The Sherwood, combination bus depot and diner in Sunrise, Colorado. Real-life situations are played against mythical backgrounds as lost and troubled people attempt to overcome their difficulties.

CAST

Grace Sherwood, the
    proprietress   Marilyn Maxwell
Elma Gahringer, the
    waitress   Joan Freeman
Will Mayberry, the
    sheriff   Rhodes Reason
Glenn Wagner, the district
    attorney   Richard Anderson
Music: Frank DeVol.

BUS STOP—60 minutes—ABC— October 1, 1961 - March 25, 1962. Syndicated.

BUTCH AND BILLY AND THEIR BANG BANG WESTERN MOVIES

Live Action-Animation. Cliff-hanger type Western adventure serials reedited from "Bronco Billy" silent features. Cartoon characters Billy Bang Bang and his brother Butch host and provide commentary.

CAST

Bronco Billy   Bob Cust
Billy Bang Bang
    (voiced by)   Steve Krieger
Butch Bang Bang
    (voiced by)   Danny Krieger

BUTCH AND BILLY AND THEIR BANG BANG WESTERN MOVIES—05 minutes—Syndicated 1961.

BUTCH CASSIDY AND THE SUNDANCE KIDS

Animated Cartoon. The global investigations of Butch Cassidy and the Sundance Kids (Stephanic, Wally, Marilee, and Freddy), U.S. government agents who pose as a Rock group under contract with the World Wide Talent Agency, a front for an international spy ring.

Gang dog: Elvis.

Voices: Cameron Arthur Clark, Henry Corden, Ronnie Schell, Hans Conried, Mickey Dolenz, Ross Martin, Alan Oppenheimer, John Stephenson, Virginia Gregg, Pamela Peters, Frank Maxwell.

Music: Hoyt Curtin.

BUTCH CASSIDY AND THE SUNDANCE KIDS—30 minutes—NBC— September 8, 1973 - August 31, 1974.

BWANA MICHAEL OF AFRICA

Documentary. Films depicting animal

behavior and African tribal customs.
Host-Narrator: George Michael (hunter and explorer).

BWANA MICHAEL OF AFRICA—30 minutes—Syndicated 1966. Also released as theatrical shorts.

BY LINE—BETTY FURNESS

Variety. Music, songs, and celebrity interviews.
Hostess: Betty Furness.
Regulars: Don Cherry, Hank Fost, Bill Stern, David Ross.
Music: The Buddy Weed Trio.

BY LINE—BETTY FURNESS—30 minutes—ABC 1950.

BY LINE—STEVE WILSON

See title: "Big Town."

BY POPULAR DEMAND

Variety. Performances by undiscovered professional talent.
Host: Robert Alda.
Orchestra: Harry Sosnick.

BY POPULAR DEMAND—30 minutes—CBS 1950.

C

CADE'S COUNTY

Modern Western. Background: The Southwestern community of Madrid County. The story of Sheriff Sam Cade and his attempts to maintain law and order in an area easily able to become a lawless wasteland. The series emphasizes relations with and acceptance of the Indian.

CAST

Sheriff Sam Cade	Glenn Ford
Deputy J.J. Jackson	Edgar Buchanan
Deputy Arlo Pritchard	Taylor Lacher
Deputy Rudy Davillo	Victor Campos
Pete, a deputy	Peter Ford
Kitty Ann Sundown, the radio dispatcher	Sandra Ego
	Betty Ann Carr

Music: Henry Mancini.

CADE'S COUNTY—60 minutes—CBS —September 19, 1971 - September 4, 1972.

CAFE De PARIS

Musical Variety.
Hostess: Sylvie St. Clair.
Featured: Jacques Arbuschon.
Music: The Stan Free Trio.

CAFE De PARIS—15 minutes—DuMont 1949.

CAFE DUBONNETT

Musical Variety.
Host: Andy Russell.
Hostess: Della Russell.
Music: The Cy Coleman Trio.

CAFE DUBONNETT—15 minutes—ABC 1950.

CAIN'S HUNDRED

Crime Drama. The story of Nicholas Cain, a former underworld attorney who teams with the U.S. authorities in an attempt to infiltrate the ranks of organized crime and bring the nation's top one hundred criminals to justice.

Starring: Mark Richman as Nicholas Cain.

Music: Jerry Goldsmith; Morton Stevens.

CAIN'S HUNDRED—60 minutes—NBC—September 19, 1961 - September 10, 1962. Syndicated.

THE CALIFORNIANS

Western. Background: San Francisco, California, 1851, during the era of its turbulent pioneering years. The story of two men, and their attempts to establish a system of law enforcement. Abandoning his original plan to seek gold, a settler, Dion Patrick, becomes a somewhat unofficial source of law and order. Following his departure, lawlessness once again prevails. Attempting to combat it, the citizens organize and hire Matt Wayne as their marshal. Episodes relate their experiences and the struggles of settlers as they attempt to establish a new life.

CAST

Dion Patrick	Adam Kennedy
Marshal Matt Wayne	Richard Coogan
Jack McGivern, the owner of the General Store	Sean McClory
Martha McGivern, his wife	Nan Leslie
R. Jeremy Pitt, a lawyer	Arthur Fleming
Wilma Fansler, a widow, the owner of the gambling house	Carol Matthews

THE CALIFORNIANS—30 minutes—NBC—September 24, 1957 - January 5, 1958 (Kennedy episodes); January 12, 1958 - September 1959 (Coogan episodes). Syndicated.

CALL MR. D

See title: "Richard Diamond, Private Detective."

CALL MY BLUFF

Game. Two competing teams each composed of three members — two studio-audience contestants and one celebrity captain. Object: to determine the correct definitions of obscure words. The Host presents a card to each member of one team. One card contains the correct meaning of the word to be guessed. Each player states a definition, but two are bluffing. The opposing team must determine the purveyor of the truth.

Host: Bill Leyden.

CALL MY BLUFF—30 minutes—NBC—March 29, 1965 - September 24, 1965.

CALL OF THE WEST

Anthology. Rebroadcasts of Western dramas that were originally aired via "Death Valley Days."

Host: John Payne.

Music: Marlen Skiles.

CALL OF THE WEST—30 minutes—Syndicated 1969.

CALL OF THE WILD

Documentary. Filmed accounts of wildlife behavior.

Host-Narrator: Arthur Jones.

CALL OF THE WILD—30 minutes—Syndicated 1970.

CALUCCI'S DEPARTMENT

Comedy. Background: New York City. The harassed life of Joe Calucci, a soft-hearted state unemployment office supervisor who constantly finds himself at odds with his position of authority as he attempts to curtail the antics of his staff of seven rude and raucous bureaucrats.

CAST

Joe Calucci	James Coco
Shirley Balukis, Joe's girlfriend, a pretty, but not-too-bright secretary	Candy Azzara
Ramon Gonzales, the assistant supervisor, Joe's protégé	Jose Perez
Oscar Cosgrove, the claims adjuster	Jack Fletcher
Elaine P. Fusco, a secretary	Peggy Pope
Jack Woods, an employee	Bill Lazarus
Mitzi Gordon, the telephone operator	Rosetta Lenore
Walter Frohler, an employee	Bernard Wexler
Mrs. Clairmont, the elderly claiment	Judith Lowry
Mrs. Calucci, Joe's mother	Vera Lockwood
The Priest	Philip Stirling

Music: Marvin Hamlisch.

CALUCCI'S DEPARTMENT—30 minutes—CBS—September 14, 1973 - December 28, 1973.

CALVIN AND THE COLONEL

Animated Cartoon. Background: A big city up North. The misadventures of two backwoods Southern animals as they struggle to cope with life: Calvin, not-too-bright bear, and his friend, the Colonel, a cunning fox. Created by Freeman Gosden and Charles Correll. Based on their "Amos and Andy" characters.

Characters' Voices

The Colonel	Freeman Gosden
Calvin	Charles Correll
Maggie Bell, the Colonel's wife	Virginia Gregg
Sue, Maggie's sister	Beatrice Kay
Oliver Wendell Clutch, the lawyer (a weasel)	Paul Frees

Additional Voices: Frank Gerstle, Barney Phillips, Gloria Blondell.

CALVIN AND THE COLONEL—30 minutes—October 3, 1961 - September 22, 1962. Syndicated.

CAMEO THEATRE

Anthology. Rebroadcasts of dramas that were originally aired via "Matinee Theatre."

CAMEO THEATRE—60 minutes—Syndicated 1959.

CAMERA THREE

Anthology. A program, unsponsored, reflecting the interests of the people producing it — "an experimental educational series, a market place of ideas from drama, literature, dance, music, and art."

Host: James Macandrew.

Included:

The Music Of A Different Drummer.
The life of author Henry David
Thoreau.

Edgar Allen Poe: Israfel. Geddeth
Smith, as Poe, discussing his life.

The World In 1984. A discussion with
guest Nigel Calder.

The Eagle, The Tiger, And The Fly. A
program depicting works of art in-
spired by these creatures.

A Salute To Stravinsky. *Orchestra:*
The New York Philharmonic, conducted by Pierre Boulet.

The Art Of The Animator. A demon-
stration, with guest Faith Hubley.

The Sorrow And The Pity. Excerpts
from the French film, with director
Marcel Ophails as guest.

CAMERA THREE—30 minutes—Pre-
miered: Local New York, WCBS-TV,
May 16, 1953; Network: CBS, 1956.
Original title: "It's Worth Knowing."

CAMOUFLAGE

Game. Two competing players. A
camouflaged cartoon drawing, containing a hidden object, is flashed on a
screen. Through correct responses during a series of general-knowledge question-answer rounds, players receive a
chance to trace the object. If they are
unable to guess it, a section of the
camouflage is removed. The game
continues until someone identifies the
object.

Host: Don Morrow.

Organist: Paul Taubman.

CAMOUFLAGE—30 minutes—ABC—
January 9, 1961 - November 16,
1962.

CAMP RUNAMUCK

Comedy. Background: Summer
camps, Runamuck for boys, and
Divine for girls. Runamuck is
slipshodly operated by Commander
Wivenhoe, a child hater, and his staff
of lamebrains: Spiffy, Pruett, Malden,
and Doc. Divine is impeccably main-
tained under the auspices of Counselor Mahalia May Gruenecker and her
beautiful assistant, Caprice
Yeudleman.

Stories relate Wivenhoe's attempts
to cope with his horde of detested
brats and the female manipulation of
his counselors into performing
burdensome tasks for Divine.

CAST

Commander Wivenhoe	Arch Johnson
Caprice Yeudleman	Nina Wayne
Mahalia May Gruenecker	Alice Nunn
Spiffy	Dave Ketchum
Pruett	Dave Madden
Malden	Mike Wagner
Doc	Leonard Stone
	Frank DeVol
Eulalia Divine, the camp owner	Hermione Baddeley

Music: Frank DeVol.

CAMP RUNAMUCK—30 minutes—
NBC—September 17, 1965 - September 2, 1966.

CANDID CAMERA

Comedy. Ordinary people, suddenly
confronted with prearranged, ludicrous situations, are filmed by hidden

Camp Runamuck. Left to right: Arch Johnson, Dave Ketchum, and Leonard Stone. © *Screen Gems.*

cameras and seen in the act of being themselves. Based on the radio program "Candid Microphone."

First Version:
CANDID CAMERA—30 minutes. ABC—December 5, 1948 - August 15, 1949; CBS—September 12, 1949 - August 19, 1951; ABC—August 27, 1951 - August 22, 1956.

Host: Alan Funt.

Featured: Jerry Lester.

Announcer: Ken Roberts.

Second Version:
CANDID CAMERA—30 minutes—CBS—October 2, 1960 - September 3, 1967.

Host: Alan Funt.

Co-Hosts: Arthur Godfrey (October 2, 1960 - September 24, 1961); Durwood Kirby (October 1, 1961 - September 4, 1966); Bess Myerson (September 11, 1966 - September 3, 1967).

Regulars: Marilyn Van de Var, the Candid Camera girl; Dorothy Collins; Joey Faye; Betsy Palmer; Al Kelly; Marge Green; Tom O'Mally; Thelma Pellmige; Fannie Flagg.

Music: Sid Ramin; Henri Rene.

Third Version: British—
CANDID CAMERA—30 minutes—ABC-TV from Manchester—1961-1967.

Host: Bob Monkhouse.

Co-Host: Jonathan Routt.

Fourth Version:
THE NEW CANDID CAMERA—30 minutes—Syndicated 1974.

Host: Alan Funt.

Announcer-Co-Host: John Bartholomew Tucker.

Music: Recorded.

CAN DO

Game. Object: For contestants to determine whether or not guest celebrities can perform certain stunts. After a series of indirect question-and-answer rounds between the contestant and the celebrity, the player is escorted to an isolation booth and given a limited amount of time to reach a decision. The guest is then asked if he is able to perform the stunt in question. If the contestant correctly guesses, he wins a cash prize.

Host: Robert Alda.

CAN DO—30 minutes—NBC—1956-1957.

CANNON

Crime Drama. Background: Los Angeles, California. The investigations of Frank Cannon, a highly paid and overweight private detective.

Starring: William Conrad as Frank Cannon.

Music: John Parker; John Cannon.

CANNON—60 minutes—CBS—Premiered: September 14, 1971.

CANNONBALL

Adventure. Background: Various areas between the United States and Canada. The experiences of Mike "Cannonball" Malone and his partner, Jerry, drivers for the International Transport Trucking Company.

CAST
Mike "Cannonball" Malone Paul Birch
Jerry   William Campbell

CANNONBALL—30 minutes—Syndicated 1958.

CAN YOU TOP THIS?

Game. Jokes, submitted by home viewers are relayed to the audience by the "Joke Teller." The response, zero to one hundred, is registered on a laugh meter. A panel of three then tries to beat the established score with other jokes in the same category.

The home viewer receives twenty-five dollars for his joke and an additional twenty-five dollars for each joke that registers a lesser response. The limit is one hundred dollars. Based on the radio program of the same title.

Versions:
ABC—30 minutes—October 3, 1950 - March 21, 1951.

Host: Ward Wilson.

Joke Teller: Senator Edward Ford.

Panel: Harry Hersfield, Joe Laurie, Jr., Peter Donald.

Syndicated — 30 minutes—1970.

Host: Wink Martindale.

Joke Tellers (alternating): Dick Gautier, Richard Dawson.

Regular Panelist: Morey Amsterdam (assisted by two guests per week).

CAPTAIN BILLY'S SHOWBOAT

Musical. Variety set against the background of an Ohio River showboat.

Host (appearing as Captain Billy Bryant): Ralph Dunne.

Regulars: Ralph Dumke, Johnny Downs, Bibi Osterwald, Juanita Hall, Betty Brewer, George Jason.

Orchestra: John Gart.

CAPTAIN BILLY'S SHOWBOAT—30 minutes—CBS 1948.

CAPTAIN DAVID GRIEF

Adventure. Background: The West Indies. The story of sloop captain David Grief, and his traveling companion, Anura. Episodes relate their search for adventure.

CAST
Captain David Grief   Maxwell Reed
Anura   Maureen Hingert

CAPTAIN DAVID GRIEF—30 minutes—Syndicated 1956.

CAPTAIN GALLANT

See title: "Foreign Legionnaire."

CAPTAIN KANGAROO

Educational. Entertainment geared to preschool children. Background: The Treasure House. Various aspects of the adult world are explained to children through cartoons, stories, songs, and sketches.

CAST
Captain Kangaroo   Bob Keeshan
Mr. Green Jeans, his
    assistant   Lumpy Brannum
Also: Ann Leonardo, Bennye Gatteys, Dr. Joyce Brothers.

Vocalists: The Kangaroos (Beverly Hanshaw, Holly Mershon, Phil Casnoff, Terrence Emanuel).

Puppets: Mr. Moose, Bunny Rabbit, Miss Worm, Miss Frog.

Characters: Dancing Bear, Grandfather Clock.

Music: Recorded.

CAPTAIN KANGAROO—60 minutes —CBS—Premiered: October 3, 1955. Based on a local New York Program, hosted by Bob Keeshan, entitled: "Tinker's Workshop." Spin-off: "Mister Mayor"—60 minutes—CBS— September 26, 1964 - September 1965. Bob Keeshan as an acting Mayor who relates various aspects of the world to children. Also cast: Jane Connell, Bill McCutcheon, and Cosmo Allegrette. Broadcast in place of the Saturday morning edition of "Captain Kangaroo."

CAPTAIN MIDNIGHT

Adventure. The story of a private citizen who devotes his life to fighting crime. Named "Captain Midnight" for his daring air tactics against the enemy during the war, Captain Albright commands the Secret Squadron, a U.S. government organization designed to combat evil. Assisted by Tut and Ickky, he battles the sinister forces threatening world security.

Based on the radio program of the

same title. After the program was dropped by network television, its syndicated title became "Jet Jackson, Flying Commando." By voice-over dubbing, the name, Captain Midnight, was also changed to Jet Jackson. Ovaltine, the sponsor and owner, reserved the right to the original name.

CAST

Captain Midnight
     (Jet Jackson)   Richard Webb
Ichabod (Ickky) Mudd, his
     mechanic   Sid Melton
Tut, a scientist   Olan Soule
Chuck Ramsey, the Captain's
     ward   Renee Beard
Marcia Stanhope,
     a Secret Squadron
     agent   Jan Shepard

Captain Midnight's plane: The *Sky King.*

Music: Don Ferris.

CAPTAIN MIDNIGHT—30 minutes—CBS—September 4, 1954 - September 1958.

CAPTAIN NICE

Comedy. Background: Big Town, U.S.A. Experimenting, Carter Nash, a mild-mannered police chemist, discovers Super Juice, a liquid, that when taken, transforms him into Captain Nice, a heroic crime fighter.

Secretly appearing as Captain Nice whenever the need arises, Nash fights an endless battle against the diabolical fiends of crime-ridden Big Town.

CAST

Carter Nash/Captain
     Nice   William Daniels
Mrs. Nash, his
     mother   Alice Ghostley
Police Sergeant Candy Kane,
     his girlfriend   Ann Prentiss
Police Chief Segal   William Zuckert
Mayor Finny   Liam Dunn
Mr. Nash, Carter's
     father   Byron Fougler

Music: Vic Mizzy.

CAPTAIN NICE—30 minutes—NBC—January 9, 1967 - September 4, 1967.

CAPTAIN SCARLET AND THE MYSTERONS

Marionette Adventure. Era: The twenty-first century. During an exploration of the planet Mars, the Mysterons, its inhabitants, misconstrue a visit by Spectrum, an international organization established to safeguard the world, as an unprovoked attack and declare a war of revenge on Earth.

Seeking a champion to their cause, the Mysterons contrive an automobile accident that claims the life of Spectrum Agent Captain Scarlet (named as all agents after the colors of the spectrum). Able to recreate any person or object after it has first been destroyed, the Mysterons restore his life. However, retaining his human force, as well as Mysteron characteristics, he fails to fulfill their expectations; instead, he becomes their indestructible enemy.

Episodes depict Spectrum's battle against the never-seen Mysterons' war of attrition. Filmed in Supermarionation. An I.T.C. presentation.

Characters' Voices
Captain Scarlet, Spectrum's chief
     operative   Francis Matthews
Colonel White, the commander of
     Spectrum   Donald Gray
Captain Grey, a Spectrum
     agent   Paul Maxwell

Captain Blue, a Spectrum
 agent   Ed Bishop
Captain Ochre, a Spectrum
 agent   Jeremy Wilkins
Captain Magenta, a Spectrum
 agent   Gary Files
Lieutenant Green, a
 Spectrum agent   Cy Grant
Doctor Fawn, the medical
 commander   Charles Tingwell
Symphony Angel, a Spectrum
 pilot   Janna Hill
Melody Angel, a Spectrum
 pilot   Sylvia Anderson
Rhapsody Angel, a Spectrum
 pilot   Liz Morgan
Harmony Angel, a Spectrum
 pilot   Lian-Shin
Destiny Angel, a Spectrum
 pilot   Liz Morgan
The Mysteron Voice   Donald Gray
The World President   Paul Maxwell

Additional characters:

Captain Black, a former Spectrum Agent, now the Mysteron Agent on Earth.

Music: Barry Gray.

Vocals: The Spectrum.

CAPTAIN SCARLET AND THE MYSTERONS—30 minutes—Syndicated 1967.

CAPTAIN VIDEO AND HIS VIDEO RANGERS

Adventure. Era: Earth, A.D. 2254. Background: A lab hidden deep in a mountain peak, the central headquarters of Captain Video, "The Guardian of the Safety of the World." Possessing amazing scientific genius and electronic weapons, he assists various world governments, and attempts to destroy persons dangerous to the safety and peace of the universe.

CAST

Captain Video
 (1949-1950)   Richard Coogan
Captain Video
 (1950-1956)   Al Hodge
The Video Ranger, a teen-
 ager (fifteen) the
 Captain hopes to one
 day carry on his vital
 work   Don Hastings
Dr. Pauli, an enemy
 seeking to secure the
 Captain's secrets   Hal Conklin
Dr. Tobor   Dave Ballard
Agent Carter   Nat Polen

Captain Video's Rocket: The *Galaxey.*

Featured: Frequent Video Ranger messages; short, inspirational communications designed to instill viewers with the spirit of fair play, antidiscrimination, and the Golden Rule.

When first begun, "Captain Video and His Video Rangers" was telecast as a continuing serial. In 1953, when it was titled "The Secret Files of Captain Video," it became a weekly adventure complete in itself. In 1956, the adventure format was dropped, and Al Hodge became the host of "Captain Video's Cartoons," a weekly presentation featuring the animated antics of "Betty Boop," voiced by Mae Questel. 1951 saw a fifteen-episode theatrical version, "Captain Video," starring Judd Holdren as the Captain.

CAPTAIN VIDEO AND HIS VIDEO RANGERS—30 minutes—DuMont—1949-1953. THE SECRET FILES OF CAPTAIN VIDEO—30 minutes—DuMont—1953-1956. CAPTAIN VIDEO'S CARTOONS—30 minutes—DuMont—1956.

CAPTAIN Z-RO

Adventure. Captain Z-Ro, the inventor of a time machine, establishes a day of crisis in the life of an individual. His young assistant, Jet, is placed in its chamber and transported to a past era. As the Captain controls his activities, the boy assists where possible and attempts to resolve encountered difficulties.

CAST
Captain Z-Ro   Roy Steffins
Jet   Bobby Trumbull

The Captain's Rocket Ship: ZX-99.

CAPTAIN Z-RO—15 minutes—Syndicated 1955.

CAPTURE

Adventure. Films depicting the capture of wild animals.

Hosts-Narrators: Bill Wilson, Arthur Jones.

CAPTURE—30 minutes—Syndicated 1965.

CAPTURED

Crime Drama. Retitled episodes of "Gangbusters."

Host-Narrator: Chester Morris.

Included:

Man From Mars. The story of a thief who dresses as a Martian to rob banks in broad daylight.
Starring: Bob Karnes, Eddie Marr.

Hogan-Yates. The story details the risks taken by a group of prisoners as they attempt to escape from jail.
Starring: Leonard Bill, Eddie Hyans.

Max Baroda. The story concerns the grim police hunt for a murderous gang of thieves.
Starring: John Seven.

CAPTURED—30 minutes—Syndicated 1954.

THE CARA WILLIAMS SHOW

Comedy. Distinguished by two formats. The background for each is Los Angeles, California.

Format One:
The story of a young bride and groom who are employed by Fenwick Diversified Industries, Incorporated, a company that prohibits the employment of married couples. Cara Wilton, a beautiful, but scatterbrained file clerk, and Frank Bridges, the effi-

The Cara Williams Show. Frank Aletter and Cara Williams.

ciency expert, resolve their problem by concealing their marriage. Episodes relate their struggles to keep their marriage a secret.

Format Two (five months following):
    Plagued by a constant fear of discovery, Cara and Frank reveal the fact of their marriage to Damon Burkhardt, the company manager. When discovering that Frank is to be discharged, Cara, whose complicated filing system makes her inexpendable, questions the company's marriage policy and convinces Mr. Fenwick, the president, to alter the rule. Stories relate the home and working lives of young marrieds.

CAST

Cara Wilton (Bridges)	Cara Williams
Frank Bridges	Frank Aletter
Damon Burkhardt, Cara and Frank's employer	Paul Reed
Fletcher Kincaid, Cara and Frank's neighbor, a hip-talking jazz musician	Jack Sheldon
Mary Hamilmyer, Mr. Burkhardt's secretary	Jeanne Arnold
Mr. Fenwick, the company president	Edward Everett Horton

Music: Kenyon Hopkins.

THE CARA WILLIAMS SHOW—30 minutes—CBS—September 23, 1964 - September 10, 1965.

CAR 54, WHERE ARE YOU?

Comedy. Background: The Bronx, the 53rd precinct on Tremont Avenue. The on-duty and off-duty lives of two fictitious New York policemen, Gunther Toody and Francis Muldoon, patrol car officers assigned to Car 54.

CAST

Gunther Toody	Joe E. Ross
Francis Muldoon	Fred Gwynne
Captain Martin Block	Paul Reed
Lucille Toody, Gunther's wife	Beatrice Pons
Patrolman Leo Schnauzer	Al Lewis
Sylvia Schnauzer, his wife	Charlotte Rae
Patrolman Ed Nicholson	Hank Garrett
Desk Sgt. Sol Abrams	Nathaniel Frey
Officer Rodrequez	Jack Healy
Officer O'Hara	Al Henderson
Officer Anderson	Nipsey Russell
Officer Steinmetz	Joe Warren
Officer Wallace	Fred O'Neal
Officer Murdock	Shelly Burton
Officer Nelson	Jim Gromley
Officer Reilly	Duke Farley
Officer Kissel	Bruce Kirby
Officer Antonnucci	Jerry Guardino
Mrs. Bronson, the Bronx troublemaker	Molly Picon
Mrs. Muldoon, Francis's mother	Ruth Masters
Peggy Muldoon, his sister	Helen Parker
Al, a friend of Toody and Muldoon	Carl Ballantine
Rose, his wife	Martha Greenhouse
Bonnie Kalsheim, Muldoon's occasional date	Alice Ghostley
Mrs. Block, the Captain's wife	Patricia Bright
Charlie, the drunk, a friend of Toody and Muldoon	Larry Storch

Theme: CAR 54, WHERE ARE YOU?

Words: Nat Hiken.

Music: John Strauss.

There's a hold-up in the Bronx,
Brooklyn's broken out in fights.
There's a traffic jam in Harlem,
That's backed up to Jackson Heights.
There's a scout troop short a child,
Krushchev's due at Idlewild—
CAR 54, WHERE ARE YOU?

Music: John Strauss.

CAR 54, WHERE ARE YOU?—30 minutes—NBC—September 17, 1961 - September 8, 1963. Syndicated.

CARIBE

Crime Drama. The cases of Ben Logan and Mark Walters, Miami-based police agents who handle special assignments fighting crime in the Caribbean.

CAST
Lt. Ben Logan	Stacy Keach
Sgt. Mark Walters	Carl Franklin
Captain Rawlings	Robert Mandan

Music: John Elizade.

CARIBE—60 minutes—ABC—February 17, 1975 - August 11, 1975.

THE CARLTON FREDERICKS SHOW

Information. Nutrition and health advice.

Host: Carlton Fredericks.

THE CARLTON FREDERICKS SHOW—30 minutes—Syn,dicated 1967.

CARNIVAL

Anthology. Rebroadcasts of dramas that were originally aired via other filmed anthology programs.

Included:

My Nephew Norville. The story of a traveler from outer space who is befriended by an amateur inventor.
Starring: Harold Peary, Gil Stratton.

Old Mother Hubbard. The story of a woman who resorts to desperate tactics to determine if her daughter's employer can be trusted.
Starring: Ellen Corby.

My Rival Is A Fiddle. The story of a school teacher and her struggles to snatch the attentions of a man whose love is his fiddle.
Starring: Hans Conried.

Never Trust A Redhead. The story of a wealthy but spoiled girl and her attempts to run her fiancé's life.
Starring: Sandra Dorn.

CARNIVAL—30 minutes—ABC—June 1953 - September 1953.

THE CAROL BURNETT SHOW

Variety. Music, comedy, songs, and dances.

Hostess: Carol Burnett.

Regulars: Harvey Korman, Vicki Lawrence, Lyle Waggoner, The Ernest Flatt Dancers.

Announcer: Lyle Waggoner.

Orchestra: Harry Zimmerman; Peter Matz.

Features:
The Opening Monologue. Carol's question and answer session with the studio audience.

Guests in solo and/or sketch performance.

The Old Timers. Seated in rocking chairs, an elderly couple (Carol and Harvey) recall the past and what might have been.

The Marriage Skit. The bickering relationship between a husband, Harry (Harvey Korman), his wife Blanche (Carol Burnett), and their liberated teen-age daughter, Chris (Vicki Lawrence).

Salutes. Programs devoted to single musical topics (e.g., Broadway and Hollywood spoofs).

THE CAROL BURNETT SHOW—60 minutes—CBS—Premiered: September 11, 1967.

CARTOON THEATRE

Children. Line sketch drawings illustrating off-stage story telling.

Yarn Spinner: Jack Lucksinger.

Artist: Chuck Lucksinger.

Organist: Rosa Rio.

CARTOON THEATRE—30 minutes—ABC 1947.

CARTOON THEATRE

Cartoons. Paul Terry's animated creations: "Heckle and Jeckle," "Gandy Goose," "Dinky Duck," and "Little Roguefort."

Host: Dick Van Dyke.

CARTOON THEATRE—30 minutes—CBS—June 13, 1956 - September 1956.

CARTOONSVILLE

See title: "Paul Winchell and Jerry Mahoney."

CASABLANCA

See title: "Warner Brothers Presents," *Casablanca* segment.

THE CASE OF THE DANGEROUS ROBIN

Mystery. The story of insurance investigators Robin Scott and Phyllis Collier. Episodes relate their attempts to expose "The Cheaters," people who defraud insurance companies with false claims.

CAST
Robin Scott	Rick Jason
Phyllis Collier	Jean Blake

Music: David Rose.

THE CASE OF THE DANGEROUS ROBIN—30 minutes—Syndicated 1961.

THE CASES OF EDDIE DRAKE

Crime Drama. Background: New York City. The investigations of Eddie Drake, a private detective, and Dr. Karen Gayle, a psychologist who assists him to acquire information for a book she is compiling on criminal behavior.

CAST
Eddie Drake	Don Haggerty
Karen Gayle	Patricia Morrison

THE CASES OF EDDIE DRAKE—30 minutes—CBS 1949 (dropped after nine episodes); Syndicated 1952.

CASEY JONES

Adventure. Background: Jackson, Tennessee, during the latter half of the nineteenth century. The saga of the famed 382 Engine, the Cannonball Express (Illinois Central Railroad) and its legendary engineer, Casey Jones.

CAST

Casey Jones	Alan Hale, Jr.
Alice Jones, his wife	Mary Lawrence
Casey Jones, Jr., their son	Bobby Clark
Red Rock, the Cannonball Conductor	Eddy Waller
Willie Sims, the Cannonball Fireman	Dub Taylor
Sam Peachpit, Casey's Indian friend	Pat Hogan
Mr. Carter, the businessman	Paul Keast

Jones family dog: Cinders.

Casey Jones. Left to right: Eddy Waller, Paul Keast, Bobby Clark, (holding Cinders), Dub Taylor, Mary Lawrence, Pat Hogan, Alan Hale, Jr. © *Screen Gems.*

CASEY JONES–30 minutes–Syndicated 1957.

CASPER, THE FRIENDLY GHOST

Animated Cartoon. The story of Casper, a ghost who struggles to befriend humans and animals.

Characters: Casper; Wendy, the Good Witch; Spooky, the mischievous ghost; Poil, Casper's girlfriend; and the Ghostly Trio.

Voices are not given screen credit.

Music: Winston Sharples.

CASPER, THE FRIENDLY GHOST–6 minute, 30-second theatrical cartoons–Syndicated 1953.

THE CATTANOOGA CATS

Animated Cartoon. The misadventures of the Cattanooga Cats (Chessie, Kitty Jo, Scootz, Groovey, and Country), a feline Rock group. A Hanna-Barbera production.

Additional segments:

It's The Wolf. The story of Mildew, a wolf who is determined to catch a decent meal: Lambsy, the poor defenseless lamb. Savior of the lamb is Bristol Hound—"Bristol Hound's my name and saving sheep's my game."

Around The World In 79 Days. The adventures of Phineas Fogg, Jr. as he attempts to travel around the world in seventy-nine days. His aides: Jenny Trent and Happy; his enemies: Crumdon and Bumbler, who plot to thwart his efforts.

Auto Cat And Motor Mouse. The story of a cat who is determined to beat a mouse in a race.

Characters' Voices

Country	Bill Galloway
Groovey	Casey Kaseem
Scoots	Jim Begg
Kitty Jo	Julie Bennett
Chessie	Julie Bennett
Mildew Wolf	Paul Lynde
Lambsy	Daws Butler
Bristol Hound	Allan Melvin
Phineas Fogg, Jr.	Bruce Watson
Jenny Trent	Janet Waldo
Happy	Don Messick
Smerky	Don Messick
Crumdon	Daws Butler
Bumbler	Allan Melvin
Motor Mouse	Dick Curtis
Auto Cat	Marty Ingles

Music: Hoyt Curtin.

THE CATTANOOGA CATS—60 minutes—ABC—September 6, 1969 - September 5, 1970; 30 minutes—September 13, 1970 - September 4, 1971.

CAVALCADE OF AMERICA

Anthology. Dramatizations based on past events. The struggles of outstanding individuals in the shaping of America.

Included:

Sunset At Appomattox. The events leading to and the men responsible for the ending of the Civil War.

CAST
William Johnstone, Henry Morgan.

Duel At The O.K. Corral. A recreation of the famed gunfight—the Earps against the outlaw Dalton Brothers.

CAST
Kenneth Tobey, Harry Morgan.

The Texas Ranger. The story of the hardships endured by the men of the Nation's oldest law enforcement agency, the Texas Rangers.

CAST
Jim Davis, William Tollman.

CAVALCADE OF AMERICA—60 minutes. NBC—October 1, 1952 - September 1953. ABC—September 29, 1953 - September 6, 1955. As "Cavalcade Theatre"—60 minutes—ABC—September 13, 1955 - September 14, 1956.

CAVALCADE OF BANDS

Musical Variety. The recreated sounds of the Big Band Era.

Host: Buddy Rogers.

Regulars: Marsha Van Dyke, The Mello-Larks, The Clark Brothers.

Orchestra: Weekly guest band leaders.

CAVALCADE OF BANDS—60 minutes—DuMont 1951.

CAVALCADE OF STARS

Variety. Music, songs, dances, and comedy routines.

Host: Jack Carter.

Regulars: Joan Edwards, Larry Storch, The Fontaines, The Arnauts.

Orchestra: Sammy Spear.

CAVALCADE OF STARS—60 minutes—DuMont—1949-1950. Broadcast from January 7, 1950 - September 3, 1952, with Jackie Gleason as its host. See title: "Jackie Gleason."

THE CBS CHILDREN'S FILM FESTIVAL

Movies. International award-winning films for and about children.

Hostess: Fran Allison.

Puppets: Kukla, a bald-headed, round-nosed little man; and Ollie, the scatterbrained dragon.

Puppeteer: Burr Tillstrom.

Included:

Skinny And Fatty. The misadventures of two boys, Fatty and his friend Skinny. Japanese.

CAST
Y. Kataoka, H. Sha, M. Saito.

Adventure In Hopfields. The story of a young girl and her attempts to earn the money she needs to replace a statue that she accidentally broke. English.

CAST
Mandy Miller, Hilda Fenemore, Russell Waters.

The Little Bearkeepers. The story of a boy and his pet bear. Czechoslovakian.

CAST
Gustav Heverle, Vojetch Rosenberg.

Stowaway In The Sky. A boy's adventures, trapped in a sixty-foot traveling balloon. French.

CAST
Andre Gille, Maurice Baquet.
Narrator: Jack Lemmon.

Lone Wolf. The story of a young boy and his attempts to prove that a German Shepherd is innocent of sheep-slaying charges. Yugoslavian.

CAST
Slavko Stimac.

John And Julie. A tale of two children and their efforts to attend the coronation of Elizabeth II. English.

CAST
Colin Gibson, Lesley Dudley, Noelle Middleton, Moira Lister, Peter Sellers.

THE CBS CHILDREN'S FILM FESTIVAL—60 minutes—CBS—Premiered: September 11, 1971. Previously, broadcast on CBS as a series of specials from 1966-1971.

THE CBS COMEDY PLAYHOUSE

Pilot Films. Proposed comedy series for the 1971-1972 season.

Included:

An Amateur's Guide To Love. A Candid Camera type of program featuring various filmed sequences involving ordinary people and their reactions to questions relating to love and courtship.

Host-Narrator: Joe Flynn.

Eddie. The story of Eddie Skinner, a conniving private patrolman who manipulates people and machines to benefit himself.

CAST
Eddie Skinner: Phil Silvers; Chief Pike: Fred Clark; Sylvia: Joanna Barnes; Callahan: Frank Faylen.

Elke. The story of a homely American

who marries a beautiful German Countess.

CAST

Elke Sommer, Peter Bonerz, Paul Peterson, Debi Storm.

My Wives Jane. The story of actress Jane Franklin—a woman, married to a doctor, and who also portrays a doctor's wife on a TV serial.

CAST

Jane Franklin: Janet Leigh; Nat Franklin: Barry Nelson; Vic Semple: John Delmer.

Shepherd's Flock. The misadventures of an ex-football player turned priest.

CAST

Jack Shepherd: Kenneth Mars; Abby Scofield: Jill Jaress; Dr. Hewitt: Don Ameche.

THE CBS COMEDY PLAYHOUSE— 30 minutes—CBS—August 1, 1971 - September 5, 1971.

CBS MOVIES

Movies. Theatrical releases.

Titles:
THE CBS SUNDAY NIGHT MOVIE —2 hours—September 19, 1971 - August 27, 1972.

Included:

The Great Race. The time: 1908. The saga of a New York-to-Paris motor race. The ill-fated attempts by the evil Professor Fate to secure the championship.

CAST

Professor Fate: Jack Lemmon; The

Great Leslie: Tony Curtis; Max: Peter Falk; Hezekiah: Keenan Wynn; Maggie DuBois: Natalie Wood; Lily Olay: Dorothy Provine.

A Fine Madness. The story of Samson Shillitoe, a Greenwich Village nonconformist.

CAST

Samson Shillitoe: Sean Connery; Rhoda Shillitoe: Joanne Woodward; Lydia West: Jean Seberg; Dr. Oliver West: Patrick O'Neal; Miss Walnicki: Sue Anne Langdon.

Gentle Ben. The story of the relationship between a boy and his pet bear.

CAST

Tom Wedloe: Dennis Weaver; Ellen Wedloe: Vera Miles; Mark Wedloe: Clint Howard.

THE CBS THURSDAY NIGHT MOVIE—2 hours—Premiered: September 16, 1965.

Included:

Butterfield 8. The story of a beautiful fashion model and her succession of ill-fated love affairs.

CAST

Gloria Wandrous: Elizabeth Taylor; Weston: Laurence Harvey; Emily: Dina Merrill; Norma: Susan Oliver.

Valley Of The Dolls. The story of three career girls and their world of distress, confronted with the hard knocks of Broadway and Hollywood.

CAST

Neely O'Hara: Patty Duke; Jennifer North: Sharon Tate; Anne Wells: Barbara Parkins.

Goodbye Charlie. Charlie Sorel, play-boy, is murdered after having an affair at a party with another man's wife. Reincarnated as a beautiful young woman, he adopts the guise of Mrs. Sorel, and seeks revenge on his murderer through blackmail.

CAST

Charlie Sorel: Debbie Reynolds; George: Tony Curtis.

Bye, Bye Birdie. A teen-age singing idol, Conrad Birdie, is drafted, striking dismay within the hearts of the world's young females. A songwriter attempts to arrange his farewell — his kissing of a typical American girl on "The Ed Sullivan Show."

CAST

Albert: Dick Van Dyke; Rosie: Janet Leigh; Kim: Ann-Margret; Hugo: Bobby Rydell; Birdie: Jesse Pearson.

THE CBS FRIDAY NIGHT MOVIE— 2 hours—September 17, 1965 - September 10, 1971. Returned: September 15, 1972.

Included:

Bonnie And Clyde. The story of gangsters, Bonnie Parker and Clyde Barrow.

CAST

Bonnie Parker: Faye Dunnaway; Clyde Barrow: Warren Beatty; Blanche: Estelle Parsons; C.W. Moss: Michael J. Pollard.

Bullit. The story of an incorruptable police detective and his attempts to apprehend syndicate killers.

CAST

Frank Bullit: Steve McQueen; Walter:

Robert Vaughn; Cathy: Jacqueline Bisset.

The Cincinnati Kid. Era: New Orleans during the 1930s. The saga of the marathon poker game between a young ace, the Cincinnati Kid, and an unbeatable pro, Lancey Howard.

CAST

Cincinnati Kid: Steve McQueen; Lancey Howard: Edward G. Robinson; Christian: Tuesday Weld; Melba: Ann-Margret; Shooter: Karl Malden; Lady Fingers: Joan Blondell.

The Graduate. The story of an insecure college graduate who is seduced by a sophisticated married woman.

CAST

Benjamin Braddock: Dustin Hoffman; Mrs. Robinson: Anne Bancroft; Elaine Robinson: Katherine Ross.

THE CBS LATE MOVIE—Times approximate depending upon the feature: one hour, thirty-five minutes, to two hours, thirty minutes.

Included:

I Love Melvin. The story of a chorus girl as she attempts to break into movies.

CAST

Judy: Debbie Reynolds; Melvin: Donald O'Connor; Mergo: Jim Backus.

The Woman Hunter. The story of a socialite as she struggles to protect a fortune in jewels from a murderous theif.

CAST

Barbara Eden, Stuart Whitman.

Live A Little, Love A Little. The story

of a free-lance photographer who is pursued by an eccentric young lady.

CAST
Elvis Presley, Michele Carey, Rudy Vallee, Dick Sargent.

Where Were You When The Lights Went Out? A series of marital mishaps attributed to the East Coast power failure of November 9, 1965.

CAST
Margaret Garrison: Doris Day; Waldo Zane: Robert Moorse; Peter Garrison: Patrick O'Neal; Ladislau Walichik: Terry-Thomas.

THE CBS NEWCOMERS

Variety. Showcased: Undiscovered professional talent.

Host: Dave Garroway.

Regulars: Rodney Winfield, Joey Garya, Cynthia Clawson, David Arlen, Paul Perez, Rex Allen, Jr., Gay Perkins, Peggy Sears, The Good Humor Company, The Californians.

Orchestra: Nelson Riddle.

THE CBS NEWCOMERS—60 minutes —CBS—July 12, 1971 - September 6, 1971.

CELEBRITY BILLIARDS

Game. Famed hustler Minnesota Fats vs. a guest celebrity, the challenger. Various games of billiards are played. Celebrities donate their winnings to charity.

Host: Rudolph Wanderone, Jr. (Minnesota Fats).

CELEBRITY BILLIARDS—30 minutes—Syndicated 1967.

CELEBRITY BOWLING

Game. Four celebrities, divided into two teams of two, play for selected studio audience members. A game based on a ten-frame score wherein the best ball doubles. Two alleys are used. The members of one team each stand on one lane. The player on Lane one bowls first. If a strike is not achieved (which would end the frame and score twenty points), his or her partner then bowls. If, again, a strike is not achieved, the player first to bowl receives a second chance. Taking one of the two lanes, he attempts to acquire the spare. Points are determined accordingly. The second team bowls in the same manner. Gifts are awarded to studio audience members according to team scores.

Host: Jed Allen.

Assistants: Bill Buneta; Bobby Cooper; Dave Davis.

Announcer: Jed Allen.

Music: Recorded.

CELEBRITY BOWLING—30 minutes —Syndicated 1971.

THE CELEBRITY GAME

Game. Nine celebrity guests, two competing players. The host reads a yes-or-no type question. The celebrities, by pressing a button, secretly lock in their answers. Contestants, in turn, select a guest and try to guess his or her answer. Each correct prediction awards a player a cash prize.

Host: Carl Reiner.

THE CELEBRITY GAME—30 minutes—CBS—April 5, 1964 - September 13, 1964. Rebroadcasts: CBS—June 1965 - September 1965.

CELEBRITY PLAYHOUSE

Anthology. Rebroadcasts of dramas that were originally aired via other filmed anthology programs.

CELEBRITY PLAYHOUSE—30 minutes—Syndicated 1956.

CELEBRITY SWEEPSTAKES

Game. Players: Six celebrities; two contestants, who each receive twenty dollars betting money; and the studio audience.
Round One: The host asks a general knowledge question; the celebrities write their answers on a card which is electronically screened backstage; the studio audience, through electronic panels before them, vote for the celebrity each feels has the correct answer. When the odds for each celebrity are established, each contestant chooses a celebrity and bets a specified amount of money (twenty, ten, five, or two dollars). If correct, the player's amount is increased in accord with the displayed odds; if incorrect, the bet amount is deducted. Celebrities' answers are tabulated on a tote board.
Round Two: Same play as round one; however, the contestant may bet any amount of his accumulated money. If he guesses correctly, he may bet the amount won on another celebrity. If he is correct again, the cash is doubled; if incorrect, the amount bet is deducted.
Round Three: All or Nothing. The host asks a question; each contestant secretly chooses a celebrity, betting all or nothing on odds determined by the track record of the stars (number of questions missed). The contestants reveal their celebrity choices; the personalities one at a time reveal their answers. Cash is awarded according to the bet.
Host: Jim McKrell.
Announcer: Bill Armstrong.
Music: Stan Worth; Alan Thicke.
Regular Panelists: Carol Wayne, Joey Bishop, Buddy Hackett.

CELEBRITY SWEEPSTAKES—30 minutes—NBC—Premiered: April 1, 1974.

CELEBRITY TENNIS

Game. Background: The West Side Racquet Club in Los Angeles, California. Two competing teams, each composed of two celebrities. Played: A two set doubles match. Teams play for selected spectators who receive prizes according to the final score.
Host: Tony Trabert.
Assisting: Guest Celebrities.
Music: Recorded.

CELEBRITY TENNIS—30 minutes—Syndicated 1973.

CENTER STAGE

Anthology. Rebroadcasts of dramas that were originally aired via other filmed anthology programs.

CENTER STAGE—30 minutes—ABC—June 1, 1954 - September 21, 1954.

CESAR'S WORLD

Documentary. The lives, work, and customs of people around the world.

Host—Narrator: Cesar Romero.

CESAR'S WORLD—30 minutes—Syndicated 1968.

CHAIN LETTER

Game. Two competing teams, each composed of a celebrity captain and a noncelebrity contestant. The host presents a category topic to the teams. One contestant has to respond with a word suitable to the subject. His or her celebrity partner then has to use the last letter of the word and name another word within the same category. Each player is afforded ten seconds in which to give another word, using his or her partner's word. Failure results in a broken chain and a loss of points. Winners are the highest point scorers.

Host: Jan Murray.

CHAIN LETTER—30 minutes—NBC —July 4, 1966 - October 14, 1966.

THE CHAMBER MUSIC SOCIETY OF LOWER BASIN STREET

Variety. Swing music dedicated to "The Three B'S—Barrelhouse, Boogie-Woogie, and the Blues." Adapted from the radio program of the same title.

Host: Orson Bean.

Vocalist: Martha Lou Harp.

Music: Henry Levine's Dixieland Octet.

THE CHAMBER MUSIC SOCIETY OF LOWER BASIN STREET—30 minutes—ABC—September 14, 1948 - September 22, 1951. NBC—30 minutes—June 15, 1952 - September 1952.

THE CHAMPIONS

Adventure. Background: Geneva, Switzerland—the headquarters of Nemesis, a powerful, top-secret organization handling sensitive, difficult international assignments.

Agents Sharron Macready, Craig Stirling, and Richard Barrett are assigned to obtain deadly bacteria specimens from Chinese scientists in Tibet. Their attempt to escape after acquiring the specimens triggers an alarm. Pursued by armed guards, the agents take off in an awaiting plane. The craft, struck by gun fire, crash lands in the forbidding Himalayas.

Found by an old man, the lifeless agents are taken to his world — a lost city inhabited by the survivors of an unknown race. There, they are healed and endowed with super powers — "their mental and physical capacities fused to computer efficiency; their sight, sense and hearing, raised to their highest, futuristic stage of mental and physical growth." Still unconscious, they are returned to the site of the crash.

Later, meeting the old man, Richard learns what has befallen them and promises that he and his friends will keep the secret of the lost city and use their gifts to benefit mankind.

Stories relate the exploits of Sharron Macready, Craig Stirling, and Richard Barrett, The Champions, as they, possessing unique powers, strive to ensure law, order, and justice throughout the world.

The Champions. Left to right: Alexandra Bastedo, Stuart Damon, William Gaunt. *Courtesy Independent Television Corporation, an ATV Company.*

CAST

Sharron Macready   Alexandra Bastedo
Craig Stirling, the American
    member of the British
    team   Stuart Damon
Richard Barrett   William Gaunt
W.L. Tremayne, the head
    of Nemesis, their
    superior   Anthony Nicholls

Music: Albert Elms; Edwin Astley.

THE CHAMPIONS—60 minutes—NBC—July 11, 1967 — September 12, 1967. Syndicated. An I.T.C. Presentation.

CHANCE OF A LIFETIME

Variety. Showcased: Undiscovered professional talent. Winners, determined through the Old Gold Star Maker, which registers studio audience applause, receive one thousand dollars and a chance of a lifetime — possible discovery.

Hosts: Dennis James; John Reed King.

Regulars: Denise Darcel, Dick Collins, Russell Arms, Liza Palmer.

Orchestra: Bernie Leighton.

CHANCE OF A LIFETIME—30 minutes—ABC 1952.

CHAN-ESE WAY

Cooking. The preparation and cooking of various Oriental meals.

Host: Titus Chan, a Hawaiian restaurateur.

CHAN-ESE WAY—30 minutes—PBS—June 4, 1973 - August 27, 1973.

CHANNING

Drama. Background: Channing University. Life in a mythical Midwestern coeducational college as seen through the eyes of Joseph Howe, English professor.

CAST

Joseph Howe	Jason Evers
Dean Fred Baker	Henry Jones

CHANNING—60 minutes—ABC—September 18, 1963 - April 8, 1964.

CHARADE QUIZ

Game. Charades, submitted by home viewers, are enacted by a stock company. A panel of three has to identify it within ninety seconds. If they are able to, the sender receives ten dollars. If unable, fifteen dollars is awarded.

Host: Bill Slater.

Panelists: Minna Bess Lewis, Herb Polesie, Bob Shepard.

Stock Company: Ellen Fenwick, Sandra Poe, Allan Frank, Richard Seff, Johnny Fester.

CHARADE QUIZ—30 minutes—DuMont 1948.

CHARGE ACCOUNT

Game. Two competing players. Object: To purchase expensive merchandise items through money earned on the program. Contestants choose a packet containing sixteen letters. The host reveals its contents to one player at a time. The players place letters into a block in a manner figured to make the most three and four letter words. Twenty-five dollars is awarded for each four letter word; ten for each three. The winner, the highest cash scorer, is permitted to purchase any previously displayed item. If he hasn't accumulated enough money, he is permitted to continue playing to seek the additional cash to purchase the item sought.

Host: Jan Murray.

Assistants: Maureen Arthur, Morgan Schmitter.

Announcer: Bill Wendell.

Orchestra: Milton DeLugg.

CHARGE ACCOUNT—30 minutes—NBC—September 5, 1960 - September 28, 1962. Also known as "The Jan Murray Show."

THE CHARLES BOYER THEATRE

Anthology. Dramatic presentations.

Host-Frequent Star: Charles Boyer.

Included:

Command. The story of a first mate on a merchant ship who yearns to command a ship of his own.

CAST
Charles Boyer, Richard Hale.

Magic Night. The story of a mild-mannered bookkeeper who embarks on a mad whirl to forget his sorrows.

CAST
Charles Boyer, Joyce Gates.

Wall Of Bamboo. The story of an American intelligence agent who attempts to end the reign of a derelict man who has risen to power in Red China.

CAST
Charles Boyer.

THE CHARLES BOYER THEATRE–30 minutes–Syndicated 1953.

CHARLIE CHAN

See titles: "The Amazing Chan and the Chan Clan"; and "The New Adventures of Charlie Chan."

THE CHARLIE CHAPLIN COMEDY THEATRE

Comedy. Reedited Charlie Chaplin silent films.

Starring: Charlie Chaplin.

Also Cast: Edna Purviance, Bud Jamison, Albert Austin, Leo White, Charles Insley.

THE CHARLIE CHAPLIN COMEDY THEATRE–30 minutes–Syndicated 1966.

THE CHARLIE FARRELL SHOW

Comedy. Background: Palm Springs, California; the Racquet Club vacation resort for Hollywood personalities. The misadventures of its owner-operator, Charlie Farrell, a retired film actor.

CAST
Charlie Farrell	Himself
Dad Farrell	Charles Winninger
Sherman Hull, the director of the club	Richard Deacon
Rodney Farrell, Charlie's nephew	Jeff Silver
Mrs. Papernow, the housekeeper	Kathryn Card
The Chef	Leo Askin
Doris Mayfield, Charlie's girlfriend	Anna Lee
The newspaper editor	Marie Windsor

THE CHARLIE FARRELL SHOW– 30 minutes–CBS–July 2, 1956 - September 24, 1956; August 1, 1960 - September 19, 1960. Syndicated.

CHARLIE WILD, PRIVATE DETECTIVE

Crime Drama. Background: New York City. The investigations of private detective Charlie Wild.

CAST
Charlie Wild	John McQuade
	Kevin O'Morrison
Effie Perrine, his secretary	Cloris Leachman

CHARLIE WILD, PRIVATE DETECTIVE–30 minutes–CBS–1951 - 1952.

CHASE

Crime Drama. Background: Los Angeles, California. The investigations of Chase, a secret unit of undercover police agents designed to crack the cases that are unable to be broken by homicide, robbery, or burglary.

CAST

Captain Chase Reddick	Mitchell Ryan
Sergeant Sam MacCray	Wayne Maunder
Officer Steve Baker	Michael Richardson
Officer Fred Sing	Brian Fong
Officer Norm Hamilton	Reid Smith
Inspector Frank Dawson	Albert Reed
Officer Ed Rice	Gary Crosby
Officer Tom Wilson	Graig Gardner

Music: Oliver Nelson.

CHASE—60 minutes—NBC—September 11, 1973 - September 4, 1974.

THE CHEATERS

Mystery. Background: London, England. The cases of John Hunter, Eastern Insurance Company investigator, as he attempts to expose "The Cheaters," people who attempt to defraud insurance companies with false claims.

CAST

John Hunter	John Ireland
Walter Allen, his assistant	Robert Ayres

THE CHEATERS—30 minutes—Syndicated 1960.

CHECKMATE

Mystery. Background: San Francisco, California. The investigations of Don Corey and Jed Sills, the owner-operators of Checkmate, Incorporated, a private detective organization.

CAST

Don Corey	Anthony George
Jed Sills	Doug McClure
Carl Hyatt, the firm's criminologist	Sebastian Cabot
Chris Devlin, a firm detective	Jack Betts

Music: Pete Rugolo; Johnny Williams; Morton Stevens.

CHECKMATE—60 minutes—CBS—September 10, 1959 - September 19, 1962. Syndicated.

CHER

Variety. Music, songs, dances, and comedy sketches.

Hostess: Cher Bono.

Featured: The Tony Charmoli Dancers.

Orchestra: Jimmy Dale.

Premiere Guests: Raquel Welch, Wayne Rogers, Tatum O'Neal.

Sketches:

"Life with Laverne." Cher as Lavern Selinsky, the obnoxious housewife who airs her views on life.

"The TV Saleswoman." Cher as Southern Belle Donna Jean Brodine in a comical spoof of television commercials.

An untitled sketch. The scene opens to establish a girl (Cher) returning home from a date. As she prepares for bed, she discusses her evening with the audience.

CHER—60 minutes—CBS—Premiered: February 16, 1975.

THE CHESTERFIELD SUPPER CLUB

See title: "Perry Como."

CHESTER THE PUP

Children. The adventures of Chester the puppy, told via off screen narration and on the air cartoon sketches.

Narrator: Art Whitefield.

Cartoonist: Sid Stone.

CHESTER THE PUP—15 minutes—ABC 1950.

CHEVROLET ON BROADWAY

Musical Variety.

Host: Snooky Lanson.

Featured: The Mello-larks.

Announcer: Bill Wendell.

Orchestra: Hal Hasting.

CHEVROLET ON BROADWAY—15 minutes—NBC—June 1956 - September 1956.

THE CHEVY SHOW

Variety. Musical salutes to cities around the country.

Hosts: Janet Blair, John Raitt.

Orchestra: Harry Zimmerman.

THE CHEVY SHOW—60 minutes—NBC—June 7, 1959 - September 20, 1959.

CHEYENNE

Western. Background: The Frontier

Cheyenne. The original logo as appearing on the Warner Brothers series. Sketched: Clint Walker.

during the 1860s. The exploits of frontier scout Cheyenne Bodie, a man of Indian descent and learned in both the ways of the White Man and the Cheyenne.

Starring: Clint Walker as Cheyenne Bodie.

Music: Stan Jones; William Lava; Paul Sawtell.

CHEYENNE—60 minutes—ABC— September 20, 1956 - August 30, 1963. Syndicated. Originally telecast as part of "Warner Brothers Presents."

CHEZ PAREE REVUE

Musical Variety.

Host: Jim Dimitri.

Regulars: Joyce Sellers, Dave Dursten, The Meadowlarks.

Orchestra: Cee Davidson.

CHEZ PAREE REVUE—30 minutes— DuMont 1950.

CHICAGOLAND MYSTERY PLAYERS

Crime Drama. Background: Chicago. The investigations of police criminologist Jeffrey Hall. Episodes depict his attempts to solve baffling, bizarre murders.

CAST
Jeffrey Hall	Gordon Urquhart
Sergeant Holland, his assistant	Bob Smith

Also: Ros Twokey, Ervin Charone, Valerie McEliory, Sidney Breese, Ilka Diehl.

CHICAGOLAND MYSTERY PLAY-ERS—30 minutes—DuMont (from Chicago)—1949-1950. Previously broadcast locally in Chicago on WGN-TV from 1947-1949.

THE CHICAGO TEDDY BEARS

Comedy. Background: Chicago during the 1920s. The clash between rival nightclub owners Linc McCray and his mobster cousin Big Nick Marr. Stories concern Linc's efforts to thwart Nick's plans to add his establishment to his list of illegal speakeasies.

CAST
Linc McCray	Dean Jones
Big Nick Marr	Art Metrano
Uncle Latzi, Linc's partner	John Banner
Marvin, Linc's accountant	Marvin Kaplan
Nick's Mob:	
Duke	Mickey Shaughnessy
Dutch	Huntz Hall
Lefty	Jamie Farr
Julius	Mike Mazurki

THE CHICAGO TEDDY BEARS—30 minutes—CBS—September 17, 1971 - December 17, 1971.

CHICO AND THE MAN

Comedy. Background: East Los Angeles. The story of two men: Ed Brown, an honest but cynical one-pump garage owner, and his partner, Chico Rodriquez, a cheerful young Chicano (Mexican-American) who fast talked Ed into taking him on and letting him live in an old truck parked in the garage. Episodes depict their continual bickering, as they, representing different cultures and the generation gap, struggle to survive the inflation of the seventies.

CAST

Ed Brown   Jack Albertson
Chico Rodriquez   Freddie Prinz
Louie, the garbage
      man   Scatman Crothers
Mondo, Chico's friend   Isaac Ruiz
Rudy, Ed's
      friend   Rodolfo Hoyos
Mabel, the letter
      carrier   Bonnie Boland

Music: Jose Feliciano.

CHICO AND THE MAN—30 minutes
—NBC—Premiered: September 13,
1974.

THE CHILDREN'S CORNER

Children. Through puppet adventures,
manners, songs, and foreign phrases
are taught.

Puppeteers-Voices: Fred Rogers, Josie
      Carey.

Characters: King Friday XIII, the wise
      old owl; Daniel S. Tiger, the
      tame beast; Henrietta, the cat;
      and Grandpere, the skunk.

THE CHILDREN'S CORNER—30
minutes—NBC—August 20, 1955 -
September 10, 1955.

CHINA SMITH

Adventure. Background: The Orient.
The story of China Smith, an American soldier of fortune. Episodes depict
his battle against the forces of injustice.

Starring: Dan Duryea as China Smith.
Music: Melvyn Lenard.

CHINA SMITH—30 minutes—Syndicated 1952.

CHOOSE UP SIDES

Children's Game. Two competing
teams, the Cowboy and the Space
Ranger (later: the Bronco Buster and
the Space Pilot). Object: For one
team to out perform the other in game
contests. Prizes are awarded with the
success of completed stunts.

Hosts: Dean Miller (CBS); Gene Ray-
      burn (NBC).

CHOOSE UP SIDES—30 minutes—
CBS—1953-1954; 30 minutes—NBC—
1954-1955.

CHOPPER ONE

Crime Drama. Background: California. The story of West California
Police Department (W.C.P.D.) officers
Gil Foley and Don Burdick, the helicopter pilots of Chopper One. Episodes depict their attempts to assist
patrol-car officers.

CAST

Officer Don Burdick   Jim McMullan
Officer Gil Foley   Dirk Benedick
Captain Ted McKeegan   Ted Hartley
Mitch, the copter
      mechanic   Lou Frizzell

Music: Dominic Frontiere.

CHOPPER ONE—30 minutes—ABC—
January 17, 1974 - July 11, 1974.

THE CHUCKLE HEADS

Comedy. Reedited silent films of the
1920s.

Starring: Snub Pollard, Ben Turpin,
      Poodles Hannaford.

THE CHUCKLEHEADS—15 minutes
—Syndicated 1963.

CIMARRON CITY

Western. Background: Cimarron City, Oklahoma during the 1880s. Events in the growth of the city as seen through the eyes of Matthew Rockford, its first citizen, then mayor, now a benevolent cattle baron.

CAST

Matthew
    Rockford   George Montgomery
Beth Purcell,
    the owner of
    the boarding
    house   Audrey Totter
Lane Temple, the town
    blacksmith   John Smith

Narrator: George Montgomery.

CIMARRON CITY—30 minutes—NBC—September 27, 1958 - September 26, 1959. Syndicated.

CIMARRON STRIP

Western. Background: Cimarron City, Oklahoma during the 1880s. The story of United States Marshal Jim Crown and his attempts to settle the question of the Cimarron Strip—land over which a range war is pending between settlers and cattlemen.

CAST

Marshal Jim Crown   Stuart Whitman
Dulcey Coopersmith, the
    operator of the Hotel
    Coffee Shop   Jill Townsend
Francis Wilde, a
    photographer   Randy Boone
MacGregor, Crown's
    Deputy   Percy Herbert

CIMARRON STRIP—90 minutes—CBS—September 7, 1967 - September 19, 1968. Rebroadcasts (CBS): July 20, 1971 - September 7, 1971.

CIRCLE

Musical Variety.

Host: Lonnie Sattin.

Hostess: Barbara McNair.

Orchestra: Richard Hayman; Richard Wess.

CIRCLE—30 minutes—Syndicated 1960-1961. Withdrawn.

CIRCLE OF FEAR

Anthology. Tales of the supernatural. A spin-off from "Ghost Story."

Music: Billy Goldenberg.

Included:

Death's Head. After a man is murdered by his wife and her lover, he returns as a moth to seek revenge.

CAST

Carol: Janet Leigh; Larry: Rory Calhoun; Steve: Gene Nelson.

Graveyard Shift. Background: Fillmore Studios, a one-time production center for horror films, now closed and for sale. A couple, Fred Colby, the studio guard, and his pregnant wife, Linda, are haunted by the spirits of varied celluloid fiends seeking immortality by possessing Linda's unborn child. The story relates Fred's attempts to save Linda and the child by burning the films.

CAST

Linda Colby: Patty Duke Astin; Fred Colby: John Astin; Johnny Horne: Joe Renteria; J.B. Fillmore: William Castle.

Legion Of Deamons. A clique of devil

worshipers attempt to obtain a new member for the purposes of a sacrifice.

CAST

Beth: Shirley Knight Hopkins; Keith: John Cypher; Janet: Kathryn Hayes; Mary: Neva Patterson; Dana: Bridget Hanley.

Spare Parts. The story of a doctor who returns from the dead to seek revenge through the hands, eyes, and vocal chords donated to others.

CAST

Ellen Pritcherd: Susan Oliver; Dr. Stephen Crosley: Rick Lenz; Chuck: Christopher Connelly; Georgia Grant: Barbara Stuart.

CIRCLE OF FEAR—60 minutes—NBC—January 5, 1973 - June 22, 1973.

CIRCLE THEATRE

See title: "Armstrong Circle Theatre."

CIRCUS

Variety. Various European circus variety acts are showcased.

Host-Narrator: Bert Parks.

Music: Performed by the various circus orchestras.

CIRCUS—30 minutes—Syndicated 1971.

CIRCUS BOY

Adventure. Background: The Frontier during the latter half of the nine-

Circus Boy. Mickey Braddock as Corky, atop Bimbo the elephant. © *Screen Gems.*

teenth century. After purchasing a bankrupt circus, Big Tim Champion discovers and unofficially adopts Corky, an orphaned and homeless boy whose parents were killed in a tragic high-wire act. Stories concern the struggles endured by the traveling one-ring Champion Circus, and the adventures of Corky, water boy to Bimbo the elephant.

CAST

Big Tim Champion	Robert Lowery
Joey the Clown	Noah Beery, Jr.
Corky	Mickey Braddock
Pete, the canvassman	Guin "Big Boy" Williams
Circus Jack, Corky's friend	Andy Clyde

CIRCUS BOY—30 minutes—NBC—September 1956 - September 1958. Syndicated.

THE CISCO KID

Western. Background: The territory of New Mexico during the 1890s. The exploits of "The Robin Hood of the Old West," The Cisco Kid and his partner, Pancho. The first television series to be filmed in color. Based on the character created by O'Henry.

CAST
The Cisco Kid   Duncan Renaldo
Pancho   Leo Carillo

Cisco's horse: Diablo.

Music: Albert Glasser.

THE CISCO KID—30 minutes—Syndicated 1951.

CITY DETECTIVE

Crime Drama. Background: New York City. The investigations of Police Lieutenant Bart Grant.

Starring: Rod Cameron as Bart Grant.

CITY DETECTIVE—30 minutes—Syndicated 1953.

CITY HOSPITAL

Drama. Background: New York's City Hospital. The infinite problems faced by a doctor in a large city.

Starring: Melville Ruick as Dr. Barton Crane.

CITY HOSPITAL—30 minutes—ABC —April 19, 1951 - November 3, 1951.

CIVILIZATION

Documentary. The history of Western Man from the fall of the Roman Empire to the twentieth century.

Host-Narrator: Kenneth Clark.

Chapters:
1. "The Frozen World." An examination of the Dark Ages.
2. "The Great Thaw." A survey of the twelfth century.
3. "Romance and Reality." France and Italy during the Middle Ages.
4. "Man, The Measure of All Things." France during the Renaissance period (the fifteenth century).
5. "A World of Giants and Heroes." Sixteenth-century Italy.
7. "Grandeur and Obedience." Rome at the time of the Protestant Reformation.
8. "The Light of Experience." Seventeenth-century inventions.
9. "The Pursuit of Happiness." A study of the music of the eighteenth century.
10. "The Smile of Reason." The Enlightment period.
11. "The Worship of Nature." The Romantic movement in eighteenth century France.
12. "The Fallacies of Hope." The Romantic movement during the nineteenth century.
13. "Heroic Materalism." A two-hundred-year survey of Europe since the Industrial Revolution.

CIVILZATION—60 minutes—PBS— October 3, 1971 - December 26, 1971.

CLAUDIA: THE STORY OF A MARRIAGE

Comedy-Drama. Background: New York City. The trials and tribulations of the Naughtons: David, an architect, and his naive eighteen-year-old wife, Claudia. Stories depict Claudia's struggles to "cut the apron strings" that bind her to her mother and adjust to marriage.

CAST

Claudia Naughton   Joan McCracken
David Naughton   Hugh Riley
Mrs. Brown, Claudia's
    Mother   Margaret Wycherly

CLAUDIA: THE STORY OF A MARRIAGE—30 minutes—NBC—January 6, 1952 - March 30, 1952.

CLEAR HORIZON

Serial. Background: The Cape Canaveral Space Center in Florida. Stories dramatize the problems faced by the first Cape Canaveral astronauts and their courageous wives. Episodes focus on the experiences of Roy Selby, a Signal Corps officer, and his wife, Ann.

CAST

Roy Selby   Edward Kemmer
Ann Selby   Phyllis Avery
Nora   Lee Meriweather
The Newspaperman   Richard Coogan
Also: Jimmy Carter, Rusty Lane, Eve McVeagh, Ted Knight, Mary Jackson, Denise Alexander, Grace Albertson, Michael Cox.

CLEAR HORIZON—30 minutes—CBS—July 11, 1960 - March 10, 1961. Returned (CBS): March 8, 1962 - June 11, 1962.

THE CLIFF EDWARDS SHOW

Variety.
Host: Cliff Edwards.
Featured: Eddie Fellows.

Music: The Tony Mottola Trio.

THE CLIFF EDWARDS SHOW—15 minutes—CBS 1949.

CLIMAX

Anthology. Suspense presentations.
Host: William Lundigan.
Hostess: Mary Costa.

Included:

A Leaf Out of the Book. The story of two women: one successful, the other ambitious.

CAST

Diana Lynn, Sylvia Sidney.

The Box of Chocolates. A much hated newspaper columnist attempts to clear himself of a murder charge.

CAST

Robert Preston, Pat O'Brien, Vanessa Brown.

The Chinese Game. After playing a Chinese game that he purchased in a curio shop, a newspaper columnist sees himself murdering his wife for another woman. He believes that the vision is a bad case of imagination and forgets about it. The story concerns the conflict and terror that enters his life when several days later he meets the woman he envisioned.

CAST

Macdonald Carey, Rita Moreno, Constance Ford, Anna May Wong.

The 13th Chair. The story of a man who attempts to find the murderer of his friend through a séance.

CAST

Ethel Barrymore, Dennis O'Keefe.

CLIMAX—60 minutes—CBS—October 7, 1954 - June 26, 1958.

CLOAK OF MYSTERY

Anthology. Rebroadcasts of dramas that were originally aired via "The Alcoa Theatre" and "The General Electric Theatre."

Included:

The Fugitive Eye. The story concerns a man's attempts to clear himself of a false murder charge.

CAST

Charlton Heston, Leo G. Carroll, Jennifer Raine.

Pattern Of Guilt. The story centers on a reporter as he attempts to uncover the murderer of several spinsters.

CAST

Ray Milland, Myron McCormick, Lucy Prentiss, Joanna Moore.

Villa Portofino. By incorporating her late husband's three best friends, a woman attempts to uncover the mysterious circumstances surrounding his death.

CAST

Janet Lake, Gene Blakely, Bobby Van.

CLOAK OF MYSTERY—60 minutes—NBC—May 11, 1965 - August 10, 1965.

THE CLOCK

Anthology. Stories of people who attempt to overcome sudden crises before time runs out. Based on the radio program of the same title.

THE CLOCK—30 minutes—CBS 1949; 30 minutes—NBC 1950.

CLUB CELEBRITY

Musical Variety.

Hostess: Ginny Simms.

Regulars: Jill Richards, Greg Mitchell, Bette Bligh, The Tune Tailors.

Announcer: Harry Von Zell.

Orchestra: Dick Peterson.

CLUB CELEBRITY—30 minutes—NBC 1950.

CLUB OASIS

See title: "Spike Jones."

CLUB 60

Musical Variety.

Hosts: Don Sherwood, Dennis James, Howard Miller.

Regulars: Mike Douglas, Nancy Wright, The Mello-Larks.

Orchestra: Joseph Gallicchio.

CLUB 60—60 minutes—NBC 1957.

CLUTCH CARGO

Animated Cartoon. The adventures of world traveler Clutch Cargo, and his companions, Spinner, a young boy, and his dog, Paddlefoot.

Music: Paul Horn.

CLUTCH CARGO—05 minutes—Syndicated 1959.

CODE THREE

Crime Drama. Background: Los Angeles County, California. The investigations of Assistant Sheriff Barrett into crimes designated Code Three (murder, robbery, kidnapping). Based on actual case files.

CAST

Sheriff Barrett	Richard Travis
Sgt. Murchison	Denver Pyle
Lt. Bill Hollis	Fred Wynn

Appearing: Eugene W. Bissculuce, the Sheriff of Los Angeles County at the time of filming.

CODE THREE—30 minutes—Syndicated 1957.

THE COLGATE COMEDY HOUR

Variety. Programs tailored to the talents of its guest hosts.

Included:

The Eddie Cantor Show.

Host: Eddie Cantor.

Guests: Yma Sumac, Lew Hearn, Joseph Buloff, Jack Albertson, Howard Smith, Bob Sari, Fay MacKenzie, Tommy Wonder, Danny Daniells, Helen Wood, Janet Gayelord, Charlotte Fayni, Lou Wills, Val Buttegnat.

Orchestra: Al Goodman.

The Dean Martin, Jerry Lewis Show.

Hosts: Dean Martin, Jerry Lewis.

Guest: Rosemary Clooney.

Orchestra: Dick Stabile.

The Abbott And Costello Show.

Hosts: Bud Abbott, Lou Costello.

Guests: Sid Fields, Joe Kirk, Bobby Barbor, Joan Shawlee.

Orchestra: Al Goodman.

The Donald O'Connor Show.

Host: Donald O'Connor.

Guests: Ben Blue, Lisa Kirk, Sid Miller, Andy Clyde, Chester Conklin.

Orchestra: Al Goodman.

The Judy Canova Show.

Hostess: Judy Canova.

Guests: Cesar Romero, Zsa Zsa Gabor, Hans Conried, Liberace.

Orchestra: Charles Dent.

Also appearing: Jimmy Durante, Bobby Clark, Spike Jones, Bob Hope, Jackie Gleason, Gordon MacRae, Fred Allen, Ethel Merman, Ezio Pinza, Gisele McKenzie, Don Ameche, Frances Langford, Ann Sheridan, Peggy Lee, Hal March, Tony Martin, The Bell Sisters, Gene Sheldon, Jayne Morgan, Sheldon Leonard, Rex Romer, Connie Russell, Tom D'Andrea, Sandy Davis, Eddie Fisher, Dorothy Loudon, Rose Marie, The Esther Junger Dancers, The Jimmy Russell Singers.

THE COLGATE COMEDY HOUR— 60 minutes—NBC—September 10, 1950 - December 25, 1955. In May of 1967, NBC presented a revival, titled same, with: Edie Adams, Kay Ballard, Carl Reiner, Mel Brooks, Phyllis Diller, Nanette Fabray, Bob Newhart, Nipsey Russell, and Dan Rowan and Dick Martin.

COLGATE THEATRE

Anthology. Rebroadcasts of dramas

that were originally aired via other filmed anthology programs.

COLGATE THEATRE—30 minutes—NBC 1958.

COLISEUM

Circus Variety Acts.

Hosting: Guest Personalities.

Performers: Guests (Show Business).

Orchestra: Bernie Green

COLISEUM—60 minutes—CBS—January 1967 - June 1, 1967.

THE COLLEGE BOWL

Variety. Background: The campus soda fountain, "The College Bowl," of a small-town university. Programs spotlight the talent performances of its youthful clientele.

Host: The College Bowl Proprietor: Chico Marx.

Clientele: Andy Williams, Paula Huston, Jimmy Brock, Evelyn Ward, Tommy Morton, Lee Lindsey, Stanley Prager, Barbara Ruick, Joan Holloway, Kenny Buffert, Vickie Barrett.

THE COLLEGE BOWL—30 minutes—ABC—October 2, 1950 - March 26, 1951.

COLONEL BLEEP

Animated Cartoon. Era: The universe a million light years from the present. An evil scientist, Dr. Destructo, "the master criminal of the universe," escapes from the planet Pheutora, and retreats to the distant planet Pluto, where he establishes a base.

Colonel Bleep, of the Pheutora Police Department and his Space Deputies, Squeak the Puppet and Scratch the Caveman, are assigned to capture him. Episodes relate their attempts to protect the universe from his power-mad plan to conquer it. Characters are nonspeaking.

Colonel Bleep's ship: The *Wonder Rocket.*

COLONEL BLEEP—06 minutes—Syndicated 1957.

COLONEL FLACK

Comedy. The story of two men, modern-day Robin Hoods — Humphrey Flack, a retired colonel, and his companion, Uthas P. (Patsy) Garvey. With larceny in their minds and charity in their hearts, they travel throughout the world and, through imaginative deceptions, con the confidence men in their attempt to assist the needy.

CAST
Colonel Humphrey
   Flack   Alan Mowbray
Uthas P. Garvey   Frank Jenks

Versions:
DuMont (Live)—30 minutes—1953-1954.
Syndicated (Filmed)—30 minutes—1958.

Also titled: "Colonel Humphrey Flack;" "Fabulous Fraud;" "The Imposter."

COLONEL MARCH OF SCOTLAND YARD

Mystery. Background: London, England. The investigations of Colonel March, an intrepid one-eye (a black patch covers the left eye) British Inspector, the head of Department D-3, the Office of Queens Complaints of the New Scotland Yard. Stories depict his attempts to solve the sinister acts of deranged criminals.

Starring: Boris Karloff as Colonel March.

COLONEL MARCH OF SCOTLAND YARD—30 minutes—Syndicated 1957.

COLONEL STOOPNAGLE'S STOOP

Comedy. Background: The front porch of Colonel Lemuel Q. Stoopnagle's home. Basis: The exchange of conversation between he and those friends and neighbors who just happen to pass by.

CAST
Colonel Lemuel Q.
    Stoopnagle   F. Chase Taylor
Friends and neighbors: Dave Ballard, Richard Collier, Gregg Mason, Eda Heinemann.

COLONEL STOOPNAGLE'S STOOP —30 minutes—CBS 1948.

THE COLORFUL WORLD OF MUSIC

Children. Interpretations of musical masterpieces by the Podrecca Piccolli Theatre Marionettes.

THE   COLORFUL   WORLD   OF MUSIC—05 minutes—Syndicated 1964.

COLT .45

Western. Background: The Frontier during the 1880s. The story of Chris Colt, a United States government agent who poses as a salesman for the Colt .45 Repeater. Episodes depict his attempts to ensure law and order.

CAST
Christopher Colt   Wayde Preston
Sam Colt, Jr. (replaced
    Preston)   Donald May
Music: Hal Happer; Douglas Heyes; Paul Sawtell.

COLT   .45—30   minutes—ABC— October 18, 1957 - October 10, 1962. Syndicated.

COLUMBO

See title: "NBC Mystery Movie," *Columbo* segment.

COMBAT

Drama. Background: Europe during World War Two. The saga of the United States Infantry, Second Platoon, K Company, followed from its D-Day landing to victory one year after.

CAST
Lt. Gil Hanley   Rick Jason
Sgt. Chip Saunders   Vic Morrow
"Wildman" Kirby   Jack Hogan
Caje   Pierre Jalbert
Littlejohn   Dick Peabody
Nelson   Tom Lowell
Doc   Conlan Carter

Music: Leonard Roseman.

COMBAT — 60 minutes — ABC — October 1962 - August 29, 1967. Syndicated.

COMBAT SERGEANT

Drama. Background: North Africa during its campaign of World War Two. Detailed: The Allied Forces battle against Rommel's Afrika Korps.

CAST
Sergeant Nelson	Michael Thomas
General Harrison	Cliff Clark
Corporal Murphy	Frank Marlowe
Corporal Harbin	Mara Corday

COMBAT SERGEANT — 30 minutes — ABC — June 29, 1956 - September 1956. Syndicated.

THE COMEBACK STORY

Interview. The lives of one-time famous personalities are recalled. The program relates the incidents that ended an individual's career and his attempt to make a comeback. The past is related through interviews with frineds of the subject and filmed highlights of his career; the present through interviews with the subject.

Host: George Jessel.

THE COMEBACK STORY — 30 minutes — ABC — October 2, 1953 - February 5, 1954.

COMEDY PLAYHOUSE

Anthology. Rebroadcasts of comedy episodes that were originally aired via other filmed anthology programs.

COMEDY PLAYHOUSE — 30 minutes — ABC — June 1958 - September 1958.

COMEDY PREVIEW

Pilot Films. Proposed comedy series for the 1970-1971 season.

The telecast order of the only three episodes aired:

Prudence And The Chief. The story of a missionary as she attempts to establish a school on an Indian Reservation.

CAST
Sally Ann Howes, Rick Jason, Cathryn Givney.

Three For Tahiti. The misadventures of three young men as they attempt to establish a life in a Tahitian paradise.

CAST
Robert Hogan, Bob Einstein, Steve Franken.

The Murdocks And The McClays. The feud that erupts between two hillbilly families when their offspring fall in love and want to be married against parental objections.

CAST
Dub Taylor, Kathy Davis, Noah Beery, Jr., Judy Canova.

COMEDY PREVIEW — 30 minutes — ABC — August 19, 1970 - September 2, 1970.

COMEDY SPOT

Pilot Films. Proposed comedy series for the 1960-1961 season.

Host: Art Gilmore.

Included:

Head Of The Family. Pilot film for "The Dick Van Dyke Show." When his son Richie feels that his father is a failure because he is only the head writer of a television show, Rob Petrie takes him to the office to show him that is is as important as his friends' fathers.

CAST

Rob Petrie: Carl Reiner; Laura Petrie: Barbara Britton; Richie Petrie: Gary Morgan; Buddy Sorrell: Morty Gunty; Sally Rogers: Sylvia Miles; Alan Sturdy (later to become Alan Brady): Jack Wakefield.

The Incredible Jewel Robbery. The misadventures of two inexperienced safecrackers.

CAST

Harry: Harpo Marx; Nick: Chico Marx.

Welcome To Washington. The misadventures of Elizabeth Harper, a newly elected congresswoman.

CAST

Elizabeth Harper: Claudette Colbert; Paul Harper: Leif Erickson.

Meet The Girls. The story of three girls: Maybelle "the shape" Perkins; Lacey "the face" Sinclair; and Charlotte "the brain" Dunning as they search for fame, fortune, and rich husbands.

CAST

Maybelle: Mamie Van Doren; Lacey: Gale Robbins; Charlotte: Virginia Field.

COMEDY SPOT—30 minutes—CBS—July 19, 1960 - September 20, 1960.

COMEDY SPOT

Pilot Films. Proposed comedy series for the 1962-1963 season.

Included:

For The Love Of Mike. The misadventures of Betty and Mike Stevens, young marrieds.

CAST

Betty Stevens: Shirley Jones; Mike Stevens: Burt Metcalfe.

Life With Virginia. The story of a young girl and her attempts to assist the distressed.

Starring: Candy Moore as Virginia.

The Soft Touch. The story of Ernestine McDougal, the beautiful, but slightly scatterbrained daughter of a loan-company owner. The episode relates her attempts to prove her intuition is better than collateral in determining the recipients of loans.

CAST

Ernestine McDougal: Marie Wilson; Mr. McDougal: Charlie Ruggles.

COMEDY SPOT—30 minutes—CBS—July 3, 1962 - September 18, 1962.

COMEDY SPOTLIGHT

Anthology. Rebroadcasts of comedy episodes that were originally aired via "The General Electric Theatre."

Included:

Miracle At The Opera. The story of a lonely, veteran music teacher who finds great pleasure in the company of his dog, Linda.

Starring: Ed Wynn.

A Blaze Of Glory. The story of a meek plumber who encounters various misadventures when he answers an emergency service call.

Starring: Lou Costello, Jonathan Harris, Lurene Tuttle, Joyce Jameson.

Platinum On The Rocks. The effect of a false robbery charge on an aging ex-vaudevillian comic.

CAST

George Burns, Fred Beir, Milton Frome.

COMEDY SPOTLIGHT—30 minutes —CBS—July 25, 1961 - September 19, 1961.

COMEDY TONIGHT

Comedy. Various sketches satirizing life.

Host: Robert Klein.

Regulars: Barbara Cason, Peter Boyle, Marty Barris, Bonnie Enten, Judy Graubart, Laura Greene, Jerry Lacey, Madeline Kahn, Lin Lipton, Macintyre Dixon.

COMEDY TONIGHT—60 minutes— CBS—July 5, 1970 - August 23, 1970.

COMMANDO CODY

Adventure. The exploits of Commando Cody, "Sky Marshall of the Universe." Episodes depict his battle against celestial, sinister forces of evil.

CAST

Commando Cody	Judd Holdren
Joan Albright, his assistant	Aline Towne
Ted Richards, his assistant	William Schallert
Retik, the commander of the moon	Greg Grey
Dr. Varney	Peter Brocco
Henderson	Craig Kelly

COMMANDO CODY—30 minutes— NBC—July 16, 1955 - October 8, 1955.

CONCENTRATION

Game. Two competing players. A large electronic board with thirty numbered, three-sided wedges is displayed on stage. The first player chooses two numbers. The wedges rotate and reveal prizes. If they match, the wedges rotate again and reveal two puzzle parts. The player is then permitted to guess what the puzzle will read (slogan, name, or place). If he is unable, he picks two more numbers.

If the numbers do not match, the wedges return to numbers and his opponent receives a chance.

The player first to identify the puzzle is the winner and receives the prizes accumulated on his side of the board.

Versions:

NBC—30 minutes—August 25, 1958 - March 23, 1973.

Hosts: Hugh Downs; Jack Barry; Art James; Bill Mazer; Ed McMahon; Bob Clayton.

Announcers: Wayne Howell; Art James; Bob Clayton.

Music: Milton DeLugg; Dick Hyman; Milton Kaye; Tony Columbia.

Syndicated—30 minutes—1973.

Host: Jack Narz.

Announcer: Johnny Olsen.

Music: Ed Kalehoff.

CONCERNING MISS MARLOWE

Serial. Background: New York City. The dramatic story of Margaret Marlowe, a middle-aged actress.

CAST

Margaret Marlowe	Louise Albritton
Jim Gavin	Efrem Zimbalist, Jr.
Louise Gavin	Jane Seymoure
Bill Cooke	John Raby

Also: John Gibson, Helen Shield, Eddie Brian, Patty Bacworth.

CONCERNING MISS MARLOWE—15 minutes—CBS—1954-1955.

CONFIDENTIAL FILE

Anthology. Dramatizations of newspaper headline stories.

Host-Narrator: Paul V. Coates.

CONFIDENTIAL FILE—30 minutes —Syndicated 1955.

CONFIDENTIAL FOR WOMEN

Serial. Dramatizations of problems faced by women.

Hostess-Narrator: Jane Wyatt.

Consultant: Dr. Theodore Rubin.

CONFIDENTIAL FOR WOMEN—30 minutes—ABC 1966.

CONGRESSIONAL INVESTIGATOR

Drama. Background: Washington, D.C. The story behind the fifth amendment is dramatized. Episodes depict the activities of a team of U.S. government investigators as they seek to uncover evidence for congressional hearings.

CAST

Investigator	Edward Stroll
Investigator	William Masters
Investigator	Stephen Roberts
Investigator	Marion Collier

CONGRESSIONAL INVESTIGATOR—30 minutes—Syndicated 1959.

CONRAD NAGEL

Listed: the television programs of actor Conrad Nagel.

Silver Theatre—Anthology Drama—30 minutes—CBS 1948.

Host: Conrad Nagel.

Celebrity Time—Panel Discussion—30 minutes—CBS 1949.

Host: Conrad Nagel.

Panel: Kitty Carlisle, Kyle McDonnell, Herman Hickman, Joe Wilson.

The Conrad Nagel Show—Celebrity Interview—30 minutes—DuMont 1953.

Host: Conrad Nagel.

Hostess: Maxine Barrett.

The Conrad Nagel Theatre—Anthology Drama—30 minutes—DuMont 1955. Young talent discoveries appear with established performers.

Host: Conrad Nagel.

Where Were You?—Celebrity Interview—30 minutes—DuMont 1955. The past lives of celebrities are recalled through films and interviews.

Host: Conrad Nagel.

Tell Us More—Documentary—30 minutes—NBC 1963. See title.

THE CONTINENTAL

Women. Setting: A bachelor's apartment — a romantic, candlelit room; a table for two, and a dashing, suave, and sophisticated host. His conversation, directed to the fairer sex, relating humor, poetry, and philosophy, is the focal point of the program.

Host: Renzo Cesana, the Continental.

Music: The Tony Mottola Trio.

Featured: His meeting with couples having their first date.

THE CONTINENTAL—30 minutes—ABC—October 11, 1952 - January 6, 1953.

CONTINENTAL SHOWCASE

Variety. Filmed in Munich and featuring the talent of performers throughout the world.

Host: Jim Backus.

Regulars: The Kessler Twins, The Hazy Osterwald Sextet, The Showcase Dancers.

Orchestra: Harry Segers.

CONTINENTAL SHOWCASE—60 minutes—CBS—June 11, 1966 - September 10, 1966.

CONVOY

Drama. Era: World War II. The saga of a convoy of two hundred heavily armed American ships slowly heading toward England. Episodes focus on the experiences of the men in charge: Dan Talbot, commander of the escort destroyer *DD181,* and Ben Foster, captain of the freighter *Flagship.*

CAST
Commander Dan Talbot	John Gavin
Captain Ben Foster	John Larch
Chief Officer Steve Kirkland	Linden Chiles
Lieutenant Ray Glasser	James McMullan
Lieutenant O'Connell	James Calahan

CONVOY—60 minutes—NBC—September 17, 1965 - December 10, 1965.

COOL MILLION

See title: "NBC Wednesday Mystery Movie," *Cool Million* segment.

COPTER PATROL

See title: "The Whirlybirds."

THE CORNER BAR

Comedy. Distinguished by two formats.

Format One:
Background: New York City, 137 Amsterdam Avenue, Manhattan, the address of Grant's Toomb, a restaurant-bar. Stories relate the misadventures of Harry Grant, its owner-operator, as he becomes involved with and struggles to solve staff and clientele problems.

CAST

Harry Grant	Gabriel Dell
Meyer Shapiro, the waiter	Shimen Ruskin
Mary Ann, the waitress	Langhorne Scruggs
Phil Bracken, a client, a henpecked Wall Street executive	Bill Fiore
Peter Panama, a client, a male fashion designer	Vincent Schiavelli
Fred Costello, a client, an Irish-American cab driver	J.J. Barry
Joe, the cook	Joe Keyes

Music: Norman Paris.

THE CORNER BAR—30 minutes—ABC—June 21, 1972 - August 23, 1972.

Format Two:
Background: New York City, 137 Amsterdam Avenue, Manhattan, the address of The Corner Bar. The harassed life of its owner-operators, Frank Flynn, the bartender, and his partner, Mae, who inherited her share with her husband's death. Episodes relate their attempts to solve staff and clientele problems.

CAST

Mae	Anne Meara
Frank Flynn	Eugene Roche
Meyer Shapiro, the waiter	Shimen Ruskin
Fred Costello, a client, a cab driver	J.J. Barry
Phil Bracken, a client, a Wall Street executive	Bill Fiore
Donald Hooten, a client, an actor	Ron Carey

Music: Norman Paris.

THE CORNER BAR—30 minutes—ABC—August 3, 1973 - September 7, 1973.

CORONADO 9

Crime Drama. Background: San Diego, California's Coronado Peninsula. The investigations of Dan Adams, a retired naval officer turned private detective. (Coronado 9: his telephone exchange).

Starring: Rod Cameron as Dan Adams.

CORONADO 9—30 minutes—Syndicated 1960.

CORONATION STREET

Serial. Background: Weatherfield, England, the Rovers Bar at Number Eleven Coronation Street. Stories dramatize the lives and problems of the working class Britons who inhabit it. Coronation Street, a low- and middle- income neighborhood, is one of many that developed shortly after the Coronation of Edward VII in 1902.

CAST

Ena Sharples	Violet Carson
Minni Caldwell	Margot Bryant
Elsie Howard	Patricia Phoenix
Albert Tatlock	Jack Howarth
Ken Barlow	William Roache
Anne Walker	Doris Speed
Dennis Maxwell	William Lucas
Bobby Walker	Kenneth Farrington
Alf Roberts	Bryan Mosley
George Greenwood	Arthur Penlow
Peter Bromley	Jonathan Adams
Ray Langton	Neville Buswall
Hilda Ogden	Jean Alexander
Stan Ogden	Bernard Youens
Betty Turpin	Betty Driver

Arnold Sheppard	Julian Somers
Frank Bradley	Alan Browning
Tommy Deacon	Paddy Joyce
Dirty Dick	Talfryn Thomas
Francois Dubois	Francois Pacal
Lucille Hewit	Jennifer Moss
Irma Barlow	Sandra Gough
Eddie Duncan	Del Henney
Jerry Booth	Graham Haberfield
Ernest Bishop	Stephen Hancock
Janet	Judith Barker
Dave Robbins	Jon Rollason
Tim	Ray Barron
Lorna	Luan Peters
Vinnie	Irene Sutcliffe
Emily	Eileen Derbyshire
Dave Smith	Reginald Marsh
Yvonne Chappell	Alexandra Marshall
Maggie Clegy	Irene Sutcliffe
Len Fairclough	Peter Adamson
Deirdre Hunt	Anne Kirkbride
Jerry Booth	Graham Haberfield
Bet Lynch	Julie Goodyear
Ron Cooke	Eric Landen
Mavis Riley	Thelma Barlow
Gordon Clegg	Bill Kenwright
Vera Hopkins	Kathy Staff
Idris Hopkins	Kathy Jones
Rita Littlewood	Barbara Mullaney
Norma Ford	Diana Davies
George Farmer	Phil McCall
Sidney Wilson	John Barrard
Megan Hopkins	Jessie Evan

Music: Eric Spear.

CORONATION STREET—30 minutes—Syndicated (PBS Network) 1972. Import begun with episode 1,082. Premiered in London, 1960. A Granada Television Production.

CORONET BLUE

Mystery. Background: New York City. Shot and believed to be dead, Michael Alden is thrown into the East River. Regaining consciousness in a hospital room, he discovers that he is suffering from amnesia. Unaware of who his attackers are, or the reason for their attempt on his life, he remembers only two words, "Coronet Blue," the phrase that holds the key to his past and is able to set him free.

Released from the hospital, he begins his investigation and attempts to discover the meaning of the phrase. Unknown to him, he is followed by his mysterious attackers who seek to right their mistake if he should come too close to discovering who he is. "Coronet Blue, no other clue. . .and so I go my lonely way. . .even to myself a stranger, wondering who am I."

Originally scheduled for a fall run, the series was shelved and aired as a summer replacement for "The Carol Burnett Show." Subsequently, an ending was never filmed.

CAST

Michael Alden	Frank Converse
Brother Anthony, a monk, his assistant	Brian Medford
Max, a friend	Joe Silver

Music: Laurence Rosenthal.

CORONET BLUE—60 minutes—CBS —July 24, 1967 - September 14, 1967.

CORRIGAN'S RANCH

Variety. Performances by Country and Western artists.

Host: Ray "Crash" Corrigan.

CORRIGAN'S RANCH—30 minutes —ABC—July 15, 1950 - August 19, 1950.

THE COUNT OF MONTE CRISTO

Adventure. Background: Eighteenth-century France. Falsely accused of bearing treasonable information, Edmond Dantes is convicted and sentenced to life imprisonment in the Chateau d'If. Learning of a buried treasure from his cellmate, he digs his way out, escapes, and retreats to the island of Monte Cristo. Uncovering the treasure, he establishes himself as a mysterious and powerful figure for justice. Stories relate his battle against the forces of corruption.

CAST

Edmond Dantes, the Count
  of Monte Cristo   George Dolenz
Princess Anne   Faith Domerque
Jacopo   Nick Cravat
Mario   Fortunio Bonanova
Minister Bonjean   Leslie Bradley

THE COUNT OF MONTE CRISTO—30 minutes—Syndicated 1955.

COUNTERPOINT

Anthology. Rebroadcasts of dramas that were originally aired via "Fireside Theatre."

COUNTERPOINT—30 minutes—Syndicated 1952.

COUNTERSPY

Spy Drama. The investigations of David Harding, a United States government counterintelligence agent. Stories depict his battle against secret enemy societies — organizations posing a threat to the security of the Free World.

Starring: Don Megowan as David Harding.

COUNTERSPY—30 minutes—Syndicated 1958.

COUNTERTHRUST

Adventure. Background: The Far East. The exploits of American espionage agents as they battle the forces of Communism.

CAST

Agent   Tod Andrews
Agent   Diane Jergens
Agent   Victor Diaz

COUNTERTHRUST—30 minutes—Syndicated 1959.

COUNTRY CARNIVAL

Variety. Performances by Country and Western entertainers.

Hosts: Billy Walker, Del Reeves.

Regulars: Jamey Ryan, Chase Webster.

Music: The Goodtime Charlies.

COUNTRY CARNIVAL—30 minutes—Syndicated 1960.

COUNTRY CLUB

Variety. Performances by Country and Western entertainers.

Host: Hugh X. Lewis.

COUNTRY CLUB—30 minutes—Syndicated 1971.

COUNTRY MUSIC CAROUSEL

Variety. Performances by Country and Western entertainers.

Host: Slim Wilson.

COUNTRY MUSIC CAROUSEL—30 minutes—Syndicated 1967.

THE COUNTRY MUSIC HALL

Variety. Performances by Country and Western entertainers.

Host: Carl Smith.

THE COUNTRY MUSIC HALL—30 minutes—Syndicated 1965.

COUNTRY MUSIC JUBILEE

See title: "Jubilee U.S.A."

THE COUNTRY PLACE

Variety. Performances by Country and Western entertainers.

Hosts: Jim Ed Brown, Black Emmons.

Regulars: Crystal Gale, The Gema.

Music: The Sound Seventies.

THE COUNTRY PLACE—30 minutes —Syndicated 1969.

COUNTRY STYLE

Variety. Performances by Country and Western entertainers.

Hostess: Peggy Anne Ellis.

Regulars: Gloria Dilworth, Emily Baines, Bob Austin, Pat Adair, The Folk Dancers.

Music: The Alvy West Band.

COUNTRY STYLE—60 minutes—Du-Mont 1950.

COUNTRY STYLE, U.S.A.

Variety. Performances by Country and Western entertainers.

Host: Charlie Applewhite.

COUNTRY STYLE, U.S.A.—15 minutes—Syndicated 1959.

COUNTY FAIR

Variety.

Host: Bert Parks.

Announcer: Kenny Williams.

Music: The Bill Gale Band.

COUNTY FAIR—30 minutes—NBC—1958-1959.

A COUPLE OF JOES

Variety. Music, songs, and comedy sketches.

Hosts: Joe Rosenfield, Joe Bushkin.

Regulars: Joan Barton, Beryl Richard, Allyn Edwards, Morgan the Wonder Dog.

Announcer: Tom Shirley.

Music: The Joe Bushkin Trio.

A COUPLE OF JOES—55 minutes—ABC—August 12, 1949 - July 22, 1950.

COURAGEOUS CAT

Animated Cartoon. Background: Empire City. The investigations of Courageous Cat and Minute Mouse, masked crusaders for justice.

Characters: Courageous Cat; Minute Mouse; the Police Chief (a dog). Their base: The Cat Cave. Mode of transportation: The *Catmobile.* Weapon: The thousand-purpose Catgun.

Villains: The Frog; Harry (a gorilla);

Rodney Rodent; The Black Cat; Professor Noodle Stroodle (the only human figure); Professor Shaggy Dog.

Music: Johnny Holiday.

COURAGEOUS CAT—05 minutes—Syndicated 1961.

COURT-MARTIAL

Drama. Background: London, England, during World War Two. The story of Captain David Young and Major Frank Whitaker, attorneys attached to the Judge Advocate General's Office. Episodes relate their defense of American military personnel.

CAST
Major Frank Whitaker   Peter Graves
Captain David
     Young   Bradford Dillman
Wendy, their secretary   Diene Clare
Sergeant MacCaskey, their
     aide   Kenneth J. Warren

COURT-MARTIAL—60 minutes—ABC—April 8, 1966 - September 2, 1966.

THE COURT OF LAST RESORT

Crime Drama. Programs designed to help people falsely accused of committing crimes. Details of actual case histories are related through private detective Sam Larsen's investigations and criminal attorney Earl Stanley Gardener's courtroom defenses.

CAST
Earl Stanley Gardener   Paul Birch
Sam Larsen   Lyle Bettger

THE COURT OF LAST RESORT—30

minutes—ABC—August 26, 1959 - February 24, 1960.

THE COURTSHIP OF EDDIE'S FATHER

Comedy. Background: Los Angeles, California. The story of the relationship between widower Tom Corbett, the editor of *Tomorrow* magazine, and his six-year-old son, Eddie, trustworthy people who seek one and other in time of need, and strive for each other's happiness.

Eddie, believing his father's happiness depends upon a wife, indulges in endless matchmaking attempts. Tom, the innocent victim, finds himself confronted by beautiful women and embarrassing situations.

CAST
Tom Corbett   Bill Bixby
Eddie Corbett   Brandon Cruz
Mrs. Livingston, their Japanese
     housekeeper   Miyoshi Umeki
Norman Tinker, the magazine's
     art editor   James Komack
Tina Rickles, Tom's
     secretary   Kristina Holland
Joey Kelly, Eddie's
     friend   Jodie Foster

Music: George Tipton; Nilsson.

THE COURTSHIP OF EDDIE'S FATHER—30 minutes—ABC—September 17, 1969 - June 14, 1972. Syndicated.

COWBOY G-MEN

Western. Background: California during the 1880s. The investigations of cowhand Pat Gallagher and wrangler Stoney Crockett, United States government undercover agents. Episodes depict their attempts of ensure law and order.

CAST

Pat Gallagher   Russell Hayden
Stoney Crockett   Jackie Coogan

COWBOY G-MEN—30 minutes—Syndicated 1952.

COWBOY IN AFRICA

Adventure. Background: Kenya, East Africa. Wing Commander Hayes undertakes a plan to guarantee the survival of wild beasts through their domestication on his wild-animal ranch. Assisted by champion rodeo rider Jim Sinclair, and a Navaho Indian, John Henry, he attempts to prove his theory that game ranching is Africa's best defense "against the ravages caused by unrestricted cattle grazing," against the objections of the Boer cattlemen who feel his plan is foolish.

Filmed on location and in California's Africa U.S.A.

CAST

Jim Sinclair   Chuck Connors
John Henry   Tom Nardini
Commander Hayes   Ronald Howard
Samson, a young native
    friend   Gerald B. Edwards
Music: Malcolm Arnold.

COWBOY IN AFRICA—60 minutes—ABC—September 11, 1967 - September 16, 1968. Syndicated.

THE COWBOYS

Western. Background: The Longhorn Ranch in Spanish Wells, New Mexico, during the 1870s. Faced with unpaid bills, a possible loss of the ranch, and a four-hundred-mile trek to Dodge City with fifteen hundred head of cattle, owner Will Andersen is reluctantly forced to hire and train eleven children, aged nine to fifteen (seven became the series regulars).

On the journey, Will is killed by rustlers who steal the herd. The boys and a range cook, Mr. Nightlinger, pursue and kill the culprits.

Returning to the ranch three months after, the eight present the money to Kate, Will's widow, and express a desire to remain as ranch hands. Assured of their education by Mr. Nightlinger, she hires them. Stories relate their attempts to maintain a cattle ranch in a turbulent era. Adapted from the movie of the same title.

CAST

Mr. Nightlinger   Moses Gunn
Kate Andersen   Diana Douglas
Marshal Bill Winter   Jim Davis
Cimarron   A. Martinez
Slim   Robert Carradine
Homer   Kerry MacLane
Steve   Clint Howard
Weedy   Clay O'Brien
Jim   Sean Kelly
Hardy   Mitch Brown
Will Andersen
   (feature)   John Wayne
Music: Johnny Williams; Harry Sukman.

THE COWBOYS—30 minutes—ABC—February 6, 1974 - August 14, 1974.

CRAFTS WITH KATY

Instruction. The preparation and making of interesting and fashionable home furnishings—items constructed from inexpensive Fantasy Film liquid plastic, wire, and assorted accessories.

Hostess/Instructress: Katy Dacus.

Music: Recorded.

CRAFTS WITH KATY—30 minutes—Syndicated 1971.

CRAIG KENNEDY, CRIMINOLOGIST

Crime Drama. Background: New York City. The investigations of criminologist Craig Kennedy, a master of scientific deduction. Episodes depict his attempts to solve gangland crimes.

Starring: Donald Woods as Craig Kennedy.

CRAIG KENNEDY, CRIMINOLOGIST—30 minutes—Syndicated 1952.

CREATIVE COOKERY

Cooking. The preparation of meals, from the simplest American to the most elaborate foreign dishes.

Host: Francois Pope.

Assistant: Bob Pope.

CREATIVE COOKERY—60 minutes—CBS 1951; ABC—1953-1954.

CRIME AND PUNISHMENT

Interview. Interviews conducted from various federal penitentiaries.

Host: Clete Roberts.

Commentator: Robert A. McGee.

CRIME AND PUNISHMENT—30 minutes—Syndicated 1961.

CRIME DOES NOT PAY

Anthology. Dramatizations based on the files of state police departments.

CRIME DOES NOT PAY—30 minutes—Syndicated 1960.

CRIME PHOTOGRAPHER

Crime Drama. Background: New York City. The investigations of Casey, a press-photographer for the *Morning Express,* a crusading newspaper. Based on the stories by George Harmon Coxe.

CAST

Casey	Richard Carlyle
	Darren McGavin
Ann Williams, his girlfriend, a reporter	Jan Miner
Ethelbert, the bartender at the Blue Note Café	John Gibson
Captain Bill Logan, N.Y.P.D.	Bernard Lenrow

Announcer: Ken Roberts.

Music: Morton Gould.

The Blue Note Café Musicians: The Tony Mottola Trio.

CRIME PHOTOGRAPHER—30 minutes—CBS—April 17, 1951 - June 19, 1952.

CRIME REPORTER

See title: "Big Town."

CRIME SYNDICATED

Documentary. True crime exposés based on the Kefauver Committee files.

Host-Narrator: Rudolph Halley.

CRIME SYNDICATED—30 minutes—
CBS—1951-1952.

CRIME WITH FATHER

Crime Drama. Background: New York
City. The investigations of a homicide
bureau chief and his self-proclaimed
assistant, his teen-age daughter.

CAST

Father   Rusty Lane
Daughter   Peggy Lobbin

CRIME WITH FATHER—30 minutes
—ABC—October 5, 1951 - February 1,
1952.

CRISIS

Anthology. Rebroadcasts of dramas
that were originally aired via "The
Bob Hope Chrysler Theatre" and
"Kraft Suspense Theatre."

CRISIS—60   minutes—Syndicated
1971.

CROSS CURRENT

See title: "Foreign Intrigue."

CROSSROADS

Anthology. Dramatizations based on
the experiences of the men of the
clergy.

Included:

The Riot. The ordeal of a priest who

becomes the unwitting accomplice in
a prison break.

CAST

Father O'Neal: Pat O'Brien; Daniels:
Roy Roberts.

The Comeback. The true story of Lou
Brissie, a pitcher who returned to
major league baseball after sustaining
injuries during World War II.

CAST

Rev. C. E. Stoney Jackson: Don
DeFore; Lou Brissie: Chuck Connors;
Whitey Martin: Grant Withers.

Johnakunga—Called   John. Background: Wisconsin, 1883. The true
story of Rev. John Stucker, a missionary who risked his life to befriend the
hostile Winnebago Indians.

CAST

Rev.   Stucker: Hugh   Marlowe;
Johnakunga: Pat Hogan.

CROSSROADS—30 ' minutes—ABC—
October 7, 1953 - September 4, 1956.
Syndicated.

CROWN THEATRE WITH GLORIA SWANSON

Anthology. Dramatic presentations.

Hostess-Frequent Performer: Gloria
Swanson.

Included:

Uncle Harry. The story of a man who
is overly generous with other people's
property.

CAST

Edgar Buchannan, Elizabeth Fraser.

A Chair In The Boulevard. An enterprising young Frenchman believes he has found the mysterious Mlle. Guard, the woman on whose identity a French newspaper has pinned a large sum of cash. Romantic complications ensue when he attempts to turn her in.

CAST

Gloria Swanson, Claude Dauphin.

The Buzzer. So she can marry her fiancé who is transferring to another city, a young girl desperately attempts to get rid of her invalid mother.

CAST

Lorna Thayer, John Oliver.

CROWN THEATRE WITH GLORIA SWANSON—30 minutes—Syndicated 1953.

CRUNCH AND DES

Adventure. Background: The Bahamas. The story of Crunch Adams and his partner, Des, the owners and operators of the charter boat service, *Poseidon.*

CAST

Crunch Adams	Forrest Tucker
Des	Sandy Kenyon
Sari Adams, Crunch's sister	Joanne Bayes

CRUNCH AND DES—30 minutes—Syndicated 1955. Also titled: "Charter Boat" and "Deep Sea Adventures."

THE CRUSADER

Adventure. The story of Matt Anders, a crusading free-lance magazine writer. Episodes relate his battle against the global forces of oppression and treachery.

Starring: Brian Keith as Matt Anders.

Music: Edmund Wilson.

THE CRUSADER—30 minutes—CBS —October 7, 1955 - December 28, 1956. Syndicated.

CRUSADER RABBIT

Animated Cartoon. The misadventures of Crusader Rabbit and his friend, Rags the Tiger.

CRUSADER RABBIT—04 minutes (theatrical cartoons)—Syndicated 1949.

CURIOSITY SHOP

Educational. Various aspects of the adult world are explained to children via sketches, cartoons, and films.

CAST

Gittel the Witch	Barbara Minkus
Pam	Pamelyn Ferdin
Gerard	John Levin
Ralph	Kerry MacLane
Cindy	Jerelyn Fields

Animated features: "Dennis The Menace"; "Big George"; "Miss Peach"; "B.C."; "Mr. Mum"; "The Bears."

Puppets: Oogle; Flip the Hippo; Eeek A. Mouse; Nostalgia the Elephant.

Voices: Mel Blanc, Bob Halt, Chuck Jones.

Orchestra: Dick Elliott.

CURIOSITY SHOP—60 minutes—ABC—September 11, 1971 - September 9, 1973.

CURT MASSEY TIME

Musical Variety.

Host: Curt Massey.

Co-Hostess: Martha Tilton.

CURT MASSEY TIME—15 minutes—CBS 1950.

CURTAIN CALL

Anthology. Dramatic presentations based on classical and contemporary short stories.

CURTAIN CALL—30 minutes—NBC—June 20, 1952 - September 1952. Also known as "Pond's Theatre."

CUT

Game. An amateurish script, suggesting an object or theme, is performed by a group of actors. An operator places a random phone call. The viewer is asked to identify the suggested theme. If correct, he is awarded a prize and receives a chance at the jackpot — to identify the portrait of a celebrity on a rapidly spun wheel.

Host: Carl Caruso.

Music: The Al Logan Trio.

CUT—60 minutes—DuMont 1949.

CYBORG BIG "X"

Animated Cartoon. The story of Arika, a cyborg with the brain of a human and the body of a robot. Armed with a special magnetic pen, his sole weapon, he combats the criminal world.

CYBORG BIG "X"—30 minutes—Syndicated 1965.

CYBORG: THE SIX MILLION DOLLAR MAN

See title: "The Six Million Dollar Man."

D

THE D.A.

Crime Drama. Background: Los Angeles, California. The story of Paul Ryan, a district attorney who functions as both a detective and a prosecutor.

CAST
Paul Ryan   Robert Conrad
H.M. "Staff" Stafford, the
    Chief Deputy   Harry Morgan
Kathy Benson, the
    Deputy Public
    Defender   Julie Cobb
Bob Ramerez, Ryan's chief
    investigator   Ned Romero

Music: Frank Comstock.

THE D.A.—30 minutes—NBC—September 17, 1971 - January 7, 1972.

THE D.A.'S MAN

Crime Drama. Background: New York City. The investigations of Shannon, a private detective working anonymously under the auspices of the district attorney.

CAST

Shannon   John Compton
Al Bonacorsi, his contact
        at the D.A.'s
        office   Ralph Manza

Music: Frank Comstock.

THE D.A.'s MAN—30 minutes—NBC
—January 3, 1959 - August 29, 1959.
Syndicated.

DAGMAR'S CANTEEN

Musical Variety. Background: A military camp. Performances by the men and women in the U.S. Armed Forces.

Hostess: Dagmar (Jennie Lewis).

Regulars: Ray Malone, Joey Faye.

Orchestra: Milton DeLugg.

DAGMAR'S CANTEEN—15 minutes—NBC 1952.

THE DAKOTAS

Western. Background: The Dakota Territory during the 1880s. The story of United States Marshal Frank Regan and his attempts to maintain law and order.

CAST

Marshal Frank Regan	Larry Ward
Deputy Del Stark	Chad Everett
Deputy J.D. Smith	Jack Elam
Deputy Vance Porter	Michael Green

Music: Frank Perkins.

THE DAKOTAS—60 minutes—ABC—January 7, 1963 - September 9, 1963. Syndicated.

DAKTARI

Adventure. Background: The Wameru Game Preserve and Research Center in Africa. The struggles of Daktari (Swahili for "doctor") Marsh Tracy and his associates to protect the endangered wildlife and ensure its future existence.

CAST

Dr. Marsh Tracy	Marshall Thompson
Paula Tracy, his teenage daughter, studying to become a scientist	Cheryl Miller
District Game Warden Headley	Headley Mattingley
Jack Dane, a zoologist	Yule Sommers
Bart Jason, a game hunter	Ross Hagen
Mike, a zoologist	Hari Rhodes
Jenny Jones, an orphan, Marsh's six-year old admirer	Erin Moran

Animals: Clarence, the cross-eyed lion; Judy, the chimp.

Music: Shelly Mann; Ruby Raksin; Harold Gelman.

DAKTARI—60 minutes—CBS—January 11, 1966 - January 15, 1969. Syndicated.

DAMON RUNYON THEATRE

Anthology. Dramatizations set against the background of old New York. Tales, as penned by Damon Runyon, detailing the soft-hearted characters of the underworld.

Host: Donald Woods.

Included:

Teacher's Pet. A young school teacher struggles to run a recently inherited bookmaking empire.

CAST

Emilie: Fay Bainter; Tony Rose: Gene Evans; Bo Peep: Adele Jergens.

The Mink Doll. Inheriting a large sum of money, a chorus girl moves to Park Avenue and struggles to be accepted by society.

CAST

Sally Bracken: Dorothy Lamour; Harry Bracken: Wayne Morris; Frankie Farrell: Joe Besser.

A Light In France. Era: World War II France. The story of two fleeing U.S. criminals and their attempts to stray from trouble.

CAST

Thaddeus: Edward Everett Horton; Packy: Hugh O'Brian; Marie: Lita Mann.

It Comes Up Money. Plans for a new skyscraper are blocked by the owner of an antique store who refuses to sell. Desperate, construction officials plot to make the man change his mind.

CAST

Sylvester: Thomas Mitchell; Abigail: Frances Bavier; Joey: Wally Vernon; Pat: Jackie Loughery.

DAMON RUNYON THEATRE—30 minutes—CBS—April 16, 1955 - June 9, 1956.

DAN AUGUST

Crime Drama. Background: Santa Luisa, California, a small, fictitious coastal community. The investigations of Detective Lieutenant Dan August, a man caught between the hatreds of the Establishment and his duty to protect.

CAST

Det. Lt. Dan August	Burt Reynolds
Sgt. Charles Wilentz	Norman Fell
Sgt. John Rivera	Ned Romero
Police Chief George Untermyer	Richard Anderson
Kathy Grant, the secretary	Ena Hartman

Music: Dave Grusin.

DAN AUGUST—60 minutes—ABC—September 23, 1970 - September 9, 1971. Rebroadcasts: CBS—April 23, 1973 - October 17, 1973.

DANCING PARTY

See title: "The Lawrence Welk Show."

DANGER

Anthology. The art of murder is explored through dramatization.

Host-Narrator: Dick Stark.

Included:

Murder On Tenth Street. The story of a young woman who overhears a murder plot, then desperately struggles to prevent it from happening.

CAST

Katherine Bard, John Baragrey.

The Face Of Fear. The story of a switchboard operator trapped by a dangerous mental patient in a deserted office building.

Starring: Lee Grant.

Pete River's Blues. The story of a jazz musician who befriends a society woman, then finds himself involved with murder.

CAST

Conrad Janis, Barbara Nichols.

DANGER—30 minutes—CBS—October 3, 1950 - December 21, 1955.

DANGER IS MY BUSINESS

Documentary. Films depicting the hazardous occupations of people.

Host-Narrator: Col. John D. Craig.

DANGER IS MY BUSINESS—30 minutes—Syndicated 1958.

DANGER MAN

Adventure. The story of John Drake, a special investigator for the North Atlantic Treaty Organization (NATO). Episodes depict his attempts to solve situations jeapardizing its objectives.

Starring: Patrick McGoohan as John Drake.

Music: Edwin Astley.

DANGER MAN—30 minutes—CBS—April 5, 1961 - September 14, 1961. Syndicated.

DANGEROUS ASSIGNMENT

Adventure. The cases of Steve Mitchell, an international trouble-shooter who investigates and solves crimes on behalf of the United States government.

Starring: Brian Donlevy as Steve Mitchell.

DANGEROUS ASSIGNMENT—30 minutes—Syndicated 1952.

DANGER ZONE

Documentary. Films depicting the hazardous work of specialized professionalists (e.g., people involved in air rescues at sea; professional divers; sea fire fighters).

Host-Narrator: Pappy Boyington, Marine Corps Ace.

DANGER ZONE—30 minutes—Syndicated 1960.

DANIEL BOONE

Adventure. Background: Boonesborough, Kentucky, during the latter eighteenth century. The exploits of legendary frontiersman-pioneer Daniel Boone.

CAST

Daniel Boone	Fess Parker
Rebecca Boone, his wife	Patricia Blair

Daniel Boone. Fess Parker and Patricia Blair.

Jemima Boone, their
  daughter   Veronica Cartwright
Israel Boone, their
  son   Darby Hinton
Yadkin, Daniel's
  sidekick   Albert Salmi
Mingo, Daniel's Oxford-
  educated friend, a
  Cherokee Indian   Ed Ames
Cincinnatus, Daniel's
  friend   Dallas McKennon
Josh Clements, a
  backwoodsman   Jimmy Dean
Gabe Cooper, runaway slave,
  Chief Canawahchaquaoo of
  The Tuscarora
  Indians   Roosevelt Grier

Music: Lionel Newman.

DANIEL BOONE—60 minutes—NBC
—September 24, 1964 - September 10,
1970. Syndicated.

THE DANNY KAYE SHOW

Variety. Music, songs, dances, and comedy sketches.

Host: Danny Kaye.

Regulars: Harvey Korman, Vikki Carr, Joyce Van Patten, Laurie Ichino, Victoria Meyerink, The Johnny Mann Singers, The Earle Brown Singers, The Tony Charmoli Dancers.

Announcer: Berne Bennett.

Orchestra: Paul Weston.

THE DANNY KAYE SHOW—60 minutes—CBS—September 25, 1963 - June 7, 1967.

THE DANNY THOMAS HOUR

Anthology. Varying presentations:

dramatic, musical and comedic.

Host-occasional performer: Danny Thomas.

Music: Earl Hagen.

Included:

The Wonderful World Of Burlesque. A musical variety hour reviving the world of burlesque.

CAST
Danny Thomas, Phil Silvers, Nanette Fabray, Cyd Charisse, Ernie Ford.

Make More Room For Daddy. A revision of the classic "Make Room for Daddy" series. Danny attempts to adjust to the prospect of losing a son when Rusty marries.

CAST
Danny Williams: Danny Thomas; Kathy Williams: Marjorie Lord; Rusty

The Danny Thomas Show. Danny Thomas and Marjorie Lord.

Williams: Rusty Hamer; Linda Williams: Angela Cartwright; Charlie Helper: Sid Melton.

The Royal Follies Of 1933. Variety depicting the music, comedy, and entertainment of 1933.

CAST

Danny Thomas, Hans Conried, Eve Arden, Shirley Jones, Gale Gordon.

Instant Money. A comedy detailing the ill-fated efforts of a man as he attempts to acquire money through gambling.

CAST

Danny Thomas, Don Adams, Sid Caesar, Abby Dalton, Richard Deacon.

THE DANNY THOMAS HOUR—60 minutes—NBC—September 11, 1967 - September 9, 1968.

THE DANNY THOMAS SHOW

See title: "Make Room for Daddy."

DAN RAVEN

Crime Drama. Background: California. The story of Dan Raven, a detective lieutenant with the Hollywood Sheriff's Office. Episodes depict his attempts to assist his clientele—show business personalities.

CAST

Det. Lt. Dan Raven   Skip Homeier
Sergeant Burke, his
    assistant   Dan Barton
Perry Levitt, a
    photographer   Quinn Redeker

DAN RAVEN—30 minutes—NBC— 1960-1961.

DANTE

Drama. Background: San Francisco, California. The exploits of Willie Dante, reformed gambler turned owner of Dante's Inferno Nightclub. Stories depict his attempts to overcome the situations that occur when his past reputation attracts unscrupulous characters. Based on the character portrayed by Dick Powell on "Four Star Playhouse."

CAST

Willie Dante   Howard Duff
Stewart Styles, the club
    maitre'd, a former
    confidence man   Alan Mowbray
Biff, his right-hand
    man   Tom D'Andrea

DANTE—30 minutes—NBC—October 3, 1960 - April 10, 1961. Syndicated.

DAN TEMPEST

See title: "The Buccaneers."

DARK ADVENTURE

Anthology. Dramatizations of people trapped in uncertain situations as the result of emotional problems.

Included:

The Second Mrs. Sands. A mother attempts to acquire her foster son's inheritance.
Starring: Hillary Brooke.

Lady With Ideas. An actress attempts

to acquire publicity by pretending to be a European star.

CAST
Pamela Britton, Gig Young.

Conqueror's Isle. A psychiatrist's probe into the story, related by a hospitalized soldier, of a mad scientist's plans to enslave the world.

Starring: Ray Montgomery.

DARK ADVENTURE—30 minutes— ABC—January 5, 1953 - July 6, 1953.

DARK OF NIGHT

Anthology. The first live suspense program to originate from locations outside a network's studios (DuMont in New York). Dramatizations set against the background of New York City.

DARK OF NIGHT—30 minutes—Du-Mont—1952-1953.

DARK SHADOWS

Serial. Background: Collinsport, a small fishing village in Maine. The story of Victoria Winters, a young woman who is hired as governess for ten-year-old David Collins. Episodes relate her involvement in the supernatural existences of the Collins family. The first daytime serial to present horror—vampires, werewolves, witches, and black magic—for its stories.

CAST

Elizabeth Collins Stoddard	Joan Bennett
Victoria Winters	Alexandra Moltke
Barnabas Collins	Jonathan Frid
Carolyn Stoddard	Nancy Barrett

Dark Shadows. Jonathan Frid.

Charity	Nancy Barrett
Roger Collins	Louis Edmonds
Edward Collins	Louis Edmonds
Dr. Julia Hoffman	Grayson Hall
Magda	Grayson Hall
Maggie Evans	Kathryn Leigh Scott
Joe Haskell	Joel Crothers
Angelique	Lara Parker
Cassandra	Lara Parker
Quentin Collins	David Selby
Willie Loomis	John Karlen
David Collins	David Henesy
Peter Bradford	Roger Davis
Sarah Collins	Sharon Smyth
Sam Evans	David Ford
Mrs. Johnson	Clarice Blackburn
Cyrus Longworth	Chris Pennock
Jeb Hawks	Chris Pennock
Burke Devlin	Anthony George
Kate Jackson	Daphne Harridge
Bruno	Michael Stroka
Amy	Denise Nickerson
Sabrina Stuart	Lisa Richards
Mrs. Collins	Diana Millay

Adam	Robert Rodan
Eve	Marie Wallace
Beth	Terry Crawford
King Johnny	Paul Richard
Hallie Stokes	Kathy Cody
Professor Elliot Stokes	Thayer David
Count Petofi	Thayer David
Reverend Trask	Jerry Lacy
Balberith, Prince of Darkness	Humbert A. Astredo
Alexander	David Jay
Rondell Drew	Gene Lindsey
Amanda Harris	Donna McKechnie
Olivia Corey	Donna McKechnie
Michael	Michael Maitland

Final Cast

During the course of the program's last year on the air, stories related incidents in the Collins family during the nineteenth century—one hundred years prior to the original twentieth-century setting. Through the use of black magic, characters were able to travel from the present to the past and observe the lives of their ancestors—people also involved with the supernatural.

Flora Collins	Joan Bennett
Barnabas Collins-Bramwell	Jonathan Frid
Julia H. Collins	Grayson Hall
Quentin Collins	David Selby
Letitia Faye	Nancy Barrett
Gabriel Collins	Chris Pennock
Carrie Stokes	Kathy Cody
Mordecai Grimes	Thayer David
Edith Collins	Terry Crawford
Valerie Collins	Lara Parker
Samantha Collins	Virginia Vestoff
Daniel Collins	Louis Edmonds
Tad Collins	David Henesy
Kate Jackson	Daphne Harridge
Desmond Collins	John Karlen
Morgan Collins	Keith Prentice
Gerald Stiles	James Storm
Reverend Trask	Jerry Lacy

Laszlo	Michael Stroka
Roxanne Drew	Donna Wandrey
Charles Dawson	Humbert A. Astredo
The Werewolf	Alex Stevens

Also: Don Briscoe, Alan Feinstein, Conrad Fowkes, Alan Yorke.

Music: Robert Cobert.

DARK SHADOWS—30 minutes—ABC—June 27, 1966 - April 2, 1971.

DASTARDLY AND MUTLEY IN THEIR FLYING MACHINES

Animated Cartoon. Era: World War One. The efforts of the evil Dick Dastardly, on orders from the General, to intercept the vital messages of the American Courier, Yankee Doodle Pigeon. His unsuccessful attempts are assisted by a fumbling, snickering dog, Mutley, and a group of misplaced misfits, The Flying Squadron (Klunk and Zilly). A Hanna-Barbera Production.

Characters' Voices

Dick Dastardly	Paul Winchell
Mutley	Don Messick
Klunk	Don Messick
Zilly	Don Messick
The General	Paul Winchell

Music: Hoyt Curtin.

DASTARDLY AND MUTLEY IN THEIR FLYING MACHINES—30 minutes—CBS—September 13, 1969 - September 3, 1971.

DATELINE: EUROPE

See title: "Foreign Intrigue."

DATELINE: HOLLYWOOD

Variety. Celebrity interviews and filmland news.

Hostesses: Joanna Barnes; Rona Barrett.

Appearing: Jayne Mansfield (her last television appearance), Patty Duke, Cornel Wilde, Dean Jones, Marlo Thomas, Efrem Zimbalist, Jr., Chad and Jeremy, Nick Adams, Victor Buono, Gloria Swanson, Bob Crane, Pat Wayne, Ann Baxter, Charles Bronson, Meredith MacRae, Bobby Vinton, Barbara Parkins, Louis Nye, Sherry Jackson, Werner Klemperer.

DATELINE: HOLLYWOOD—30 minutes—ABC 1967.

A DATE WITH THE ANGELS

Comedy. Background: Los Angeles, California. The trials and tribulations of young marrieds: Gus Angel, a bright and determined insurance salesman, and his attractive, level-headed wife, Vickie.

CAST

Vickie Angel	Betty White
Gus Angel	Bill Williams
George Clemson, their neighbor	Roy Engle
Wilma Clemson, his wife	Natalie Masters
George Neise, a friend	Karl Koening
Dottie Neise, his wife	Joan Banks
Adam Henshaw, Gus's employer	Russell Hicks
Mary Henshaw, his wife	Isobel Elsom
Mr. Finley, the Angels' crusty neighbor	Bert Mustin

A DATE WITH THE ANGELS—30 minutes—ABC—May 10, 1957 - January 29, 1958.

A DATE WITH JUDY

Comedy. Background: Santa Barbara, California. The misadventures of Judy Foster, an unpredictable teenage girl. Based on the radio program of the same title.

CAST

Judy Foster	Patricia Crowley
	Mary Lynn Beller
Melvyn Foster, her father, president of the Foster Canning Company	Judson Rees
	John Gibson
Dora Foster, her mother	Anna Lee
	Flora Campbell
Randolph Foster, her brother	Gene O'Donnell
	Peter Avramo
Oogie Pringle, Judy's boyfriend	Jimmie Sommers

Also: Patty Pope.

A DATE WITH JUDY—30 minutes—ABC—June 2, 1951 - September 30, 1953.

A DATE WITH LIFE

Serial. Background: The town of Bay City. Life in a small American town as seen through the eyes of Jim Bradley, the editor of the *Bay City News.*

CAST

Jim Bradley	Logan Field
His brother	Mark Roberts
Jennifer, the school teacher	June Dayton
David, her boyfriend	Dean Harens

Also: Dolores Sulton, Billy Redfield,

Barbara Britton, Anthony Eisley, Irene Hubbon.

A DATE WITH LIFE—30 minutes— NBC—October 10, 1955 - June 29, 1956.

A DATE WITH REX

Variety. Celebrity interviews.

Host: Rex Marshall.

Hostess: Sondra Deel.

A DATE WITH REX—30 minutes— DuMont—1950 - 1951.

THE DATING GAME

Game. Three handsome young men vie for a date with a lovely young bachelorette. Seated on opposite sides of a stage-separating wall, she asks them specially prepared questions designed to reveal the romantic nature of each individual. By their answers, she chooses the one she would most like to have as her date. The program furnishes the couple an all-expenses-paid romantic date. Also played in reverse—three girls, one bachelor.

Host: Jim Lange.

Announcer: Johnny Jacobs.

Music: Frank Jaffe.

THE DATING GAME—30 minutes— ABC—October 6, 1966 - July 6, 1973.

DAVE AND CHARLEY

Comedy. The misadventures of a pair of cronies—Charley, a senile oldster, and Dave, his friend, an unemployed clerk.

CAST

Dave Willock	Dave Willock
Charley Weaver	Cliff Arquette

DAVE AND CHARLEY—15 minutes —NBC 1952.

DAVE ELMAN'S CURIOSITY SHOP

Discussion. Guests and discussions on hobbies.

Host: Dave Elman.

DAVE ELMAN'S CURIOSITY SHOP —30 minutes—Syndicated 1952.

DAVE GARROWAY

Listed: The television programs of Dave Garroway.

Garroway At Large—Variety—30 minutes—NBC—April 16, 1949 - June 24, 1951.

Host: Dave Garroway.

Regulars: Connie Russell, Jack Haskell, Betty Shetland, Aura Vainio, Cliff Norton, James Russell, Betty Chapel, The Songsmiths.

Announcer: Jack Haskell.

Orchestra: Joseph Gallechio.

The Today Show—Information—2 hours—NBC—1952-1962 (Dave Garroway's run as host). See title.

The Dave Garroway Show—Variety— 30 minutes—NBC—October 2, 1953 - June 25, 1954.

Host: Dave Garroway.

Regulars: Jack Haskell, Jill Corey, Cliff Norton, Shirley Hammer.

Announcer: Jack Haskell.

Orchestra: Skitch Henderson.

Wide Wide World—News (diverse views on topical issues)—90 minutes—NBC —October 16, 1955 - June 8, 1958.

Host: Dave Garroway.

Announcer: Bill Wendell.

Orchestra: David Broekman.

Garroway—Discussion and Variety— 60 minutes—Live from Boston—Syndicated 1969.

Host: Dave Garroway.

The CBS Newcomers—Variety—30 minutes—CBS—July 12, 1971 - September 6, 1971. See title.

THE DAVE KING SHOW

Musical Variety.

Host: Dave King, "The British Como."

Regulars: The Jerry Packer Singers, The Bill Foster Dancers.

Announcer: Ed Herlihy.

Orchestra: Vic Schoen.

THE DAVE KING SHOW—30 minutes—NBC—May 1958 - September 1958; May 26, 1959 - September 23, 1959. Summer replacement for "The Kraft Music Hall." Official title: "Kraft Music Hall Presents Dave King."

THE DAVID FROST REVUE

Satire. Sketches based on various topical issues (e.g., food, sex, health, money).

Host: David Frost.

Regulars: Jack Gilford, Marcia Rodd, George Irving, Lynne Lipton, Larry Moss, Jim Catusi, Cleavon Little.

THE DAVID FROST REVUE—30 minutes—Syndicated 1971.

THE DAVID FROST SHOW

Discussion-Variety.

Host: David Frost.

Announcer: Wayne Howell.

Orchestra: Billy Taylor.

THE DAVID FROST SHOW—90 minutes—Syndicated 1969-1972.

THE DAVID NIVEN THEATRE

Anthology. Dramatic presentations.

Host—Occasional Performer: David Niven.

Included:

The Lady From Winnetka. Background: A Mediterranean island. Vacationing and meeting a handsome guide, a woman seeks the romance that is lacking in her marriage.

CAST
Ellen Baird: Joanne Dru; Tavo: Jacques Bergerac; Mr. Baird: Carleton G. Young.

Good Deed. A newspaper reporter attempts to arrange the surrender of a cop killer.

CAST
Gentry: Keefe Brasselle; Simms: James Best; Hazel: Virginia Grey.

Fortune's Folly. The story centers on

the struggles of a man as he attempts to overcome gambling fever.

CAST

Hal Shattuck: Cameron Mitchell.

Portrait. Background: Germany, World War II. A group of American soldiers, taking refuge in a home, are intrigued by the portrait of a beautiful woman. Each envisions what she is really like.

CAST

Woman: Carolyn Jones; Max: Otto Woldis; Private Dennis: Bob Nichols; Private Menoti: Joseph Tuckel; Private Boland: James Best.

THE DAVID NIVEN THEATRE–30 minutes–NBC–April 7, 1959 - September 15, 1959.

THE DAVID STEINBERG SHOW

Variety. Various comedy sketches designed to satirize the world and its problems.

Host: David Steinberg.

Announcer: Bill Thompson.

Orchestra: Artie Butler.

Guests: Carol Wayne, Patty Duke, John Astin, Burns and Schreiber, Ed McMahon, Carly Simon.

THE DAVID STEINBERG SHOW–60 minutes–CBS–July 19, 1972 - August 16, 1972.

THE DAVID SUSSKIND SHOW

Discussion. A roundtable discussion on various topical issues with appropriate guests.

Host: David Susskind.

Music: Recorded.

THE DAVID SUSSKIND SHOW–2 hours–Syndicated 1967. Original title: "Open End"–60 minutes–Syndicated–1958-1967.

DAVY AND GOLIATH

Animated Religious Cartoon. The adventures of a young boy, Davy Hanson, and his talking dog, Goliath. Stories depict Davy's attempts to relate the meaning of God's Word in the solving of everyday problems.

Characters: Davy Hanson; Goliath; John Hanson, Davy's father; Mary Hanson, Davy's mother; Alice Hanson, Davy's sister; Miss Lindsey, the school teacher; Pastor Miller; and Tom, Davy's friend.

Voices: Richard Belar, Hal Smith, Nancy Wible, Norma MacMillan.

Music: John Seely Associates.

DAVY AND GOLIATH–15 minutes –Syndicated 1963.

DAVY CROCKETT

Adventure. The life of legendary frontiersman-pioneer Davy Crockett. Originally broadcast via the "Disneyland," *Frontierland* series.

Titles:
Davy Crockett, Indian Fighter (12/15/54). Background: Tennessee, 1813, during the era of the Creek Indian Uprising, the slaughter of settlers by Indians seeking to protect their land. Joining a small band of volunteers, Davy and his friend, George Russell, attempt to keep officials posted on Indian activities

Davy Crockett. Left to right: Nick Cravat,
Fess Parker, Buddy Ebsen, and Hans
Conried. © *Walt Disney Productions.*

and convince the chief of the Black-
feet, Red Stick, to end his war.
Confronting and defeating Red Stick
in a tomahawk battle, Davy convinces
him to join the other chiefs in a peace
treaty.

**Davy Crockett Goes To Congress
(1/26/55).** Shortly after their return
home, Davy and George seek land on
which to settle. Attempting to file a
claim, they encounter the wrath of a
bigoted, self-imposed magistrate, Big
Foot Mason. After learning of Mason's
practices of selling Indian land to
settlers, Davy opposes him and ends
his reign. Seeking representation in
Nashville, the settlers elect Davy as
their state legislator. The episode
depicts his experiences as an elected
senator in Washington, D.C.

**Davy Crockett At The Alamo
(2/23/55).** Era: 1836, the beginning
of the Western March. Learning of the
Texas struggle for independence, Davy
and George, assisted by friends
Thimbelrig and Bustedluck, journey
to the Alamo where two hundred
men, under the command of Jim
Bowie, have established a stronghold
against thousands of Santa Anna's
Mexican soldiers. The episode depicts
the final defense before the Alamo is
captured by Santa Anna.

Davy Crockett's Keelboat Race (11/16/55). Background: The Ohio and Mississippi Rivers during the 1830s. The story of the keelboat race between Davy Crockett, his partner, George Russell, and Mike Fink, "King of the River."

Davy Crockett And The River Pirates (12/14/55). Background: Illinois, during the 1830s. Davy, George, and Mike Fink attempt to end the reign of the Ohio River Cave-In-Rock Den of pirates.

CAST

Davy Crockett	Fess Parker
George Russell	Buddy Ebsen
Polly Crockett, Davy's wife	Helen Stanely
Billy Crockett, their son	Eugene Brindle
Johnny Crockett, their son	Ray Whiteside
Chief Red Stick	Pat Hogan
Thimbelrig	Hans Conried
Bustedluck	Nick Cravat
Jim Bowie	Kenneth Tobey
Mike Fink	Jeff York
Big Foot Mason	Mike Mazurki

Davy's Rifle: Betsy.
Theme: "The Ballad Of Davy Crockett."
　　　　Words: Tom Blackburn.
　　　　Music: George Burns.
　　　　"Copyright 1954 Walt Disney Music Company. Reprinted by permission."

Born on a mountain top in Tennessee,
Greenest state in the Land of the Free
Raised in the woods so's he knew every tree
Kilt him a b'ar when he was only three.
Davy, Davy Crockett, King of the wild frontier.

Off through the woods he's a marchin' along
Makin' up yarns an' a singin' a song,
Itchin' fer fightin' an' rightin' a wrong.
He's ringy as a b'ar an' twict as strong.
Davy, Davy Crockett, the buck-skin buccaneer!

His land is the biggest an' his land is best,
From grassy plains to the mountain crest,
He's ahead of us all meetin' the test,
Followin' his legend into the West.
Davy, Davy Crockett, King of the wild frontier!

DAYDREAMING WITH LARAINE

Variety. Dramatic vignettes, interviews, music and current events.
Hostess: Laraine Day.
Vocalist: Ruth Woodner.
Music: The Bill Harrington Trio.

DAYDREAMING WITH LARAINE—30 minutes—ABC—May 3, 1951 - July 5, 1951. Daily, as titled above; Saturday afternoons as: "The Laraine Day Show"—30 minutes—ABC—May 5, 1951 - July 28, 1951.

DAY IN COURT

Courtroom Drama. Reenactments of city and state criminal and civil hearings.
Judge: Edgar Allan Jones Jr.; William Gwinn.

DAY IN COURT—30 minutes—ABC—1958-1965.

DAYS OF OUR LIVES

Serial. "Like sands through the hour glass, so are the days of our lives. . . ."
Background: Salem, Massachusetts. The life of Dr. Thomas Horton, Pro-

fessor of Medicine at University Hospital; and his family. Stories relate the events that befall and alter their daily existences.

CAST

Dr. Thomas Horton	Macdonald Carey
Alice Horton	Frances Reid
Marie Horton	Marie Cheatham
Dr. Laura Spencer	Susan Flannery
Mickey Horton	John Clarke
Sandy Horton	Heather North
Dr. Thomas Horton, Jr.	John Lupton
Michael Horton	Alan Decker
	John Amour
	Dick DeCort
Dr. William Horton	Edward Mallory
Craig Merritt	David McLean
David Banning	Jeffrey Williams
John Martin	Robert Brubaker
Helen Martin	K.T. Stevens
Susan Martin	Denise Alexander
Addie Olson	Patricia Huston
	Patricia Barry
Dr. Greg Peters	Peter Brown
Kim Douglas	Helen Funai
Doug Williams	Bill Hayes
Jim Phillips	Victor Holchak
Cliff Patterson	John Howard
Scott Banning	Robert Hogan
	Ryan Macdonald
	Mike Farrell
Linda Peterson	Margaret Mason
Julie Olson	Charla Doherty
	Kathy Dunn
	Susan Seaforth
	Cathy Ferrar
Rick	Myron Natwick
Phyllis Anderson	Nancy Wickwire
	Corinne Conley
Eric Peters	Stanley Kamel
Anne Peters	Jeanne Bates
Phil Peters	Herb Nelson
Mary Anderson	Brigid Bazlen
	Karen Wolfe
Wilbur Austin	Arlund Schubert
Diane Hunter	Coleen Gray
Richard Hunter	Terry O'Sullivan
Susan Peters	Bennye Gatleys

Bob Anderson	Mark Tapscott
Don Craig	Jed Allen
Meg Hansen	Suzanne Rogers
Hank	Frederick Downs
Dr. Neil Curtis	Joe Gallison
Ben Olsen	Robert Knapp
Steve Olsen	Flip Mark
Jim Fisk	Burt Douglas
Tony Merritt	Dick Colla
	Ron Husmann
Letty Lowell	Ivy Bethune
Jeri Clayton	Kaye Stevens
Mrs. Jackson	Pauline Myers

Music: Tommy Boyce, Bobby Hart, Barry Mann, Charles Albertine.

DAYS OF OUR LIVES—30 minutes—NBC—Premiered: November 8. 1965.

A DAY WITH DOODLES

Comedy. Short slapstick sketches relating the misadventures of Doodles Weaver, as he attempts to cope with life's endless problems. Starring, as himself and everyone else in the cast: Doodles Weaver.

A DAY WITH DOODLES—05 minutes—Syndicated 1965.

DEADLINE

Anthology. Dramatizations depicting the work of newspapermen throughout the country.

Host-Narrator: Paul Stewart.

Music: Fred Howard.

Included:

Thesis For Murder. The story of a

mentally disturbed student who develops the perfect crime.

CAST
Robert Morris, Tony Franke.

Exposure. A reporter attempts to expose a photography racket that is operating in his city.

CAST
Patricia Englund, Henrietta Moore.

Massacre. The story of a newspaper reporter as he attempts to trap a berserk killer.

CAST
William Johnstone.

DEADLINE—30 minutes—Syndicated 1959.

DEADLINE FOR ACTION

Adventure. The investigations of Dan Miller, Wire Service reporter for *Trans Globe News*. Episodes were originally aired via "Wire Service."

Starring: Dane Clark as Dan Miller.

DEADLINE FOR ACTION—60 minutes—ABC—February 8, 1959 - September 20, 1959.

DEALER'S CHOICE

Game. Three competing contestants. Basis: Various games based on gambling.

Round One. Any Pair Loses. Two cards are placed on a board. Each player bets up to ten chips as to whether the next card will make a pair. Deductions or accumulations depend on the failure or success of the bet.

Round Two. Wheel of Chance. The four card suits, each represented by different odds (from one to one, to eleven to one) are displayed on a large electronic spinning wheel. Players are permitted to choose one and wager up to twenty-five chips. The wheel is spun and chips are added or deducted accordingly.

Round Three. Blackjack. A contestant is chosen from the studio audience. The bet limit is fifty. Two cards are dealt to each player. Players are then permitted to either freeze their score or receive another card. The player closest to or hitting an exact twenty-one is the winner and receives the bet amount. The chip total of the losers is the amount awarded to the studio-audience contestant who is able to trade his chips for a merchandise prize.

The Last Chance Round. Dealer's Derby. Three horses, each represented by different odds (one to one; three to one; five to one) are displayed on a board. The odds are determined by the corresponding number of numbered ping pong balls contained in a large air machine. Players secretly wager a bet, risking any part of their chips. The machine is turned on and balls are ejected one at a time. Each ball moves the horse one furlong in a five furlong race. The player with the highest chip total is the winner and trades his chips for a merchandise prize.

Host: Bob Hastings; Jack Clark.

Assistant: Jane Nelson.

Announcer: Jim Thompson.

Music: John La Salle.

DEALER'S CHOICE—30 minutes—Syndicated 1974.

DEAN MARTIN PRESENTS MUSIC COUNTRY

Musical Variety. Newcomers and established singers perform against the background of various Tennessee locales.

Regularly appearing: Loretta Lynn, Donna Fargo, Mac Davis, Jerry Reed, Lynn Anderson, Tom T. Hall, Kris Kristofferson, Marty Robbins, Ray Stevens, Tammy Wynette, Doug Kershaw, Doug Dillard.

Music: Jonathan Lucas.

Music Supervision: Doug Gilmer.

Music Co-ordinator/Arranger: Ed Hubbard.

DEAN MARTIN PRESENTS MUSIC COUNTRY—60 minutes—NBC—July 26, 1973 - September 6, 1973.

DEAN MARTIN'S COMEDY WORLD

Variety. Performances by new comedy talent. Taped on locations throughout the United States and England.

Host: Jackie Cooper.

Locational Hosts: Barbara Feldon, Nipsey Russell.

Regularly appearing: Eric Morecomb, Ernie Wise, Lonnie Shorr, Rich Little, Jud Strunk, Don Rickles, Phyllis Diller, Jack Benny, Ruth Buzzi, The Committee, and acts from the British television series, "Monty Python's Flying Circus."

DEAN MARTIN'S COMEDY WORLD—60 minutes—NBC—June 6, 1974 - August 8, 1974.

THE DEAN MARTIN SHOW

Variety. A varying format featuring comedy and song and dance performances.

Host: Dean Martin.

Regulars: Ken Lane, Kay Medford, Marian Mercer, Lou Jacoby, Tom Bosley, Inga Nielson, Dom DeLuise, Nipsey Russell, Rodney Dangerfield, The Golddiggers, The Ding-a-ling Sisters (Lynn Latham, Tara Leigh, Helen Funai, Jayne Kennedy), The Krofft Marionettes.

Announcer: Frank Barton.

Orchestra: Les Brown.

Included Features:

Celebrity Roastings. A guest of honor, seated among friends, is comically insulted.

"At The Barbershop." A discussion on various world affairs by barbers Dom DeLuise and Nipsey Russell.

Musical salutes to MGM films.

The middle aged romance between a diner owner (Lou Jacobi) and his waitress (Kay Medford).

THE DEAN MARTIN SHOW—60 minutes—NBC—September 16, 1965 - May 24, 1974.

DEAR PHOEBE

Comedy. Background: California, the city office of a newspaper, the *Los Angeles Daily Blade.* The misadventures of Bill Hastings, an ex-college professor employed as Phoebe Goodheart, the male advice-to-the-lovelorn columnist. Stories relate the romantic rivalries that occur between he, seeking a reporter's position, and his girl-friend, Mickey Riley, the female sportswriter.

CAST

Bill Hastings (Phoebe
    Goodheart)   Peter Lawford
Mickey Riley   Marcia Henderson
Mr. Fosdick, the managing
    editor   Charles Lane
Humphrey, the copy
    boy   Josef Corey
Also   Jamie Farr

DEAR PHOEBE—30 minutes—NBC—September 10, 1954 - September 2, 1955.

DEATH VALLEY DAYS

Western Anthology. Background: Various areas between Nevada and California during the latter half of the nineteenth century. Dramatizations depicting the pioneers journeying West and their struggles in establishing a new homeland.

Hosts: Stanley Andrews, the Old
    Ranger (twelve years).
    Ronald Reagan (three years).
    Robert Taylor (two years).
    Dale Robertson (three years).

Music: Marlen Skiles.

Commercial Spokeswoman: Rosemary
    DeCamp.

Included:

Death And Taxes. A young tenderfoot attempts to collect taxes from a murderous gang of outlaws.

CAST

Wes Hudman, Jean Lewis, Vernon Rich.

The Lost Pegleg Mine. The desert search of two people attempting to find the famed lost Pegleg Mine.

CAST

Gloria Eaton, Gilbert Frye, Andy Clyde.

Sequoia. The true story of the self-sacrificing Cherokee Indian who spent twelve years developing an alphabet for his people.

Starring: Lane Bradford.

California's First Schoolmarm. A school teacher attempts to assemble her first class in the ruins of an old mission.

Starring: Dorothy Granter.

A Woman's Rights. The story of the first woman judge; and her fight against corruption.

CAST

Bethel Leslie, Dan Harens.

A Calamity Named Jane. The story of the relationship between Calamity Jane and Wild Bill Hickok.

CAST

Fay Spain, Rhodes Reason.

The Lady Was An M.D. A woman struggles to establish a medical practice.

Starring: Yvonne DeCarlo.

DEATH VALLEY DAYS—30 minutes—Syndicated 1952.

DEBBIE DRAKE'S DANCERCIZE

Weight-reducing exercise. Dance steps combined with exercise movement.

Hostess: Debbie Drake.

DEBBIE DRAKE'S DANCERCIZE—
30 minutes—Syndicated 1968.
Original title: "The Debbie Drake
Show"—30 minutes—Syndicated
1961.

THE DEBBIE REYNOLDS SHOW

Comedy. Background: 804 Devon
Lane, Los Angeles, California, the
residence of Jim Thompson, sportswriter for the *Los Angeles Sun;* and
his beautiful and unpredictable wife,
Debbie, who yearns for a career as a
newspaper feature writer. Reluctant
to have two newspaper writers in the
family, Jim wants her to remain as she
is: "a loving and beautiful housewife
devoting herself to making her lord
and master happy." Stories depict
Debbie's attempts to prove her abilities and achieve her goal; and Jim's
struggles to discourage her.

The Debbie Reynolds Show. Debbie
Reynolds.

CAST
Debbie Thompson   Debbie Reynolds
Jim Thompson   Don Chastain
Charlotte Landers, her married
    sister   Patricia Smith
Bob Landers, Charlotte's husband,
    an accountant   Tom Bosley
Bruce Landers, their son, publisher
    of a neighborhood gossip
    sheet   Bobby Riha
Mr. Crawford, Jim's
    employer   Herbert Rudley
Music: Tony Romeo.

THE DEBBIE REYNOLDS SHOW—
30 minutes—NBC—September 16,
1969 - September 8, 1970.

DECEMBER BRIDE

Comedy. Background: Los Angeles,
California. The trials and tribulations
of Ruth and Matt Henshaw, a couple
married eight years; and the life and
romantic misadventures of Lily
Ruskin, Ruth's mother, a widow who
lives with them.

CAST
Lily Ruskin   Spring Byington
Matt Henshaw   Dean Miller
Ruth Henshaw   Frances Rafferty
Hilda Crocker, Lily's
    friend   Verna Felton
Peter Porter, the
    Henshaw's nextdoor
    neighbor   Harry Morgan
Music: Wilbur Hatch.

DECEMBER BRIDE—30 minutes—
CBS—October 4, 1954 - September
1959. Syndicated. Spin-off series:
"Pete and Gladys" (see title).

DECISION

Pilot Films. Proposed programs for the 1958-1959 season.

Included:

The Virginian. Western. The Virginian's investigation into a series of mysterious events that have been plaguing a judge's attempts to build a railroad spur to his ranch. Unsold as a half-hour series. Remade, four years later, as a ninety-minute pilot, the series was sold to NBC.

CAST
The Virginian: James Drury; Judge: Robert Burton; Dora: Jeanette Nolan.

Fifty Beautiful Girls. Mystery. A chorus girl attempts to solve the murders of three dancehall girls.
Starring: Barbara Bel Geddes.

The Danger Game. Adventure. A U.S. government undercover agent, posing as a singer, attempts to protect an American scientist.
Starring: Ray Danton as Stagg.

The Tall Man. Western. Background: Clayton City. A special investigator attempts to apprehend a gang of outlaws who robbed a train and killed the expressman.

CAST
Col. T.J. Allan: Michael Rennie; Leslie Henderson: William Phillips; Dawson: Dean Stanton.

DECISION—30 minutes—NBC—July 6, 1958 - September 1958.

DECISION—THE CONFLICTS OF HARRY S. TRUMAN

Documentary. Detailed via film clips: The decisions and conflicts of former U.S. President, Harry S. Truman.

DECISION—THE CONFLICTS OF HARRY S. TRUMAN—30 minutes—Syndicated 1964.

DECOY

Crime Drama. Background: New York City. The investigations of Casey Jones, a beautiful and daring police woman.
Starring: Beverly Garland as Casey Jones.

DECOY—30 minutes—Syndicated 1957. Also known as "Police Woman Decoy."

THE DEFENDERS

Crime Drama. Background: New York City. The investigations and courtroom defenses of trial lawyer Lawrence Preston, and his son, attorney Kenneth Preston.

CAST
Lawrence Preston	E.G. Marshall
Kenneth Preston	Robert Reed
Joan, the secretary	Polly Rowles
	Rosemary Forsythe

Music: Leonard Rosenman.

THE DEFENDERS—60 minutes—CBS—September 16, 1961 - September 9, 1965. Syndicated.

DELLA

Variety. Music, guests and interviews.

Hostess: Della Reese.

Co-Host: Sandy Baron.

DELLA—60 minutes—Syndicated 1970.

THE DELPHI BUREAU

See title: "The Men," *The Delphi Bureau* segment.

DEMI-TASSE TALES

Anthology. Rebroadcasts of dramas that were originally aired via other filmed anthology series. Also featured: first-run airings of theatrical shorts of the 1930s and 1940s.

DEMI-TASSE TALES—30 minutes—CBS 1953.

THE DENNIS DAY SHOW

Variety. Music, comedy, songs and dances.
Sketch: Background: Hollywood, California. The misadventures of Dennis Day, a swinging young bachelor.

CAST

Dennis Day   Himself
Charley Weaver, the apartment-
    house super   Cliff Arquette
Susan, Dennis's young
    admirer   Jeri Lou James
Marion, Dennis's
    girlfriend   Carol Richards
                        Lou Butler
Lavinia, the
    landlady   Minerva Urecal
                        Ida Moore

Hal, Dennis's
    friend   Hal March
Also: Verna Felton, Katy Phillips.

Dancers: Tom and Jean Mahoney.

Orchestra: Charles "Bud" Dante.

THE DENNIS DAY SHOW—30 minutes—NBC—February 8, 1952 - August 2, 1954. Also known as: "The R.C.A. Victor Show."

DENNIS JAMES CARNIVAL

Variety.

Host: Dennis James.

Regulars: Dagmar (Jennie Lewis), Victoria Rone, Leonardo and Zola.

DENNIS JAMES CARNIVAL—30 minutes—CBS—October 3, 1948 - November 7, 1948.

THE DENNIS JAMES SHOW

Variety. Interviews, audience participation, and discussions.

Host: Dennis James.

Assistant: Julia Meade.

THE DENNIS JAMES SHOW—30 minutes—ABC—February 8, 1952 - August 2, 1954.

DENNIS THE MENACE

Comedy. Background: 627 Elm Street, Hillsdale, the residence of the Mitchell family: Henry, an engineer with Trask Engineering; his wife, Alice; and their son, Dennis, a very mischievous young boy. Stories depict Dennis's disastrous attempts to assist people he believes are in trouble.

CAST

Dennis Mitchell   Jay North
Henry Mitchell   Herbert Anderson
Alice Mitchell   Gloria Henry
George Wilson, neighbor, avid
    gardener and bird
    watcher   Joseph Kearns
Martha Wilson, his
    wife   Sylvia Field
John Wilson, his
    brother   Gale Gordon
Eloise Wilson, John's
    wife   Sara Seeger
Tommy Anderson, Dennis's
    friend   Tommy Booth
Seymour, Dennis's
    friend   Robert John Pitman
Margaret Wade, Dennis's
    friend, "That dumb
    old girl"   Jeannie Russell
Sgt. Theodore Mooney, the
    neighborhood police-
    man   George Cisar
Mr. Quigley, supermarket
    owner   Willard Waterman
Mr. Finch, drugstore
    owner   Charles Lane
Joey MacDonald, Dennis's
    friend   Gil Smith
Esther Cathcart, Dennis's
    friend, a woman des-
    perately seeking a
    husband   Mary Wickes
Mr. Dorfman, the
    postman   Robert B. Williams
James Trask, Henry's
    employer   Henry Norell
Mr. Timberlake, president, the
    National Birdwatchers
    Society   Byron Foulger
June Wilson, George's
    sister   Nancy Evans
Mr. Merivale, the
    florist   Will Wright
Mr. Hall, Henry's
    employer   J. Edward McKinley
Mayor Yates   Charles Watts
Mr. Krinkie, the newspaper
    editor   Charles Seel

George Wilson's Dog: Freemont.

Music: Irving Friedman.

DENNIS THE MENACE—30 minutes —CBS—September 1959 - September 1963. Syndicated.

THE DENNIS O'KEEFE SHOW

Comedy. Background: Los Angeles, California. The home and working life of widowed newspaper columnist Hal Towne. Stories focus on his struggles to raise his young son, Randy.

CAST

Hal Towne   Dennis O'Keefe
Randy Towne   Rickey Kelman
Sarge, their
    housekeeper   Hope Emerson
Karen Hadley   Eloise Hardt
Eliot   Eddie Ryder

THE DENNIS O'KEEFE SHOW—30 minutes—CBS—1959-1960.

DEPARTMENT S

Mystery. Background: Paris, France — the headquarters of Department S, a special investigative branch of Interpol that undertakes the task of resolving the unsolved baffling crimes of any law enforcement organization in the world. Director: Sir Curtis Seretse; operatives: Jason King, the successful author of Mark Cain Mystery Novels; Annabell Hurst, a pretty scientific-minded young woman; and Stewart Sullivan, the American member of the British team. Stories relate their investigations with Jason solving each case as if it were a plot for one of his books.

CAST

Jason King   Peter Wyngarde

Department S. Left to right: Peter Wyngarde, Joel Fabiani, and Rosemary Nichols. *Courtesy Independent Television Corp.; an ATV Company.*

Annabell Hurst   Rosemary Nichols
Stewart Sullivan   Joel Fabiani
Sir Curtis Seretse Dennis Alaba Peters

Music: Edwin Astley.

DEPARTMENT S–60 minutes–Syndicated 1971.

THE DEPUTY

Western. Background: Silver City, Arizona during the 1880s. The story of U.S. Marshal Simon Fry and his deputy, Clay McCord, and their attempts to maintain law and order.

CAST

Marshal Simon Fry	Henry Fonda
Deputy Clay McCord	Allen Case
Fran McCord, Clay's sister	Betty Lou Keim
Sergeant Tasker, a U.S. Cavalry agent assigned to duty in Silver City	Read Morgan
Herb Lamson, the owner of the general store	Wallace Ford

Music: Jack Marshall.

THE DEPUTY—30 minutes—NBC—September 12, 1959 - September 16, 1961. Syndicated.

DEPUTY DAWG

Animated Cartoon. Background: Mississippi. The misadventures of Deputy Dawg, a simple-minded lawman, as he attempts to maintain law and order.

Additional characters: The near-sighted Vincent Van Gopher; Muskie the Muskrat; Ty Coon, the Raccoon; Pig Newton, the hombre seeking to rob the corn fields; and the Sheriff, Deputy Dawg's superior, the only human figure.

Voice of Deputy Dawg: Dayton Alan.

DEPUTY DAWG—30 minutes—Syndicated 1960. NBC—September 11, 1971 - September 2, 1972.

DESILU PLAYHOUSE

Anthology. Dramatic presentations.

Host: Desi Arnaz.

Music: Wilbur Hatch.

Included:

Meeting At Apalachin. Background: The small town of Apalachin, New York. The conflicts and tensions that arise from a gangland convention.

CAST
Midge Rospond: Cara Williams; Gino Rospond: Cameron Mitchell; Joe Rogarti: Jack Warden; Sol Raimondi: Luther Adler.

Dr. Kate. After their mother is wounded and their father arrested, a country doctor attempts to care for a deaf boy, aged six, and his hostile ten-year-old sister.

CAST
Dr. Kate: Jane Wyman; Sally: Karen Lee; Buddy: Bobby Buntrock.

Trial At Devil's Canyon. A sheriff attempts to apprehend a band of outlaws who robbed an army payroll and killed the stage passengers.

CAST
El Jefe: Lee J. Cobb; Farnsworth: Barry Kelly; Colonel Simmons: Edward Platt; Rose: Carol Thurston; Doc: Paul Bryar.

Change Of Heart. A blind detective, aided by a seeing-eye dog, seeks to track down a murderer.

CAST
Duncan McLain: Robert Middleton; Dick Sprague: Dick Sargent; Bill Wood: Donald May.

DESILU PLAYHOUSE—60 minutes—CBS—1958-1961. Syndicated.

THE DES O'CONNOR SHOW

Variety. Songs, dances, music, and comedy sketches. Taped in London, England.

Host: Des O'Connor.
Regulars: Connie Stevens, Jack Douglas, The Bonnie Birds Plus Two, The New Faces, Charlie Callas, Joe Baker, The Paddy Stone Dancers, The Mike Sammes Singers.
Announcers: Paul Griffith (from

London); Ed Herlihy (for the sponsor).

Orchestra: Jack Parnell.

Sketches:

"Dandy Sandy." Background: A make-believe toy land. The story of Little Dandy Sandy (Des O'Connor) and Pretty Little Lucie Loose (Connie Stevens) and their attempts to get rid of the overgrown Teddy Bear (Jack Douglas), who constantly interferes in their love life.

"I Say, I Say, I Say." Des's determined efforts to recite despite constant interruptions by people singing, telling jokes, or relating riddles.

"At the Principal's Office." The story of the fear that befalls two mischievous boys as they await to see the school principal.

THE DES O'CONNOR SHOW—60 minutes—NBC—June 1970 - September 1970; June 21, 1971 - September 1, 1971. Summer replacement for "The Kraft Music Hall."

DESTINY

Anthology. Dramatizations of fate's intervention in the lives of ordinary people. Rebroadcasts of episodes that were originally aired via other filmed anthology programs.

Host-Narrator: Francis C. Sullivan.

Included:

Killer's Pride. The story of a college student who joins a posse to track down a killer.

CAST
Fay Wray, John Kerr, Mae Clarke.

Doctors Of Pawnee Hill. The story of two brothers, doctors, and their attempts to maintain law and order in a small frontier town.

CAST
Lee Marvin, Kevin McCarthy, Margaret Hayes.

Foreign Wife. The story of a group of enemy agents who try to blackmail the Viennese wife of a U.S. army officer into obtaining secret documents.

CAST
Phyllis Kirk, Stephen McNally, Larry Dobkin.

DESTINY—30 minutes—CBS—July 5, 1957 - September 1957; July 25, 1958 - September 1958.

DESTRY

Western. Background: The Frontier, 1860s. Harrison Destry, the peace-loving son of rugged gunfighter Tom Destry, is framed and falsely accused of a robbery charge. Stories relate his attempts to find the man responsible and clear his name.

Starring: John Gavin as Harrison Destry.

DESTRY—60 minutes—ABC—February 14, 1964 - May 9, 1964.

THE DETECTIVES

Crime Drama. Background: New York City. The assignments of an elite team of N.Y.P.D. plainclothes detectives.

CAST
Captain Matt Holbrook   Robert Taylor

Lt. Johnny Russo — Tige Andrews
Sgt. Steve Nelson — Adam West
Sgt. Chris Ballard — Mark Goddard
Lisa Bonay, a police
  reporter — Ursula Thiess
Lt. Lindstrom — Russ Thorson
Lt. Conway — Lee Farr

Music: Herschel Burke Gilbert.

THE DETECTIVES—30 minutes—ABC—October 16, 1959 - September 22, 1961. Syndicated. 60 minutes—ABC—September 29, 1961 - September 21, 1962. Syndicated.

THE DETECTIVE'S WIFE

Crime Drama. Background: New York City. The investigations of Adam Conway, a private detective whose assignments are complicated by the intervention of his meaningful but troubleprone wife, Connie.

CAST
Adam Conway — Donald Curtis
Connie Conway — Lynn Bari

THE DETECTIVE'S WIFE—30 minutes—CBS—July 7, 1950 - September 29, 1950.

DEVLIN

Animated Cartoon. The story of three orphans, Ernie, Tod, and Sandy Devlin, and their attempts to support themselves by performing as a motorcycle stunt team.

Voices: Norman Alden, Michael Bell, Philip Clarke, Don Diamond, Mickey Dolenz, Sarina Grant, Bob Hastings, David Jolliffe, Robie Lester, Stan Livingston, Derrell Maury, Barney Phillips, Michele Robinson, Fran Ryan, John Stephenson, John Tuell, Ginny Tyler, Don Weiss, Jesse White.

Music: Hoyt Curtin.

DEVLIN—30 minutes—ABC—Premiered: September 7, 1974.

DIAGNOSIS: UNKNOWN

Crime Drama. Background: New York City. The cases of pathologist Dr. Daniel Coffe. Stories relate his attempts to solve unusual crimes through the use of scientific technology.

CAST
Dr. Daniel Coffe — Patrick O'Neal
Doris Hudson, the lab
  technician — Phyllis Newman
Dr. Matilal, a visiting
  colleague from
  India — Carl Bellini
Link, an
  associate — Martin Houston
Lieutenant Ritter,
  N.Y.P.D. — Chester Morris

DIAGNOSIS: UNKNOWN—60 minutes—CBS—July 5, 1960 - September 20, 1960.

DIAL 999

Crime Drama. Background: London, England. The investigations of Inspector Michael Maguire, a Royal Canadian Mounted Policeman assigned to study British methods of crime detection at the New Scotland Yard. (999: The Scotland Yard emergency telephone number.)

Starring: Robert Beatty as Inspector Michael Maguire.

DIAL 999—30 minutes—Syndicated 1959.

DIANA—30 minutes—NBC—September 10, 1973 - January 7, 1974.

DIANA

Comedy. Background: New York City. The trials and tribulations of Diana Smythe, a beautiful young divorcée newly arrived in Manhattan from London.

Stories depict her home life at 4 Sutton Place, Apartment 11-B, a bachelor flat that is owned by her brother, Roger, an anthropologist who is presently in Equador; her work as a fashion illustrator at Buckley's Department Store; and her attempts to reclaim the numerous keys given out by her brother to his friends, acquaintances, and drinking companions—people, who are unaware of his absence and seek to use his apartment at all hours.

CAST
Diana Smythe   Diana Rigg
Norman Brodnik, the president
    of Buckley's Department
    Store   David Sheiner
Norma Brodnik, his wife, the
    merchandising department
    head   Barbara Barrie
Howard Tolbrook, the
    copywriter   Richard B. Shull
Marshall Tyler, the window
    dresser   Robert Moore
Holly Green, a friend of Diana's,
    a model   Carol Androsky
Jeff Harmon, a mystery writer,
    a friend of
    Diana's   Richard Mulligan
Smitty, the Sutton Place
    Bellboy   Liam Dunn
Diana's dog (Roger's Great Dane):
Gulliver.

Music: Jerry Fielding.

DICK AND THE DUCHESS

Comedy. Background: London, England. The investigations of Dick Starrett, an insurance claims detective, and his wife and assistant, Jane, a British duchess. Situations are played comically.

CAST
Dick Starrett   Patrick O'Neal
Jane Starrett   Hazel Court
Inspector Stark, a Scotland Yard
    investigator   Michael Shepley
Peter Jamison, Dick's
    boss   Richard Wattis

DICK AND THE DUCHESS—30 minutes—CBS—September 28, 1957 - May 16, 1958.

DICK CAVETT

Listed: The television programs of Dick Cavett.

This Morning—Discussion-Variety—90 minutes—ABC—April 1, 1968 - January 24, 1969.

Host: Dick Cavett.

Announcer: Fred Foy.

Orchestra: Bobby Rosengarden.

The Dick Cavett Show—Discussion-Variety—60 minutes—ABC—May 26, 1969 - September 19, 1969.

Host: Dick Cavett.

Announcer: Fred Foy.

Orchestra: Bobby Rosengarden.

The Dick Cavett Show—Disscussion-

Variety—90 minutes—ABC-December 12, 1969 - January 1, 1975.

Host: Dick Cavett.

Announcer: Fred Foy.

Orchestra: Bobby Rosengarden.

The Dick Cavett Show—Talk-Variety —60 minutes—CBS—August 16, 1975 - September 6, 1975.

Host: Dick Cavett.

Series Regular: Leigh French.

Orchestra: Stephen Lawrence.

DICK CLARK PRESENTS THE ROCK AND ROLL YEARS

Variety. A nostalgic backward glance into the music and personalities of the fifties, sixties, and seventies via live appearances, tape, film, and newsreel footage.

Host: Dick Clark.

Orchestra: Billy Strange.

Appearing: Danny and the Juniors, Herman's Hermits, Leon Russell, Paul Revere and the Raiders, Big Bopper, The Righteous Brothers, Freddie Cannon, The Diamonds, Pat Boone, Bo Diddly, Melanie, Peter and Gordon, Dick and Dee Dee, Bobby Sherman, Chuck Berry, The Drifters, Duane Eddy, Tommy James, Jan and Dean, Del Shannon, Johnny Tillotson, Sal Mineo, The Byrds, Paul Anka, Rod Stewart, Raquel Welch, Gene Vincent, Brenda Lee, Johnnie Ray, B.B. King, The Shirelles.

DICK CLARK PRESENTS THE ROCK AND ROLL YEARS—30 minutes—ABC—November 28, 1973 - January 9, 1974.

THE DICK CLARK SATURDAY NIGHT BEECHNUT SHOW

Variety. Performances by the top Rock and Roll personalities.

Host: Dick Clark.

Appearing: Connie Francis, The Royal Teens, Jerry Lee Lewis, Chuck Willis, Pat Boone, The Chordettes, Billie and Lillie, Danny and the Juniors, Chuck Berry, Teresa Brewer, Eddie Platt, The Chantels, John Zacherle, Anne Reynolds, The Four Dates, Fats Domino, The Four Lads, Don Gibson, The Voxpoppers, Vic Damone, Paul Anka, The Everly Brothers, Tommy Sands, The Shirelles, Dale Hawkins, The Four Preps, The Monotones, The Aquatones, Somethin' Smith and the Red-heads, The Chordettes, Valerie Carr, Wally Lewis, Jimmy Rogers, Dickie Doo and the Donts, Jan and Arnie, Mickey and Sylvia, Tony Bennett, Duane Eddy and the Rebels, Little Booker, Jodie Reynolds, Lee Andrews and the Hearts, The Diamonds, The Kalin Twins, Fabian Forte, Bobby Darin, Jack Scott, The DeJohn Sisters, George Hamilton IV; Annette Funicello.

THE DICK CLARK SATURDAY NIGHT BEECHNUT SHOW—30 minutes—ABC—February 15, 1958 - September 1959.

DICK CLARK'S WORLD OF TALENT

Discussion-Variety. Discussions, with two professional guests, based on the merits of material performed by young hopefuls.

Host: Dick Clark.

Permanent Panelist: Jack E. Leonard.

DICK CLARK'S WORLD OF TALENT—30 minutes—ABC—1959-1960.

THE DICK POWELL THEATRE

Anthology. Dramatic presentations.

Host-Occasional Performer: Dick Powell.

Hostess: June Allyson (Mrs. Powell). When Syndicated in 1966 under the title "Hollywood Showcase."

Music: Herschel Burke Gilbert; Joseph Mullendore; Hans Salter; Richard Shores.

Included:

Days Of Glory. The story of a power struggle involving a Latin-American dictator and an army colonel.

CAST
Morell: Charles Boyer; Marta: Suzanne Pleshette; Volera: Lloyd Bochner.

Doyle Against The House. A Blackjack dealer, needing five thousand dollars for his daughter's operation, attempts to rig a game against his employer.

CAST
Eddie Doyle: Milton Berle; Chris: Jan Sterling; Victor: Ludwig Donath.

Killer In The House. A man, faced with a vicious threat, attempts to help his brother, an escaped convict, evade a police dragnet.

CAST
Sid Williams: Edmond O'Brien; Paul Williams: Earl Holliman.

Thunder In A Forgotten Town. Returning home after serving ten years in a Red Chinese prisoner-of-war camp, a man struggles to readjust to life.

CAST
Jackie Cooper, Susan Oliver, David Janssen, Dewey Martin.

THE DICK POWELL THEATRE—60 minutes—NBC—September 26, 1961 - September 17, 1963. Syndicated.

DICK POWELL'S ZANE GREY THEATRE

Western Anthology.

Host-Occasional Performer: Dick Powell, introducing the evening's drama, with interesting facts about the Old West.

Music: Herschel Burke Gilbert; Joseph Mullendore.

Included:

Welcome From A Stranger. Returning from the Civil War, a lawman struggles to adopt the changing methods of law enforcement.

CAST
Ben Sanderson: Dick Powell.

Seed of Evil. A woman attempts to avenge the death of her son.

CAST
Irene: Cara Williams; West: Raymond Massey; Lance: Charles Maxwell.

Fearful Courage. After her husband is

killed by a gunman, a woman attempts to return home and readjust to life.

CAST

Louise Brandon: Ida Lupino; Jeb: James Whitmore.

The Setup. Seeking his property, two land barons force Mike Bagley to marry a girl. When the ceremony is completed, he is forced to sign a paper relinquishing the property to her. After a fist beating, Mike is urged to leave or face death by the gun. Returning years following, Mike attempts to regain his property.

CAST

Mary Ann: Phyllis Kirk; Mike Bagley: Steve Forrest.

Hang The Heart High. A woman, discontent with her marriage, attempts to persuade a gunfighter to kill her husband.

CAST

Regan Moore: Barbara Stanwyck; Dix Porter: David Janssen; Regan's husband: Paul Richards.

DICK POWELL'S ZANE GREY THEATRE—30 minutes—CBS—October 10, 1956 - September 19, 1962. Syndicated.

DICK TRACY

Crime Drama. Background: New York City. The investigations of Dick Tracy, a dauntless plainclothes police detective, and his assistant, Sam Catchem.

CAST

Dick Tracy   Ralph Byrd

Sam Catchem   Joe Devlin
Police Chief Murphy   Dick Elliott

DICK TRACY—30 minutes—ABC—September 11, 1950 - April 7, 1951.

On October 12, 1931, Dick Tracy, the brainchild of Chester Gould, made its first appearance in comic strip form. Originally, the strip, submitted to the *Chicago Tribune-New York News* Syndicate, was entitled "Plainclothes Tracy," but was changed when Joseph Patterson, publisher of the *News* ran them as "Dick Tracy," since all cops are called "Dicks."

The popularity of the comics fostered movie interest, and in 1937, the first filmed version appeared, Republic's fifteen-episode serial, *Dick Tracy,* starring Ralph Byrd as Tracy in hot pursuit of the evil Spider. Byrd played Tracy in all but two films. 1939 saw *Dick Tracy's G-Men,* with Tracy pitted against the International Spy, Zarnoff. Two years later, 1941, the final Dick Tracy serial appeared, *Dick Tracy vs. Crime Incorporated,* with Tracy in battle against the evil Ghost.

In 1945, R.K.O. Pictures starred Morgan Conway as Tracy in two of four full-length features, *Dick Tracy* and *Dick Tracy vs. Cueball.* Ralph Byrd replaced Morgan for the remaining two, *Dick Tracy's Dilemma* and *Dick Tracy Meets Gruesome.*

1950-1951 saw the half-hour filmed television series, "Dick Tracy."

On August 18, 1952, Ralph Byrd's death ended the legend of a live Dick Tracy.

In 1961, U.P.A. Pictures distributed a syndicated version, "The Dick Tracy Show," an animated series of five-minute films designed to include a local market host acting as the Chief.

Characters:

Law Enforcers: Dick Tracy; Hemlock Holmes; The Retouchables Squad; Joe Jitsu; Speedy Gonzolez; and Heap O'Calorie.

Criminals: Sketch Paree and the Mole; Prune Face and Itchy; Flattop and Bee Bee Eyes; Stooge Villa and Mumbles; The Brow and Oodles.

Voices: Everett Sloane (Tracy), Mel Blanc, Benny Rubin, Paul Frees.

The sixth and latest version became, again in animation, a part of "Archie's TV Funnies." See title: "The Archie Show."

The **Dick Van Dyke Show.** Left to right: Mary Tyler Moore, Dick Van Dyke, and Larry Matthews.

THE DICK VAN DYKE SHOW

Comedy. Background: 485 Bonnie Meadow Road, New Rochelle, New York, the residence of the Petric family; Rob, the head writer of "The Alan Brady Show"; his wife, Laura; and their son, Richie. Stories relate the incidents that befall and complicate his life, and the lives of his friends and family.

Recurring story line: incidents in the lives of Rob and Laura before and shortly after their marriage. Flashbacks are used and first show Rob Petrie, a sergeant in the U.S. Army, and Laura Meeker (also referred to as Laura Mean), a dancer in a U.S.O. show, meeting when the show arrives at the Camp Crowder Base in Joplin, Missouri.

Later episodes relate the comical escapades of their courtship, marriage, and struggles as newlyweds in Ohio. The final sequence of flashbacks focus on Rob's securing employment as the head writer for "The Alan Brady Show"; the Petries move from Ohio to New Rochelle; the birth of their son, Richie; and Rob's hectic first days as a comedy writer.

CAST

Rob Petrie	Dick Van Dyke
Laura Petrie	Mary Tyler Moore
Buddy Sorrell, Rob's co-worker	Morey Amsterdam
Sally Rogers, Rob's co-worker	Rose Marie
Millie Helper, the Petrie's neighbor	Ann Morgan Guilbert
Jerry Helper, her husband, a dentist	Jerry Paris
Mel Cooley, the producer	Richard Deacon
Alan Brady, the neurotic star	Carl Reiner
Richie Petrie	Larry Matthews
Pickles Sorrell, Buddy's wife, former showgirl, Pickles Conway	Joan Shawlee

Freddie Helper, Millie and
    Jerry's son   Peter Oliphant
                     David Fresco

Sam Petrie, Rob's
    father   Tom Tully
                  J. Pat O'Malley

Clara Petrie, his
    wife   Isabel Randolph

Ben Meehan, Laura's
    father   Carl Benton Reid

Mrs. Meehan, his
    wife   Geraldine Wall

Herman Gilmcher, Sally's
    mother-dominated boy
    friend   Bill Idelson

Stacy Petrie, Rob's
    brother   Jerry Van Dyke

Music: Earl Hagen.

THE DICK VAN DYKE SHOW—30 minutes—CBS—October 3, 1961 - September 7, 1966. Syndicated.

DINAH SHORE

Listed: The television programs of singer-actress Dinah Shore.

The Dinah Shore Chevy Show—Musical Variety—15 minutes—NBC—1950 - 1954. Also called: "The Dinah Shore Show."

Hostess: Dinah Shore.

Regulars: The Notables, The Skylarks.

Announcer: Art Baker.

Orchestra: Vic Schoen; Harry Zimmerman.

The Dinah Shore Show—Musical Variety—30 minutes—NBC—1954 - 1956.

Hostess: Dinah Shore.

Featured: The Skylarks (Gilda Maiken, Jackie Joslin, Earl Brown, Joe Hamilton, George Becker).

Announcer: Art Baker.

Orchestra: Harry Zimmerman.

The Dinah Shore Show—Musical Variety—60 minutes—NBC—1956 - 1962.

Hostess: Dinah Shore.

Featured: The Tony Charmoli Dancers.

Orchestra: Harry Zimmerman; David Rose; Frank DeVol.

Dinah's Place—Variety—30 minutes—NBC—August 3, 1970 - July 26, 1974.

Format: An informal gathering of guests, lively talk, fashion, cooking, songs, decorating ideas, health, and beauty tips.

Hostess: Dinah Shore.

Regulars: Jerry Baker, gardening; Carol Board, sewing; Carol Owen, nutrition; Mary Ann Ryan, shopping advice; David Horowitz, auto advice; Bill Toomey, health; Merle Ellis, food.

Frequently appearing: Karen Valentine, beauty tips and advice; Lyle Waggoner, home decorating.

Music: The John Rodby Group.

Dinah—Variety—90 and 60 minutes versions (depending on individual local stations)—Syndicated 1974.

Hostess: Dinah Shore.

Music: The John Rodby Group.

DINAH'S PLACE

See title: "Dinah Shore."

DING DONG SCHOOL

Educational. Preschool instruction.

Art, finger painting, and games.

Hostess-Instructress: Dr. Frances Horwich (Miss Frances).

Organist: Helen Morton.

Versions:
NBC—60 minutes—November 24, 1952 - December 28, 1956.

Syndicated—30 minutes—1959.

DIRTY SALLY

Western Comedy. Era: The 1880s. Sally Fergus, a ragged, tough, gray-haired, redeye drinkin', tobacco chewin' collector of prairie junk, and Cyrus Pike, an ornery young outlaw, a former ex-gunfighter regarded as the son she never had, join forces and become traveling companions destined for the gold fields of California. Stories relate one aspect of their journey—their attempts to assist the distressed.

CAST
Sally Fergus   Jeanette Nolan
Cyrus Pike   Dack Rambo
Sally's mule: Worthless.

Music: John Parker.

DIRTY SALLY—30 minutes—CBS—January 11, 1974 - July 19, 1974.

THE DISCOPHONIC SCENE

Musical Variety. Performances by Rock personalities.
Host: Jerry Blavat, "America's teen-age music idol."

THE DISCOPHONIC SCENE—60 minutes—Syndicated 1966.

DISCOVERY

Educational. Explored: Various cultures and events of the world. Purpose: To familiarize children with an appreciation of history through filmed observations.
Hosts: Virginia Gibson; Frank Buxton; Bill Owen.

DISCOVERY—30 minutes—ABC—September 8, 1963 - September 5, 1971.

DISNEYLAND

See title: "Walt Disney's Wonderful World of Color."

DIVER DAN

Children's Adventure. Live action with marionettes. "He walks among creatures of frightening features, that's where you'll find Diver Dan. . . ." Background: The Sargasso Sea. The exploits of Diver Dan, a fearless explorer. Stories relate his efforts to aid the good fish and protect their watery domain from the rule of the evil Baron—a barracuda who is bent on controlling life amid King Neptune's world.

Characters: Diver Dan; Miss Minerva, the Mermaid; Baron Barracuda; Trigger Fish, the Baron's striped accomplice; Finley Haddock; Skipper Kipper; Scout Fish, reminiscent of an Indian—complete with tomahawk and feather; Killer Squid; Saw Fish Sam; Goldie the Goldfish; Hermit the Crab; Georgie Porgy; Gill-Espie, the bongo beating beatnick fish.

DIVER DAN—07 minutes—Syndicated 1961.

DIVORCE COURT

Drama. Staged courtroom sessions of divorce hearings.

Judge: Voltaire Perkins.

Announcer/Commentator: Bill Walsh.

DIVORCE COURT—30 minutes—Syndicated 1957.

DIVORCE HEARING

Drama. Staged courtroom sessions of divorce hearings.

Host: Dr. Paul Popenoe.

DIVORCE HEARING—30 minutes—Syndicated 1958.

DOBIE GILLIS

See title: "The Many Loves of Dobie Gillis."

DOC

Comedy. Background: New York City. The trials and tribulations of Dr. Joe Bogert, a general practitioner who lives in a rundown neighborhood and strives to treat his patients like human beings.

CAST
Dr. Joe Bogert	Barnard Hughes
Annie Bogert, his wife	Elizabeth Wilson
Beatrice Tully, his nurse	Mary Wickes
Happy Miller, Joe's friend	Irwin Corey
Laurie Fenner, Joe's married daughter	Judy Kahan
Fred Fenner, Laurie's husband	John Harkins
Mr. Goldman, a patient of Doc's	Herbie Faye

Music: Pat Williams.

DOC—30 minutes—CBS—Premiered: September 13, 1975.

DOC CORKLE

Comedy. The misadventures of Doc Corkle, a neighborhood dentist.

CAST
Doc Corkle	Eddie Mayehoff
Pop Corkle	Chester Conklin
Doc's Daughter	Connie Marshall

Also: Arnold Stang, Hope Emerson.

DOC CORKLE—30 minutes—NBC—October 5, 1952 - October 26, 1952.

DOC ELLIOT

Medical Drama. Benjamin R. Elliot, M.D., rejecting a lack of personal involvement and caring, resigns his position on the staff of Bellevue Hospital, New York, and retreats to the backwoods of Southern Colorado. There, in the Alora Valley, he is the only available doctor. Armed with a medically equipped camper and a citizens' band radio, he attempts to treat the inhabitants, who are suspicious of modern medicine and modern medical technology. Slowly, he wins acceptance by them.

CAST

Dr. Benjamin
　　Elliot　　　　　James Franciscus
Barney Weeks, the owner/
　　operator of the general
　　store　　　　　Noah Beery, Jr.
Margaret "Mags" Brimble,
　　Ben's landlady　　Neva Patterson
Eldred McCoy, a bush pilot
　　who assists Ben in
　　emergencies　　　　Bo Hopkins

Music: Earle Hagen.

DOC ELLIOT—60 minutes—ABC—October 10, 1973 - August 14, 1974.

THE DOCTOR

Anthology. Dramatizations of people confronted with mentally disturbing situtions.

Host-Narrator: Warner Anderson.

Included:

Song For A Banker. When his future son-in-law wants to invest heavily in a music publishing company, a banker seeks to prove it a fraud.

CAST

Roland Young, Henry Jones, Isobel Elsom.

Googan. The story of a baseball manager who is helped to improve his team by the advice of his son's imaginary friend.

CAST

Ernest Truex, Virginia Gilmore, Thomas Coley.

The World Of Nancy Clark. The story of a young girl who attempts to prevent the marriage of her governess.

CAST

Lydia Reed, Rosemary Harris.

THE DOCTOR—30 minutes—NBC—1952-1953. Syndicated title (1956): "The Visitor."

DOCTOR CHRISTIAN

Medical Drama. Background: The town of Rivers End. After Dr. Paul Christian retires, his nephew, Dr. Mark Christian, assumes control of his practice. Stories relate the infinite problems faced by a doctor in a small town. Based on the radio program.

CAST

Dr. Mark Christian　　Macdonald Carey
Dr. Paul Christian　　　Jean Hersholt
Nurses　　　　　　　　Jan Shepard
　　　　　　　　　　　Cynthia Baer
　　　　　　　　　　　Kay Faylen

DOCTOR CHRISTIAN—30 minutes—Syndicated 1956.

DOCTOR DOLITTLE

Animated Cartoon. The world travels of Dr. Dolittle, a veterinarian who possesses the ability to talk to and understand animals. Stories relate his attempts to overcome the evils of Sam Scurvy, a fiend bent on learning his secrets to control animals for purposes of world domain. Based on the stories by Hugh Lofting.

Additional characters: Tommy Stubbins, Dolittle's assistant; Dum Dum, his pet duck; Chee Chee, his pet monkey; and

Cyclops and Featherhead, Scurvy's cohorts.

Voices: Lennie Weinrib, Hal Smith, Barbara Towers, Robert Holt.

Music: Arthur Leonardi, Doug Goodwin, Eric Rogers.

DOCTOR DOLITTLE—30 minutes—NBC—September 12, 1970 - September 2, 1972. Syndicated.

DOCTOR FU MANCHU

See title: "The Adventures of Fu Manchu."

DOCTOR HUDSON'S SECRET JOURNAL

Medical Drama. Background: Center Hospital. The problems faced by Dr. Wayne Hudson, neurosurgeon, in the pioneering of new methods of treatment.

CAST
Dr. Wayne Hudson	John Howard
Nurses	Jean Howel
	Frances Mercer

DOCTOR HUDSON'S SECRET JOURNAL—30 minutes—Syndicated 1955.

DOCTOR IN THE HOUSE

Comedy. Background: Saint Swithin's Teaching Hospital in London, England. The struggles and misadventures of seven young medical students. In later episodes: Of young doctors seeking to establish a practice. Based on the "Doctor" books by Richard Gordon. Produced by London Weekend Television.

CAST
Michael Upton, intern	Barry Evans
Geoffrey Loftus, Professor of Surgery	Ernest Clark
Duncan Waring, intern	Robin Newdell
Paul Collier, intern	George Layton
Huw Evans, intern	Martin Shaw
Dick Stuart-Clark, intern	Geoffrey Davis
Danny Wholey, intern	Jonathan Lynn
Dave Briddock, intern and part-time photographer	Simon Cuff
Helga, his live-in model	Yvette Stengaard
The Dean	Ralph Michael
Mr. Upton, Michael's father	Peter Brathurst
Mrs. Loftus, the Professor's wife	Joan Benham
Valerie Loftus, their daughter	Lynn Dalby

Music: Recorded.

DOCTOR IN THE HOUSE—30 minutes—Syndicated 1971.

DOCTOR I.Q.

Game. A contestant is chosen from the studio audience. Dr. I.Q., the mental banker, asks him a question. If he correctly answers it he receives twenty silver dollars, plus a chance to earn additional silver dollars via a continuation of the question-answer rounds. The contestant plays until he is defeated by an incorrect response.

Hosts (Dr. I.Q.s): James McLain; Jay Owen; Tom Kennedy.

Assistants: Mimi Walters, Kay Christopher, Tom Reddy, Ed

Michaels, Art Fleming, George Ansboro.

DOCTOR I.Q.—30 minutes—ABC—November 4, 1953 - January 7, 1954; January 15, 1958 - March 23, 1959.

DOCTOR JOYCE BROTHERS

Listed: The television programs of psychologist Dr. Joyce Brothers.

Format: An informal look into the world of modern psychology; discussions on the problems confronting many in terms that are understandable to the layman.

Dr. Joyce Brothers—Advice—30 minutes—Local New York (WRCA-TV)—1958.

Hostess: Dr. Joyce Brothers.

Consult Dr. Brothers—Advice—30 minutes—Syndicated 1961.

Hostess: Dr. Joyce Brothers.

Tell Me, Dr. Brothers—Advice—30 minutes—Syndicated 1964.

Hostess: Dr. Joyce Brothers.

Appointment With Dr. Brothers—Advice—05 minutes—Syndicated 1969.

Hostess: Dr. Joyce Brothers.

Living Easy—Variety—30 minutes—Syndicated 1973. Guests, interviews, fashion, cooking, decorating tips, music, and songs.

Hostess: Dr. Joyce Brothers.

Announcer: Mike Darrow.

Orchestra: Bernie Green.

DOCTOR KILDARE

Medical Drama. Background: Blair General Hospital. The experiences, struggles, defeats, and victories of a young intern (later resident physician), James Kildare.

CAST

Dr. James Kildare	Richard Chamberlain
Dr. Leonard Gillespie, his mentor	Raymond Massey
Nurse Zoe Lawton	Lee Kurtz
Mrs. Salt	Cynthia Stone
Dr. Gerson	Jud Taylor
Dr. Lowry	Steven Bell
Dr. Agurski	Eddie Ryder
Dr. Kapish	Ken Berry
Nurse Conant	Jo Helton

Music: Jerry Goldsmith; Pete Rugolo; Harry Sukman.

DOCTOR KILDARE—60 minutes—NBC—September 27, 1961 - September 9, 1965. 30 minutes—NBC—September 13, 1965 - August 29, 1966. Syndicated.

Doctor Kildare. Richard Chamberlain and Raymond Massey.

THE DOCTORS

Serial. Background: Hope Memorial Hospital. The conflicts and tensions, the working and personal lives of doctors and nurses. Originally, it was an anthology series dramatizing medical cases in thirty-minute segments. Nine months later, the program was revamped and became a serial.

Original Cast (Alternating Daily)

Dr. Jerry Chandler	Richard Roat
Dr. Elizabeth Hayes	Margot Moses
Dr. William Scott	Jack Gaynor
Rev. Samuel Shafter, the hospital chaplin	Fred J. Scollay

Serial Cast

Dr. Matt Powers	James Pritchett
Brock Hayden	Adam Kennedy
Dr. Maggie Fielding	Bethel Leslie
	Kathleen Murray
	Ann Williams
	Lydia Bruce
Nora Hansen	Joan Alexander
Jackie	Louise Lasser
Mr. Fielding	Fred Stewart
Steve	Craig Huebing
Dr. Althea Davis	Elizabeth Hubbard
	Virginia Vestoff
Kate	Ellen MacRae
Jessie	Joselyn Somers
Willard	Court Benson
Peter Bonds	Gerald S. O'Loughlin
Gloria	Nancy Berg
Nurse Kathy Ryker	Nancy Barrett
	Holly Peters
Dr. Mike Powers	Peter Burnell
Nurse Carolee Simpson	Carolee Campbell
Dr. Hank Iverson	Palmer Deane
Dr. Nick Bellini	Gerald Gordon
Martha Allen	Sally Gracie
Dr. John Morrison	Patrick Horgan
Dr. Vito McCray	Paul Itkin
Dr. Karen Werner	Laryssa Lauret
Dr. Steve Aldrich	David O'Brien
Ginny	Greta Rae
Emma Simpson	Katherine Squire
Toni Ferra	Anna Stuart
Dr. John Rice	Terry Kiser
Dr. Bill Winters	James Noble
Mrs. Winters	Ann Whiteside
Kate Harris	Denise Nickerson
Dr. Ann Larimer	Geraldine Court
Margo Stewart	Mary Denham
Dr. Alan Stewart	Gil Gerard
Eric Aldrich	Keith Blanchard
Lauri James	Marie Thomas
Dr. Gil Lawford	Dale Robinette
Nurse	Susan Adams
Kurt Van Olsen	Byron Sanders
Simon Gross	Luis Van Rooten
Nurse Brown	Dorothy Blackburn
Keith Wilson	Morgan Sterne
Penny Davis	Julia Duffy
Anna Ford	Zaida Coles
Ed Stark	Conrad Roberts
Dr. Simon Harris	Mel Winkler
Mr. Stark	P. Jay Sidney
Mrs. Stark	Clarissa Gaylor
Dr. Powers Son	Rex Thompson
	Harry Packwood
	Robert La Tourne
	Peter Burnell
Ma Thatcher	Madeleine Sherwood
Pa Thatcher	John Cullum
Dr. George Mitchell	Staats Cotsworth
Nora Harper	Muriel Kirkland
Margaret Liggett	Jean Sullivan
Mrs. Murtrie	Ruth McDevitt
Judy Stratton	Joanna Pettet
Dr. Johnny McGill	Scott Graham
Billy Allison	Bobby Hennessey
Dr. DeSales	Thomas Connolloy
Greta Powers	Jennifer Houlton
	Eileen Kearney
Shana Golan	Marta Heflin
Jody Lee Bronson	C.C. Courtney
Dr. Nancy Bennett	Nancy Donahue
Mona Aldrich	Meg Mundy
Liz Wilson	Pamela Toll
Theodora Rostand	Clarice Blackburn

Also: Nancy Fox, Ed Kemmer, Katherine Meskill, Court Benson, Robert Gentry, Angus Duncan.

Music: John Geller.

THE DOCTORS—30 minutes—NBC—Premiered: April 1, 1963.

THE DOCTORS AND THE NURSES

See title: "The Nurses."

DOCTORS HOSPITAL

Medical Drama. Life in the neurological wing of Lowell Memorial Hospital as seen through the eyes of Jake Goodwin, the chief neurosurgeon.

CAST

Dr. Jake Goodwin	George Peppard
Dr. Norah Purcell	Zohra Lampert
Dr. Felipe Ortega	Victor Campos
Dr. Jonas Varga	Albert Paulsen

Music: Don Ellis.

DOCTORS HOSPITAL—60 minutes—NBC—Premiered: September 10, 1975.

DOCTOR'S HOUSE CALL

Medical Advice.

Host: Dr. James Fox, specialist in internal and occupational medicine.

DOCTOR'S HOUSE CALL—05 minutes—Syndicated 1965.

DOCTOR SIMON LOCKE

Medical Drama. Background: Dixon Mills, Canada. Andrew Sellers, an aging doctor unable to properly care for his patients, places an ad for assistance in the medical journal. Simon Locke, a young doctor disgusted with his lucrative but unrewarding city practice, responds. Stories relate their attempts to assist the people of a poor community.

CAST

Dr. Simon Locke	Sam Groom
Dr. Andrew Sellers	Jack Albertson
Nurse Louise Wynn	Nuala Fitzgerald
Police Chief Dan Palmer	Len Birman

Music: Score Productions.

DOCTOR SIMON LOCKE—30 minutes—Syndicated 1971. Spin-off series: "Police Surgeon" (see title).

DOCTOR SPOCK

Discussion. Two sets of patients discuss topics relating to children.

Host: Dr. Benjamin Spock, pediatrician.

DOCTOR SPOCK—30 minutes—NBC 1955.

DOCTOR WHO

Science Fiction Serial. The adventures of Dr. Who, scientist, the inventor of Tardis (Time And Relative Dimension In Space), a time machine that is capable of transporting him to any time or any place in the past or future or to any planet in the endless heavens. Episodes relate his battle against the sinister forces of evil. Created by Terry Nation. Produced by the B.B.C. Theatrical versions, culled from the serial: *Dr. Who and the Daleks* (1965); and *Invasion Earth, 2150 A.D.* (1966).

CAST

Dr. Who	Peter Cushing
	Jon Pertwee
Barbara, his niece	Jennie Linden
Susan, his granddaughter	Roberta Tovey
Tom	Bernard Cribbins
Ian	Roy Castle

Also: Andrew Keir, Barrie Ingham, Geoffrey Toone.

Music: Bill McGuffie; Barry Gray; Malcolm Lockyear.

DOCTOR WHO—30 minutes—Syndicated (U.S.) 1973.

DODO—THE KID FROM OUTER SPACE

Animated Cartoon. Dodo, an inhabitant of the atomic planet Hena Hydo, and his pet, Compy, are dispatched to Earth to assist Professor Fingers with his research. Stories relate their attempts to resolve scientific mysteries.

DODO—THE KID FROM OUTER SPACE—30 minutes—Syndicated 1967.

DO IT YOURSELF

Home repairs and maintenance. Comical and serious treatment is given to do-it-yourself projects.

Hosts: Dave Willock, Cliff Arquette.

Assistants: Mary McAdoo, Steve Woolton.

DO IT YOURSELF—30 minutes—NBC—June 26, 1955 - September 18, 1955.

DOLLAR A SECOND

Game. A humiliating stunt is announced at the beginning of the program. A contestant, chosen from the studio audience, competes in a series of rapid-fire general knowledge question-answer rounds. The player receives one dollar a second for each second of correct responses. He continues upon his own discretion and stops when he feels safe. However, if the announcer should interrupt the proceedings, and the player has not stopped, he loses all his accumulated money. The player then receives a chance to earn money by performing the stunt that was announced at the beginning of the program.

A ticking clock is set to establish a specific amount of money. The contestant then performs the stunt. For each second that the clock ticks before the player completes the stunt, one dollar is deducted from the established amount. His final cash prize depends on his swiftness in performing the stunt.

Host: Jan Murray.

Assistants: Patricia White, Bernard Martin, Stuart Mann.

Announcers: Ken Roberts, Terry O'Sullivan.

DOLLAR A SECOND—30 minutes—DuMont—September 20, 1953 - September 1954; ABC—October 1, 1954 - August 31, 1956.

THE DOM DeLUISE SHOW

Variety. Music, songs, and comedy sketches.

Host: Dom DeLuise.

Regulars: Peggy March, Carol Arthur, Paul Dooley, Dick Lynn, Bill McCutcheon, Marian Mercer, The Gentry Brothers, The June Taylor Dancers.

Announcer: Johnny Olsen.

Orchestra: Sammy Spear.

THE DOM DeLUISE SHOW—60 minutes—CBS—June 1968 - September 18, 1968.

THE DON ADAMS SCREEN TEST

Game. One contestant, chosen from three finalists, receives the opportunity to star in a screen test. The contestant is brought on stage where he meets his celebrity partner and views a scene from a film that he and his partner must reenact. The actors are then sent to makeup where they are permitted to study their scripts and review the film clip. After a commercial break, the outtakes (mistakes) of the contestant's screen test are seen. A second round, played in the same manner, but involving different contestants and a different film reenactment, follows. At the end of the second screen test, the final, edited versions of both tests are seen. A guest producer or director then selects the contestant he feels was best. His decision awards the amateur a part in a movie or television series.

The Donald O'Connor Show. Host Donald O'Connor and guest Shari Lewis.

Host-Director of the Screen Tests: Don Adams.

Announcer: Dick Tufel.

Music: Hal Mooney.

THE DON ADAMS SCREEN TEST— 30 minutes—Syndicated 1975.

DONALD O'CONNOR

Listed: The television programs of actor Donald O'Connor.

The Donald O'Connor Show—Musical Variety—60 minutes—NBC—1951.

Host: Donald O'Connor.

Regulars: Sid Miller, Walter Catlett, The Unger Twins.

Orchestra: Al Goodman.

The Donald O'Connor Show—Musical Variety—30 minutes—NBC—October 9, 1954 - September 10, 1955.

Host: Donald O'Connor.

Regulars: Sid Miller, Regina Gleason, Jan Arvan, Joyce Smight, Laurette Luez, Nestor Paiva, Olan Soule, Chief Santini, Phil Garris, Fritz Fields, Joyce Holden, Marcia Moe, Eilene Janssen.

Orchestra: Al Goodman.

The Donald O'Connor Show—Talk-Variety—90 minutes—Syndicated 1968.

Host: Donald O'Connor.

Announcer: Joyce Jameson.

Orchestra: Alan Copeland.

THE DON AMECHE THEATRE

Anthology. Rebroadcasts of dramas that were originally aired via other filmed anthology programs.

Host: Don Ameche.

Included:

Trapped. A wife and her money-hungry lover attempt to murder her shrewd husband.

CAST
Dan O'Herlihy, Jerry Hayas.

Across The Dust. Though feeling incapable, a frontier scout attempts to lead a wagon train to California.

Starring: Lloyd Nolan.

Hour Of Truth. A bullfighter attempts to regain his reputation after a serious goring.

Starring: Ricardo Montalban.

THE DON AMECHE THEATRE—30 minutes—Syndicated 1958.

DON KIRSHNER'S ROCK CONCERT

Variety. Performances by Rock personalities.

Host: Don Kirshner.

DON KIRSHNER'S ROCK CONCERT—90 minutes—Syndicated 1973.

THE DON KNOTTS SHOW

Variety. Various comedy sketches.
Host: Don Knotts.
Regulars: Elaine Joyce, John Dehner, Gary Burghoff, Eddy Carroll, Kenneth Mars, Mickey Deems, Frank Welker, Bob Williams, and his dog, Louis.

Announcer: Dick Tufel.

Orchestra: Nick Perito.

THE DON KNOTTS SHOW—60 minutes—NBC—September 15, 1970 - July 6, 1971.

DON McNEILL'S TV CLUB

Variety. Music, comedy, songs, and conversation. Broadcast from the Terrace Casino of the Hotel Motel in Chicago. Based on the radio program: "Breakfast Club."

Host: Don McNeill.

Regulars: Fran Allison (Aunt Fanny), Johnny Desmond, Sam Cowling, Eileen Parker, Patsy Lee, Cliff Peterson, Jack Owen.

Announcer: Ken Nordine.

Orchestra: Eddie Ballantine.

DON McNEILL'S TV CLUB—60 minutes—ABC—September 5, 1950 - December 19, 1951; February 22, 1954 - February 25, 1955.

DON MESSER'S JUBILEE

Musical Variety. Performances by Country and Western entertainers.

Host: Don Messer.

Regulars: Don Tremaine, Mary Osburne, Charlie Chamberlain.

DON MESSER'S JUBILEE—30 minutes—Syndicated 1960. Produced in Canada.

THE DONNA REED SHOW

Comedy. Background: The town of Hilldale. The dreams, ambitions, and frustrations of the Stone family: Alex, a pediatrician; his wife, Donna; and their children, Mary and Jeff. Trisha, their unofficially adopted daughter, appears in later episodes. An orphan, she follows them home from a picnic. Through an arrangement with her uncle-guardian, she is permitted to remain with the Stones.

CAST

Donna Stone	Donna Reed
Alex Stone	Carl Betz
Mary Stone	Shelley Fabares
Jeff Stone	Paul Peterson
Midge Kelsey, Donna's friend	Ann McCrea
Dr. David Kelsey, her husband	Bob Crane
Smitty, Jeff's friend	Darryl Richard
Herbie Bailey, Mary's boyfriend (early eipisodes)	Tommy Ivo
Scotty Simpson, Mary's boyfriend (later episodes)	Jerry Hawkins
Karen, Jeff's girlfriend	Janet Languard
Bibi, Jeff's girlfriend	Candy Moore
Susanna, Smitty's girlfriend	Sandy Descher
Trisha	Patty Peterson

THE DONNA REED SHOW—30 minutes—ABC—September 24, 1958 - September 3, 1966. Syndicated.

The Donna Reed Show. Bottom, left: Patty Peterson, Carl Betz. Top, left: Donna Reed, right: Paul Peterson. © *Screen Gems*.

DON QUIXOTE

Adventure. Background: Seventeenth-century Spain. Believing himself to be the knight errant described in books of chivalry, Don Quixote, a gaunt country gentleman of La Mancha, teams with his friend, Sancho Panza, and undertakes a crusade to defend the oppressed, avenge the injured, and capture the heart of his beloved Dulcinea. Based on the novel by Cervantes.

CAST

Don Quixote	Josef Meinrad
Sancho Panza	Roger Carrel
Dulcinea	Maria Saavedra

DON QUIXOTE—30 minutes—Syndicated 1965.

DON RICKLES

Listed: The television programs of insult comedian Don Rickles.

The Don Rickles Show—Variety—30

minutes—ABC—September 27, 1968 - January 31, 1969.

Format: Guests, interviews and comedy sketches.

Host: Don Rickles.

Announcer: Pat McCormick.

Orchestra: Vic Mizzy.

The Don Rickles Show—Comedy—30 minutes—CBS—January 14, 1972 - May 26, 1972.

Background: Great Neck, Long Island, New York, the residence of the Robinson family — Don, an account executive with the advertising firm of Kingston, Cohen, and Vanderpool; his wife, Barbara, and their daughter, Janie. Stories depict the harassed life of Don Robinson, a man at odds with all and struggling to survive the red tape and the mechanizations of a computerized society.

CAST

Don Robinson	Don Rickles
Barbara Robinson	Louise Sorel
Janie Robinson	Erin Moran
Tyler Benedict, Don's friend, neighbor, co-worker	Robert Hogan
Jean Benedict, his wife	Joyce Van Patten
Audrey, Don's secretary	Judy Cassmore
Conrad Musk, the agency's hip advertising man	Barry Gordon
Arthur Kingston, Don's employer	Edward Andrews
	M. Emmet Walsh
Mr. Vanderpool, Don's employer	Parley Baer

DON'S MUSICAL PLAYHOUSE

Musical Comedy. Background: A sum-

mer theatre. The lives and struggles of the performers.

Host: Don Ameche.

Regulars: Dorothy Greener, Betty Brewer, The June Graham Dancers, The Don Craig Chorus, The Charles Faler Dancers, The Myer Rappaport Chorus.

Orchestra: Bernie Green.

DON'S MUSICAL PLAYHOUSE—30 minutes—ABC—July 5, 1951 - September 1951. Also known as "The Don Ameche Show."

DON'T CALL ME CHARLIE

Comedy. Background: Paris, France, a United States Army Veterinary post under the command of Colonel Charles Baker, a man who fraternizes with the troops, but detests being called "Charlie." Stories relate the misadventures of Private Judson McKay, a simple, backwoods Iowa veterinarian who refuses to let the sophistication of Europe or the attempts of his fellow officers change his square but innocent ways.

CAST

Private Judson McKay	Josh Peine
Colonel U. Charles Baker	John Hubbard
First Sergeant Wozniah	Cully Richard
Patricia Perry, the general's secretary	Linda Lawson
General Steele	Alan Napier
Corporal Lefkowitz	Artie Johnson
Selma Yassarian, a secretary	Louise Glenn
Madame Fatime, the landlady	Penny Santon

DON'T CALL ME CHARLIE—30 minutes—NBC—September 28, 1962 - January 25, 1963.

THE DOODLES WEAVER SHOW

Variety. Music, songs, dances, and comedy sketches.

Host: Doodles Weaver.

Regulars: Lois Weaver (Mrs.), Rex Marshall, Peanuts Mann, Dick Dana, Mariam Colby.

Announcer: Rex Marshall.

Orchestra: Milton DeLugg.

THE DOODLES WEAVER SHOW— 30 minutes—NBC—June 9, 1951 - September 1951.

DOORWAY TO DANGER

Adventure. The U.S. government's battle against international intrigue as seen through the secret missions of undercover agents.

CAST
John Randolph, the chief	Roland Winters
Agent Doug Carter	Stacy Harris

Announcer: Ernest Chapell.

DOORWAY TO DANGER—30 minutes—NBC—July 4, 1952 - October 1, 1953.

THE DOOR WITH NO NAME

Spy Drama. Background: Washington, D.C. Dramatizations based on the secret activities of The Door With No Name, an unidentified portal through which presumably pass the most intrepid of spies and spy fighters.

CAST
The Intelligence Chief	Mel Ruick
The Undercover Agent	Grant Richards

Narrator: Westbrook Van Voorhis.

Music: Charles Paul.

THE DOOR WITH NO NAME—30 minutes—NBC—July 6, 1951 - September 1951.

THE DORIS DAY SHOW

Comedy. Distinguished by four formats.

Format One: September 24, 1968 — September 16, 1969.

Background: Mill Valley, California. Dissatisfied with the congestion of the big city, Doris Martin, widow and mother of two children, relinquishes her career as a singer and returns to her father's ranch. Stories depict her attempts to raise her children, Billie and Toby, and her involvement in local community affairs.

The Doris Day Show. Doris Day.

Format Two: September 22, 1969 - September 7, 1970.

Feeling a need to assist with the growing expenses on the ranch, Doris acquires a job in San Francisco as the executive secretary to Michael Nicholson, the editor of *Today's World Magazine.* Episodes relate her home and working life.

Format Three: September 14, 1970 - September 6, 1971.

With occasional reporting assignments and difficulty commuting from country to city, Doris relocates and rents apartment 207 at 965 North Parkway over Pallucci's Italian Restaurant. Her children reside with her; and her father, Buck Webb, and his handyman, Leroy B. Simpson, continue to operate the ranch.

Format Four: September 13, 1971 - September 3, 1973.

A complete change in format and cast. Background: San Francisco, California. The working and romantic life of a beautiful young bachelorette, Doris Martin, General News Reporter for *Today's World Magazine.*

CAST
September 24, 1968 - September 6, 1971 (formats one, two, and three).

Doris Martin	Doris Day
Buck Webb	Denver Pyle
Billy Martin	Philip Brown
Toby Martin	Tod Starke
Leroy B. Simpson	James Hampton
Aggie, their housekeeper (early episodes)	Fran Ryan
Juanita, their housekeeper (later episodes)	Naomi Stevens
Michael Nicholson	McLean Stevenson
Ron Harvey, the associate editor	Paul Smith
Myrna Gibbons, his secretary	Rose Marie

Willard Jarvis, Doris's perfectionist neighbor	Billy DeWolfe
Angie Pallucci, the owner of the restaurant; Doris's landlady	Kaye Ballard
Louie Pallucci, her husband	Bernie Kopell
Colonel Fairburn, the publisher of *Today's World Magazine*	Edward Andrews
Ethel, Billy and Toby's babysitter	Carol Worthington
Duke Farentino, Doris' friend, a boxer	Larry Storch

Martin family sheep dog: Lord Nelson.

Music: Jimmie Haskel.

CAST
September 13, 1971 - September 4, 1972 (first year of format four).

Doris Martin (Miss)	Doris Day
Cyril Bennett, the editor of *Today's World Magazine*	John Dehner
Jackie Parker, his secretary	Jackie Joseph
Willard Jarvis	Billy DeWolfe
Angie Pallucci	Kaye Ballard
Louie Pallucci	Bernie Kopell
Dr. Peter Lawrence, Doris's romantic interest	Peter Lawford

Music: Jimmie Haskell.

CAST
September 11, 1972 - September 3, 1973 (final year of format four).

Doris Martin (Miss)	Doris Day
Cyril Bennett	John Dehner
Jackie Parker	Jackie Joseph
Jonathan Rusk, Doris's romantic interest, a foreign correspondent	Patrick O'Neal
Detective Broder, San Francisco Police	

Department   Ken Lynch

Music: Jimmie Haskell.

THE DORIS DAY SHOW—30 minutes—CBS—September 24, 1968 - September 3, 1973.

DOTTO

Game. Two competing contestants. Displayed on a large frame are fifty dots that, when connected, represent a famous person. The host states a general knowledge type of question. The player first to identify himself through a buzzer signal receives a chance to answer. If his answer is correct, a connection is made between two of the dots and he receives a chance to identify the drawing. If he is unable, the game continues. Correct identifications earn players large sums of cash. Contestants compete until defeated by another player.

Host: Jack Narz.

Announcer: Wayne Howell.

DOTTO—30 minutes—CBS—January 6, 1958 - August 15, 1958.

THE DOTTY MACK SHOW

Variety. Pantomimed renditions of hit recordings.

Hostess: Dotty Mack.

Regulars: Bob Braun, Colin Male.

Music: Recorded.

THE DOTTY MACK SHOW—15 minutes—ABC—August 31, 1953 - September 3, 1956.

DOUBLE EXPOSURE

Game. Two competing contestants. Object: The identification of a famous celebrity or event that is hidden under a jigsaw puzzle. Contestants, in turn, choose a puzzle piece that, when removed, reveals a picture part, and a varying amount of cash or a merchandise prize that is placed on his side of a board. If neither player is able to identify it, the game continues. The first player to correctly identify the photograph is the winner and receives the prizes that are on his side of the board.

Host: Steve Dunne.

DOUBLE EXPOSURE—30 minutes—CBS 1961.

THE DOUBLE LIFE OF HENRY PHYFE

Comedy. Background: Washington, D.C. Henry Wadsworth Phyfe, a mild-mannered accountant and the exact double of foreign spy, U-31, is recruited by Central Intelligence to replace the spy, who was killed by a hit-and-run before he was able to reveal vital secrets.

Stories relate Henry's reluctant and fumbling investigations as he struggles to carry out U-31's vital missions.

CAST

Henry Phyfe	Red Buttons
Sub Chief Hannahan	Fred Clark
Judy, Henry's girl-friend	Zeme North
Florence, Henry's land-lady	Marge Redmond
Hamble, Henry's employer	Parley Baer
Sandy, a C.I. Agent	Rob Kilgallen
Larry, a C.I. Agent	Ed Faulkner

Music: Vic Mizzy.

THE DOUBLE LIFE OF HENRY PHYFE—30 minutes—ABC—January 13, 1966 - September 1, 1966.

DOUBLE OR NOTHING

Game. Five contestants, working as a team, start with a specific amount of money. The host questions each on various category topics. Players receive additional cash for each correct response. Incorrect responses deduct the "at stakes" amount from their total. With each correct response players option to either stop or continue and risk. If risking, they may double their money by correctly answering three questions. If they fail, the money is deducted from the team's score. Final cash earnings are divided equally.

Host: Bert Parks.

Assistant: Joan Meinch.

Announcer: Bob Williams.

Orchestra: Ivan Ditmars.

DOUBLE OR NOTHING—30 minutes—CBS 1952.

DOUGH RE MI

Game. Three competing players, who each receive two hundred dollars betting money. Object: To identify song titles after hearing only the first three notes. If players are unable, they bid for the next note. The highest bidder receives it, and a chance to identify the song title. If he correctly guesses the title, he receives the "at stakes" cash. If incorrect, the player is permitted to challenge the remaining players to guess it. If the tune still remains a mystery, bidding begins on the next note. Winners are the highest cash scorers.

Host: Gene Rayburn.

DOUGH RE MI—30 minutes—NBC—February 4, 1958 - December 30, 1960.

DOUGLAS FAIRBANKS JR. PRESENTS

Anthology. Dramatizations of people caught in unusual circumstances.

Host: Douglas Fairbanks, Jr.

Included:

The Refugee. Background: Berlin. A British officer attempts to discover which member of a group of refugees from the Eastern Zone is a Russian spy.

Starring: Dennis O'Dea.

Someone Outside. An artist attempts to avenge the death of his wife; his victim is the fiancée of the doctor who operated on her.

Starring: Maurice Kaufman.

The Man Who Wouldn't Escape. Background: South America. The brother of a ruthless dictator attempts to begin a resistance movement.

CAST
Karel Slephanek, Christopher Lee.

Second Wind. With their daughter about to have a baby, a married couple attempt to overcome their feeling of growing old.

CAST
Michael Shepley, Nora Swimburne.

DOUGLAS FAIRBANKS JR. PRE-
SENTS–30 minutes–NBC–
1953-1957.

THE DOW HOUR OF
GREAT MYSTERIES

Anthology. Dramatizations depicting
the plight of people confronted with
uncertain situations.

Host: Joseph N. Welch.

Included:

The Datchet Diamonds. The story of
Cyril Paxton, a handsome British con
artist who suddenly loses Lady Luck,
his money, and his beautiful fiancée,
Daisy, who has given up on him. The
drama centers on the changes in his
life when he picks up the wrong valise
and discovers he is in possession of
stolen gems–the Datchet Diamonds.

CAST
Cyril Paxton: Rex Harrison; Daisy
Strong: Tammy Grimes; Laurence:
Robert Fleming.

The Bat. The story concerns a series
of mysterious events that occur in a
country house that a woman has
rented for the summer.

CAST
Helen Hayes, Jason Robards, Jr.,
Margaret Hamilton, Bethel Leslie,
Martin Brooks, Shepperd Strudwick.

THE DOW HOUR OF GREAT
MYSTERIES–60 minutes–NBC
1960. Broadcast as a series of specials.

DOWN YOU GO

Game. Four regular panelists compete.

The moderator presents a cryptic clue
representing a popular slogan, quota-
tion, or phrase, which is indicated by
a line of dashes, one per letter, on a
large board. Players, informed of the
mystery expression, receive one free
guess. If the phrase is not identified,
each panelist suggests a letter of the
alphabet. If an incorrect letter is
posed, that player is disqualified from
that round and forfeits five dollars to
the sender (home viewer) of the
phrase.
Moderator: Dr. Bergen Evans.

Panelists: Robert Breer, Fran
Coughlin, Toni Gilmar, Carmelita
Pope.

DOWN YOU GO–30 minutes–ABC–
September 16, 1953 - September 8,
1956.

DO YOU KNOW?

Educational Quiz. Geared to children.
Basis: The testing of knowledge
acquired through the reading of
specific books. After the quiz segment, authors and guest experts discuss the books' contents with the
children.
Host: Bob Maxwell.

DO YOU KNOW?–30 minutes–CBS
–1963-1964.

DO YOU TRUST YOUR WIFE?
WHO DO YOU TRUST?

Game. Married couples, chosen for
their unusual backgrounds, compete.
The host asks each couple two sets of
questions for a total of twelve
hundred dollars. The husband may
either answer them or trust his wife to
do so. The couple correctly answering

the most questions is the winner and receives the additional prize of one hundred dollars a week for a year. Couples compete until defeated, and, if successful long enough, can win one hundred dollars a week for life. Retitled one year following its premiere: "Who Do You Trust?"

Host ("Do You Trust Your Wife?"): Edgar Bergen.

Assistants (Dummies): Charlie McCarthy, Mortimer Snerd, Effie Klinger.

Announcer: Ed Reimers.

Orchestra: Frank DeVol.

Host ("Who Do You Trust?"): Johnny Carson; Woody Woodbury.

Announcer: Del Sharbutt; Ed McMahon.

DO YOU TRUST YOUR WIFE?—30 minutes—CBS—January 3, 1956 - March 26, 1957.
WHO DO YOU TRUST?—30 minutes—ABC—July 14, 1958 - December 23, 1963.

DRAGNET

Crime Drama. Background: Los Angeles, California. The assignments of Police Sergeant Joe Friday. A realistic approach to the battle against crime as undertaken by the Los Angeles Police Department. Based on actual case histories.

CAST
Det. Sgt. Joe Friday
   (Badge: 714)   Jack Webb
Partners:
Detective Sergeant Ben Romero
   (1951)   Barton Yarborough
Sergeant Jacobs
   (1952)   Barney Philips

Officer Frank Smith
   (1952-1959)   Ben Alexander
Officer Bill Gannon
   (1967-1970)   Harry Morgan
Ann Baker, Joe's
   fiancée   Dorothy Abbott
Captain Mack   Byron Morrow
Captain Brown   Art Balinger

Narrator: Jack Webb.

Announcers: George Fenneman; Hal Gibney.

Music: Frank Comstock; Walter Schumann; Nathan S. Scott; Lynn Murray.

Program close: The results of the trials or hearings of the involved criminals are given.

DRAGNET—30 minutes—NBC—December 16, 1951 - September 6, 1959. Syndicated as "Badge 714." Returned: NBC—30 minutes—January 12, 1967 - September 10, 1970. Syndicated.

DRAW ME A LAUGH

Game. An artist draws a cartoon from an idea submitted by a home viewer. Simultaneously, the gag line, but not the cartoon idea, is given to a contestant who must, within a two minute time limit, draw a sketch. A panel of four studio audience members judge the funniest of the two drawings. If the contestant wins, he receives a prize.

Host: Walter Hurley.

Cartoonist: Mel Casson.

DRAW ME A LAUGH—30 minutes—ABC—January 5, 1949 - February 5, 1949.

DRAW TO WIN

Game. Four regular panelists. Object: The identification of persons, names, objects, or slogans based on an artist's sketchings. If, within a specified time limit, the charade remains unidentified, the sender (home viewer) receives cash (twenty-five dollars, maximum).

Host: Henry Morgan.

Panelists: Abner Dean, Bill Halman, Eve Hunter, Sid Hoff.

DRAW TO WIN—30 minutes—CBS—April 22, 1952 - June 10, 1952.

DREAM GIRL OF '67

Beauty Contest. Single girls compete for the title of "Dream Girl of '67." Contestants, twenty per week, are judged on their beauty, charm, and talent.

Stages:
The Daily Dream Girl Competition. Four of the twenty girls are judged daily. Each day, Monday through Thursday, one is selected and crowned "Dream Girl of the Day."

The Weekly Dream Girl Competition. The four daily winners compete in the

Dream Girl of '67. Four contestants in the evening-gown competition and host Dick Stewart.

Friday judging. One is crowned "Dream Girl of the Week."

The Year End Competition. Weekly winners vie for the title of "Dream Girl of '67." Prizes: A trip around the world, a film contract, five thousand dollars in cash, and a new car.

Hosts: Dick Stewart; Wink Martindale; Paul Peterson.

Judges: Guest celebrities.

DREAM GIRL OF '67—30 minutes—ABC—December 19, 1966 - December 29, 1967.

DREAM HOUSE

Game. Three competing husband-and-wife couples vie for their dream house, worth up to forty thousand dollars, and built for them anywhere in the United States.

Rounds:
The Preliminary Round: One couple is to be eliminated. Basis: General knowledge question-answer rounds. The team first to identify themselves by sounding a buzzer receives a chance to answer. If correct, points are awarded. Winners are the two highest scoring couples.

The Championship Round: Rapid-fire question-answer rounds. Winners, the highest scoring couple, receive one room and the chance to compete again and earn additional rooms. Teams compete until defeated ,or until they furnish their dream house by winning seven straight games.

Host: Mike Darrow.

Announcer: Chet Gould.

Music: Recorded.

DREAM HOUSE—30 minutes—ABC—April 1, 1968 - January 2, 1970.

DROODLES

Game. Object: For a celebrity panel to identify droodles, nonsense drawings either submitted by home viewers or drawn by the host. Home viewers who stump the panel receive cash prizes.

Host: Roger Price.

Panelists: Denise Lor, the Looker; Carl Reiner, the Cut-up; Marc Connelly, the Thinker.

DROODLES—30 minutes—NBC—June 21, 1954 - September 1954.

THE DUDLEY DO-RIGHT SHOW

Animated Cartoon. Era: The early twentieth century. Dudley Do-Right, a simple-minded and naive young man, departs from home for the movies. After three miserable hours, he realizes that he has fallen through an open manhole and is sitting in a sewer. Believing he is guilty of tresspassing, and with a proud family tradition, "a Do-Right must always do right," he turns himself into the North Alberta Mountie Camp in Canada—five hundred miles from his home.

Shocked when learning of his foul deed, Inspector Ray K. Fenwick is prompted to ask Dudley if he would consider becoming a Mountie. Noticing the string that is attached to the Inspector's pistol, Dudley becomes hooked, signs up, and ninety minutes later completes his training.

Stories relate his attempts to apprehend Snively Whiplash, the most diabolical of fiends.

Characters' Voices

Dudley Do-Right   Bill Scott
Nell Fenwick, the Inspector's
      daughter   June Foray
Snively Whiplash   Hans Conried
Inspector Ray K.
      Fenwick   Paul Frees

Narrator: Paul Frees.

Dudley's horse: Steed.

Additional segments:

The Hunter. A beagle detective, The Hunter, dispatched by Officer Flim Flanagan, attempts to apprehend the cunning Fox.

The World Of Commander McBragg. The tall tales of a retired naval officer.

Tutor The Turtle. The story of Tutor, a turtle who becomes what he wishes through the magic of Mr. Wizard, the lizard.

Voices: Bill Conrad, Walter Tetley, Skip Craig, Barbara Baldwin.

Music: Sheldon Allman; Stan Worth.

THE DUDLEY DO-RIGHT SHOW— 30 minutes—ABC—April 27, 1969 - September 6, 1970. Syndicated.

DUFFY'S TAVERN

Comedy. Background: Duffy's Tavern, a run-down restaurant-bar on Third Avenue in New York City. The misadventures and dealings of Archie, a con artist who operates and manages the tavern for the never-seen Mr. Duffy. Duffy's Tavern, "Where the elite meet to eat," and where, with a beer, the free lunch costs fifteen cents. Based on the radio program of the same title.

CAST

Archie, the
      manager   Ed Gardner
Clifton Finnegan, Archie's
      simple-minded
      friend   Alan Reed
Miss Duffy, Duffy's
      unmarried daughter,
      seeking a husband—
      "Nature's revenge on
      Peeping Toms"   Patte Chapman
Charley, the
      waiter   Jimmy Conlin

Orchestra: Peter Van Steeden.

DUFFY'S TAVERN—30 minutes— NBC—April 5, 1954 - September 1954.

THE DUKE

Comedy. Background: New York City. Believing himself meant for the finer things in life, prize fighter Duke Zenlee discovers a love of the arts and oil painting. Impulsively, he decides to quit the ring and with a friend, Claude Stroud, opens a night club. Stories depict his attempts to enjoy his newly adopted life style against the wishes of his former trainer, Johnny, who schemes to get him to return to the ring.

CAST

Duke Zenlee   Paul Gilbert
Johnny   Allen Jenkins
Gloria, Duke's girl-
      friend   Phyllis Coates
Claude Stroud   Rudy Cromwell

Orchestra: Lou Bring.

THE DUKE—30 minutes—NBC—July 2, 1954 - September 24, 1954.

DUNDEE AND THE CULHANE

Western. Background: The Frontier of the 1870s. The story of Dundee, a sophisticated adverse-to-violence, trail-riding British barrister; and the Culhane, his assistant, an apprentice lawyer, rugged and fast with his fists and guns. Episodes relate their self-proclaimed mission to establish law and order throughout the West.

CAST

Dundee   John Mills
The Culhane   Sean Garrison

DUNDEE AND THE CULHANE—60 minutes—CBS—September 6, 1967 - December 13, 1967.

DUNNINGER

Listed: The television programs of mentalist Joseph Dunninger.

Format: Demonstrations of mind reading ability.

Dunninger And Winchell—Variety—30 minutes. NBC—October 14, 1948 - September 28, 1949; CBS—October 5, 1949 - December 28, 1949.

Hosts: Paul Winchell, Jerry Mahoney.
Starring: Joseph Dunninger.

The Dunninger Show—Variety—30 minutes—Syndicated 1953.
Host: John K.M. McCaffrey.
Starring: Joseph Dunninger.
Featured: Orson Bean.

The Amazing Dunninger—Variety—30 minutes—Syndicated 1968.
Host: Hank Stohl.
Starring: Joseph Dunninger.

THE DuPONT SHOW OF THE MONTH
THE DuPONT SHOW OF THE WEEK

Anthology. Dramatizations based on real-life incidents.

Included:

Windfall. After purchasing a nineteenth-century day sink in an antique shop, Frank Foster finds ninety-two thousand dollars hidden in it. He and his wife struggle over the decision of what to do with the money.

CAST
Frank Foster: Eddie Albert; Emily Foster: Glynis Johns; Bob Foster: Murray Hamilton.

Holdup. The efforts of a bright accountant and a top flight safe cracker to pull a million dollar heist, the proceeds from an amusement park's holiday activities.

CAST
Charles Hamilton: Hans Conried; Max Von Ritter: Hal March; Rudy Schrieber: Gerald Hickes.

The Winslow Boy. Background: Osborne, England. A Defense counselor attempts to defend a boy falsely accused of forging a five shilling postal order.

CAST
Arthur Winslow: Frederic March; Grace Winslow: Florence Eldridge; Ronnie Winslow: Rex Thompson; Sir Robert Morton: Noel Willman.

The Shadowed Affair. A journalist probes into the mysterious relationship between a famed novelist and his wife.

CAST

Juliette Harben: Greer Garson; Hans Harben: Douglas Fairbanks; Jennifer Graham: Lois Nettleton.

THE DuPONT SHOW OF THE MONTH—90 minutes—CBS—1957-1962.

THE DuPONT SHOW OF THE WEEK—60 minutes—NBC—1962-1964.

DUSTY'S TRAIL

Western Comedy. Era: The 1880s. A wagon train, destined for California, begins its long, hazardous journey. Through the efforts of a dim-witted scout, a stage and a wagon are separated from the main body and lost. Stories relate the wagon master's efforts to safely deliver his passengers to the Promised Land.

CAST

Mr. Callahan, the wagon
    master   Forrest Tucker
Dusty, the trail
    scout   Bob Denver
Lulu, a beautiful young
    dancehall girl hoping
    to open a saloon in
    California   Jeannine Riley
Betsy, a beautiful young
    teacher hoping to estab-
    lish a school in
    California   Lori Saunders
Carter Brookhaven, a wealthy
    banker   Ivor Francis
Daphne Brookhaven,
  his wife   Lynn Wood
Andy, a well-educated, resourceful
    pioneer   Bill Cort

Callahan's horse: Blarney.

Dusty's horse: Freckles.

Music: Sherwood Schwartz; Frank DeVol; Jack Plees.

DUSTY'S TRAIL—30 minutes—Syndicated 1973.

E

THE EARL WRIGHTSON SHOW

Musical Variety.

Host: Earl Wrightson.

Vocalist: Betty Jane Watson.

Music: The Buddy Weed Trio.

THE EARL WRIGHTSON SHOW—15 minutes—ABC 1948.

EARN YOUR VACATION

Game. A question, "Where on earth would you like to go and why?" is posed to the studio audience. Those with the best responses are selected as contestants and receive the opportunity to win an all-expenses-paid vacation to their place of desire. The player selects a subject category and answers questions of ascending difficulty within four plateaus. Each plateau represents a segment of the vacation. A player is defeated if he incorrectly answers any part of the plateau.

Host: Johnny Carson.

Assistants: Jackie Lougherty, Millie Sinclair.

EARN YOUR VACATION—30 minutes—CBS—May 23, 1954 - September 1954.

EARTH LAB

Educational. Contemporary views of

the physical sciences; geared to children eight to fourteen years of age.

Instructor: Tex Trailer.

EARTH LAB—60 minutes—Syndicated 1971.

EAST SIDE COMEDY

Movies. Background: New York City. The story of a group of lower East Side kids who just manage to stay on the right side of the law.

From 1937 to 1943, wherein thirty-six feature films and three twelve-chapter serials were released, the group has been billed as the Dead End Kids (Leo Gorcey, Huntz Hall, Billy Halop, Gabe Dell, Bobby Jordan, Bernard Punsley), the Little Tough Guys (Billy Halop, Gabe Dell, Huntz Hall, Bernard Punsley, Hally Chester, David Gorcey), and the East Side Kids (see Cast).

Between 1945 and 1956, forty-two Bowery Boys films were made (see Cast). 1956 to 1957 saw the final era, the six remaining Bowery Boys films (see Cast).

1946 to 1948 saw the appearance of another group, the Gas House Kids (Carl "Alfalfa" Switzer, Bennie Bartlett, Rudy Wissler, Tommy Bond) in a three-feature series that failed to re-create the style of the original.

Today, via television, the 1937 to 1957 parade of tough guys finds renewed life and popularity as local stations endlessly air their antics under such titles as "East Side

East Side Comedy. Huntz Hall and Leo Gorcey as Bowery Boys Sach and Slip.

Comedy" (New York); and "West Side Comedy" (Los Angeles).

CAST:
THE EAST SIDE KIDS

Ethelbert "Muggs" McGinnis	Leo Gorcey
Glimpy	Huntz Hall
Danny	Bobby Jordan
Scruno	Sunshine Sammy Morrison
Benny	Bennie Bartlett
	Billy Benedict
Skinny	Dave Durand
	Donald Haines
Stash	Stanley Clements
Skid	Gabe Dell
Sniffy	Jack Raymond
Sleepy	Bill Bates
Dave	Bobby Stone
Pee Wee	David Gorcey

Also: Hally Chester, Harris Berger, Frankie Burke, Donald Haines, Eddie Brian.

CAST:
THE BOWERY BOYS

Terrence Aloysius Mahoney (Slip)	Leo Gorcey
Horace DeBussy Jones (Sach)	Huntz Hall
Louis Xavier Dumbrowsky (Louie), the owner of Louie's Sweet Shop	Bernard Gorcey
Chuck Anderson	David Gorcey
Dave Marino	Gabe Dell
Gabe Marino	Gabe Dell
Whitey	Billy Benedict
Bobby	Bobby Jordan
Butch	Bennie Bartlett

CAST:
NEW EPISODES 1956-1957

Duke Stanislaus Kovilesky	Stanley Clements
Horace DeBussy Jones	Huntz Hall
Chuck Anderson	David Gorcey
Blinkey	Eddie LeRoy
Myron	Jimmy Murphy

Mike Clancy, the owner of the Sweet Shop	Percy Helton
	Dick Elliott
Mrs. Kelly, the owner of the boarding house at which the boys reside	Queenie Smith

EAST SIDE KIDS

See title: "East Side Comedy."

EAST SIDE/WEST SIDE

Drama. Background: New York City. The role of social workers in coping with the aged, the poor, and the desperate of a large metropolis. Stories depict the problems and their handling as seen through the eyes of Neil Brock, a Manhattan social worker.

CAST

Neil Brock	George C. Scott
Fredia "Hecky" Hechlinger, the agency director	Elizabeth Wilson
Jane Foster, the office secretary	Cicely Tyson

Music: Kenyon Hopkins.

EAST SIDE/WEST SIDE—60 minutes —CBS—1963-1964. Syndicated.

EASY ACES

Comedy. Events in the lives of the Aces: Jane, the Dumb Dora type; and Goodman, her husband, the recipient of her unpredictable antics. Based on the radio program of the same title.

CAST

Goodman Ace	Himself

Jane Ace	Herself
Dorothy, Jane's friend	Betty Garde

EASY ACES—30 minutes—DuMont—1949-1950.

EASY CHAIR THEATRE

Anthology. Dramatic presentations.

EASY CHAIR THEATRE—30 minutes—DuMont 1952.

ED ALLEN TIME

Exercise.

Host: Ed Allen.

Assisting: Alice, his "talking dog."

ED ALLEN TIME—30 minutes—Syndicated 1967.

THE EDDIE CANTOR COMEDY THEATRE

Variety. Music, songs, and comedy sketches.

Host: Eddie Cantor.

Regulars: Helen O'Connell, Billie Burke, Ralph Peters, Frank Jenks, Pierre Watkin.

Orchestra: Ray Anthony.

THE EDDIE CANTOR COMEDY THEATRE—30 minutes—Syndicated 1955.

EDDIE FISHER

Listed: The television programs of singer Eddie Fisher.

Coke Time—Musical Variety—15 minutes—NBC—April 29, 1953 - June 1957.

Host: Eddie Fisher.

Regulars: Jaye P. Morgan, Don Ameche, Fred Robbins.

Orchestra: Alex Stordahl; Carl Hoff.

The Eddie Fisher Show—Musical Variety—60 minutes—NBC—October 1, 1957 - March 17, 1959 (on an alternating basis with "The George Gobel Show").

Host: Eddie Fisher.

Regulars: George Gobel (his permanent guest), Debbie Reynolds (an occasional guest), Erin O'Brien, The Johnny Mann Singers.

Orchestra: Buddy Bergman.

EDDY ARNOLD

Listed: The television programs of singer Eddy Arnold.

The Eddy Arnold Show—Country—Western Musical Variety—15 minutes—CBS—July 14, 1952 - September 1952.

Host: Eddy Arnold.

Featured: Chet Atkins.

Music: Paul Mitchell's Instrumental Quintet.

The Eddy Arnold Show—Country-Western Musical Variety—15 minutes—NBC 1953.

Host: Eddy Arnold.

Vocalists: The Dickens Sisters.

Music: An unidentified combo.

Eddy Arnold Time—Country-Western

Musical Variety—30 minutes—NBC—April 20, 1956 - July 19, 1956.

Host: Eddy Arnold.

Regulars: Betty Johnson, The Gordonaires Quartet.

Orchestra: Russ Case.

THE EDGAR WALLACE MYSTERY THEATRE

Anthology. Mysteries as penned by author Edgar Wallace.

Included:

Ricochet. A woman attempts to clear herself of a false murder charge.

CAST
Richard Leech, Maxine Audley.

Man At The Carlton Tower. Police efforts to apprehend a notorious murderer/jewel thief.

CAST
Maxine Audley, Nigel Green, Lee Montague.

Locker Sixty-Nine. A detective attempts to find his employer's murderer.

CAST
Walter Brown.

Death Trap. A girl attempts to prove that her sister's recorded suicide was actually murder.

CAST
Mercy Haystead, Albert Lieven, Barbara Shelly.

THE EDGAR WALLACE MYSTERY THEATRE—60 minutes—Syndicated 1963. Originally produced in England as theatrical releases.

THE EDGE OF NIGHT

Serial. Background: The turbulent Midwestern city of Monticello. Stories depict the lives of ordinary people driven by intense feeling and difficult circumstances. Emphasis is placed on crime detection methods and courtroom proceedings.

CAST

Mike Karr	John Larkin
	Lawrence Hugo
	Forest Compton
Sarah Lane	Teal Ames
Nancy Pollock	Ann Flood
Grace O'Leary	Maxine Stuart
Jackie Lane	Don Hastings
Adam Drake	Donald May
Dr. Kevin Reed	Stanley Grover
Nicole Travis	Maeve McGuire
Cookie Christopher	Fran Sharon
Winston Grimsley	Walter Greza
Ed Gibson	Larry Hagman
Ron Christopher	Burt Douglas
Kate Sloane	Jan Farrand
Elly Jo Jamison	Dorothy Lyman
Phil Caprice	Ray MacDonnell
	Robert Webber
Ken Emerson	Alan Manson
Joe Pollock	Alan Nourse
	John Gibson
Tango	Lynn Ann Redgrave
Steve Prentiss	Conrad Fowkes
Dr. Katherine Lovell	Mary Fickett
Ruth Tuttle	Barbara Hayes
Ernie Hall	George Hall
Bart Fletcher	James Ray
Harry Constable	Dolph Sweet
Julie Jamison	Millette Alexander
Dr. Jim Fields	Alan Feinstein
Liz Hillyer	Alberta Grant
Frank Sloane	Sam Grey
Martha Marceau	Teri Keane

Bill Marceau	Alan Feinstein	Ben Travis	Cec Linder
	Carl Frank	Mr. LePage	William Post Jr.
	Mandel Kramer	Danny	Lou Criscuolo
Laurie Ann Karr	Emily Prager	Betty Jean Lane	Mary Moor
Orin Hillyer	Lester Rawlins	The Detective Sergeant	Ian Martin
Simon Jessep	Hugh Riley	The Police Department	
Vic Lamont	Ted Tinling	secretary	Maxine Stuart
Nurse Hubbell	Frances Beers	Mattie Lane	Betty Garde
Trudy	Mary Hayden	Harry Lane	Lauren Gilbert
Lobo Haines	Fred J. Scollay	Harry's wife	Sarah Burton
Fred Burns	William Kiehl	Harry's secretary	Mary Alice Moore
Celia Burns	Carol Teitel	Andre Lazor	Val Dufor
Corky	Joy Claussen	Malcolm Thomas	Edward Kemmer
Doug Hastings	Hal Studer	John Barnes	Barry Newman
Angela Morgan	Valerie French	Rick Oliver	Keith Charles
Jack Berman	Ward Costello	Laurie Ann Karr	Emily Prager
Dr. Warner	Richard Buck	Gerry McGrath	Milee Taggart
Jessica Webster	Rita Lloyd	The Police Captain's	
Jason Everett	Barry Ford	secretary	Teri Keane
Phoebe Smith	Renne Jarrett	Mrs. Thatcher	Billie Lou Watt
	Johanna Leister		
	Hedi Vaughn		
Pamela Stuart	Irene Dailey		
Geraldine Whitney	Lois Kibbee		
Gordon Whitney	Allan Gifford		
Senator Colin Whitney	Anthony Call		
Tiffany Whitney	Lucy Martin		
Dr. Charles Weldon	David Hooks		
Keith Whitney	Bruce Martin		
Rose Pollock	Kay Campbell		
	Virginia Kaye		
Louise Caprice	Mary K. Wells		
	Lisa Howard		
Tracy Carroll	Kendall March		
Eric Morgan	John Lehve		
Lennie Small	Mike Minor		
Lee Pollock	Tony Roberts		
Kevin Jameson	Dick Schoberg		
John	George Hall		
Laurie Lamont	Jeanne Ruskin		
Lt. Luke Chandler	Herb Davis		
D.A. Peter Quinn	George Petrie		
Mr. Lamarti	James Gallery		
Kaye Reynolds	Elizabeth Farley		
Babs	Leslie Ray		
Dr. Lacy	Brooks Rogers		
Johnny Dallas	John LaGioa		
Sam English	Edward Moore		
Floyd	James Ray		

Also: Janet Margolin, Barbara Sharma, Ruby Dee, Jan Miner, Martin Rudy, Ann Minot, Audra Lindley, Charles Baxter, David Ford, Carl Low, Kathleen Cody, Eva Marie Saint, Wesley Addy, Nancy Wickwire, Karen Thorsell, Ruth Mattheson, Kathleen Bracken, Peggy Allenby, Ronnie Welsch, Peter Kastner, Joan Harvey, Anthony Ponzini, Robert Dryden, Priscilla Gillette, Jeremy Slate, Sam Groom, Diana Van derVlis, Nancy Pinkerton.

Announcer: Hal Simms.

Music: Paul Taubman.

THE EDGE OF NIGHT—30 minutes —CBS—Premiered: April 2, 1956.

THE ED NELSON SHOW

See title: "The Morning Show."

THE ED SULLIVAN SHOW

Variety. Lavish, top-rated entertainment acts.

Host: Ed Sullivan.

Regulars: The Toastettes Chorus Line; The Hugh Lambert Dancers.

Commercial Spokeswoman: Julia Meade.

Announcer: Ralph Paul.

Orchestra: Ray Bloch.

Appearing: The Beatles, Elvis Presley, Ingrid Bergman, The Moiseyev Dancers (Russian Folk Troupe), Judy Garland, Petula Clark, Van Cliburn, Englebert Humperdinck, Tom Jones, Janis Joplin, Dean Martin, Jerry Lewis, Bob Hope, Bing Crosby, Red Skelton, Ethel Merman, Richard Burton, Julie Andrews, Bert Lahr, Elsa Lanchester, Evelyn Knight, Roy Campanella, Jackie Robinson, Gil Hodges, Ted Williams, Robert Merrill, Anna Maria Alberghetti, Rudy Vallee, Alfred Drake, Stan Kenton, Matt Monro, Eydie Gorme, Count Basie, Stiller and Meara, Sandy Baron, Victor Borge, Tony Bennett, Leslie Uggams, Van Hefflin, Sidney Blackmer, Ann-Margret, Carol Lawrence, Eddy Arnold, Totie Fields, Jimmy Durante, Vaughn Monroe, Patti Page, Jean Carroll, Liza Minnelli, Ray Charles, Jack E. Leonard, Vikki Carr, Wayne and Shuster, Robert Goulet, Joan Rivers, The Rolling Stones, Rip Taylor, Diahann Carroll, Topo Gigio (mechanical Italian mouse), Anthony Newley, Connie Francis, Wayne Newton, Jackie Vernon, Morty Gunty, Georgia Brown, Tessie O'Shea, Frank Gorshin, Gordon MacRae, Shelia MacRae, The McGuire Sisters, Harry James, Henny Youngman, John Byner, Kate Smith, Jackie Mason, Roger Williams, Eartha Kitt, Phil Foster, Pat Henning, Teresa Brewer, Dorothy Dandridge, Jack Carter, Myron Cohen, Earl Grant, Alan King, Nancy Sinatra, Jaye P. Morgan, Mickey Rooney, Burt Lancaster, Shelly Berman, Bobby Van, Leslie Gore, Buddy Hackett, Eddie Fisher, Debbie Reynolds, The Young Rascals.

Opening Night Guests: Dean Martin, Jerry Lewis, Jim Kirkwood, Richard Rodgers, Oscar Hamerstein II, Ruby Goldstein (a fight referee), Lee Goodman.

Closing Night Performers: Carol Channing, Sid Caesar, Jerry Vale, Peter Nero, Robert Klein, Pat Henning, Gladys Knight and the Pips.

THE ED SULLIVAN SHOW—60 minutes—CBS—September 25, 1955 - June 6, 1971. Broadcast as "Toast of the Town"—60 minutes—CBS—June 20, 1948 - September 18, 1955.

ED WYNN

Listed: The television programs of comedian Ed Wynn.

The Ed Wynn Show—Variety—30 minutes—NBC—October 6, 1949 - July 4, 1950.

Host: Ed Wynn.

Regulars: Ben Wrigley, Edith Praf, The Hannaford Family, The Merriel Abbott Dancers.

Orchestra: Lud Gluskin.

The Ed Wynn Show—Comedy—30

minutes—NBC—September 25, 1958 - January 1, 1959.

Background: A small Midwestern college town. The trials and tribulations of John Beamer, widower and retired businessman. Stories focus on his struggles to raise his orphaned granddaughters, Midge and Laurie.

CAST

John Beamer	Ed Wynn
Laurie Beamer	Jacklyn O'Donnell
Midge Beamer	Sherry Alberoni
Ernie Hinshaw, his friend, an attorney	Herb Vigran
Mayor Brandon	Clarence Straight

THE EGG AND I

Comedy Serial. Background: New York State. The struggles of Bob and Betty MacDonald, the owners and operators of a run-down chicken farm. Based on the book by Betty Mac-Donald.

CAST

Betty MacDonald	Patricia Kirkland
Bob MacDonald	Frank Craven
Jed Simmons, their handyman	Grady Sutton
Ma Kettle, their neighbor	Doris Rich
Pa Kettle, her lazy husband	Frank Twedell

THE EGG AND I—15 minutes—CBS —September 3, 1951 - August 1, 1952.

THE EIGHTH MAN

Animated Cartoon. Era: The twenty-first century. Background: Metro City, the headquarters of Metro International, the futuristic police force. After agent Peter Brady is killed attempting to apprehend Saucer Lip, the most wanted of criminals, Professor Genius embodies Brady's life force into that of Tobor the Eighth Man, an indestructible robot that appears in the image of the mild-mannered Brady. Stories relate Brady's battle, as Tobor, against evil and his attempts to apprehend his killer, Saucer Lip.

THE EIGHTH MAN—30 minutes— Syndicated 1965.

87th PRECINCT

Crime Drama. Background: New York City. The grim day-to-day activities of plainclothes detectives, the men of Manhattan's 87th police precinct.

CAST

Detective Steve Carella	Robert Lansing
Teddy Carella, his deaf-mute wife	Gena Rowlands
Detective Bert Kling	Ron Harper
Detective Meyer Meyer	Norman Fell
Detective Roger Havilland	Gregory Walcott

Music: Morton Stevens.

87th PRECINCT—60 minutes—NBC— September 25, 1961 - September 10, 1962. Syndicated.

THE ELECTRIC COMPANY

Educational. Second to fourth graders. Objectives: To enable slow readers to increase their speed and to reinforce skills. The specifics of whole words and complete sentences are presented through cartoons, sketches, and/or musical numbers.

Regulars: Judy Graubart, Skip Hinnant, Rita Moreno, Bill Cosby, Jimmy Boyd, Lee Chamberlain, Morgan Freeman.

Announcer: Ken Roberts.

Music: The Joe Roposo Combo.

Characters: Julia Grownup (Judy); Madame Rosalie, Gladys Glowworm (Lee); The Ice Cream Man (Bill); Easy Reader, Mel Mel Mounds (Morgan); Fargo North, Norman Neat (Skip); J. Arthur Crank (Jimmy).

THE ELECTRIC COMPANY—30 minutes—PBS—Premiered: October 25, 1971.

THE ELEVENTH HOUR

Drama. Background: New York City. The work of psychiatrist Theodore Bassett, court alienist and advisor to the state board of correction, as he attempts to assist people overcome by the turmoil of human emotion.

CAST
Dr. Theodore Bassett   Wendell Corey
Dr. Paul Graham, his assistant,
   a clinical
   psychologist   Jack Ging
Dr. Richard Starke (replaced
   Bassett)   Ralph Bellamy

Music: Harry Sukman.

THE ELEVENTH HOUR—60 minutes—NBC—October 3, 1962 - September 9, 1964. Syndicated.

ELGIN HOUR

Anthology. Dramatic presentations.

Included:

Crime In The Streets. Having grown up in a tough neighborhood, a social worker attempts to prevent two boys from facing a possible life of crime.

CAST
Ben Wagner: Robert Preston; Mrs. Dorne: Glenda Farrell; Frankie Dorn: John Cassavettes; Richard Dorn: Van Dyke Parks.

Days Of Grace. Discharged after twenty years service, an advertising executive attempts to reconstruct his life.

CAST
William L'Hommedieu: Franchot Tone; Madge L'Hommedieu: Peggy Conklin; Gloria L'Hommedieu: Nancy Malone.

Family Meeting. Never allowed a voice in family disputes, a young woman attempts to assert her opinion.

CAST
Father: Alan Bunce; Mother: Polly Rowles; Daughter: Kaye Margery; Lyman Poole: William Redfield.

ELGIN HOUR—60 minutes—ABC—1954-1955.

ELLERY QUEEN

Crime Drama. Background: New York City. The investigations of Ellery Queen, a suave, cynical, rugged, and incorruptable gentleman detective and writer.

Versions:

Ellery Queen—30 minutes—DuMont—1950-1955.

CAST

Ellery Queen	Richard Hart
	Lee Bowman
	Hugh Marlowe
Inspector Richard Queen, his father, with the N.Y.P.D.	Florenz Ames
Nikki Porter, Ellery's secretary	Charlotte Keane

The Further Adventures Of Ellery Queen—60 minutes—NBC—September 1958 - September 1959.

CAST

Ellery Queen	George Nader
	Lee Philips

Ellery Queen—60 minutes—NBC—Premiered: September 11, 1975.

CAST

Ellery Queen	Jim Hutton
Inspector Richard Queen	David Wayne
Sergeant Velie, the inspector's assistant	Tom Reese
Frank Flannigan, a reporter on the *New York Gazette*	Ken Swofford
Simon Brimmer, a criminologist	John Hillerman

Music: Elmer Bernstein, Hal Mooney.

The format allows the viewer to match wits with Ellery Queen. The viewer sees the murder being committed, is told who the suspects are, and is presented with all the clues—none are withheld from him and nothing extra is given to Ellery. Before the last commercial, Ellery faces the camera and asks viewers to identify the murderer. After the commercial break, all the suspects are gathered and Ellery reveals the guilty party.

EMERGENCY!

Drama. Background: California. The work of the paramedics of Squad 51 of the Los Angeles County Fire Department Rescue Division.

CAST

Dr. Kelly Brackett	Robert Fuller
Dr. Joe Early	Bobby Troup
Nurse Dixie McCall	Julie London
Fireman Roy DeSoto	Kevin Tighe
Fireman John Gage	Randolph Mantooth
Fire Captain Henderson	Dick Hammer
Fire Captain Stanley	Michael Norell
Fireman Marco Lopez	Marco Lopez
Fireman Kelly	Tim Donnelly
Fireman Mike Woiski	Jack Kruschen
Nurse Carol Williams	Lillian Lehman
Fireman Stoker	Mike Stoker
Dr. Morton	Ron Pinkard
Squad 51 dog: Boots.	

Music: Nelson Riddle; Billy May.

EMERGENCY!—60 minutes—NBC—Premiered: January 22, 1972.

EMERGENCY PLUS FOUR

Animated Cartoon. A spin-off from "Emergency." Assisted by four youngsters, Sally, Matt, Jason, and Randy (the "Plus Four"), John Gage and Roy DeSoto, paramedics with the Squad 51 Rescue Division of the Los Angeles County Fire Department, continue their work, rescuing people trapped in life-and-death situations.

Characters' Voices

Roy DeSoto	Kevin Tighe
John Gage	Randolph Mantooth
Sally	Sarah Kennedy
Matt	David Joliffe
Jason	Donald Fullilove
Randy	Peter Haas

Plus Four pets: Flash the dog; Bananas the monkey; Charlmayne the bird.

Music: The Sound Track Music Company.

EMERGENCY PLUS FOUR—30 minutes—NBC—Premiered: September 8, 1973.

EMPIRE

Drama. Background: The one-half million acre Garrett Ranch in Santa Fe, New Mexico. Stories focus on the work of Jim Redigo, the foreman, as he struggles to solve difficulties within the Garrett empire.

CAST

Jim Redigo	Richard Egan
Lucia Garrett, the owner of the ranch	Anne Seymour
Connie Garrett, her daughter	Terry Moore
Tal Garrett, Lucia's son	Ryan O'Neal
Paul Moreno, a ranch hand	Charles Bronson
Chuck, a ranch hand	Warren Vanders

EMPIRE—60 minutes—NBC—September 25, 1962 - September 17, 1963. ABC—60 minutes—March 22, 1964 - September 6, 1964. Spin-off series: "Redigo" (see title).

ENCORE THEATRE

Anthology. Rebroadcasts of dramas that were originally aired via other filmed anthology programs.

Included:

The Silence. The story of an engineer who falls in love with another man's wife.

CAST
Carolyn Jones, Rod Cameron.

Exit Laughing. After he promises his wife he will take her to Honolulu for a vacation, a television comic discovers that his manager has arranged bookings for him that will interfere with his plans. The story relates his wife's efforts to see that he keeps his promise.

CAST
Pat O'Brien, Fay Wray, John Baragen.

The Boy With The Beautiful Mother. The story of a foreign boy who struggles to adjust to a new life after he is adopted by an American couple.

CAST
Jean Byron, Natalie Norwick, Peter Votrian.

ENCORE THEATRE—30 minutes— NBC—July 7, 1956 - September 1956.

ENCOUNTER

Anthology. Dramatizations featuring both American and Canadian performers.

ENCOUNTER—60 minutes (Simultaneous broadcast)—U.S.—ABC; Canada —CBC—October 5, 1958 - October 26, 1958.

THE ENGELBERT HUMPERDINCK SHOW

Musical Variety.

The Engelbert Humperdinck Show.
Engelbert Humperdinck.

Host: Engelbert Humperdinck (Arnold Dorsey).
Featured: The Irving Davies Dancers.
Orchestra: Jack Parnell.

THE ENGELBERT HUMPERDINCK SHOW—60 minutes—January 21, 1970 - September 19, 1970. Syndicated.

ENSIGN O'TOOLE

Comedy. Background: The South Pacific. The misadventures of the men and officers of the U.S. Navy Destroyer USS *Appleby*. Stories focus on a bickering relationship between two men: Commander Homer Nelson, a man with a penchant for adhering to the rules, which has earned him the antagonism of the crew; and morale officer Ensign O'Toole, a man whose philosophy is to take life as it comes, worry about the present, and dream of the future. Knowledgeable in all fields, lazy in his approach to work, and unable to be found when needed, he has earned the respect of the crew. Because of his carefree attitude and influence on the crew, he struggles to solve the problems that arise when they follow his leadership.

CAST
Ensign O'Toole	Dean Jones
Captain Homer Nelson	Jay C. Flippen
Lt. Rex St. John	Jack Mullaney

Lt. Cdr. Virgil Stoner	Jack Albertson
Seaman Gabby Di Julio	Harvey Lembeck
Seaman Spicer	Beau Bridges
Seaman White	Bob Sorrells

Music: Frank Comstock.

ENSIGN O'TOOLE—30 minutes—NBC—September 23, 1962 - September 15, 1963. Syndicated.

THE ENTERTAINERS

Variety. Music, song, dance, and comedy presented in the style of a revue.

Hosts: Bob Newhart, Carol Burnett, Caterina Valente.

Repertoire Company: John Davidson, Tessie O'Shea, Art Buchwald, Jack Burns, Dom DeLuise, Tony Hendra, Nic Ullet, The Lee Hale Singers, The Ernie Flatt Dancers, The Peter Gennaro Dancers.

Orchestra: Harry Zimmerman.

THE ENTERTAINERS—60 minutes—CBS—September 25, 1964 - March 27, 1965.

THE ERN WESTMORE SHOW

Women. Beauty tips and advice.

Host: Ern Westmore.

Regulars: Betty Westmore (Mrs.); Dick Hyde.

THE ERN WESTMORE SHOW—30 minutes—ABC—August 7, 1955 - September 11, 1955.

ERNIE KOVACS

Listed: The television programs of comedian Ernie Kovacs. Developing visual trickery, he was the first to make full use of television's potential through the skilled use of cameras and technical equipment.

Format: Split-second blackouts; pantomimed sketches; and satirizations on life.

Deadline For Dinner—Satire—30 minutes—DuMont—1950.

Host: Ernie Kovacs.

Kovacs On The Corner—Satire—60 minutes—NBC—January 7, 1951 - March 28, 1952.

Host: Ernie Kovacs.

Regulars: Edie Adams, his wife, Miss U.S. Television, 1950; Peter Boyle, the Irish cop on the beat.

Music: The Dave Appel Trio.

It's Time For Ernie—Satire—15 minutes—NBC—May 14, 1951 - June 29, 1951.

Host: Ernie Kovacs.

Regulars: Edie Adams, Hugh Price.

Ernie In Kovacsland—Satire—30 minutes—NBC—July 21, 1951 - August 24, 1951.

Host: Ernie Kovacs.

Regulars: Edie Adams, Hugh Price.

Kovacs Unlimited—Satire—60 minutes—Local New York (WCBS-TV)—1952.

Host: Ernie Kovacs.

Regulars: Edie Adams, Andy McKay, Trig Lund, Peter Hanley.

Orchestra: Eddie Hatrak.

The Ernie Kovacs Show—Satire—30 minutes—NBC—December 12, 1955 - July 27, 1956.

Host: Ernie Kovacs.

Regulars: Edie Adams, Matt Dennis, Kenny Delmar, Harry Lascoe, Al Keith.

Music: The Hamilton Trio.

The Ernie Kovacs Show—Satire—30 minutes—ABC—1958-1959.

Host: Ernie Kovacs.

Featured: Edie Adams.

Orchestra: Harry Geller.

Take A Good Look—Game—30 minutes—ABC—1959 - 1960. See title.

The New Ernie Kovacs Show—Satire—30 minutes—ABC—1961-1962.

Host: Ernie Kovacs.

THE ERROL FLYNN THEATRE

Anthology. Dramatic presentations.

Host-Occasional performer: Errol Flynn.

Included:

The Girl In Blue Jeans. The romance that develops when an actor-producer catches a beautiful girl breaking into his home.

CAST
The girl: Glynis Johns; the producer: Herbert Lom.

The 100th Night Of Don Juan. The story concerns Don Juan's efforts to prove his love for a woman.

CAST
Don Juan: Errol Flynn; the woman: Jean Kent.

Rescued. After Lord Alston is wounded on the battlefields and held prisoner by one of Cromwell's officers, his friends attempt to rescue him.

CAST
Errol Flynn, Andrew Keir.

Out Of The Blue. A stewardess on a flight to London agrees to take care of an infant child. When the plane lands in Rome, the baby is kidnapped. The episode relates her struggles to find the baby.

Starring: Rosanna Rory.

The Duel. The story of the duel between an arrogant lord and his ward's sweetheart.

CAST
Errol Flynn, Ann Silvers.

THE ERROL FLYNN THEATRE—30 minutes—DuMont 1957.

ESCAPE

Anthology. Dramatizations depicting the fate of people caught in life and death situations. Tales designed "to free you from the four walls of today for a half-hour of high adventure." Based on the radio program of the same title.

ESCAPE—30 minutes—CBS 1950.

ESCAPE

Anthology. True stories of people caught in life-and-death situations.

Narrator: Jack Webb.

Music: Frank Comstock.

Included:

(Episode untitled). Background: The South Pacific, World War II. The story of a U.S. submarine caught in enemy waters by a Japanese destroyer. Partially crippled by depth charges, the sub sinks to the bottom. Unable to resurface to recharge its batteries, the crew is caught in a deadly game of waiting—to suffocate below or be shelled above.

After five hours, and out of oxygen, the sub surfaces. The enemy is gone. "Had they gone because they were sure they had made a hit? Or had they run out of depth charges? The answer will never be known."

CAST
Captain Frank Wyatt: Ed Nelson; Mike Coles: Ron Hayes; Murphy: Dennis Rucker; Kurczak: Kip Niven.

(Episode untitled). Background: California. On a family picnic, the McGowan children (Matthew, age nine, and Kate, age six) stray from camp and wander into dangerous mountain lion country while chasing a butterfly. Unknowingly stalked by a cougar, Matthew and Kate constantly change their position, making it difficult for rescuers to locate them. Confronted by the cougar, Kate's screams alert the searchers who scare away the beast and rescue the children.

CAST
Larry McGowan: Glenn Corbett; Matthew McGowan: Lee H. Montgomery; Kate McGowan: Dana Laurita; Fran McGowan: Marion Ross.

(Episode untitled). Era: The Korean War. Shortly after the village of Myling is destroyed by bombings, leaving one survivor, a little girl, the patrol helicopter of congressional investigator Brian Collyer is hit by enemy fire and crash lands behind enemy lines. Blinded by the accident, Collyer begins his journey south toward American lines. Stopping to rest, he comes upon the little girl. Not able to communicate because of the language barrier, but sensing he will not hurt her, she leads him through enemy lines to an American camp. Although he had lost his sight on the battlefields of Korea, congressional investigator Brian Collyer found something important.

CAST
Brian Collyer: John Ericson; the Korean Girl: Charlene Wong.

ESCAPE—30 minutes—NBC—February 11, 1973 - April 1, 1973. Rebroadcasts: NBC—August 19, 1973 - September 9, 1973.

E.S.P.

Variety. The sixth sense of extrasensory perception (E.S P., the ability to predict the future) is tested. Two people, screened by psychiatrists, are placed in separate isolation booths. Various experiments are conducted to determine the possessor of the higher degree of E.S.P.

Host: Vincent Price.

Consultant: Carroll B. Nash, Director of Parapsychology at St. Joseph's College in Philadelphia.

E.S.P.—30 minutes—ABC—July 11, 1958 - August 1, 1958.

E.S.P.

Anthology. Stories of people endowed with extrasensory perception, the ability to predict the future.

Host: Vincent Price.

E.S.P.—30 minutes—ABC—August 7, 1958 - August 22, 1958.

ESPECIALLY FOR YOU

See title: "The Roberta Quinlan Show."

ESPIONAGE

Anthology. Dramatizations based on the activities of international undercover agents. Through documented accounts and actual newsreel footage, events are covered from the American Revolution to the Cold War. Filmed in Europe.

Included:

A Covenant With Death. The story of two Norwegian resistance fighters who are tried for the wartime slaying of an elderly couple.

CAST
Mangus Anderson: Bradford Dillman; Ivar Kolstrom: Don Borisenko.

A Camel To Ride. Background: Arabia. The story of Father James, a Catholic priest who, by leading demonstrations, attempts to end the nation's repressive regime.

CAST
Father James: Bill Travers; Bishara: Marne Maitland; Gebal: Roger Delgado.

The Incurable One. Era: The years following World War II. Having been trained as an espionage agent during the war, a Danish countess attempts to recapture the excitement of wartime life.

CAST
Celeste: Ingrid Thulin; Andrew Evans: Steven Hill.

Do You Remember Leo Winters? The story of a frogman who is incorporated by British Intelligence to observe suspicious waterfront activities.

CAST
Leo Winters: George A. Cooper; Davenport: Peter Madden; Jane Vesey: Rhoda Lewis; Frank Vesey: Victor Platt.

ESPIONAGE—60 minutes—NBC—October 2, 1963 - July 1964. Syndicated.

ETHEL AND ALBERT

Comedy. Background: The small town of Sandy Harbor. The trials and tribulations of Ethel and Albert Arbuckle, a happily married couple.

CAST
Ethel Arbuckle	Peg Lynch
Albert Arbuckle	Alan Bunce
Aunt Eva	Margaret Hamilton

Also: Helen Ray, Harrison Dowd, Nelson Olmstead.

Announcer: Lee Gordon.

ETHEL AND ALBERT—30 minutes—CBS—June 20, 1955 - September 26, 1955. ABC—30 minutes—October 4, 1955 - July 6, 1956.

THE ETHEL BARRYMORE THEATRE

Anthology. Dramatic presentations.
Hostess: Ethel Barrymore.

Included:

The Victim. A courtroom drama concerning the regeneration of a once-brilliant lawyer.

Starring: Edward Arnold.

Dear Miss Lovelace. The story of an advice-to-the-lovelorn columnist who becomes involved with gangsters.

Starring: Anita Louise.

The Duke. The story of a clever thief who must prove his innocence in a jewel robbery he did not commit.

Starring: K. T. Stevens.

Winter In Spring. The misadventures of an elderly man as he takes a job as a baby-sitter.

Starring: Charles Coburn.

THE ETHEL BARRYMORE THEATRE—30 minutes—DuMont 1956.

THE EVA GABOR SHOW

Variety. Guests, interviews, beauty tips, and advice.

Hostess: Eva Gabor.

THE EVA GABOR SHOW—15 minutes—ABC—November 10, 1950 - October 22, 1951.

THE EVE ARDEN SHOW

Comedy. Background: Los Angeles, California. The misadventures of Liza Hammond, mother, widow, and traveling lecturer, as she struggles to divide her time among work, home, and her twin daughters, Jenny and Mary.

CAST

Liza Hammond	Eve Arden
Jenny Hammond	Gail Stone
Mary Hammond	Karen Greene
George Howell, her agent	Allyn Joslyn
Nora, her housekeeper and baby-sitter	Frances Bavier

THE EVE ARDEN SHOW—30 minutes—CBS—September 17, 1957 - March 26, 1958.

EVENING AT POPS

Music. The presentation of all styles and forms of music.

Host: Arthur Fiedler.

Soloists: Guests.

Music: The Boston Pops Orchestra conducted by Fiedler.

EVENING AT POPS—60 minutes—PBS 1970.

THE EVERGLADES

Adventure. Background: Southern Florida. The investigations of Lincoln Vail, a law-enforcement officer with the Everglades County Patrol.

CAST

Lincoln Vail	Ron Hayes
Chief Anderson	Gordon Cosell

THE EVERGLADES—30 minutes—Syndicated 1961.

THE EVERLY BROTHERS SHOW

Musical Variety.

Hosts: Phil Everly, Don Everly.

Regulars: Ruth McDevitt (as Aunt Hattie), Joe Higgins, Dick Clair, Jenna McMahon.

Announcer: Mike Lawrence.

Orchestra: Jack Elliott, Allyn Ferguson.

THE EVERLY BROTHERS SHOW—60 minutes—ABC—July 8, 1970 - September 16, 1970. Official title: "Johnny Cash Presents The Everly Brothers Show."

EVERYBODY'S TALKING

Game. Two competing contestants. A film sequence that features the man-in-the-street talking about a famous personality, place, or thing is played and stopped prior to the denouncement. Players, who receive only one guess per film sequence, are permitted to guess at any time during the film. If the subject is still unidentified when the film stops, a celebrity panel then provide clues to its identity. Players then have to each hazard a guess. The film is played to reveal the answer. Correct identifications award players points. The first player to score one hundred points is the winner and receives merchandise prizes.

Host: Lloyd Thaxton.

Music: Score Productions.

EVERYBODY'S TALKING—30 minutes—ABC—February 6, 1967 - October 25, 1968.

EVERYTHING'S RELATIVE

Game. Two four-member families compete, each composed of a father, a mother, and two children. The host places one member of one family in a specific situation, and asks the remaining members of that family to predict the individual's outcome. The individual is then asked to perform a stunt or answer a question. Correct predictions award one point. Each member of each family has to face an individual task. Winners are the highest point scorers.

Host: Jim Hutton.

EVERYTHING'S RELATIVE—30 minutes—Syndicated 1965.

EVIL TOUCH

Anthology. Dramatizations depicting the plight of people who, possessing the deadly seed of evil, are driven to frustration.

Host: Anthony Quayle.

Music: Laurie Lewis.

Included:

The Lake. After his wife of twenty years refuses to grant him a divorce so he can marry another woman, Arthur Randall kills her. Justice is achieved when her spirit lures him to the murder site and kills him.

CAST
Arthur Randall: Rober Lansing; Ellen Randall: Anne Hardy; Sylvia: Ann Bowden.

Dr. McDermit's New Patients. The story of a doctor who devises an ingenious plan to steal from the dead.

CAST
Tom McDermit: Richard Lupino; Jill McDermit: Kim Hunter; Nona: Pandora Bronsen.

Dear Cora, I'm Going To Kill You. The story of a woman who plots the almost perfect murder of her husband.

CAST

Cora Blake: Carol Lynley; Harry Winston: Charles McCallum; Lt. Brennan: Dennis Clinton.

A Game Of Hearts. The story of a doctor who is haunted by the original owner of a heart he transplanted.

CAST

Doctor: Darren McGavin; Marshall: Colin Croft; Anne: Judi Far.

Marci. A woman attempts to prevent her hostile stepchild from destroying her life.

CAST

Elizabeth: Susan Strasberg; Marci: Elizabeth Crosby; John: Peter Gwynne.

Happy New Year, Aunt Carrie. The story of an invalid who witnesses a gangland murder and becomes the killer's next quarry.

Starring: Julie Harris.

Program closing: (Host) "This is Anthony Quayle reminding you that there is a touch of evil in all of us. Goodnight. Pleasant dreams."

EVIL TOUCH—30 minutes—Syndicated 1973.

EXCLUSIVE

Anthology. Dramatizations based on the experiences of the members of the Overseas Press Club of America.

EXCLUSIVE—30 minutes—Syndicated 1960.

EXERCISE WITH GLORIA

Exercise. Acrobatics coupled with nutritional guidance.

Hostess: Gloria Roeder.

Assistants: Her six daughters.

EXERCISE WITH GLORIA—30 minutes—Syndicated 1964.

EXPEDITION

Documentary. Films depicting the hazardous expeditions of modern-day adventurers.

Host-Narrator: Colonel John D. Craig.

EXPEDITION—30 minutes—ABC—September 1960 - June 20, 1961. Syndicated.

THE EXPLORERS

Documentary. Films depicting the exploits of modern-day adventurers.

Host-Narrator: Leslie Nielsen.

THE EXPLORERS—30 minutes—Syndicated 1972.

EXPLORING

Educational. Through films, songs, and sketches, various aspects of the adult world are explained to children.

Host: Dr. Albert Hibbs.

Regulars: The Ritts Puppets, The Gus Soloman Dancers.

Orchestra: Fred Karlin.

EXPLORING—60 minutes—NBC—1962 - 1965.

EYE GUESS

Game. Two competing players. Tested: The ability to observe and memorize. The "Eye Guess" game board, which contains eight numbered answers, is revealed for eight seconds. At the end of the time, the answers are hidden by overlaying corresponding numbers. The host then questions the players, one at a time, by reading questions relating to the hidden answers. Each answer that is remembered by a player awards him a merchandise prize. The first player to score seven correct answers is the winner. The loser receives his choice of any prize that is on his side of the board. The winner, who receives all the prizes that are contained on his side of the board, is escorted to the "Eye Guess Risk Board." The board contains eight numbered squares, seven of which contain the word "Go;" the other "Stop." The player, who receives twenty-five dollars, chooses numbers randomly. Each "Go" that is picked doubles his cash. If "Stop" is selected he is defeated and loses all his cash. Winners compete until defeated.

Host: Bill Cullen.

Announcer: Don Pardo.

Music: Recorded.

EYE GUESS—30 minutes—NBC—January 3, 1966 - September 26, 1969.

EYE WITNESS

Anthology. Stories of people who witness accidents or crimes and come forward to testify.

Host-Narrator: Richard Carlson.

Included:

The Baby-Sitter. The story concerns a police search for a baby-sitter—the only witness to the murder of a young mother.

CAST

Evelyn Varden, Sallie Brophy, Jean Carson.

My Father's A Murderer. The story of a young girl who tries to convince her stepmother that her father murdered his first wife.

CAST

Janet Parker, Mary Stuart, Wesley Addy.

Statement Of The Accused. The story of an attorney who prosecutes a murderer on the testimony of an eyewitness.

CAST

Carl Schiller.

EYE WITNESS—30 minutes—NBC 1953.

EYE WITNESS TO HISTORY

Documentary. In-depth coverage of the single most important news story of the week.

Host: Charles Kuralt.

Narrator: Walter Cronkite.

EYE WITNESS TO HISTORY—30 minutes—CBS 1960.

ℐ

FABULOUS FRAUD

See title: "Colonel Flack."

FACE THE FACTS

Game. A criminal case is redramatized and stopped prior to conclusion. Contestants, acting as judges, bet a specific amount of points and state a verdict. The film is played and correct predictions award the bet amount of points. Winners, highest scorers, receive merchandise prizes.

Host: Red Rowe.

FACE THE FACTS—30 minutes—CBS 1961.

THE FACE IS FAMILIAR

Game. Two competing teams each composed of one celebrity captain and one noncelebrity contestant. Object: The identification of famous personalities who are shown in scrambled photographs. The host states a question. The team first to identify themselves through a buzzer signal receive a chance to answer. If the response is correct, a picture piece is placed in its appropriate position and the team receives a chance to identify the person. The game continues until the photograph is identified.

Host: Jack Whitaker.

THE FACE IS FAMILIAR—30 minutes—CBS—May 7, 1966 - September 3, 1966.

FACE THE MUSIC

Musical Variety. An entertainment session featuring two singers who alternate on the performances of current tunes.

Hosts: Johnny Desmond, Shaye Cogan.

Music: The Tony Mottola Trio.

FACE THE MUSIC—15 minutes—CBS 1949.

FACE OF DANGER

Anthology. Rebroadcasts of dramas that were originally aired via other filmed anthology programs.

Included:

Midnight Kill. A lawyer attempts to find the gangster who is responsible for the death of a policeman.

CAST
James Whitmore, Carl Benton Reid, Phyllis Avery.

Strange Defense. A lawyer attempts to discover whether a woman accused of murder is his wife who supposedly died while she was overseas, or her twin sister.

CAST
David Brian, Constance Ford.

Weapon Of Courage. The story of a disabled war veteran who struggles to overcome the feeling that he is now useless.

CAST
Kevin McCarthy, Victor Jory, Maxine Cooper.

FACE OF DANGER—30 minutes—CBS—April 18, 1959 - May 30, 1959.

FACES AND PLACES

Travel. Filmed interviews; explorations of areas about the globe.

Hosts-Narrators: Don and Bettina Shaw.

FACES AND PLACES—30 minutes—Syndicated 1965. Titled in 1967: "Travel with Don and Bettina."

FAIR EXCHANGE

Comedy. Background: New York City and London, England. Basic plot: Two families, American and British, exchange their teenage daughters for one year. Stories emphasize the girls' struggles to adjust to a foreign country and a new family; and the fathers' struggles to adjust to the temporary loss of their daughters.

American family: Eddie Walker, a World War II veteran; his wife, Dorothy; their son, Larry; and their daughter, Patty, who hopes to become an actress and wants to study at London's Royal Academy of Dramatic Arts.

British family: Tommy Finch, a World War II veteran, a friend of Eddie's; his wife, Sybil; their son, Neville; and their daugher, Heather, who wants to acquaint herself with the American way of life.

CAST

Eddie Walker	Eddie Foy, Jr.
Dorothy Walker	Audrey Christie
Patty Walker	Lynn Loring
Larry Walker	Flip Mark
Tommy Finch	Victor Maddern
Sybil Finch	Diana Chesney
Heather Finch	Judy Carne
Neville Finch	Dennis Waterman
Willie Shorthouse, Tom's friend	Maurice Dallimore

FAIR EXCHANGE—60 minutes—CBS—September 21, 1962 - March 21, 1963. 30 minutes—CBS—March 28, 1963 - September 19, 1963. Filmed in both New York and London.

FAIRMEADOWS, U.S.A.

Serial. Background: The town of Fairmeadows. The trials and tribulations of an American family.

CAST

The father	Howard St. John
His wife	Ruth Matheson
Their twenty-one-year-old son	Tom Tyler
Their nineteen-year-old daughter	Hazel Dawn, Jr.
Their thirteen-year-old daughter	Mimi Stragin

FAIRMEADOWS, U.S.A.—30 minutes—NBC 1950.

FAIR WINDS TO ADVENTURE

Travel. Films exploring little-known areas of the world.

Host-Narrator: Dr. Frank Baxter.

FAIR WINDS TO ADVENTURE—30 minutes—Syndicated 1966.

FAITH BALDWIN ROMANCE THEATRE

Anthology. Dramatizations depicting the problems faced by people in their everyday lives.

Hostess: Faith Baldwin.

FAITH BALDWIN ROMANCE THEATRE—30 minutes—ABC—January 20, 1951 - October 20, 1951.

THE FALCON

Adventure. The story of Michael Waring, a United States government undercover agent know as the Falcon. Episodes depict his battle against the global forces of injustice.

Starring: Charles McGraw as Michael Waring, The Falcon.

THE FALCON—30 minutes—Syndicated 1955. Also known as "Streets of Danger."

FAMILY AFFAIR

Comedy-Drama. Background: New York City, 600 East 32nd Street, Manhattan. When his brother and sister-in-law are killed in an automobile accident, Bill Davis, the president of the Davis and Gaynor Construction Company, agrees to raise his brother's children rather than split them up among the relatives who don't want them.

Assisted by his gentleman's gentleman, Jiles French, he attempts to provide love and security to one teenager and two lonely, disillusioned children (Catherine, known as Cissy, and twins, Buffy and Jody).

Realistically presenting children's needs and feelings, and showing that adults are capable of making mistakes, "Family Affair" distinguishes itself from other family comedies by its heartwarming, sentimental, and at times sad stories.

CAST

Bill Davis	Brian Keith
Giles French	Sebastian Cabot
Cissy Davis	Kathy Garver
Jody Davis	Johnnie Whitaker
Buffy Davis	Anissa Jones
Miss Faversham, a friend of Jiles	Heather Angel
Nigel French, Jiles's brother	John Williams
Gregg Bartlett, Cissy's boyfriend	Gregg Fedderson
Sharon James, Cissy's girlfriend	Sherry Alberoni
Emily Turner, Bill's inept maid	Nancy Walker
Ted Gaynor, Bill's partner	Philip Ober
Miss Cummings, the twin's school teacher	Joan Vohs

Music: Frank DeVol.

FAMILY AFFAIR—30 minutes—CBS —September 12, 1966 - September 9, 1971.

FAMILY CLASSICS THEATRE

Serial. The overall title for three television adaptations of literary masterpieces: *The Black Tulip; Ivanhoe; Little Women.*

The Black Tulip (serialized in six chapters). Background: Seventeenth-century Holland. Against disbelievers, Cornelius attempts to perfect his dream, a black tulip.

CAST

Cornelius	Simon Ward
Cornelius de Wit	John Phillips
Isaac	Wolfe Morris
Rosa	Tessa Wyatt
Dirk	John Cater

Ivanhoe (serialized in ten chapters). Background: England, 1194. Provoking Norman hatreds, Prince John usurps the throne from his brother, Richard the Lionhearted, while he is leading a Crusade to the Holy Land. Returning from the Crusades, a young Saxon knight, Ivanhoe, finds that he has been disowned by his father for taking part in them. The story describes in detail Ivanhoe's struggles to procure his country's crown for the rightful king, regain his inheritance, and win the hand of Lady Rowena. Based on the story by Sir Walter Scott.

CAST

Ivanhoe	Eric Flynn
Sir Brian de Bois-Guilbert, the Templar Knight	Anthony Bate
Lady Rowena	Clare Jenkins
Richard the Lion-hearted	Bernard Horsfall
Prince John	Tim Preece
Preceptor	Eric Woofe
Rebecca	Vivian Brooks
Isaac	John Franklyn Robbins

Little Women (serialized in nine chapters). Background: New England 1860s. The joys and sorrows of four young women, the March Sisters—Beth, frail and sickly; Meg, pragmatic; Jo, an aspiring writer; and Amy, feminine and flirtatious. A detailed insight into nineteenth-century life. Based on the story by Louisa May Alcott.

CAST

Mrs. March (Marmie)	Stephanie Bidmead
Beth March	Sarah Craze
Meg March	Jo Rowbottom
Amy March	Janina Faye
Jo March	Angela Down
Aunt March	Jean Anderson
Laurie	Stephanie Turner
Professor Bhaer	Frederick Jaeger

FAMILY CLASSICS THEATRE—30 minutes—Syndicated 1971.

THE FAMILY GAME

Game. Three families compete, each composed of the father, the mother, and two children. Questions, which were asked of the children prior to the broadcast, are restated with their answers in mixed order. The parents of each team then have to match the correct answers with the children who said them. Each correct match awards that family one point. The winners, the highest point scorers, receive merchandise prizes.

Host: Bob Barker.

THE FAMILY GAME—30 minutes—ABC—June 19, 1967 - July 2, 1968.

THE FAMILY HOLVAK

Drama. Background: The small Southern town of Benfield during the Depression of the 1930s. The life of Reverend Tom Holvak as he struggles to feed his family and maintain the faith of his congregation.

CAST

Rev. Tom Holvak	Glenn Ford
Elizabeth Holvak, his wife	Julie Harris
Ramey Holvak, their son	Lance Kerwin
Julie Mae Holvak, their daughter	Elizabeth Cheshire
Jim Shanks, the police deputy	William McKinney
Chester Purdle, the owner of the general store	Ted Gehring
Ida, Chester's assistant	Cynthia Hayward.

Music: Dick De Benedicks; Lee Holdridge; Hal Mooney.

THE FAMILY HOLVAK—60 minutes—NBC—September 7, 1975 - October 27, 1975.

THE FAMOUS ADVENTURES OF MR. MAGOO

Animated Cartoon. Video adaptations

of legendary tales and figures of past history and literature.

Host-Story Teller-Star: Quincy Magoo (Voiced by Jim Backus).

Additional Voices: Marvin Miller, Howard Morris, Julie Bennett, Shepard Menkin, Joe Gardner, Paul Frees.

Music: Charles Brandt.

THE FAMOUS ADVENTURES OF MR. MAGOO—30 minutes—NBC— September 19, 1964 - August 21, 1965. Syndicated.

FAMOUS CLASSIC TALES

Animated Cartoon. Adaptations of literary works. Produced in Australia.

Voices: Elizabeth Crosby, Barbara Frawley, Tim Elliot, Richard Meikle, Ron Haddrick, Bob Frawley, Don Pascoe.

Music: Richard Bowden.

Included:

The Prince And The Pauper. Background: Sixteenth-century England. The story of the begger boy who changes places with his double, the Prince of Wales. Based on the novel by Mark Twain.

The Legend Of Robin Hood. The story of Robin Hood, who stole from the rich to give to the poor. Based on the minstrel ballads, which tell of his skill as an archer.

Twenty Thousand Leagues Under The Sea. Jules Verne's classic tale of the submarine *Nautilus* and its deranged scientist-captain, Nemo.

Swiss Family Robinson. The story of the Robinson family's struggle for survival after being shipwrecked on a deserted island. Based on the story by Robert Louis Stevenson.

FAMOUS CLASSIC TALES—60 minutes—CBS—September 23, 1973 - December 2, 1973.

FAMOUS JURY TRIALS

Drama. Background: A simulated courtroom. A case, usually murder, is in progress when an episode begins. The on-the-spot battle between the prosecutor and the defense attorney is depicted. Both present their briefs and the incidents of actual cases are reenacted through flashbacks.

Versions:

Famous Jury Trials—30 minutes—DuMont 1949.

Prosecutor: Jim Bender.

Defense Attorney: Truman Smith.

Famous Jury Trials—30 minutes—Syndicated 1971.

CAST
Donnelly Rhodes, Allen Doremus, Tim Henry, Joanna Noyers, Cec Linder.

FANFARE

Anthology. Rebroadcasts of dramas that were originally aired via other filmed anthology programs.

Host: Richard Derr.

Included:

For Better Or For Worse. Unable to accept the fact that his former law partner is guilty of destroying evidence in a blackmail case, for which he was arrested, Jim Pierson, now governor, attempts to clear his name.

CAST

Jim Pierson: Mark Stevens.

The Break Off. Because of his ability to keep himself under control in adverse conditions, pilot Duke Cavannaugh is selected to test an experimental supersonic jet. The story focuses on the conflict that arises when tragedy affects his personal life hours before the scheduled test.

CAST

Duke Cavannaugh: Ralph Meeker; Jim Mitchell: Barry Atwater; Dr. Temple: Barney Phillips

Operation Snowball. A wife is suspected of having an affair with her husband's best friend. Innocent, the wife decides to remedy the situation and attempts to find her supposed lover a wife.

CAST

Virginia Mayo, Lee Goodman, Art Fleming, Chris White.

Seed From The End. The true story of the Holt family, people who have devoted their lives to helping Korean-American war orphans find foster homes in the U.S.

CAST

Dean Jagger, Virginia Christine, Donna Boyce.

FANFARE—30 minutes—CBS—June 1959 - September 1959.

FANFARE

Musical Variety.

Host: Al Hirt.

Featured: The Don McKayle Dancers.

Orchestra: Mort Lindsey.

FANFARE—60 minutes—CBS—June 1965 - September 11, 1965.

THE FANTASTIC FOUR

Animated Cartoon. When their rocket ship penetrates a strange radioactive belt that is encircling the Earth, four people acquire fantastic powers. Scientist Reed Richards acquires the ability to stretch like taffy; Sue Richards, his wife, possesses the ability to become invisible at will; Ben Grimm becomes "The Thing," a beast with the strength of a thousand men; and Johnny Storm, who acquires the ability to turn to fire, becomes "The Human Torch." Stories relate their battle against the sinister forces of evil. A Hanna-Barbera production.

Characters' Voices

Reed Richards	Gerald Mohr
Sue Richards	Jo Ann Pflug
Johnny Storm	Jack Flounders
Ben Grimm	Paul Frees

Music: Hoyt Curtin.

THE FANTASTIC FOUR—30 minutes—ABC—September 9, 1967 - March 15, 1970.

FANTASTIC VOYAGE

Animated Cartoon. Background: C.M.D.F. (Combined Miniature Defense Force), a secret United States government organization possessing the ability to reduce people to microscopic size. Agents: Commander Jonathan Kidd; biologist Erica Stone; scientist Cosby Birdwell; and The

Guru, "the master of mysterious powers." Reduced in size the team travels in the *Voyager,* a microscopic plane. Stories relate their battle against the unseen, unsuspecting enemies of the free world (criminal and germinal matter). Based on the movie of the same title.

Voices: Marvin Miller, Jane Webb, Ted Knight.

Music: Gordon Zahler.

FANTASTIC VOYAGE—30 minutes —ABC—September 14, 1968 - September 5, 1970. Syndicated.

FARADAY AND COMPANY

See title: "NBC Wednesday Mystery Movie," *Faraday and Company* segment.

FARAWAY HILL

Serial. Television's first dramatic serial. Background: New York. The story of a woman who, after the death of her husband, seeks an escape from the memories of their life together. The action is bridged by an off-stage voice talking to the lead and revealing her thoughts.

CAST

The Woman   Flora Campbell
Also: Ann Stell, Mel Brandt, Lorene Scott, Frederick Meyer, Melville Gilliart, Jacqueline Waite, Ben Low, Jack Holloran, Vivian King, Bill Gale, Eve Meagh, Julie Christy, Hal Studer, Barry Doig, Munia Gabler.

FARAWAY HILL—30 minutes— DuMont 1946.

THE FARMER'S DAUGHTER

Comedy. Background: 307 Marshall Road, Washington, D.C., the residence of the Morley family: Glen, widower and congressman; his mother, Agatha; and his children, Steven and Danny.

Seeking a government job teaching underprivileged children in the Congo, Katy Holstrum, a beautiful Minnesota farm girl, approaches Glen and requests his help and endorsement. His offer to assist her results in the unexpected delay of red tape and application approval.

Residing with the Morleys, she quickly wins over the affections of Steve and Danny. Impressed with her beauty, and ability to handle his sons, Glen offers her the position of governess, which she accepts.

Stories depict: the home and working life of a congressman; and the attempts of a Swedish country girl to adjust to both political and city life.

The Farmer's Daughter. Inger Stevens and William Windom. © *Screen Gems.*

Based on the movie, *The Farmer's Daughter,* which stars Loretta Young.

CAST

Katy Holstrum	Inger Stevens
Glen Morley	William Windom
Agatha Morley	Cathleen Nesbitt
Steven Morley	Mickey Sholdar
Danny Morley	Rory O'Brien
Chester Cooper, Glen's associate	Philip Coolidge
Senator Charles Ames, Glen's friend	David Lewis
Lars Holstrum, Katy's father	Walter Sande
Mama Holstrum, his wife	Alice Frost
Clemmy Hoyle, Katy's friend	Emmaline Henry
Margaret, Katy's friend	Nancy Rennick
	Barbara Bostock
Charlotte, Katy's friend	Marilyn Lovell
Molly, Katy's friend	Shelly Morrison

Music: Dave Grusin.

THE FARMER'S DAUGHTER—30 minutes—ABC—September 20, 1963 - September 2, 1966. Syndicated.

FAR OUT SPACE NUTS

Comedy. While loading food aboard a moon rocket at a NASA space center, ground crewmen Junior and Barney accidentally launch the ship and are propelled into the vast regions of outer space. Stories relate their misadventures on unknown planets and their attempts to return to Earth.

CAST

Junior	Bob Denver
Barney	Chuck McCann
Honk, their pet space creature	Patty Maloney
Lantana, their alien friend	Eve Bruce
Crakor, Lantana's robot	Stan Jenson

Music: Michael Lloyd.

FAR OUT SPACE NUTS—25 minutes—CBS—Premiered: September 6, 1975.

FASHION

Women. Fashion previews. Guests and interviews.

Hostess: Arlene Francis.

FASHION—15 minutes—CBS 1951.

FASHION MAGIC

Women. Fashion previews. Guests and interviews.

Hostess: Ilka Chase.

Music: Provided by guests.

FASHION MAGIC—30 minutes—CBS 1950.

FASHION PREVIEW

Women. Fashion trends as reported by the designers themselves. Filmed in cooperation with the leading women's magazines.

FASHION PREVIEW—12 minutes—Syndicated 1951.

FASHION SHOW

Variety. Fashion previews coupled

with music, songs, and interviews.

Hosts: Marilyn Day, Carl Reiner.

Regulars: Pamela O'Neill, Doris Lane, Patsy Davis, Elaine Joyce, Don Saxon.

FASHION SHOW—30 minutes—NBC 1949.

FAST DRAW

Game. Two competing teams of two, each composed of one celebrity captain and one noncelebrity contestant. The host presents one member of each team with a secret phrase (book, movie, or song). Players, one at a time, within a fifteen second time limit, have to draw cartoon charades to identify it. The teammate has to identify the charade. Winners, the team that identify the most charades, receive merchandise prizes.

Host: Johnny Gilbert.

Announcer: Fred Scott.

FAST DRAW—30 minutes - Syndicated 1968.

FAST GUNS

See title: "Stories of the Century."

FAT ALBERT AND THE COSBY KIDS

Animated Cartoon. Background: Nothern Philadelphia. The fond recollections of Bill Cosby's childhood buddies—Fat Albert, Rudy, Weird Harold, Edward, Mush Mouth, Donald, Bucky, and Russell (Bill's brother). Characters and situations are designed, through their acitvities, to educate and entertain children as to the meanings of topics in everyday life.

Host: Bill Cosby.

Voices: Bill Cosby, Keith Allen, Gerald Edwards, Pepe Brown, Jon Crawford, Lane Vaux.

FAT ALBERT AND THE COSBY KIDS—30 minutes—CBS—Premiered: September 9, 1972.

FATHER KNOWS BEST

Comedy. Background: 607 South Maple Street, Springfield. The dreams, ambitions and frustrations of the Anderson family: Jim, manager of the General Insurance Company; his wife Margaret; and their children, Betty, Bud, and Kathy. Stories tenderly mirror their lives. Based on the radio program of the same title.

CAST

Jim Anderson	Robert Young
Margaret Anderson	Jane Wyatt
Betty Anderson (Princess)	Elinor Donahue
Bud Anderson (James Anderson, Jr.)	Billy Gray
Kathy Anderson (Kitten)	Lauren Chapin
Miss Thomas, Jim's secretary	Sarah Selby
Claude Messner, Bud's friend	Jimmy Bates
Kippy Watkins, Bud's friend	Paul Wallace
Joyce Kendell, Bud's girlfriend	Roberta Shore
Ralph Little, Betty's boyfriend	Robert Chapman
Ed Davis, the Anderson's neighbor	Robert Foulk
Myrtle Davis, his wife	Vivi Jannis

Father Knows Best. Bottom, left to right:
Billy Gray, Lauren Chapin, Elinor Donahue.
Top, left: Jane Wyatt. Right: Robert Young.
© *Screen Gems.*

Dottie Snow, Betty's
    friend   Yvonne Lime
Patty Davis, Kathy's
    friend   Tina Thompson
                                    Reba Waters
April Adams, Bud's
    girlfriend   Sue George
Burgess Vale, Kathy's boyfriend
    (early episodes)   Richard Eyer
Grover Adams, April's brother,,
    Kathy's boyfriend (later
    episodes)   Richard Eyer
Hubert Armstead, the high
    school principal   Sam Flint
Emily Vale, Margaret's
    friend   Lenore Kingston

Joe Phillips, Bud's
    friend   Peter Heisser
Music: Irving Friedman.

FATHER KNOWS BEST—30 minutes.
CBS—October 3, 1954 - March 27,
1955; NBC—August 31, 1955 - September 17, 1958; CBS—September 22,
1958 - September 17, 1962; ABC
(rebroadcasts)—September 30, 1962 -
February 3, 1967. Syndicated.

FATHER OF THE BRIDE

Comedy.   Background: 24   Maple

Drive, Fairview Manor, Connecticut. The trials and tribulations of attorney Stanley Banks, the father of the bride from the first shock of his daughter, Kay, becoming engaged through the meeting of the families, the wedding preparations, the ceremony, and the first months of marriage. Also detailed are the struggles of the newlyweds, Kay and Buckley Dunston, from the first spats and the threats to go home to mother through their new roles as parents. Based on the movie of the same title.

CAST

Stanley Banks	Leon Ames
Ellie Banks, his wife	Ruth Warrick
Kay Banks (Dunston)	Myrna Fahey
Buckley Dunston	Burt Metcalfe
Tommy Banks, Kay's brother	Rickie Sorensen
Delilah, the Banks' housekeeper	Ruby Dandridge
Gloria Bellamy, Stanley's secretary	Shelly Ames
Herbert Dunston, Buckley's father	Ransom Sherman
Doris Dunston, Buckley's mother	Lurene Tuttle

FATHER OF THE BRIDE—30 minutes—CBS—1961-1962.

FAVORITE STORY

Anthology. Dramatizations based on stories selected by guests.

Host: Adolphe Menjou.

Included:

The Gold Bug. Adapted from the story by Edgar Allen Poe. The story of two Confederate soldiers who take up residence on a desolate island to brood over their impoverishment.

Starring: Neville Brand.

Canterville Ghost. Adapted from the story by Oscar Wilde. The story of a ghost who is doomed to haunt his family home because of a cowardly act in his past.

Starring: John Qualen.

Strange Valley. Adapted from the story by H. G. Wells. The story of an adventurer who finds himself in the strange valley of the blind.

Starring: Kenneth Tobey, Carla Balenda.

FAVORITE STORY—30 minutes—Syndicated 1952.

FAY

Comedy. Background: San Francisco, California. The joys, sorrows, and romantic misadventures of Fay Stuart, a middle-aged divorcée.

CAST

Fay Stuart, a legal secretary	Lee Grant
Jack Stuart, her philandering ex-husband	Joe Silver
Lillian, Fay's neighbor	Audra Lindley
Linda Baines, Fay's married daughter	Margaret Willock
Dr. Elliott Baines, Linda's husband	Stewart Moss
Danny Messina, Fay's employer, a crusading young lawyer	Bill Gerber
Al Cassidy, Danny's	

conservative part-
ner   Norman Alden
Letty Gilmore, Al's
    secretary   Lillian Lehman

Music: George Tipton.

Theme Vocal: Jaye P. Morgan.

FAY—30 minutes—NBC—September 8, 1975 - October 23, 1975.

FAYE AND SKITCH

See title: "Faye Emerson."

FAYE EMERSON

Listed: The television programs of actress Faye Emerson.

Paris Cavalcade Of Fashion—Fashion Highlights—15 minutes—NBC—August 13, 1948 - December 16, 1948.

Narrator: Faye Emerson.

The Faye Emerson Show—Interview—15 minutes—CBS—October 4, 1949 - April 12, 1952.

Hostess: Faye Emerson.

Regulars: Mary Bennett, Kenneth Banghart.

Orchestra: Skitch Henderson.

Wonderful Town—Variety—30 minutes—CBS 1951.

Format: A U.S. city is selected and interviews are conducted with outstanding individuals.

Hostess: Faye Emerson.

Vocalists: The Don Large Chorus.

Orchestra: Skitch Henderson.

Strictly Skitch—Musical Variety-Interview—15 minutes—NBC—1952-1953.

Broadcast on ABC as "Faye and Skitch"—15 minutes—1953-1954.

Hostess: Faye Emerson.

Co-Host: Skitch Henderson.

Music (NBC): The NBC Symphony Orchestra; ABC: Skitch Henderson Orchestra.

Of All Things—Musical Variety—30 minutes—CBS—July 23, 1956 - August 20, 1956.

Hostess: Faye Emerson.

Regulars: Ilehe Woods, Jack Haskell.

Announcer: Del Sharbutt.

Orchestra: Billy Clifton.

THE F.B.I.

Crime Drama. Case dramatizations based on the files of the Federal Bureau of Investigation.

The F.B.I. Lynn Loring (center), Stephen Brooks, and Efrem Zimbalist, Jr.

CAST

Inspector Lewis
    Erskine   Efrem Zimbalist, Jr.
Arthur Ward, the assistant
    director   Philip Abbott
Jim Rhodes, Erskine's
    assistant   Stephen Brooks
Barbara Erskine, the Inspector's
    daughter   Lynn Loring
Agent Tom Colby   William Reynolds
Agent Chris Daniels   Shelly Novack
Agent Chet Randolph Anthony Eisley

Narrator: Marvin Miller.

Music: Richard Markowitz; John Elizade.

THE F.B.I.—60 minutes—ABC—September 19, 1965 - September 1, 1974. Syndicated.

F.D.R.

Documentary. The life and administration of former president Franklin D. Roosevelt is traced through newsreel footage.

Host-Narrator: Arthur Kennedy.

F.D.R.'s writings read by: Charlton Heston.

F.D.R.—30 minutes—ABC—January 8, 1965 - September 10, 1965.

FEAR AND FANCY

Anthology. Dramatizations of people involved with supernatural happenings.

FEAR AND FANCY—30 minutes—ABC—May 13, 1953 - September 5, 1953.

FEATHER YOUR NEST

Game. Various household furnishings are displayed on stage. Two couples select desired pieces. Within a specified time limit, one member of each team has to find a hidden feather in chosen articles. The questions contained by the feather are answered by the other teammate. Each correct answer awards the couple the represented merchandise.

Host: Bud Collyer.

Assistants: Lou Prentiss, Janis Carter, Joan Williams.

FEATHER YOUR NEST—30 minutes—CBS—1954-1956.

THE FELONY SQUAD

Crime Drama. Background: Los Angeles, California. The investigations of L.A.P.D. detectives Sam Stone and Jim Briggs.

CAST

Detective Sam Stone   Howard Duff
Detective Jim Briggs   Dennis Cole
Sergeant Dan Briggs, Jim's
    father   Ben Alexander

THE FELONY SQUAD—30 minutes—ABC—September 12, 1966 - January 31, 1969. Syndicated.

FELIX THE CAT

Animated Cartoon. The story of Felix, a cat who possesses a magic black bag that can grant its owner any wish. Cliff-hanger-type episodes relate the ill-fated attempts of the Professor and his accomplices, Rock Bottom and Poindexter, to acquire the bag for

The Felony Squad. Left to right: Dennis Cole, Kevin Hagen (guest), Howard Duff.

the power it will afford them. Voices and music are not given screen credit.

FELIX THE CAT—04 minutes—Syndicated 1960.

FESTIVAL OF FAMILY CLASSICS

Animated Cartoon. Video adaptations of classic fairy tales.

Voices: Carl Banas, Peg Dixon, Keith Hampshire, Len Birman, Peggi Loader, Donna Miller.

Music: Maury Laws.

Included:

Hiawatha. Henry Wadsworth Longfellow's story of the strength and courage of an Indian warrior.

Snow White And The Seven Dwarfs. An adaptation wherein the Seven Dwarfs attempt to save Snow White from her cruel stepmother.

Around The World In 80 Days. The story of Phineas Fogg, who attempts to travel around the world in eighty days.

20,000 Leagues Under The Sea. Jules Verne's classic tale of Captain Nemo as he journeys to the ocean's depths.

FESTIVAL OF FAMILY CLASSICS —30 minutes—Syndicated 1972.

FESTIVAL OF STARS

Anthology. Rebroadcasts of episodes of "The Loretta Young Theatre" that do not star Loretta Young.

Host: Jim Ameche.

Included:

Incident In Kawi. Background: Africa. The story of a big-game hunter who attempts to adjust to new responsibilities when he is put in charge of his recently orphaned nephew.

CAST
Don O'Herlihy, Vanessa Brown, Frederick Worlock.

My Uncles O'Moore. Era: The 1920s. When a schoolmarm is imported for the sole purpose of marriage to one of the O'Moore boys, she finds herself rejected because she is considered too frail for ranch life. The story concerns her efforts to prove her ability.

CAST
Teresa Wright.

The Wise One. The story of a prospector who seeks a legendary silver mine to help a needy tribe of Indians.

CAST
Stephen McNally, Joy Page.

FESTIVAL OF STARS—30 minutes —NBC—June 30, 1956 - September 1956; July 2, 1957 - September 1957.

FIBBER McGEE AND MOLLY

Comedy. Background: The town of Wistful Vista. The trials and tribulations of the McGees: Fibber, amateur inventor, the world's greatest liar; and his tolerant wife, Molly, who reside at 79 Wistful Vista. Based on the radio program of the same title.

CAST

Fibber McGee	Bob Sweeny
Molly McGee	Cathy Lewis
Mayor Charles La Trivia	Hal Peary
Roy Norris, Fibber's friend and neighbor	Paul Smith
Hazel Norris, his wife	Elizabeth Fraser
Doctor John Gamble, the town physician	Addison Richards
Teeny, the little girl next door	Barbara Beaird
Mrs. La Trivia, the mayor's wife	Dorothy Neumann
Mrs. Driscoll, Molly's mother	Reta Shaw

FIBBER McGEE AND MOLLY—30 minutes—NBC—1959 - 1960.

54th STREET REVUE

Musical Variety. Background: The 54th Street Theatre in New York City.

CAST
Jack Sterling, Carl Reiner, Joey Faye, Joe Silver, Marilyn Day, Tommy Wonder, Jordan Bentley, Virginia Gorski, Mort Marshall, Billy Vine, Joan Diener, Russell Arms, Patricia Bright, Bambi Linn, Annabell Lyons, Count Reno, Jonathan Lucas, Jimmy Spitarny.

Music: Albert Selden.

54th STREET REVUE—60 minutes— CBS 1949.

THE FIGHT FOR LIFE

Medical Discussion. Interviews between doctors and their patients who have made near-miraculous recoveries.

Hostess: Kathryn Crosby, R.N.

THE FIGHT FOR LIFE—30 minutes —Syndicated 1967.

THE FILES OF JEFFREY JONES

Crime Drama. Background: New York City. The confidential investigations of private detective Jeffrey Jones.

CAST

Jeffrey Jones	Don Haggerty
Michele "Mike" Malone, his girlfriend, a newspaper reporter	Gloria Henry

THE FILES OF JEFFREY JONES— 30 minutes—Syndicated 1955.

FILM ODYSSEY

Movies. Foreign and American film classics.

Host: Charles Champlin, Movie critic for the *Los Angeles Times.*

Included:

M (German; 1931). A psychological chiller. The grim police search for Franz Becker, a demented child killer terrorizing Berlin.

CAST

Franz Becker: Peter Lorre; Child: Inge Landgut; Mother: Ellen Widmann.

The Blue Angel (German, 1930). The destruction of a respected school

master, Professor Roth, as depicted through his marriage to a beautiful cabaret entertainer, Lola.

CAST

Lola: Marlene Dietrich; Professor Roth: Emil Jannings.

Our Daily Bread (U.S., 1934). Era: The 1930s. The struggles of a young city couple who resort to farming to survive the Depression.

CAST

Karen Morley, Tom Keens, Barbara Pepper, Addison Richards.

The Cabinet Of Dr. Caligari (German, 1919). The tale of the evil hypnotist, Caligari, and of the murders committed by his ghoulish sleepwalker, Cesare.

CAST

Caligari: Werner Krauss; Cesare: Conrad Veidt.

FILM ODYSSEY—2 hours—PBS—January 15, 1972 - July 3, 1973.

FIREBALL FUN FOR ALL

Variety. Music, songs, and slapstick comedy.

Hosts: John "Ole" Olsen (tall and thin); Harold "Chic" Johnson (short and fat)—insult comics.

Regulars: Pat Donahue, Marty May, June Johnson, Bill Hays, The Lyn Dudley Singers.

Orchestra: Charles Sanford.

FIREBALL FUN FOR ALL—60 minutes—NBC—1949-1950.

FIREBALL XL-5

Marionette Adventure. Era: Twenty-first-century Earth. Background: Space City, the headquarters of the Galaxy Patrol, the futuristic police force. Stories relate its attempts to protect the planets of a united solar system from the sinister forces bent on destroying its truce. Filmed in Supermarionation.

Characters:
Colonel Steve Zodiac, the pilot of Fireball XL-5.
Venus, his co-pilot.
Commander Zero, the Space City controller.
Lieutenant 90, a Space Patrol pilot.
Professor Matic, the scientific genius.
Robert the Robot, the electronic brain.
Mr. and Mrs. Superspy, notorious villains of the universe.
The Briggs Brothers, saboteurs, enemies of Space City.

Voices: Paul Maxwell, Sylvia Anderson, David Graham, John Bluthal.

Music: Barry Gray.

FIREBALL XL-5—30 minutes—NBC —1963-1965. Syndicated.

FIREHOUSE

Drama. Background: California. The work of the men of Engine Company Number 23 of the Los Angeles County Fire Department.

CAST

Captain Spike Ryerson	James Drury
Hank Myers	Richard Jaeckel
Sonny Capito	Mike Delano
Cal Dakin	Bill Overton
Scotty Smith	Scott Smith
Billy Del Zel	Brad David

Music: Billy Goldenberg.

FIREHOUSE—30 minutes—ABC—January 17, 1974 - August 1, 1974.

FIRESIDE THEATRE

Anthology. Dramatic presentations.

Hosts: Gene Raymond; Jane Wyman (under title: "Jane Wyman's Fireside Theatre").

Included:

I Cover Korea. Possessing vital enemy information acquired from a prisoner, war correspondent Wanda Brown must decide whether to release it to the press or inform United Nations officials.

CAST
Wanda Brown: Marguerite Chapman; Steve Trent: Donald Woods.

His Name Is Jason. The story of an illiterate wife who devotes her life to her educated but alcoholic husband.

CAST
Gertrude Michtal, John Warburton.

Grey Gardens. After escaping the bounds of his Oriental jailers, a secret service agent returns to his home in the South and struggles to find peace.
Starring: Arthur Franz.

We'll Never Have A Nickel. The story of the unknown force behind a successful producer.

CAST
Gerry Warren: Hayden Rorke; Eva: Ann Doran; Penny: Gloria Talbot; Ben Morris: Taylor Holmes.

Mirage. Fleeing from police, a circus roustabout finds refuge at the farmhouse of a former circus performer, now housewife. Without arousing his suspicions, she seeks a way to acquire help.

CAST
Marjorie Lord, Bill Henry.

FIRESIDE THEATRE—30 minutes—NBC—1949-1955. Syndicated.

FIRING LINE

Discussion. Public officials are interviewed on topical issues.

Host: William F. Buckley, Jr., conservative spokesman.

FIRING LINE—60 minutes—Syndicated 1971; PBS—60 minutes—Premiered: May 26, 1971.

THE FIRST HUNDRED YEARS

Serial. Background: New York City. The dramatic story of young marrieds Chris and Connie Thayer.

CAST
Chris Thayer	Jimmy Lydon
Connie Thayer	Anne Sargent
	Olive Stacey
Mr. Thayer, Chris's father	Don Tobin
Mrs. Thayer, his wife	Valerie Cassort
Mr. Martin, Connie's father	Robert Armstrong
Mrs. Martin, his wife	Nana Bryant

Also: Nancy Malone, Larry Haines.

Announcer: Cy Harris.

Organist: Clark Morgan.

THE FIRST HUNDRED YEARS—15 minutes—CBS—December 4, 1950 - June 27, 1952.

FIRST LOVE

Serial. The dramatic story of young marrieds Laurie and Zachary James.

CAST
Laurie James	Patricia Barry
Zachary James	Val Dufour
Bruce McKee	Jay Barney
Penny Hughes	Rosemary Prinz

Also: Frederic Downs, Hal Currier, Henrietta Moore, Joe Warren, Scotty McGregor, Henry Slanton, Howard Smith.

FIRST LOVE—15 minutes—NBC—July 5, 1954 - December 30, 1955.

FIRST PERSON SINGULAR

Anthology. Dramatizations incorporating the subjective camera—a technique developed by Fred Coe for the feature film *Lady in the Lake* (1946). The television camera becomes the eyes of the characters; and unseen actor or actress provides the voice and sets the emotional tone.

Included:

I'd Rather Be a Squirrel. The story of a man who, when situations become difficult, retreats to a tree.

Starring: Wally Cox.

August Heat. A tale of the supernatural; a man envisions his own doom.

Starring: Francis L. Sullivan, Nelson Olmstead.

Tears Of My Sister. The story of a woman who is forced to marry a man she does not love. The problems of the marriage arranged by their families is seen through the eyes of the woman's younger sister.

Starring: Kim Stanley, Lenka Patterson.

One Night Stand. A young man attempts to prove to his depressed father that he is a success as a jazz-band leader.

Starring: James Dunn, Conrad Janis.

Comeback. An agent attempts to trick a fading, but once glamorous, actress into accepting a role she doesn't want.

Starring: Jessie Royce Landis, Jack Warden, Murray Hamilton, John Fletcher.

FIRST PERSON SINGULAR—30 minutes—NBC—June 1953 - September 1953. The subjective camera technique was also encompassed in "The Plainclothesman." (See title.)

FIVE FINGERS

Mystery.   Background: Europe. The story of United States counterintelligence agent Victor Sebastian. Episodes relate his attempts to infiltrate and inform authorities of the activities of Soviet espionage rings.

CAST
Victor Sebastian   David Hedison
Simone Genet, his
    assistant   Luciana Paluzzi

Music: David Raskin.

FIVE FINGERS—60 minutes—NBC—October 3, 1959 - January 6, 1960. Syndicated.

FIVE STAR COMEDY

Comedy. Geared to children and featuring the performances of five comedians.

Hosts for the five-week run of the series: Ben Blue; Jerry Colona; Ole Olsen and Chic Johnson; Senior Wences; Paul Winchell and Jerry Mahoney.

FIVE STAR COMEDY—30 minutes—ABC—May 18, 1957 - June 15, 1957.

FLASH GORDON

Adventure. Era: Twenty-first-century Earth. The exploits of Flash Gordon, the resourceful son of a famous scientist; Dale Arden, "the beautiful blonde always in distress"; and Dr. Alexis Zarkov, the scientific genius who invented Earth's first rocket ship. Stories relate their efforts to preserve peace in outer space.

TV CAST
Flash Gordon   Steve Holland
Dale Arden   Irene Champlin
Dr. Alexis Zarkov   Joseph Nash

FLASH GORDON—30 minutes—Syndicated 1953.

Based on the comic strip by Alex Raymond, which appeared in 1934, three theatrical series were also produced: *Flash Gordon,* 1936; *Flash Gordon's Trip To Mars,* 1939; and *Flash Gordon Conquers the Universe,* 1940.

THEATRICAL CAST
Flash Gordon   Larry "Buster" Crabbe
Dale Arden   Jean Rogers
              Carol Hughes
Dr. Zarkov   Frank Shannon

Emperor Ming ("Ming
   the Merciless")Charles Middleton
Princess Aura   Priscilla Lawson

FLATT AND SCRUGGS

Musical Variety. Performances by Country and Western artists.

Hosts: Earl Flatt and Lester Scruggs (singer-musicians).

FLATT AND SCRUGGS—30 minutes —Syndicated 1966.

FLIGHT

Anthology. Dramatizations based on true stories from the files of the United States Air Force.

Host: Gen. George C. Kenney, USAF (Ret.)

FLIGHT—30 minutes—Syndicated 1958.

THE FLINTSTONES

Animated Cartoon. The life style of the twentieth century is depicted in the Stone Age era of the one million forties, B.C. Background: The town of Bedrock, 345 Stone Cave Road, the residence of the Flintstones: Fred, a dino operator for the Slaterock Gravel Company; and his wife, Wilma. With

The Flintstones. Left to right: Fred Flintstone, Wilma Flintstone, Barney Rubble, Betty Rubble. *Courtesy Hanna-Barbera Productions.*

their friends and neighbors, Barney and Betty Rubble, they struggle to make ends meet and enjoy a few luxuries.

Produced by Joseph Hanna and William Barbera, "The Flintstones" became television's first "adult cartoon," a situation comedy in animated form, wherein a Stone Age family is beset by problems similar to the protagonists in "The Honeymooners" (see title). Fred and Barney are the prototypes of Ralph and Norton; and Wilma and Betty are the prototypes of Alice and Trixie. Similarities include their struggles to better their lives, and their association with lodges—Ralph and Norton belong to The Raccoon Lodge; Fred and Barney to The Royal Order of Water Buffalos.

Characters' Voices

Fred Flintstone	Alan Reed
Wilma Flintstone	Jean VanderPyl
Barney Rubble	Mel Blanc
Betty Rubble	Bea Benaderet
	Gerry Johnson
Dino, the Flintstone pet dinosaur	Chips Spam
Pebbles Flintstone, Fred and Wilma's daughter	Jean VanderPyl
Bamm Bamm Rubble, Barney and Betty's son	Don Messick
Hoppy, the Rubble family pet	Don Messick
George Slate, Fred's employer	John Stephenson

Additional characters: Arnold, the newspaper boy; Mrs. Flaghoople, Wilma's mother; the Gazoo, a space creature dispatched from the planet Zetox and ordered to assist deserving underdogs Fred and Barney.

Music: Hoyt Curtin; Ted Nichols.

Spin-Offs:

Pebbles And Bamm Bamm. The story of the teenage Flintstone and Rubble children, Pebbles and Bamm Bamm. Episodes revolve around their activities while attending Bedrock High School.

Characters' Voices

Pebbles Flintstone	Sally Struthers
Bamm Bamm Rubble	Jay North
Moonrock	Lennie Weinrib
Fabian	Carl Esser
Penny	Mitzi McCall
Cindy	Gay Hartwig
Wiggy	Gay Hartwig

Music: Hoyt Curtin.

The Flintstones Comedy Hour; The Flintstones Show. Continued events in the lives of the Flintstones and the Rubbles.

Characters' Voices

Fred Flintstone	Alan Reed
Barney Rubble	Mel Blanc
Wilma Flintstone	Jean VanderPyl
Betty Rubble	Gay Hartwig
Pebbles Flintstone	Mickey Stevens
Bamm Bamm Rubble	Jay North
Moonrock	Lennie Weinrib
Penny	Mitzi McCall
Fabian	Carl Esser
Schleprock	Don Messick
Wiggy	Gay Hartwig
Bronto	Lennie Weinrib
Zonk	Mel Blanc
Noodles	John Stephenson
Stub	Mel Blanc

Music: Hoyt Curtin.

THE FLINTSTONES—30 minutes—ABC—September 30, 1960 - September 2, 1966. Syndicated. Rebroadcasts, NBC: September 2, 1967 - September 5, 1970. Syndicated.

PEBBLES AND BAMM BAMM—30 minutes—CBS—September 11, 1971 - September 2, 1972.

THE FLINTSTONES COMEDY

HOUR—60 minutes—CBS—September 9, 1972 - September 1, 1973.

THE FLINTSTONES SHOW—30 minutes—CBS—September 8, 1973 - January 26, 1974.

FLIPPER

Adventure. Background: Coral Key Park in Florida. The story of Porter Ricks, widower, the marine preserve ranger; his sons, Sandy and Bud; and their pet dolphin, Flipper, who assists them in patrolling and protecting the park.

CAST
Ranger Porter Ricks	Brian Kelly
Sandy Ricks	Luke Halpin
Bud Ricks	Tommy Norden
Ulla Norstrand, a research chemist	Ulla Stromstedt
Hap Gorman, a friend of the boys	Andy Devine
Flipper	Susie

Porter family pets: Pete the pelican; and Spray the dog.

Music: Henry Vars; Samuel Motlovsky.

FLIPPER—30 minutes—NBC—September 19, 1964 - May 14, 1967. Syndicated.

THE FLIP WILSON SHOW

Variety. Various comedy sketches.

Host: Flip Wilson.

Dancers: The Flipettes: Marguerite DeLain, Ka Ron Brown, Jaki Morrison, Edwetta Little, Bhetty Waldron, Mary Vivian.

Orchestra: George Wyle.

THE FLIP WILSON SHOW—60 minutes—NBC—September 17, 1970 - June 27, 1974.

FLOOR SHOW

Music. Performances by jazz musicians.

Host: Eddie Condon.

Regulars: Wild Bill Davison, Cutty Cuttshall, Sidney Bechet, Joe Bushkin, Billy Butterfield, Pee-wee Russell.

FLOOR SHOW—30 minutes—NBC 1949.

THE FLORIAN ZaBACH SHOW

Musical Variety.

Host: Florian ZaBach (a violinist).

Vocalist: Leila Hyer.

Music: Performed by an unidentified orchestra.

THE FLORIAN ZaBACH SHOW—15 minutes—CBS—March 10, 1951 - June 9, 1951.

THE FLYING DOCTOR

Adventure. Background: Australia. The story of an American physician who, by using an airplane, struggles to serve those far removed from society —from the remote ranchers to the Bushmen.

CAST
Greg, the flying doctor	Richard Denning
Mary, his nurse	Jill Adams
Dr. Harrison	Peter Madden
Charley, the pilot	Alan White

THE FLYING DOCTOR—30 minutes—Syndicated 1959.

THE FLYING FISHERMAN
THE OUTDOORSMAN

Sport.

The Flying Fisherman (also known as "Gadabout Gaddis"). Fishing instruction and advise.

Host-Narrator: Roscoe Vernon (nicknamed Gadabout Gaddis by an employer who could never find him).

The Outdoorsman. Hunting instruction and advice.

Host-Narrator: Joe Foss.

History: "The Flying Fisherman" first appeared in 1939 via W2XAD, General Electric's experimental television station in Schenectady, N.Y. The program, which ended its run after several months, returned in 1944 over station WRGB (formerly W2XAD). From the late 1940s to the early 1960s, the series appeared on several stations around the U.S. In 1965, under the sponsorship of the Liberty Mutual Insurance Company, it was syndicated nationally. In 1969, the thirty-minute series began alternating weekly with "The Outdoorsman," its spin-off series.

THE FLYING NUN

Comedy. Impressed by her missionary aunt, Elsie Ethrington decides to devote her life to helping the less fortunate and joins a convent. Ordained as Sister Bertrille, she is assigned to the Convent San Tanco in San Juan, Puerto Rico.

Shortly after beginning her duties she discovers the ability to fly. The coronets, the headgear worn by the nuns of her order, possess sides that resemble wings; and San Juan is an area affected by trade winds. Weighing only ninety pounds, she is able to soar above the ground when caught by strong gales. Through the manipulation of her coronets she acquires some control over flight, but not all, and landings become difficult.

Youthful, exuberant, with a knack for finding trouble, and a sincere desire to do good, Sister Bertrille seeks to use her gift of flight to benefit her poor community.

CAST

Sister Bertrille (Elsie Ethrington)	Sally Field
Sister Jacqueline	Marge Redmond
The Reverend Mother Plaseato (Mother Superior)	Madeleine Sherwood
Carlos Ramirez, a playboy, the owner of the Casino Carlos, a discotheque	Alejandro Rey
Sister Ana	Linda Dangcil
Sister Sixto	Shelley Morrison
Sister Teresa	Naomi Stevens
Captain Fomento, the fumbling police supersleuth	Vito Scotti
Jennifer Ethrington, Elsie's sister	Elinor Donahue

Music: Dominic Frontiere; Warren Barker; Harry Geller.

THE FLYING NUN—30 minutes—ABC—September 7, 1967 - September 11, 1969. Syndicated.

FOLLOW THE LEADER

Game. Two three-minute sketches are enacted by the Hostess. Selected studio audience members have to re-enact the same situation. Those who achieve a performance as close to the original as possible receive a merchandise prize.

Hostess: Vera Vague.

FOLLOW THE LEADER—30 minutes—CBS—June 1953 - September 1953.

FOLLOW THE SUN

Adventure. Background: Honolulu, Hawaii. The experiences of free-lance magazine writers Ben Gregory and Paul Templin.

CAST
Ben Gregory	Barry Coe
Paul Templin	Brett Halsey
Eric Jason, the legman for their ship, the *Scuber*	Gary Lockwood
Katherine Ann Richards, their part-time secretary, a Honolulu University student	Gigi Perreau
Frank Roper, a lieutenant, Honolulu Police Department	Jay Sanin

Music: Sonny Burke.

FOLLOW THE SUN—60 minutes—ABC—September 17, 1961 - September 9, 1962. Syndicated.

FOLLOW THAT MAN

See title: "Man Against Crime."

FOLLOW YOUR HEART

Serial. A girl's efforts to break set traditions in her wealthy family. Unhappily engaged to a man her mother has chosen for her, she struggles to gain the right to choose her own spouse outside her social scale.

CAST
Julie Fielding	Sallie Brophy
Her boy friend	Louis Hallister
Julie's mother	Nancy Sheridan

Also: Anne Seymour, Maxine Stuart.

FOLLOW YOUR HEART—15 minutes—NBC—1953-1954.

FOODINI THE GREAT

Marionettes. The misadventures of Foodini the magician and his assistant, Pinhead.

Hostess: Ellen Parker; Doris Brown.

Puppet Characters and Voices: Hope Bunin, Mory Bunin.

FOODINI THE GREAT—15 minutes—ABC—August 23, 1951 - November 17, 1951.

FOOTLIGHT THEATRE

Anthology. Dramatic presentations.

Included:

National Honeymoon. The story of a bride who drags her unwilling husband onto a national television show to reveal the details of their courtship in return for a houseful of furniture.

CAST
Diana Lynn, Dick Haymes, Alan Mowbray.

The Sum Of Seven. The story of a college professor who discovers that a student has stolen a copy of an exam.

CAST
Victor Jory.

The Time Of Day. The story of a socialite who falls in love with a man with a dubious past — a relationship that threatens her family with unfavorable publicity.

CAST

Peggy Ann Garner.

FOOTLIGHT THEATRE—30 minutes—CBS—July 4, 1952 - September 1952.

FOR ADULTS ONLY

Interview. Guests in informative discussions on topical issues.

Hostesses: Joyce Susskind, Barbara Howar.

Music: Recorded.

FOR ADULTS ONLY—30 minutes—Syndicated 1970. Also known as "Joyce and Barbara: For Adults Only."

FOR BETTER OR WORSE

Serial. Dramatizations of marital difficulties. Based on actual case histories. Guests appear in stories that last from one to two weeks.

Host-Narrator: Dr. James A. Peterson, a marriage counselor and teacher at the University of Southern California.

FOR BETTER OR WORSE—30 minutes—CBS—June 29, 1959 - June 24, 1960.

FORD FESTIVAL

Variety. Music, songs, dances, and comedy sketches.

Host: James Melton.

Orchestra: David Brokeman.

FORD FESTIVAL—60 minutes—NBC 1951.

FORD STAR JUBILEE

Variety. Entertainment specials.

Included:

The Judy Garland Show (9/24/55). Musical Variety. Miss Garland's television debut. Basically, a one-woman show featuring the songs associated with Judy's career.

Hostess: Judy Garland.

Guest: David Wayne.

Dancers: The Escorts.

Orchestra: Jack Catheart.

High Tor (3/10/56). A musical fantasy based on Maxwell Anderson's play.

Starring: Bing Crosby, Nancy Olson, and Julie Andrews (her television debut).

The Wizard Of Oz (11/3/56). The television debut of the 1939 feature film based on the story by L. Frank Baum.

Opening scene: Kansas. A young girl, Dorothy Gale, with her dog, Toto, is rushing home to seek shelter from a tornado. Hit by a flying window, she is knocked unconscious. The wooden house is lifted from its foundation, and she and Toto are transported to the fantasy kingdom of Munchkin Land. They land on and kill the Wicked Witch of the East, making them heroes to the little people and enemies to the Wicked Witch of the West.

Wishing to return home, Dorothy is told to seek the Wizard of Oz in Emerald City. Following the Yellow Brick Road, she meets and befriends the Scarecrow, the Tin Woodman, and the Cowardly Lion—each seeking a desire: a brain, a heart, and courage.

Adventure abounds in the Haunted Forest as the Wicked Witch of the West captures Dorothy and Toto. A dramatic rescue is made by the daring trio of Scarecrow, Woodman, and Lion.

Despair overwhelms them when they discover the wizard to be a fraud. But all ends well when the good witch, Glinda, shows Dorothy the secret of the way home.

Closing scene: Dorothy awakening in bed; her family hovering above; her land over the rainbow, just a dream.

CAST

Dorothy Gale	Judy Garland
The Scarecrow	Ray Bolger
The Cowardly Lion	Bert Lahr
The Tin Woodman	Jack Haley
The Wicked Witch of the West	Margaret Hamilton
The Wizard of Oz	Frank Morgan
Glinda, the Good Witch	Billie Burke
Uncle Henry	Charlie Grapewin
Aunt Emily	Clara Blandick
The Munchkins	The Singer Midgets

Music: Harold Arlen.

FORD STAR JUBILEE—60 minutes to 2 hours (pending production)—CBS—September 24, 1955 - November 3, 1956.

FORD STAR REVUE

Variety. Music, songs, dances, and comedy routines.
Host: Jack Haley.

Regulars: Mindy Carson, The Continentals, The Mellow-Larks.

Orchestra: David Brockman.

FORD STAR REVUE—60 minutes—NBC—July 6, 1950 - September 1950.

FORD STARTIME

Anthology. Musical, dramatic, and comedic productions.

Included:

The Rosalind Russell Show. A musical revue tracing the changes in show business.
Hostess: Rosalind Russell.

CAST
Polly Bergen, Maurice Chevalier, Eddie Foy, Jr., Eddie Hodges, Ernie Kovacs, Arthur O'Connell, Jack Paar, Kate Smith.
Orchestra: Harry Sosnick.

The Jazz Singer. Drama. A father attempts to persuade his son, who wants to become a comedian, to carry on the family tradition and become a cantor.

CAST
Joey Robbins: Jerry Lewis; Ginny Gibbons: Anna Maria Alberghetti; Sarah: Molly Picon; Cantor: Edward Franz.

Turn Of The Screw. Suspense Drama. An adaptation of the Henry James novel. A governess attempts to protect a young girl and her brother from a spirit who seeks to possess them.

CAST
Governess: Ingrid Bergman (her American television debut); Miles: Hayward Morse; Flora: Alexandra Wagner.

Music: David Amron.

The Dean Martin Show. Musical Variety.

Host: Dean Martin.

Guests: Frank Sinatra, Mickey Rooney.

Orchestra: David Rose.

George Burns In The Big Time. Variety. The music, song, dance, and comedy of vaudeville.

Host: George Burns.

Guests: Jack Benny, Eddie Cantor, George Jessel, Bobby Darin.

Orchestra: Jeff Alexander.

Merman On Broadway. Variety. A program tracing the highlights of Ethel Merman's Broadway career.

Hostess: Ethel Merman.

Guests: Tab Hunter, Fess Parker, Tom Poston, Bobby Sherwood.

Orchestra: Jack Kane.

FORD STARTIME—60 to 90 minutes (pending the production)—NBC— October 6, 1959 - May 31, 1960.

FORD THEATRE

Anthology. Dramatic presentations.

Included:

A Touch Of Spring. The story of a summer romance between a married woman and a young bachelor.

CAST
Maria Clark: Irene Dunn; Bill Hannagin: Gene Barry.

Deception. A mother attempts to prepare a happy homecoming after learning that her son, once reported dead in Korea is alive.

CAST
Laura Blake: Sylvia Sidney; Paul Blake: John Howard.

Sunday Morn. Returning to his peaceful hometown, a former gunfighter struggles to adjust to a nonviolent life.

CAST
Mano: Brian Keith; Sally Carter: Marilyn Maxwell.

FORD THEATRE—30 and 60 minute versions—NBC—1950-1955.

FOREIGN INTRIGUE

Mystery-Adventure. Distinguished by three formats.

Format One (1951- 1953):
Background: Paris. The experiences of Robert Cannon and Helen Davis, Foreign Correspondents for *Consolidated News.* Stories relate their attempts to infiltrate and expose espionage rings. Syndicated under the title: "Dateline: Europe."

CAST
Robert Cannon	Jerome Thor
Helen Davis	Sydna Scott

Music: Charles Norman; Ervin Drake.

Format Two (1953-1954):
Background: Europe. The experiences of Michael Powers and Patricia Bennett, Foreign Correspondents for *Associated News.* Syndicated under the title: "Overseas Adventures."

CAST
Michael Powers	James Daly
Patricia Bennett	Ann Preville

Their aid in Paris   Nikole Milinaire

Music: Charles Norman; Ervin Drake.

Format Three (1954-1955):
Background: Vienna. The story of Christopher Storm, a hotel owner who aides the distressed against the international underworld. Syndicated under the title: "Cross Current."

CAST
Christopher Storm   Gerald Mohr

Music: Charles Norman; Ervin Drake.

FOREIGN INTRIGUE—30 minutes—NBC—1951-1955. Also titled "Foreign Assignment."

FOREIGN LEGIONNAIRE

Adventure. Background: The French Foreign Legion headquarters in North Africa. The story of Captain Michael Gallant and his ward, Cuffy Sanders, the son of a slain officer. Episodes relate the struggles of men as they attempt to uphold the causes of freedom and justice.

CAST
Captain Michael Gallant	Buster Crabbe
Cuffy Sanders	Cullen Crabbe
First Class Private Fuzzy Knight	Fuzzy Knight
Sergeant DuVal	Gilles Queant
Carla, Fuzzy's girlfriend	Norma Eberhardt
The Colonel	Roger Trevielle

FOREIGN LEGIONNAIRE—30 minutes—NBC—February 13, 1955 - February 7, 1957; 30 minutes—ABC—June 6, 1960 - September 24, 1960; NBC—30 minutes—October 1, 1960 - September 21, 1963. Syndicated. Also known as "Captain Gallant" and "Captain Gallant of the Foreign Legion."

THE FOREST RANGERS

Adventure. Background: The Canadian North Woods. Stories realistically relate the experiences of the members of the Junior Ranger Club, four boys and two girls, as they assist the forest rangers. Produced in Canada.

CAST
Ranger Keeley	Graydon Gould
Joe Two Rivers	Michael Zenon
Sergeant Scott	Gordon Pinset
Chub	Ralph Endersby
Mike	Peter Tully
Steve	Don Mason
Peter	Rex Hagen
Kathy	Susan Conway
Denise	Barbara Pierce
Ted	George Allen

THE FOREST RANGERS—30 minutes—Syndicated 1965.

FOR LOVE OR MONEY

Game. Three competing players. Each states his preference for a visible prize or an unknown series of cash awards. The host begins the game with a series of question-answer rounds. The player first to identify himself through a buzzer signal receives a chance to answer. Correct answers award points; incorrect responses deduct points. Winners, the highest scorers, receive their previous selection.

Host: Bill Nimmo.

FOR LOVE OR MONEY—30 minutes—CBS 1958.

THE FORSYTE SAGA

Serial. The intrigues, loves, and financial dealings of the Forsyte family. Stories span over a half-century beginning in Victorian England. Produced by the B.B.C. Based on the novels by John Galsworthy.

CAST

Jo Forsyte	Kenneth More
Soames Forsyte	Eric Porter
Old Jolyon Forsyte	Joseph O'Connor
Irene	Nyree Dawn Porter
Monty	Terence Alexander
Mrs. Heron	Jenny Laird
Frances	Ursula Howells
June	June Barry
Bosinney	John Bennett
Swithin	George Woodbridge
Helen	Lana Morris
Winnifred	Margaret Tyzack
Annette	Dallia Penn
Val	Jonathan Burn
Fleur Forsyte	Susan Hampshire
Jon Forsyte	Martin Jarvis
Michael Mont	Nicholas Pennell
Holly	Suzanne Neve
Lord Charles Ferrar	Basil Dingnam
Sir Lawrence Mont	Cyril Lukham
Marjorie	Caroline Blakiston
Bicket	Terry Scully
Mac Gowan	John Phillips
Francis Wilmot	Hal Hamilton

THE FORSYTE SAGA—60 minutes—NET—October 5, 1969 - April 4, 1970.

FOR THE PEOPLE

Drama. Background: New York. The work of Assistant District Attorney David Koster as he attempts to prosecute all crimes within the state.

CAST

David Koster	William Shatner
Phyllis Koster, his wife	Jessica Walter
Anthony Celese, his superior	Howard DaSilva
Frank Malloy, a detective assigned to the D.A.'s office	Lonny Chapman

FOR THE PEOPLE—60 minutes—CBS—January 31, 1965 - May 1965.

FOR YOUR PLEASURE

Musical Variety.

Hostess: Kyle MacDonnell.

Featured: Jack and Jill.

Music: The Norman Paris Trio; The Earl Sheldon Orchestra.

FOR YOUR PLEASURE—15 minutes—NBC 1948; 30 minutes—NBC 1949.

FOUR-IN-ONE

Drama. The overall title for four individual rotating series: "McCloud"; "Night Gallery"; "The Psychiatrist"; and "San Francisco International Airport."

McCloud. Background: New York City. The investigations of Sam McCloud, a deputy marshall from New Mexico who is assigned to Manhattan's twenty-seventh precinct to study crime-detection methods.

CAST

Sam McCloud	Dennis Weaver
Peter B. Clifford, the chief of detectives	J.D. Cannon
Sergeant Joe Broadhurst	Terry Carter
Chris Coughlin, Sam's romantic interest	Diana Muldaur

Music: Lee Holdridge.

Night Gallery. Supernatural tales of the horrifying confrontation between nightmare and reality.

Host: Rod Serling—Guide through a bizarre Night Gallery whose exhibits hold beneath their canvasses twisted tales of another dimension.

Music: Eddie Sauter.

Included (three examples listed):

THE DIARY. Background: Hollywood, California. A one-time glamorous actress seeks revenge when she is insulted by a vicious television reporter. She presents her with a diary that writes its own bizarre entries that come true. Seeking to escape the foreboding diary, the reporter enters a sanitarium. Revenge is achieved when the reporter goes insane.

CAST

Holly Schaefer, the reporter: Patty Duke; Carrie Crane, the actress: Virginia Mayo; Dr. Mill: David Wayne.

THE BIG SURPRISE. Three boys, walking home from school, are approached by a farmer and told they will find a surprise if they dig a four-foot hole on a certain piece of his property. Thinking to find buried treasure, they eagerly begin to dig. Two boys leave as the hour grows late, but the third perseveres. Tension mounts when he uncovers and opens a large box. The dim light reveals the farmer in the box—"Surprise!"

CAST

The Farmer: John Carradine.

PROFESSOR PEABODY'S LAST LECTURE. Background: A college classroom. Lecturing to his students on the ancient Gods, a professor begins to ridicule them. Suddenly the skies darken, the clouds grow black, and the heavens become angry. Unable to stand his insults any further the Gods transform him into a hideous fiend.

CAST

Professor Peabody: Carl Reiner.

The Psychiatrist. Background: Los Angeles, California. The story of James Whitman, a young psychiatrist who practices the new but controversial techniques of modern mental therapy.

CAST

Dr. James Whitman   Roy Thinnes
Dr. Bernard Altman, his friend, a
    psychiatrist   Luther Adler

San Francisco International Airport. Background: San Francisco, California. Dramatizations based on the problems that plague large airports.

CAST

Jim Conrad, the
    manager   Lloyd Bridges
Bob Hatten, the security
    chief   Clu Gulager
Suzie Conrad, Jim's
    daughter   Barbara Sigel
June, Jim's
    secretary   Barbara Werle

FOUR-IN-ONE—60 minutes—NBC—September 16, 1970 - September 8, 1971. Spin-offs: "McCloud"—90 minutes—NBC—Premiered: September 16, 1971 (as a part of the "NBC Sunday Mystery Movie"); "Rod Serling's Night Gallery"—60 minutes—NBC—September 15, 1971 - September 6, 1972; 30 minutes—NBC—September 17, 1972 - January 14, 1973. Rebroadcasts—30 minutes—NBC—May

13, 1973 - August 12, 1973. Syndicated.

FOUR JUST MEN

Adventure. Four men, friends during World War II, but having gone their separate ways since, are summoned together in England by the last request of their former commander. Tim Collier, American newspaper journalist; Ben Manfred, English private investigator; Ricco Poccari, Italian hotel owner; and Jeff Ryder, French attorney, form a union of Four Just Men who travel about the world and combat injustice. Stories relate their experiences on a rotational basis.

CAST

Tim Collier	Dan Dailey
Ben Manfred	Jack Hawkins
Ricco Poccari	Vittorio De Sica
Jeff Ryder	Richard Conte

FOUR JUST MEN—30 minutes—Syndicated 1957.

FOUR STAR PLAYHOUSE

Anthology. Dramatic presentations. The title, "Four Star Playhouse," took its name from the four stars who created Four Star Studios and its first series, the aforementioned "Playhouse." They were: Dick Powell, Charles Boyer, Rosalind Russell, and Joel McCrea. As two later dropped out (Russell and McCrea), two joined (Ida Lupino and David Niven). By 1955, the four became three as Miss Lupino parted.

Included:

Village In The City. After he finds the body of a woman in his Greenwich Village apartment, a man attempts to find her murderer.

CAST

David Niven.

Lost Kid. A grandmother attempts to prevent her juvenile delinquent grandson from embarking on an adult life of crime.

CAST

Elizabeth Patterson, Mary Field, Harry Harvey, Jr.

Death Makes A Pair. The story centers on the struggles faced by a businessman as he attempts to overcome gambling fever.

CAST

Lloyd Corrigan, Jay Novello, Margia Dean.

The Watchers And The Watched. A suspense drama that details a woman's carefully laid plot to drive a man insane.

CAST

Faye Roope.

FOUR STAR PLAYHOUSE—60 minutes—CBS—September 25, 1952 - September 27, 1956.

THE FOUR-STAR REVUE

See title: "The All-Star Revue."

FOURSQUARE COURT

Interview. A panel of masked, paroled convicts discuss their past crimes and their present struggles for reformation.

Host: Norman Brokenshire.

FOURSQUARE COURT—30 minutes
—ABC 1957.

FRACTURED FLICKERS

Comedy. A satirization of Hollywood's Golden Era. Silent films are seen with added synchronized, zany dialogue.

Host: Hans Conried.

Creator: Jay Ward.

Featured: Interviews with past and present celebrities.

FRACTURED FLICKERS—30 minutes—Syndicated 1963.

FRACTURED PHRASES

Game. Selected studio-audience members compete. Slogans or song or book titles phonetically written are flashed on a screeen. The player first to identify himself through a buzzer signal receives a chance to answer. If correct, one point is awarded. Winners, the highest point scorers, receive merchandise prizes.

Host: Art James.

FRACTURED PHRASES—30 minutes—NBC—1965-1966.

THE FRANCES LANGFORD-
DON AMECHE SHOW

Variety. Songs, dances, musical numbers, guests, and interviews.

Host: Don Ameche.

Hostess: Frances Langford.

Orchestra: Tony Romano.

Sketch: "The Couple Next Door" (Jack Lemmon, Cynthia Stone). A domestic comedy depicting the struggles that make up a marriage.

Features: Excerpts from Miss Langford's diary, *Purple Heart;* and a studio audience participation segment wherein selected members compete in a current-events question-answer session.

THE FRANCES LANGFORD-DON AMECHE SHOW—60 minutes—ABC —1951-1952.

FRANKENSTEIN JR.
AND THE IMPOSSIBLES

Animated Cartoon. The exploits of Frankenstein Jr., a thirty-foot mechanical robot, and The Impossibles, Coil Man, Fluid Man, and Multi Man, United States government agents who pose as a Rock and Roll group. Stories depict their battle against the sinister forces of evil. A Hanna-Barbera production.

Characters' Voices

Frankenstein Jr.	Ted Cassidy
Buzz	Dick Beals
Father	John Stephenson
Multi Man	Don Messick
Fluid Man	Paul Frees
Coil Man	Hal Smith

Music: Hoyt Curtin.

FRANKENSTEIN JR. AND THE IMPOSSIBLES—30 minutes—CBS—September 10, 1966 - September 7, 1968.

THE FRANKIE CARLE SHOW

Musical Variety.

Host: Frankie Carle, pianist.

Musical Backing: Perry Bodkin; The Carle Combo.

THE FRANKIE CARLE SHOW—15 minutes—NBC—August 7, 1956 - October 29, 1956.

FRANKIE LAINE

Listed: The television programs of singer Frankie Laine.

The Frankie Laine Show—Musical Variety—15 minutes—CBS—July 20, 1955 - September 7, 1955.

Host: Frankie Laine.

Regulars: Connie Harris, Jud Conlon, Jack Toegander, Mitchell Choirloy, The James Starbuch Dancers, The Rhythmaires.

Announcer: Tony Marvin.

Orchestra: Hank Sylvern; Jimmy Carroll.

Premiere Guests: Connie, Russell, Shirley MacLaine, Dick Van Dyke, Duke Ellington.

Frankie Laine Time—Musical Variety—30 minutes—CBS—July 1955 - September 1955; August 1956 - September 1956.

Host: Frankie Laine.

Featured: The Lyn Duddley Chorus.

Announcer: Tony Marvin.

Orchestra: Jimmy Carroll.

FRANK SINATRA

Listed: The television programs of singer-actor Frank Sinatra.

The Frank Sinatra Show—Musical Variety—30 minutes—CBS—October 7, 1950 - April 1, 1952.

Host: Frank Sinatra.

Regulars: Erin O'Brien, Ben Blue, The Blue Family, Sid Fields, The Whipoorwills.

Orchestra: Alex Stordah.

The Frank Sinatra Show—Variety—30 minutes—ABC—October 18, 1957 - June 27, 1958. A series capitalizing on all of his talents, from acting to singing.

Host (and occasional performer in anthology productions): Frank Sinatra.

Orchestra: Nelson Riddle.

Included:

Face of Fear. A governess attempts to discover the reason for a young child's state of shock.

CAST
Christie Nolan: Glynis Johns; Paul Dupree: Michael Pate; Claude: Eugene Martin.

That Hogan Man. A cab driver struggles to raise his children after the death of his wife.

CAST
Hogan: Frank Sinatra; Marty Potter: Jesse White; Michele: Reba Waters; Gaby: Johnny Crawford; Miss Douglas: Susan Cummings.

Brownstone Incident. A wife attempts to convince her city-born husband to move to the suburbs.

CAST
Al Wesson: Frank Sinatra; Helen Wesson: Cloris Leachman.

A Gun In His Back. Dissatisfied with

a police investigation, a cabbie attempts to locate his own stolen car.

CAST
Sam Hatter: Frank Sinatra; Grace Hatter: Patricia Crowley.

THE FREDDY MARTIN SHOW

Musical Variety.

Host: Freddy Martin.

Regulars: Merv Griffin, Murray Arnold, Judy Lynn.

Orchestra: Freddy Martin.

THE FREDDY MARTIN SHOW—30 minutes—NBC—July 12, 1951 - September 1951.

FRED WARING

Listed: The television programs of bandleader Fred Waring.

The Fred Waring Show—Musical Variety—60 minutes—CBS—April 17, 1947 - May 30, 1954.

Host: Fred Waring.

Regulars: Jane Wilson, Stuart Churchill, Joe Marine, Joanne Wheatley, Daisey Bernier, Gordon Goodman, Keith and Sylvia Textor, Virginia and Livingston Gearhart, Bob Sands, Nadine Gae, Frances Wyatt, Suzanne Lovell, Hugh Brannum, Leonard Kranendonk, Joan Woodward, The Waring Glee Club, The Marc Breaux Dancers.

Announcer: Red Barber.

Orchestra: The Pennsylvanians, conducted by Waring.

The Fred Waring Show—Musical Variety—30 minutes—CBS—July 22, 1957 - September 6, 1957.

Host: Fred Waring.

Orchestra: The Pennsylvanians.

FREEDOM RINGS

Game. Selected female studio-audience members have to solve various homemaker problems that are enacted and complicated by a cast of regulars. Contestants, judged by the studio audience, receive prizes according to their satisfaction (applause). The title, "Freedom Rings," stresses the sponsor's theme of freedom from the drudgery of housework.

Host: John Beal.

Cast: Alice Ghostley, Ted Telles, Chuck Taylor, Malcolm Broderick, Jay Hitton.

Announcer: Vince Williams.

Orchestra: Ben Ludlow.

FREEDOM RINGS—30 minutes—CBS 1953.

THE FRENCH CHEF

Cooking. The preparation of gourmet meals.

Hostess: Julia Child.

THE FRENCH CHEF—30 minutes. NET—1963-1970; PBS—1970-1974.

FRIENDS AND LOVERS

Comedy. Background: Boston, Mass. The life, fantasies, and romantic misadventures of a young bachelor, Robert Dreyfuss, a bass violist with the Boston Symphony Orchestra.

CAST

Robert Dreyfuss	Paul Sand
Charlie Dreyfuss, his brother	Michael Pataki
Janis Dreyfuss, Charlie's wife	Penny Marshall
Fred Myerback, Robert's friend	Steve Landesberg
Jack Reardon, the orchestra manager	Dick Wesson
Mason Woodruff, the orchestra conductor	Craig Richard

Music: Pat Williams.

FRIENDS AND LOVERS—30 minutes—CBS—September 14, 1974 - January 4, 1975. Original title: "Paul
Sand in Friends and Lovers."

THE FRITOS SPORTS CLUB

Sport Instruction. Through representative guests, a basic introduction
is given to the rules of various sports.

Host: Charlie Jones.

Music: Recorded.

THE FRITOS SPORTS CLUB—05
minutes—Syndicated 1971.

FROM A BIRD'S EYE VIEW

Comedy. Background: London,
England. The misadventures of two
International Airline stewardesses:
Millie Grover, British, meddlesome,
and scatterbrained; and Maggie
Ralston, her partner, a level-headed
American on loan from the U.S. to
International's European division.
Stories relate Millie's continual inter-
ference in people's affairs and her and
Maggie's efforts to resolve the chaos
before customer complaints reach the
office of Clyde Beauchamp, the per-
sonnel director.

CAST

Millie Grover	Millicent Martin
Maggie Ralston	Pat Finley
Clyde Beachamp	Peter Jones
Bert Grover, Millie's uncle	Robert Cawdron
Miss Fosdyke, Beachamp's secretary	Noel Hood

Music: Frank Barber.

FROM A BIRD'S EYE VIEW—30
minutes—NBC—March 29, 1971 -
August 16, 1971.

FROM THESE ROOTS

Serial. Background: The town of
Strathfield. The life and struggles of
the Frasers: Ben, a widower, the
sixty-five-year-old editor-owner of the
Strathfield Record; Liz, his youngest
daughter, a writer living in Washington, D.C., and engaged to journalist
Bruce Crawford; Emily, his eldest
daughter, happily married to her
high-school sweetheart, Jim Benson, a
mill foreman; and Ben Fraser, Jr., his
son, who married the wealthy Rose
Corelli and decided not to follow in
his father's footsteps.

CAST

Ben Fraser Sr.	Joseph Macauley
Liz Fraser	Ann Flood
	Susan Brown
Bruce Crawford	David Sanders
Jim Benson	Henderson Forsythe
Ben Fraser, Jr.	Frank Marth
Dr. Buck Weaver	Tom Shirley
Podge	Freeman Hammond
Maggie Barker	Billie Lou Watt
Lyddy Benson	Sarah Hardy
Emily Fraser	Helen Shields
Rose Fraser	Julie Bovasso
David Allen	Bob Mandan
Laura Tompkins	Audra Lindley
Lynn	Barbara Berjer
Gloria	Millette Alexander

Tom Jennings   Craig Huebing
Also: John Calenbeck, Mae Munroe,
      Grant Code, Vera Allen, John
      Stewart, Herb Shields, Sarah
      Burton, Mary Alice Moore,
      Charles Egelston, Dan White,
      Gary Morgan, Sam Gray.

FROM THESE ROOTS—30 minutes
—NBC—1958-1962.

FRONTIER

Anthology. Western dramatizations
based on actual newspaper files.
Host: Walter Coy.

Included:

Tomas And The Widow. The story of
a widow who plans revenge against the
man who killed her husband.

CAST
Tomas: Mike Connors; Shona: Laura
Elliot; Gavin: Sean McClory.

Shame Of A Nation. Background:
Denver, 1864. The court-martial trial
of J. M. Chivington, a U.S. Cavalry
colonel accused of the needless slaying
of Indians.

CAST
Scott Forbes, George Keyman,
Hayden Rorke, Barry Atwater.

In Nebraska. The beginning of settlement in what is now the city of
Omaha.

CAST
Sallie Brophy, Jeff Morrow, Ken
Tobey.

FRONTIER—30 minutes—NBC—
1955-1956.

FRONTIER CIRCUS

Drama. Background: The Frontier
during the 1880s. The saga of the
traveling one-ring T and T (Thompson
and Travis) Combined Circus. Stories
relate the struggles involved and the
dangers braved in presenting a frontier
circus.

CAST
Colonel Casey Thompson, the
        owner   Chill Wills
Ben Travis, his
        partner   John Derek
Tony Gentry, the trail
        scout   Richard Jaeckel
Music: Jeff Alexander

FRONTIER CIRCUS—60 minutes—
CBS—October 5, 1961 - September
1962. Syndicated.

FRONTIER DOCTOR

Western. Background: Rising Springs,
Arizona during the early 1900s. The
role of a doctor during the early
settlement days of the twentieth century is dramatized. Stories relate the
experiences of Dr. Bill Baxter as he
struggles to enforce neglected medical
laws and assist pioneers.
Starring: Rex Allen as Dr. Bill Baxter.

FRONTIER DOCTOR—30 minutes—
Syndicated 1958. Also known as:
"Man of the West" and "Unarmed."

FRONTIER JUSTICE

Anthology. Rebroadcasts of western
dramas that were originally aired via
"Dick Powell's Zane Grey Theatre."
Hosts: Lew Ayres; Melvyn Douglas.
Music: Herschel Burke Gilbert; Joseph
        Mullendore.

Included:

Legacy Of A Legend. The story of a drifter who claims to be a famous lawman.

CAST
Lee J. Cobb, John Dehner.

Black Creek Encounter. The story of a man who must face the challenge from a gunfighter or ignore it and shame himself in the eyes of his son.

CAST
Jim Morrison: Ernest Borgnine; Kelly: Norma Crane; Davey Harper: Jan Merlin; Billy Morrison: Billy Chapin.

Fearful Courage. The story of a woman who attempts to return to her husband—a gunfighter.

CAST
Ida Lupino, James Whitmore.

FRONTIER JUSTICE—30´minutes— CBS—June 1958 - September 1958; June 1959 - September 1959.

FRONT PAGE DETECTIVE

Crime Drama. Background: New York City. The investigations of David Chase, a newspaper columnist and amateur sleuth—a man possessing an eye for beauty, a nose for news, and a sixth sense for danger.

CAST
David Chase   Edmund Lowe
The homicide detective   Frank Jenks
Also   Paula Drew

FRONT PAGE DETECTIVE—30 minutes—ABC—1951-1953; DuMont 1953.

FRONT PAGE STORY

Anthology. Dramatizations depicting the 1950s front-page stories.
Host-Narrator: Paul Stewart.

Included:

The Cave. The story of Robert J. Billeter of the *Preston* (W. Va.) *Times* as he attempts to rescue two boys who are trapped in a cave.

CAST
Robert Billeter: Carlton Colyer.

Birthday Present. A father and son playing catch in the yard follow the ball under the porch and discover a woman's body. The story relates the police investigation into her mysterious death.

CAST
Wayne: David Brenner; Charles Linden: John McGovern.

Hit And Run. A driver flees from the scene of a fatal accident. Reporter Nye Beaman of the *Waterburn* (Conn.) *American* attempts to track down the driver.

CAST
Nye Beaman: Allen Nourse.

FRONT PAGE STORY—30 minutes —Syndicated 1959.

FRONT ROW CENTER

Musical Revue.
Starring: Hal Loman, Monica Moore, Phil Leeds, Joan Fields, Marian Bruce, Cass Franklin.

FRONT ROW CENTER—60 minutes —DuMont 1950.

FRONT ROW CENTER

Anthology. Adaptations of works by noted authors.

Host: Fletcher Markle.

Included:

Dark Victory. The story of Judith Traherne, a flighty woman who becomes a woman of courage when she discovers that she faces blindness and almost certain death.

CAST
Judith Traherne: Margaret Field; Dr. Steele: Kent Smith; Aldin Blaine: Kay Stewart.

Outward Bound. The story of several people who find themselves aboard a strange ship that is leaving the land of the living.

CAST
Tom Prior: Wilfred Knapp; Rev. Thompson: Alan Napier; Mrs. Cliveden-Banks: Isobel Elsom.

Tender Is The Night. The story of Dr. Dick Diver, a psychoanalyst who violates professional ethics by marrying his lovely and wealthy patient.

CAST
Dr. Diver: James Daly; Michele Warren: Mercedes McCambridge; Rosemary: Olive Sturgiss.

FRONT ROW CENTER—30 minutes —CBS—1955 - 1956.

F TROOP

Comedy. In an unidentifed Union camp during the closing months of the Civil War, Wilton Parmenter of the

F Troop. Left to right: Larry Storch, Forrest Tucker, Ken Berry, and Melody Patterson.

Quarter Masters Corps, a private in charge of officers' laundry, encounters an excess of pollin, sneezes, and blurts out what sounds like "CHARGE!" Troopers, on stand-by, are prompted into action—an action that foils Confederate objects and fosters a complete Union victory. Promoted to captain and awarded the Medal of Honor, Wilton Parmenter is assigned to command F Troop at Fort Courage.

Kansas, 1866. Arriving and assuming command, Captain Wilton Parmenter meets those he will become closely associated with: Sergeant Morgan O'Rourke, the head of the illegal O'Rourke Enterprises—a business dealing in Indian souvenirs made by the friendly Hekawi (prounced: Ha-cow-we) Indians and the town saloon; Corporal Randolph Agarn, his vice president; Private Hannibal Shirley Dobbs, the inept company bugular; Trooper Duffy, survivor of the Alamo; and Trooper Vanderbuilt, the almost blind look-out.

Dismissing the troops, he meets and befirends the beautiful, marriage-minded Jane Angelica Thrift (Wrangler Jane), the proprietress of the fort general store and U.S. Post Office.

Stories relate the misadventures of Captain Wilton Parmenter, "The Scourge of the West," as he struggles to maintain the peace, adjust to frontier life, and escape the matrimonial plans of his girlfriend. Complicating matters are Sgt. O'Rourke and Cpl. Agarn, who constantly devise schemes to conceal and expand their illegal enterprises.

CAST

Sgt. Morgan O'Rourke	Forrest Tucker
Cpl. Randolph Agarn	Larry Storch
Capt. Wilton Parmenter	Ken Berry
Wrangler Jane	Melody Patterson
Wild Eagle, the Hekawi Chief	Frank DeKova
Pvt. Hannibal Dobbs	James Hampton
Private Duffy	Bob Steele
Crazy Cat, the Chief's aide	Don Diamond
Private Vanderbuilt	Joe Brooks
Private Hoffenmeuller, the German recruit, the man unable to speak English	John Mitchum
Papa Bear, an Hekawi Indian	Ben Frommer
Private Dudleson	Irving Bell
Roaring Chicken, the Hekawi Medicine Man	Edward Everett Horton

Other Troopers (screen credit is not given): McIntosh, Ashby, Hightower, Swenson, Hogan, Stanley, Livingston, Holmes, Watson, Franklin, Gilbert, Sullivan, Lewis, Clark.

Music: William Lava; Richard LaSalle.

F TROOP—30 minutes—ABC—September 14, 1965 - September 7, 1967. Syndicated.

THE FUGITIVE

Drama. Indiana, the home of Dr. Richard Kimble. Preparing for dinner, Richard and his wife, Helen, begin to discuss the prospect of adopting children. Unable to have her own children, Helen refuses to adopt any, feeling it would be living with a lie. Failing in an attempt to convince her otherwise, Richard leaves and drives to a nearby lake. Reviewing his actions and believing them a mistake, he returns to apologize.

Entering the driveway, the car headlights catch the figure of a one-armed man running from the house. Rushing inside, Kimble finds Helen, dead, the victim of a burgular whom she caught in the act. Unable to prove his innocence, he is arrested and later charged with murder.

Numerous attempts by police to find the mysterious one-armed man fail. A long courtroom trial ends, and based on circumstantial evidence, Richard Kimble is sentenced to death.

Enroute to the state penitentiary, the train derails and Kimble escapes the bounds of Indiana Police Lieutenant Philip Gerard. Though free, he is relentlessly pursued by Gerard, the man who is determined to apprehend his escaped prisoner. Assuming numerous identities, Kimble involves himself in the lives of troubled people and assists where possible, hoping that one will lead him to the one-armed man and freedom.

After four years, Johnson, the one-

The Fugitive. David Janssen.

armed man is apprehended. Certain the news will bring Kimble, Gerard releases the story to the press. As Gerard had anticipated, Kimble surrenders. However, as Kimble is being taken into custody, Johnson escapes. Pleading with his cold-hearted pursuer, Kimble is released and granted the opportunity to find Johnson. Investigating, Kimble tracks Johnson to a closed amusement park. Fighting on the ledge of a water tower, Johnson, who has Kimble pinned to the floor, admits killing Helen. In an extremely tense and dramatic moment, Gerard, who had been following Kimble, enters the park. Faced with a dilemma, whether to believe Kimble's story or not, Gerard decides in favor of Kimble. A bullet, fired from his rifle, strikes Johnson, whose final words clear Richard Kimble of all suspicions.

CAST

Richard Kimble	David Janssen
Lt. Philip Gerard	Barry Morse
Johnson, the one-armed man	Bill Raisch
Helen Kimble (flashbacks)	Diane Brewster
Donna Kimble, Richard's sister	Jacqueline Scott

Narrator: William Conrad.

Music: Pete Rugolo.

THE FUGITIVE—60 minutes—ABC—September 17, 1963 - August 29, 1967. Syndicated.

FULL CIRCLE

Serial. The story of Gary Donovan, a footloose wanderer who remains in one place only long enough to earn the resources he needs to continue his travels. The only story line presented: Background: Maryland. Donovan's involvement with Lisa Crowder and the mystery surrounding the death of her first husband.

CAST

Gary Donovan	Robert Fortier
Lisa Crowder	Dyan Cannon
Dr. Kit Aldrich	Jean Byron
Beth Perce	Amzie Strickland
David Talton	Bill Lundmark
Virgil Denker	Michael Ross
Roy Pollard	Andrew Colman
The Deputy	Sam Edwards

Also: John McNamara.

FULL CIRCLE—30 minutes—CBS—June 27, 1960 - March 1, 1961.

FUN AND FORTUNE

Game. The contestant must identify, within four clues, a piece of merchandise hidden on stage behind the "Magic Curtain." Cash prizes are awarded based on the number of clues used: beginning with fifty dollars and diminishing with each successive clue.

Host: Jack Lescoulie.

FUN AND FORTUNE—30 minutes—ABC 1949.

THE FUNKY PHANTOM

Animated Cartoon. East Muddlemore, New England, 1776, the era of the Revolutionary War. Pursued by Red Coats, Jonathan Muddlemore runs into a deserted mansion and hides in a large grandfather clock. The door locks and traps him.

   Almost two hundred years later (1971), three teenagers, April, Skip, and Augie, caught in a thunderstorm, seek shelter in the deserted mansion. Seeing the clock and resetting it to its correct time, Muddlemore, the Spirit of '76, emerges. Teaming, the four travel about the country and crusade against the forces of evil.

Characters' Voices
Jonathan Muddlemore
      ("Musty")   Daws Butler
April Stewart   Tina Holland
Skip   Mickey Dolenz
Augie   Tommy Cook

Additional voices: Jerry Dexter, Julie Bennett.

The gang dog: Elmo.

Musty's cat: Boo.

Music: John Sangster.

THE FUNKY PHANTOM—30 minutes—ABC—September 11, 1971 - September 1, 1972.

FUNNY BONERS

Game. Children compete. The host states a question. The player first to identify himself through a buzzer signal receives a chance to answer. If the response is correct, he is awarded points; if incorrect, he pays the penalty by performing a stunt. Winners, the highest point scorers, receive merchandise prizes.

Host: Jimmy Weldon, ventriloquist.

His Dummy: Webster Webfoot the duck.

FUNNY BONERS—30 minutes—NBC 1954.

THE FUNNY BUNNY

Children's Variety. Game contests and cartoons.

Host: Dick Noel.

Assistant: Dick West (costumed as The Funny Bunny).

THE FUNNY BUNNY—30 minutes—DuMont 1954.

FUNNY FACE

Comedy. Background: Los Angeles, California. The misadventures of Sandy Stockton, a student teacher enrolled at U.C.L.A. and a part-time actress employed by the Prescott Advertising Agency. Stories relate her attempts to divide her time between school and work.

CAST
Sandy Stockton   Sandy Duncan
Alice MacRaven, her
      friend   Valorie Armstrong
Pat Harwell, the land-
      lord   Henry Beckman
Kate Harwell, his
      wife   Kathleen Freeman

Maggie Prescott, the
    advertising agency
    head   Nita Talbot

Music: Pat Williams.

FUNNY FACE—30 minutes—CBS—
September 18, 1971 - December 11,
1971.

THE FUNNY MANNS

Comedy. Reedited theatrical comedy
shorts. Eight-minute segments are in-
tegrated with the antics of the Funny
Manns and his relatives: Milk Mann,
Mail Mann, Fire Mann, Police Mann,
Rich Mann, etc.

Starring: Cliff Norton as The Funny
    Manns.

Featuring: Ben Turpin, the Keystone
    Kops, Harry Langdon.

THE FUNNY MANNS—30 minutes—
Syndicated 1961.

THE FUNNY SIDE

Satire. The funny side of everyday life
as seen through the eyes of five
couples—from money, to sex, to self
improvement.

Host: Gene Kelly.

Couples:

The Blue Collar Couple: Warren
    Berlinger, Pat Finley.
The Sophisticated Couple: Jenna
    McMahon, Dick Clair.
The Young Couple: Michael Lembeck,
    Cindy Williams.
The Middle Class Black Couple:
    Teresa Graves, John Amos.
The Senior Citizen Couple: Bert
    Mustin, Queenie Smith.

THE FUNNY SIDE—60 minutes—

NBC—September 14, 1971 - December 28, 1971.

FUNNY YOU SHOULD ASK

Game. Before air time, five celebrity
guests are asked specific questions. On
stage, the host presents the same
questions to three competing contestants and states their answers in
·mixed order. Object: For each player
to pair the celebrity with what he or
she said. Each correct match awards
one point. Winners, the highest point
scorers, receive merchandise prizes.

Host: Lloyd Thaxton.

Music: Score Productions.

FUNNY YOU SHOULD ASK—30
minutes—ABC—October 28, 1968 -
September 5, 1969.

FURY

Adventure. Background: Capitol City.
Engaging in a game of baseball, a
group of boys accidentally break a
window. Fearing punishment, they
place the blame on Joey, an innocent
youngster who is suspected of being a
troublemaker. Witnessing the act,
rancher Jim Newton clears the boy's
name. Learning that Joey is an orphan, Jim takes him home to the
Broken Wheel Ranch and begins
adoption procedures.

    In an effort to acquire the boy's
affections, Jim presents him with
Fury, a recently captured black stallion. Given a sense of responsibility,
Joey finds home and love.

    Stories concern an orphan boy's
growth into manhood.

CAST

Jim Newton   Peter Graves

Joey Newton	Bobby Diamond
Pete, Jim's top hand	William Fawcett
Helen Watkins, the school teacher	Ann Robinson
Pee Wee, Joey's friend	Jimmy Baird
Packey Lambert, Joey's friend	Roger Mobley
Harriet Newton, Jim's sister	Nan Leslie
The sheriff	James Seay
The deputy sheriff	Guy Teague
Fury	Gypsy

FURY—30 minutes—NBC—October 15, 1955 - September 3, 1966. Syndicated. Also known as "Brave Stallion."

g

THE GABBY HAYES SHOW

Children. Background: The Double Bar M Ranch. Tales of the American West.

Host-Story Teller: Gabby Hayes.

Regulars: Clifford Sales, Lee Graham, Robert Simon, Michael Strong, Irving Winter, Malcolm Keer.

Featured, via film clips: Hoot Gibson, Buster Crabbe, Tim Holt, Roy Rogers, Dale Evans, Tex Ritter, Gene Autry, Lash LaRue.

THE GABBY HAYES SHOW—30 minutes —ABC—May 12, 1956 - July 14, 1956.

GADABOUT GADDIS

See title: "The Flying Fisherman."

THE GALE STORM SHOW

Comedy. The misadventures of Susanna Pomeroy, the trouble-prone social director of the luxury liner, S.S. *Ocean Queen.*

CAST

Susanna Pomeroy	Gale Storm
Miss Nugent (Nugey), her friend, the beauty-salon operator	ZaSu Pitts
Captain Huxley, the ship's commander	Roy Roberts
Cedric, the cook-waiter	James Fairfax
Dr. Reynolds, the ship's physician	Ralfe Sedan

Music: Alan Bergman

THE GALE STORM SHOW—30 minutes—CBS—August 30, 1956 - April 11, 1959. ABC—30 minutes—April 13, 1959 - April 1962. Syndicated. Original title: "Oh! Susanna."

THE GALLANT MEN

Drama. Background: Salerno, Italy during the Italian Campaign of World War II (1943). The story of Conley Wright, a foreign correspondent assigned to the 36th Infantry of the American fifth army. Scared and unsure of himself, he accompanies the squad on suicide missions and reports the experiences of men desperately struggling to end the war and return home.

CAST

Captain James Benedict	William Reynolds
Conley Wright	Robert McQueeny

THE SQUAD:

Gibson, the radio
     operator   Roger Davis
D'Angelo   Eddie Fontaine
McKenna   Richard X. Slattery
Hanson   Robert Cothie
Lucavich   Roland La Starza
Kimbro   Robert Ridgley

THE GALLANT MEN—60 minutes—ABC—September 1962 - September 14, 1963. Syndicated.

THE GALLERY OF MADAME LIU TSONG

Drama. Distinguished by two formats.

Format One:

The Gallery Of Mme. Liu Tsong—30 minutes—DuMont 1951 - 1952.

The experiences of Madame Liu Tsong, the beautiful Chinese proprietress of an art gallery, as she ventures forth in search of treasured art objects.

Starring: Anna May Wong as Madame Liu Tsong.

Format Two:

Madame Liu Tsong—30 minutes—DuMont 1952.

The story of Madame Liu Tsong, a Chinese exporter, "a good girl against bad men. . . .A combination of the daughter of Fu Manchu, the daughter of Shanghai, and the daughter of the Dragon."

Starring: Anna May Wong as Madame Liu Tsong.

THE GALLOPING GOURMET

Cooking. The preparation and making of gourmet meals. Spiced with light humor.

Host: Graham Kerr, international culinary expert.

Assistants: Patricia Burgess, Wilemina Meerakker.

Music: Champ Champagne.

THE GALLOPING GOURMET—30 minutes—Syndicated 1969. Produced in Canada.

GAMBIT

Game. Two married couples compete. Basis: Blackjack (twenty-one). The dealer, standing between the four seated players, opens a sealed deck of fifty-two oversized cards. The first card is revealed. The host then asks a general-knowledge question. The team first to sound a buzzer signal receives a chance to answer. If correct, they choose to keep or pass the exposed card to their opponents. Questions continue with each team seeking to score as close as possible to twenty-one without going over. Winning couples receive one hundred dollars per game and compete until defeated.

Existing rules: No ties. Should one team "freeze" their score, for example at twenty, the other team must beat it to win. An exact twenty-one in any combination of cards earns five hundred dollars.

Card values: Ace, one or ten points, depending on the situation; picture cards, ten points; other cards, face values.

Host: Wink Martindale.

Dealer: Elaine Stewart.

Announcer: Kenny Williams.

Music: Mort Garson.

GAMBIT—30 minutes—CBS—Premiered: September 4, 1972.

Host: Jim McKrell.

Announcer: Johnny Jacobs.

Music: Frank Jaffe.

GAMBLE ON LOVE

Game. Three married couples compete. Each is interviewed and quizzed via "The Wheel of Fortune." One member of one team spins the wheel and the mate answers its specific category questions. The winning team, the couple correctly answering the most questions, receive a chance to win a mink stole via "The Cupid Question."

Hostess: Denise Darcell.

GAMBLE ON LOVE—30 minutes—DuMont—July 9, 1954 - September 1954.

THE GAME GAME

Game. Three guest celebrities who comprise the panel; and one non-celebrity contestant. Basis: A psychological examination that is conducted through one question (e.g., "Should you be single?") that contains five parts. Before the game begins the contestant predicts whether he will score higher or lower than the panel. The host states question one and reveals four possible answers. Players answer in turn. The host then reveals the answers, which are validated by the Southern Institute of Psychology. Each answer is designated by points—From five to twenty. Points are scored to each player according to his choice. The remaining four questions are played in the same manner. The contestant receives money according to his prediction-twenty-five dollars for each celebrity he beats; one hundred dollars if he beats all three.

THE GAME GAME—30 minutes—Syndicated 1969.

GANGBUSTERS

Anthology. True crime exposés. Based on the files of local, state and federal law enforcement agencies. Adapted from the radio program of the same title.

Hosts-Narrators: Guest police chiefs.

Creator-Writer: Phillips H. Lord.

Included:

Tri State Gang. Police efforts to end a hijacking ring that is operating on Maryland highways.

Starring: Tim Garez, Michael Grainger.

Chinatown. A depiction of how the murders of two Chinese are solved from an insignificant strand of hair.

Starring: Harold Craig.

Gnatz-Franx. The story of a criminal who used hypnosis to commit robberies.

Starring: Lou Polan, Thomas Nello.

The Paul Hilton Story. The reporting of the Phantom of Long Island, an elusive ghostlike killer.

GANGBUSTERS—30 minutes—NBC —1951-1953. Syndicated title: "Captured."

THE GARLUND TOUCH

See title: "Mister Garlund."

GARRISON'S GORILLAS

Adventure. Background: Europe, World War II. A group of convicts from various federal penitentiaries is assembled in France under the command of Lt. Craig Garrison, U.S. Army: Casino, master thief; Goniff, expert pickpocket; Actor, master con-artist; and Chief, professional switchblade artist. Their assignment: to harass the Germans. Their reward: full pardons.

CAST

Craig Garrison	Ron Harper
Casino	Rudy Solari
Actor	Cesare Danova
Coniff	Christopher Cary
Chief	Brendon Boone

Music: Leonard Rosenman.

GARRISON'S GORILLAS—60 minutes—ABC—September 5, 1967 - September 10, 1968. Syndicated.

GARROWAY AT LARGE

See title: "Dave Garroway."

GARRY MOORE

Listed: The television programs of comedian Garry Moore.

The Garry Moore Show—Variety—30, 45, and 60 minute versions—CBS—October 16, 1950 - June 27, 1958.

Host: Garry Moore.

Regulars: Ken Carson, Denise Lor,

Durwood Kirby, Hattie Colbert.

Announcer: Durwood Kirby.

Music: Hank Jones; The Howard Smith Quartet.

I've Got A Secret—Game—CBS—1952-1964 Garry's run as Host. (See title.)

The Garry Moore Show—Variety—60 minutes—CBS—September 30, 1958 - June 16, 1964.

Host: Garry Moore.

Regulars: Durwood Kirby, Ron Martin, Carol Burnett, Denise Lor, Dorothy Loudon, Ken Carson.

Announcer: Durwood Kirby.

Orchestra: Irwin Kostal; Howard Smith.

The Garry Moore Show—Variety—60 minutes—CBS—September 11, 1966 - January 29, 1967.

Host: Garry Moore.

Regulars: Durwood Kirby, Jackie Vernon, Carol Corbett, Pete Barbutti, John Byner, Ron Carey, Eddie Lawrence, Dick Davey, Patsey Elliott, The Bob Hamilton Dancers.

Announcer: Durwood Kirby.

Orchestra: Bernie Green.

To Tell The Truth—Game—30 minutes—Syndicated 1970. (See title.)

THE GAS HOUSE GANG

See title: "East Side Comedy."

THE GAY COED

Variety. Era: The 1920s. A musical

comedy depicting the life of a college coed during America's most reckless, carefree era.

CAST

The Coed	Sandra Barkin
Her romantic interest	Gary McHugh
The football star	Bernie Barrow
His girlfriend	Evelyn Bennett

Also: Chuck Tranum, Melvin Nodell.

THE GAY COED—25 minutes—DuMont 1947.

GAYELORD HAUSER

Women. Beauty tips, advice, and nutritional guidance.

Host: Gayelord Houser, Phd.

GAYELORD HAUSER—15 minutes —ABC—November 21, 1951 - April 25, 1952.

GAY NINETIES REVUE

Musical Variety. A revue set against the background of the 1890s.

Host: Joe Howard, Gus Van.

Regulars: Pat O'Mally, Lulu Bates, Loraine Fontaine, Romona Lang, The Townsmen Quartet.

Orchestra: Ray Bloch.

GAY NINETIES REVUE—30 minutes—ABC—August 11, 1948 - January 12, 1949.

THE GENE AUTRY SHOW

Western. Background: The Melody Ranch. The exploits of Gene Autry, a daring defender of range justice.

CAST

Gene Autry	Himself
Pat Buttram, his partner	Himself

Also: Gail Davis.

Gene's horse: Champion.

THE GENE AUTRY SHOW—30 minutes—Syndicated 1950.

THE GENERAL ELECTRIC COLLEGE BOWL

Game. "Match wits with the champions in America's favorite question and answer game, live from New York, The General Electric College Bowl." Competing are two four-member varsity scholar teams, representatives of two colleges. Basis: Difficult liberal arts questions. The game begins with the Toss Up Round. The host asks a question. The first team to sound a buzzer receives a chance to answer and earn points (five to ten, depending on the question) and the opportunity to increase their score twenty-five to thirty points via a four-part bonus question. The game continues with Toss Up Rounds and Bonus Questions. Winners are the highest point scorers. Prizes: first place—a $3,000 scholarship grant and the right to return to defend their title; the runner-up—a $1,000 grant.

Hosts: Allen Ludden (CBS); Robert Earle (NBC).

THE GENERAL ELECTRIC COLLEGE BOWL—30 minutes—CBS—1957-1960; NBC—1960-1970.

THE GENERAL ELECTRIC GUEST HOUSE

Panel Variety. Hollywood celebrities are interviewed and quizzed on various aspects of the entertainment industry.

Host: Durwood Kirby; Oscar Levant.

Appearing: Connee Boswell, Valeries Bettis, William Gaxton, Eddie Mayehoff, Jean Barlrymple, Cornelia Otis Skinner, Binnie Barnes, Isabel Bigley. Dean Murphy, Felix Greenfield, Whitney Bolton, Norman Levin, John C. Holm.

THE GENERAL ELECTRIC GUEST HOUSE—60 minutes—CBS—July 1, 1951 - September 1951.

GENERAL ELECTRIC SUMMER ORIGINALS

Anthology. Original dramatic productions.

Included:

It's Sunny Again. A musical comedy depicting the struggles of a popular singer who can't get bookings.

Starring: Vivian Blaine, Jules Munshin.

The Unwilling Witness. The story of a man, the only witness to a murder, who refuses to give a defense counselor the information that might save his client.

Starring: Zachary Scott, Frances Rafferty.

The Green Parrot. Assigned to deliver a parrot named Cleopatra to the U.S. War Department, a representative of the French government struggles to complete his mission and protect the bird from foreign agents who seek it for the atomic secrets it carries in its head.

Starring: Claude Dauphin.

GENERAL ELECTRIC SUMMER ORIGINALS—30 minutes—ABC—July 3, 1956 - September 17, 1956.

THE GENERAL ELECTRIC THEATRE

Anthology. Original productions.

Host-Occasional Star: Ronald Reagen.

Music: Elmer Bernstein, Melvyn Lenard; Johnny Mandell.

Included:

The Girl With The Flaxen Hair. The story of a lonely, girl-shy accounting clerk who yearns for the company of a beautiful saleslady in the department store where he is employed.

Starring: Ray Bolger.

The Web Of Guilt. The story of a famous trial lawyer who suddenly finds himself forced to defend his own life.

Starring: Arthur Kennedy.

The Stone. The dramatic retelling of the biblical story of David, a young poet-shepherd and his encounter with the giant Goliath.

Starring: Tony Curtis.

Robbie And His Mary. The dramatic story of Scottish poet Robert Burns's first love, Mary Campbell.

Starring: Dan O'Herlihy, Pippa Scott.

Man On A Bicycle. Background: The French Riviera. A luxury-loving opportunist attempts to help a young French girl in her work with a group of orphans.

Starring: Fred Astaire.

THE GENERAL ELECTRIC THEATRE—30 and 60 minute versions—CBS—February 1, 1953 - September 1961.

GENERAL ELECTRIC TRUE

Anthology. Dramatizations based on stories appearing in *True Magazine.*

Host-Narrator-Occasional Performer: Jack Webb.

Included:

U.X.B. (Unexploded bomb). Background: London, 1962. The attempts of the Suicide Squad to disarm a live and ticking bomb.

CAST
Major Arthur Hartly: Michael Evans; Lt. Keith Allison: David Frankham.

Code Name Christopher. Background: Norway, 1944. An American captain attempts to sabotage Nazi attempts in the production of heavy water, the essential ingredient of the atom bomb.

CAST
Captain John Burke: Jack Webb; Erik Lund: Gunner Hilstrom; Sigrid Lund: Anna-Lisa.

V-Victor Five. Background: New York City. An off-duty patrolman attempts to apprehend five wanted criminals.

CAST
John Egan: Karl Held; Jean Egan: Barbara Wilkins; Eddy: John Sebastian.

The Handmade Private. Whenever their superior, Lt. Bronner, is out tracking missing soldiers, Corporals Coogan and Bailey have the easy life. In order to get him off their backs, Coogan and Bailey invent an A.W.O.L. soldier. The story depicts the U.S. Army's actual global search to find a mythical soldier.

CAST
Cpl. Bailey: Jerry Van Dyke; Cpl. Coogan: Arte Johnson; Lt. Bronner: James Milhollin.

GENERAL ELECTRIC TRUE—30 minutes—CBS—September 30, 1962 - September 22, 1963. Syndicated title: "True."

THE GENERAL FOODS SUMMER PLAYHOUSE

Pilot Films. Proposed comedy series for the 1965-1966 season.

Included:

Hello Dere. The misadventures of two television news reporters.
Starring: Marty Allen, Steve Rossi.

Young In Heart. The story of a newly hired Kappa Phi sorority housemother and her clash with the student president.
Starring: Barbara Bain, Mercedes McCambridge, Lou Foster.

Kibbie Hates Finch. The bickering relationship between two firemen, Kibbie and Finch, once friends until Kibbie was promoted to the position of Captain of Hook and Ladder Company 23.

CAST

Kibbie: Don Rickles; Finch: Lou Jacobi.

Take Him—He's All Yours. The story of an American travel-agency manager in England and her attempts to adjust to a new homeland.

Starring: Eve Arden, Cindy Carol, Jeremy Lloyd.

THE GENERAL FOODS SUMMER PLAYHOUSE—30 minutes—CBS— July 1965 - September 1965.

GENERAL HOSPITAL

Serial. Background: General Hospital. Intimate glimpses into the personal and professional lives of doctors and nurses.

CAST

Dr. Steve Hardy	John Beradino
Audrey March	Rachel Ames
Nurse Iris Fairchild	Peggy McKay
Brooke Clinton	Indus Arthur
Al Weeks	Tom Brown
Sharon Pinkham	Sharon DeBord
Carol Murray	Nancy Fisher
Howie Dawson	Ray Girardin
Lee Baldwin	Peter Hansen
Jane Dawson	Shelby Hiatt
Mrs. Dawson	Phyllis Hill
Dr. Peter Taylor	Craig Huebing
Eddie Weeks	Doug Lambert
Dr. Henry Pinkham	Peter Kilman
Nurse Jessie Brewer	Emily McLaughlin
Nurse Kendell Jones	Joan Tompkins
Dr. Thomas Baldwin	Paul Savior
Diana Maynard	Valerie Starrett
Nurse Lucille March	Lucille Wall
Peggy Mercer	K. T. Stevens
Angie Costello	Jana Taylor
Dr. Phil Brewer	Roy Thinnes
	Martin West
	Robert Hogan

Dr. Lyons	Martin Blaini
Randy	Mark Miller
Dr. Leslie Williams	Denise Alexander
Meg Bentley	Patricia Breslin
Mary Briggs	Anne Helm
Clampett	Robin Blake
Scotty	Tony Campo
Beverly Cleveland	Sue Bernard
Mrs. Nelson	Ann Morrison
The District Attorney	Ivan Bonar
Lieutenant Adams	Don Hammer
Denise Wilson	Julie Adams
Mrs. Bailey	Florence Lindstrom
Polly Prentice	Jennifer Billingsley
Nurse Linda Cooper	Linda Cooper
Augusta McLeod	Judith McConnell
Dr. James Hobart	James Sikking
Gordon Gray	Eric Server
Florence Gray	Ann Collings
Mr. Chamberlain	Ed Platt
Papa Costello	Ralph Manza
Marge	Mae Clark
Johnny	Butch Patrick
Dr. Miller (early role)	Ed Platt
Secretary	Iris Fairchild
Janie Dawson	Shelly Hiatt
Ling Wang	George Chiang
Mailin	Virginia Ann Lee
Ann Coheen	Virginia Grey
Dr. Joel Stratton	Rod McCarey
Owen Stratton	Joel Mareden
Kira Faulkner	Victoria Shaw
Wallace Baxter	Len Wayland

Musical Director: George Wright.

GENERAL HOSPITAL—30 minutes —ABC—Premiered: April 1, 1963.

THE GENERATION GAP

Game. The younger generation is pitted against the older. Intent: To discover how much each knows about the other; how wide or narrow the gap may be. The younger contestants answer questions regarding the past; the older, the present.

Two three-member teams compete. Basis: Six rounds composed of three generation questions directed to specific members of each team (twenty-five points for each correct response) and three cross-generation rapid-fire questions with both teams competing (ten additional points for each correct response). The first person to sound the buzzer is the only one permitted to answer. Ten points are deducted if incorrect. Winners are the highest point scorers. The points are transferred into dollars and each member of the winning team receives that amount; losing team members divide their earnings.

Hosts: Dennis Wholey; Jack Barry.

Announcer: Fred Foy.

Orchestra: Norman Paris.

THE GENERATION GAP—30 minutes—ABC—February 7, 1969 - May 23, 1969.

GENTLE BEN

Adventure. Exploring the Bear River Game Reserve, young Mark Wedloe stumbles upon a baby cub. Suddenly, confronted by its angry mother, he climbs to the safety of a tree. As the bear approaches her cub, she is killed by Fog Hanson, a hunter. Unaware of Mark's presence, Fog takes the cub.

The next day, Mark discovers the bear cub concealed in Fog's waterfront shack. Sneaking in to feed the cub, he befriends him and names him Ben.

Months later, when Mark overhears Fog talking about killing the bear, now fully grown, and selling the meat, he becomes desperate and takes the bear to the safety of the woods. As

the afternoon hour grows late, Ellen, Mark's mother, begins to search for him. Finding Mark with the bear, she discovers its gentleness, but after learning of Mark's act, she demands that he take Ben back. That evening, Mark speaks to his father, Tom, and asks him to purchase the six hundred pound bear from Hanson.

After accepting the position of game warden in the Florida Everglades, Tom complies with Mark's desire and purchases Ben. Stories depict Tom's experiences as a game warden; and the adventures shared by a boy and his pet bear.

CAST

Tom Wedloe	Dennis Weaver
Ellen Wedloe	Beth Brickell
Mark Wedloe	Clint Howard
Boomhauer, a friend	Rance Howard
Willie, a friend	Angelo Rutherford
Ellen Wedloe (pilot episode)	Vera Miles
Fog Hanson (pilot episode)	Ralph Meeker

GENTLE BEN—30 minutes—CBS—September 10, 1967 - August 31 1969. Syndicated.

THE GEORGE BURNS AND GRACIE ALLEN SHOW

Comedy. Background: 312 Maple Street, Beverly Hills, California, the residence of comedian George Burns, a tolerant man who accepts life as it comes; and his scatterbrained wife, comedienne Gracie Allen, a woman who possesses the talent to complicate situations that are seemingly uncomplicatable.

Stories relate the home lives and misadventures of a show business

The George Burns and Gracie Allen Show.
Left to right: Bea Benaderet, Larry Keating,
Gracie Allen, and George Burns. © *Screen
Gems.*

couple. George, who creates the program as it is being viewed, is the only person that is aware of a viewing audience. He interrupts the plots, comments, delivers monologues, and explains the situations that result due to Gracie's harebrained activities.

The series, which is now a television classic, is distinguished by two endings. In early years by public service announcements; in later years by a recreation of their vaudeville routines: comments between man and wife, George being the straight-man. Episodes conclude with George saying, "Say goodnight Gracie." Her inevitable response: "Goodnight Gracie."

The series ended with Gracie's retirement from show business in 1958. With a revised format, George continued the series via "The George Burns Show" (see title).

CAST

George Burns	Himself
Gracie Allen	Herself
Harry Von Zell, George's Announcer	Himself
Ronnie Burns, George and Gracie's son	Himself
Blanche Morton, Gracie's friend and neighbor	Bea Benaderet
Harry Morton, Blanche's husband, a C.P.A.	Hal March
	Bob Sweeny
	Fred Clark
	Larry Keating

Bonnie Sue McAfee, Ronnie's
girlfriend   Judi Meredith
Ralph Grainger, Ronnie's
friend   Robert Ellis
Imogene Reynolds, Ralph's
girlfriend   Carol Lee
Jane Adams,
Gracie's wardrobe
girl   Elva Allman
Frank Adams, her
husband   James Flavan
Edie Westlip, the eleven-year
old president of the
Ronnie Burns Fan
Club   Anna Maria NaNasse
Malcolm Rogers, Edie's
boyfriend   Stevie Tursman
Verna Mason, an aspiring
actress, a friend of
Ronnie's   Valerie Allen
Vickie Donavan, the Hat
Check Girl at the MaCombo
Club, a friend of
Ronnie's   Jackie Loughery
Al Simon, the Burns's business
manager   Lyle Talbot
Professor Ainsworth, Ronnie's
Ancient History instructor at
U.C.L.A.   Howard Guendell
Gloria Gallagher, one of Harry
Von Zell's girlfriends,
employed at the Sunrise
laundry   Barbara Stuart
Mr. Jentzen, the
plumber   Howard McNair
His daughters   Yvonne Lime
Mary Ellen Kay
Jody Warner
Mr. Beasley, the
mailman   Ralph Seadan
Chester Vanderlip, a society
friend   Brandon Rhodes
Detective Soyer, a Los Angeles
cop plagued by
Gracie   James Flavan
Clara Bagley, a friend of
Gracie's   Irene Hervey
Joey Bagley, her
son   Garry Marshall

Announcers: Bill Goodwin (early, not syndicated episodes); Harry Von Zell.

THE GEORGE BURNS AND GRACIE ALLEN SHOW—30 minutes—CBS—October 12, 1950 - September 1958. Syndicated (years '52-'58).

THE GEORGE BURNS SHOW

Comedy. Background: Beverly Hills, California. The life of George Burns, a comedian-turned-theatrical-producer. Stories relate his attempts to overcome the chaotic situations that arise from auditions, performer tantrums, his son, Ronnie's, romantic entanglements, the antics of his secretary, Blanche Morton, and the attempts of his anouncer, Harry Von Zell, to convince George that he is capable of any role asssignment.

CAST

George Burns   Himself
Ronnie Burns   Himself
Harry Von Zell   Himself
Blanche Morton   Bea Benaderet
Harry Morton, her husband, a
C.P.A.   Larry Keating
Lily, the waitress   Barbara Stuart

Announcer: Harry Von Zell.

THE GEORGE BURNS SHOW—30 minutes—NBC—October 21, 1958 - April 5, 1959.

GEORGE GOBEL

Listed: The television programs of comedian George Gobel.

The George Gobel Show—Variety—60 minutes—NBC—October 2, 1954 - June 29, 1957.

Host: George Gobel.

Regulars: Jeff Donnell (as Alice, his wife in sketches), Peggy King.

Orchestra: John Scott Trotter.

The George Gobel Show—Variety—60 minutes—NBC—September 4, 1957 - March 10, 1959. On alternating basis with "The Eddie Fisher Show."

Host: George Gobel.

Regulars: Eddie Fisher, Phyllis Avery (as Alice), Peggy King, The Johnnie Mann Singers.

Orchestra: John Scott Trotter.

THE GEORGE HAMILTON IV SHOW

Musical Variety. Performances by Country and Western entertainers.

Host: George Hamilton IV.

Regulars: Mary Klick, Buck Ryan, Roy Clark, Clint Miller, Elton Britt, Jack French, Billy Gibson, Joe Williams, Joe Davis, Jan Crockett, Smitty Irvin, The Country Lads.

Music: Alec Houston and The Texas Wildcats.

THE GEORGE HAMILTON IV SHOW—60 minutes—ABC—April 13, 1959 - May 29, 1959.

GEORGE JESSEL'S SHOW BUSINESS

Variety. Testimonial dinners honoring personalities of the entertainment world. Celebrity friends, seated about a banquet table, roast the honored guests.

Host: George Jessel, Toastmaster General.

Appearing:

George Burns, roasted by Jack Benny, Edward G. Robinson, Pat Boone, Roberta Sherwood, Della Reese.

Carol Burnett, roasted by Rory Calhoun, Rod Serling, Jean Pierre Aumont, Marty Ingles, Joey Adams, Rich Little, Jan Daley, Mickey Shaughnessy.

Edward G. Robinson, roasted by Tony Bennett, Polly Bergen, Alice Ghostley.

Laurence Harvey, roasted by Liberace, Jim Backus, Henny Backus, Norm Crosby, Marty Ingles, France Nuyen, Morgana King.

Lorne Green, roasted by Gypsy Rose Lee, Frankie Avalon, Shari Lewis, David Canary.

Debbie Reynolds, roasted by Gig Young, Ann Sothern, Agnes Moorehead, Norm Crosby, Paul Gilbert.

Jimmy Stewart, roasted by Ed Begley, Agnes Moorehead, Frankie Avalon, Morey Amsterdam, Rich Little.

Don Rickels, roasted by Al Martino, Jan Daley, Pat McCormick, Henny Youngman.

Versions:

GEORGE JESSEL'S SHOW BUSINESS—60 minutes—ABC—1953-1954.

GEORGE JESSEL'S SHOW BUSINESS—60 minutes—Syndicated 1958.

HERE COME THE STARS—60 minutes—Syndicated 1968.

GEORGE OF THE JUNGLE

Animated Cartoon. Background: The Imgwee Gwee Valley in Africa. The exploits of George, the king of the jungle, a tree-crashing-prone, simpleminded klutz who aids people in distress.

Additional characters: Friends—Bella and Ursula, native girls; Ape, his overgrown gorilla; Shep, his elephant; Seymour, the man-eating plant; Wiggy, the rhino. Enemies—Tiger and Weavel, fiends out to foil George's mission of good.

Additional Segments:

Super Chicken. The story of Henry Cabot Henhouse III, a mild-mannered scientist who discovers Super Sauce, a liquid that when taken transforms him into the daring crime fighter Super Chicken. Episodes relate his battle against the forces of evil. He is assisted by Fred, the rooster.

Tom Slick. The misadventures of Tom Slick, a simple-minded racing car driver.

His aide: Marigold; his car: *The Thunderbolt Grease Slapper.*

Voices: Bill Scott, June Foray, Paul Frees, Bill Conrad, Walter Tetley, Skip Craig, Barbara Baldwin.

Music: Sheldon Allman, Stan Worth.

GEORGE OF THE JUNGLE—30 minutes—ABC—September 9, 1967 - September 6, 1970.

THE GEORGE RAFT CASEBOOK

See title: "I'm the Law."

THE GEORGE SANDERS MYSTERY THEATRE

Anthology. Mystery presentations.

Host-Occasional Performer: George Sanders.

Included:

The Call. Plagued by mysterious phone calls in the night, a nurse attempts to uncover the caller's identity.

CAST

Ann: Toni Gerry; Lewis: James Gavin; Tom: Adam Williams.

Last Will And Testament. An amnesiac, told he resembles a missing heir, joins forces with a couple in attempt to claim the inheritance. The deal is to divide the money; his plan, however, is to kill the man and marry the woman.

CAST

George Cook: Robert Horton; Milo Davenport: Herb Butterfield; Felice: Dolores Dinlon.

Man In The Elevator. A married couple, planning to spend the weekend in the country, are about to leave when the wife remembers that she left her watch in the apartment. The husband returns for it. While he is in the elevator, she removes the fuse, trapping him between floors. The story concerns his frantic efforts to escape.

CAST

Don Haggerty, Dorothy Green.

THE GEORGE SANDERS MYSTERY THEATRE—30 minutes—NBC—June 22, 1957 - September 1957.

GEORGIA GIBBS MILLION RECORD SHOW

Variety. The presentation of songs

that have sold over a million copies.

Hostess: Georgia Gibbs.

Orchestra: Eddie Safronski.

GEORGIA GIBBS MILLION RE-CORD SHOW–30 minutes–NBC–July 1, 1957 - September 1957.

GERALD McBOING-BOING

Animated Cartoon. The misadventures of a young boy, Gerald McCloy, who speaks in sound effects ("Boing! Boing!") rather than words.

Additional characters: The Twirlinger Twins; Dusty of the Circus.

Featured segments: "Meet the Inventor"; "Meet the Artist"; "Legends of Americans in the World."

Off-screen commentator and interpreter of Gerald's sounds: Bill Goodwin.

Voices: Marvin Miller.

Music: Ernest Gold.

GERALD McBOING-BOING–30 minutes–CBS (U.P.A. Theatrical Shorts) –December 16, 1956 - October 3, 1958.

GET CHRISTIE LOVE!

Crime Drama. Background: Los Angeles, California. The investigations of Christie Love, an undercover police agent who encompasses beauty, charm, wit, and an understanding of human nature as her weapons. Working for the L.A.P.D., she is assigned to a special investigative division consisting of eight men and two women. Hating to wear a uniform, she uses various disguises and is determined not to be hindered by procedures.

CAST

Christie Love	Teresa Graves
Lt. Matthew Reardon	Charles Cioffi
Captain Arthur P. Ryan	Jack Kelly
Lt. Steve Belmont	Dennis Rucker
Lt. Joe Caruso	Andy Romano
Officer Pete Gallagher	Michael Pataki

Music: Luchi de Jesus; Jack Elliott, Allyn Ferguson.

GET CHRISTIE LOVE!–60 minutes –ABC–September 11, 1974 - July 18, 1975.

GET IT TOGETHER

Musical Variety. Performances by Rock personalities.

Hosts: Sam Riddle, Cass Elliott.

Announcer: Sam Riddle.

Music: Recorded.

GET IT TOGETHER–30 minutes– ABC–January 3, 1970 - September 6, 1970.

GET THE MESSAGE

Game. Two competing teams, each composed of three members—two celebrities and one studio audience contestant. The host presents an expression to the celebrities (title, name, place, or slogan). Contestants have to identify it through word-association clues. The first to acquire three identifications is the winner and receives one hundred dollars and the chance to compete again.

Hosts: Frank Buxton; Robert Q. Lewis.

GET THE MESSAGE—30 minutes—
ABC—March 30, 1964 - December 25,
1964.

GET SMART

Comedy. Background: 123 Main
Street, Washington, D.C., the headquarters of C.O.N.T.R.O.L., an international spy organization dedicated
to destroying the diabolical objectives
of K.A.O.S., an international organization of evil.

Stories relate the investigations of
two C.O.N.T.R.O.L. agents: Maxwell
Smart, Secret Agent 86, a bumbling
klutz; and his partner, Agent 99, a
beautiful, level-headed woman.

Max and The Chief, to protect their
identities in the presence of 99's
mother, adopt the guises of Maxwell
Smart, a salesman for the Pontiac
Greeting Card Company and the
Chief, Howard Clark, his employer.

Get Smart. Don Adams and Barbara Feldon.

Unaware of her daughter's activities as
a spy, 99's mother believes she is The
Chief's secretary.

CAST

Maxwell Smart	Don Adams
Agent 99 (real name not revealed)	Barbara Feldon
Thaddeus, The Chief	Edward Platt
Conrad Siegfried, the head of K.A.O.S.	Bernie Kopel
Larrabee, a C.O.N.T.R.O.L. agent	Robert Karvelas
C.O.N.T.R.O.L. Agent 44	Victor French
Admiral Harold Harmon Hargrade, the former C.O.N.T.R.O.L. Chief	William Schallert
Dr. Steele, head of C.O.N.T.R.O.L.'s lab, located in a burlesque theatre	Ellen Weston
Hymie, a C.O.N.T.R.O.L. robot	Dick Gautier
Charlie Watkins, a beautiful and shapely blonde C.O.N.T.R.O.L. agent (supposedly a man in disguise)	Angelique
Professor Windish, a C.O.N.T.R.O.L. scientist	Robert Cornthwaite
Charlson, a C.O.N.T.R.O.L. scientist	Kasey Steach
Dr. Bascomb, the head of C.O.N.T.R.O.L.'s crime lab	George Ives
Starker, Siegfried's aide	King Moody
99's mother	Jane Dulo

C.O.N.T.R.O.L.'s dog agent: Fang
(Agent K-13).

Music: Irving Szathmary.

GET SMART—30 minutes—NBC—
September 18, 1965 - September 13,
1969. CBS—September 26, 1969 -
September 11, 1970. Syndicated.

GETTING TOGETHER

Comedy. Background: Los Angeles, California. The misadventures of composer Bobby Conway and lyricist Lionel Poindexter, songwriters anxiously awaiting success.

CAST

Bobby Conway	Bobby Sherman
Lionel Poindexter	Wes Stern
Jenny Conway, Bobby's sister	Susan Neher
Rita Simon, their landlady, a beautician	Pat Carroll
Rudy Colcheck, a police officer, Rita's boyfriend	Jack Burns

GETTING TOGETHER—30 minutes —ABC—September 18, 1971 - January 8, 1972.

GHOST

Game. Distinguished by two formats.

Format One:
Four regular competing players. Words are supplied by home viewers. The host states the number of letters contained in a particular word. Players, one at a time, state a letter. If a correct letter is guessed, it appears in its appropriate place on a board. The object is for players to spell the word without supplying the last letter. If the last letter is given before the word is known, the sender receives fifty dollars. If the word is guessed before the last letter appears, the sender receives twenty-five dollars.

Format Two:
Three competing players. The host states the amount of letters contained in a word. Players, in turn, contribute letters to its formation. For each letter that is correct, beyond the first three, money is awarded. However, should a player supply the last letter he is disqualified. The player first to identify the word is the winner of that round. Players compete until defeated.

Host: Dr. Bergen Evans.

Panelist (format one): Robert Pallock, Shirley Stern, Gail Compton, Hope Ryder.

GHOST—30 minutes—NBC—July 27, 1952 - September 1952. Also known as "Super Ghost."

THE GHOST AND MRS. MUIR

Comedy. Background: Schooner Bay, New England. Determined to reconstruct her life after the death of her husband, free-lance magazine writer Carolyn Muir moves into Gull Cottage, a cottage haunted by the spirit of its nineteenth-century owner, Cap-

The Ghost And Mrs. Muir. Hope Lange.

tain Daniel Gregg. Having passed away before he was able to complete his plans for its development, he is determined to maintain his privacy and continue with his original goal.

Stories relate Carolyn's efforts to make Gull Cottage her home despite the protests of the Captain.

CAST

Carolyn Muir	Hope Lange
Captain Daniel Gregg	Edward Mulhare
Jonathan Muir, her son	Harlen Carraher
Candy Muir, her daughter	Kellie Flanagan
Martha Grant, the housekeeper	Reta Shaw
Claymore Gregg, the Captain's nephew	Charles Nelson Reilly
Peevy, Martha's boyfriend	Guy Raymond
Noorie Coolidge, the owner of the town lobster house	Dabbs Greer

Muir family dog: Scruffy.

Music: Dave Grusin; Warren Barker.

THE GHOST AND MRS. MUIR—30 minutes—NBC—September 21, 1968 - September 6, 1969. ABC—30 minutes —September 18, 1969 - September 18, 1970. Syndicated.

THE GHOST BUSTERS

Comedy. The comic escapades of Kong and Spencer, Ghost Busters, and their assistant, Tracy, a gorilla, as they battle and attempt to dematerialize the ghosts of legendary fiends (e.g., Frankenstein's Monster, Dracula, the Mummy, the Werewolf, etc.).

CAST

Kong	Forrest Tucker
Eddie Spencer	Larry Storch
Tracy	Bob Burns

Music: Yvette Blais, Jeff Michael, The Horta-Mahana Corporation.

THE GHOST BUSTERS—25 minutes —CBS—Premiered: September 6, 1975.

GHOST STORY

Anthology. Suspense dramas relating the plight of people suddenly confronted with supernatural occurrences.

Host: Sebastian Cabot, appearing as Winston Essex, a mysterious psychic gentleman who introduces stories.

Music: Billy Goldenberg.

Included:

At The Cradle Foot. A glimpse into the world of the future when a man envisions, in 1992, the murder of his daughter.

CAST

Paul: James Franciscus; Karen: Elizabeth Ashley; Emily, as a girl: Lori Busk; Emily, as a woman: Lisa James.

The Summer House. Alone in their summer home, Martha Alcot is caught in a world between nightmare and reality when she envisions her husband murdering her by pushing her into an open well in the celler. That evening, her husband lures her to the celler; and, in the attempt to murder her, he himself is killed when he falls into the well.

CAST

Martha Alcott: Carolyn Jones;

Andrew Alcott: Steve Forrest; Charlie Pender: William Windom.

Alter Ego. Wishing to have a play-mate, a bedridden student's dream becomes a reality when an exact double appears. However, he destroys everything he likes. The story concerns his teacher's efforts to return it from whence it came

CAST

Miss Gideon: Helen Hayes; Robert: Michael James Wixted.

The Dead We Leave Behind. The story of Elliot Brent, a man unable to control events in his life—tragic events that are forecast by his television set.

CAST

Elliot Brent: Jason Robards; Joann Brent: Stella Stevens.

GHOST STORY—60 minutes—NBC—September 15, 1972 - December 29, 1972. Spin-off series: "Circle of Fear." (See title.)

THE GIANT STEP

Game. Three youngsters, seven to seventeen years of age, compete. After selecting a subject category, contestants answer questions increasing in difficulty on each plateau they reach. Players vie for the top prize, a college education, which is earned by retaining the championship for a specified number of weeks.

Host: Bert Parks.

Orchestra: Jerry Bresler.

THE GIANT STEP—30 minutes—NBC—November 7, 1956 - May 29, 1957.

GIDEON, C.I.D.

Crime Drama. Background: London, England. The investigations of Commander George Gideon, the Chief Inspector of the Criminal Investigation Division (C.I.D.) of Scotland Yard.

Starring: John Gregson as Commander George Gideon.

GIDEON, C.I.D.—60 minutes—Syndicated 1966. Also known as "Gideon's Way."

GIDGET

Comedy. Background: Santa Monica, California. Swimming and befelled by a cramp, fifteen-and-a-half-year-old Frances Lawrence is rescued by surfer Jeff Matthews, called Moon Doogie by

Gidget. Don Porter and Sally Field. © *Screen Gems.*

other surfers. Nicknamed "Gidget,"* she befriends Jeff and discovers a new life: the world of surfing.

Stories relate her experiences as she and her friends become actively involved in the exciting world of surfing. Based on the movie, *Gidget,* which stars Sandra Dee.

CAST

Frances "Gidget" Lawrence	Sally Field
Russell Lawrence, her father, a widower, an English Professor	Don Porter
Anne, her married sister	Betty Conner
John, Anne's husband, a psychiatrist	Peter Deuel
Jeff Mathews	Steven Miles

Gidget's Friends:

Larue	Lynette Winter
Treasure	Beverly Adams
Becky	Heather North
Sally	Bridget Hanley
Mel	Ron Rifkin
Betty	Barbara Hershey
Ken	Tim Rooney
Ellen	Pam McMyler
Randy	Rickie Sorensen
Siddo	Mike Nader

Music: Howard Greenfield; Jack Keller.

GIDGET—30 minutes—ABC—September 15, 1965 - September 1, 1966. Syndicated.

*According to the movie, a reference to height for a girl who is approximately five feet two; not tall, yet not a midget.

GIGANTOR

Animated Cartoon. Era: Twenty-first-century Earth. The battle against interplanetary evil as depicted through the activities of Gigantor, an indestructible robot; his twelve-year-old master, Jimmy Sparks; and police inspector Blooper.

Music: Lou Singer.

GIGANTOR—30 minutes—Syndicated 1966. Produced in Japan.

GILLIGAN'S ISLAND

Comedy. Background: An uncharted island in the South Pacific. Shipwrecked after a tropical storm at sea, the seven members of the sight-seeing charter boat, the S.S. *Minnow,* develop a community after all attempts to contact the outside world fail. Stories relate their struggle for survival, and their endless attempts to be rescued despite their constant foiling by the bumbling actions of the first-mate, Gilligan.

CAST

Jonas Grumby, the skipper	Alan Hale, Jr.
Gilligan, the first- mate	Bob Denver
Ginger Grant, a beautiful movie actress	Tina Louise
Thurston Howell III, a multimillionaire	Jim Backus
Lovey Howell III, his wife	Natalie Schafer
Mary Ann Summers, a pretty general store clerk from Kansas	Dawn Wells
Roy Hinkley, the professor, a brilliant research scientist	Russell Johnson

Music: Sherwood Schwartz; Johnny Williams; Herschel Burke Gilbert; Lyn Murray; Gerald Fried; Morton Stevens.

GILLIGAN'S ISLAND—30 minutes—CBS—September 26, 1964 - September 3, 1967. Syndicated. Spin-off series: "The New Adventures of Gilligan." (See title.)

GIRL ABOUT TOWN

Variety. Interviews and entertainment performances set against the background of a staged dress rehearsal.

Hostess: Kyle MacDonnell.

Announcer: Johnny Downs.

Music: The Norman Paris Trio.

GIRL ABOUT TOWN—20 minutes—NBC—April 15, 1948 - January 19, 1949.

The Girl From U.N.C.L.E. Stefanie Powers and Noel Harrison.

THE GIRL FROM U.N.C.L.E.

Adventure. Background: New York City. A dry-cleaning establishment, Del Florias Taylor Shop, is the front for the headquarters of U.N.C.L.E.—the United Network Command for Law Enforcement—an international organization responsible for the welfare of peoples and nations against the subversive objectives of THRUSH, an international organization bent on world domination.

Stories relate the investigations of April Dancer and Mark Slate, U.N.C.L.E. agents battling the global forces of crime and corruption as influenced by THRUSH. A spin-off from "The Man From U.N.C.L.E." (See title.)

CAST

April Dancer	Stefanie Powers
Mark Slate	Noel Harrison
Alexander Waverly, the head of U.N.C.L.E.	Leo G. Carroll
Randy Kovacs, an U.N.C.L.E. Agent	Randy Kirby

Music: Jerry Goldsmith.

THE GIRL FROM U.N.C.L.E.—60 minutes—NBC—September 13, 1966 - September 5, 1967. Syndicated.

THE GIRL IN MY LIFE

Testimonial. Recognition of that "special girl in everyone's life" who has been kind, unselfish, and undemanding. The format unites or reunites the recipient of the good deed with the woman who performed it. Gifts are presented to that special girl.

Host: Fred Holliday.

Announcer: John Harlen; Bob Warren.

Music: Ed Kaleoff.

THE GIRL IN MY LIFE—30 minutes —ABC—July 9, 1973 - December 20, 1974.

GIRL TALK

Discussion. Setting: A living room. Guests, mainly women, discuss their thoughts, fears, joys, sorrows, aspirations, and confessions.

Versions:

Girl Talk—30 minutes—DuMont 1955.
Hostess: Wendy Barrie.

Girl Talk—30 minutes—Syndicated 1962-1970.
Hostesses: Virginia Graham; Gloria DeHaven; Betsy Palmer.

In 1969, contract difficulties forced Miss Graham to leave the program. Gloria DeHaven was hired to replace her, but a heavy schedule, including her own New York program, "Prize Movie," forced her to relinquish hosting duties. Betsy Palmer replaced her and continued with the series until it ended in September of 1970.

THE GIRL WITH SOMETHING EXTRA

Comedy. Background: Los Angeles, California. The trials and tribulations of young marrieds: John Burton, an attorney with the firm of Metcalf, Klein, and Associates; and his wife, Sally, who possesses E.S.P. and is able to preceive his every thought. Stories relate John's attempts to cope with the situations that develop when Sally inadvertently meddles into his private thoughts.

CAST

Sally Burton	Sally Field
John Burton	John Davidson
Jerry Burton, John's brother, a bachelor musician	Jack Sheldon
Anne, Sally's friend, operates a variety shop, "The Store"	Zohra Lampert
Owen Metcalf, John's employer	Henry Jones
Angela, John's secretary	Stephanie Edwards
Stewart Klein, John's employer	William Windom

Music: Dave Grusin.

THE GIRL WITH SOMETHING EXTRA—30 minutes—NBC—September 14, 1973 - May 24, 1974.

THE GISELE MacKENZIE SHOW

Musical Variety.
Hostess: Gisele MacKenzie.
Vocalists: The Double Daters.
Orchestra: Alex Stordah.

THE GISELE MacKENZIE SHOW— 30 minutes—NBC—September 28, 1957 - March 29, 1958.

GLADYS KNIGHT AND THE PIPS

Variety. Music, songs, dances, and comedy sketches.
Hostess: Gladys Knight.
Co-Hosts: The Pips, her backup trio: Edward Patten, William Guest,

and Merald "Bubba" Knight (Gladys's brother).

Choreographer: Tony Charmoli.

Orchestra: George Wyle.

Additional Orchestrations: Sid Feller.

GLADYS KNIGHT AND THE PIPS—60 minutes—NBC—July 10, 1975 - July 31, 1975.

THE GLEN CAMPBELL GOODTIME HOUR

Variety. Music, songs, and comedy set against a Country and Western atmosphere.

Host: Glen Campbell.

Regulars: Jerry Reed, Eddie Mayehoff, Larry McNeely, R.G. Brown, John Hartford, Pat Paulsen, Mel Tellis, The Mike Curb Congregation.

Announcer: Roger Carroll.

Orchestra: Marty Paich.

THE GLEN CAMPBELL GOODTIME HOUR—60 minutes—CBS—June 23, 1968 - September 8, 1968. Returned: CBS—60 minutes—January 22, 1969 - June 13, 1972.

GLENCANNON

Adventure. Background: Various Caribbean Islands. The experiences of Colin Glencannon, the skipper of the freighter, *Inchcliffe Castle.* Based on the stories by Guy Gilpatrick.

Starring: Thomas Mitchell as Colin Glencannon.

GLENCANNON—30 minutes—Syndicated 1958.

GLENN MILLER TIME

Musical Variety. A recreation of the Glenn Miller sound.

Hosts: Ray McKinley, drummer, and Johnny Desmond, singer—both members of the Miller orchestra.

Regulars: Patty Clark, The Castle Sisters.

Music: The Glenn Miller Orchestra.

GLENN MILLER TIME—60 minutes—CBS—July 10, 1961 - September 11, 1961.

THE GLENN REEVES SHOW

Musical Variety. Performances by Country and Western artists.

Host: Glenn Reeves.

Music: The Glenn Reeves Band.

THE GLENN REEVES SHOW—30 minutes—Syndicated 1966.

GLOBAL ZOBEL

Travel. Various aspects of countries around the world.

Host-Narrator: Myron Zobel, photographer.

GLOBAL ZOBEL—30 minutes—Syndicated 1961.

THE GLORIA DeHAVEN SHOW

Musical Variety.

Hostess: Gloria DeHaven.

Featured: Bobby Hackett.

Orchestra: Tony Mottola.

THE GLORIA DeHAVEN SHOW—15

minutes—ABC—October 9, 1953 - January 25, 1954.

THE GLORIA SWANSON SHOW

See title: "Crown Theatre with Gloria Swanson."

GLYNIS

Comedy. Background: San Diego, California. The misadventures of Glynis Granville, mystery-story authoress and amateur sleuth. Episodes detail her investigations as she attempts to solve crimes to acquire story material.

CAST

Glynis Granville	Glynis Johns
Keith Granville, her husband, an attorney	Keith Andes

Glynis. Glynis Johns.

Chick Rogers, her consultant, a retired policeman   George Mathews

GLYNIS—30 minutes—CBS—September 25, 1963 - December 18, 1963. Rebroadcasts: CBS—July 1965 - September 6, 1965.

THE GO GO GOPHERS

Animated Cartoon. Background: Gopher Gulch, 1860s. The efforts of two Indians (who resemble gophers), the double talking Ruffled Feather, and his interpreter, Running Board, to safeguard their domain from army colonel Kit Coyote as he attempts to rid the West of Indians.

THE GO GO GOPHERS—24 minutes —CBS—September 14, 1968 - September 6, 1969. Syndicated.

GO LUCKY

Game. Two competing contestants. A group of performers enact a common phrase through charades. Players have to identify it within a two-minute time limit. The most correct identifications award a player a one-hundred-dollar bond. A fifty-dollar bond is awarded to the runner-up.

Host: Jan Murray.

GO LUCKY—30 minutes—CBS—July 15, 1951 - September 2, 1951.

GOING MY WAY

Comedy-Drama. Background: New York City. Father Charles O'Mally, a young Catholic Priest with progressive ideas, is assigned to Saint Dominic's Parrish and its conservative pastor, the aging Father Fitzgibbons. Stories relate his struggles to assist the needy, modernize the church, and reform its stubborn pastor. Based on the movie of the same title.

CAST
Father Charles O'Mally   Gene Kelly
Father Fitzgibbons   Leo G. Carroll
Tom Colwell, the community
     center director   Dick York
Mrs. Featherstone   Nydia Westman

Music: Leo Shuken.

GOING MY WAY—60 minutes—ABC —October 3, 1962 - September 11, 1963.

THE GOLDBERGS

Comedy. Background: 1030 East Tremont Avenue, Bronx, New York, Apartment 3-B. Rent: $78.00 per month. Occupants: The Goldbergs— Molly, Jake, Rosalie, Sammy, and Uncle David. The trials and tribulations of a poor Jewish family who are guided through their difficult times by a warm, compassionate, and understanding woman. Molly is the typical mother trying to raise her children and run her home; the "yenta" talking through the window to her neighbor ("Yoo-hoo, Mrs. Bloom!"); the philosopher who has a theory and a solution for all problems. Based on the radio program.

Revised format. After twenty-five years, Molly uproots her family and moves from the Bronx to the mythical town of Haverville, U.S.A. Stories mirror the lives of the Goldbergs.

CAST
Molly Goldberg   Gertrude Berg

Jake Goldberg   Philip Leob
     Robert H. Harris
Rosalie Goldberg   Arlene McQuade
Sammy Goldberg   Larry Robinson
     Tom Taylor
Uncle David   Eli Mintz
Mrs. Bloom   Olga Fabian
Also: Betty Walker, Dora Weissman, Henry Sharp.

THE GOLDBERGS—30 minutes— CBS—January 17, 1949 - September 25, 1953. Revised version: 30 minutes—Syndicated 1955.

THE GOLDDIGGERS

Variety. Music, songs, dances, and comedy sketches. The Golddiggers are a group of beautiful and talented young ladies, between eighteen and twenty-two years of age, assembled by producer Gregg Garrison through open auditions.

The Golddiggers: Michelle Della Fave, Rosetta Cox, Lucy Codham, Paula Cinko, Peggy Hansen, Nancy Bonetti, Susan Lund, Barbara Sanders, Patricia Mickey, Francie Mendenhall, Loyita Chapel, Lee Crawford, Jimmie Cannon, Tanya Della Fave, Nancy Reichert, Janice Whitby, Jackie Chidsey, Liz Kelley, Karen Cavenaugh, Rebecca Jones.

Programs:

Dean Martin Presents The Golddiggers—Musical Variety—60 minutes— NBC—July 1968 - September 12, 1968.

Hosts: Frank Sinatra, Jr., Joey Heatherton.

Regulars: Paul Lynde, Barbara Heller,

Stanley Myron Handleman, Stu Gilliam, The Times Square Two, Avery Schrieber, Skiles and Henderson, Gail Martin.

Orchestra: Les Brown.

Dean Martin Presents The Golddiggers—Musical Variety—60 minutes—NBC—July 17, 1969 - September 11, 1969. The program features the music, comedy, song, and dance of the 1930s and 40s.

Hosts: Gail Martin, Paul Lynde, Lou Rawls.

Regulars: Stanley Myron Handleman, Tommy Tune, Albert Brooks, Danny Lockin, Darleen Carr, Fiore and Eldridge, Allison McKay, Joyce Ames.

Orchestra: Les Brown.

The Golddiggers In London—Musical Variety—60 minutes—NBC—July 1970 - September 10, 1970.

Host: Charles Nelson Reilly.

Regulars: Marty Feldman, Tommy Tune, Julian Chagrin.

Orchestra: Jack Parnell.

The Golddiggers—Variety—30 minutes—Syndicated 1971.

Hosts: Male Guests of the week: Van Johnson, Glenn Ford, Doug McClure, Rosey Grier, Buddy Hackett, Dom DeLuise, Steve Allen, John Davidson, Hugh O'Brian, Martin Milner.

Regulars: Larry Storch, Alice Ghostley, Charles Nelson Reilly, Jackie Vernon, Lonnie Shorr, Barbara Heller, Don Rice, Jennifer Buriner.

Orchestra: Van Alexander.

GOLDEN WINDOWS

Serial. Juliet Goodwin, a singer, leaves her home in Maine and struggles to further her career in New York City. Her actions are opposed by her boyfriend, Tom Anderson, and her foster father who has always sheltered her.

CAST
Juliet Goodwin	Leila Martin
Tom Anderson	Grant Sullivan
Juliet's foster father	Herb Patterson
	Eric Dressler

GOLDEN WINDOWS—15 minutes—NBC—July 5, 1954 - September 28, 1954.

GOLDEN VOYAGE

Travel. Filmed explorations, narrated by the traveler, to areas about the globe.

Host: Jack Douglas.

GOLDEN VOYAGE—30 minutes—Syndicated 1968. Before being syndicated, the program was produced and aired in Los Angeles for eleven years.

GOLDIE

See title: "The Betty Hutton Show."

GOLF FOR SWINGERS

Game. Background: The Talabasses Park Country Club in Southern California. Involved: Two guest celebrities; host, Lee Trevino; and several condensed versions of golf, "a stroke play match over three par four holes." By the flip of a coin, one player tees off. He may either hit the ball by himself or incorporate Lee, who may hit two shots for each celebrity on each hole. After four holes are played, the winning celebrity receives a check for one thousand dollars, which he donates to the charity of his choice.

Host: Lee Trevino.

Music: Recorded.

GOLF FOR SWINGERS—30 minutes —Syndicated 1972.

GOMER PYLE, U.S.M.C.

Comedy. Background: Camp Henderson, a marine base in Los Angeles, California. The life of Gomer Pyle, a simple-minded and naive private with the Second Platoon, B Company. Stories depict the chaos that ensues when he unconsciously diverges from the set rules of the system and complicates matters; and the efforts of his superior, Sergeant Vincent Carter, a man constantly plagued by Pyle's antics, to resolve the situations.

A spin-off from "The Andy Griffith Show," wherein Gomer Pyle was depicted as a gas-station attendant before he decided to join the marines.

CAST
Private Gomer Pyle	Jim Nabors
Sgt. Vincent Carter	Frank Sutton
Private Duke Slatter	Ronnie Schell
Private Frankie Lombardi	Ted Bessell
Bunny, Carter's girlfriend	Barbara Stuart
Sgt. Charles Hacker	Allan Melvin
Lou Anne Poovie, a friend of Gomer's, a singer at the Blue Bird Cafe	Elizabeth MacRae
Corporal Charles Boyle, Carter's aide	Roy Stuart
Colonel Edward Gray, the Commanding officer	Forrest Compton
Private Hummel	William Christopher
Anderson	Craig Huebing

Music: Earle Hagen.

GOMER PYLE, U.S.M.C.—30 minutes—CBS—September 25, 1964 - March 24, 1972. Syndicated.

GOOBER AND THE GHOST CHASERS

Animated Cartoon. Background: Los Angeles, California. The investigations of Ted, Tina, and Gillie, the staff members of *Ghost Chasers* magazine. Assisted by Goober, a dog who is able to become invisible when he is scared, they incorporate scientific evaluation in their attempt to expose the frauds who perpetrate ghostly occurrences.

Characters' Voices
Goober	Paul Winchel
Ted	Jerry Dexter
Tina	Jo Anne Harris
Gillie	Ronnie Schell

Additional voices: Alan Diehard Jr., Alan Oppenheimer.

Music: Hoyt Curtin.

GOOBER AND THE GHOST CHASERS—30 minutes—ABC—September 8, 1973 - August 31, 1975.

GOOD COMPANY

Interview. Celebrities are interviewed in their homes via remote pickup. The format follows that of "Person to Person." Cameras are placed in the homes and the host, seated in the studio, conducts the interview.

Host: F. Lee Bailey, attorney.

Music: Recorded.

GOOD COMPANY—30 minutes—ABC—September 7, 1967 - December 21, 1967.

THE GOOD GUYS

Comedy. Background: Los Angeles, California. Seeking to better their lives, Bert Gramus and Rufus Butterworth, life-long friends, pool their resources and purchase a diner. Assisted by Claudia, Bert's wife, they attempt to run "Bert's Place" and live the "good life."

CAST

Rufus Butterworth	Bob Denver
Bert Gramus	Herb Edleman
Claudia Gramus	Joyce Van Patten
Big Tom, Rufus's friend, a truck driver	Alan Hale
Gertie, Tom's girl-friend	Toni Gilman
Hal, a friend	George Furth

Music: Jerry Fielding.

THE GOOD GUYS—30 minutes—CBS—September 25, 1968 - January 23, 1970.

THE GOOD LIFE

Comedy. Albert and Jane Miller, plagued by life's endless problems and expenses—a home in the process of repair, a broken car, numerous unpaid bills—seek a better life. An idea of how occurs to Al when their car breaks down in the country and they are befriended by a butler. After seeing the mansion and the style in which he lives, Al thinks "maybe there is a better way."

Donning the guise of a butler, and convincing Jane to pose as a cook, the Millers answer an ad for experienced help at the thirty-two room mansion of Charles Dutton, the head of Dutton Industries. They are invited to spend the night in the servant's quarters while they ponder their decision. Jane is hesitant but Al convinces her that they "can fake it." Their fate is sealed when Al quits his job as a stockbroker and sells their house.

Previously overhearing their discussion through an open intercom button, Nick Dutton, Charles's son by his third wife, promises to keep their secret and assist with the masquerade. Stories relate the Miller's struggles to maintain their cover, attend household duties, and enjoy "The Good Life."

CAST

Albert Miller	Larry Hagman
Jane Miller	Donna Mills
Charles Dutton	David Wayne
Grace Dutton, Charles's sister	Hermione Baddeley
Nick Dutton	Danny Goldman

Music: Sacha Distel.

THE GOOD LIFE—30 minutes—NBC—September 18, 1971 - January 8, 1972.

GOOD MORNING, AMERICA

News-Information. A spin-off from "A.M. America." Broadcast from 7:00 a.m.-9:00 a.m., E.S.T.

Hosts: David Hartman, Nancy Dussault.

Regulars: Rona Barrett, Jonathan Winters, John Lindsay, Geraldo Rivera, Jack Anderson, Erma Bombeck, Nena and George O'Neill.

Newscasters: Steve Bell, Margaret Osmer.

Music Theme: Marvin Hamlisch.

GOOD MORNING, AMERICA—2 hours—ABC—Premiered: November 3, 1975.

GOOD MORNING WORLD

Comedy. Background: Los Angeles, California. The home and working lives of disc jockeys Dave Lewis, married, shy, and retiring, and Larry Clark, a swinging young bachelor, the hosts of "The Lewis and Clark Show," a radio program aired from 6-10 A.M.

CAST

Dave Lewis	Joby Baker
Larry Clark	Ronnie Schell
Linda Lewis, Dave's wife	Julie Parrish
Roland B. Hutton, Jr., the station manager	Billy DeWolfe
Sandy, the Lewis's gossipy neighbor	Goldie Hawn

GOOD MORNING WORLD—30 minutes—CBS—September 5, 1967 - September 17, 1968.

GOOD TIMES

Comedy. Background: A housing project in Chicago. The struggles of the poor black Evans family in rough times when jobs are scarce.

CAST

James Evans, the husband	John Amos
Florida Evans, his wife	Esther Rolle
James Evans, Jr. their oldest son	Jimmie Walker
Thelma Evans, their teenage daughter	BernNadette Stanis
Michael Evans, their son	Ralph Carter
Willona, their friend and neighbor	Ja'net DuBois
Monty, a friend	Stymie Beard

Music: Marilyn Bergman, Alan Bergman, Dave Grusin.

GOOD TIMES—30 minutes—CBS—Premiered: February 8, 1974.

THE GOODYEAR SUMMERTIME REVUE

Musical Variety. Summer replacement for "The Paul Whiteman Revue."

Host: Earl Wrightson.

Regulars: Maureen Cannon, The Ray Porter Chorus.

Orchestra: Glenn Osser.

THE GOODYEAR SUMMERTIME REVUE—30 minutes—ABC—July 1951 - August 1951.

GOODYEAR THEATRE

Anthology. Rebroadcasts of dramas that were originally aired via "The General Electric Theatre."

Included:

You Should Meet My Sister. Adapted from the movie *My Sister Eileen.* Leaving their home in Ohio, sisters Ruth and Eileen Sherwood arrive in New York to further their careers. While Ruth pursues her career as a writer, the city's eligible males pursue would-be actress Eileen.

CAST

Elaine Strich, Anne Helm, Joey Forman.

Squeeze Play. A truck driver attempts to prove that he is not guilty of an accident caused by a speeding white car with only one headlight.

CAST

Dick Shannon, William Campbell.

Marked Down For Connie. The story of Connie Peters, a salesgirl who decides to drum up extra business for the department store by advertising cut-rate cuckoo clocks.

CAST

Elinor Donahue, Tony Travis, Howard McNair.

GOODYEAR THEATRE—30 minutes—NBC—July 1960 - September 1960.

THE GORDON MacRAE SHOW

Musical Variety.
Host: Gordon MacRae.
Vocalists: The Cheerleaders.
Orchestra: Van Alexander.

THE GORDON MacRAE SHOW—60 minutes—NBC—March 5, 1956, - August 27, 1956.

THE GOURMET

Cooking. The preparation and cooking of gourmet meals.
Host: David Wade—"The Rembrandt of the Kitchen, the Edison of the cookbook. . . ."
Announcer: Jack Harrison.

Music: Recorded.

THE GOURMET—30 minutes—Syndicated 1969.

THE GOURMET CLUB

Cooking. Step-by-step methods in the preparation of gourmet meals.
Hostess: Dione Lucas.
Assisting: Guest celebrities.

THE GOURMET CLUB—30 minutes —Syndicated 1958.

GOVERNMENT STORY

Documentary. The history and operation of the U.S. Federal Government is detailed through films and interviews.
Narrators: E. G. Marshall, Paul Long.
Music: Recorded.

GOVERNMENT STORY—30 minutes—Syndicated 1969.

THE GOVERNOR AND J.J.

Comedy. Background: A small, unidentified Midwestern state. The story of its governor, William Drinkwater, a widower, and his twenty-three-year-old daughter, his first lady, Jennifer Jo (J.J.), the curator of the local children's zoo, a woman who possesses the uncanny knack for getting him into and out of political hot water.

CAST

Governor William
    Drinkwater   Dan Daily

Jennifer Jo
Drinkwater   Julie Sommers
George Callison,
the governor's press
secretary   James Callahan
Maggie McCloud,
the governor's
secretary   Neva Patterson
Sara, the house-
keeper   Nora Marlowe

Music: Jerry Fielding.

THE GOVERNOR AND J.J.—30 minutes—CBS—September 23, 1969 - January 6, 1971. Rebroadcasts: CBS—June 1, 1972 - August 11, 1972.

THE GRAND JURY

Crime Drama. Case dramatizations based on the files of the Los Angeles Grand Jury. Episodes depict the work of Harry Driscoll, an ex-F.B.I. agent, and his partner John Kennedy, Grand Jury investigators.

CAST
Harry Driscoll   Lyle Bettger
John Kennedy   Harold J. Stone
Grand Jury investi-
gator   Richard Travis
Grand Jury investi-
gator   Douglas Dumbrille

Program Open; Announcer: "The forework of liberty, protecting the inalienable rights of free people, serving unstintingly and without prejudice to maintain the laws of our land, the Grand Jury."

THE GRAND JURY—30 minutes—Syndicated 1958.

THE GRAND OLE OPRY

Musical Variety. Performances by Country and Western entertainers.

Host: Red Foley.

Regulars: Judy Lynn, Les Paul and Mary Ford, Hank Snow, Chet Atkins, Minnie Pearl, Ernest Tubb, Jimmy Dickens, Goldie Hull, Cal Smith, Lonzo and Oscar, The Lovin' Brothers, The Grand Ole Opry Square Dancers.

THE GRAND OLE OPRY—60 minutes—ABC—October 15, 1955 - September 15, 1956.

THE GRAY GHOST

Adventure. Background: Virginia during the Civil War, 1860s. In a desperate attempt to infiltrate the Confederacy, the Union army recruits a woman spy. However, she becomes a double agent when she reveals their plans to Confederate Major John Singleton Mosby.

Returning, she is exposed, apprehended, and sentenced to death by the Union. Learning of her fate, Mosby affects a dramatic raid on the Union camp and rescues her. He is proclaimed their enemy—The Gray Ghost.

Episodes depict Mosby's daring and cunning raids against the Union army in the hopes of fostering a Confederate victory.

CAST
Major John Mosby   Tod Andrews
Lieutenant Saint
Clair   Phil Chambridge

THE GRAY GHOST—30 minutes—Syndicated 1957.

GREAT ADVENTURE

Anthology. Dramatizations of events that shaped America's past.

Narrator: Van Heflin.

Included:

The Testing Of Sam Houston. The early years of his life from his days as lieutenant under Andrew Jackson through the start of his political life.

CAST
Sam Houston: Robert Culp; Andrew Jackson: Victor Jory.

Six Wagons To Sea. Background: California. Using a horse-drawn wagon, a raisin grower attempts to deliver his crop to San Francisco against railroad objections.

CAST
Misok Bedrozian: Lee Marvin; Mercer: Gene Lyons; Elissa: Ellen Madison.

The Story Of Nathan Hale. Era: The American Revolution. The events leading to the conviction and hanging of Nathan Hale, found guilty of spying.

CAST
Nathan Hale: Jeremy Slate; Jenny: Nancy Malone.

GREAT ADVENTURE—60 minutes —CBS—September 23, 1963 - May 8, 1964.

GREAT ADVENTURE

Travel. Films exploring various areas around the world.

Host-Narrator: Jim Dooley.

GREAT ADVENTURE—60 minutes —Syndicated 1972.

GREAT ADVENTURES

Travel. Films exploring various areas around the world.

Host-Narrator: Ray Forrest.

GREAT ADVENTURES—30 minutes —Syndicated 1958. Canadian title: "Adventure Theatre."

THE GREAT AMERICAN DREAM MACHINE

Satire. A television magazine format designed "to make significant statements about the good and bad trends in our society." A satirization of everyday life from true love, to politics, to purchasing a frozen dinner at the supermarket.

Semiregulars: Marshall Efron, Ken Shapiro, Chevy Chase, Lee Meredith, Nicholas Van Hoffman, Andrew Rooney, Robert Townsend.

THE GREAT AMERICAN DREAM MACHINE—60 minutes—PBS— October 6, 1971 - February 9, 1972.

GREAT BANDS

Music: The re-created sound of the Big Band Era.

Host: Paul Whiteman, the Dean of American Music.

Appearing, with their orchestras: Xavier Cugat, Gene Krupa, Johnny Long, Ralph Marterie, Buddy Rogers, Percy Faith.

GREAT BANDS—60 minutes—CBS 1954.

THE GREATEST GIFT

Serial. The dramatic story of a woman doctor, who, after serving as a nurse in Korea, returns home to assume control of her late uncle's practice. Ultimately, she must decide whether to remain there or fulfill her desire for a large, city practice.

CAST
Dr. Eve Allen   Ann Burr
Dr. Phil Stone   Philip Foster

THE GREATEST GIFT—15 minutes —NBC—August 30, 1954 - September 28, 1954.

THE GREATEST MAN ON EARTH

Game. Tested: Male superiority. Five men compete for the title "The Greatest Man." Each contestant is nominated by five women who assist him in various stunts and question-answer rounds. One couple is eliminated in each round. Winners are the last remaining couple.

Host: Ted Brown.

Assistant: Pat Conway.

THE GREATEST MAN ON EARTH —30 minutes—ABC—December 3, 1952 - December 31, 1952.

THE GREATEST SHOW ON EARTH

Drama. Background: The Ringling Brothers Barnum and Bailey Circus. Stories dramatize the problems of the circus performers, and the struggles endured in presenting "The Greatest Show on Earth."

CAST
Johnny Slate, the working
  boss   Jack Palance
Otto King, the business
  manager   Stu Erwin
Music: Jeff Alexander.

THE GREATEST SHOW ON EARTH —60 minutes—ABC—September 17, 1963 - September 8, 1964. Syndicated.

GREAT GHOST TALES

Anthology. Mystery and suspense presentations.

Host: Frank Gallop.

Included:

William Wilson. The story of a man plagued by his exact double— a man out to kill him.

CAST
William Wilson: Robert Duval; Whispers: Peter Brandon.

Lucy. The story of an actress who discovers a strange talent—what she wishes for comes true.

CAST
Lucy Morrison: Lee Grant. Also: Kevin McCarthy.

Shredni Vashtar. The tale of a young boy, Conradin, and his pet ferret, Shredni Vashtar.

Starring: Richard Thomas as Conradin.

GREAT GHOST TALES—30 minutes

−NBC−July 6, 1961 - September 1961.

THE GREAT GILDERSLEEVE

Comedy. Background: The town of Summerfield, 217 Elm Street, the residence of Throckmorton P. "The Great" Gildersleeve, the water commissioner, and his wards, his orphaned niece and nephew, Marjorie and Leroy Forrestor. Stories relate the home, working, and romantic life of the bachelor uncle of two children. Based on the radio program of the same title.

CAST

Throckmorton P. Gildersleeve (Gildy)	Willard Waterman
Marjorie Forrestor	Stephanie Griffin
Leroy Forrestor	Ronald Keith
Leila Ransom, Gildersleeve's former girlfriend, a Southern belle eagerly awaiting his marriage proposal	Shirley Mitchell
Lois, Gildersleeve's girlfriend	Doris Singleton
Birdie Lee Coggins, the Gildersleeve housekeeper	Lillian Randolph

THE GREAT GILDERSLEEVE−30 minutes−NBC−1955-1956.

THE GREAT WAR

Documentary. A filmed history of British and American participation in the Second World War.

Host-Narrator: Sir Michael Redgrave.

THE GREAT WAR−30 minutes−Syndicated 1964.

GREEN ACRES

Comedy. Yearning to be a farmer all his life, attorney Oliver Wendell Douglas purchases, sight unseen, the 160-acre Haney farm in Hooterville. Much to the objections of his glamorous and sophisticated wife, Lisa, they relinquish their life of luxury in New York City, and retreat to a shabby, broken-down, unfurnished nightmare−Oliver's Green Acres dream.

Agreeing only to try farm life for six months, Lisa has a change of heart after discovering that their cow, Elinor, and chicken, Alice will be destroyed when they leave. Stories relate the struggles of two city slickers as they attempt to cope with the numerous trials and tribulations of farming and country living.

CAST

Oliver Douglas	Eddie Albert
Lisa Douglas	Eva Gabor
Eb Dawson, their handyman	Tom Lester
Mr. Haney, a conniving salesman	Pat Buttram
Hank Kimball, the agricultural representative	Alvy Moore
Fred Ziffel, a pig farmer	Hank Patterson
Doris Ziffel, his wife	Fran Ryan
	Barbara Pepper
Sam Drucker, the general store owner	Frank Cady
Newt Kiley, a farmer	Kay E. Kicter
Alf Monroe, a carpenter hired by Oliver to repair their house	Sid Melton
Ralph Monroe, his partner (his sister)	Mary Grace Canfield
Joe Carson, the Shady Rest Hotel Manager	Edgar Buchanan

Unis Douglas, Oliver's
    mother   Eleanor Audley
Darlene, Eb's girl-
    friend   Judy McConnell
Also: Arnold the Pig, Fred Ziffel's
    intelligent pet pig, the animal
    considerd to be his son.

Music: Vic Mizzy.

GREEN ACRES—30 minutes—CBS—
September 15, 1965 - September 7,
1971. Syndicated.

THE GREEN HORNET

Adventure. Background: Washington,
D.C. Building the *Daily Sentinel* into
America's greatest publication, editor
Dan Reid turns over the management
of the paper to his playboy bachelor
son, Britt, hoping the responsibility
will mature him, and hires an ex-cop,
Mike Axford to secretly watch over
Britt's activities.

The Green Hornet. Left to right: Bruce Lee,
Beth Brickell (guest), Van Williams.

Instilled with his father's goal,
Britt, like his great-grand-uncle, John
Reid (the Lone Ranger), undertakes a
crusade to protect the rights and lives
of decent citizens. Adopting the guise
of the Green Hornet (the symbol of
the insect that is the most deadly
when aroused) he establishes a base in
an abandoned building, and reveals his
true identity to only three people—
Kato, his Oriental houseboy; Frank
Scanlon, the district attorney; and his
secretary, Lenore Case.

Considered criminal and wanted by
police, the Green Hornet and Kato
avenge crimes as semifugitives rather
than as a law-enforcement organization, always disappearing before
authorities take over. Based on the
radio program of the same title.

CAST
Britt Reid/The Green
    Hornet   Van Williams
Kato   Bruce Lee
Lenore Case (Casey)   Wende Wagner
Frank Scanlon   Walter Brooke
Mike Axford   Lloyd Gough

The Hornet's mode of transportation:
    The *Black Beauty.*

Music: Billy May.

THE GREEN HORNET—30 minutes
—ABC—September 9, 1966 - July 14,
1967. Syndicated.

GRIFF

Crime Drama. Background: Los
Angeles, California. The investigations
of Wade "Griff" Griffin, a former
police captain turned private detective.

CAST
Wade Griffin   Lorne Greene

Mike Murdoch, his
    partner   Ben Murphy
Gracie Newcombe, their
    secretary   Patricia Stich
Police Captain Barney
    Marcus   Vic Tyback

Music: Elliot Kaplan; Mike Post, Pete Carpenter.

GRIFF—60 minutes—ABC—September 29, 1973 - January 4, 1974.

GRINDL

Comedy. Background: New York City. The misadventures of Grindl, a maid with the Foster Employment Agency. Stories depict her attempts to successfully complete her assigned duties.

CAST

Grindl   Imogene Coca
Anson Foster, her
    employer   James.Millhollin

GRINDL—30 minutes—NBC—September 15, 1963 - September 13, 1964.

THE GROOVIE GOOLIES

Animated Cartoon. Background: Horrible Hall, an ancient, spider-web-covered castle. The antics of its residents, the Groovie Goolies, practical-joke playing, musically inclined creatures who resemble celluloid monsters of the 1930s and 40s.

Characters: Frankenstein, Dracula, the Mummy, the Werewolf, Bella, the female Vampire, the two-headed Dr. Jekyll and Mr. Hyde, witches, warlocks, and walking and talking skeletons.

Voices: Larry Storch, Don Messick, Howard Morris, Jane Webb, Dallas McKennon, John Erwin.

Music: The Horta-Mahana Corporation.

THE GROOVIE GOOLIES—30 minutes—CBS—September 12, 1971 - September 17, 1972.

GUESS AGAIN

Game. Three competing contestants are assisted by three guest celebrities. A skit is performed on a stage by a repertoire company. Contestants, through its clues, have to answer questions related to it.

Host: Mike Wallace.

Repertory Company: Joey Faye, Mandy Kaye, Bobbie Martin.

GUESS AGAIN—30 minutes—CBS 1951.

GUESS WHAT?

Game. Four celebrity panelists compete. The host relates short quotations or statements that refer to a famous person, place, or thing. Panelists, who are permitted to ask "yes" or "no" type questions, have to identify the subject within an allotted time limit. A cash prize, which is donated to charity, is awarded for each correct identification.

Host: Dick Kollmar.

Panelists: Virginia Peine, Quenton Reynolds, Mark Hanna, Cliff Norton, Audrey Christie, Lisa Fenaday.

GUESS WHAT?—30 minutes—Dumont—July 8, 1952 - September 1952.

GUESS WHAT HAPPENED?

Game. Object: For a panel to discover via question-answer probe rounds the stories behind their guests—people involved in unusual news stories.

Hosts: John Cameron Swayze; Ben Grauer.

Panelists: Neva Patterson, Roger Price, H. Allen Smith, Maureen Stapleton, Frank Gallop, Jack Norton.

GUESS WHAT HAPPENED?—30 minutes—NBC 1952.

GUEST SHOT

Interview. Films revealing little-known aspects of Hollywood celebrities.

Hosts—Interviewers: Army Archard, Vernon Scott, Earl Wilson, Joe Hyams, Hank Grant, Dan Jenkins.

Appearing: Jayne Mansfield, demonstrating her physical fitness program; Tina Louise, doing gymnastics; Rod Comeron, sailing his forty-two-foot Ketch; Jeffrey Hunter, skiing; Mamie Van Doren, motorcycling; Fess Parker, playing polo; Monique Van Vooren, ice skating; Robert Horton, flying; Fabian Forte, lion hunting.

GUEST SHOT—30 minutes—two fifteen minute segments—Syndicated 1962. Withdrawn.

GUESTWARD HO

Comedy. Dissatisfied with life in New York, advertising executive Bill Hoot-in purchases Guestward Ho, a dude

Guestward Ho. Left to right: Mark Miller, J. Carroll Naish, Joanne Dru, Earl Hodgins.

ranch in New Mexico. Stories relate the attempts of he and his family—his wife, Babs, and their son, Brook—to adjust to new responsibilities and acquire paying customers.

CAST

Bill Hootin	Mark Miller
Babs Hootin	Joanne Dru
Brook Hootin	Flip Mark
Chief Hawkeye, the owner of the local trading post; an Indian on a campaign to win back the American continent for his people	J. Carrol Naish
Lonesome, their wrangler	Earl Hodgins
Pink Cloud, Hawkeye's assistant	Jolene Brand
Rocky, a friend	Tony Montenaro

GUESTWARD HO—30 minutes—

ABC—September 29, 1960 - September 21, 1961. Syndicated.

THE GUIDING LIGHT

Serial. Background: The town of Springfield. The dramatic story of the Bauer family. Episodes relate the conflicts and tensions that arise from the interactions of the characters.

CAST

Papa Bauer	Theo Goetz
Dr. Edward Bauer	Martin Hulswit
	Robert Gentry
Michael	Glenn Walker
	Don Stewart
Meta Roberts	Ellen Demming
Mark Holden	Whitfield Connor
Anne Benedict	Joan Gray
Dr. Paul Fletcher	Bernard Grant
Susan Carver	Judy Lewis
Leslie Jackson	Barbara Rodell
	Lynne Adams
Bertha Bauer	Charita Bauer
Don Peters	Paul Gallantyne
Dick	James Lypton
Kathy	Susan Douglas
Joe Roberts	Herb Nelson
George Hayes	Philip Sterling
Jane Hayes	Chase Crosley
Tracy Delmar	Victoria Wyndham
Dianah Buckley	Courtney Sherman
Kit Vested	Nancie Addison
Dr. Sara McIntyre	Millette Alexander
	Patricia Roe
Barbara Norris	Barbara Berjer
Deborah Mehren	Olivia Cole
Holly Norris	Lynn Deerfield
Peter Wexler	Michael Durrell
Charlotte Waring	Melinda Fee
David Vested	Dan Hamilton
Marion Conway	Kate Harrington
Hope Bauer	Elissa Leeds
Janet Mason	Caroline McWilliams
Peggy Dillman Fletcher	Fran Myers
Ken Norris	Roger Newman
Linell Conway	Christine Pickles
Stanley Norris	William Smithers
Dr. Stephen Jackson	Stefan Schnabel
Karen Martin	Tudi Wiggins
Roger Thorpe	Mike Zaslow
Dr. Joe Werner	Ed Zimmerman
Ellen Mason	Jeanne Arnold
Gil Mehren	David Pendleton
Flip Malone	Paul Carpinelli
Mrs. Herbert	Rosetta LeNoire
Baby Fred Fletcher	Albert Zungalo III
Baby Billy Fletcher	James Long
Adam Thorpe	Robert Milli
Marie Wallace Grant	Lynne Rogers
Dr. John Fletcher	Don Scardino
	Erik Howell
Betty Eiler	Madeline Sherwood
Charles Eiler	Graham Jarvis
Captain Jim Swanson	Lee Richardson
Dr. Bruce Banning	Barnard Hughes
Bill Bauer	Lyle Surdow
	Ed Bryce
Dr. Jim Frazier	James Earl Jones
Martha Frazier	Cecily Tyson
	Ruby Dee
Claudia Dillman	Grace Matthews
Ann Fletcher	Elizabeth Hubbard
Alex Bowden	Ernest Graves
	Tom Klunis
Helene Benedict	Kay Campbell
Sir Clayton Olds	Myles Easton
Karl	Richard Morse
Victoria Ballinger	Carol Teitel
Lincoln Yates	Peter MacLean
Trudy Bauer	Actress Unknown
Dr. Wilson Frost	Jack Bels
Robin Holden	Zina Bethune
	Gillian Spencer

Also: Betty Lou Gerson, Jone Allison, Willard Waterman, Ned LeFeore, Sandy Dennis, Adelaide Klein, Joseph Campanella, Diana Hyland, Ethel Everett, Charles Baxter, Carl Low, Anthony Call, Eric Howell, Sydney Walker, Kathryn Hays.

Announcer: Hal Simms.

Music: Charles Paul.

THE GUIDING LIGHT—15 and 30 minute versions—CBS—Premiered: June 30, 1952.

GULF PLAYHOUSE

Anthology. Dramatic presentations.

GULF PLAYHOUSE—30 minutes—NBC 1952.

GUMBY

Children. Background: Scotty McKee's Fun Shop. The misadventures of a boy, Gumby, and his horse, Pokey—animated clay figures.

Host (portraying Scotty McKee): Bob Nicholson.

GUMBY—30 minutes—NBC 1957. Segments, five minutes each, are syndicated separately.

GUNSLINGER

Western. Background: Fort Scott in Los Flores, New Mexico, 1860s. The story of Cord, a United States Cavalry undercover agent who poses as a gunslinger. Episodes depict his attempts to apprehend criminals wanted by the army.

CAST
Cord	Tony Young
Captain Zachary Scott, the Commanding Officer	Preston Foster
Amber Hollister, Cord's romantic interest	Midge Ware
Pico McGuire, an undercover agent	Charles Gray
Billy Urchin, an undercover agent	Dee Pollock
Murdock, an undercover agent	John Pickard

Music: Dimitri Tiomkin.

GUNSLINGER—60 minutes—CBS—February 9, 1961 - September 5, 1961.

THE GUNS OF WILL SONNETT

Western. Background: Wyoming during the 1880s. The travels of ex-cavalry scout Will Sonnett and his twenty-year-old grandson, Jeff, as they seek to find James Sonnett, Jeff's father, a wanted gunman and killer who deserted his family during the 1860s.

CAST
Will Sonnett	Walter Brennan
Jeff Sonnett	Dack Rambo
James Sonnett	Jason Evers

THE GUNS OF WILL SONNETT—30 minutes—ABC—September 8, 1967 - September 15, 1969. Syndicated.

GUNSMOKE

Western. Background: Dodge City, Kansas during the 1880s. A realistic and tensely dramatic series that focuses on the lives and experiences of five people: Matt Dillon, a dauntless and fearless United States Marshal; Kitty Russell, proprietress of the Longbranch Saloon, a woman with a heart of gold and eyes for Matt; Chester Goode, Matt's deputy, a man who walks with a limp and "brews a mean pot of coffee" (half-hour episodes); Galen Adams, the kindly and dedicated physician; and Festus

Gunsmoke. Left to right: James Arness, Burt Reynolds, Milburn stone, Amanda Blake, Ken Curtis.

Haggen, the comic relief, Matt's unkempt, hillbilly deputy (hour episodes).

CAST

Marshal Matt Dillon	James Arness
Kitty Russell	Amanda Blake
Dr. Galen Adams (Doc)	Milburn Stone
Chester Goode	Dennis Weaver
Festus Haggen	Ken Curtis
Newly O'Brien, the gunsmith	Buck Taylor
Sam, the Longbranch bartender	Glenn Strange
	Robert Brubaker
Quint Asper, the blacksmith	Burt Reynolds
Nathan Burke, the freight agent	Ted Jordan
Hank Patterson, the stableman	Hank Patterson
Thad Greenwood, a friend of Matt's	Roger Ewing
Mr. Jones, the general-store owner	Dabbs Greer
Barney, the telegraph operator	Charles Seel
Ma Smalley, the owner of the Dodge City Boarding House	Sarah Selby
Mr. Bodkin, the town banker	Roy Roberts
Howie, the hotel clerk	Howard Culver
Percy Crump, the town undertaker	John Harper
Lathrop, the storekeeper	Woody Chambliss
Halligan, a friend of Matt's	Charles Wagenheim
Ed O'Connor, a rancher	Tod Brown
Louis Pheeters, the town drunk	James Nusser
Dr. John Chapman	Pat Hingle

Matt's horse: Marshal.

Festus's mule: Ruth.

Music: Richard Shores; John Parker.

GUNSMOKE—30 and 60 minute versions—CBS—September 10, 1955 - September 1, 1975. Syndicated. Half-hour episodes are also known as "Marshal Dillon."

GUY LOMBARDO

Listed: The television programs of orchestra leader Guy Lombardo.

Guy Lombardo And His Royal Canadians—Musical Variety—30 minutes—Syndicated—1954 - 1956.

Host: Guy Lombardo.

Regulars: Lebert Lombardo, Carmen Lombardo, Victor Lombardo,

Kenny Gardner, Bill Flannigan, Toni Arden.

Orchestra: The Royal Canadians.

Guy Lombardo's Diamond Jubilee—Musical Variety—CBS 1956.

Host: Guy Lombardo.

Regulars: Lebert Lombardo, Carmen Lombardo, Victor Lombardo.

Orchestra: The Royal Canadians.

Featured Segment: "The Song of Your Life." Letters sent in by home viewers describe how certain songs influenced their lives. The authors of selected songs receive one thousand dollars, appear on stage, and, as an off-stage voice reads the letter, the song is played in the background.

A New Year's Eve Party With Guy Lombardo—Annually—90 minutes. Stations vary, broadcast both by networks and on a syndicated basis. Guy, his Royal Canadians Orchestra, and guests ring out the old and welcome in the new. Began on radio in 1930.

THE GUY MITCHELL SHOW

Musical Variety.

Host: Guy Mitchell.

Regulars: The Guy Mitchell Singers, The Ted Cappy Dancers.

Orchestra: Van Alexander.

THE GUY MITCHELL SHOW—30 minutes—NBC—1957-1958.

GYPSY ROSE LEE

Listed: The television programs of actress Gypsy Rose Lee.

The Gypsy Rose Lee Show—Talk-Variety—90 minutes—Syndicated 1958.

Hostess: Gypsy Rose Lee.

Regulars: Earl Wrightson, Stan Freeman, Mary Ellen Terry.

Gypsy—Talk-Variety—30 minutes—Syndicated 1966.

Hostess: Gypsy Rose Lee.

Music: Recorded.

H

HAGGIS BAGGIS

Game. Four competing contestants. Object: The identification of concealed photographs. Contestants, one at a time, pick a category from a large board. The host reads a related question that, if correctly answered, will enable the player to see a small portion of the photograph. Winners are the players with the most number of correct identifications. With the runner-up, he receives a choice of one of two sets of prizes: The Haggis (Luxury) or the Baggis (Utility). The champion secretly locks in his choice; the runner-up chooses verbally. If his choice matches he loses and receives nothing; if he selects the other, he receives the prizes.

Hosts (afternoon version): Fred Robbins; Bert Parks.

Hosts (evening version): Jack Linkletter; Dennis James.

Assistant: Lillian Naud.

HAGGIS BAGGIS—30 minutes—NBC. Evening version: June 20, 1958 - September 20, 1958; Afternoon (daily): June 30, 1958 - June 19, 1959.

HAIL THE CHAMP

Game. Six children chosen from the studio audience compete in various original athletic stunts. The winners are crowned "Champ of the Week" and receive accompanying prizes.

Hosts: Herb Allen; Howard Roberts.

Assistants: Angel Casey; Jim Andelin.

HAIL THE CHAMP—30 minutes—ABC—September 22, 1951 - June 13, 1953.

HALF-HOUR THEATRE

Anthology. Dramatic presentations.

Included:

The Housekeeper. The story of a psychiatrist who believes that he has found a cure for neurotics.

CAST
Albert Dekker, Dorothy Adams.

Foo Young. A Chinese detective attempts to clear an innocent man accused of murder.

CAST
Richard Loo, Ed Gargan, Iris Adrian.

When The Devil Is Sick. The story of a man who believes he has only a short time to live and resolves to reform.

CAST
Larry Blake, Dorothy Adams.

HALF-HOUR THEATRE—30 minutes—ABC—June 19, 1953 - September 25, 1953.

HALF THE GEORGE KIRBY COMEDY HOUR

Variety. Sketches coupled with music and songs.

Host: George Kirby.

Regulars: Connie Martin, Jack Duffy, Julie Amato, Steve Martin, Joey Hollingsworth, The Walter Painter Dancers.

Orchestra: Hank Marr.

HALF THE GEORGE KIRBY COMEDY HOUR—30 minutes—Syndicated 1972.

THE HALLMARK HALL OF FAME

Anthology. Classical and serious dramas, period plays, and musical adaptations.

Hostess-Performer-Narrator (early years): Sarah Churchill.

Frequently Cast: Julie Harris, Dame Judith Anderson, Maurice Evans.

Included:

The Country Girl. The story of three people: Frank Elgin, a matinee idol drowning in self pity and alcohol; Georgie, his long-suffering wife; and Bernie Dodd, an ambitious film director.

CAST
Frank Elgin: Jason Robards; Georgie Elgin: Shirley Knight Hopkins; Bernie Dodd: George Grizzard.

The Littlest Angel. A musical adaptation of Charles Tazewell's Christmas story about a boy's attempts to adjust to heaven.

CAST

Michael: Johnnie Whitaker; Patience: Fred Gwynne; God: E.G. Marshall; Gabriel: Cab Calloway; Angel of Peace: John McGiver; Flying Mistress: Connie Stevens.

Brief Encounter. Noel Coward's play about two married strangers who meet by chance and fall in love.

CAST

Anna Jesson: Sophia Loren (her American TV debut); Alec Harvey: Richard Burton; Mrs. Gaines: Rosemary Leach.

Give Us Barabbas. A period drama that explores the reason for Pontius Pilate's decision to free the thief, Barabbas, and crucify Jesus Christ. The story also explains the evaluation of Barabbas "from a cold criminal to a man of awakening conscience."

CAST

Barabbas: James Daly; Pontius Pilate: Dennis King; Mara: Kim Hunter.

THE HALLMARK HALL OF FAME —90 minutes to 2 hours (depending on the production)—NBC—Premiered: December 24, 1951.

THE HALLS OF IVY

Comedy. Background: Number One Faculty Row of Ivy College in Ivy, U.S.A., the residence of Professor William Todhunter Hall, the president, and his wife, Vicky. Stories relate the incidents that befall a mythical college, its students, and its faculty.

CAST

Dr. William Todhunter Hall	Ronald Coleman
Vicky Hall, a former stage performer, Victoria Cromwell	Benita Hume
Alice, their housekeeper	Mary Wickes
Clarence Wellman, the Chairman of the Board of Ivy College	Herb Butterfield
Mrs. Wellman, his wife	Sarah Selby
Professor Warren	Arthur Q. Bryan

Music: Les Baxter.

THE HALLS OF IVY—30 minutes— CBS—October 19, 1954 - September 19, 1955.

HANDLE WITH CARE

Anthology. Dramatization disclosing the problems encountered by the United States Postal Service in its handling of the mails. Stories relate the cases of postal investigators who attempt to curtail the misuse of mail.

HANDLE WITH CARE—30 minutes —ABC—October 7, 1954 - December 30, 1954. Original title: "The Mail Story."

HANDS OF DESTINY

Anthology. Dramatizations depicting the plight of people caught in a web of supernatural intrigue.

HANDS OF DESTINY—30 minutes— DuMont—1949-1951. Also titled: "Hands of Murder" and "Hands of Mystery."

HANK

Comedy. Background: Western State University. The story of Hank Dearborn, an enterprising young businessman who is determined to obtain the college education that he was denied when his parents were killed in an automobile accident and he was forced to quit high school and care for his younger sister, Tina.

Supporting himself by operating several campus concessions, he attends classes unregistered and under various aliases, struggling to achieve a long-awaited dream.

CAST

Hank Dearborn	Dick Kallman
Tina Dearborn	Katie Sweet
Doris Royal, his girl-friend	Linda Foster
Dr. Lewis Royal, her father, the registrar	Howard St. John
Professor McKillup	Lloyd Corrigan
Coach Weiss	Dabbs Greer
Franny, Tina's baby sitter	Kelly Jean Peters
Miss Mittleman, an instructress	Dorothy Neumann
Ralph, Hank's friend	Don Washbrook
Kim, a friend	Judy Parker
Loretta, a friend	Margaret Blye
Arlene Atwater, the social worker	Lisa Gaye
Mrs. Weiss, the coach's wife	Sheila Bromley

Music: Frank Perkins.

HANK—30 minutes—NBC—September 17, 1965 - September 2, 1966.

THE HANK McCUNE SHOW

Comedy. The misadventures of Hank McCune, a kind-hearted bumbler who seeks but inevitably fails to achieve success.

CAST

Hank McCune	Himself
Lester, his friend	Hanley Stafford

Also: Sara Berner, Arthur Q. Bryan, Larry Keating.

THE HANK McCUNE SHOW—30 minutes—NBC—1949 - 1950. Syndicated. Withdrawn.

HANS CHRISTIAN ANDERSON

Anthology. Dramatizations based on the magical kingdom of fantasy created by Hans Christian Anderson, a cobbler and spinner of stories.

HANS CHRISTIAN ANDERSON—30 minutes—DuMont 1955.

HAPPENING '68

Musical Variety. Performances by Rock personalities.

Hosts: Paul Revere, Mark Lindsay.

Regulars: Freddie Welles, Keith Allison, The Raiders.

Features: The weekly band contest; undiscovered professional talent.

Music: The Raiders; Recorded.

HAPPENING '68—30 minutes—ABC —January 6, 1968 - September 20, 1969.

HAPPY

Comedy. Background: The Desert Palm Hotel in Palm Springs, California. The story of Sally and Chris Day, the owners and operators. As they struggle to successfully operate the hotel, their infant son, Christopher Hapgood (Happy) Day, observes and, through the voice-over technique, comments on their activities.

CAST

Sally Day	Yvonne Lime
Chris Day	Ronnie Burns
Christopher Hapgood Day	David Born
	Steven Born
Charley Dooley, Sally's uncle	Lloyd Corrigan
Clara Mason, the woman out to change Charley's bachelor status	Doris Packer

HAPPY—30 minutes—NBC—June 6, 1960 - September 2 , 1960; Also: NBC—January 13, 1961 - September 1961. Syndicated.

HAPPY DAYS

Variety. The music, dance, song, and comedy of the 1930s and 40s.

Host: Louis Nye.

Regulars: Chuck McCann, Laara Lacey, Julie McWhirter, Clive Clerk, Bob Elliott, Ray Goulding, Alan Copeland, The Happy Days Singers, The Wisa D'Orso Dancers.

Orchestra: Jack Elliott.

Features: "The Great Voodini"—Chuck McCann as the world's most fumbling escape artist.

"A Visit With Eric Von Director"—Louis Nye as the famed Hollywood director interviewing one-time greats.

"The Radio Spot"—Brief recordings from actual programs.

Comic variations on old radio programs by Bob and Ray— "Jack Armstrong, the All-American American"; and "Mary Backstayge, Noble Wife."

HAPPY DAYS—60 minutes—CBS— June 1970 - September 10, 1970.

HAPPY DAYS

Comedy. Background: Milwaukee, Wisconsin. Era: The latter 1950s (1956). Life in the nostalgic Eisenhower era as seen through the eyes of Richie Cunningham, a shy, naive teenager, and his friend, the wordly wise Warren "Potsie" Weber, Jefferson High School students.

CAST

Richie Cunningham	Ron Howard
Potsie Weber	Anson Williams
Howard Cunningham, Richie's father, the owner of a hardware store	Tom Bosley
Marion Cunningham, Richie's mother	Marion Ross
Chuck Cunningham, Richie's oldest brother	Gavan O'Herlihy
Joanie Cunningham, Richie's sister	Erin Moran
Arthur Fonzerelli (Fonzie), a friend, the respected, know-it-all drop-out; a mechanic at Otto's Auto Orphanage	Henry Winkler
Ralph Malph, Richie's friend	Donny Most
Marsha Simms, a waitress at Arnolds, the after-school hangout	Beatrice Colen
Trudy, a friend	Tita Bell
Gloria, Richie's girl-friend	Linda Purl
Wendy, a waitress at Arnolds	Misty Rowe

Moose, a friend   Ralph Greenberg

Background Music: Pete King; Recordings of the fifties.

HAPPY DAYS—30 minutes—ABC—Premiered: January 15, 1974.

HARBOR COMMAND

Crime Drama. Dramatizations based on incidents in the lives of the men of the U.S. Harbor Police Command. Stories relate the work of Ralph Baxter, a harbor police chief.

Starring: Wendell Corey as Captain Ralph Baxter.

HARBOR COMMAND—30 minutes—Syndicated 1957.

HARBOURMASTER

Adventure. Background: Scott Island, Cape Ann, Massachusetts. The story of David Scott, the captain of the *Blue Chip II.* Episodes relate his attempts to curtail coastal crime in a small New England community.

CAST

Captain David Scott	Barry Sullivan
Jeff Kitredge, his partner	Paul Burke
Anna Morrison, a friend	Nina Wilcox
Professor Wheeler	Murray Matheson
Captain Dan, a retired naval officer	Mike Keene
Danny Morrison, Anna's son	Evan Elliot

HARBOURMASTER—30 minutes—CBS—September 26, 1957 - December 26, 1957. Syndicated title: "Adventures at Scott Island."

THE HARDY BOYS

Animated Cartoon. The global adventures of The Hardy Boys, a Rock and Roll group. Based on the mystery stories by Franklin W. Dixon.

Characters: Joe Hardy, Frank Hardy (brothers), Wanda Kay Breckenridge, Pete, and Chubby.

Voices: Dallas McKennon, Jane Webb, Byron Kane.

Vocals: The real-life Rock group, The Hardy Boys.

Music: Gordon Zahler.

THE HARDY BOYS—30 minutes—ABC—September 6, 1969 - September 4, 1970. Syndicated.

THE HARLEM GLOBETROTTERS

Animated Cartoon. The comedy adventures of the Harlem Globetrotters, basketball magicians who use their talents both on the court and off to help good defeat evil. A Hanna-Barbera production.

Characters' Voices

Meadowlark Lemon	Scatman Crothers
Freddie "Curly" Neal	Stu Gilliam
Gip	Richard Elkins
Bobby Joe Mason	Eddie Anderson
Geese	Johnny Williams
Pablo	Robert Do Qui
Granny	Nancy Wible

Music: Hoyt Curtin.

THE HARLEM GLOBETROTTERS—30 minutes—CBS—September 12, 1970 - May 13, 1973.

THE HARLEM GLOBETROTTERS POPCORN MACHINE

Children's Variety. Varied musical

numbers and comedy sketches designed to relate social messages (e.g., good behavior, good manners).

Starring: The Harlem Globetrotters (a basketball team comprising: Meadowlark Lemon, Curley, Geese, Tex, Bobby Jo, Marques, John, Theodis, and Nate).

Regulars: Avery Schreiber (as Mr. Evil), Rodney Allen Rippy.

Orchestra: Jack Elliott, Allyn Ferguson.

THE HARLEM GLOBETROTTERS POPCORN MACHINE—25 minutes—CBS—1947-1975 Season.

HARRIGAN AND SON

Comedy. Background: New York City, the law firm of Harrigan and Harrigan. The story of James Harrigan, Senior, its founder, a conservative attorney who insists on the human angle in defending clients; and his son, James Harrigan, Junior, a recent Harvard graduate who disagrees with him and believes in defending clients strictly according to the book. Episodes depict the clash that ensues as each attempts to prove his theory correct.

CAST

James Harrigan, Sr.   Pat O'Brien
James Harrigan, Jr.   Roger Perry
Gypsy, the elder's glamorous
    secretary   Georgine Darcy
Miss Claridge, the younger's
    sedate secretary   Helen Kleeb

HARRIGAN AND SON—30 minutes—ABC—October 14, 1960 - September 29, 1961. Syndicated.

HARRIS AGAINST THE WORLD

See title: "Ninety Bristol Court," *Harris Against the World* segment.

HARRY O

Crime Drama. Background: San Diego, California. The investigations of private detective Harry Orwell, an ex-cop who was forced to retire when shot in the back and disabled. (The background in later episodes is Los Angeles, California.)

CAST

Harry Orwell   David Janssen
Detective Lt. Manuel (Manny)
    Quinn, S.D.P.D. (San
    Diego-based epi-
    sodes)   Henry Darrow
Lt. K.C. Trench, L.A.P.D.
    (Los Angeles-based
    episodes)   Anthony Zerbe

Harrigan and Son. Left to right: Georgine Darcy, Pat O'Brien, Roger Perry.

Betsy, Harry's neighbor
(Los Angeles-based
episodes)   Katherine Baumann

Music: Kim Richmond; Billy Goldenberg.

HARRY O—60 minutes—ABC—Premiered: September 12, 1974.

HARRY'S GIRLS

Comedy. Background: Europe. The romantic misadventures of Harry's Girls, a vaudeville type song-and-dance act that is touring the Continent.

CAST
Harry Burns, the
    manager   Larry Blyden
The Troup:
Lois   Dawn Nickerson
Rusty   Susan Silo

Harry's Girls. Dawn Nickerson (left), Diahn Williams (center), Larry Blyden (behind Diahn), Susan Silo (right).

Terry   Diahn Williams

HARRY'S GIRLS—30 minutes—NBC —September 13, 1963 - January 3, 1964.

THE HARTMANS

Comedy. Background: Suburban New York. The trials and tribulations of Paul and Grace Hartman.

CAST
Paul Hartman   Himself
Grace Hartman   Herself
The brother-in-law   Loring Smith
The handyman   Harold Stone

THE HARTMANS—30 minutes—NBC 1949.

THE HATHAWAYS

Comedy. Background: Los Angeles, California. The trials and tribulations of the Hathaways: Walter, a real-estate salesman, and his wife, Elinor, the manager-ower of three theatrical chimpanzees: Enoch, Charlie, and Candy.

CAST
Walter Hathaway   Jack Weston
Elinor Hathaway   Peggy Cass
Jerry Roper, the chimps'
    agent   Harvey Lembeck
Enoch, Candy, and
    Charlie   The Marquis Chimps

THE HATHAWAYS—30 minutes— ABC—October 8, 1961 - August 3, 1962.

HAVE A HEART

Game. Four competing contestants

who comprise two teams of two. The host reads a general-knowledge type of question. The player who is first to identify himself through a buzzer signal receives a chance to answer. If correct, cash is scored. Winners, the highest scoring teams, donate their earnings to home-town charities.

Host: John Reed King.

HAVE A HEART—30 minutes—DuMont 1955.

HAVE GUN—WILL TRAVEL

Western. Background: San Francisco during the 1870s. The story of Paladin, a former army officer turned professional gunman who hires his guns and experience to people who are unable to protect themselves. Operating from the Hotel Carlton, he is distinguished by two trademarks: a black leather holster that bears the symbol of a Paladin, the white chess knight; and a calling card that reads: "Have Gun—Will Travel. Wire Paladin, San Francisco."

CAST

Paladin   Richard Boone
Hey Boy, his
     servant   Kam Tong
Hey Girl, his
     servant   Lisa Lu
Mr. McGunnis, the hotel
     manager   Olan Soulé

Music: Leith Stevens; Jeff Alexander; Fred Steiner; Wilbur Hatch; Bernard Herrmann; Rene Garriguenc; Jerry Goldsmith; Lud Gluskin; Lucien Moraweck.

Theme: "The Ballad of Paladin" sung by Johnny Western.

HAVE GUN—WILL TRAVEL—30 minutes—CBS—September 14, 1957 -

September 21, 1963. Syndicated.

HAWAIIAN EYE

Mystery. Background: Honolulu, Hawaii. The investigations of Tom Lopaka, Tracy Steele, and Gregg MacKenzie, the owner-operators of Hawaiian Eye, a private detective organization. Assisted by Cricket Blake, a beautiful singer at the Hawaiian Village Hotel, they strive to eliminate the sources of trouble that invade a tropical paradise.

CAST

Cricket Blake   Connie Stevens
Tracy Steele   Anthony Eisley
Tom Lopaka   Robert Conrad
Gregg MacKenzie   Grant Williams
Kim, the taxicab
     driver   Poncie Ponce

Hawaiian Eye. Connie Stevens. Background: The Arthur Lyman Band.

Philip Barton, the hotel
    social director   Troy Donahue
Monk   Doug Mosam
Quon   Mel Prestidge

Music, Miss Stevens's accompaniment: The exotic sounds of Arthur Lyman.

Music, background: Frank Perkins, Paul Sawtell.

HAWAIIAN EYE—60 minutes—ABC —October 7, 1959 - September 10, 1963. Syndicated.

Detective
    Che Fong   Harry Endo
Doc, the medical
    examiner   Al Eben
May, a secretary   Maggi Parker
Jenny, a secretary   Peggy Ryan
The attorney
    general   Morgan White
Wo Fat, a wanted
    criminal   Khigh Dhiegh

Music: Morton Stevens; Pete Rugolo.

HAWAII FIVE-O—60 minutes—CBS— Premiered: September 26, 1968.

HAWAII CALLS

Music. The music, song, and dance of Hawaii as performed by various artists.

Host-Narrator: Webley Edwards.

HAWAII CALLS—30 minutes—Syndicated 1966.

HAWAII FIVE-O

Crime Drama. Background: Honolulu, Hawaii. The cases of Steve McGarrett, a plainclothes detective with Hawaii Five-O, a special computerized branch of the Hawaiian Police Force (based in the Lolani Palace, the fictitious headquarters of the Hawaiian government.)

CAST
Detective
    Steve McGarrett   Jack Lord
Detective
    Danny Williams   James MacArthur
Detective
    Chin Ho Kelly   Kam Fong
Detective Kono   Zulu
The governor   Richard Denning
Detective
    Ben Kokua   Al Harrington

HAWK

Crime Drama. Background: New York City. The investigations of John Hawk, a plainclothes detective with the Manhattan district attorney's special detective squad—an elite team designed to corrupt the workings of gangland. Part Iroquois Indian and a prowler of the night, Hawk excels in solving crimes perpetrated by those who find darkenss their specialty.

CAST
John Hawk   Burt Reynolds
Detective Carter   Wayne Grice
Gorten, the Manhattan
    newsstand owner, Hawk's
    information man   Leon Janney

HAWK—60 minutes—ABC—September 15, 1966 - December 1966.

HAWKEYE AND THE LAST OF THE MOHICANS

Adventure. Background: New York State, 1750s. The founding and growth of America as seen through the adventures of Nat Cutler, also known as Hawkeye and the Long

Rifle, and Chingachgook, his blood brother, the Last of the Mohicans—fur traders and frontier scouts who assist the pioneers in settling and the army in its battle against the constant Huron uprisings.

CAST

Hawkeye	John Hart
Chingachgook	Lon Chaney, Jr.

HAWKEYE AND THE LAST OF THE MOHICANS—30 minutes—Syndicated 1957.

HAWKINS

Crime Drama. Background: West Virginia. The cases and courtroom defenses of Billy Jim Hawkins, a shrewd, common-sense criminal attorney.

CAST

Billy Jim Hawkins	James Stewart
R. J. Hawkins, his cousin, his investigative assistant	Strother Martin

Music: George Duning; George Romanos.

HAWKINS—90 minutes—CBS—October 2, 1973 - September 3, 1974.

HAWKINS FALLS, POPULATION 6200

Serial. Background: The town of Hawkins Falls. Personality sketches of life in a small American town as seen through the eyes of Clate Weathers, the newspaper editor.

CAST

Clate Weathers (The Narrator)	Frank Dane

Also: Sam Gray, Arthur Peterson, Norm Sottschalk, Alice Dinsen, Jean Mowry, Viola Berwick, Les Spears, Hope Summers, Alma DuBus, Anozia Kukaki, Mary Frances Desmond, Bill Snary, Bernadene Flynn, Win Strackle, Jim Bannon.

HAWKINS FALLS, POPULATION 6200—15 minutes—NBC—1950-1952.

HAZEL

Comedy. Distinguished by two formats.

Format One:
Background: 123 Marshall Road, Hydsberg, New York, the residence of the Baxter family: George, an attorney with the firm of Butterworth, Hatch, and Noell; his wife, Dorothy; their son, Harold; and their maid, Hazel Burke. Stories depict Hazel's misadventures as she attempts to solve arising crises, both household and legal, which result from meddling in George's business affairs.

Format Two (by storyline, thirteen years following):
Background: 325 Sycamore Street, Hydsberg, New York, the residence of Steve Baxter, George's younger brother, a real-estate salesman; his wife, Barbara; and their daughter, Susie. Transferred to the Middle East on business, George and Dorothy relocate and leave Harold in the care of Steve and Barbara to prevent interference to his education. Hazel becomes their maid and stories follow the original format, with Steve plagued by Hazel's intervention in his business affairs.
Based on the cartoon character

Hazel. Michael Callan (guest) and Shirley Booth. © *Screen Gems.*

appearing in the *Saturday Evening Post.*

CAST
1961-1965 (format one):

Hazel Burke	Shirley Booth
George Baxter	Don DeFore
Dorothy Baxter	Whitney Blake
Harold Baxter	Bobby Buntrock

Harriet Johnson, the helpless next-door neighbor — Norma Varden

Herbert Johnson, her husband, an interpreter of dead languages, a rich investor who had cornered the market on whale bones (427 tons) — Donald Foster

Rosie Hamicker, Hazel's friend, a maid — Maudie Prickett

Harvey Griffin, President of Griffin Enterprises, a client of George's — Howard Smith

Deidre Thompson, George's sister — Cathy Lewis

Harry Thompson, her husband — Robert P. Lieb

Nancy Thompson, their daughter — Davey Davison

Eddie Burke, Hazel's nephew — John Washbrook

Barney Hatfield, the mailman — Robert B. Williams

Mitch Brady, the owner of the Checkerboard Cab Company, Hazel's friend — Dub Taylor

Stan Blake, the Baxter's neighbor — John Newton

Linda Blake, his daugher — Brenda Scott

Mavis Blake, his daughter — Judy Erwin

Don Blake, his son — Paul Engle

Miss Scott, George's secretary — Molly Dodd

Gus Jenkins, Hazel's boyfriend — Patrick McVey

Clara, a maid, a friend of Hazel's — Alice Backus

Miss Sharp, Mr. Griffin's secretary — Mary Scott

Baxter family dog: Smiley.

Music: Van Alexander.

1965-1966 (format two).

Hazel Burke — Shirley Booth

Steve Baxter, head of the Baxter Realty Company — Ray Fulmore

Barbara Baxter — Lynn Borden

Susie Baxter, their daughter — Julia Benjamin

Harold Baxter — Bobby Buntrock

Mona Williams, Barbara's friend — Mala Powers

Fred Williams, her husband — Charles Bateman

Jeff Williams, their son — Pat Cardi

Millie Ballard, Steve's part-time secretary — Ann Jillian

Deidre Thompson	Cathy Lewis
Harry Thompson	Robert P. Lieb
Bill Fox, Steve's salesman	Lawrence Haddon
Ted Drake, Millie's boyfriend	Harvey Grant
Gus Jenkins	Patrick McVey

Music: Van Alexander; Howard Blake; Charles Albertine.

HAZEL—30 minutes—NBC—September 28, 1961 - September 6, 1965. CBS—30 minutes—September 10, 1965 - September 5, 1966. Syndicated.

THE HAZEL SCOTT SHOW

Musical Variety.

Hostess: Hazel Scott.

Announcer: Gloria Lucas.

Music: Hazel Scott (pianist).

THE HAZEL SCOTT SHOW—15 minutes—DuMont 1950.

HEADLINE STORY

See title: "Big Town."

HEADMASTER

Comedy-Drama. Background: Concord, a small, private, coeducational high school in California. A tender portrayal of student-teacher relationships and their problems; both scholastic and personal, as seen through the eyes of Andy Thompson, the headmaster.

CAST

Andy Thompson	Andy Griffith
Margaret Thompson, his wife	Claudette Nevins
Jerry Brownell, the athletic coach	Jerry Van Dyke
Mr. Purdy, the school custodian	Parker Fennelly
Judy, Andy's student helper	Lani O'Grady

Music: Dick Williams.

HEADMASTER—30 minutes—CBS—September 18, 1970 - January 1, 1971. Rebroadcasts: CBS—June 25, 1971 - September 10, 1971.

HE AND SHE

Comedy. Background: New York City. The trials and tribulations of the Hollisters: Richard, a cartoonist, the creator of the comic-strip-turned-television-series, "Jetman"; and his wife, Paula, a beautiful, but scatterbrained traveler's-company aide. Stories depict Dick's struggles to survive Paula's meaningful but misguided attempts to assist others; the pressures of work and the complications of a computerized society.

CAST

Richard Hollister	Richard Benjamin
Paula Hollister	Paula Prentiss
Oscar North, the egotistical star of "Jetman"	Jack Cassidy
Andrew Humble, the building's not-so-handyman	Hamilton Camp
Harry, their friend, a fireman	Kenneth Mars
Norman Nugent, Dick's employer	Harold Gould
Murray Mouse, Dick's Accountant	Alan Oppenheimer

HE AND SHE—30 minutes—CBS—September 6, 1967 - September 18, 1968. Rebroadcasts, CBS—June 1970 - September 1970.

HEAVEN FOR BETSY

Comedy. Background: New York. The struggles that make up a marriage as depicted through the activities of newlyweds Peter and Betsy Bell.

CAST

Peter Bell	Jack Lemmon
Betsy Bell	Cynthia Stone

HEAVEN FOR BETSY—15 minutes —CBS—1952-1953.

HEAVENS TO BETSY

Comedy. Background: New York City. The struggles of two young Broadway hopefuls seeking a career in show business.

CAST

Betsy	Elizabeth Cote
Her friend	Mary Best
The cabdriver	Russell Nype
Their landlord	Nick Dennis

HEAVENS TO BETSY—30 minutes— NBC 1949.

THE HECKLE AND JECKLE SHOW

Animated Cartoon. The misadventures of Heckle and Jeckle, mischievous, talking magpies.

Additional segments: "Andy Pandy"; "Dinky Duck"; "Little Roquefort"; and "The Teddy Bears."

Voice characterizations: Paul Frees.

Music: Paul A. Scheib.

THE HECKLE AND JECKLE SHOW —30 minutes. Syndicated 1955; CBS—1956 - 1957; CBS—September 1965 - September 3, 1966; NBC—September 6, 1969 - September 7, 1971.

HEC RAMSEY

See title: "NBC Sunday Mystery Movie, *Hec Ramsey* segment.

THE HECTOR HEATHCOTE SHOW

Animated Cartoon. The misadventures of Hector Heathcote, a scientist who has invented the means by which to travel back through history. Stories relate his intrusion into the major events which have shaped the world.

THE HECTOR HEATHCOTE SHOW —30 minutes—NBC—October 1963 - September 1964.

HEE HAW

Variety. Performances by Country and Western artists coupled with short skits and running gags played against the Nashville Sound.

Hosts: Buck Owens, Roy Clark.

Regulars: Archie Campbell, Grandpa Jones, Sheb Wooley, The Hagers, Gordie Tapp, Jeannine Riley, Stringbean, Don Harron, Susan Raye, Cathy Baker, Jennifer Bishop, Lulu Roman, Zella Lehr, Gunilla Hutton, Lisa Todd, Minnie Pearl, Alvin "Junior" Samples, Claude Phelps, Jimmy Riddle, Don Rich, Ann Randall, Misty Rowe, Nancy Baker, Mary Ann Gordon, The Buckaroos, The Inspiration, Beauregard the Wonder Dog.

Musical Direction: George Richey.

HEE HAW—60 minutes—CBS—June 15, 1969 - July 13, 1971. Syndicated.

THE HELEN O'CONNELL SHOW

Musical Variety.

Hostess: Helen O'Connell.

THE HELEN O'CONNELL SHOW—15 minutes—NBC—May 29, 1957 - September 1957.

THE HELEN REDDY SHOW

Musical Variety. A format tailored to the talents of guests.

Hostess: Helen Reddy.

Featured: The Jaime Rogers Dancers.

Orchestra: Nelson Riddle.

THE HELEN REDDY SHOW—60 minutes—NBC—June 28, 1973, - August 16, 1973.

HELP! IT'S THE HAIR BEAR BUNCH

Animated Cartoon. Background: Cave Block Number 9 at the Wonderland Zoo, the residence of the Hair Bear Bunch: Hair, Square, and Bubi. Stories relate their misadventures as they attempt to improve living conditions. A Hanna-Barbera production.

Characters' Voices

Hair Bear	Daws Butler
Bubi Bear	Paul Winchell
Square Bear	Bill Calloway

Help! It's the Hair Bear Bunch. The Hair Bear Bunch. *Courtesy Hanna-Barbera Productions.*

Mr. Peevley, the zoo-
keeper   John Stephenson
Botch, his
assistant   Joe E. Ross
Additional voices: Hal Smith,
Jeannine Brown, Joan Gerber,
Vic Perrin, Janet Waldo, Lennie
Weinrib.

Music: Hoyt Curtin.

HELP! IT'S THE HAIR BEAR
BUNCH—30 minutes—CBS—September 11, 1971 - September 2, 1972.

HENNESSEY

Comedy. Background: San Diego,
California. The misadventures of
Lieutenant Charles J. "Chick"
Hennessey, a doctor assigned to the
San Diego Naval base.

CAST

Lt. Chick Hennessey   Jackie Cooper
Nurse Martha Hale, his
romantic interest   Abby Dalton
Harvey Spencer Blair III,
a dentist waiting out a
million-dollar inheri-
tance   James Komack
Chief Corpsman Max
Bronsky   Henry Kulky
Captain Shafer   Roscoe Karns
Commander Wilker   Steve Roberts
Dr. King   Robert Gist
Chief Branman   Ted Fish

Music: Sonny Burke.

HENNESSEY—30 minutes—CBS—
October 4, 1959 - September 17,
1962. Syndicated.

HENNY AND ROCKY

Variety. Music, songs, and comedy
sketches. Presented following the ABC
network fights.

Hosts: Henny Youngman, Rocky
Graziano.

Vocalist: Marion Colby.

Music: The Jazz Combo of Bobby
Hackett, trumpeter; Morrey
Feld, drummer; Buddy Weed,
pianist; Peanuts Hucko,
clarinetist.

Features: Henny and Rocky's recap of
the preceding bout; and
"Henny's Ribber's Digest"—a
satire on current events.

HENNY AND ROCKY—15 minutes
(approximately)—ABC—June 1, 1955
- September 1955.

HENRY FONDA PRESENTS THE STAR AND THE STORY

Anthology. Dramatizations of stories
selected by guests.

Host: Henry Fonda.

Included:

Another Harvest. The honest young
wife of a fugitive crook attempts to
pay off his creditors.

CAST
Ruth Warrick, Philip Reed.

Malaya Incident. Background: Malaya.
A plantation owner attempts to
supply rubber to the free world
against armed Red guerrillas.

CAST
Ann Sheridan, Richard Egan.

Call Me Irving. The story of a meek
and mild-mannered actor who dons

the guise of a vicious killer in order to land a part in a play.

CAST
Johnny Johnston, Jean Byron.

Valley Of The Shadows. Defying the gang that is terrorizing his town, a storekeeper attempts to end their reign by helping an enemy of the gang leader.

CAST
Dabbs Greer, Jeff York.

HENRY FONDA PRESENTS THE STAR AND THE STORY—30 minutes—Syndicated 1954. Also known as: "Star and Story."

HENRY MORGAN

Listed: The television programs of comedian Henry Morgan.

On The Corner—Variety—30 minutes —ABC—April 18, 1948 - May 16, 1948.

Host: Henry Morgan.

Regulars: George Guest, Virginia Austin, Roy Davis, The Clark Sisters.

Henry Morgan's Talent Hunt—Satire— 30 minutes—NBC 1951.

Format: Unusual talent acts and performers are presented.

Host: Henry Morgan.

Regulars: Arnold Stang, Dorothy Jarnac, Dorothy Claire, Art Carney, Kaye Ballard.

Here's Morgan—Satire—30 minutes— ABC 1953. Syndicated in 1959 under the title: "Henry Morgan and Company."

Format: Unusual talent acts are presented.

Host: Henry Morgan.

A Man's World—Discussion—30 minutes—DuMont 1955.

Format: Discussions on topics of interest primarily to men.

Host: Henry Morgan.

Music: The Three Bars.

HERB SHRINER TIME

Variety. Music, songs, and comedy sketches.

Host: Herb Shriner.

Regulars: Lenka Peterson, Peggy Allenby, Biff McGuire, Eda Heineman, Joseph Sweeny, Paul Huber.

Orchestra: Milton DeLugg; Bernie Greene.

HERB SHRINER TIME—30 minutes —CBS—November 7, 1949 - February 4, 1950.

THE HERCULOIDS

Animated Cartoon. Background: Futuristic space. The story of the Herculoids, animals as strong as they are invincible, whose function is to protect their king, Zandor, and the inhabitants of their peaceful and utopian planet from creatures from other galaxies. A Hanna-Barbera Production.

Characters' Voices

Zandor	Mike Road
Tarra	Virginia Gregg
Zok, the lazor dragon	Mike Road

Dorno, the ten-legged rhinoceros	Teddy Eccles
Gloop, a shapeless blob	Don Messick
Gleep, a shapeless blob	Don Messick
Igoo, a come-to-life rock	Mike Road

Music: Hoyt Curtin.

THE HERCULOIDS—30 minutes—CBS—September 9, 1967 - September 6, 1969.

HERE COMES THE BRIDE

Wedding performances. Actual ceremonies performed on TV.

Host: John Weigel.

Vocalist: Richard Paige.

Organist: Adele Scott.

HERE COMES THE BRIDE—30 minutes—DuMont 1951.

HERE COMES THE GRUMP

Animated Cartoon. A magic fantasy land is put under the Curse of Gloom by the evil Grump. Unaffected, Princess Dawn is the kingdom's lone savior. A young boy, Terry, and his dog, Bib, are magically transported from America to her domain. Informing Terry of the situation, she also tells him about the Land of a Thousand Caves. In the Cave of Whispering Orchids, the Grump has hidden the Crystal Key, which, if found, will lift the dreaded curse. Boarding a balloon car, Terry and the Princess begin their search. Stories depict their adventures and the Grump's efforts, traveling aboard his fumbling Jolly Green Dragon, to thwart their attempts and keep secret the location of the Cave of Whispering Orchids.

HERE COMES THE GRUMP—30 minutes—NBC—September 6, 1969 - September 4, 1971.

HERE COME THE BRIDES

Adventure. Background: Seattle, Washington, 1870, the dreary, and muddy logging camp of the Bolt brothers, Jason, Joshua, and Jeremy. Populated by men, with the exception of a few dancehall girls, the love-and-affection-starved loggers threaten to walk out. Agreeing to meet their demands and provide women, Jason begins preparations for a journey to New England. Faced with a lack of resources, he is approached by Aaron Stemple, the sawmill owner, who offers him a proposition. The agreement: in return for his financial backing, Jason must recruit one hundred respectable and marriageable women and keep them in Seattle for one full year. If, however, he should fail, he must forfeit Bridal Veil Mountain, the legacy left to the Bolts by their parents.

With the help of Captain Fred Clancy, one hundred women, mostly Civil War widows, are transported from Massachusetts to Washington. Episodes depict the adjustment of refined city women to rugged pioneer life and men.

CAST

Jason Bolt	Robert Brown
Joshua Bolt	David Soul
Jeremy Bolt	Bobby Sherman
Lottie Hatfield, the owner of the saloon	Joan Blondell
Candy Pruitt, Jeremy's romantic interest	Bridget Hanley

Aaron Stemple	Mark Lenard
Captain R. Fred Clancy	Henry Beckman
Corky Sam McGee, the Swede, the camp foreman	Bo Svenson
Biddie Gloom, one of the brides	Susan Tolsky
Miss Essie, the school teacher	Mitzi Hoag
Ben Jenkins, a logger	Hoke Howell
Molly Pruitt, Candy's sister	Patti Coohan
Christopher Pruitt, her brother	Eric Chase

Music: Warren Barker, Hugo Montenegro.

HERE COME THE BRIDES—60 minutes—ABC—September 25, 1968 - September 18, 1970. Syndicated.

HERE COME THE DOUBLE DECKERS

Comedy. Background: A junkyard in England where a double-decker London bus is parked and reconstructed into the clubhouse of seven young children—Scooper, Spring, Billie, Brains, Doughnut, Sticks, and Tiger. Stories relate their misadventures and attempts to solve problems without help from the adult world.

CAST

Scooper	Peter Firth
Spring	Brinsley Forde
Billie	Gillian Bailey
Brains	Michael Auderson
Doughnut	Douglas Simmonds
Sticks	Bruce Clark
Tiger	Debbie Russ
Albert, their adult friend	Melvyn Hayes

HERE COME THE DOUBLE

DECKERS—30 minutes—ABC—September 12, 1970 - September 3, 1972. British produced.

HERE COME THE STARS

Testimonial dinners honoring guests. See title: "George Jessel's Show Business."

HERE'S BARBARA

Interview. Fashion, politics, and people—"an insider's look at Washington society."

Hostess: Barbara Coleman.

Music: Recorded.

HERE'S BARBARA—30 minutes—Syndicated 1969. Also known as: "The Barbara Coleman Show."

HERE'S EDIE

Variety. Music, songs, and comedy sketches.

Hostess: Edie Adams.

Orchestra: Peter Matz.

HERE'S EDIE—30 minutes—ABC—September 26, 1963 - March 19, 1964.

HERE'S HOLLYWOOD

Interview. Intimate aspects of celebrities lives are revealed through in-person interviews.

Host: Dean Miller.

Hostess: Joanne Jordan.

Appearing: Judy Garland, Gregory Peck, Telly Savalas, Robert

Mitchum, Lori Martin, Jack Benny, Bob Hope, Polly Bergen.

HERE'S HOLLYWOOD—30 minutes —NBC—1960 - 1961.

HERE'S LUCY

Comedy. Background: 4863 Valley Lawn Drive, Los Angeles, California, the residence of Lucille Carter, widow, the nosey, overzealous secretary to Harrison Otis Carter, her brother-in-law, the owner of the Unique Employment Agency— "Unusual Jobs For Unusual People." Stories depict: her home life with her children, Kim and Craig; and her office life wherein she plagues Harry with her scatterbrained antics.

CAST

Lucille Carter	Lucille Ball
Harrison Otis Carter (Harry)	Gale Gordon
Kim Carter	Lucie Arnaz
Craig Carter	Desi Arnaz, Jr.
Mary Jane Lewis, Lucy's friend	Mary Jane Croft

Music: Marl Young.

HERE'S LUCY—30 minutes—CBS— September 23, 1968 - September 2, 1974.

HERE WE GO AGAIN

Comedy. Background: Encino, California. A story of love, divorce, and remarriage.

Richard Evans, an easy-going architect, and his bossy and formidably efficient wife, Judy, the editor of *Screen World* magazine, terminate their relationship after seventeen years. They have one son, Jeff.

Jerry Standish, a philandering ex-quarterback for the Los Angeles Rams, now the owner of the Polynesia Paradise Cafe, and his wife Susan, end their marriage of ten years due to his endless romantic involvements. They have two children, Cindy and Jan.

Seeking information concerning the development of a research center for underprivileged children, Susan and Richard meet, fall in love, marry, and establish housekeeping in the Standish home. Jerry Standish maintains a bachelor apartment one block away; and Judy Evans and Jeff live one-half mile away.

Episodes relate the struggles of newlyweds to find serenity in a neighborhood where they are plagued by the constant intrusion of their former spouses.

CAST

Richard Evans	Larry Hagman
Susan Evans (Standish)	Diane Baker
Judy Evans	Nita Talbot
Jerry Standish	Dick Gautier
Jeff Evans	Chris Beaumont
Cindy Evans (Standish)	Leslie Graves
Jan Evans (Standish)	Kim Richards

Music: Al DeLory.

HERE WE GO AGAIN—30 minutes— ABC—January 20, 1973 - June 23, 1973.

THE HERO

Comedy. Background: Hollywood, California. The home and working life of Sam Garrett, a bumbling klutz who portrays a fearless and dauntless law enforcer on the fictitious television series, "Jed Clayton, U.S. Marshall."

Episodes depict his attempts to conceal his real life from his fans.

CAST

Sam Garrett	Richard Mulligan
Ruth Garrett, his wife	Mariette Hartley
Paul Garrett, their son	Bobby Horan
Fred Gilman, their neighbor	Victor French
Burton Gilman, his son	Joe Baio

THE HERO—30 minutes—NBC—September 8, 1966 - January 5, 1967.

HE SAID, SHE SAID

Game. Four celebrity couples compete, playing for selected married couples from the studio audience. The husbands are before camera and the wives are isolated backstage in a soundproof room. The host reveals a topic. The men have to state a personal association that will hopefully trigger a response from the individual's wife, to recognize it as what "He Said."

The wives are aired and seen through four monitors that are built into the set and placed before their mates. The topic is restated and one answer is revealed. The first to recognize the answer sounds a buzzer. If she matches her husband, she receives points. The second round is played in the same manner. Rounds three and four are reversed. He has to recognize what "She Said."

Points. Each couple begins with one hundred. Matching answers add twenty-five; misses deduct ten. The highest-scoring team earns their selected studio audience couple two hundred and fifty dollars and a seven-day vacation at a Holiday Inn.

Host: Joe Garagiola.

Announcer: Johnny Olsen.

Music: Score Productions.

HE SAID, SHE SAID—30 minutes—Syndicated 1969.

HEY, JEANNIE!

Comedy. Background: New York City. The story of Jeannie MacLennan, a young lass newly arrived in the States from Scotland. Stories depict her misadventures as she struggles to adjust to the American way of life.

CAST

Jeannie MacLennan	Jeannie Carson
Al Murray, her guardian, a cab driver	Allen Jenkins
Liz Murray, his sister	Jane Dulo

HEY, JEANNIE!—30 minutes—CBS—September 8, 1956 - May 4, 1957. Rebroadcasts: ABC—June 30, 1960 - September 22, 1960.

HEY, LANDLORD!

Comedy. Background: New York City. The misadventures of bachelors Woodrow "Woody" Banner, an aspiring writer; and Chuck Hookstratten, an aspiring comedian, the landlords of a ten-room apartment house in Manhattan.

CAST

Woody Banner	Will Hutchins
Chuck Hookstratten	Sandy Baron
Jack Ellenhorn, a tenant, a photographer	Michael Constantine

Timothy, a glamorous upstairs
tenant   Pamela Rodgers
Kyoko, her room-
mate   Miko Mayama
Mrs. Henderson, a
tenant   Ann Morgan Guilbert
Mrs. Teckler, a
tenant   Kathryn Minner
Bonnie Banner, Woody's
sister   Sally Field
Lloyd Banner, Woody's
father   Tom Tully
Marcy Banner, Woody's
mother   Ann Doran

HEY, LANDLORD!—30 minutes—
NBC—September 11, 1966 - May 14,
1967. Syndicated.

HEY MULLIGAN

Comedy. Background: Los Angeles,
California. The misadventures of
Mickey Mulligan, a page at the fictitious International Broadcasting Company. Undecided about his future, he
attends the Academy of Dramatic
Arts and by taking various part-time
jobs, he struggles to discover his goal
in life.

CAST
Mickey Mulligan   Mickey Rooney
Mrs. Mulligan, his mother,
a former burlesque
star   Claire Carleton
Mr. Mulligan, his father,
a policeman attached to
the 23rd precinct   Regis Toomey
Patricia, his girlfriend,
a secretary at
I.B.C.   Carla Balenda
Freddie, his friend   Joey Forman
Mr. Brown, his
employer   John Hubbard
Mickey's drama
instructor   Alan Mowbray
Also   Pauline Drake
                       Fred E. Sherman

HEY MULLIGAN—30 minutes—NBC
—August 28, 1954 - June 4, 1955.
Also known as: "The Mickey Rooney
Show."

HI MOM

Information. Advice and entertainment tailored to young mothers.

Hosts: Shari Lewis (1957-1959), ven-
triloquist. Puppets: Lamb Chop,
Hush Puppy, and Charlie Horse.
Johnny Andrews, Paul and Mary
Ritts (1959).

Cooking authority: Josephine
McCarthy.

Medical advice: Jane Palmer, R.N.

Features: Guests, stories, and films
concerning children.

HI MOM—60 minutes—NBC—September 15, 1957 - March 20, 1959.

HIDDEN FACES

Serial. The dramatic story of Arthur
Adams, a lawyer in a small, Midwestern town. Emphasis is placed on
the methods incorporated to solve
crimes.

CAST
Arthur Adams   Conrad Fowkes
Mimi Jaffe   Rita Gam
Also: Louise Shaffer, Stephen Joyce,
Mark Curran, Roy Scheider,
Gretchen Walther, Tony
LoBianco, Joe Daly.

HIDDEN FACES—30 minutes—NBC
—December 30, 1968 - June 30, 1969.

HIGH ADVENTURE WITH
LOWELL THOMAS

Travel. The people and the customs of

lands untouched by civilization.

Host: Lowell Thomas.

HIGH ADVENTURE WITH LOWELL THOMAS—30 minutes—CBS—1957-1958. Syndicated—60 minutes—1960.

HIGH AND WILD

Travel. Filmed hunting and fishing adventures.

Host: Don Hobart.

Music: George Wasch.

HIGH AND WILD—30 minutes—Syndicated 1968.

THE HIGH CHAPARRAL

Western. Background: Tucson, Arizona during the 1870s. The saga of the Cannon family as they struggle to maintain and operate the High Chaparral Ranch in an era of violence and lawlessness.

CAST

John Cannon	Leif Erickson
Buck Cannon, his brother	Cameron Mitchell
Victoria Sebastian Cannon, John's wife	Linda Cristal
Billy Blue Cannon, John's son, by a former marriage	Mark Slade
Don Sebastian, a Mexican land baron, the owner of the Montoya Ranch	Frank Silvera
Manolito Sebastian, Don's son	Henry Darrow
Ranch Hands:	
Sam, the forman	Don Collier
Ted Reno	Ted Markland
Pedro	Roberto Contreras
Wind	Rudy Ramos
Joe	Bob Hoy
Vasquero	Rodolfo Acosta

Music: Harry Sukman.

THE HIGH CHAPARRAL—60 minutes—NBC—September 10, 1967 - September 10, 1971. Syndicated.

HIGH FINANCE

Game. Contestants, selected from various cities across the country, are quizzed on news items that appear in their local papers. Question-and-answer rounds, consisting of three levels, are played one per week. The winner of the first round, the highest cash scorer, receives the choice of either keeping his accumulated earnings or returning and attempting to earn additional cash in level two. If he succeeds again he may choose as before—keep his earnings or attempt level three. At this level the player may win his secret desire (up to $35,000 value), but he stands the chance of losing everything won previously if he fails.

Host: Dennis James.

Announcers: Jay Simms; Jack Gregson.

HIGH FINANCE—30 minutes—CBS—July 7, 1956 - September 1956.

HIGH LOW

Game. Object: For a contestant to challenge a panel of three experts by offering to answer one or more parts of questions containing several segments. The challenge: the player has to match the panelist claiming to have the most answers (High) or the one with the fewest (Low). If he matches the High expert, his five hundred dollars betting money is tripled; if he matches Low, his money is doubled. Failure to match either High or Low results in the loss of everything and a new challenger is introduced.

Host: Jack Barry.

HIGH LOW—30 minutes—NBC—1957 - 1958.

HIGH ROAD

Travel. Films exploring the people and the customs of distant lands.

Host-Narrator: John Gunther.

HIGH ROAD—30 minutes—Syndicated 1959. Also known as "John Gunther's High Road."

HIGH ROAD TO ADVENTURE

Travel. Films exploring the people and customs of various countries around the world.

Hosts-Narrators: Bill Burrud; Bob Stevenson.

HIGH ROAD TO ADVENTURE—30 minutes—Syndicated 1964.

HIGH ROAD TO DANGER

Documentary. Films relating the exploits of men who challenge Nature.
Host-Narrator: Steve Brodie.

HIGH ROAD TO DANGER—30 minutes—Syndicated 1957.

HIGH ROLLERS

Game. Two competing contestants. The host reads a general-knowledge type of question. The player first to identify himself through a light signal receives a chance to answer. If correct, he receives control of two dice. He is permitted to either pass or keep the roll. The dice are rolled by a girl and, according to the number that appears, he is permitted to select any combination of numbers that total the rolled number from a large number board (top line: 6,7,8,9,; bottom line: 1,2,3,4,5). Each number contains a prize that is placed on his side of the board. The remaining numbers, as they appear on the board, are the only active numbers. Any inactive numbers that are rolled automatically disqualify the player that acquires them. Winners are determined by the roll of the dice and receive the prizes that are accumulated on their side of the board.

Host: Alex Trebek.
Assistants (rolling the dice): Ruta Lee; Linda Kaye Henning.
Announcer: Kenny Williams.
Music: Recorded.
First Champion: Phyllis Matson.

HIGH ROLLERS—30 minutes—NBC —Premiered: July 1, 1974.

HIGH TENSION

Anthology. Dramatic ventures into the world of the possible but improbable.

HIGH TENSION—30 minutes—Syndicated 1953.

HIGHWAY PATROL

Crime Drama. Dramatizations based on the experiences of Highway Patrol officers in all forty-eight states (at the time of filming).

CAST

Dan Matthews, chief
   of the Highway
   Patrol   Broderick Crawford
Sergeant Williams, his
   assistant   William Boyett

Music: Richard Llewelyn.

HIGHWAY PATROL—30 minutes—Syndicated 1956.

HIPPODROME

Variety. Showcased: European circus acts.

Hosts: Weekly guests including Allen Sherman, Woody Allen, Tony Randall, Eddie Albert, Merv Griffin.

Orchestra: Peter Knight.

HIPPODROME—60 minutes—CBS—July 5, 1966 - September 6, 1966.

HIRAM HOLLIDAY

See title: "The Adventures of Hiram Holliday."

THE HIS AND HER OF IT

Discussion-Variety. A topical-issues discussion revealing the male and female points of view—the His and Her of It.

Hosts: Geoff and Suzanne Edwards.

Premiere guests: Dick and Linda Smothers.

THE HIS AND HER OF IT—90 minutes—Syndicated 1969.

HIS HONOR, HOMER BELL

Comedy. Background: Spring City. The trials and tribulations of Homer Bell, the understanding and respected Justice of the Peace.

CAST

Homer Bell   Gene Lockhart
Cassandra "Casey"
   Bell   Mary Lee Dearing
Maude, their
   housekeeper   Jane Moutrie

HIS HONOR, HOMER BELL—30 minutes—Syndicated 1956.

HOBBY LOBBY

Variety. People and their usual or unusual hobbies are showcased. Celebrities appear to lobby their hobbies.

Host: Cliff Arquette, portraying Mount Idy hillbilly Charlie Weaver.

Announcer: Tom Reddy.

Orchestra: John Gart.

Premiere guest: Maureen O'Hara.

HOBBY LOBBY—30 minutes—ABC—September 30, 1959 - April 23, 1960.

HOBBIES IN ACTION

Variety. People and their usual or unusual hobbies are showcased.

Host: Steve Booth.

HOBBIES IN ACTION—30 minutes—Syndicated 1958.

HOGAN'S HEROES

Comedy. Background: Stalag 13, a

German prisoner-of-war camp officially run by the naive and inept Colonel Wilhelm Klink and his obese, bumbling assistant, Sergeant Hans Schultz. Unofficially, events and camp life are manipulated by Colonel Robert Hogan, U.S. Air Force, senior officer in the camp.

Assisted by inmates LeBeau, Newkirk, Carter, Kinchloe, and Baker, Hogan, under the code name Papa Bear, conducts vital missions for the Allies. Through phone taps, underground escape routes, radio contacts, and custom tailoring, the prisoners assist Allied fugitives and secure top-secret information for their superiors.

Often Schultz becomes an unwitting and reluctant accomplice to their schemes. Fear of betrayal and transfer to the Russian front keeps him silent—"I know no—thing!"

Stalag 13—a prison camp paradise with all the comforts of a good but dangerous life.

CAST

Col. Robert Hogan   Bob Crane
Col. Wilhelm
    Klink   Werner Klemperer
Sgt. Hans Schultz   John Banner
Louis LeBeau, the French
    corporal   Robert Clary
Newkirk, the English
    corporal   Richard Dawson
Andrew Carter, the American
    sergeant   Larry Hovis
James Kinchloe, the American
    corporal   Kenneth Washington
Helga, the Commandant's
    secretary (early
    episodes)   Cynthia Lynn
Hilda, the Commandant's
    secretary (later
    episodes)   Sigrid Valdis
Colonel Crittendon, Hogan's
    nemesis, the Commandant of
    Stalag 16   Bernard Fox
Marya, the beautiful
    Russian spy   Nita Talbot

Major Hockstedder, the Gestapo
    commander   Howard Caine
Music: Jerry Fielding.

HOGAN'S HEROES—30 minutes—CBS—September 17, 1965 - July 4, 1971. Syndicated.

HOLD IT PLEASE

Game. A telephone call is placed at random to a viewer. If he is able to correctly answer a question, he is awarded a prize and receives a chance at the jackpot, which consists of valuable merchandise prizes. To win he must identify the portrait of a celebrity that is located on a spinning wheel.

Host: Gil Fates.

Regulars: Cloris Leachman, Bill McGraw, Mort Marshall, Evelyn Ward.

Orchestra: Max Showalter.

HOLD IT PLEASE—30 minutes—CBS 1949.

HOLD THAT CAMERA

Game. Two competing contestants—a studio player and a home participant. The viewer, whose voice is amplified over the telephone, directs the studio player through a series of shenanigans. The player who performs the stunt in the least amount of time receives prizes for himself and the home viewer.

Host: Jimmy Blaine.

Orchestra: Ving Merlin.

HOLD THAT CAMERA—30 minutes—DuMont 1951.

HOLIDAY HOTEL

Variety. Background: New York City. Entertainment performances set against the background of the Pelican Room of the fashionable but fictitious Holiday Hotel on Fifth Avenue.

Hosts (the hotel managers for the unseen Mr. Holiday): Edward Everett Horton; Don Ameche.

Regulars: Betty Brewer, Dorothy Greener, Lenore Longergan, The June Graman Dancers, The Don Craig Chorus.

Orchestra: Bernie Green.

HOLIDAY HOTEL—30 minutes— ABC—July 12, 1951 - October 4, 1951.

HOLIDAY LODGE

Comedy. Background: The plush Holiday Lodge Hotel in Upper New York State. The misadventures of social directors Johnny Miller and Frank Boone. Stories depict their efforts to provide interesting entertainment despite an encounter with ever-present obstacles.

CAST
Johnny Miller	Johnny Wayne
Frank Boone	Frank Shuster
J. W. Harrington, the hotel manager	Justice Watson
Dorothy Johnson, the hotel receptionist	Maureen Arthur
Woodrow, the bellboy and general handy-man	Charles Smith

HOLIDAY LODGE—30 minutes— CBS—June 21, 1961 - September 1961.

HOLLYWOOD A GO GO

Musical Variety. Performances by Rock personalities.

Host: Sam Riddle.

Regulars: The Sinners, The Gazzarri Dancers.

Music: Recorded.

HOLLYWOOD A GO GO—60 minutes—Syndicated 1965.

HOLLYWOOD AND THE STARS

Documentary. The behind-the-scenes story of Hollywood—its stars and its celluloid accomplishments.

Host-Narrator: Joseph Cotten.

Music: Jack Tiller.

HOLLYWOOD AND THE STARS— 30 minutes—NBC—September 30, 1963 - September 28, 1964. Syndicated.

HOLLYWOOD BACKSTAGE

Variety. A behind-the-scenes report on Hollywood, showcasing the people, the parties, and the premieres.

Host: John Willis.

Music: Recorded.

HOLLYWOOD BACKSTAGE—30 minutes—Syndicated 1965.

HOLLYWOOD FILM THEATRE

Movies. Theatrical releases.

Included:

Race Street. A murder by the syndicate results in a bookie's attempts to avenge the death of their victim— a friend.

CAST

George Raft, Marilyn Maxwell, William Bendix.

Mr. Blandings Builds His Dream House. A man's costly attempts to construct a country home to escape from the crowded city.

CAST

Cary Grant, Myrna Loy.

Experiment Perilous. A doctor attempts to save a woman from the machinations of her psychotic husband.

CAST

George Brent, Hedy Lamarr, Paul Lukas, Albert Dekker.

Walk Softly, Stranger. The story of a fortune-hunting gambler who becomes romantically involved with 'a wealthy but crippled girl.

CAST

Joseph Cotten, Valli, Spring Byington.

HOLLYWOOD FILM THEATRE—90 minutes—ABC 1957.

HOLLYWOOD JR. CIRCUS

Circus Variety Acts.

Ringmaster: Paul Barnes.

Regulars: George Cesar, Max Bronstein, Marie Louise, Bill Hughes, The Hanneford Family, Boffo the Clown, Zero the Candyman, Blackie the Talking Crow.

Orchestra: Bruce Chase.

HOLLYWOOD JR. CIRCUS—30 minutes—ABC—1951.

HOLLYWOOD OFF BEAT

Crime Drama. Background: Hollywood, California. The story of private detective Steve Randall, an unjustly disbarred attorney who seeks to find those responsible for framing him and regain his right to practice law.

Starring: Melvyn Douglas as Steve Randall.

HOLLYWOOD OFF BEAT—30 minutes—ABC—May 24, 1953 - August 11, 1953. Also: ABC—August 7, 1955 - September 11, 1955.

HOLLYWOOD OPENING NIGHT

Anthology. Comedy and drama presentations. The first anthology series to originate from the West Coast.

Included:

Let George Do It. A personal-service-bureau operator attempts to help a young chemist learn the art of wooing.

Starring: Ann Sothern.

Terrible Tempered Tolliver. The comic tale of a baseball umpire who never reverses decisions. Feature version: *Kill the Umpire.*

Starring: William Bendix.

Quite A Viking. A tomboy's reaction to her first kiss.

Starring: Ann Harding, James Dunn.

30 Days. The story concerns a brilliant lawyer and his attempts to clear an innocent man.

Starring: Edward Arnold, Robert Stack.

Hope Chest. To win the affections of a pretty girl, an interior decorator helps her find a job.

Starring: Macdonald Carey.

The Housekeeper. A psychiatrist attempts to rectify a mistake made in the diagnosis of an important case.

Starring: Albert Dekker.

HOLLYWOOD OPENING NIGHT—60 minutes—ABC 1952.

THE HOLLYWOOD PALACE

Variety. Music, songs, dances, and comedy sketches set against the background of the Hollywood Palace Theatre. Guest artists perform.

Hosting: Weekly Guests.

Regulars: Raquel Welch (The Hollywood Palace Card Holder), The Ray Charles Singers, The Buddy Schawb Dancers.

Announcer: Dick Tufel.

Orchestra: Mitchell Ayres.

Appearing: Bing Crosby, Mickey Rooney, Gary Crosby, Bob Newhart, Nancy Wilson, Judy Garland (re-creating, in a tramp costume, the songs made famous at the original Palace Theatre in New York), Vic Damone, Avery Schreiber, Jack Burns, Chita Rivera, Tony Martin, Cyd Charisse, Cesar Romero, Vikki Carr, Norm Crosby, Rowan and Martin, Kate Smith, Ben Blue, Mort Sahl, Trini Lopez, Martha Raye, Chad and Jeremy, Ann Miller, Allan and Rossi, Jack Benny, Liza Minelli, Sammy

Davis, Jr., Fred Astaire, Beverly Washburn, Ethel Merman, Marcel Marceau, Jack Jones, Roy Rogers and Dale Evans, Debbie Reynolds, Sid Caesar, Imogene Coca, Edie Adams, Milton Berle, Jimmy Durante, Steve Allen and Jayne Meadows, Don Adams, Phyllis Diller, Don Rickles, The Lennon Sisters (Kathy, Janet, Dianne, Peggy).

THE HOLLYWOOD PALACE—60 minutes—ABC—January 4, 1964 - February 7, 1970.

HOLLYWOOD SCREEN TEST

Anthology. Dramatic productions. Young theatrical hopefuls appear with established performers.

Host: Neil Hamilton.

Hostess: Betty Furness.

Assistant: Martha Wayne.

Announcer: Ted Campbell.

HOLLYWOOD SCREEN TEST—30 minutes—ABC—August 15, 1948 - September 26, 1949.

HOLLYWOOD SHOWCASE

See title: "The Dick Powell Theatre."

THE HOLLYWOOD SQUARES

Game. Two competing contestants—Player X and Player O. Nine guest celebrities each occupy a square on a huge Tic-Tac-Toe board. Object: To win two out of three Tic-Tac-Toe games.

The first player begins by choosing one celebrity who is then asked a question by the host. The player must determine whether the answer given is correct or a bluff, i.e., agree or disagree. If the player is correct, the appropriate letter is lit on the board; incorrect, the opponent receives the square. Exception: Should the square complete a Tic-Tac-Toe game for the opponent, he does not receive it. Players have to earn essential squares by themselves. Winners, those acquiring three squares in a row, up and down or diagonally, receive two hundred dollars. Two wins earns the championship. Players compete until defeated or until reaching the game limit of ten at which time he wins two thousand dollars and a new car.

One game per show is a jackpot round. If the player chooses "The Secret Square" (one of the squares designated before the game but unknown to the players or the celebrities), a special question is asked. If the player is correct in agreeing or disagreeing with the celebrity, he receives valuable merchandise prizes.

Host: Peter Marshall.

Announcer: Kenny Williams.

Music: Recorded.

Regulars Wally Cox, Cliff Arquette as Charlie Weaver, Paul Lynde, Rose Marie.

Frequently Appearing: Jan Murray, Joey Bishop, Abby Dalton, Karen Valentine, Vincent Price, Artie Johnson, Arthur Godfrey, Nanette Fabray, Jo Anne Worley, Stu Gilliam, Gypsy Rose Lee, Michael Landon, Della Reese, Janet Leigh, Jack Cassidy, Charles Nelson Reilly, Harvey Korman, McLean Stevenson, Charo, George Gobel, Roddy McDowell, Florence Henderson, Connie Stevens, Rich Little, Joan Rivers, John Davidson, Pearl Bailey.

THE HOLLYWOOD SQUARES—30 minutes—NBC—Premiered: October 17, 1966.

HOLLYWOOD'S TALKING

Game. Involved: Three competing contestants and approximately fifteen Hollywood celebrities. A video tape, divided into three cash segments ($150, $100, and $50) is played, showing celebrities expressing their opinions on people, places, or things. Contestants have to determine exactly what's being talked about. A press on a button automatically stops the tape. If the player guesses correctly, he receives cash according to the amount of tape run; if incorrect, he is disqualified from that particular round.

The first player to score two hundred and fifty dollars is the winner and receives a chance to earn additional cash via "The Bonus Round." The format follows the same as the game. Five short subjects are discussed. The player must identify as many as possible within a sixty-second time limit. Each correct identification earns cash equal to the amount won in the preceeding game. Players compete until defeated.

Host: Geoff Edwards.

Announcer: Johnny Jacobs.

Music: Recorded.

Premiere Week Celebrities: Mary Tyler Moore, Ross Martin, Pearl Bailey, Milton Berle, Sally Struthers, Rich Little, Lloyd Haines, Jo Anne Worley, John Forsythe, Fess Parker, Judy Carne, Doc Severnson, Dean Jones, Joan Rivers, Sebastian Cabot, Red Buttons, David Janssen.

First champion: Gail Silverton.

HOLLYWOOD'S TALKING—30 minutes—CBS—March 26, 1973 - June 23, 1973.

HOLLYWOOD TALENT SCOUTS

Variety. Performances by undiscovered professional talent presented by celebrity guests.

Versions:

CBS—60 minutes—August 1, 1960 - September 26, 1960.

Host: Sam Levenson.

Orchestra: Harry Sosnick.

Premiere Guests: Ann Sheridan, Phil Silvers, Audrey Meadows.

CBS—60 minutes—July 3, 1962 - September 1962.

Host: Jim Backus.

Orchestra: Harry Sosnick.

Premiere Guests: Carol Burnett, Van Johnson, Robert Goulet.

CBS—60 minutes—July 2, 1963 - September 17, 1963.

Host: Merv Griffin.

Orchestra: Harry Sosnick.

Premiere Guests: Lauren Bacall, George Maharis, Hugh O'Brien.

CBS—60 minutes—June 12, 1965 - September 6, 1965.

Host: Art Linkletter.

Orchestra: Harry Zimmerman.

Premiere Guests: Debbie Reynolds, Ann Miller, Roy Rogers and Dale Evans.

CBS—60 minutes—December 20, 1965 - September 5, 1966.

Host: Art Linkletter.

Orchestra: Harry Zimmerman.

Premiere Guests: Debbie Reynolds, Ann Miller, Jack Carter, Roy Rogers and Dale Evans.

Also known as "Celebrity Talent Scouts."

HOLLYWOOD TELEVISION THEATRE

Anthology. Original dramatic productions.

Included:

Lemonade. On a country road, two middle-aged women selling lemonade recall times past and what might have been if things had been different.

CAST
Mabel: Martha Scott; Edith: Eileen Herlie.

The Typists. The lives of two losers—a spinster and self-pitying married man.

CAST
Anne Jackson, Eli Wallach.

The Plot To Overthrow Christmas. A television adaptation of Norman Corwin's radio play about the devil's plot to kill Santa Claus.

CAST
Devil: John McIntire; Nero: Karl Swenson; Santa Claus: Allen Reed, Sr.; Simon Legree: Parley Baer; Lucrezia Borgia: Jeanette Nolan.

Awake And Sing. Background: The Bronx, New York 1930s. A Jewish family struggles to survive the Depression.

CAST
Walter Matthau, Ruth Storey, Felicia Farr, Robert Lipton.

Birdbath. The story of a young woman who seeks help after committing a murder.

CAST
Velma Sparrow: Patty Duke; Frankie Basta: James Farentino.

HOLLYWOOD TELEVISION THEATRE—60 minutes—PBS—Premiered: October 7, 1971. Originally broadcast as a series of monthly specials from 1970-1971 before becoming a weekly series.

HOLLYWOOD TODAY

Interview. A behind-the-scenes look at Hollywood during the mid-1950s.

Hostess: Sheila Graham.

HOLLYWOOD TODAY—30 minutes —NBC 1955.

HOME

Information-Variety. A woman's television magazine of the air.

Hostess, Leisure Activities Editor, Shopping Guide Expert: Arlene Francis.

Decorating Editor: Sydney Smith.

Women's Interest, Fashion and Beauty Editor: Eve Hunter.

Food Editor: Poppy Cannon.

Fix-It-Shop and Home Gardening Editor: Will Peiglebeck.

Children's Problem Editor: Rose Frangblau.

Special Projects Editor: Estelle Parsons.

Variety Editor (Vocalist): Johnny Johnston.

Music Editors: The Norman Paris Trio.

HOME—60 minutes—NBC (Daily)— March 1, 1954 - August 9, 1957.

HOMEMAKERS' EXCHANGE

Women. Cooking, decorating, household tips, and shopping advice.

Hostess: Louise Leslie.

HOMEMAKERS' EXCHANGE—30 minutes—CBS 1950.

HOMICIDE

Crime Drama. Background: Australia. The life and problems faced by detectives attached to the Melbourne Police Force.

CAST
Detective   George Fairfax
Detective   Joe McCormick

HOMICIDE—50 minutes—Produced and syndicated in the early 1960s. (The exact production and syndicated year is unknown.)

HOMICIDE SQUAD

See title: "Mark Saber."

HONDO

Western. Background: The Arizona Territory, 1869. The exploits of Hondo Lane, a United States Army troubleshooter. Episodes relate his attempts to resolve the bloodthirsty conflict between settlers and Apache Indians over the possession of land.

CAST

Hondo Lane	Ralph Taeger
Buffalo Baker	Noah Beery, Jr.
Angie Daw, a settler, the woman Hondo saved from her murdering husband	Kathie Brown
Johnny Daw, her son	Buddy Foster
Apache Chief Vittoro	Michael Pate
Captain Richards, Hondo's superior	Gary Clarke
Hondo's dog: Sam.	

HONDO—60 minutes—ABC—September 8, 1967 - December 29, 1967.

HONESTLY, CELESTE!

Comedy. Background: Manhattan. The misadventures of Celeste Anders, a college teacher from Minnesota as she struggles to acquire journalism experience through her job as a reporter for the *New York Express*.

CAST

Celeste Anders	Celeste Holm
Mr. Wallace, the editor	Geoffrey Lumb
Bob Wallace, his son	Scott McKay
Marty, her friend, a cab driver	Mike Kellin
Mr. Wallace's secretary	Mary Finny
The Obit Editor	Henry Jones
Also	Fred Worlock

HONESTLY, CELESTE!—30 minutes —CBS—October 10, 1954 - December 12, 1954.

THE HONEYMOONERS

Comedy. Era: The 1950s. Background: 328 Chauncey Street, Bensonhurst, Brooklyn, New York, the apartment residences of the Kramdens and the Nortons, people, fifteen years after the Depression, still struggling to make ends meet, save some money, and move into larger, more modern apartments.

Meeting while working for the WPA, Ralph Kramden and Alice Gibson married following his acquiring employment as a bus driver with the Gotham Bus Company.

Ed Norton, a sewer worker for the New York City Department of Water Works, and his wife, Trixie, live above the Kramdens.

Stories depict the sincere attempts of two men to better their lives and the ensuing frustrations when their schemes to strike it rich inevitably backfire.

The success of "The Honeymooners" stems not only from its sensitive portrayal of the struggles that make up a marriage in difficult times, but from the verbal interactions of the characters. Ralph, loud mouthed, impulsive and quick tempered; Alice, logical and tolerant, a constant source of his aggravation when she questions many of his ventures; Ed, calm and sensitive, representing Ralph's complement; and Trixie, undemanding and seemingly content, a woman who is totally devoted to Ed.

CAST

Ralph Kramden	Jackie Gleason
Alice Kramden	Audrey Meadows
Ed Norton	Art Carney
Trixie Norton	Joyce Randolph

Additional characters (not given screen credit): Mrs. Gibson, Alice's mother; Mrs. Manicotti, a tenant; Mr. Marshall, Ralph's employer; Mr. Johnson, the landlord; Morris Fink, the Grand High Exaulted Ruler of the Raccoon Lodge, Ralph and Norton's fraternity; Mr. Monahan, the president of the bus company.

Announcer: Jack Lescoulie.

Orchestra: Sammy Spear.

THE HONEYMOONERS—30 minutes—CBS—October 1, 1955 - September 22, 1956. Syndicated.

History: "The Honeymooners" first appeared as a short segment on "Cavalcade of Stars" (DuMont 1950, wherein Pert Kelton portrayed Alice). After switching to CBS the following year, the series, titled "The Jackie Gleason Show" continued the *Honeymooners* segment. From 1955-1956 a weekly thirty-minute series, "The Honeymooners," was filmed at the Park Sheraton Hotel on the DuMont Electronicam System.* The series, failing to establish itself on its own, continued via short segments of "The Jackie Gleason Show" (CBS, 1956-1959).

After an absence of seven years, new episodes in the lives of the Kramdens and the Nortons appeared, first in short fifteen-minute segments, then later as full sixty-minute musical productions, also aired via "The Jackie Gleason Show" (CBS, 1966-1970). The final network appearance to date were rebroadcasts of the hour long *Honeymooners* episodes that were aired on CBS, January 3, 1971 - May 16, 1971.

*A system wherein the performance is filmed before a live audience to create the illusion of a live telecast when it is later aired.

CAST (New Version)

Ralph Kramden	Jackie Gleason
Alice Kramden	Sheila MacRae
Ed Norton	Art Carney
Trixie Norton	Jane Kean

Featured: The June Taylor Dancers.

Announcer: Johnny Olsen.

Orchestra: Sammy Spear.

THE HONEYMOON GAME

Game. Six engaged couples compete in contests of skill and knowledge.

Segments:

The Qualifying Round. Three couples at a time compete; two are to be eliminated. Basis: The identification of persons, places, objects, occupations, or actions. The host states a category (e.g., "A Living Woman") and proceeds to ask the women related questions which serve as clues (e.g., "What is her profession?"). If the woman answers correctly, her partner receives a chance to identify the subject of the category, and thus score one point. If incorrect, a second clue is given. Six clues are given for each identification. Four segments are played, two of which are in reverse (clues are given to the men while the ladies have to identify subjects). Winners are the four highest-scoring couples.

The Semi-Final Round. Four couples, two at a time, compete, two to be defeated. Each team has before them a lever, which when pulled activates a large spinning wheel. The wheel contains three glass windows that reveal three celebrity-picture categories (e.g. Jaye P. Morgan representing show business; Don Drysdale representing sports). Five guest celebrities are present. Each team receives a chance to activate the wheel. One player of that team then chooses one window. The corresponding guest asks a question. If it is correctly answered, the team receives one point.

If a celebrity appears in two windows, the point value is doubled. If in three, it is tripled. Ten points wins the round. Should the word "Bonus" appear with any picture, the question, if correctly answered, earns one extra point; if it appears three times, on one spin, the round is automatically won. Off-stage couples compete in the same manner.

The Final Round. Two couples. The levers are pulled and players in turn answer the category questions that appear. The highest scoring team is the winner and receives their point value in dollars.

Grand Finale. The winning couple has the chance to win merchandise prizes and an all-expense-paid honeymoon. The spinning wheel, containing prizes, is incorporated. One member is permitted to pull the lever. The wheel, when stopping, pinpoints three prizes. The couple, if not satisfied, receives another chance to activate the spinning wheel. If still not pleased, they are allowed a final third spin and must keep what then appears.

As their gifts are established, three windows are revealed, each containing a honeymoon varying in luxury and elegance. The couple, aften ten seconds, select and receive the honeymoon of their choice.

Host: Jim McKrell.

Announcer: Harry Blackstone, Jr.

Music: Recorded.

THE HONEYMOON GAME—90 minutes—Syndicated 1971.

THE HONEYMOON RACE

Game. Three newlywed couples compete. Background: The Hollywood Mall Shopping Center in Hollywood, Florida. Basis: A scavenger hunt. A specific amount of time is established. Players, who each receive a series of clues, have to find the items that they represent. The couple who find the most items are the winners and receive these articles as their prize.

Host: Bill Malone.

THE HONEYMOON RACE—30 minutes—ABC—July 20, 1967 - April 1, 1968.

HONEY WEST

Mystery. Background: Los Angeles, California. The investigations of Honey West, owner and operator of H. West and Company, a private

Honey West. Anne Francis, "Television's loveliest private detective."

detective organization. Stories relate her attempts to solve crimes through advanced scientific technology.

CAST

Honey West	Anne Francis
Sam Bolt, her partner	John Ericson
Meg West, Honey's aunt	Irene Hervey

Honey's pet ocelot: Bruce.

Music: Joseph Mullendore.

HONEY WEST—30 minutes—ABC—September 17, 1965 - September 2, 1966. Syndicated.

HONG KONG

Adventure. Background: Hong Kong. The experiences of Glenn Evans, an American foreign correspondent assigned to cover the Cold War.

CAST

Glenn Evans	Rod Taylor
Neil Campbell, the police chief	Lloyd Bochner
Tully, the owner of the Golden Dragon Night-club	Jack Kruschen
Ching Mei, a cocktail waitress	Mai Tai Sing
Fong, Evans's houseboy (1960)	Harold Fong
Ling, Evans's houseboy (1961)	Gerald Jann

Music: Lionel Newman.

HONG KONG—60 minutes—ABC—October 28, 1960 - September 27, 1961. Syndicated.

HONG KONG PHOOEY

Animated Cartoon. The story of Henry, a meek police station janitor who possesses the ability to transform himself into the disaster prone Hong Kong Phooey, "America's secret weapon against crime." Episodes relate his fumbling attempts to solve baffling acts of criminal injustice. A Hanna-Barbera Production.

Characters' Voices

Henry/Hong Kong Phooey	Scatman Crothers
Sergeant Flint	Joe E. Ross
Rosemary, the switchboard operator	Jean VanderPyl

Additional Voices: Richard Dawson, Ron Feinberg, Kathy Gori, Casey Kaseem, Jay Lawrence, Peter Leeds, Allan Melvin, Don Messick, Alan Oppenheimer, Bob Ridgley, Fran Ryan, Hal Smith, Lee Vines, Franklin Welker, Janet Waldo, Paul Winchell, Lennie Weinrib.

Music: Hoyt Curtin.

Henry's pet cat: Spot.

Hong Kong's car: The *Phooeymobile.*

HONG KONG PHOOEY—30 minutes—ABC—Premiered: September 7, 1974.

HOOTENANNY

Musical Variety. Performances by Folk singers. Filmed on college campuses throughout the country.

Host: Jack Linkletter.

Featured: Glenn Yarbrough of The Limeliters.

Music: The Chad Mitchell Trio.

HOOTENANNY—60 minutes—ABC—April 6, 1963 - September 21, 1963.

HOPALONG CASSIDY

Western. Background: The Bar 20 Ranch in Crescent City. The exploits of Hopalong Cassidy, a daring defender of range justice.

CAST

Hopalong Cassidy (Hoppy)	William Boyd
Red Connors, his partner	Edgar Buchanan

Hoppy's horse: Topper.

HOPALONG CASSIDY—30 minutes —Syndicated 1948.

In 1935 producer Harry Sherman bought the screen rights to Clarence E. Mulford's *Hopalong Cassidy* stories. Offered a chance to star in the first film, William Boyd accepted, but refused to play the part of the ranch foreman. His insistance awarded him the role of Cassidy. As written, Cassidy was originally an illiterate, "tabacco-chewin', hard-drinkin', able-swearin' son of the Old West who got his nickname because of a limp." However, when the first film, *Hop-a-Long Cassidy*, was released by Paramount, Boyd dropped everything that the original literary character had possessed, including the limp, with an explanation, in the second film, that the wound had healed.

Between 1935 and 1948, sixty-six Hopalong Cassidy films were made. A half-hour television series appeared in 1948; and a thirty-minute radio series, starring William Boyd, appeared on Mutual in 1949.

HOPPITY HOOPER

Animated Cartoon. The comic escapades of three talking animals: Hoppity Hooper, the frog; Uncle Waldo, the fox; and Fillmore, the bear.

Characters' Voices

Hoppity Hooper	Chris Allen
Uncle Waldo	Hans Conried
Fillmore	Bill Scott
The Narrator	Paul Frees

HOPPITY HOOPER—30 minutes— Syndicated 1962. Also known as: "Uncle Waldo."

THE HORACE HEIDT SHOW

Musical Variety. Performances by undiscovered professional talent.

Host: Horace Heidt.

Announcer: Bud Collyer.

Orchestra: Horace Heidt.

THE HORACE HEIDT SHOW—30 minutes—CBS 1950.

HOT DOG

Educational. Filmed explorations of the technological mysteries surrounding the making of everyday items, e.g., footballs, rope, bricks, pencils, hot dogs, blue jeans, felt tip pens, baseballs, plywood, license plates, the canning of sardines, cuckoo clocks, and paper.

Regulars: Jonathan Winters, Woody Allen, Jo Anne Worley (tackling chosen subjects in a comical fashion).

Music: The Youngbloods.

HOT DOG—30 minutes—NBC—September 12, 1970 - September 4, 1971.

HOTEL BROADWAY

Musical Variety.

Hostess: Jerri Blanchard.

Regulars: Avon Long, Rose and Rana, The Striders.

Music: The Harry Ranch Sextet.

HOTEL BROADWAY—30 minutes—DuMont 1949.

HOTEL COSMOPOLITAN

Serial. Background: The Cosmopolitan Hotel in New York City. Dramatizations based on incidents in the lives of people frequenting the hotel as seen through the eyes of television actor Donald Woods.

CAST
Donald Woods   Himself
The House
    Detective   Henderson Forsythe
Also: Dinnie Smith, John Holmes, Wesley Larr, Walter Brooke, Tom Shirley.

HOTEL COSMOPOLITAN—15 minutes—CBS—August 19, 1957 - April 11, 1958.

HOTEL de PAREE

Western. Background: George Town, Colorado, 1870s. The saga of the West's most colorful gathering place, the Hotel de Paree, and its legendary proprietor, a gunslinger turned law enforcer (upon his release from prison), the Sundance Kid.

CAST
Sundance (distinguished by
    a black Stetson with a
    hatband of polished silver
    discs)   Earl Holliman
Annette Devereaux, the hotel
    operator   Jeanette Nolan

Hotel de Paree. Left to right: Peggy Joyce (guest), Earl Holliman (Sundance), and Kathleen Hughes (guest). Episode: "The Only Wheel in Town."

Monique Devereaux, her
    niece   Judi Meredith
Aaron Donager, a
    friend   Strother Martin
Sundance's dog: Useless.

HOTEL de PAREE—30 minutes—CBS—1959-1960.

HOT L BALTIMORE

Comedy. Background: Baltimore, Maryland. Life in the seedy Hotel Baltimore (the E in the neon sign has burned out) as seen through the activities of the eleven people who live like a family in the decaying establishment. Based on the Broadway play of the same title.

CAST

Bill Lewis, the desk clerk	James Cromwell
Suzy Madaraket, a prostitute	Jeannie Linero
April Green, a prostitute	Conchata Ferrell
Clifford Ainsley, the hotel manager	Richard Masur
Winthrop Morse, the cantankerous old man	Stan Gottlieb
Charles Bingham, the young philosopher	Al Freeman, Jr.
Jackie, a young, unemployed woman	Robin Wilson
Millie, the waitress	Gloria LeRoy
George, a homosexual	Lee Bergere
Gordon, a homosexual	Henry Calvert
Mrs. Esmee Belotti, the mother of the never-seen psychotic youngster, Moose	Charlotte Rae

Music: Marvin Hamlisch.

HOT L BALTIMORE—30 minutes—ABC—January 24, 1975 - June 13, 1975.

HOT LINE

Discussion. Two guests and panelists discuss topical issues.

Host: Gore Vidal.

Panelists: Dorothy Killgallen, David Susskind.

HOT LINE—90 minutes—Syndicated 1964.

HOT WHEELS

Animated Cartoon. Background: Metro City. The experiences of responsible young teenage drivers, members of the Hot Wheels automobile racing car club. Intent: To establish and explain, through the recklessness of rival gangs, the dangers of racing; and to advocate automotive safety.

Characters:

The Hot Wheels Club: Jack Wheeler, its organizer, owner of the Wheeler Motors Garage; Janet Martin, Skip Frasier, Bud Stuart, Mickey, Tag, Art, and Kip.

Rival Racing Car Clubs: Dexter Carter and His Demons; Stuff Haley and His Bombers.

Music: Jack Fascinato.
Theme: "Hot Wheels."
 Words: Ken Snyder.
 Music: Jack Fascinato.
 Copyright 1969 by Ken Snyder Properties, Inc. Reprinted by permission.

Hot Wheels, Hot Wheels, keep a turnin' now,
Keep a burnin' now, Keep a turnin'
 Hot Wheels, Hot Wheels,
Keep a turnin' now, Keep a burnin' now,
 Hot Wheels...

HOT WHEELS—30 minutes—ABC—September 6, 1969 - September 4, 1971.

THE HOUNDCATS

Animated Cartoon. Background: The Western United States. The investigations of the Houndcats, bumbling government cat and dog agents organized to combat evil. A spin-off from "Mission: Impossible."

Characters' Voices

Studs, the leader   Daws Butler
Muscle Mut, the strong
         dog   Aldo Ray
Rhubarb, the
         inventor   Artie Johnson
Puddy Puss, the cat of-a-thousand
         faces   Joe Besser
Ding Dog, the dare
         devil   Stu Gilliam

Their car: Sparkplug.

Music: Doug Goodwin.

THE HOUNDCATS—30 minutes—
NBC—September 9, 1972 - September
1, 1973.

THE HOUR GLASS

Anthology. Dramatizations of people
confronted with sudden, unexpected
situations.

Included:

One Night With You. The romantic
story of an Italian teenager's chance
meeting with a girl in a railroad
station.

CAST

Giulio: Nino Martine; Mary: Patricia
Roc.

Turn The Key Softly. Three women,
released from prison, attempt to readjust to the outside world.

CAST

Monica: Yvonne Mitchell; Stella: Joan
Collins; Joan: Dorothy Alison.

Another Shore. The story of a young
man who believes that if he rescues an
elderly man or woman he will receive
a substantial sum of money as a
reward, which will enable him to
travel to a South Seas island. The
episode relates his attempts to find
someone in distress.

CAST

Gulliver Shields: Robert Beatly;
Jennifer: Morra Lister; Alastair:
Stanley Holloway.

THE HOUR GLASS—60 minutes—
ABC—December 3, 1952 - September
30, 1953. Also: ABC—June 21, 1956 -
September 1956.

HOUR OF STARS

Anthology. Rebroadcasts of dramas
that were originally aired via "The
Twentieth Century Fox Hour."

Host: John Conte.

Included:

The People Against McQuade. A
soldier attempts to clear himself of a
false homicide charge.

CAST

Tab Hunter, James Garner.

Men Against Speed. A female photographer tries to bring her two bickering
brothers together again.

CAST

Mona Freeman, Farley Granger.

The Magic Brew. In his attempt to
fleece the citizens, a medicine show
huckster runs a contest for the "most
popular girl in town."

CAST

Jim Backus, Fay Spain, Will Hutchins.

Deadlock. A father tries to hide the

fact that he's a wanted criminal from his young daughter.

CAST
Charles McGraw.

HOUR OF STARS—60 minutes—Syndicated 1958.

THE HOUSE ON HIGH STREET

Serial. Background: Los Angeles, California. The cases of defense attorney John Collier. Based on actual records from the Domestic Relations Court. The series, which involves people in trouble with the law, is episodic, with stories running from three to five installments.

CAST
John Collier	Philip Abbott
Judge James Gehrig	Himself
Dr. Harris B. Peck	Himself

THE HOUSE ON HIGH STREET—30 minutes—NBC—September 29, 1959 - February 5, 1960.

HOUSE PARTY

See title: "Art Linkletter."

THE HOWARD MILLER SHOW

Musical Variety.

Host: Howard Miller.

Regulars: Mike Douglas, Barbara Becker, The Mello-Larks, The Art Van Damme Quintet.

Orchestra: Joseph Gallicchia.

THE HOWARD MILLER SHOW—30 minutes—CBS 1957.

HOW DO YOU RATE

Game. Selected studio-audience members compete. Tested: Hidden aptitudes. Players compete in rounds designed to test intelligence and reasoning power. The first to successfully complete the problems (mathematics, observation, logic, mechanics, etc.) is the winner and receives merchandise prizes.

Host: Tom Reddy.

HOW DO YOU RATE—30 minutes—CBS—March 3, 1958 - June 26, 1958.

HOWDY DOODY

Children. Early history: Doodyville, Texas. On December 27, 1941, the wife of a ranch hand named Doody gave birth to twins, boys named Howdy and Double. The years swiftly passed and the boys enjoyed growing up on the ranch where their parents earned a living by performing chores for the owner.

At the age of six, their rich uncle, Doody, died and bequeathed Howdy and Double a small plot of land in New York City. (Striking oil near Doodyville, the citizens named the town after him. Traveling east before the twins were born, he had always regretted the fact that he had never returned to see them).

Howdy cherished a dream of operating a circus. Double wished to remain in Texas. When NBC offered to purchase the land to construct a television studio, Mr. Doody arranged the deal to provide for Howdy to have his circus. NBC built the circus grounds, surrounded it with TV cameras and appointed Buffalo Bob Smith as Howdy's guardian.

After a tearful farewell, Howdy departed Texas for New York. Arriving and befriending Buffalo Bob, the two began their television show in 1947.

Set against the background of Doodyville, and surrounded by "The Peanut Gallery" (children) the program depicts the efforts of a circus troupe to perform against the wishes of Phineas T. Bluster, an old man opposed to people having fun.

Characters:

Buffalo Bob Smith, an adventurer dressed in a pioneer costume, supposedly descended from Buffalo Bill — Bob Smith

Clarabell Hornblow, a highly skilled clown hired by Howdy when no other circus would stand for his constant playing of practical jokes. He remains silent and "speaks" through his honking of a "Yes" or "No" horn — Bob Keeshan, Bob Nicholson, Lou Anderson

The Story Princess — Alene Dalton

Tim Tremble — Don Knotts

Chief Thunderthud, a descendent of Chief Bungathud (a supposed founder of Doodyville), a friend of Phineas T. Bluster's — Bill Lecornec

Princess Summer-Fall-Winter-Spring — Judy Tyler

Lowell Thomas, Jr., the traveling lecturer — Himself

Additional Characters: Doctor Sing-a-Song; Grandpa Doody.

Puppets:

Howdy Doody (voiced by Bob Smith), a red-haired, freckle-faced (72 freckles), blue-eyed boy with an enormous grin who dresses in dungarees, a plaid work shirt, and a large bandana.

Phineas T. Bluster (voiced by Dayton Allen), the terror of Doodyville. Seventy years of age and as spry as a pup. An old man who is forever undermining Bob and Howdy and causing trouble.

Dr. Jose Bluster, Phineas's twin brother, the opposite in character and not very bright, living most of his life in South America. He sides with Howdy and Bob against Phineas.

Double Doody, Howdy's twin brother.

Heidi Doody, Howdy's cousin.

Ugly Sam, Doodyville's wrestler, always trying to win a bout.

Lanky Lou, a talkative cowboy until someone asked him a question at which time he clammed up.

Trigger Happy, a notorious bad man.

Spin Platter, the disc jockey.

The Flubadub, the main circus attraction—a creature with a dog's ears, a duck's head, cat's whiskers, a giraffe's neck, a raccoon's tale, an elephant's memory, and a feather-covered body who craves meatballs and spaghetti.

Inspector John, the chief of police, a top-notch investigator.

Captain Scuttlebut, an old sea captain whose boat is docked in Doodyville Harbor.

The Bloop, an invisible, but sometimes visible creature.

Dilly Dally, a nervous chap who is able to wiggle his ears.

Sandy McTavish, a visitor from Scotland who is in Doodyville trying to build a factory.

Andy Handy, the business tycoon.

Doc Ditto, an old toymaker.

Sandra, the witch.

Voices: Bob Smith, Dayton Allen, Allen Swift, Herb Vigran.

Puppeteers: Rhoda Mann, Lee Carney.

Music: Edward Kean.

HOWDY DOODY—60 and 30 minute versions—NBC—Decmeber 27, 1947 - September 24, 1960. 2,543 performances. Original title: "Puppet Playhouse."

HOW'S YOUR MOTHER-IN-LAW

Game. Object: For three guest celebrities, acting as lawyers for the defense, to judge, through a series of question and answer rounds on behavior, which of three contestants are the best mothers-in-law. Prizes are awarded to the winner.

Host: Wink Martindale.

HOW'S YOUR MOTHER-IN-LAW— 30 minutes—ABC—October 2, 1967 - March 1, 1968.

HOW TO

Discussion. A person with a problem is brought on stage. The host and panelists then attempt to resolve the difficulties.

Host: Roger Price.

Panelists: Anita Martell, Leonard Stern, Stapley Adams.

Announcer: Bob Lemond.

HOW TO—30 minutes—CBS 1951.

HOW TO MARRY A MILLIONAIRE

Comedy. Background: New York City. The story of three beautiful career girls: Loco Jones, a model; Michele (Mike) Page, a secretary; and Greta Lindquist, a secretary—bachelorettes sharing a Manhattan apartment and each desiring to marry a millionaire. Episodes depict their

individual pursuits and attempts to secure a dream. Based on the movie of the same title.

CAST
Loco Jones	Barbara Eden
Michele (Mike) Page	Merry Anders
Greta Lindquist	Lori Nelson
Gwen Laurel (replaced Greta)	Lisa Gaye
Jessie, the elevator operator	Jimmy Cross

HOW TO MARRY A MILLIONAIRE —30 minutes—Syndicated 1958.

HOW TO SURVIVE A MARRIAGE

Serial. Background: Los Angeles, California. The series, which is aimed primarily at young marrieds and divorcées, dramatizes the problems of marriage, divorce, separation, and readjustment.

CAST
Dr. Julie Franklin	Rosemary Prinz
Monica Courtland	Joan Copeland
Sandra Henderson	Lynn Lowry
Maria McGhee	Lauren White
Chris Kirby	Jennifer Harmon
Rachel Bachman	Elissa Leeds
David Bachman	Allan Miller
Fran Bachman	Fran Brill
Joan Willis	Tricia O'Neil
Lori Ann Kirby	Suzanne Davidson
	Cathy Greene
	Lori Lowe
Terry Courtland	Peter Brandon
Dr. Max Cooper	James Shannon
Dr. Tony DeAngelo	George Webles
Neil Abbott	George Shannon
Dr. Brady	Don Keyes
Larry Kirby	Michael Landrum
Dr. Charles Maynard	Paul Vincent
Jerry Nelson	Dino Narizzano
Joshua T. Browne (J. B.)	F. Murray Abraham

Johnny McGhee	Armand Assante
Dr. Robert Monday	Gene Bua
Susan Pritchett	Veleka Gray
Peter Willis	Steve Elmore
	Berkeley Harris
Moe Bachman	Albert Ottenheimer
Greg Bachman	Richie Schectman
Lt. Bowling	Al Fann

Music: Score Productions.

Music Supervision: Sybil Weinberger.

Orchestrations: William Goldstein.

HOW TO SURVIVE A MARRIAGE—
30 minutes—NBC—January 7, 1974 -
April 17, 1975.

H. R. PUFNSTUF

Children's Adventure. Playing near the edge of a river, Jimmy and his talking gold flute, Freddie, board a boat that suddenly materializes. As it drifts out to sea, the evil Miss Witchiepoo, seeking Freddie, the world's only talking flute, for her collection, casts a spell and makes the boat vanish.

Swimming to the shore of Living Island, they are rescued by its mayor, H.R. Pufnstuf.

Taken to the home of Dr. Blinkey, they learn about Judy the Frog, the only creature knowing the secret of the way off the island through the Secret Path of Escape.

Finding Judy, they are led to the path—and unknowingly followed by Miss Witchiepoo. Casting a spell, she makes it vanish and is angered when Jimmy refuses to trade the path for Freddie.

Overshadowed by the schemes of the evil Miss Witchiepoo, Jimmy and Freddie, assisted by the inhabitants of Living Island, struggle to find the secret of the way home to their world and safety.

CAST

Jimmy	Jack Wild
Miss Witchiepoo	Billie Hayes

Also: Joan Gerber, Felix Silla, Jerry Landon, John Linton, Angelo Rosetti, Hommy Stewart, Buddy Douglas.

Characters (The Sid and Marty Krofft Puppets): H.R. Pufnstuf; Judy the Frog; Dr. Blinkey; Cling and Clang, friends of the Mayor's; Dumb, Stupid, Orville and Seymoure, the Witch's aides; Grandfather Clock; Ludicrous Lion; The Four Winds (North, East, South, and West).

Vocals: The Pufnstuf.

Orchestra: Glen Paige, Jr.

H.R. PUFNSTUF—30 minutes—NBC —September 6, 1969 - September 4, 1971. ABC—September 9, 1972 - September 1, 1973.

THE HUCKLEBERRY HOUND SHOW

Animated Cartoon. The misadventures of Huckleberry Hound, a slow-thinking and slow-talking animal who tackles various occupations in his struggle to discover his goal in life. A Hanna-Barbera production.

Additional Segments:
"Pixie and Dixie." The misadventures of two mischievous mice.
"Mr. Jinks." The story of a cantankerous cat.
"Hokey Wolf." The life of a mischievous wolf.

Characters' Voices

Huckleberry Hound	Daws Butler
Pixie	Don Messick
Dixie	Don Messick

The Huckleberry Hound Show. Huckleberry Hound. *Courtesy Hanna-Barbera Productions.*

Mr. Jinks   Daws Butler
Hokey Wolf   Daws Butler
Ding   Doug Young
Music Supervision: Hoyt Curtin.

THE HUCKLEBERRY HOUND SHOW—30 minutes—Syndicated 1958.

THE HUDSON BROTHERS

Listed: The television programs of the Hudson Brothers.

The Hudson Brothers Show—Variety—60 minutes—CBS—July 31, 1974 - August 28, 1974.

Format: Various sketches, spoofs, and musical numbers.

Hosts: The Hudson Brothers: Bill, Mark, and Brett.

Regulars: Stephanie Edwards, Ronne Graham, Gary Owens, Ron Hull, The Jimmie Rogers Dancers.

Announcer: Gary Owens.

Orchestra: Jack Eskrew.

Special Musical Material: Earl Brown.

The Hudson Brothers Razzle Dazzle Comedy Show—Children's Variety—25 minutes—CBS—Premiered: September 7, 1974.

Format: Varied songs, sketches, and

musical numbers designed to convey value-related messages.

Hosts: Bill, Brett, and Mark Hudson.

Regulars: Billy Van, Peter Cullen, Ted Zeigler, Murray Langston, Rod Hull, Scott Fisher.

Announcer: Peter Cullen.

Orchestra: Jimmy Dale.

HULLABALOO

Variety. A weekly excursion into the world of Rock music.

Hosts: Guests of the week.

Regulars: Sheila Forbes, Lada Edmonds, Jr. (the caged Go Go Dancer), The Hullabaloo Dancers, The David Winters Dancers.

Orchestra: Peter Matz.

HULLABALOO—60 and 30 minute versions—NBC—1965-1966.

THE HUMAN JUNGLE

Drama. Background: London, England. The work of psychiatrist Roger Corder. Stories depict his attempts to assist people overcome by the turmoil of human emotion.

Starring: Herbert Lom as Dr. Roger Corder.

Hullabaloo. The Hullabaloo Dancers.

THE HUMAN JUNGLE—60 minutes
—Syndicated 1964.

THE HUNTER

Adventure. The exploits of Bart Adams, a United States government undercover agent known as The Hunter. Adopting the guise of a wealthy American playboy, he attempts to corrupt the forces of communism in the Western world.

Starring: Barry Nelson as Bart Adams.

THE HUNTER—30 minutes—CBS 1952.

HUNTER

Adventure. Background: Southeast Asia. The exploits of John Hunter, a top operative of C.O.S.M.I.C. (the Office of Security and Military Intelligence), a British government organization. Unassisted by law enforcement officials, he and his partner, Eve Halliday, battle the sinister elements of C.U.C.W., an enemy organization bent on dominating the world.

CAST
John Hunter	Tony Ward
Eve Halliday	Fernande Glyn
Undercover Chief Blake	Nigel Lovell

HUNTER—60 minutes—Syndicated 1968.

THE HUNTLEY-BRINKLEY REPORT

News Report.

Anchor Men: Chet Huntley, David Brinkley.

Music: Recorded.

THE HUNTLEY-BRINKLEY REPORT—15 and 30 minute versions—NBC—October 29, 1956, - August 3, 1971.

HURDY GURDY

Variety. The music, song, and dance of the Gay 90s era.

Host: Pete Lofthouse.

Regulars: Barbara Kelly, The Sportsmen, The Hurdy Gurdy Girls.

Music: The Second Story Men.

HURDY GURDY—30 minutes—Syndicated 1967.

THE HY GARDNER SHOW

Discussion-Interview.

Host: Hy Gardner, newspaper columnist.

THE HY GARDNER SHOW—90 minutes—Syndicated 1965.

I

THE IAN TYSON SHOW

Variety. Performances by U.S. and Canadian Folk and Country and Western entertainers.

Host: Ian Tyson.

Featured: Sylvia Tyson (Mrs.)

Music: The Great Speckled Bird.

THE IAN TYSON SHOW—30 minutes—Syndicated 1970. Also known as: "Nashville Now."

THE ICE PALACE

Variety. Entertainment acts set against the background of a mythical Ice Palace.

Hosts: Weekly Guests (for its eight program run): Roger Miller, The Lennon Sisters (Peggy, Janet, Dianne, and Kathy), Leslie Uggams, Jack Jones, Vickki Carr, Johnny Mathis, John Davidson, Dean Jones.

Regulars (skating personalities): Tim Wood, Linda Carbonetto, Billy Chappell, Gisela Head, Don Knight, Tim Noyers, Roy Powers, Sandy Parker, The Bob Turk Ice Dancers.

Orchestra: Alan Copeland.

THE ICE PALACE—60 minutes—CBS—May 23, 1971 - July 25, 1971.

ICHABOD AND ME

Comedy. Background: Phippsboro, a small New England community. Discontent with life in New York, Bob Major, widower, businessman, quits his job and purchases the *Phippsboro Bulletin,* the town newspaper. Becoming the editor, and assisted by Ichabod Adams, the former owner, now the traffic commissioner, he struggles to learn the ropes and publish a weekly newspaper.

CAST

Bob Major	Robert Sterling
Ichabod Adams	George Chandler
Abby Adams, his daughter	Christine White
Benjie Major, Bob's son	Jimmy Mathers
Aunt Lavinnia, Bob's house-keeper	Reta Shaw
Jonathan, a friend	Jimmy Hawkins
Colby, a friend	Forrest Lewis
Martin, a friend	Guy Raymond
Olaf, a friend	Bert Mustin

Music: Pete Rugolo.

ICHABOD AND ME—30 minutes—CBS—September 26, 1961 - September 18, 1962.

I COVER TIMES SQUARE

Crime Drama. Background: New York City. The investigations of Johnny Warren, a crusading Broadway newspaper columnist. His beat is the out-of-town newsstand on Second Avenue in Times Square.

Starring: Harold Huber as Johnny Warren.

Music: Ethel Stevens.

I COVER TIMES SQUARE—30 minutes—ABC 1951.

THE IDA LUPINO THEATRE

Anthology. Dramatic presentations.

Hostess-Star: Ida Lupino.

Included:

With All My Heart. A tender drama revealing the feelings of an overweight woman as she watches the man she has loved since childhood marry another woman.

Starring: Ida Lupino, Walter Coy.

Woman Afraid. The story of a woman who is constantly spoiled by her husband's affections.

Starring: Ida Lupino.

The Case Of Emily Cameron. The story of a man who devotes his life to caring for his bedridden wife.

Starring: Ida Lupino, Scott Forbes.

Eddie's Place. The story of a beautiful parolee who jeopardizes her chances of reform when she becomes involved in a murder.

Starring: Ida Lupino.

THE IDA LUPINO THEATRE—30 minutes—Syndicated 1956.

I DREAM OF JEANNIE

Comedy. Early history: Jeannie was born in Baghdad, Iraq, April 1, 64 B.C. When she reached the age of marriage, her hand was sought by the Blue Djin, the most powerful and the most feared of all genies. When she refused his proposal, he became enraged; and in retribution turned her into a genie, placed her in a bottle, and sentenced her to a life of loneliness on a desert island.

The centuries passed and the girl in the bottle remained unaffected by time.

The 20th century. Saturday, September 18, 1965. Captain Tony Nelson, an astronaut on a flight from the NASA Space Center, Cape Kennedy, Cocoa Beach, Florida, crash lands on a desert island in the South Pacific. Seeking material with which to make an S.O.S. signal, he finds a strange green bottle. Upon opening it, pink smoke emerges and materializes into a beautiful girl dressed as a harem dancer — a genie.

"Thou may ask anything of thy slave, Master," she informs him; and with her hands crossed over her chest and a blink of her eyes, she proceeds to provide a rescue helicopter for him.

I Dream of Jeannie. Barbara Eden (left), Larry Hagman, and guest Spring Byington. © *Screen Gems.*

Realizing the problems her presence and powers will cause him at NASA, he sets her free, despite her desire to remain with him. Blinking herself back into smoke, and into her bottle, she places herself in Tony's survival kit without his knowledge.

Returning home, 1020 Palm Drive, and discovering Jeannie, Tony, realizing that she is determined to remain, makes her promise to conceal her presence, curtail her powers, and grant him no special treasures. Though reluctant she agrees, but secretly vows to always ensure his safety.

Accidentally stumbling upon Tony's secret, astronaut Roger Healey, his friend, becomes the only other person to know of Jeannie's existence. Caught in a web of mysterious, inexplicable situations that result from Jeannie's magic, he and Tony become the fascination of Dr. Alfred Bellows, a NASA psychiatrist who observes, records, and ponders their activities, determined to uncover the cause.

Stories depict the attempts of a jealous genie to protect her master from harm and from the influx of feminine admirers; and a master's efforts to control and conceal the presence of a beautiful, fun-loving genie.

CAST

Jeannie	Barbara Eden
Jeannie II, her sister, a genie who wanted Tony for herself, but lost	Barbara Eden
Captain Anthony Nelson (Tony), later promoted to major	Larry Hagman
Captain Roger Healey, later promoted to major	Bill Daily
Dr. Alfred Bellows	Hayden Rorke
Amanda Bellows, his wife	Emmaline Henry
General Martin Peterson	Barton MacLane
General Winfield Schaffer	Vinton Hayworth
Hadji, the Master of all genies	Abraham Safaer
Habib, Jeannie's sister's master	Ted Cassidy
Various roles, including The Blue Djin	Michael Ansara

Jeannie's dog, a genie: Gin Gin.

Music: Hugo Montenegro; Richard Wess; Buddy Kaye.

I DREAM OF JEANNIE—30 minutes —NBC—September 18, 1965 - September 8, 1970. Syndicated. Spin-off series: "Jeannie" (see title).

IF YOU HAD A MILLION

See title: "The Millionaire."

THE IGOR CASSINI SHOW

Interview. Artists, businessmen, and scientists are interviewed via the "Person to Person" format (cameras are placed in the homes; and via remote pickup, the host, seated in the studio, conducts the interview).

Host: Igor Cassini.

THE IGOR CASSINI SHOW—30 minutes—DuMont 1953.

I LED THREE LIVES

Drama. The story of Herbert Philbrick, the man who led three lives—private citizen, undercover agent, and F.B.I. counterspy. Episodes depict his life as a counterspy and his attempts to infiltrate the American Communist Party and inform U.S. government officials of the Red military movement.

CAST

Herbert Philbrick	Richard Carlson
Ann Philbrick, his wife	Virginia Steffan
The F.B.I. agent	John Beradino

I LED THREE LIVES—30 minutes— Syndicated 1953.

I'LL BET

Game. Two married couples compete. A question is asked of one team member via telephone (to prevent other players from hearing it). He or she then silently bets points—twenty-five to one hundred—as to whether or not his partner "Can" or "Can't" answer it. The host then reads the question aloud. The partner's answer determines the score. If it is in accord with the prediction, the team wins the points; if incorrect, their opponents receive the points. Winners, the highest point scorers, receive merchandise prizes.

Host: Jack Narz.

I'LL BET—30 minutes—NBC 1965. Revised as "It's Your Bet" (see title).

I'LL BUY THAT

Game. Contestants, chosen from the studio audience, are assisted by four celebrity panelists. Object: The identification of articles submitted by home viewers and that are up for sale. The celebrities ask questions of the host regarding the article's identity. Each question raises the purchase price from five dollars to a limit of one hundred dollars. Players then receive a chance to identify the article. If one is successful, he receives the established purchase price of the article and the chance to possibly triple it by answering three questions. If the player fails to correctly respond to all three, the article becomes his parting prize.

Host: Mike Wallace.

Panelists: Vanessa Brown, Hans Conried, Robin Chandler, Albert Mooreland.

Commercial Spokeswoman: Robin Chandler.

I'LL BUY THAT—30 minutes—CBS—1953-1954.

THE ILONA MASSEY SHOW

Musical Variety. Background: A Continental supper club atmosphere.

Hostess: Ilona Massey.

Music: The Irving Fields Trio.

THE ILONA MASSEY SHOW—30 minutes—DuMont—1954-1955.

I LOVE LUCY

Comedy. Background: 623 East 68th Street, New York City, Apartment 3-B, the residence of Ricky Ricardo, an orchestra leader at the Tropicanna Club (later episodes, The Ricky Ricardo Babalu Club) and his wife Lucy. Stories depict the basic, most often copied premise: a husband plagued by the antics of his well-meaning, but scatterbrained wife. In this case, by a wife who longs for a career in show business, but encounters the objections of a husband who sees her as his housewife, not as an entertainer. Mirroring the trials and tribulations of marriage, "I Love Lucy" has become a television classic.

CAST

Lucy Ricardo	Lucille Ball
Ricky Ricardo	Desi Arnaz
Fred Mertz, their friend, the landlord	William Frawley
Ethel Mertz, his wife	Vivian Vance
Little Ricky Ricardo, Lucy and Ricky's son	The Mayer Twins Richard Keith
Betty Ramsey, their neighbor (Connecticut-based episodes)	Mary Jane Croft
Ralph Ramsey, her husband	Frank Nelson
Mrs. Trumbal, the Ricardos' neighbor	Elizabeth Patterson

Music: Wilbur Hatch, conducting the Desi Arnaz Orchestra.

I LOVE LUCY—30 minutes—CBS—October 15, 1951 - September 1956. Prime time rebroadcasts: CBS—September 1956 - September 1959.

Spin-offs:

The Lucille Ball-Desi Arnaz Show—60 minutes—CBS—November 6, 1957 - September 1958. Also titled: "The Luci-Desi Comedy Hour." Syndicated.

Continued events in the lives of Ricky and Lucy Ricardo, and their friends Fred (now Ricky's band manager) and Ethel Mertz.

Lucy In Connecticut—30 minutes—CBS—July 3, 1960 - September 25, 1960.

Retitled episodes of "I Love Lucy" wherein Ricky and Lucy purchase a home in Westport, Connecticut, and, with their boarders, Fred and Ethel Mertz, struggle to find a life of peace and quiet, despite Lucy's constant knack for finding trouble.

I MARRIED JOAN

Comedy. Background: Los Angeles, California. The trials and tribulations of the Stevens: Bradley, a sophisticated domestic-relations court judge; and his well-meaning but scatterbrained wife, Joan.

CAST

Joan Stevens	Joan Davis
Judge Bradley Stevens	Jim Backus
Charlie, their neighbor	Hal Smith
Mabel, his wife	Geraldine Carr
Janet Tobin, Joan's friend	Sheila Bromley
Kerwin Tobin, her husband	Dan Tobin
Mildred Webster, Joan's friend	Sandra Gould
Beverly Grossman, Joan's sister	Beverly Wills
Alan Grossman, her husband	Himself
Helen, Joan's friend	Mary Jane Croft

I MARRIED JOAN—30 minutes—NBC—October 15, 1952 - April 6, 1955. Rebroadcasts: NBC—May 5, 1956 - March 9, 1957. Syndicated.

I'M DICKENS. . .HE'S FENSTER

Comedy. Background: Los Angeles, California. The misadventures of carpenters Harry Dickens, married and henpecked; and Arch Fenster, a swinging young bachelor.

CAST

Harry Dickens	John Astin
Arch Fenster	Marty Ingles
Kate Dickens, Harry's wife	Emmaline Henry
Mr. Bannister, their employer	Frank DeVol
Mel Warshaw, a friend and co-worker	Dave Ketchum
Mulligan, a friend and co-worker	Henry Beckman

Music: Frank DeVol; Irving Szathmary.

I'M DICKENS. . .HE'S FENSTER—30 minutes—ABC—September 28, 1962 - September 13, 1963. Syndicated.

THE IMMORTAL

Adventure. Seriously injured when his plane passes through an electrical turbulence area, aged and dying billionaire Jordan Braddock, the owner of Braddock Industries, is given a transfusion of Type O blood donated earlier by Ben Richards, an employee in the automotive division. Shortly after, Braddock miraculously recovers, feeling and looking younger.

Baffled, Dr. Matthew Pearce conducts tests and discovers that Richards, through a freak of nature is immortal, possessing a rare blood type that grants him immunity to old age and disease. Further tests reveal that Braddock's rejuvenation is only temporary; and that to sustain it, periodic transfusions are necessary. Ben, who is advised to leave with his fiancée, Sylvia Cartwright, and begin life anew elsewhere—to get away from the greedy who will seek a second or third lifetime—refuses, and chooses to remain and work with researchers until they discover a means by which to duplicate his blood.

Hoping to secure financial backing, Richards approaches Braddock. However, Braddock, who is obsessed with the idea of a new life, kidnaps Richards and imprisons him.

Discovering that as infants Ben and his brother Jason were separated after their parent's death, Braddock, who believes that Jason may also possess the same blood antibodies, begins a search for him.

Assisted by Braddock's wife, Janet, who opposes her husband's obsession, Richards escapes from the Braddock mansion. Angered, Jordan orders his apprehension.

After months of separation, Ben arranges a reunion with Sylvia. Though careful in her preparations to leave, she is followed by Braddock's men. Shortly after he and Sylvia meet, Braddock's men close in. In the ensuing chase and struggle, Sylvia is shot and critically injured.

Saved by a transfusion of his blood, Ben reluctantly leaves Sylvia. Driven by a constant thought that sooner or later Braddock will die and he and Sylvia will have their life together, he struggles to live free. "Sylvia, I love you. . .I'll always think about you.

Even if Braddock wasn't after me, there would be others by now. . . .It's only a matter of time before other people find out. Dr. Pearce was right, I've got to run far and fast. While I'm doing it, I'm going to try to find my brother. Wherever he is, he's got to be warned. Warned that Braddock is looking for him, ready to throw him in a cage and drain him dry. Whatever happens to me finally, Sylvia, wherever I go, I want you to know I'm gonna miss you. I'm gonna miss you for as long as I live."

CAST

Ben Richards	Christopher George
Jordan Braddock	Barry Sullivan
Sylvia Cartwright	Carol Lynley
Fletcher, Braddock's right-hand man	Don Knight
Janet Braddock	Jessica Walter
Dr. Matthew Pearce	Ralph Bellamy
Jason Richards	Michael Strong

Music: Dominic Frontiere; Leith Stevens.

THE IMMORTAL—60 minutes—ABC —September 24, 1970 - September 8, 1971.

THE IMOGENE COCA SHOW

Variety. Various comedy sketches.

Hostess: Imogene Coca.

Regulars: Billy DeWolfe, Ruth Donnelly, Hal March, David Burns, Bibi Osterwald.

Orchestra: George Bassman.

Featured Sketch: "The Newlyweds." The incidents abounding in the lives of Betty and Jerry Crane, a young married couple struggling to survive the difficult first years.

CAST

Betty Crane	Imogene Coca

Jerry Crane — Hal March
Harry Millican,
    their friend and
    neighbor — David Burns
Helen Millican, his
    wife — Bibi Osterwald

THE IMOGENE COCA SHOW—60 minutes—NBC—October 2, 1954 - June 25, 1955.

THE IMPOSTER

See Title: "Colonel Flack."

I'M THE LAW

Crime Drama. Background: New York City. The investigations of Lieutenant George Kirby, a plainclothes police detective. Stories relate his attempts to infiltrate and corrupt the ranks of organized crime.

Starring: George Raft as Lt. George Kirby.

I'M THE LAW—30 minutes—Syndicated 1953. Also known as "The George Raft Casebook."

THE INA RAY HUTTON SHOW

Musical Variety. Female guests (a no-men-allowed policy) coupled with a bevy of beautiful hostesses.

Hostess: Ina Ray Hutton.

Regulars: Dee Dee Ball, Helen Smith, Margaret Rinker, Janice Davis, Harriet Blackburn, Judy Var Buer, Mickey Anderson, Evie Howeth, Helen Wooley, Lois Cronen, Peggy Fairbanks, Helen Hammond, Zoe Ann Willy.

Announcer: Diane Brewster.

Music: The shapely Ina Ray Hutton All-Girl Orchestra.

THE INA RAY HUTTON SHOW—30 minutes—NBC—July 4, 1956 - August 31, 1956.

INCH HIGH PRIVATE EYE

Animated Cartoon. The investigations of Inch High, the world's smallest man, a master detective employed by the Finkerton Organization.

Characters:
Inch High; Laurie, his niece; Gator, his aide, a master of a thousand faces; Braveheart, his coward dog; Mr. Finkerton, Inch High's employer; Mrs. Finkerton his wife.

Inch High's car: The *Hugemobile.*

Voices: Lennie Weinrib, Ted Knight, Kathy Gori, Don Messick, Jamie Farr, John Stephenson, Allan Oppenheimer, Janet Waldo, Vic Perrin.

Music: Hoyt Curtin.

INCH HIGH PRIVATE EYE—30 minutes—NBC—September 8, 1973 - August 31, 1974.

IN COMMON

Game. Three specially selected contestants who have never met, but who each have something in common, compete. Each has three minutes to question the other and determine the common denominator. Merchandise prizes are awarded to successful players.

Host: Ralph Story.

IN COMMON—30 minutes—CBS 1954.

INFORMATION PLEASE

Game. Three panelists, assisted by guests, attempt to answer questions submitted by home viewers. Prizes are awarded to those which stump the experts, the Brain Panel.

Host: Clifton Fadiman.

Brain Panel: Franklin P. Adams, Oscar Levant, John Kiernan.

INFORMATION PLEASE—30 minutes—CBS—June 29, 1952 - September 1952.

THE INFORMER

Crime Drama. Background: London, England. The activities of Alexander Lambert, a disbarred barrister who has become a police informer.

CAST
Alexander Lambert   Ian Hendry
Also: Jean Marsh, Heather Sears.

THE INFORMER—43 minutes—Syndicated 1965.

IN THE MORGAN MANNER

Musical Variety.

Host: Russ Morgan.

Orchestra: Russ Morgan.

IN THE MORGAN MANNER—30 minutes—ABC 1950.

THE INNER FLAME

See title: "Portia Faces Life."

THE INNER SANCTUM

Anthology. Mystery presentations. Tales of people confronted with sudden, perilous situations.

Host: Paul McGrath (as the unseen, only heard, Raymond).

Included:

The Third Fate The story of a young woman plagued by nightmares of a psychopathic killer.

CAST
Louise Horton, Donald Woods.

Family Skeleton. After discovering a skeleton in the basement of a home owned by a wealthy family, two moving men attempt blackmail.

CAST
Murray Hamilton, Edward Binns, Steve Elliot.

The Yellow Parakeet. Two confidence men attempt to dupe a lonely old man into stealing money for them.

CAST
Ernest Truex.

INNER SANCTUM—30 minutes—Syndicated 1954. Based on the radio program of the same title.

IN THE NEWS

Children's Documentary. Newsreel presentations designed to acquaint young audiences with national and world events and people making headlines.

Narrator: Christopher Glen.

IN THE NEWS—02 minutes, 30

seconds—CBS—Premiered: September 12, 1970. Presented four minutes to the hour throughout the network's Saturday morning cartoon schedule.

INSIDE N.B.C.

Documentary. A behind-the-scenes look into the past, the present, and future of the National Broadcasting Company. Features: visits to program rehearsals, interviews, and previews of forthcoming events.

Host: Bill Cullen.

INSIDE N.B.C.—15 minutes—NBC—December 12, 1955 - June 1, 1956.

INSIDE U.S.A.

Variety. Music, songs, guests, and interviews.

Hosts: Peter Lind Hayes, Mary Healy.

Regulars: Sheila Bond, Marian Colby.

Orchestra: Jay Blacton.

INSIDE U.S.A.—30 minutes—CBS 1949.

INSPECTOR FABIAN OF SCOTLAND YARD

Crime Drama. Background: England. The investigations of Inspector Robert Fabian, the Superintendant of Detectives of the New Scotland Yard. Stories stress the use of scientific evaluation and modern techniques in solving crimes.

Starring: Bruce Seton as Inspector Robert Fabian.

INSPECTOR FABIAN OF SCOTLAND YARD—30 minutes—NBC 1955.

INSPECTOR MARK SABER

See title: "Mark Saber."

INTERLUDE

Anthology. Dramatic presentations.

Included:

Myrt And Marge. A video adaptation of the 1930s radio classic. The story of a stage-struck woman in New York.

CAST
Franklin Pangborn, Lyle Talbot.

Sadie And Sally. Background: New York City. The misadventures of two beautiful young career girls.

CAST
Sadie: Joi Lansing; Sally: Lois Hall.

The Puddle Patch Club. The efforts of two boys to establish a club.

CAST
Ed Gargen, Billy Gray.

Battsford's Beanery. A restaurant owner attempts to prevent gangsters from establishing a gambling concession in his establishment.

CAST
Joe Sawyer.

INTERLUDE—30 minutes—ABC 1953.

INTERNATIONAL DETECTIVE

Crime Drama. The global investigations of Ken Franklin, a private detective for the William J. Burns Detective Agency. Based on actual clientele files.

Starring: Arthur Fleming as Ken Franklin.

Music: Sidney Shaw, Leroy Holmes.

INTERNATIONAL DETECTIVE–30 minutes–Syndicated 1959.

INTERNATIONAL PERFORMANCE

Variety. International entertainment programs, opera, ballet, and concert, performed especially for television. English subtitles are incorporated where appropriate.

Host: Robert Merrill.

Included:

Les Brigands. Italy, nineteenth century. The efforts of bandits, masquerading as royal escorts, to rob the coffers of the Duke of Mantua.

CAST
Falsacappa: Dominique Tirmont; Fiorella: Elaine Manchet; Duke of Mantua: Andre Mallabera; Princess of Granada: Nicole Fallien.

La Sylphide. The story of a young Scottish nobelman's love for a captured woodland sprite. Enacted by the Paris Opera Ballet.

CAST
La Sylphide: Ghislaine Thesmar; James: Michael Denard; Effie: Laurence Nerval.

Salome. The biblical story of Salome, the daughter of Herod, and her lust for and the ultimate destruction of John the Baptist.

CAST
Salome: Ludmilla Tcherina; Herod: Michael Auclaire; John the Baptist: Jean Paul Zehnocker.

A Beethoven Concert.

Performers: Zino Francescatti, violinist; Claudio Arau, pianist; Robert Casadesus, pianist.

An Evening Of Tchaikovsky And Wagner.

Performing: The French ORTF TV Orchestra conducted by George Sebastian and Charles Dutoit.

İNTERNATIONAL PERFORMANCE–60 minutes–PBS–October 5, 1972 - January 10, 1973.

INTERNATIONAL PLAYHOUSE

Anthology. Internationally produced dramas.

INTERNATIONAL PLAYHOUSE–30 minutes–Syndicated 1953.

INTERNATIONAL SHOWTIME

Variety. Highlights of various European circuses.

Host-Interpreter: Don Ameche.

Music: Performed by the various circus orchestras.

INTERNATIONAL SHOWTIME–60 minutes–NBC–September 15, 1961 - September 10, 1965.

THE INTERNS

Medical Drama. Background: New North Hospital in Los Angeles, California. The personal and professional lives of interns Greg Pettit, Lydia Thorpe, Pooch Hardin, Sam Marsh, and Cal Barrin.

The Interns. Left to right: Hal Frederick, Sandra Smith, Stephen Brooks, Mike Farrell, and Christopher Stone. © *Screen Gems.*

CAST

Dr. Peter Goldstone, the interns' supervisor	Broderick Crawford
Dr. Pooch Hardin	Christopher Stone
Dr. Lydia Thorpe	Sandra Smith
Dr. Sam Marsh	Mike Farrell
Dr. Greg Pettit	Stephen Brooks
Dr. Cal Barrin	Hal Frederick
Bobbe Marsh, Sam's wife	Elaine Giftos
Dr. Jacoby	Skip Homeier

THE INTERNS—60 minutes—CBS— September 18, 1970 - September 10, 1971.

THE INVADERS

Adventure. Driving home on a deserted country road, architect David Vincent witnesses the landing of a craft from another galaxy. Its inhabitants, aliens who appear in human form and who plan to make the Earth their world, fail in their initial attempt to destroy Vincent. Witnessing the destruction of a young alien couple before his eyes (disintegrating in a glowing light) and learning of their one flaw, a crooked finger on the right hand, he becomes their mortal enemy.

Stories depict Vincent's lone attempts to thwart alien objectives and convince a disbelieving world "that the nightmare has already begun."

CAST

David Vincent	Roy Thinnes
Edgar Scoville, his one believer and assistant	Kent Smith

Music: Dominic Frontiere.

THE INVADERS—60 minutes—ABC —January 10, 1967 - September 17, 1968. Syndicated.

THE INVESTIGATOR

Crime Drama. Background: New York City. The investigations of private detective Jeff Prior.

CAST

Jeff Prior	Lonny Chapman
Lloyd Prior, his father, a retired newspaper reporter; his occasional assistant	Howard St. John

THE INVESTIGATOR—30 minutes— NBC—June 30, 1958 - September 1958.

THE INVESTIGATORS

Crime Drama. Background: New York City. The cases of crime specialists Steve Banks and Russ Andrews, highly paid and highly skilled private insurance investigators.

CAST

Steve Banks	James Philbrook
Russ Andrews	James Franciscus
Maggie Peters, their assistant	Mary Murphy
Bill Davis, their assistant	Al Austin
June Polly, their secretary	June Kenny

THE INVESTIGATORS—60 minutes —CBS—September 21, 1961 - December 28, 1961.

THE INVISIBLE MAN

Adventure. Background: London, England. Experimenting with the problems of optical density (the refraction of light), Peter Brady, a young British scientist, is exposed to a leaking conductor and rendered invisible when the gasses mix with the oxygen.

Learning of his plight, the Ministry considers him a national menace (fearing panic to result if the existence of an invisible man is known) and imprison him.

When a rival experimentor fails to secure Brady's formula for invisibility, the Ministry is convinced otherwise and permits Brady to continue with his research.

Lacking the knowledge to become visible, Brady agrees to use his great advantage to assist the British government and undertakes hazardous missions throughout the world. Continuing his experiments, he struggles to discover the unknown formula into the realm of reality. Based on the stories by H. G. Wells.

CAST

Peter Brady, the Invisible Man	?*

*Though seen and heard, the actor's name has been withheld by the series producer, Ralph Smart, for reasons that are purely his own. One can only assume that perhaps it is to create the illusion of authenticity.

Diane Brady, his
sister   Lisa Daniely
Sally Brady, his
niece   Deborah Walting
Sir Charles, the Cabinet
Minister   Ernest Clark

THE INVISIBLE MAN—30 minutes—
Syndicated 1958.

THE INVISIBLE MAN

Science Fiction Adventure. Background: Los Angeles, California. While working on a formula to transfer matter from one place to another through the use of lazer beams, Daniel Weston, a scientist employed by the KLAE Corporation, a research center that undertakes government contracts, injects himself with a newly developed serum that renders him invisible. When he discovers that his serum is to be used for military purposes, he destroys the process and his only means by which to become visible. By wearing a special plastic face mask and hands developed by a friend, Weston appears as he did before the experiment. Stories detail Weston's investigations into highly dangerous national and international assignments on behalf of the KLAE Corporation. Based on the story by H.G. Wells.

CAST
Daniel Weston   David McCallum
Kate Weston, his
wife   Melinda Fee
Walter Carlson, his
employer   Craig Stevens
Music: Henry Mancini; Pete Rugolo.

THE INVISIBLE MAN—60 minutes—
NBC—Premiered: September 8, 1975.

INVITATION TO MURDER

Anthology. Dramatizations of stories penned by mystery writer Edgar Wallace. Later titled, with additional episodes, "The Edgar Wallace Mystery Theatre." (See title.)

INVITATION TO MURDER—60 minutes—Syndicated 1962.

I REMEMBER MAMA

Comedy-Drama. Background: San Francisco, California, 1910. The story of the Hansons, parents Marta and Lars, and their children, Katrin, Dagmar, and Nels, a Norwegian family living busily in a large American city. Events in their lives are seen through the sentimental eyes of Katrin, the older daughter, an aspiring writer who records their daily activities in her diary. Episodes focus on Mama, warm, wise, compassionate, and loving, the guiding light through their difficult times. Based on the book, *Mama's Bank Account,* by Kathryn Forbes.

CAST
Marta Hanson (Mama)   Peggy Wood
Lars Hanson (Papa), a
carpenter   Judson Laire
Katrin Hanson   Rosemary Rice
Dagmar Hanson   Robin Morgan
                    Toni Campbell
Nels Hanson   Dick Van Patten
Jenny, Mama's older
sister   Ruth Gates
Trina, Mama's younger
sister   Alice Frost
Uncle Gunnar   Carl Frank
T.R. Ryan   Kevin Coughlin
Also: Abby Lewis.
Music: Billy Nalle.

Program open:

Katrin: "I remember the big white house on Elm Street, and my little sister Dagmar, and my big brother Nels, and Papa. But most of all, I Remember Mama."

I REMEMBER MAMA—30 minutes—CBS—July 1, 1949 - March 17, 1957.

IRON HORSE

Western. Background: Wyoming during the 1870s. Ben Calhoun, a rugged gentleman cowboy, wins a near-bankrupt railroad in a poker game. Assuming control, he attempts to acquire customers, pay off overanxious creditors, replenish a lacking fund, and establish a successful operation.

CAST

Ben Calhoun	Dale Robertson
Dave Tarrant, his assistant	Gary Collins
Barnabas Rogers, his assistant	Bob Random
Nils Torvald, his assistant	Roger Torrey

Ben's horse: Hannibal.

Ben's pet raccoon: Ulysses.

IRON HORSE—60 minutes—ABC—September 12, 1966 - January 6, 1968.

IRONSIDE

Crime Drama. Background: San Francisco, California. Vacationing, Robert T. Ironside, San Francisco Police Chief, is shot by a would-be assassin. The bullet, shattering a spinal nerve junction, causes permanent paralysis.

Determined to continue his life, and his crusade against crime, he is appointed the special consultant to the San Francisco Police Department and is assigned a staff of crime fighters: Detective Sergeant Ed Brown and Policewoman Eve Whitefield (later replaced by Policewoman Fran Belding); and Mark Sanger, an ex-con who later becomes a lawyer, is "his legs" and general helper.

Stories depict their case investigations.

CAST

Chief Robert Ironside	Raymond Burr
Policewoman Eve Whitefield	Barbara Anderson
Det. Sgt. Ed Brown	Don Galloway
Mark Sanger	Don Mitchell
Policewoman Fran Belding	Elizabeth Baur
Diana Sanger, Mark's wife	Jane Pringle

Music: Marty Paich; Oliver Nelson.

IRONSIDE—60 minutes—NBC—September 14, 1967 - January 16, 1975. Syndicated title: "The Raymond Burr Show."

I SEARCH FOR ADVENTURE

Documentary. Films depicting man's quest for adventure.

Host-Narrator: Jack Douglas.

I SEARCH FOR ADVENTURE—30 minutes—Syndicated 1954.

ISIS

Adventure. Early history: Background: Ancient Egypt. Presented with a magic amulet by the Royal Sorcerer, the queen and her descendants were endowed by the power of Isis (the Egyptian goddess of Fertility) and received the ability to soar, the power of the animals, and control over the elements of earth, sea, and sky.

Three thousand years later, Andrea Thomas, a young high school science teacher on an expedition, uncovers the lost amulet and becomes heir to the secrets and powers of Isis.

Series background: The town of Lockspur. Stories relate Andrea's battle against crime as the mysterious Isis, "dedicated foe of evil, defender of the weak, and champion of truth and justice." (When holding the amulet, which she wears as a necklace, and speaking the words, "Oh mighty Isis," Andrea becomes Isis.)

The Islanders. James Philbrook (left), William Reynolds, Diane Brewster (right), and Daria Massey.

CAST

Andrea Thomas/
  Isis   JoAnna Cameron
Rick Mason,
  Andrea's friend,
  a teacher   Brian Cutler
Cindy Lee,
  Andrea's friend,
  a student at
  Lockspur High
  School   Joanna Pang
Dr. Barnes,
  the head of
  the science
  department   Albert Reed

Andrea's pet crow: Tut.

Music: Yvette Blais, Jeff Michael.

ISIS—25 minutes—CBS—Premiered: September 6, 1975.

Indies. The experiences of Sandy Wade and Zack Malloy, the pilots of the *Islander,* a two-man, one-plane airline based in the Spice Islands.

CAST

Zack Malloy   James Philbrook
Sandy Wade   William Reynolds
Whilhelmina "Steamboat Willie"
  Vandeveer, the business
  manager   Diane Brewster
Naja, a friend   Daria Massey
Shipwreck Callahan, a
  friend   Roy Wright

THE ISLANDERS—60 minutes—ABC —October 2, 1960 - January 1961. Syndicated.

THE ISLANDERS

Adventure. Background: The West

ISLANDS IN THE SUN

Travel. Visits to various tropical

islands via the sailing ship *Islanda*.

Host-Narrator: Bill Burrud.

Assistant: Minzie the Mermaid.

ISLANDS IN THE SUN—30 minutes —Syndicated 1969.

I SPY

Anthology. Tales of intrigue and espionage spanning the 16th to 20th centuries.

Host-Story Teller: Raymond Massey, appearing as Anton, the spy master.

Included:

The Amateur. The story of a girl who becomes a spy for General Stonewall Jackson when Union troops take over her father's hotel.

Starring: Mary Linn Beller.

The Baby Spy. The story of an eight-year-old boy who unknowingly does spying for the Japanese at Pearl Harbor years before World War II.

Starring: Jacques Aubochan, Richie Andrusco, Abby Lewis.

Betrayal At West Point. The events that led Benedict Arnold to betray his country.

Starring: Otto Hulett, Louis Edmonds.

I SPY—30 minutes—Syndicated 1956.

I SPY

Spy Drama. The investigations of U.S. government undercover agents Kelly Robinson and Alexander Scott. Kelly,

under the guise of an international tennis champion, and Scott, as his trainer-masseur, battle the destructive counterforces of democracy throughout the world.

CAST

Kelly Robinson	Robert Culp
Alexander Scott (Scotty)	Bill Cosby

Music: Earle Hagen; Carl Brandt.

I SPY—60 minutes—NBC—September 15, 1965 - September 9, 1968. Syndicated.

IT COULD BE YOU

Game. Contestants selected from the studio audience compete by performing stunts. Winners receive a prize that they had always wanted (stated before the game begins), but could never afford to purchase. Featured: Friend and family reunions.

Host: Bill Leyden.

Announcer: Wendell Niles.

IT COULD BE YOU—30 minutes—NBC—June 4, 1956 - September 1956.

IT HAPPENS IN SPAIN

Crime Drama. Background: Spain. The investigations of Joe Jones, a private detective who assists distressed American tourists.

CAST

Joe Jones	Scott McKay
Tina, his secretary	Elena Barra

IT HAPPENS IN SPAIN—30 minutes —Syndicated 1958.

IT PAYS TO BE IGNORANT

Comedy Game. Involved: Three regular panelists and two contestants. Each player, in turn, picks a question from "The Dunce Cap" and reads it aloud (e.g., "From what state do we get Hawaiian canned pineapple?"). The panelists provide comic answers while evading the correct response. Object: For the contestant, if at all possible, to get a word in and extract the right answer. Prizes are awarded accordingly—basically for attempting to face the panel.

Host: Tom Howard.

Panelists: Harry McNaughton, George Shelton, Lulu McConnell.

Announcer: Dick Stark.

Vocalists: The Townsmen Quartet.

Orchestra: Ray Morgan.

IT PAYS TO BE IGNORANT—30 minutes—CBS—June 6, 1949 - April 28, 1950. Based on the radio program of the same title.

IT PAYS TO BE MARRIED

Interview-Quiz. Interview segment: Married couples converse with the host and relate their marital difficulties and how they overcame them. Quiz Segment: The host reads a general-knowledge question. The couple who are first to identify themselves through a buzzer signal, receive a chance to answer. If correct, points are scored. Winners, the highest point scorers, receive three hundred and fifty dollars.

Host: Bill Goodwin.

Announcer: Jay Stewart.

IT PAYS TO BE MARRIED—30 minutes—NBC—July 4, 1955 - October 28, 1955.

IT'S ABOUT TIME

Game. Competing: Selected studio-audience members. Through clues provided by the host, contestants have to identify incidents from the past. Highest scorers (most correct responses) receive merchandise prizes.

Host: Dr. Bergen Evans.

IT'S ABOUT TIME—30 minutes—ABC 1954.

IT'S ABOUT TIME

Comedy. Distinguished by two formats.

Format One:
A rocket, launched from the NASA Space Center in Florida, penetrates a turbulence area and breaks the time barrier. Crash landing in a swamp, its astronauts, Mac and Hector, escape unharmed.

Exploring the surrounding area, they discover and rescue a young boy, Breer, trapped on a ledge. Through him they discover they have landed in the Prehistoric Era. Befriending his family, his father, Gronk, his mother, Shad, and his sister, Mlor, the astronauts, through their strange dress, customs, and inventions, are believed by others to be evil spirits and ordered killed by the Cave Boss. Relating the story of Breer's rescue, Gronk persuades the Cave Boss to spare their lives. Stories relate the astronauts attempts to adjust to a past era and locate copper to repair their disabled spacecraft.

Format Two (five months later):

Discovering a copper mine, Mac and Hector repair the rocket. However, the Cave Boss, uneasy over the astronauts presence, orders them and Gronk and his family destroyed for aiding evil spirits. Learning of their plans, Mac and Hector prepare for blast off. The Cave Family, with no where else to turn, sneak aboard the craft.

Rebreaking the time barrier and landing in present day Los Angeles, California, the Cave Family is concealed in Mac's apartment. Stories relate the Cave Family's attempts to master the ways of modern society; and Mac and Hector's efforts to conceal their presence from NASA officials.

CAST

Mac	Frank Aletter
Hector	Jack Mullaney
Gronk	Joe E. Ross
Shad	Imogene Coca
Mlor	Mary Grace
Breer	Pat Cardi
The Cave Boss	Cliff Norton
Clon, the Boss's aide	Mike Mazurki
Mrs. Boss	Kathleen Freeman
Dr. Hamilton	Jan Arvan
General Tyler	Alan DeWitt

Music: Sherwood Schwartz; Gerald Fried; George Wyle.

IT'S ABOUT TIME—30 minutes—CBS—September 11, 1966 - September 3, 1967.

IT'S A BUSINESS

Variety. Background: New York City during the 1900s. A musical comedy revolving around the operating difficulties of the Broadway Music Publishing Company. Stories depict the lives of song pluggers in an era when the performer visited the publisher to find material.

CAST

Song Plugger	Bob Haymes
Song Plugger	Leo de Lyon
The Secretary	Dorothy Loudon

IT'S A BUSINESS—30 minutes—DuMont—March 26, 1952 - May 27, .1952.

IT'S A GREAT LIFE

Comedy. Background: Hollywood, California. Recently discharged from the service, ex-G.I.s Denny David and Steve Connors answer an ad for a furnished room at the Morgan Boarding House. Renting the room, they meet and befriend Uncle Earl, the unemployed and conniving brother of its owner, Amy Morgan. A saga of three men plagued by financial matters and their harebrained attempts to terminate monetary burdens.

CAST

Denny David	Michael O'Shea
Steve Connors	William Bishop
Uncle Earl	James Dunn
Amy Morgan (widow)	Frances Bavier
Katy Morgan, her daughter	Barbara Bales

Music: David Rose.

IT'S A GREAT LIFE—30 minutes—NBC—September 7, 1954 - June 3, 1956. Syndicated.

IT'S ALWAYS JAN

Comedy. Background: New York City. The home and working lives of three career girls: Janis Stewart,

It's Alway's Jan. Left to right: Merry Anders, Janis Paige, and Patricia Bright.

widow, nightclub entertainer, and hopeful Broadway actress; Valerie Malone, a shapely blonde model; and Patricia Murphy, a secretary with a heart of gold—women sharing a Manhattan apartment. Stories depict Jan's attempts to raise her ten-year-old-daughter, Josie, and provide for her a life without the hardships of her own.

CAST

Janis Stewart	Janis Paige
Valerie Malone	Merry Anders
Patricia Murphy	Patricia Bright
Josie Stewart	Jeri Lou James
Stanley Schrieber, the delivery boy	Arch Johnson
Harry Cooper, Jan's agent	Sid Melton

IT'S ALWAYS JAN—30 minutes—CBS—September 10, 1955 - September 1, 1956.

IT'S A MAN'S WORLD

Comedy. Background: Cordella, an Ohio river town. The story of three young men, Tom Tom DeWitt, Vern Hodges, and Wes Macauley, college students residing in a houseboat docked at the water's edge. Recently orphaned when their parents were killed in an automobile accident, Wes's younger brother, Howie, also lives with them. Episodes relate their experiences as they attempt to cope with life and prove it to be a man's world.

CAST

Wes Macauley	Glenn Corbett
Tom Tom DeWitt	Ted Bessell
Vern Hodges	Randy Boone
Howie Macauley	Michael Burns
Nora	Ann Schuyler
Irene	Jan Norris
Scott	Harry Harvey
Mrs. Dodson	Kate Murtagh
Alma Jean	Jeannie Cashell
Mrs. Meredith	Mary Adams

IT'S A MAN'S WORLD—60 minutes—NBC—September 17, 1962 - January 28, 1963.

IT'S MAGIC

Children. Performances by guest magicians.

Host: Paul Tripp.

Orchestra: Hank Sylvern.

IT'S MAGIC—30 minutes—CBS—July 31, 1955 - September 1955.

IT'S NEWS TO ME

Game. Involved: Five celebrity

panelists and two competing contestants, each of whom receive thirty dollars starting money. The panelists are presented with a prop or picture relating to a news event. Four of the celebrities give false identifications of the object; the fifth states the actual newsworthiness. Contestants, vying for additional cash (ten dollars per round) have to determine which one is telling the truth. One round per game involves a dramatic reenactment of a news event with the game continuing in the same manner.

Hosts: John Daly; Walter Cronkite; Quincy Howe.

Panelists: Nina Foch, Quenton Reynolds, John Henry Faulk, Constance Bennett, Anna Lee.

Performing Reenactments: Frank Wayne.

IT'S NEWS TO ME—30 minutes— CBS—1951 - 1955.

IT'S A WONDERFUL WORLD

Travel-Documentary. Films depicting specific customs and life styles of various countries throughout the world.

Host: John Cameron Swayze.

IT'S A WONDERFUL WORLD—30 minutes—Syndicated 1963.

IT'S YOUR BET

Game. Two celebrity couples play for studio-audience members. A small, movable wall is placed between each player. One partner is asked a question via telephone to prevent the other from hearing it. He then bets points (twenty-five to one hundred) as to whether his partner "Can," or

"Can't" correctly answer it. The host then reads the question aloud. If the answer corresponds with the prediction, the team is awarded the points; if it does not, the points are awarded to their opponents. Winners: The first team scoring three hundred. The participating studio-audience members receive merchandise prizes.

Hosts, in order: Hal March; Tom Kennedy; Dick Gautier; Lyle Waggoner.

Announcer: John Harlan.

Music: Recorded.

IT'S YOUR BET—30 minutes—Syndicated 1969.

IT'S YOUR MOVE

Game. Four competing contestants comprising two teams of two. One team member acts out a charade; the other must guess it in a specified time limit. The amount of time is determined through bidding—both teams bid for the charade. The team bidding the lowest time limit receives it. If they are successful, they receive merchandise prizes.

Host: Jim Perry.

IT'S YOUR MOVE—30 minutes—Syndicated 1967.

IT TAKES A THIEF

Adventure. Through an arrangement with S.I.A. Chief Noah Bain, Alexander Mundy, a sophisticated and cunning cat burglar, is granted a pardon from prison when he agrees to become a spy for the United States government. Posing as an international playboy, he attempts to perform

It Takes a Thief. Robert Wagner and Malachi Throne.

necessary but highly dangerous feats of thievery through the use of his unique skills.

CAST
Alexander Mundy	Robert Wagner
Noah Bain	Malachi Throne
Alister Mundy, Alex's father, a master thief	Fred Astaire
S.I.A. Agent Dover	John Russell

Music: Benny Golson; Ralph Ferraro.

IT TAKES A THIEF—60 minutes—ABC—January 9, 1968 - September 9, 1969. Syndicated.

IT TAKES TWO

Game. Three competing celebrity couples. The host asks a question (e.g., "What was the total distance in feet of the Wright Brothers first flight at Kitty Hawk?"). Players, who are seated on revolving platforms, are separated. They then write their answers on a card. The platforms return and the responses are revealed. Team totals, excluding fractions, are automatically calculated. The announcer, stationed in the studio audience, selects someone who then chooses the couple he believes has come closest to the correct figure. If correct, the contestant receives an expensive merchandise prize; if incorrect, a less expensive gift is awarded.

Host: Vince Scully.

Announcer: John Harlan.

IT TAKES TWO—30 minutes—NBC—
March 31, 1969 - August 1, 1970.

IT WAS A VERY GOOD YEAR

Variety. The past is recalled through
film—the music, fads, sports, politics,
movies, radio, and television programs, and the sensational and tragic
moments of the years 1918 through
1968.

Host-Narrator: Mel Tormé.

Included:

1933—Prohitition repealed; gangster
headlines; the Model B Ford;
an interview with Sally Rand, a
hit at the Chicago World's Fair.
1939—The German invasion of
Poland; *The Wizard Of Oz* and
Gone With The Wind pre-
mieres; the opening of the New
York World's Fair.
1949—The rise of television.
1953—The ceremonies surrounding
the premiere of the 3-D movie,
The House Of Wax; the Coronation of Elizabeth II; the
Korean armistice.
1959—A review of TV's long running
"Your Hit Parade"; the Edsel;
Alaska and Hawaii celebrating
statehood; a tribute to Billie
Holliday.
1961—John F. Kennedy's inaugura-
tion; the fashion style as set by
Jackie Kennedy; paintings by
Grandma Moses.
1964—The invasion of the Beatles; the
Ranger 7 moon survey; Robert
Kennedy's appearance at the
Democratic National Conven-
tion.

IT WAS A VERY GOOD YEAR—30
minutes—ABC—May 10, 1971 -
August 30, 1971.

IVANHOE

Adventure. Background: England during the 1190s. The exploits of
Ivanhoe, a young Saxon knight, as he
battles the forces of injustice. Based
on the character created by Sir Walter
Scott.

CAST
Ivanhoe	Roger Moore
The Monk, his aide	Robert Brown
King Richard	Bruce Seton
Sir Maverick	Paul Whitsun

Music: Edwin Astley.

IVANHOE—30 minutes—Syndicated
1957. British produced.

I'VE GOT A SECRET

Game. Through question-and-answer
probe rounds, celebrity panelists have
to guess the secret of a guest contestant. Contestants receive both cash
and merchandise prizes.

Versions:

CBS—30 minutes—June 26, 1952 -
September 3, 1967.

Hosts: Garry Moore; Steve Allen.

Regular Penelists: Jayne Meadows,
Bill Cullen, Henry Morgan, Betsy
Palmer, Faye Emerson, Steve
Allen.

Announcers: John Cannon; Johnny
Olsen.

Syndicated—30 minutes—1972.

Host: Steve Allen.

Regular Panelists: Pat Carroll, Richard
Dawson, Nanette Fabray, Gene
Rayburn, Anita Gilette, Henry
Morgan, Jayne Meadows.

Announcer: Johnny Olsen.

g

THE JACK BENNY PROGRAM

Variety. A situation comedy series focusing on the home and working life of comedian Jack Benny.

CAST

Jack Benny	Himself
Mary Livingston, his wife	Herself
Rochester, Jack's valet	Eddie Anderson
Dennis Day, Jack's vocalist	Himself
Don Wilson, Jack's announcer	Himself
Professor LeBlanc, Jack's violin teacher	Mel Blanc
Harlow Wilson, Don's awkward son	Dale White
Lois Wilson, Don's wife	Lois Corbett
Schlepperman	Sam Hearn

Also: Joyce Jameson, Benny Rubin, Beverly Hills, Frank Nelson, Joe Besser, Barbara Nichols, Barbara Pepper.

Vocalists: Dennis Day; The Sportsman Quartet.

Announcer: Don Wilson.

Orchestra: Mahlon Merrick.

Format: Jack's opening monologue; followed by guests in solo and/or sketch performances.

Recurring Comedy bits: Jack's stinginess; an impenetrable underground vault; Professor LeBlanc's efforts to teach the "inept" violinst, Benny.

THE JACK BENNY PROGRAM—30 minutes—CBS—October 29, 1950 - September 15, 1964. Syndicated.

NBC—30 minutes—September 25, 1964 - September 10, 1965.

THE JACK CARSON SHOW

Variety. Music, songs, dances, and comedy sketches.

Host: Jack Carson.

Regulars: Don Ameche, Connie Towers, Kitty Kallen, Donald Richards, Peggy Ryan, Ray McDonald, The Asia Boys.

Announcers: Ed Peck; Bud Heistand.

Orchestra: Harry Sosnick; Vic Schoen.

THE JACK CARSON SHOW—60 and 30 minute versions—NBC—1950-1955.

JACK CARTER AND COMPANY

Variety. Music, songs, and comedy sketches.

Host: Jack Carter.

Regulars: Elaine Stritch, Rowena Rollin, Sonny King, Jack Albertson, Paul Castle.

JACK CARTER AND COMPANY—30 minutes—ABC—April 5, 1949 - April 21, 1949.

JACKIE GLEASON

Listed: The television programs of comedian Jackie Gleason.

The Life Of Riley—Comedy—30 minutes—DuMont—October 4, 1949 - March 28, 1950. See title.

Cavalcade Of Stars—The Jackie Gleason Show—Variety—60 minutes—DuMont—January 7, 1950 - September 13, 1952.

Host: Jackie Gleason.

Regulars: Art Carney, Pert Kelton, Audrey Meadows, Patricia Morrison, Zomah Cunningham, Joyce Randolph, The June Taylor Dancers.

Announcer: Jack Lescoulie.

Orchestra: Ray Bloch.

Characters portrayed by Jackie: Joe the Bartender—monologue with the unseen Mr. Dunahee about Crazy Guggenhiemer, Moriarty the undertaker, Duddy Duddleson, and Bookshelf Robinson; Charlie Barton the loudmouth; The Poor Soul, the well-meaning lad in an uphill battle with life; Reginald Van Gleason III, the playboy philosopher; Fenwick Babbitt, the man out for revenge against people who annoy him; Rudy, the helpless repairman; Pedro, the Mexican; Father and Son; Rum Dum, the drunk; Stanley R. Sogg.

Format: Songs, dances, and comedy sketches.

Sketch: "The Honeymooners"—the trials and tribulations of Ralph (Jackie) and Alice (Pert Kelton) Kramden (See title).

The Jackie Gleason Show—Variety—60 minutes—CBS—September 20, 1952 - June 18, 1955. "Cavalcade Of Stars" retitled after a network switch. Format/performers, same.

The Honeymooners—Comedy—30 minutes—CBS—1955-1956. (see title.)

The Jackie Gleason Show—Variety—30 minutes—CBS—1957-1959.

Host: Jackie Gleason.

Regulars: Art Carney, Audrey Meadows, Joyce Randolph,

George Petrie, Buddy Hackett, The Gleason Girls, The June Taylor Dancers, The Lyn Diddy Singers.

Announcer: Jack Lescoulie.

Orchestra: Ray Bloch.

You're In The Picture—Game—30 minutes—CBS—January 20, 1961-March 24, 1961 (see title.)

Jackie Gleason And His American Scene Magazine—Variety—60 minutes—CBS—September 29, 1962 - June 4, 1966. Sketches based on topics drawn from newspapers and weekly journals.

Host: Jackie Gleason.

Regulars: Frank Fontaine (Crazy), Sid Fields, Alice Ghostley, Sue Anne Langdon, Jan Crockett, Helen Curtis, Barbara Heller (as Christine Clam, who introduces the segments), Peter Gladke, Patricia Wilson, Phil Burns, Elizabeth Allen (the "Away We Go" girl), The Glea Girls, The June Taylor Dancers.

Announcer: Johnny Olsen.

Orchestra: Sammy Spear.

The Jackie Gleason Show—Variety—60 minutes—CBS—September 17, 1966 - September 12, 1970. Taped in Miami Beach, Florida.

Host: Jackie Gleason.

Regulars: Art Carney (as Ed Norton), Sheila MacRae (Alice Kramden), Jane Kean (Trixie Norton), and Jackie as Ralph Kramden in the rebirth of "The Honeymooners"; Lanita Kent, Jami Henderson, Andrea Duda, Carlos Bas, The Glea Girls, The June Taylor Dancers.

Announcer: Johnny Olsen.

Orchestra: Sammy Spear.

THE JACK La LANNE SHOW

Exercise. The benefits of daily systematic exercise coupled with nutritional guidance.

Host-Instructor: Jack La Lanne, physical fitness expert.

Assistant: Elaine La Lanne (Mrs.)

Dogs: Happy and Walter.

THE JACK La LANNE SHOW—30 minutes—Syndicated—1951-1960; 1961-1965; 1966-1970.

JACK PAAR

Listed: The programs of comedian Jack Paar.

I've Got News For You—Game—30 minutes—NBC—July 28, 1952 - September 26, 1952.

Host: Jack Paar.

Format: Three competing players answer questions based on articles appearing in newspapers.

Bank On The Stars—Game—30 minutes—CBS—1953. (See title.)

The Jack Paar Show—Variety—30 minutes—CBS—November 11, 1953 - May 24, 1956.

Host: Jack Paar.

Regulars: Edie Adams, Richard Hayes, Martha Wright, Betty Clooney, Johnny Desmond, Jose Melis.

Announcer: Hal Simms.

Orchestra: Pupi Campo.

The Morning Show—Variety—CBS—1954. (See title.)

The Jack Paar Show—Variety—30 minutes—CBS—August 16, 1954 - July 1, 1955.

Host: Jack Paar.

Regulars: Edie Adams, Jack Haskell.

Announcer: Jack Haskell.

Orchestra: Jose Melis.

The Tonight Show—Variety—105 minutes—NBC—July 29, 1957 - April 30, 1962 (Jack's run as host). (See title.)

The Jack Paar Show—Variety—60 minutes—NBC—September 21, 1962 - September 10, 1965.

Host: Jack Paar.

Orchestra: Jose Melis.

Jack Paar Tonight—Variety—90 minutes—ABC—January 8, 1973 - November 16, 1973. Broadcast as part of "The ABC Wide World of Entertainment" series. Seen five times each month.

Host: Jack Paar.

Co-Host: Peggy Cass.

Announcer: Peggy Cass.

Orchestra: Charles Randolph Grean.

JACKPOT

Game. Sixteen contestants, competing for one week, vie for the opportunity to win up to $50,000 in cash. Each player possesses a different riddle, one the "Jackpot Riddle," worth from five to two hundred dollars. A target number (e.g., five hundred) is established and becomes the cash amount for the jackpot. One player, designated as "The Expert" calls on other players one at a time. The chosen player states the cash value of his riddle, then reads it. The money is calculated on a board; if the player solves it, he remains; if he fails to solve it, he trades places with the person who stumped him. Each riddle that is solved increases the money in the jackpot, but two plateaus have to be overcome before a player can win it. First, the jackpot amount has to be equaled or surpassed by answering riddles; and secondly, only by selecting the person possessing the "Jackpot Riddle" and correctly answering it. If successful, the expert and the player divide the money and a new game begins. If unsuccessful, the game still ends, but players do not receive anything. Should the "Jackpot Riddle" be selected before the target number is equaled, it is voided until the amount is reached. After the "Jackpot Riddle" has been selected, it can be answered at any time as determined by the expert who will either increase the money in the jackpot by continuing to answer riddles or stop when feeling safe and attempt to answer it. "The Super Jackpot." After the target number is established (e.g., five-hundred) a multiplication figure from five to fifty is established (e.g., ten). If the expert matches the target number exactly through riddles, or if the last three digits of the jackpot match the target number, he receives a chance to answer the "Super Jackpot Riddle," which is possessed by the host. If it is correctly answered, the expert receives the money that figures when the target number is multiplied by the random multiplication figure (e.g., $5000).

Host: Geoff Edwards.

Announcer: Don Pardo.

Music: Recorded.

JACKPOT—30 minutes—NBC—January 7, 1974 - September 26, 1975.

THE JACKSON FIVE

Animated Cartoon. The misadventures of the Jackson Five, a Motown rock group.

Voices: The Jackson Five (brothers): Tito, Jackie, Michael, Marion, Jermaine.

Additional voices: Paul Frees, Edmund Silvers, Joe Cooper.

Background Music: Maury Laws.

THE JACKSON FIVE—30 minutes—ABC—September 11, 1971 - September 1, 1973.

THE JACQUELINE SUSANN SHOW

Women. Fashion previews, guests, and interviews.

Hostess: Jacqueline Susann.

Announcer: John McNight.

THE JACQUELINE SUSANN SHOW —30 minutes—DuMont 1951; 30 minutes—ABC 1953.

JACQUES FRAY'S MUSIC ROOM

Musical Variety.

Host: Jacques Fray.

Regulars: Bess Myerson, Jeri Nagle, Conrad Thibault, Bob Calder, Joan Francis, Russell & Aura, Fredo Gordoni.

Orchestra: Charles Stark.

JACQUES FRAY'S MUSIC ROOM—30 minutes—ABC 1949.

JAMBO

Adventure. Stories of African wildlife.

Host-Storyteller: Marshall Thompson.

Assistant: Judy the Chimp.

JAMBO—30 minutes—NBC—September 6, 1969 - September 4, 1971.

JAMBOREE

Musical Variety.

Hostess: Gloria Van.

Regulars: Danny O'Neill, Jane Brockman, Bud Tygett, Jimmy McPartland, Dick Edwards, "Woo Woo" Stevens, Paula Raye, John Dolie.

Orchestra: Julian Stockdale.

JAMBOREE—60 minutes—DuMont 1950.

JAMES BEARD

Women. The preparation of gourmet meals; fashion, decorating ideas, and related subjects of interest to housewives.

Host: James Beard, gourmet, chef, cookbook author.

JAMES BEARD—30 minutes—Syndicated 1963.

JAMES GARNER AS NICHOLS

See title: "Nichols."

JAMIE

Comedy. The story of Jamieson John Francis McHummer (Jamie), an orphan who comes to live with his relatives (his grandfather, Cousin Liz, and Aunt Laurie) after the death of his parents. The focal point of the series is the relationship between a young boy (Jamie) and an old man (his grandfather).

CAST
Jamie McHummer	Brandon De Wilde
Grandpa McHummer	Ernest Truex
Liz McHummer	Kathleen Nolan
Laurie McHummer	Polly Rowles
Annie Moakum, Laurie's assistant in her catering business	Alice Pearce

Music: Jacques Press.

JAMIE—30 minutes—ABC—September 28, 1953 - October 4, 1954. The pilot was broadcast as part of "ABC Album" shown April 26, 1953.

THE JAN MURRAY SHOW

Variety. Presented following the NBC network fights.

Host: Jan Murray.

Regulars: Tina Louise, Fletcher Peck, The Novelettes.

THE JAN MURRAY SHOW—15 minutes (approx.)—NBC 1955.

JANE FROMAN'S U.S.A. CANTEEN

Variety. Entertainment set against the background of an armed-services canteen. Performances by men and women in military service.

Hostess: Jane Froman, "The girl with a song in her heart."

Featured: The Peter Birch Dancers.

Announcer: Allyn Edwards.

Orchestra: Alfredo Antonini; Hank Sylvern.

JANE FROMAN'S U.S.A. CANTEEN —15 minutes—CBS—October 18, 1952 - July 2, 1953. As "The Jane Froman Show"—15 minutes—CBS—September 1, 1953 - June 23, 1955.

THE JANE PICKENS SHOW

Musical Variety.

Hostess: Jane Pickens.

Featured: The Vikings.

THE JANE PICKENS SHOW—15 minutes—ABC—January 31, 1954 - April 11, 1954.

JANET DEAN, REGISTERED NURSE

Drama. Background: New York City. The cases of Janet Dean, a private-duty nurse. Incorporating applied psychology, she seeks the facts behind patients' problems and attempts to attribute most illnesses as psychosomatic.

Starring: Ella Raines as Janet Dean.

JANET DEAN, REGISTERED NURSE—30 minutes—Syndicated 1954.

JANE WYMAN'S SUMMER PLAYHOUSE

Anthology. Rebroadcasts of dramas that were originally aired via "The Jane Wyman Theatre."

Hostess: Jane Wyman.

JANE WYMAN'S SUMMER PLAYHOUSE—30 minutes—CBS—June 1957 - September 1957.

THE JANE WYMAN THEATRE

Anthology. Tense, highly dramatic presentations.

Hostess: Jane Wyman.

Music: Melvyn Lenard.

Included:

Helpmate. A wife attempts to help her detective husband solve a case.

CAST
Janet Blaine: Imogene Coca; Henry Blaine: Dabbs Greer; Dino: Vincent Barnett.

The Girl On The Drum. The difficulties that arise from a respectable married businessman's involvement with a nightclub dancer.

CAST
Guy Whitman: Jack Kelly; Lonita: Lita Baron; Kenneth Neville: Carleton G. Young.

The Black Road. The effect of a black-sheep member on his family.

CAST
David Ederly: Robert Horton; Jenny: Judith Ames; Mrs. Ederly: Dorothy Adams.

The Wildcatter. A hotel owner attempts to strike oil after borrowing money from a woman cattle rancher.

CAST
Stella Gates: Virginia Grey; Jack: Claude Atkins; Germine: Dabbs Greer.

A Place On The Bay. Dissatisfied with life on a houseboat, a wife attempts to convince her husband, an author, that the atmosphere is not necessary for writing best-selling novels.

CAST
Hal Robertson: Gene Barry; Laura Robertson: Gloria Talbot.

THE JANE WYMAN THEATRE—30 minutes—ABC—1956 - 1961.

The Jaye P. Morgan Show. Jaye P. Morgan.

THE JAYE P. MORGAN SHOW

Musical Variety.

Hostess: Jaye P. Morgan.

Regulars: The Morgan Brothers (Dick, Bob, Charlie, and Duke—Jaye's real-life brothers).

Orchestra: Joel Herron.

THE JAYE P. MORGAN SHOW—15 minutes—NBC—June 13, 1956 - September 1956. The Summer replacement for "Eddie Fisher's Coke Time."

JAZZ ALLEY

Music. The Jazz music of Chicago during the 1920s coupled with interviews and representative guests.

Host: Art Hodes.

Music: The Hodes Combo.

JAZZ ALLEY—30 minutes—NET—September 3, 1969 - October 9, 1969.

THE JEAN ARTHUR SHOW

Comedy. Background: Los Angeles, California. The investigations and courtroom defenses of a mother-and-son legal team, Patricia and Paul Marshall (Marshall & Marshall, attorneys at law).

CAST

Patricia Marshall (a widow)	Jean Arthur
Paul Marshall	Ron Harper
Mr. Morton	Leonard Stone
Richie Wells, a reformed hood	Richard Conte

Music: Johnny Keating.

THE JEAN ARTHUR SHOW—30 minutes—CBS—September 12, 1966 - December 12, 1966.

THE JEAN CARROLL SHOW

See title: "Take It from Me."

JEANNIE

Animated Cartoon. A spin-off from "I Dream of Jeannie." Background: Center City. Surfing, Corey Anders, a high school senior, is overcome by a wave that washes him upon the shore and exposes a bottle that was buried in the sand. Upon opening it, a beautiful young genie, named Jeannie, and her friend, an inept apprentice genie, Babu, emerge and become his slaves.

Stories depict Corey's attempts to conceal their presence and live the normal life of a teenager; and Jeannie's efforts to adjust to life in the 1970s and to protect Corey from the wiles of other girls.

Unlike Barbara Eden's portrayal of Jeannie ("I Dream of Jeannie"), whose powers are evoked by crossing her hands over her chest and blinking her eyes, the animated Jeannie's powers are in her pony tail.

Additional characters: Henry Glopp, Corey's friend, the only other person aware of Jeannie's presence; S. Melvin Fathinggale, a friend; Mrs. Anders, Corey's mother; Hadji, the master of all genies.

Voices: Julie Bennett, Joe Besser, Guy Autterson, Indira Danks, Ginny Tyler, John Stephenson, Don Messick, Sherry Alberoni, Vincent Van Patten, Judy Strangis, Hal Smith, Tommy Cook, Bob Hastings.

Music: Hoyt Curtin, Paul DeKorte.

JEANNIE—30 minutes—CBS—September 8, 1973 - August 30, 1975.

Jefferson Drum. Karen Steele (guest), star Jeff Richards.

JEFFERSON DRUM

Western. Background: The ruthless, lawless gold-mining town of Jubilee during the 1850s. The story of Jefferson Drum, widower, an embittered newspaper publisher struggling to establish peace through the power of the press.

CAST

Jefferson Drum	Jeff Richards
Joey Drum, his son	Eugene Martin
Lucius Coin, his type- setter	Cyril Delevanti
Big Ed, a friend	Robert J. Stevenson

JEFFERSON DRUM—30 minutes—NBC—April 25, 1958 - April 23, 1959. Original title: "The Pen and the Quill."

THE JEFFERSONS

Comedy. Background: A fashionable East Side apartment in Manhattan. The trials and tribulations of the Jefferson family: George, the snobbish, pompous, and wealthy owner of several dry cleaning establishments; Louise, his tolerant, long-suffering wife; and Lionel, their twenty-two-year-old son. A spin-off from "All in the Family."

CAST

George Jefferson	Sherman Hemsley
Louise Jefferson	Isabel Sanford
Lionel Jefferson	Mike Evans
	Damon Evans
Tom Willis, their neighbor	Franklin Cover
Helen Willis, his wife	Roxie Roker
Jenny Willis, their daughter	Berlinda Tolbert

Harry Bentley,
  the Jefferson's
  neighbor   Paul Benedict
Mrs. Jefferson, George's
  mother   Zara Cully

Music: Jeff Berry, Ja'net DuBois.

THE   JEFFERSONS—30   minutes—
CBS—Premiered: January 17, 1975.

JEFF'S COLLIE

See title: "Lassie."

JENNIE:
LADY RANDOLPH CHURCHILL

Biography. A seven-part series that
dramatizes the life of Winston
Churchill's American mother, Lady
Randolph Churchill (nee Jeannie
Jerome, 1854-1921).

CAST
Lady Randolph
  Churchill   Lee Remick
Lord Randolph
  Churchill   Ronald Pickup
Mr. Jerome   Dan O'Herlihy
Mrs. Jerome   Helen Horton
Leonie   Barbara Parkins
Clara   Linda Lilies
Duke of
  Marlborough   Rachel Kempson
Prince of Wales   Thorley Walters
Montie Porch   Charles Kay
Sir Henry James   John Barley
George Cornwallis-
  West   Christopher Cazenove
Bertha   Barbara Laurenson

Music Theme: Andre Previn.

Music Score: Tom McCall.

JENNIE: LADY   RANDOLPH

CHURCHILL—60   minutes—PBS—
October 8, 1975 - November 19
1975.

JEOPARDY

Game. Three competing players, a
champion and two challengers. Object: To supply questions to given
answers. A large board is revealed
containing six subject categories (e.g.,
Say When, Television, Presidents,
Movies, Alphabet, The Color Blue,
Opera). Each one has five answers
with monetary values increasing as the
questions increase in difficulty. The
champion chooses a subject and an
amount. The host then states the
answer as it is revealed on the board
(e.g., Subject, Movies: "A musical
spoof of the old West starring Doris
Day."). The first player to sound his
buzzer receives the chance to supply
the question ("What is *Calamity
Jane?*"). If correct, he earns its cash
value; if incorrect, the amount is
deducted. The person with the last
correct answer chooses the next category and amount.

Round One: Single Jeopardy. Question values of ten, twenty, thirty,
forty, and fifty dollars.

Round Two: Double Jeopardy. Cash
values double from twenty to one
hundred dollars.

Round Three: Final Jeopardy. One
category topic is stated. Players are
permitted to wager any amount of
their accumulated earnings. The
answer is stated and each player is
allotted thirty seconds to write down
the question. The players' questions
are revealed and cash is added or

deducted accordingly. Winners are the highest cash scorers.

Bonus: The Daily Double. Round one contains one Daily Double hidden somewhere on the board; round two features two. When a Daily double sign appears, the player may wager any or all of his earnings. The answer is given; and only the one player may answer. Cash is added or deducted accordingly.

Host: Art Fleming.

Announcer: Don Pardo.

Music: Recorded.

JEOPARDY—30 minutes—NBC—April 30, 1964 - January 3, 1975.

JERICHO

Adventure. Background: Europe during World War II. The exploits of three Allied agents: Franklin Sheppard, American, Nicholas Gage, Englishman, and Jean-Gatson André, Frenchman. Stories relate their attempts to infiltrate enemy lines and sabotage and discredit the Germans. (Jericho is the code name under which they operate.)

CAST
Franklin Sheppard	Don Francs
Nicholas Gage	John Leyton
Jean-Gaston André	Marino Maśe

JERICHO—60 minutes—CBS—September 15, 1966 - January 1967. Also known as: "Code Name Jericho."

THE JERRY COLONNA SHOW

Variety. Music, songs, and comedy sketches.

Host: Jerry Colonna.

Regulars: Barbara Ruick, Gordon Polk, Frankie Laine, Arthur Duncan, Isobel Randolph, Louis Colonna.

Announcer: Del Sharbutt.

Orchestra: The Cookie Fairchild Band.

THE JERRY COLONNA SHOW—30 minutes—ABC—May 28, 1951 - September 1951.

THE JERRY LESTER SHOW

Variety. Music, songs, and comedy sketches.

Host: Jerry Lester.

Regulars: Nancy Walker, Betty George, Bobby Sherwood, Lorenzo Fuller, Leon Belasco, Kathy Callin, Ellie Russell.

Orchestra: Buddy Weed.

THE JERRY LESTER SHOW—60 minutes—Syndicated 1953.

JERRY LEWIS

Listed: The television programs of comedian Jerry Lewis.

The Jerry Lewis Show—Talk-Variety—2 hours—ABC—September 21, 1963 - December 22, 1963.

Format: Guests, conversation, and entertainment acts.

Host: Jerry Lewis.

Announcer: Del Moore.

Orchestra: Lou Brown.

The Jerry Lewis Show—Variety—60 minutes—NBC—September 12, 1967 - May 26, 1969.

Format: Music, songs, and comedy sketches.

Host: Jerry Lewis.

Regulars: Bob Harvey, Debbie Macomber, The Osmond Brothers, The George Wyle Singers, The Nick Castle Dancers.

Orchestra: Lou Brown.

Will The Real Jerry Lewis Please Sit Down—Animated Cartoon—30 minutes—ABC—September 12, 1970 - September 2, 1972. (See title.)

The Jerry Lewis Labor Day Telethon. A twenty-four-hour fund-raising telethon for muscular dystrophy. What started twelve years ago as a small local telethon is now a national event that raised over sixteen million dollars Labor Day 1974.

THE JERRY REED
WHEN YOU'RE HOT,
YOU'RE HOT HOUR

Variety. Music, songs, and comedy sketches played against a Country and Western background.

Host: Jerry Reed.

Regulars: Cal Wilson, Spencer Quinn, Merie Earle, John Twomey, Norman Alexander, The Lou Regas Dancers.

Announcer: Bill Thompson.

Orchestra: George Wyle.

Premiere Guests: The Lennon Sisters—Kathy, Peggy, Janet and Diane; Artie Johnson.

THE JERRY REED WHEN YOU'RE HOT, YOU'RE HOT HOUR—60 minutes—CBS—June 20, 1972 - July 25, 1972.

JERRY VISITS

Interview. Hollywood celebrities open their homes to television cameras and reveal their dreams, their ambitions, and aspects of their private and public lives.

Host: Jerry Dunphy, Los Angeles newsman.

Appearing: Glenn Ford, Barbara Feldon, Barbara Eden and Michael Ansara (Mr. and Mrs.), Sue Anne Langdon, Carroll O'Connor, Phyllis Diller, Elke Sommer, Amanda Blake, Eva Gabor, Rod Steiger, Greg Morris, Jerry Lewis, Irene Ryan, Dennis Weaver, Mike Connors.

An announcer and music are not used.

JERRY VISITS—30 minutes—Syndicated 1971.

JET JACKSON,
FLYING COMMANDO

See title: "Captain Midnight."

THE JETSONS

Animated Cartoon. Background: Twenty-first-century Earth. The trials and tribulations of the Jetsons, an ultramodern family: George, an employee of Spacely Space Sprockets; his wife Jane; and their children, Judy and Elroy. A Hanna-Barbera production.

Characters' Voices

George Jetson	George O'Hanlon
Jane Jetson	Penny Singleton
Judy Jetson	Janet Waldo
Elroy Jetson	Daws Butler
Mr. Spacely, George's	

THE JIM BACKUS SHOW— HOT OFF THE WIRE

Comedy. The misadventures of John Michael O'Toole, editor-reporter of the *Headline Press Service,* a newspaper in financial trouble. Episodes depict his efforts to dodge creditors, acquire major stories, and improve circulation to obtain needed resources.

CAST

John Michael O'Toole	Jim Backus
Dora, his assistant	Nita Talbot
Sidney, the office boy	Bobs Watson

THE JIM BACKUS SHOW—HOT OFF THE WIRE—30 minutes—Syndicated 1960.

JIMMIE RODGERS

Listed: The television programs of singer Jimmie Rodgers.

The Jimmie Rodgers Show—Musical Variety—30 minutes—NBC—March 31, 1959 - September 7, 1959.

Host: Jimmie Rodgers.

Regulars: Connie Francis, The Kirby Stone Four, The Clay Warnick Singers.

Orchestra: Buddy Morrow.

The Jimmie Rodgers Show—Musical Variety—60 minutes—CBS—June 16, 1969 - September 8, 1969.

Host: Jimmie Rodgers.

Regulars: Vicki Lawrence, Lyle Waggoner, Nancy Austin, Don Crichton, Bill Fanning, The Burgundy Street Singers.

Announcer: Lyle Waggoner.

Orchestra: Harry Zimmerman.

The Jetsons. The Jetson family (left to right): Elroy, Jane, George, and Judy. *Courtesy Hanna-Barbera Productions.*

employer	Mel Blanc
Astro, the Jeston family dog	Don Messick
Rosie, the Jetson electronic maid	Jean VanderPyl

Additional Voices: Shepard Menkin, Howard Morris.

Music: Hoyt Curtin.

THE JETSONS—30 minutes. ABC—September 1962 - September 1964; CBS—September 4, 1965 - September 3, 1966; NBC—September 10, 1966 - September 2, 1967; CBS—September 13, 1969 - September 5, 1970; NBC—September 11, 1971 - September 1975.

JIGSAW

See title: "The Men," *Jigsaw* segment.

JIMMY DEAN

Listed: The television programs of singer Jimmy Dean.

The Jimmy Dean Show—Country-Western Musical Variety—CBS. 6C minutes—April 8, 1957 - November 23, 1957; 45 minutes—June 1957 - August 1958; 30 minutes—September 15, 1958 - January 26, 1959.

Host: Jimmy Dean.

Regulars: Jeri Miyazaki, Mary Kluck, Joan Crockett, Jo Davis, Herbie Jones, The Double Daters, The Country Lads, The Noteworthies, Alec Houston's Wildcats.

Orchestra: Joel Herron.

The Jimmy Dean Show—Country-Western Musical Variety—60 minutes

The Jimmy Dean Show. Left to right: Guest Jaye P. Morgan, host Jimmy Dean, and guest Jane Morgan.

—ABC—September 19, 1963 - April 1, 1966.

Host: Jimmy Dean.

Regulars: Molly Bee; Rowlf, the hound dog muppet; The Grass Roots Band; The Doerr Hutchinson Dancers, The Chuck Cassey Singers.

Orchestra: Peter Matz; Al Pellegrini; Don Sebesky.

The Jimmy Dean Show—Country-Western Musical Variety—30 minutes—Syndicated 1974.

Host: Jimmy Dean.

Vocalists: The Imperials.

JIMMY DURANTE

Listed: The television programs of comedian Jimmy Durante.

The Buick Circus Hour—Variety—60 minutes—NBC—October 7, 1952 - June 6, 1953. (See title.)

The Texaco Star Theatre—Comedy-Variety—60 minutes—NBC—October 2, 1954 - September 24, 1955.

Host: Jimmy Durante.

Regulars: Eddie Jackson, Jack Roth, Jules Buffano, The Durante Girls.

Orchestra: Allen Roth; Roy Bargy.

The Jimmy Durante Show—Variety—30 minutes—CBS—June 1957 - September 1957. Featured: Kinescope highlights of "Star Theatre."

Host: Jimmy Durante.

Regulars: Eddie Jackson, Jack Roth, Jules Buffano.

Orchestra: Roy Bargy.

Jimmy Durante Presents the Lennon Sisters Hour. The Lennon Sisters: (left to right) Dianne, Kathy, Peggy, and Janet.

Jimmy Durante Presents The Lennon Sisters Hour—Musical Variety—60 minutes—ABC—September 26, 1969 - July 4, 1970. (See title.)

JIMMY DURANTE PRESENTS THE LENNON SISTERS HOUR

Variety. Music, songs, dances, and comedy sketches.

Host: Jimmy Durante.

Hostesses: The Lennon Sisters: Diane, Peggy, Cathy, and Janet.

Regulars: Edna O'Dell, Bernie Kukoff.

Announcers: Charlie O'Donnell; Jay Stewart.

Orchestra: George Wyle.

Format:

The Lennons' opening song, an up-tempo of a current hit.

Jimmy's solo, seated at the piano.
Guests in solo and/or sketch performance.
"At Home." The girls relate aspects of their private lives.
"City Salute." A weekly musical tribute to cities around the country.

Closing (The Lennons, singing):
    "...May the Good Lord bless you, and may He always send you a happy day. Goodnight."

JIMMY DURANTE PRESENTS THE LENNON SISTERS HOUR—60 minutes—ABC—September 26, 1969 - July 4, 1970.

JIMMY HUGHES, ROOKIE COP

Crime. Drama. Background: New York City. Returning home from service in Korea, and learning that his father, a policeman, has been killed in the performance of duty, Jimmy Hughes joins the force in an attempt to apprehend the slayers. Learning to serve for reasons other than revenge and finding that teamwork and concern for others are more important than individual action or motivation, he is presented with his father's badge.

Stories concern the life and problems faced by Jimmy Hughes, a rookie cop.

CAST
Jimmy Hughes	Billy Redfield
His sister	Wendy Drew
Inspector Ferguson	Rusty Lane

JIMMY HUGHES, ROOKIE COP—30 minutes—DuMont—May 8, 1953 - July 3, 1953.

THE JIMMY STEWART SHOW

Comedy. Background: 35 Hillview Drive, Easy Valley, California, the residence of three generations of Howards: James K., an anthropology professor at Josiah Kessel College; Martha, his wife of thirty years; Teddy, their eight-year-old son; Peter Jacob (P.J.), their twenty-nine year old married son, a construction engineer; his wife, Wendy; and their eight-year-old son, Jake.

Stories depict the home and working life of James Howard, and the problems that ensue when generations clash.

CAST

James Howard	Jimmy Stewart
Martha Howard	Julie Adams
P.J. Howard	Jonathan Daly
Wendy Howard	Ellen Geer
Teddy Howard	Dennis Larson
Jake Howard	Kirby Furlong
Luther Quince, a wealthy friend, the Chemistry Professor	John McGiver

Music: Van Alexander.

THE JIMMY STEWART SHOW—30 minutes—NBC—September 19, 1971 - September 3, 1972.

THE JIM NABORS HOUR

Variety. Music, songs, dances, and comedy sketches.

Host: Jim Nabors.

Regulars: Frank Sutton, Ronnie Schell, Karen Morrow, The Tony Mordente Dancers, The Nabors Kids.

Orchestra: Paul Weston.

Segments: "The Brothers-In-Law." Jim as Loomis; Frank as Harry, his quarrelsome brother-in-law; Karen as Blanche, Harry's wife; and Ronnie as Audie, the boarding house drunk.

"Bruce Baroque." Ronnie Schell as a mod interior decorator decorating the most unlikely places and/or object, e.g., caves, submarines, motorcycles.

THE JIM NABORS HOUR—60 minutes—CBS—September 25, 1969 - May 20, 1971.

THE JIM STAFFORD SHOW

Variety. Music, songs, dances, and comedy sketches.

Host: Jim Stafford.

Regulars: Valerie Curtin, Richard Stahl, Phil MacKenzie, Deborah Allen, Jeannie Sheffield, Tom Byner.

Announcers: Dick Tufel; Bill Thompson.

Orchestra: Eddie Karam.

THE JIM STAFFORD SHOW—60 minutes—ABC—July 30, 1975 - September 3, 1975.

JOANNE CARSON'S V.I.P.'s

Variety. Guests, interviews, cooking and household hints.

Hostess: Joanne Carson.

Announcer: Hugh Douger.

Music: Recorded.

JOANNE CARSON'S V.I.P.'s—30 minutes—Syndicated 1972.

JOE AND MABEL

Comedy. Background: New York City. The story of two young lovers: Joe Spartan, a cab driver who feels he is not ready to take on the responsibilities of marriage, and Mabel Spooner, a manicurist who yearns to become his wife. Episodes depict her attempts to change his mind by demonstrating her wifely interests; and Joe's attempts to avoid the paths of matrimony and retain a single life.

CAST
Joe Spartan	Larry Blyden
Mabel Spooner	Nita Talbot
Mrs. Spooner, Mabel's mother	Luella Gear
Sherman Spooner, Mabel's younger brother	Michael Mann
Mike, Joe's friend, a cabbie	Norman Field

JOE AND MABEL—30 minutes—CBS —September 20, 1955 - September 25, 1956.

JOE AND SONS

Comedy. Background: Erie, Pennsylvania. The trials and tribulations of widower Joe Vitale, a sheet metal worker, as he struggles to raise his teenage sons, Mark and Nick.

CAST
Joe Vitale	Richard Castellano
Mark Vitale	Barry Miller
Nick Vitale	Jimmy Baio
Gus, Joe's wise-cracking friend	Jerry Stiller
Josephine, Joe's sister	Florence Stanley
Estelle, Joe's neighbor, a cocktail waitress	Bobbi Jordan

Music: David Shire.

JOE AND SONS—30 minutes—CBS— September 9, 1975 - January 13, 1976.

JOE FORRESTER

Crime Drama. Background: An unidentified American City. The story of Joe Forrester, a veteran policeman who rejects a desk job and chooses to remain in uniform to walk his old beat—a rundown neighborhood that he now wants to build up again.

CAST
Officer Joe Forrester	Lloyd Bridges
Sgt. Bernie Vincent, his superior	Eddie Egan
Georgia Cameron, Joe's girlfriend, a cocktail lounge hostess	Patricia Crowley
Jolene, Joe's informant	Dawn Smith

Music: Richard Markowitz; Robert Dransin.

JOE FORRESTER—60 minutes— NBC—Premiered: September 9, 1975.

THE JOE FRANKLIN SHOW

Variety. Interviews with show business personalities; undiscovered professional talent; and films—the trip down memory lane—rarely or never before seen on television.

Basically, aired locally in New York; certain tribute programs (e.g., Louis Armstrong), are syndicated.

Host: Joe Franklin.

Appearing: Marilyn Monroe, George

The Joe Franklin Show. Guest George Jessel (left) and host Joe Franklin. *Courtesy of Joe Franklin.*

Jessel, Ruta Lee, Bobby Darin, Hugh O'Brian, Connie Stevens, Ray Anthony, Kay Stevens, Tony Sandler, Ralph Young, Bill Cosby, Woody Allen, Flip Wilson.

Music: Recorded (theme: "12th Street Rag").

THE JOE FRANKLIN SHOW—Various running times, but most often 60 minutes—WABC-TV (Ch. 7); WOR-TV—1954 - Present (1975).

THE JOE NAMATH SHOW

Interview. Interviews with sports and show-business personalities.

Host: Joe Namath.

Co-Host: Dick Schaap.

Announcer-Assistant: Louisa Moritz.

Music: Recorded.

Artist: LeRoy Neiman (sketches guests).

THE JOE NAMATH SHOW—30 minutes—Syndicated 1969.

THE JOE PALOOKA STORY

Comedy-Drama. Background: New York City. The fictitious story of heavyweight boxer Joe Palooka, a clean living, moral champ ignorant of gambling, fixed fights, blonde sirens, and nightclubs. Based on the character created by Ham Fisher.

CAST

Joe Palooka	Joe Kirkwood, Jr.
Ann Howe, his girl-friend	Cathy Downs
Knobby Walsh, his manager	Luis Van Rooten
	Sid Tomack
Humphrey Pennyworth, Joe's trainer	Maxie Rosenbloom

THE JOE PALOOKA STORY—30 minutes—Syndicated 1954.

THE JOE PYNE SHOW

Discussion. A controversial-issues debate.

Host: Joe Pyne.

Music: Recorded.

THE JOE PYNE SHOW—2 hours—Syndicated 1966.

JOEY AND DAD

Variety. Music, songs, dances, and comedy sketches.

Hostess: Joey Heatherton.

Host: Ray Heatherton (her father).

Regulars: Pat Paulsen, Henny Youngman, Pat Proft, Bob Einstein, Nick Nicholas.

Announcer: Peter Cullen; Roger Carroll.

Orchestra: Lex de Azevedo.

Special Musical Material: David Black.

JOEY AND DAD—60 minutes—CBS—July 6, 1975 - July 27, 1975.

JOEY BISHOP

Listed: The television programs of comedian Joey Bishop.

The Joey Bishop Show—Comedy—30 minutes—NBC—September 20, 1961 - June 20, 1962. Pilot aired via "The Danny Thomas Show."

Background: Hollywood, California. The life of Joey Barnes, a trouble-prone public-relations man with the advertising firm of Wellington, Willoughby, and Jones.

CAST

Joey Barnes	Joey Bishop
Stella Barnes, his stage-struck sister	Marlo Thomas
Mrs. Barnes, his widowed mother	Madge Blake
Larry Barnes, his younger brother	Warren Berlinger
Betty Barnes, his older sister	Virginia Vincent
Frank, his brother-in-law	Joe Flynn
Barbara, Joey's girl-friend	Nancy Hadley
J.R. Willoughby, Joey's employer	John Briggs
Peggy, J.R.'s secretary	Jackie Russell

Music: Earle Hagen.

The Joey Bishop Show—Comedy—30 minutes. NBC—September 15, 1962 - September 20, 1964. CBS—September 27, 1964 - September 7, 1965.

Background: New York City. The home and working life of nightclub comedian Joey Barnes.

CAST

Joey Barnes	Joey Bishop
Ellie Barnes, his wife	Abby Dalton

Jillson, the land-
　　lord　　　　　　Joe Besser
Freddie, Joey's
　　manager　　　　Guy Marks
Larry, Joey's
　　writer　　　　Corbett Monica
Hilda, the Barnes's baby's
　　nurse　　　　　Mary Treen
Dr. Nolan, the baby's
　　doctor　　　　　Joey Froman
Joey Barnes, Jr., Joey and
　　Ellie's son　Matthew David Smith
Music: Earle Hagen.

The Joey Bishop Show—Talk-Variety
—90 minutes—ABC—April 17, 1967 -
December 20, 1969.

Host: Joey Bishop.

Announcer: Regis Philbin.

Orchestra: Johnny Mann.

THE JOHN BYNER COMEDY HOUR

Variety. Music, songs, and comedy
sketches.

Host: John Byner.

Regulars: Patty Deutsch, Linda Sub-
lette, R. G. Brown, Gary Miller,
Dennis Flannigan, The Lori
Regas Dancers.

Announcer: Bill Thompson.

Orchestra: Ray Charles.

Premiere Guests: Annette Funicello,
Frankie Avalon.

Segments:
"Dr. Felix Fosididde." John as a
strange-voiced vet attempting to
solve field-related problems.
"The Blant Family." A comical take-
off on soap operas.
"Father John." John as a Catholic
priest facing the problems of a
modern world.

THE JOHN BYNER COMEDY
HOUR—60 minutes—CBS—August 1,
1972 - August 29, 1972.

THE JOHN DAVIDSON SHOW

Variety. Music, songs, dances, and
comedy sketches.

Host: John Davidson.

Regulars: Rich Little, Mireille Mathieu
(French songstress), Amy
McDonald (comedienne).

Orchestra: Jack Parnell.

THE JOHN DAVIDSON SHOW—60
minutes—ABC—May 30, 1969 - September 12, 1969. Produced in
England.

THE JOHN FORSYTHE SHOW

Comedy. Background: The Foster
School for Girls in California. The
trials and tribulations of John Foster,
its headmaster, a former U.S. Air
Force major who inherited the school
from its founder, his late aunt. Stories
relate his struggles as he attempts to
adjust to new responsibilities and
solve the problems that stem from one
hundred and twenty teenage girls.

CAST
John Foster　　　　　John Forsythe
Sergeant Edward Robbins,
　　an Air Force friend, his
　　assistant　　　　　Guy Marks
Miss Culver, the
　　principal　　　Elsa Lanchester
Miss Wilson, the physical education
　　instructress　　　Ann B. Davis
Joanna　　　　　　Peggy Lipton
Marcia　　　　　　Page Forsythe
Kathy　　　　　　Darleen Carr
Pamela　　　　　Pamelyn Ferdin

Janice	Sara Ballantine
Susan	Tracy Stratford
Norma Jean	Brook Forsythe

THE JOHN FORSYTHE SHOW—30 minutes—NBC—September 13, 1965 - August 29, 1966.

JOHN GARY

Listed: The television programs of singer John Gary.

The John Gary Show—Musical Variety—60 minutes—CBS—June 22, 1966 - September 7, 1966.

Host: John Gary.

Regulars: The Jimmy Joyce Singers, The Jack Regas Dancers.

Orchestra: Mitchell Ayres.

The John Gary Show—Variety—60 minutes—Syndicated 1968.

Host: John Gary.

Orchestra: Sammy Spear.

JOHN GUNTHER'S HIGH ROAD

See title: "High Road."

THE JOHNNY CASH SHOW

Musical Variety. Taped at the Nashville Grand Ole Opry.

Host: Johnny Cash.

Regulars: June Carter, The Carter Family, Carl Perkins, The Statler Brothers, The Tennessee Three.

Announcer: Mike Lawrence.

Music: The Nashville Orchestra, conducted by Billy Walker.

The Johnny Cash Show. Johnny Cash and June Carter.

THE JOHNNY CASH SHOW—60 minutes—ABC—June 7, 1969 - September 6, 1969; 60 minutes—ABC—January 21, 1970 - May 21, 1971.

JOHNNY CARSON

Listed: The television programs of comedian Johnny Carson.

Carson's Celler—Variety—30 minutes—Local Los Angeles (KNXT-TV, Ch. 2)—1953.

Host: Johnny Carson.

Music: The New Yorkers.

Earn Your Vacation—Game—30 minutes—CBS—1954. (See title.)

The Johnny Carson Show—Satire—30 minutes—CBS—1954.

Host: Johnny Carson.

Regulars: Barbara Ruick, Virginia Gibson, Jana Ekelund.

Orchestra: Lud Gluskin.

The Johnny Carson Daytime Show—Variety—30 minutes—CBS—1955.

Host: Johnny Carson.

Regulars: Laurie Carroll, Jill Corey, Glenn Turnbull.

Music: Cal Gooden's Six Piece Combo.

Format: Studio-audience interviews; offbeat guests; casual humor; and spoofs of television programs and commercials.

Who Do You Trust?—Game—30 minutes—ABC—1958. (See title: "Do You Trust Your Wife?").

The Tonight Show—Variety—90 minutes—NBC—1962. (See title.)

JOHNNY CYPHER IN DIMENSION ZERO

Animated Cartoon. Experimenting, a scientist, Johnny Cypher, discovers Dimension Zero, the ability to travel through time and space. Using its power, he attempts to combat the sinister forces of evil.

JOHNNY CYPHER IN DIMENSION ZERO—06 minutes—Syndicated 1967.

THE JOHNNY DUGAN SHOW

Musical Variety.

Host: Johnny Dugan.

Vocalist: Barbara Logan.

THE JOHNNY DUGAN SHOW—30 minutes—DuMont 1952.

THE JOHNNY JOHNSTON SHOW

Musical Variety.

Host: Johnny Johnston.

Vocalist: Rosemary Clooney.

THE JOHNNY JOHNSTON SHOW—45 minutes—CBS 1951.

JOHNNY JUPITER

Fantasy. Distinguished by two story-line formats.

Format One:
  Background: The Frisbee General Store. Ernest P. Duckweather, clerk and amateur inventor, accidentally discovers interplanetary television and contacts the people of Jupiter. Stories relate the life-styles of Earth people as seen through the eyes of the inhabitants of another planet.

Format Two:
  Ernest P. Duckweather, a milquetoastish television station janitor, dreams of becoming a video producer. One day, after hours, he sneaks into the control room and, while playing producer, he accidentally discovers interplanetary television when he views and talks to the people of Jupiter. Befriending Johnny Jupiter, he relates information about life on Earth.

CAST

Ernest P. Duckweather	Wright King
Mr. Frisbee, the store owner	Vaughn Taylor
	Cliff Hall
Also	Gilbert Mack

Characters (puppets): Johnny Jupiter; B-12; Reject the Robot; Katherine; Mr. Frisley; Dynamo.

JOHNNY JUPITER—30 minutes—DuMont—March 21, 1953 - May 29, 1954.

JOHNNY MANN'S STAND UP AND CHEER

Variety. A program presenting America in a musical revue.

Host: Johnny Mann.

The Johnny Mann Singers: Marty McCall, Diane Bellis, Richard Brettiger, Thurl Ravenscroft (voice of Kellogg's Tony the Tiger), Mike Redman, Merry Vernon, Sharalle Beard, Errol Horne, Rob Stevens, Lyn Dolin, Steve Sweetland, Barbara Harris, Pat Corbett, Cathy Cahill, Tony Quinn, Freeman Celmente, Erroll Rorigwynne, Ken Prymus, Marcia Darcangelo.

Orchestra: Johnny Mann.

Music Co-ordinator: Paul Suter.

Musical Conductor: Dave Pell.

JOHNNY MANN'S STAND UP AND CHEER—30 minutes—Syndicated 1971.

JOHNNY MIDNIGHT

Crime Drama. Background: New York City. The investigations of Johnny Midnight, an actor turned private detective.

CAST
Johnny Midnight   Edmond O'Brien
Sergeant Sam Olivera,
       N.Y.P.D.   Arthur Batanides
Lieutenant Geller,
       N.Y.P.D.   Barney Phillips
Aki, Johnny's house-
       boy   Yuki Shemoda

Music: Joe Bushkin; Stanley Wilson.

JOHNNY MIDNIGHT—30 minutes—Syndicated 1960.

JOHNNY OLSEN'S RUMPUS ROOM

Variety. Music, songs, dances, comedy sketches, and audience participation. Game segment: Selected studio audience members compete for merchandise prizes by performing various stunts.

Host: Johnny Olsen.

Regulars: Kay Armen, Hal McIntyre, Gene Kirby.

Music: The Buddy Weed Trio; The Hank D'Amico Orchestra.

JOHNNY OLSEN'S RUMPUS ROOM —30 minutes—ABC 1946.

JOHNNY RINGO

Western. Background: Velardi, Arizona, 1870s. The story of Johnny Ringo, an ex-gunfighter turned law enforcer, and his deputy, Cully Charlcey, and their attempts to maintain law and order.

CAST
Johnny Ringo   Don Durant
Cully "Kid Adonas"
       Charlcey   Mark Goddard
Cason "Case" Thomas, the
       owner of the general
       store   Terrence DeMarney
Laura Thomas, his
       daughter   Karen Sharpe

Music: Herschel Burke Gilbert; Rudy Schrager.

JOHNNY RINGO—30 minutes—CBS —October 1, 1959 - September 29, 1960. Syndicated.

Johnny Ringo. Left to right: Karen Sharpe, Don Durant, and Mona Freeman (guest).

JOHNNY SOKKO AND HIS FLYING ROBOT

Adventure. Era: Twenty-first-century Earth. The battle against alien, sinister forces of evil as undertaken by Unicorn, an international defense organization.

Characters:

Johnny Sokko, a young boy, Agent U (Unicorn)-7.

Giant Robot, a computerized, flying robot controlled by Johnny.

Marne, a Unicorn agent.

U-3.

U-6.

The Commander.

Guillotine, a Unicorn enemy, a being bent on controlling the world.

Performers are not given screen credit.

JOHNNY SOKKO AND HIS FLYING

ROBOT—30 minutes—Syndicated 1968.

JOHNNY STACCATO

Crime Drama. Background: New York City. The investigations of Johnny Staccato, a jazz musician turned private detective.

CAST
Johnny Staccato   John Cassavetes
Waldo, his friend, the
       owner of a Greenwich
       Village café, his
       hangout   Eduardo Cianelli
Music: Elmer Bernstein.

JOHNNY STACCATO—30 minutes—NBC—1959 - 1960. Syndicated. Also known as: "Staccato."

THE JOKER'S WILD

Game. Two competing contestants. Displayed on stage is a large slot machine that contains five category topics. Contestants, in turn, pull levers to activate the machine, and then answer appropriate questions for varying cash prizes.

Values:

Each time the machine stops, three categories are revealed and players choose one to answer. If three separate topics appear, each is a single and worth $50. If two of the same topics appear, it is a pair and worth $100 if chosen and correctly answered. Should a triple appear (the same category across the board) the question has to be taken and is worth $150.

Also contained within the categories are Jokers. If one Joker appears with two singles, it (the Joker) is wild and allows the contestant to make a pair with any one category topic. If two Jokers and one single appears, it then becomes a triple. Should three Jokers appear, the game is automatically won.

Winners are the contestants first to score five hundred dollars. Players then decide whether to continue or depart. If continuing, he vies for the "Joker's Jackpot," worth up to $25,000 by winning four straight games. Should he fail to win the four games, all his money is forfeited and addcd to the jackpot, which begins at $2,500, to a maximum of $25,000.

Host: Jack Barry.

Announcer: Johnny Jacobs.

Music: Recorded.

THE JOKER'S WILD—30 minutes—CBS—Premiered: September 4, 1972.

JONATHAN WINTERS

Listed: The television programs of comedian Jonathan Winters.

Here's The Show—Variety—30 minutes—NBC—July 9, 1955 - September 24, 1955.

Host: Jonathan Winters; Ransom Sherman.

Regulars: Stephanie Antie, Tommy Knox, Kay O'Grady, Ted Carpenter Singers, The Double Daters.

Orchestra: John Scott Trotter.

The Jonathan Winters Show—Variety—15 minutes—NBC—1956.

Host: Jonathan Winters.

Regulars: The Platters.

Orchestra: Eddie Shfronski.

Characters (portrayed by Jonathan): Elwood P. Suggins, Brooks Bixford, Baby Elizabeth, Granny Hopps.

The Jonathan Winters Show—Variety—60 minutes—CBS—December 27, 1967 - May 1969.

Host: Jonathan Winters.

Regulars: Dick Curtis, Paul Lynde, Alice Ghostley, Cliff Arquette, Pamela Rodgers, Abby Dalton, Debi Storm, Diane Davis, Georgene Barnes, Jerry Reneau, The Establishment, The Wisa D'Orso Dancers, The Andre Tayer Dancers.

Announcer: Bern Bennett.

Orchestra: Paul Weston.

Characters portrayed by Jonathan: Chester Hunihugger, Maynard Tetlinger, Maudie Frickett, Winslow G. Flydipper, Elwood P. Suggins, Lance Loveguard.

Segments:
"Face The Folks." "The program that brings people in the news to people in their homes." Interviews with strange people (Jonathan).

"Jack Armstrong, The All-American Boy." A comic adaptation of the radio serial. Jonathan as Jack; Georgene Barnes and Jerry Reneau as Betty and Billy Fairchild; and Cliff Arquette as Uncle Charlie.

"The Information Lady." The wisdom of a beautiful but dumb blonde (Pamela Rodgers).

"The Domestic Sketch." Jonathan as the husband, and Abby Dalton as the complaining wife.

"The Improvisation Spot." Jonathan's reactions to topics given him by the announcer.

Hot Dog—Educational—30 minutes—

NBC—September 12, 1971 - September 4, 1972. (See title.)

The Wacky World Of Jonathan Winters—Comedy—30 minutes—Syndicated 1972.

Host: Jonathan Winters.

Regulars: Marian Mercer, Mary Gregory, Ronnie Graham, The Soul Sisters.

Orchestra: Van Alexander.

Premiere Guest: Debbie Reynolds.

Format: Utilizes Jonathan's greatest gift his ability to create on the spot. Cast regulars and guests appear in unrehearsed skits.

THE JOSEPH COTTEN SHOW

See title: "On Trial."

JOSEPHINE McCARTHY

Cooking. The preparation of foreign and American meals.

Hostess: Josephine McCarthy.

Assistant-Host-Announcer: Bob Kennedy.

JOSEPHINE McCARTHY—15 minutes—NBC 1953.

JOSEPH SCHILDKRAUT PRESENTS

Anthology. Dramatic productions.

Host-Occasional Performer: Joseph Schildkraut, stage and screen personality.

JOSEPH SCHILDKRAUT—30 minutes—DuMont—1953-1954.

JOSIE AND THE PUSSYCATS

Animated Cartoon. The global misadventures of Josie and the Pussycats, an all-girl Rock group. A Hanna-Barbera production.

Characters' Voices
Josie, the group leader   Janet Waldo
Melody, the drummer, the
    beautiful-but-dumb-blonde
    type   Jackie Joseph
Valerie, the guitarist   Barbara Pariot
Alan, a friend   Jerry Dexter
Alexander Cabot, the group
    manager   Casey Kaseem
Alexandra Cabot, his sister, in
    love with Alan, scheming to
    get his attention away from
    Josie   Sherry Alberoni
Sebastian, their pet
    cat   Don Messick

Vocals: The real life Rock group, Josie and the Pussycats: Cathy Douglas (Josie); Patricia Holloway (Valerie); Cherie Moore (Melody).

Music: Hoyt Curtin.

JOSIE AND THE PUSSYCATS—30 minutes—CBS—September 12, 1970 — September 2, 1972. Retitled: "Josie and the Pussycats in Outer Space."

JOSIE AND THE PUSSYCATS IN OUTER SPACE

Animated Cartoon. The Rock group Josie and the Pussycats are posing for publicity pictures atop a space craft at NASA. Alexandra, standing to the side and unable to be seen clearly, walks forward and accidentally knocks the others off balance. As they fall backward into the open capsule hatch, Alexandra's arm hits and activates the blast-off mechanism, sending the craft and its passengers into the far reaches of outer space. Descending upon unexplored planetoids, they encounter and battle the sinister forces of evil. A Hanna-Barbera Production.

Characters' Voices

Josie	Janet Waldo
Melody	Jackie Joseph
Valerie	Barbara Pariot
Alan	Jerry Dexter
Alexandra Cabot	Sherry Alberoni
Alexander Cabot	Casey Kaseem
Sebastian	Don Messick

Bleep, their mascot, a space
    creature befriended by
    Melody on the planet
    Zelcor   Don Messick

Vocals: The Rock group, Josie and the Pussycats: Cathy Douglas, Patricia Holloway, Cherie Moore.

Music: Hoyt Curtin.

JOSIE AND THE PUSSYCATS IN OUTER SPACE—30 minutes—CBS—September 9, 1972 – January 26, 1974.

THE JO STAFFORD SHOW

Musical Variety.

Hostess: Jo Stafford.

Vocalists: The Starlighters.

Orchestra: Paul Weston.

THE JO STAFFORD SHOW—15 minutes—CBS 1954.

JOURNEY THROUGH LIFE

Interview. Married couples relate anecdotes drawn from their personal experiences.

Host: Tom Reddy.

JOURNEY THROUGH LIFE—30 minutes—ABC 1954.

JOURNEY TO ADVENTURE

See title: "World Adventures."

JOURNEY TO THE CENTER OF THE EARTH

Animated Cartoon. Uncovering the long-lost trail of Arnie Saccnuson, a lone explorer who made a descent to the earth's center, but died with its secret when breaking his leg, Professor Oliver Lindenbrook organizes an expedition. With his niece Cindy, student Alec Hewit, a guide Lars, and his pet duck Gertrude, Professor Lindenbrook begins a journey to the center of the earth.

Unbeknownst to them, the evil Count Saccnuson, the last living descendent of the once-noble family, follows them. Possessing a power-mad scheme to claim the earth's core for his own sinister purposes, he instructs his servant, Torg, to set off an explosion. However, when detonated, the blast seals the entrance and traps them all.

Stories relate their adventures as they struggle to find the secret of the way back to the earth's surface. Based on the novel by Jules Verne.

Voices: Ted Knight, Pat Harrington, Jane Webb.

Music: Gordon Zahler.

JOURNEY TO THE CENTER OF THE EARTH—30 minutes—ABC—September 9, 1967 - September 6, 1969. Syndicated.

JOURNEY TO THE UNKNOWN

Anthology. Mystery and suspense stories. Tales of the slender thread between nightmare and reality.

Included:

Matakitas Is Coming. A crime reporter in 1968 is mysteriously transported to a library in the year 1927, the scene of an employee's murder. She finds herself in the slain girl's place when the fatal night is re-created. Through her efforts, the killer, previously undiscovered, is brought to justice; the reporter is mysteriously returned to the present.

CAST

June: Vera Miles; Matakitas: Leon Lissek; Sylvia: Fay Hamilton; Tracy: Lyn Pinkney.

Eve. Background: A department store in London, England. Pressured by society, Albert Baker, an employee, retreats to a world of fantasy in which a beautiful manequin, Eve, lives and breathes. When he discovers that she, as well as other plaster creations, are to be destroyed and replaced by fiberglass models, he loses all sense of reality. Kidnapping her, he escapes to the woods. There, they are spotted by motorcycle hoods. In an attempt to acquire Eve, they kill Albert and discover Eve was only alive in his eyes.

CAST

Eve: Carol Lynley; Albert: Dennis Waterman.

The Madison Equation. An insurance investigator attempts to prove that a woman murdered her husband by programming a computer to destroy him.

CAST

Inga Madison: Barbara Bel Geddes; Adam Frost: Jack Hedley; Barbara Rossiter: Sue Lloyd.

The Last Visitor. Plagued by the shadowy figure of a man, a girl seeks to uncover its sinister presence.

CAST

Barbara: Patty Duke; Mrs. Walker: Kay Walsh.

Girl In My Dreams. The story of a girl who possesses the ability to predict people's deaths through dreams.

CAST

Greg Richards: Michael Callan; Carrie Clark: Zena Walker

JOURNEY TO THE UNKNOWN—60 minutes—ABC—September 26, 1968 - January 30, 1969. Produced in England.

JOYCE AND BARBARA: FOR ADULTS ONLY

See title: "For Adults Only."

JUBILEE U.S.A.

Musical Variety. Performances by Country and Western entertainers.

Host: Red Foley.

Regulars: Wanda Jackson; Bobby Lord and His Timberjack Trio; Leroy Van Dyke; Uncle Cyp and Aunt Sap Brasfield; Marvin Rainwater; Suzi Arden; Slim Wilson and His Jubilee Band; The Promenaders; Chuck Bowers; The Marksman; Bill Wimberly and His Country Rhythm Boys.

Featured: "The Junior Jubilee." Performances by young hopefuls (e.g., Brenda Lee).

JUBILEE U.S.A.—60 minutes—ABC— January 22, 1955 - November 21, 1961. Also known as: "Ozark

Jubilee" and "Country Music Jubilee."

JUDD, FOR THE DEFENSE

Drama. Background: Texas. The cases and courtroom defenses of attorneys Clinton Judd and his partner Ben Caldwell.

CAST

Clinton Judd	Carl Betz
Ben Caldwell	Stephen Young

Music: Harry Geller; Lionel Newman.

JUDD, FOR THE DEFENSE—60 minutes—ABC—September 8, 1967 - September 19, 1969. Syndicated.

JUDGE FOR YOURSELF

Game. Six players, three studio-audience members and three guest celebrities. Object: To rate the performances of undiscovered professional acts. Cash prizes are awarded to the laymen panelists whose ratings correspond with those of the celebrities.

Hosts: Fred Allen; Dennis James.

Announcer: Dennis James.

Orchestra: Milton DeLugg.

JUDGE FOR YOURSELF—30 minutes—NBC 1953.

Judd, For the Defense. Carl Betz and Stephen Young.

JUDGE ROY BEAN

Western. Background: Langtry, Texas during the 1870s. The story of Judge Roy Bean (self-appointed), a storekeeper, and his attempts to maintain law and order in "America's most lawless region."

CAST

Judge Roy Bean	Edgar Buchanan
Jeff Taggard, his deputy	Jack Beutel
Letty Bean, the Judge's niece	Jackie Loughery
Steve, a Texas Ranger	Russell Hayden

Program open:

Announcer: "During the 1870s, the wildest spot in the United States was the desolate region west of the Pecos River, an area virtually beyond the reach of the authorities. The railroads, then pushing their way West, attracted the most vicious characters in the country. It was said that civilization and law stopped at the east bank of the Pecos. It took one man, a lone storekeeper who was sick of the lawlessness, to change all this. His name was Judge Roy Bean."

JUDGE ROY BEAN—30 minutes—Syndicated 1956.

THE JUDY GARLAND SHOW

Musical Variety.

Hostess: Judy Garland.

Featured: Jerry Van Dyke (supposedly teaching her the ropes of television production).

Special Musical Material: Mel Tormé.

Orchestra: Mort Lindsey.

Premiere Guest: Mickey Rooney.

THE JUDY GARLAND SHOW—60 minutes—CBS—September 29, 1963 - March 29, 1964.

THE JUDY LYNN SHOW

Musical Variety. Performances by Country and Western entertainers.

Hostess: Judy Lynn.

Music: The eight-piece all-male Judy Lynn Band.

THE JUDY LYNN SHOW—30 minutes—Syndicated 1969.

JULIA

Comedy. Background: Los Angeles, California. The story of Julia Baker, widow, a registered nurse with the Inner Aero-Space Center (an industrial health office). Episodes relate her struggles as she attempts to readjust to life after the death of her husband (an Air Force captain killed in Vietnam) and raise her young son, Corey.

CAST

Julia Baker	Diahann Carroll
Dr. Morton Chegley, Julia's employer	Lloyd Nolan
Corey Baker	Marc Copage
Earl J. Waggedorn, Corey's friend	Michael Link
Marie Waggedorn, his mother	Betty Beaird
Earl Waggedorn, her husband	Hank Brandt
Hannah Yarby, the head nurse	Lurene Tuttle
Carol Deering, Julia's part-time mother's helper	Alison Mills
Sol Cooper, Julia's landlord	Ned Glass

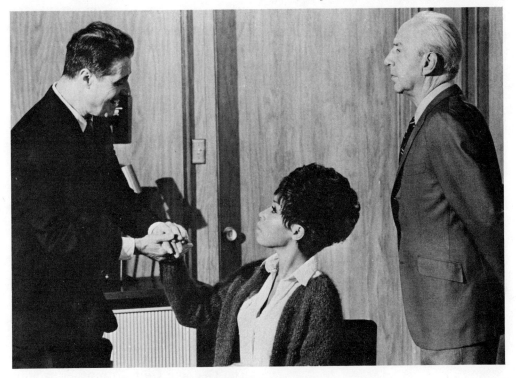

Julia. Left to right: Don Ameche (guest), Diahann Carroll, Lloyd Nolan. Episode: "The Grass Is Sometimes Greener."

Mrs. Deering, Carol's mother	Virginia Capers
Ted Neuman, Julia's boyfriend	Don Marshall
Paul Carter, Julia's boyfriend	Chuck Wood Paul Winfield
Steve Bruce, Julia's boyfriend, a student lawyer	Fred Williamson
Roberta, Corey's baby sitter	Jenear Hines
Lou, Julia's uncle, an exvaudevillian	Eugene Jackson

Music: Van Alexander.

JULIA–30 minutes–NBC–September 17, 1968, - May 25, 1971.

THE JULIE ANDREWS HOUR

Variety. Music, songs, dances, and comedy sketches.

Hostess: Julie Andrews.

Regulars: Rich Little, Alice Ghostley, The Tony Charmoli Dancers, The Dick Williams Singers.

Announcer: Dick TuFel.

Orchestra: Nelson Riddle.

THE JULIE ANDREWS HOUR–60 minutes–ABC–September 13, 1972 - April 28, 1973.

The Julie Andrews Hour. Julie Andrews. *Courtesy Independent Television Corporation; an ATV Company.*

JULIUS La ROSA

Listed: The television programs of singer Julius La Rosa.

The Julius La Rosa Show—Musical Variety—15 minutes—NBC—June 27, 1955 - September 22, 1955.

Host: Julius La Rosa.

Regulars: The Debutones—all-girl quartet—Sherry Ostrus, Connie Desmond, Bix Brent, Irene Carroll.

Orchestra: Russ Case.

The Julius La Rosa Show—Musical Variety—60 minutes—NBC—July 14, 1956 - August 4, 1956.

Host: Julius La Rosa.

Regulars: George De Witt, The Mariners, The Spellbinders, The Four Evans (Dancers).

Orchestra: Mitchell Ayres.

Perry Como Presents The Julius La Rosa Show—Musical Variety—60 minutes—NBC—June 15, 1957 — September 1957.

Host: Julius La Rosa.

Regulars: Steve Ashton, Lou Cosler, The Louis Da Pron Dancers, The Artie Malvin Chorus.

Orchestra: Mitchell Ayres.

THE JUNE ALLYSON THEATRE

Anthology. Dramatic presentations.

Hostess-Occasional Performer: June Allyson.

Music: Herschel Burke Gilbert; Hans Salter.

Included:

The Opening Door. A mother, lacking finances, attempts to enroll her mentally retarded daughter into a special school.

CAST
Dr. Gina Kerstas: Irene Dunne; Falk: Harry Townes.

The Tender Shoot. Kay Neilson, a successful young novelist, and Gary Stevens, a struggling young writer, meet. Infatuated with her, he reveals his ideas for a novel, unaware of her plan to use them as her own.

CAST
Kay Neilson: Ginger Rogers; Gary Stevens: Paul Carr; Jamie Bowers: Jan Norris.

Love Is A Headache. A young girl, infatuated with a young singer, attempts to impress him.

CAST

Ellie: Denise Alexander; Tony: Akim Tamiroff.

Child Lost. A nurse attempts to locate a missing child.

CAST

Nurse Vivian Wadron: June Allyson; Sgt. Lederman: Steve Brodie; Wim Wegless: Ronny Howard; Mrs. Wegless: Kathleen Mulqueen.

A Summer's Ending. The story of a summer romance involving a couple married, but not to each other.

CAST

Sharon Foster: June Allyson; Paul Martin: Dick Powell.

THE JUNE ALLYSON THEATRE—30 minutes—CBS—September 1959 — September 1961.

THE JUNE HAVOC SHOW

Interview.
Hostess: June Havoc.
Guests: Show-business personalities.
Music: Recorded.

THE JUNE HAVOC SHOW—60 minutes—Syndicated 1964.

JUNGLE BOY

See title: "The Adventures of a Jungle Boy."

JUNGLE JIM

Adventure. Background: Nairobi, Africa. The experiences of jungle guide Jungle Jim. Based on the character created by Alex Raymond.

CAST
Jungle Jim   Johnny Weissmuller
Skipper, his son   Martin Huston
Kaseem, his Hindu
    servant   Norman Fredric
Jim's chimpanzee: Tamba.
Skipper's dog: Trader.

JUNGLE JIM—30 minutes—Syndicated 1955.

JUNIOR HIGH JINKS

Children. Puppets, sketches, and film shorts.
Host: Warren Wright.
His Puppet: Willie the Worm.

JUNIOR HIGH JINKS—15 minutes—CBS 1952.

JUNIOR RODEO

Children. Western variety acts.
Host: Bob Atcher.

JUNIOR RODEO—30 minutes—ABC —January 15, 1952 — February 27, 1952.

JUST FOR LAUGHS

Pilot Films. Proposed comedy series for the 1974-1975 season. The complete series:

Ernie, Madge, and Artie. The story of a middle-aged newlywed couple who are plagued by the ghost of the bride's first husband.

CAST
Madge: Cloris Leachman; Ernie: Frank Sutton; Artie: Dick Van Patten; Blanche: Susan Sennett.

The Life And Times of Captain Barney Miller. The story of a compassionate policeman.

CAST
Barney Miller: Hal Linden; Elizabeth Miller: Abby Dalton; Rachel Miller: Anne Wyndham.

Ann In Blue. The story of Ann Neal, the head of a four-woman police unit.

CAST
Ann Neal: Penny Fuller; Bea Russo: Mary Elaine Monte; Elizabeth Jensen: Maybeth Hart; Jessie Waters: Hattie Winston.

The Barbara Eden Show. The story of a beautiful toy designer whose father wants to keep her under wraps and away from male suitors. Scheduled but never aired.

Starring: Barbara Eden.

JUST FOR LAUGHS—30 minutes— ABC—August 8, 1974 - August 29, 1974.

JUSTICE

Drama. Background: New York City. The investigations of Richard Adam and Jason Tyler, attorneys for the Legal Aide Society. Based on official files.

CAST
Richard Adam   Dane Clark
                    William Prince
Jason Tyler   Garry Merrill
Narrator: Westbrook Van Voorhis.

JUSTICE—30 minutes—NBC—1952 - 1955.

JUVENILE JURY

Children's Panel. "Out of the mouths of babes oft time come gems." (The host's closing words). A panel of five children give their opinion as to the solving of or coping with a problem sent in by a home viewer or presented by an in-person guest.

Host-Announcer: Jack Barry.

Panelists, including: Patricia Bruder, Angela Bell, Jeff Silver, Veronique DeAllo, Paul Jackson, Ricky Cordell, Sean Masterson, Monique Althouse, Jeff Philips, Steve Andrews, Glena Sargent, Bobby Hull, Christine Hare, Wayne Chestnut, Paul Lazott, Curtis Helm, Neil Buller, Melanie Freeman, Joe Ward, Michele Fogel, Douglas Stewart.

Music: Joe Diamond.

VERSIONS:
NBC—30 minutes—April 3, 1947 - October 3, 1953.
CBS—30 minutes—October 11, 1953 - September 14, 1954.
NBC—30 minutes—January 2, 1955 - March 27, 1955.
Syndicated—30 minutes—1971.

K

THE KAISER ALUMINUM HOUR

Anthology. Dramatic presentations.

Included:

A Fragile Affair. Switzerland, World

War II. The wife of a bitter delicatessen owner attempts to provide comfort and happiness to young soldiers.

CAST

Cristoff: Eli Wallach; Mary Cristoff: Gaby Rogers; Pip: Woodrow Parfrey.

Man On A White Horse. The story of an elderly sheriff who fears he's lost his ability to maintain law and order.

CAST

Sheriff Adam Griffith: James Barton; Dan Royal: Barton MacLane.

Army Game. A reluctant college draftee attempts to seek a psychiatric discharge.

CAST

Danny: Paul Newman; Berman: Edward Andrews; Manken: Philip Abbott.

THE KAISER ALUMINUM HOUR— 60 minutes—NBC—1956 - 1957.

KAREN

See title: "Ninety Bristol Court," *Karen* segment.

KAREN

Comedy. Background: Washington, D.C. The trials and tribulations of Karen Angelo, a young idealist staff worker for Open America, a Capitol Hill citizens' lobby.

CAST

Karen Angelo	Karen Valentine
Dale W. Bush, the founder of Open America	Denver Pyle Charles Lane
Dena Madison, a staff worker at Open America	Dena Dietrich
Cissy Peterson, Karen's roommate	Aldine King
Adam Cooperman, a staff worker at Open America	Will Seltzer
Jerry Siegle, a tenant in Karen's rooming house	Oliver Clark
Cheryl Siegle, Jerry's wife	Alix Elias
Senator Bob Hartford, Karen's friend	Edward Winter
Ernie, Karen's friend	Joseph Stone

Music: Benny Golson.

KAREN—30 minutes—ABC—January 30, 1975 - June 19, 1975.

KATE McSHANE

Drama. Background: California. The cases and courtroom defenses of Kate McShane, an uninhibited and unorthodox Irish-American lawyer.

CAST

Kate McShane	Anne Meara
Pat McShane, her father, an excop who is now her investigator	Sean McClory
Ed McShane, her brother, a Jesuit priest and professor of law	Charles Haid
Julie, her secretary	Rachel Malkin

Music: Charles Bernstein.

KATE McSHANE—60 minutes—CBS
—September 10, 1975 - November 12,
1975.

KATE SMITH

Listed: The television programs of singer Kate Smith.

The Kate Smith Hour—Variety—60 minutes—NBC—September 25, 1950 - June 18, 1954.

Format: Music, songs, dances, sketches, cooking, guests, interviews, fashion, panel discussions, and news.

Hostess: Kate Smith.

Regulars: Jeff Clark, Jimmy Nelson (Ventriloquist; his dummy: Danny O'Day), Peggy Ryan, Ray MacDonald, Evalyn Tyner, Richard and Flora Stuart, Fran Barber, Billy Mills, Robert Maxwell, Claire Frim, Virginia McCurdy, Diane Carol, Peg Lynch, Alan Bunce, Charlie Ruggles, Ruth Mattheson, Glenn Walker, Hal Le Roy, Adolph Dehm, Barry Wood, Dorothy Day, The McGuire Sisters, Louren Gilbert, Tim Taylor, Monica Lovett, Mimi Stongin, James Vickery, Arlene Dalton, The Showtimers, The John Butler Ballet Group, The Jack Allison Singers.

Announcer: Andre Baruch.

Orchestra: Jack Miller.

Featured Segments:
"Ethel And Albert." A domestic comedy starring Peg Lynch and Alan Bunce. (See Title.)
"The World Of Mr. Sweeny." A comedy starring Charlie Ruggles and Glenn Walker. (See title.)
"The Talent Showcase." Performances by young hopefuls.

"The House in the Garden." A drama of life in a small town.

The Kate Smith Evening Hour—Musical Variety—60 minutes—NBC—1951-1952.

Hostess: Kate Smith.

Regulars: Ted Collins, Paul Lukas, Susan Douglas, Ann Thomas, Kay Thompson, The Williams Brothers, The Stuart Morgan Dancers, The John Butler Dancers, The Jack Allison Singers.

Announcer: Bob Warren.

Orchestra: Harry Sosnick.

The Kate Smith Show—Musical Variety—30 minutes—CBS—January 25, 1960 - July 18, 1960.

Hostess: Kate Smith.

Featured: The Harry Simeone Chorale.

Orchestra: Neal Hefti; Bill Stegmeyer.

KAY KYSER'S KOLLEGE OF MUSICAL KNOWLEDGE

Variety-Quiz. Musical numbers are interspersed with a quiz segment situated against a college format. Contestants compete in tests of musical questions divided into midterms and final exams. The professor (host) leads the orchestra in a selection that the player must identify. If he is correct, a cash prize is awarded; if he is unable to answer, the song title is relayed by the studio audience (students).

Hosts: Kay Kyser, The Old Professor; Tennessee Ernie Ford (after Mr. Kyser's retirement in 1954).

Regulars: Mike Douglas, Sylvia Michaels, Diana Sinclair, Liza Palmer, Sue Bennett, Ish Kabbible (the comic relief, a member of

Kay's band, on sax), Kenny Spaulding, The Honeydreamers, The Cheerleaders (Donna Brown, Maureen Cassidy, Spring Mitchell).

Announcer: Verne Smith (The Dean).

Orchestra: Carl Hoff; Kay Kyser; Frank DeVol.

KAY KYSER'S KOLLEGE OF MUSICAL KNOWLEDGE—30 minutes—NBC—1949 - 1955.

THE KAY STARR SHOW

Musical Variety.

Hostess: Kay Starr.

Orchestra: Pete King.

THE KAY STARR SHOW—30 minutes—NBC 1957.

THE KEEFE BRASSELLE SHOW

Musical Variety.

Host: Keefe Brasselle.

Regulars: Rocky Graziano, Ann B. Davis, Noelle Adam, The Style Sisters, The Bill Foster Dancers.

Orchestra: Charles Sanford.

THE KEEFE BRASSELLE SHOW—60 minutes—CBS—June 25, 1963 : September 17, 1963.

KEEP IT IN THE FAMILY

Game. Two families, each composed of five members, the father, mother, and three children, compete. General-knowledge questions are asked of each member of each family, beginning with the youngest. Each correct response earns points. Winners, the highest point scorers, receive merchandise gifts.

Hosts: Bill Nimmo; Keefe Brasselle.

Announcer: Johnny Olsen.

KEEP IT IN THE FAMILY—30 minutes—ABC—October 12, 1957 - February 8, 1958.

KEEP ON TRUCKIN'

Comedy. A potpourri of broad comedy sketches and freewheeling spoofs and blackouts.

Starring: Fred Travalena, Larry Ragland, Richard Lee Sung, Rhonda Bates, Gailard Sartain, Marion Ramsey, Franklyn Ajaye, Kathryn Bauman, Jennine Burnier, Dee Dee Kahn, Rilo, Charles Flascher, Welland Flowers, Jack Riley.

Musical Director: Marvin Larlaird.

KEEP ON TRUCKIN'—60 minutes—ABC—July 12, 1975 - August 2, 1975.

KEEP TALKING

Game. Four celebrity players compete (three regulars and one guest), composing two teams of two. One member on each team receives a secret phrase that he then must work into an ad-libbed conversation. A bell sounds the end of the round. Opponents then have to identify the concealed phrase. If successful, they receive points. Winners are the highest point scorers. Prizes are awarded to home and studio-audience members represented by the celebrities.

Hosts: Monty Hall (CBS); Merv Griffin (ABC).

Regular Panelists: Ilka Chase, Joey Bishop, Danny Dayton, Morey Amsterdam, Paul Winchell, Peggy Cass, Pat Carroll.

KEEP TALKING—30 minutes. CBS—July 8, 1958 - September 22, 1959; ABC—September 29, 1959 - May 3, 1960.

THE KEN BERRY WOW SHOW

Variety. A nostalgic look at yesterday through music, song, dance, and comedy. The thirties, forties, fifties, and sixties are re-created through sketch, animation, and imaginative effects.

Host: Ken Berry.

Regulars: Laara Lacey, Billy Van, Steve Martin, Carl Gotlieb, Teri Garr, Barbara Joyce, Don Ray, Cheryl Stufflemoore, The New Seekers, The Jaime Rogers Dancers.

Orchestra: Jimmy Dale.

Premiere Guests: Patty Duke, John Astin, The Lennon Sisters, Dr. Joyce Brothers, Monty Hall, Don Knotts, Dick Clark, Cass Elliott.

THE KEN BERRY WOW SHOW—60 minutes—ABC—July 15, 1972 - August 12, 1972.

THE KEN MURRAY SHOW

Variety. Blackouts, music, songs, dances, dramatic skits, and novelty acts.

Host: Ken Murray.

Regulars: Laurie Anders, Darla Jean Hood, Joe Besser, Annie Skelton, Betty Lou Walters, Art Lund, Jack Marshall, Richard Webb, Johnny Johnston, Anita Gordon, Herbert Marshall, Joan Shea, Lillian Farmer, Cathy Hild, Tommy Labriola (as Oswald), The Ken Murray Chorus, The Ken Murray Dancers, The Glamour Lovelies.

Announcer: Nelson Chase.

Orchestra: David Brockman; Jane Bergmeler.

THE KEN MURRAY SHOW—60 minutes—CBS—1948 - 1953.

KEN MURRAY'S HOLLYWOOD

Variety. Home movies of celebrities. Presented as a fill-in when an NBC network movie ended early.

Host-Narrator-Photographer: Ken Murray.

KEN MURRAY'S HOLLYWOOD—10 minutes (approx.)—NBC—1964-1967.

KENTUCKY JONES

Drama. Background: The Jones Ranch in California, a forty-acre spread owned by Kenneth (Kentucky) Yarborough Jones, a widowed professional horse trainer turned veterinarian.

Several weeks following the death of his wife, Jones receives notice informing him of the arrival of the Chinese orphan he and his wife had planned to adopt. Feeling himself no longer qualified to raise the child, he tries to halt the adoption but is unsuccesful and soon finds himself the foster father of a ten-year old boy, Dwight Eisenhower Wong (Ike).

Stories depict the efforts of Kentucky Jones and his partner, Seldom

Kentucky Jones. Dennis Weaver.

Jackson, to raise a young refugee; and Ike's attempts to secure the affections of his foster father.

CAST

Kentucky Jones	Dennis Weaver
Seldom Jackson, a former jockey who rarely brought in a winner	Harry Morgan
Dwight Eisenhower Wong (Ike)	Rickey Der
Annie Ng, a friend of Ike's	Cherylene Lee
Thomas Wong, a friend	Keye Luke

Music: Vic Mizzy.

KENTUCKY JONES—30 minutes—NBC—September 19, 1964 - September 11, 1965.

KEY CLUB PLAYHOUSE

Anthology. Rebroadcasts of dramas that were originally aired via "Ford Theatre."

Included:

Bet The Queen. A gambler wins two tickets on the last boat to leave Fort Benton before the river freezes. The story relates the efforts of the wife of the man who lost the tickets to retrieve them.

CAST
Rory Calhoun, Gale Robbins, Donald Curtis.

A Past Remembered. Attending his twentieth-year college reunion, a middle-aged man discovers that he is the only one who is not a financial success. The story relates his attempts to acquire a job through one of his classmates by pretending to be a successful businessman.

CAST
William Bendix, Lyle Talbot, Joan Banks.

Passage to Yesterday. The story of an American captain and a British army nurse who meet and fall in love during the London Blitz of World War II.

CAST
Joanne Dru, Guy Madison, James Fairfax.

KEY CLUB PLAYHOUSE—30 minutes—ABC—June 1956 - September 1956; May 1957 - September 1957.

KEYHOLE

Documentary. Films showcasing the unusual occupations or experiences of people.
Host-Narrator: Jack Douglas.

KEYHOLE—30 minutes—Syndicated 1962.

KHAN!

Crime Drama. Background: San Francisco's Chinatown. The investigations of Khan, a Chinese private detective.

CAST

Khan	Khigh Dhiegh
Ann Khan, his daughter	Irene Yah-Ling Sun
Kim Khan, his son	Evan Kim
Lt. Gubbins, S.F.P.D.	Vic Tayback

Music: Morton Stevens; Bruce Broughton.

KHAN!—60 minutes—CBS—February 7, 1975 - February 28, 1975.

KID GLOVES

Children. Two contestants. Format: A series of three thirty-second boxing bouts that follow the rules of the professionals. Between rounds (thirty seconds), question and answer sessions are conducted with audience members by John Da Groza, the Pennsylvania Boxing Commissioner.

Host (presenting the blow-by-blow commentary): Bill Sears.

Referee: Frank Goodman.

KID GLOVES—30 minutes—CBS 1951.

KID POWER

Animated Cartoon. Background: The Rainbow Club—an anywhere club in an anywhere city or town. The story of its members, all children, who are struggling to save the environment and better the world. Object: To show kids of different ethnic backgrounds sharing thoughts on prejudice, teamwork, and responsibility.

Characters: Wellington, Oliver, Nipper, Diz, Connie, Jerry, Albert, Ralph, Sybil; Polly, Wellington's parrot; General Lee, Nipper's dog; and Tom, Ralph's cat.

Voices: John Gardiner, Jay Silverheels, Jr., Allan Melvin, Michele Johnson, Charles Kennedy, Jr., Carey Wong, Jeff Thomas, Gregg Thomas, Gary Shiparo.

Music: Perry Bodkin, Jr.

KID POWER—30 minutes—ABC—September 16, 1972 - September 1, 1974.

KID TALK

Discussion. Four child panelists and two guest celebrities discuss topical issues.

Host: Bill Adler.

Panelists: Mona Tera (age seven), Andy Yamamoto (ten), Nellie Henderson (twelve), Alan Winston (twelve).

Announcer: Johnny Olsen.

Music: Recorded.

KID TALK—30 minutes—Syndicated 1972.

THE KILLY STYLE

Ski Instruction. The performances of professional skiers.

Starring: Jean-Claude Killy (champion skier).

Narrator-Announcer: Bob Landers.

THE KILLY STYLE—30 minutes—Syndicated 1969.

KIMBA, THE WHITE LION

Animated Cartoon. Early history: Egypt, four thousand years ago. Squandering the country's wealth, the evil Pharoah, King Tut Tut, causes the kingdom to lose its prosperity. In an attempt to curtail the king's spending, Fradies, the King's Minister, develops a special wisdom formula that he feeds to his pet, a rare white lion. Sending the animal into the village, the people believe it to be the Spirit of the Sphinx, and follow its leadership. The lion teaches them economy and the development of strong bodies and minds. As Egypt prospers once again, the king extends good will to all African tribes.

Overwhelmed by the performance of one such tribe, the Kickapeels, the king offers them any treasure in his kingdom. The leader chooses and receives the white lion.

Returning to Africa, the Kickapeels are blessed with prosperity as the white lion becomes their king. Thus, generation after generation, the white lion has been in rule of Africa.

Africa, 1960s. Caesar, the ruler, old and dying, bestows upon his son Kimba, the rare white lion, the sacred throne. Stories relate Kimba's struggles to safeguard his homeland from evil.

Additional characters: Dan'l Baboon, Samson, Pauley Cracker, Tadpole, Roger Ranger, Kitty, King Speckle Rex, and Claw, an enemy determined to foil Kimba's plans.

Voice of Kimba: Billie Lou Watt.

Music: Bernie Baum, Bill Grant, Florence Kaye.

KIMBA, THE WHITE LION—30 minutes—Syndicated 1966. Produced in Japan.

THE KING FAMILY

Listed: The television programs of the King Family.

The King Family Show—Variety—60 minutes—ABC—January 23, 1965 - January 8, 1966.

Orchestra: Mitchell Ayres; Ralph Carmichael; Alvino Rey.

The King Family Show—Variety—30 minutes—ABC—March 12, 1969 - September 10, 1969.

Orchestra: Alvino Rey.

The original eight members of the King Family: William King, Karlton King, Alyce King (married name: Alyce Clark), Luise King (married name: Luise Rey), Donna King (married name: Donna Conklin), Maxine King (married name: Maxine Thomas), Yvonne King (married name: Yvonne Birch), Marilyn King (married name: Marilyn Larsen).

The thirty-six-member King family at the time of their first series:

William King. Wife: Phyllis. Three children: Steve, Della, and Jonathan.

Karlton King. Two children: William (wife: Barbara; children: Tammy and Todd), Don (wife: Cheryl Crawley; children: Don and Ray).

Alyce Clark. Husband: Bob Clark (first married to Sydney de Azevedo, deceased); two children: Lex (married; children: Linda, Julie, and Carrie), and Cameron.

Luise Rey. Husband: Alvino Rey; two children: Liza and Robi.

Donna Conkling. Husband: James Conkling; four children: Candice (husband: Robert Wilson; children: Kristen and Brook), Jamie, Alexander (Xan), and Chris.

Maxine Thomas. Husband: La Varn Thomas; one child: Thomas (wife: Donna; one child: Carolyn, husband: Bill Brennan).

Yvonne Birch. Husband: Bill Birch (first married to Buddy Cole, deceased); two children: Tina Cole (husband: Volney Howard; parents of Volney IV), Cathy Birch (husband: Jim Greene).

Marilyn Larsen. Husband: Kent Larsen. Three children: Jennifer, Lloyd, and Susannah.

KING FEATURES TRILOGY

Animated Cartoon. An adaptation of three King Features comic strips: "Barney Google"; "Beetle Bailey"; and "Krazy Kat."

Voices: Howard Morris, Penny Phillips, Allan Melvin, Paul Frees.
Music: Winston Sharples.

Barney Google. The misadventures of Barney Google, a simple-minded hillbilly.

Additional characters: Snuffy Smith, his friend; Louisa May Smith, Snuffy's wife; Jughead Smith, Snuffy's nephew; and Clem Cutplug, a feuding enemy.

Beetle Bailey. Background: Camp Swampy. The trials and tribulations of Beetle Bailey, a dim-witted private.

Additional characters: Sergeant Snorkel; General Halftrack.

Krazy Kat. The misadventures of the love-sick Krazy Kat.

Additional characters: Offissa Pup; Ignatz Mouse.

KING FEATURES TRILOGY—05 minutes (each cartoon)—Syndicated 1963.

KING KONG

Animated Cartoon. Background: The remote prehistoric island of Mondo in the Java Sea. After Professor Bond, an American scientist, establishes a research base, his young son Bobby, discovers and befriends the sixty-foot-tall gorilla, King Kong, a creature the professor believes is intelligent and an important clue in the study of anthropology. Stories relate the struggles of the professor, his children, Bobby and Susan, and Kong, as they battle the evil influences of Dr. Who, a power-mad scientist who seeks Kong for his own diabolical plan to control the world. Very loosely based on the film classic.

Also presented:

TOM OF T.H.U.M.B. Background: The secret U.S. government offices of T.H.U.M.B. (Tiny Humans Underground Military Bureau). The investigations of agents Tom and his Oriental assistant, Swinging Jack.
Music: Maury Laws.

KING KONG—30 minutes—ABC—September 10, 1966 - August 31, 1969.

KING LEONARDO

Animated Cartoon. Background: Bongoland, a mythical African kingdom ruled by King Leonardo, a lion, and his assistant, the real power behind the throne, Odie Calognie. Stories depict their battle against the evil influences of Itchy Brother and Biggy Rat.

Voices: Don Adams, Kenny Delmar, Jackson Beck, George S. Irving, Sandy Becker, Mort Marshall.

KING LEONARDO—30 minutes—NBC—October 15, 1960 - September 1963. Syndicated title: "The King and Odie."

KING OF DIAMONDS

Adventure. The cases of John King, an investigator for the diamond industry.

CAST
John King	Broderick Crawford
Casey O'Brien, his assistant	Ray Hamilton

Music: Frank Ortega.

KING OF DIAMONDS—30 minutes—Syndicated 1961.

KING'S CROSSROADS

Film Shorts.
Host-Narrator: Carl King.

KING'S CROSSROADS—60 minutes—ABC—October 10, 1951 - July 20, 1952.

KING'S ROW

See title: "Warner Brothers Presents," *King's Row* segment.

THE KINGDOM OF THE SEA

Documentary. Films exploring the seas and oceans of the world.

Host-Narrator: Robert J. Stevenson.

THE KINGDOM OF THE SEA—30 minutes—Syndicated 1957.

KIT CARSON

See title: "The Adventures of Kit Carson."

KITTY FOYLE

Serial. The dramatic story of Kitty Foyle, a teenage girl "just discovering life."

CAST
Kitty Foyle	Kathleen Murray
Edward Foyle	Bob Hastings
Pop Foyle	Ralph Dunn
Molly Scharf	Judy Lewis
Molly Scharf, as a girl	Patty Duke
Wyn Stafford	Billy Redfield
Kenneth	Jan Merlin
Rosie Rittenhouse	Les Damon
Oliva Strafford	Valerie Cassart
Stacylea	Marie Worsham
Mac	Lany Robinson
Ma Balla	Casey Allen
Myrtle	Mae Barnes
Carter Hamilton	Martin Newman
Joe Gaines	Arnold Robinson
Flip	Conrad Fowkes
Sophie	Kay Medford
George Harvey	Karl Webber

KITTY FOYLE—30 minutes—NBC—January 13, 1958 - June 27, 1958.

THE KITTY WELLS/JOHNNY WRIGHT FAMILY SHOW

Musical Variety. Performances by Country and Western artists.

Hosts: Kitty Wells, Johnny Wright.

Regulars: Carol Sue Wright, Bobby Wright, Bill Phillips, Rudy Wright.

THE KITTY WELLS/JOHNNY WRIGHT FAMILY SHOW—30 minutes—Syndicated 1969.

KLONDIKE

Adventure. Background: Alaska during the 1890s. Stories dramatize the struggles of Kathy O'Hara as she attempts to maintain an honest hotel in a lawless territory; and the exploits of adventurer Mike Holliday as he struggles to find gold in the beautiful but dangerous Ice Palace of the Northland.

CAST
Kathy O'Hara	Mari Blanchard
Mike Holliday	Ralph Taeger
Jeff Durain, a con artist	James Coburn
Goldie, his assistant	Joi Lansing

Music: Vic Mizzy.

KLONDIKE—30 minutes—NBC—October 10, 1960 - February 13, 1961.

KLONDIKE KAT

Animated Cartoon. The misadventures of Klondike Kat, an incompetent police feline who, on orders from the chief, Major Minor, struggles to apprehend the notorious rodent Savoir Faire.

KLONDIKE KAT—05 minutes—Syndicated 1965.

KOBB'S CORNER

Musical Variety. Background: The Shufflebottom General Store, a southern business establishment that sponsors a musical-comedy get-together on Wednesday evenings.

Hostess: Hope Emerson (as the General Store owner).

Regulars: Jo Hurt, Stan Fritter, Jimmy Allen, Joan Nobles, The Korn Kobblers.

KOBB'S CORNER—30 minutes CBS 1948.

KODAK REQUEST PERFORMANCE

Anthology. Rebroadcasts of dramas that were originally aired via other filmed anthology programs.

Included:

Afraid To Live. Background: The Fiji Islands. The effect of an old man's wisdom and contentment on a wealthy young woman.

CAST
Dorothy Malone, Charles Drake.

Girl In Flight. Background: A small French town. A lawyer attempts to free a woman accused of murder.

CAST
Joan Leslie, Tom Drake, Hugo Haas.

Sgt. Sullivan Speaking. The son of a

widow attempts to match his mother with a police sergeant.

CAST
William Bendix, Joan Blondell, William Fawcett, Sarah Selby, June Kenny, Jon Provost.

Trouble With Youth. Tale of a middle-aged theatrical producer who attempts to recapture his youth through the association of a young woman.

CAST
Paul Douglas, Constance Moore, Lucy Marlow, June Vincent.

K O D A K   R E Q U E S T   P E R-FORMANCE—30 minutes—NBC—April 13, 1955 - September 28, 1955.

KODIAK

Crime Drama. Background: Alaska. The cases of Cal "Kodiak" McKay, a member of the Alaska State Police Patrol. (McKay is named "Kodiak" by the natives after a great bear that roams the area.)

CAST
Cal "Kodiak" McKay   Clint Walker
Abraham Lincoln Imhook, his
   assistant   Abner Biberman
Mandy, the radio
   dispatcher   Maggie Blye
Music: Morton Stevens.

KODIAK—30 minutes—ABC—September 13, 1974 - October 11, 1974.

KOJAK

Crime Drama. Background: New York City. The investigations of Lieutenant

Theo Kojak, a plainclothes detective with the Manhattan South Precinct. One of the more realistic police dramas dealing with current and sometimes controversial topics and crimes.

CAST
Lt. Theo Kojak   Telly Savalas
Frank McNeil, Chief of
   Detectives   Dan Frazer
Lt. Bobby Crocker   Kevin Dobson
Detective Stavros   Demosthenes
Detective Rizzo   Vince Conti
Detective Saperstein   Mark Russell
Music: Billy Goldenberg; Kim Richmond; John Cacavas.

KOJAK—60 minutes—CBS—Premiered: October 24, 1973.

KOLCHAK: THE NIGHT STALKER

See title: "The Night Stalker."

THE KOPYKATS

Variety. Songs, dances, and comedy sketches featuring impersonations of show-business personalities.

Hosts: Weekly Guests: Tony Curtis, Raymond Burr, Debbie Reynolds, Robert Young, Steve Lawrence, Ed Sullivan.

The Kopykats: Rich Little, Marilyn Michaels, Frank Gorshin, George Kirby, Charlie Callas, Joe Baker, Fred Travalena.

Featured: The Norman Maen Dancers.

Orchestra: Jack Parnell.

THE KOPYKATS—60 minutes—ABC (Rebroadcasts)—June 21, 1972 - August 10, 1972. Originally broadcast as part of the "The ABC Comedy Hour"–60 minutes–ABC–January 12, 1972 - April 5, 1972. Syndicated. First appeared as two one-hour segments of "The Kraft Music Hall," "The Kopykats," and "The Kopykats Copy TV."

KORG: 70,000 B.C.

Adventure. Background: Earth, 70,000 B.C. The struggle for survival in a primitive world as seen through the experiences of a Neanderthal family. Based on assumptions and theories drawn from artifacts.

CAST

Korg	Jim Malinda
Bok	Bill Ewing
Mara	Naomi Pollack
Tane	Christopher Man
Tor	Charles Morted
Ree	Janelle Pransky

Narrator: Burgess Meredith.

Music: Hoyt Curtin.

KORG: 70,000 B.C.–30 minutes–ABC–September 7, 1974 - August 31, 1975.

THE KRAFT MUSIC HALL

Versions:

The Kraft Music Hall–Musical Variety–30 minutes–NBC–1958 - 1962.

Hosts: Milton Berle; Perry Como; Dave King.

Regulars: Ken Carpenter, The Bill Foster Dancers, The Jerry Packer Singers.

Announcer: Ed Herlihy.

Orchestra: Billy May.

The Kraft Music Hall– Musical Variety–60 minutes–NBC–September 13, 1967 - September 8, 1971. Varying format; different presentations weekly.

Hosts: Weekly guests, including Don Rickles, Wayne Newton, Mitzi Gaynor, Jack Jones, Alan King, Debbie Reynolds, Don Knotts, Herb Alpert, Roy Rogers & Dale Evans, Mike Douglas, Rock Hudson, Eddie Arnold.

Regulars: The Peter Gennaro Dancers, The Michael Bennett Dancers.

Announcer: Ed Herlihy.

Orchestra: Peter Matz.

The Kraft Summer Music Hall–Musical Variety–60 minutes–NBC–June 1966 - September 1966.

Host: John Davidson.

Regulars: The Five King Cousins, The Lively Set, Jackie and Gayle.

Announcer: Ed Herlihy.

Orchestra: Jimmie Haskell.

The Kraft Summer Music Hall–Musical Variety–60 minutes–NBC–June 11, 1969 - September 10, 1969. Taped in London.

Hosts: Tony Sandler, Ralph Young, Judy Carne.

Featured: The Paddy Stone Dancers.

Announcer: Paul Griffith.

Orchestra: Jack Parnell.

THE KRAFT MYSTERY THEATRE

Anthology. Suspense presentations. Produced in England.

Host: Frank Gallop.

Included:

The Professionals. Posing as detectives, four criminals attempt a million-dollar bank robbery.

CAST
William Lucas, Andrew Faulds, Colette Wilde.

Account Rendered. Police efforts to apprehend a woman's murderer.

CAST
Honor Blackman, Griffith Jones, Ursula Howlls.

The House On Rue Rivera. A detective attempts to clear his name after finding himself the prime suspect in a woman's death.

CAST
Jayne Mansfield, Diana Trask, John Erickson.

THE KRAFT MYSTERY THEATRE —60 minutes—NBC—July 1961 - September 1961.

THE KRAFT SUMMER MUSIC HALL

See title: "The Kraft Music Hall."

THE KRAFT SUSPENSE THEATRE

Anthology. Mystery and suspense presentations.

Included:

That Time In Havana. A woman teams with a reporter to locate her husband who supposedly is in possession of a million dollars.

CAST
Mike Taggart: Steve Forrest; Ann Palmer: Dana Wynter; Conrad Easter: Victor Jory; Captain Santos: Frank Silvera.

The Trains Of Silence. After investing time and money in a friend's multimillion-dollar project, a tycoon attempts to uncover the secret behind it.

CAST
Fred Girard: Jeffrey Hunter; Lee Anne Wickheimer: Tippi Hedren; Mark Wilton: Warren Stevens.

Leviathan Five. Four scientists and a guard are trapped by an underground lab explosion. Air is calculated to last until rescue—but for only four. The episode depicts the desperate struggle for life before rescue arrives.

CAST
Dr. Walter Taylor: Arthur Kennedy; Dr. Nat Kaufman: Harold J. Stone; Dr. Adam Winters: Andrew Duggan; Dr. Eduardo Lenzi: John Van Dreelen; Arthur Jensen: Frank Maxwell.

The Case Against Paul Ryker. Pilot film for the series "Court-Martial." A captain's defense of a sergeant accused of treason.

CAST
David Young: Bradford Dillman; Maj. Frank Whitaker: Peter Graves; Paul Ryker: Lee Marvin; Ann Ryker: Vera Miles.

THE KRAFT SUSPENSE THEATRE —60 minutes—NBC—October 10, 1963 - September 9, 1965. Syndicated title: "Suspense Theatre."

THE KRAFT TELEVISION THEATRE

Anthology. Dramatic and comedic productions adapted from the stories of famous writers and featuring Broadway veterans and unknown performers. Television's first hour-long anthology program to be broadcast to the Midwest over the coaxial cable (1949).

Included:

My Son The Doctor. The widow of a European doctor comes to the U.S. to fulfill a powerful wish that her two sons should be trained as doctors.

CAST
Seymour: Martin Newman; Joe: Woodrow Parfrey; Professor: Hans Schumann.

A Child Is Born. An adaptation of Stephen Vincent Benet's blank verse Christmas play. The story of the arrival of Mary and the infant Jesus as seen through the eyes of the innkeeper and his wife.

CAST
Innkeeper: Harry Townes; Innkeeper's wife: Mildred Dunnock; Joseph: Alan Shayne; Mary: Nancy Marchand.

Death Takes A Holiday. Death attempts to learn why mortals fear him by visiting Earth.

CAST
Death: Joseph Wisemann; The Baron: Malcolm Lee Beggs; The Duke: Stiano Broggiotti; The Princess: Lydia Clair.

Professor Jones And The Missing Link. Comedy. The complications that ensue when a professor, a fish specialist, about to be married is recruited to head a secret ichthyologist mission to discover the missing link between fish and mammal.

CAST
Prof. Jones: Roger Price; Cecil: Bill Palfrey; Elizabeth: Eva Leonard-Boyne.

THE KRAFT TELEVISION THEATRE—60 minutes—NBC—May 7, 1947 - October 1, 1958. For four months it also appeared on ABC with a different first-run drama than the one telecast on NBC. ABC—60 minutes—October 15, 1953 - February 11, 1954.

THE KUBA BUX SHOW

Variety. Demonstrations depicting the powers of mind reading.

Host: Kuba Bux, Indian Mystic.

Featured: Janet Tyler.

Announcer: Rex Marshall.

THE KUBA BUX SHOW—30 minutes —CBS 1950.

KUKLA, FRAN, AND OLLIE

Children's Fantasy. Background: The Kuklapolitan Theatre puppet stage. The antics of its inhabitants, the Kuklapolitans.

Characters: Kukla, the bald-headed, round-nosed little man; Ollie, his friend, a scatterbrained dragon (distinguished by one large tooth on the upper part of his mouth); Beulah the Witch; Madam Ooglepuss; Colonel Crockie; Cecil Bill; Dolores Dragon; Mercedes Rabbit; Fletcher Rabbit.

Hostess: Fran Allison, the "straight

man," conversing with the puppets and involved in their antics.

Puppeteer-Voices: Burr Tillstrom.

Versions:

Kukla, Fran, And Ollie—15 minutes. Premiered locally in Chicago, WBKB-TV: October 13, 1947. Premiered on the Midwest network: November 29, 1948. Became national via NBC: November 12, 1949 - June 13, 1954. ABC—September 6, 1954 - August 30, 1957.

Regulars: Carolyn Gilbert, Casear Giovannini.

Announcer: Hugh Downs.

Orchestra: Jack Fascinato; Billy Goldenberg; Caesar Giovannini.

Burr Tillstrom's Kukla, Fran, And Ollie—05 minutes—NBC 1961.

Kukla, Fran, And Ollie—30 minutes—NET—1969-1970; PBS—1970-1971.

KUNG FU

Drama. Background: China (flashbacks) and the American Frontier during the 1870s. The story of Kwai Chang Caine, a Shaolin priest who wanders across the Frontier during the early days of social injustice and discrimination searching for an unknown brother.

Early history: Background: The Who Nun Province in China. An orphan, and not of full Chinese blood (a Chinese mother and an American father), Caine is accepted into the Temple of Shaolin to study the art of Kung Fu, the medieval Chinese science of disciplined combat developed by Taoist and Buddhist monks. Instructed, he learns of the knowledge of the inner strength, a disciplining of the mind and body to remove conflict from within one's self and "discover a harmony of body and mind in accord with the flow of the universe."

Still a young boy, he befriends one of the Masters, Po, his mentor, the old blind man who nicknames him "Grasshopper." One day, while speaking with Master Po, Caine learns of his great ambition to make a pilgrimage to the Forbidden City.

Completing his training, Caine leaves the temple with the final words of Master Teh: "Remember. The wise man walks always with his head bowed, humble, like the dust."

Recalling Master Po's dream, and desiring to help him celebrate it, Caine meets the old man on the Road to the Temple of Heaven. As they journey, the body guards of the Royal Nephew pass, pushing people aside. One is tripped by the old man. A ruckus ensues and Master Po is shot. At the request of his mentor, Caine picks up a spear and kills the Royal Nephew. Before he dies, Master Po warns his favorite pupil to leave China and begin life elsewhere.

The Emperor dispatches men to seek Caine; and the Chinese Legation circulate posters—"Wanted for murder, Kwai Chang Caine. $10,000 alive; $5,000 dead."

Though seen taking the life of another in the pilot film, the series depicts Caine as humble, just, and wise, with a profound respect for human life.

Episodes depict his search, his battle against injustice, and his remembrances back to his days of training (seen via flashbacks) while a student in China. Situations he encounters parallel those of the past; and through the use of flashbacks, the viewer learns of Caine's strict training and of the wisdom of his Masters as he disciplines himself to face circumstances as a respected Shaolin priest.

Unique in its approach, the photography adds power to the drama, and through slow motion, heightens and enhances the strength and discipline of the young priest.

CAST

Kwai Chang Caine	David Carradine
Master Po (flashbacks)	Keye Luke
Master Kan (flashbacks)	Philip Ahn
Master Teh (flashbacks)	John Leoning
Caine, as a boy (flashbacks)	Radames Pera

Also, various character roles: Beulah Quo, James Hong, Benson Fong, Victor Sen Yung, David Chow.

Music: Jim Helms.

KUNG FU—60 minutes—ABC—Premiered: October 14, 1972.